GREEK AND LATIN LITERATURE OF THE ROMAN EMPIRE

From Augustus to Justinian

Albrecht Dihle

Translated by Manfred Malzahn

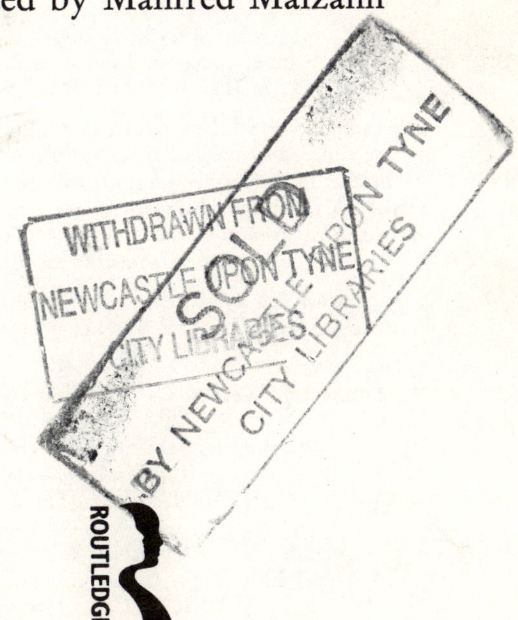

London and New York

+870.9

First published 1989
by C. H. Beck'sche Verlagsbuchhandlung

This edition in English first published 1994
by Routledge
11 New Fetter Lane, London EC4P 4EE

Simultaneously published in the USA and Canada
by Routledge
29 West 35th Street, New York, NY 10001

© C. H. Beck'sche Verlagsbuchhandlung (Oscar Beck),
München 1989
English translation © Routledge 1994

Phototypeset in Garamond by
Intype, London
Printed and bound in Great Britain by
T. J. Press (Padstow) Ltd, Padstow, Cornwall

All rights reserved. No part of this book may be reprinted or reproduced or utilised in any form or by any electronic, mechanical, or other means, now known or hereafter invented, including photocopying and recording, or in any information storage or retrieval system, without permission in writing from the publishers.

British Library Cataloguing in Publication Data
A catalogue record for this book is available from the British Library

Library of Congress Cataloging in Publication Data
Dihle, Albrecht.
[Griechische Literaturgeschichte. English]
History of Greek literature: from Homer to the Hellenistic Period/Albrecht Dihle.
p. cm.
Includes bibliographical references and index.
1. Greek literature—History and criticism. I. Title.
PA3057.D513 1994
880.9—dc20 93–45284

ISBN 0–415–06367–1

CONTENTS

PREFACE

This book is an attempt to realise a project announced in the preface to my history of Greek literature up to the reign of Augustus. The intention is to define the literary legacy of the Roman Empire's bilingual culture from its beginning to the last, brief restoration during the reign of Justinian as a coherent entity; to describe this entity and to explain it historically. If my attempt has been successful the result is a natural continuation, true to the course of historical events, of the literary histories of Rome and Greece, which may be described separately up to the Augustan era. But there should be no doubt as to the cultural unity of the period I have just outlined, in spite of all the changes which the countries around the Mediterranean Sea suffered in the long years between Augustus and Justinian.

What follows is the result of my efforts to deal with this task; it is not meant to serve as a work of reference, nor as a contribution to historical research. In view of the fragmentation and specialisation of Classical studies and the abundance of scholarly articles published every year, it seems that today information on individual issues can better be gained from encyclopaedic collections and from bibliographies than from historical accounts. In the latter the basic concept should remain recognisable as the essential feature, and not get snowed under by too much detail. Neither should the reader expect to find the latest results of specialised research presented and debated in a work which tries to put a unified historical perspective on a subject matter so wide-ranging and disparate that it comes under the domain of several academic disciplines.

Accordingly, my book is meant as an overview which should provide a motivation for studying some of the works discussed. The literary epoch I have dealt with contains relatively few writings which may be counted among the major products of world literature. Thus the reader should not be disturbed by the fact that my account does not focus exclusively on a small number of important works but discusses a large number of marginal texts also. The heritage of Classical literature from Hellas and Rome had to go through the filter of a Classicising educational tradition, beginning as early as the first century BC, a tradition which admitted only a tiny number of works of a very high quality. On the other hand a vast number of literary and subliterary texts gives us evidence of the upholders of this Classicising tradition during the Roman Empire, and especially of those Christian authors who adopted and adapted this tradition. It is the very diversity of the material which invites the attempt to define the relationship between the wide-ranging literary life which had blossomed through centuries and tenaciously preserved its inheritance and, on the other hand, the linguistic circumstances of the period in question, its intellectual life, and its social and political conditions. If the literature of the Empire was known to us only from a few works of exceptionally high quality, this task of historical interpretation would be much more difficult.

During the Imperial age, the area where Greek and Latin were spoken was, despite regional variations, a political and cultural unit. It was not until the third century AD that those tendencies could be felt which would lead to the formation of the individual cultural physiognomies of the Latin West and the Greek East, as they can be observed in the High Middle Ages. But even then, and much more so in the Late Classical age, there were far-reaching mutual influences. Those influences could hardly have had such lasting effects without that cultural unity of the entire region which was achieved in the High Empire. As the Latin Middle Ages cannot be understood without a perception of those elements in its intellectual life which it inherited directly or belatedly from the unbroken tradition of the Greek world, the culture of the Byzantine Empire and those eastern European states which succeeded it cannot be appreciated without reference to the living heritage of Rome.

The mutual interpenetration of Greek and Roman culture during the Empire, and especially during the period of Christianisation, made it possible for a Classical culture which had been moulded into a unit to remain intensely influential up to the present day. Both sources fed the flow of one tradition which kept their heritage alive. This is why, in the West as well as in the East, the Classical culture of both Rome and Greece could be rediscovered and revived repeatedly during the history of Europe; and why the Classical legacy could bear fruit under the most varied historical conditions in the Middle Ages and the Modern age. This should suffice to explain the importance of my attempt to illustrate the unity of Graeco-Roman culture during the Empire by a study of its literature.

A greater problem, however, is the following. If one is to take a historical view of the literature of an epoch, meaning to establish a correlation between literature and other contemporary phenomena, the range of works analysed must not be too narrow, and especially not limited to what is called *belles-lettres*. The most important works from the Empire, as far as their documentary value and historical influence are concerned, are of philosophical and theological content. They must not be left out in a portrayal of literary culture, but can only be adequately dealt with within the frame of reference of the academic disciplines to which they belong.

Here lies the limitation of literary history, and of the author's competence. I could do no more than try to transcend the categories of a literary historian by pointing out important insights which were characteristic of the period and influential beyond it, as far as those insights are expressed in the kind of writings referred to; I hope that in this way I have not done an injustice to the multi-faceted intellectual life of which the literature is evidence. Something very similar may be said of the references to the general historical conditions under which the works discussed came into being. If the same observations concerning the extra-literary background recur now and again, it is because I have tried to cater also for those who wish to consult individual chapters, rather than reading this book straight through.

As this work is the result of long years of study of a very diverse subject matter, I am unable to name individually all those teachers, friends, colleagues, and students who have provided me with instruction, inspiration, and criticism. This does not mean that I am any less grateful to them. For their kind help in producing the manuscript and the index, I thank Ms Karin Harmon and Ms Eeva-Marja Heidt, as well as Mr Alexiou and Mr Vollmer. My wife has shared all my toils and deserves the greatest thanks.

This book is meant for readers of the kind described by Cicero, in his dialogue *About the Orator*: Neque doctissimi neque indoctissimi, sed viri boni et non illiterati – Neither very learned nor very ignorant, but good men, and not illiterate.

1

INTRODUCTION

1 GENERAL REMARKS

After his decisive victory in the last of those civil wars which had gone on for about a century, Augustus brought peace and a new order to all the countries surrounding the Mediterranean Sea. But for those who lived in the part of the world where Greek culture dominated, for the citizens of Athens, Ephesus, Antioch, or Alexandria, this new order did not have the same features as it presented to people of the Romano-Italic tradition. It is true that on both sides of the linguistic divide, this man's astounding political success was seen as a superhuman achievement; and the apostrophising of the Emperor as a divine being, which was fairly common to the Augustan writers of Rome, could not simply be dismissed as the flattery of courtier-poets.

On the other hand Augustus tried very hard to make the new order which he gave to his world empire – an order we would not see as anything else than monarchic – appear to the Italians and to the Latin world as a restoration of the Roman Republic. He was reluctant to permit the worship of the living Emperor in the West; he was anxious to construe his manner of wielding almost absolute political power as the exercising of limited Republican control; he insisted on a show of equality with the other Roman Senators, among whom his claim to leadership was to be based solely on personal 'authority'; and finally, he encouraged the revival of countless institutions and customs which had degenerated or had been completely forgotten. These facts are evidence enough to prove that Augustus with good reason avoided presenting himself as a monarch in the public and religious life of the Roman milieu. In his day the political tradition of Rome was staunchly Republican, as his adoptive father Caesar had found out to his own detriment. It was no less an authority than Theodor Mommsen who described the political order of the Empire in its early and its high period as a dyarchy, that is a system where government is divided between Senate and Emperor. Untrue as this is with regard to the real distribution of power in state and society, it is certainly an accurate definition in terms of the political constitution.

Things looked entirely different from an eastern, Greek point of view. Here the Roman Emperor was always perceived as the successor to the Hellenistic Kings; this is to say as a monarch who like them was entitled on religious grounds to a position above the law which bound other humans. However, there was a difference between Augustus and the rulers of all those states which had emerged between Greece, Egypt, and India after the dissolution of Alexander's empire. There, power was legitimised by an ideology which saw the King as an earthly counterpart of the highest God and ruler of the world. But none of the monarchs of the Hellenistic world after Alexander had ever attained the fullness of power that could have supported the claim to world rule which has always been at least potentially linked to the cult and the ideology of the royal sovereign. With his victory at Actium Augustus had truly attained the position of world ruler. And more: he had succeeded in putting a definite end to the unrest, uncertainty, and exploitation which for several generations had accompanied the dissolution of the system of Hellenistic states under Roman pressure, and which had reached their peak during the final phase of the Roman civil wars. Thus he had proved to be the *Soter*, the Saviour, the good world ruler who was to restore the bliss of the golden age which had preceded all human sin and transgression at the dawn of time.

Consequently there is no need to be surprised by the enthusiasm with which the Greek East celebrated Augustus as world redeemer and world ruler, or by its readiness to recognise his divine status by acts of worship, the construction of temples, celebrations in his honour, or naming months after him. This shows how quickly and how smoothly, in the eyes of the Greek East, Augustus had assumed the part of King and world ruler without the slightest need to present his rule as the product of the authority bestowed by a Republican office.

The age of Alexander had already seen the clarification of the relationship between the monarch and the Greek city in its nature as an independent, free community with elected officials, its own calendar, its own dating system, its own legislation and jurisdiction, and above all, its own forms of worship. The god-like position of the ruler was the very reason why his messages or directions did not have to affect the formal independence of an urban community any more than the sayings of a divine oracle. In military terms and with regard to foreign relations such a city was, of course, in a dependent position. But as for all other aspects of its status, it must be noted that the Graeco-Macedonian rulers, not to mention the Oriental rulers of eastern territorial states, made it their particular concern to encourage the municipal independence of Greek cities as economic and cultural centres. In this manner, those monarchs were promoting the civilisation and the economic viability of their countries.

Greek civilisation, superior to oriental cultures, thrived in the cities, and it was an obvious way of social climbing for a native rural Phrygian or Syrian to become an inhabitant or even a citizen of such a city, and finally to become a Greek. The cities fostered intense social activity, expressed in the form of worship and festivals, schools and other places of education, sports and clubs, health care and poor relief, but above all public building, often financed by private benefactors. There could hardly have been a single one among those hundreds of communities between Sicily, Afghanistan, and Egypt which did not have theatres and grammar schools, baths and libraries, market halls and water installations, not to mention the temples. Here was the reason for the attraction which a city held for the rural people, underprivileged throughout the Romano-Hellenistic world. To the Greek population, the self-assurance and the far-reaching autonomy of the cities were a continuation of the tradition of city-states in the Classic period, the only difference being an arrangement – not too insulting to municipal pride – with the superior power of territorial rulers, which only very few cities (for example, Rhodes) could escape for any length of time.

The accession to power of a Roman monarch who established a modern administration with officials whom he trusted did not signify a rupture; on the contrary, Augustus could build on existing circumstances. In contrast, the Roman Republic had put the countries conquered and ruled by Rome under the command of members of the Senatorial aristocracy, changing yearly, and uncontrolled by any other authority; all of them people who saw this step in their political career as a welcome means of accumulating personal wealth for themselves and for their friends and their clientele, from whom they recruited their staff for their year of office, and on whom they relied for their further political campaigns.

Augustus introduced a varied administration to the Empire. The older provinces, being under no military threat from outside, remained in the domain of the Senate, and were governed by the respective former holders of higher offices in the Republican tradition, even if those offices were losing their importance, and finally came to be mere titles. The other provinces, where a large part of the army was stationed, were brought under the personal authority of the Emperor on the basis of the position he had attained as the supreme military commander. These provinces were administered by civil servants who came from the second order of Roman society, the knighthood, and who were directly answerable to the Emperor; although in the highest ranks there were also some members of the Senatorial class. Unlike the Republican governors and their entourage, these professional officers and civil servants, who had not attained their positions by making a mark in the hurly-burly of politics but by proving their competence and efficiency in a career in public service, guaranteed a regular, controlled, and legal administration after the model of Hellenistic kingdoms. Naturally the superior quality of the Imperial bureaucracy also provided a new yardstick for the Senatorial provinces.

In addition to the two types of provincial government, the Emperor kept a sizeable administration in his domains, most of which he acquired by taking over the property of the crown from previous dynasties to which the Roman Emperor monarch considered himself the legitimate successor. This category included all of Egypt, the richest country and the most vital one for the supply of grain to the capital. Here Augustus ruled as successor to the Ptolemies and the Pharaohs, almost a law unto himself. No Senator, that is to say no member of a class which in the fixed social order of Rome included the Emperor himself, was allowed to enter Egypt without his permission, being a potential rival for the highest position in the state.

Egypt, where a Greek state had managed to survive in the face of Roman power until 31 BC, was a special case in the Hellenistic world. On the one hand it contained Alexandria, the biggest and proudest city of the Orient; but in the rest of the country the Greek part of the population, which was culturally and economically dominant, did not live in autonomous municipal communities. Those Greeks, living according to their own civil law, were commonly called 'the people of the gymnasium' because they could not be immediately recognised as Greeks, as was the case elsewhere, through their attachment to a city.

The label shows that in Egypt, and not only there, the Greeks were regarded as what the nineteenth-century Germans came to call *eine Kulturnation*: a truly civilised nation, defined by its culture. All over the world the most characteristic expression of the Greek way of life was the practice of sports, and serious cultivation of the literary tradition in the Greek language. And because the Romans, especially the upper classes, knew that their own civilisation was largely founded on the Greek model, the cultural self-confidence which united the Greeks around the eastern Mediterranean was at the same time a decisive factor in that consciousness which was slowly growing in East and West alike: the consciousness of being part of a huge community containing the entire civilised world. This community, however, could be entered by all who embraced Graeco-Roman civilisation.

The Imperial order of Rome, which foresaw such a development, had created yet another type of government for dependent territories. This concerned native monarchies on the periphery of the Empire – for example, Mauritania in western north Africa, Cappadocia in eastern Anatolia, or Judaea. The Romans trusted in the ability of their respective rulers to civilise those countries by measures such as the foundation of cities to an extent which would enable them one day, after the end of a dynasty, to enter into provincial status.

Of course the members of such dynasties themselves had to undergo a more or less thorough process of Hellenisation or, in the West, of Romanisation, spreading and strengthening the status of their newly acquired civilisation by the foundation of cities. This corresponded exactly to Roman policy in territories with an uncivilised population such as Gaul which had to be taken into firm provincial administration immediately for security reasons. But here also, the cultural and linguistic adaptation of the upper classes (i.e. of the chieftains and local dignitaries) was encouraged and eventually rewarded by the award of citizenship, or even elevation to knighthood. There was a constant flow, mainly via a long period of military service, of Gauls and Syrians, people from Asia Minor and Mauritania, Germans and Libyans, who came to be Greek- and Latin-speaking holders of Roman citizenship.

Naturally social structures varied a lot within the vast area of the Empire. Beside the urbanised regions of Italy, Greece, western Anatolia or southern Spain, central Anatolia, for instance, had huge temple estates with peasants living in bondage; Egypt had a social order which was based entirely on the village as the fundamental unit of an agricultural economy; central and northern Gaul still had an intact system of rural tribes, with a nobility, freemen, and slaves. As trade and administrative activity increased, the religious centres and places of assembly in the tribal areas slowly assumed the character of cities and were granted the status of *coloniae* or *municipia*, with independent municipal administrations.

This had been the avowed aim of Imperial Roman policy for centuries: the penetration of urban culture into the dependent territories, regardless of their different native traditions. For this purpose, colonies were most frequently founded on the military frontiers of the Empire, along the Rhine, the Danube, and the Euphrates. The existence of civic communities established by former soldiers with twenty or twenty-five years of service and their families strengthened the structure of the Empire and accelerated its Romanisation in the West and its Hellenisation in the East.

The strengthening and the promulgation of municipal culture within the framework of a secure legal order gave meaning as well as substance to the policy of this global state. Its long stability as well as its civilising influence, which outlasted the Empire's existence by many centuries, prove the success of this endeavour.

In the East as well as in the West, the prime upholders and the prime beneficiaries of this urban culture were the upper-class burghers. The socio-historical research of the famous historian Michael Rostovzev has shed ample light on the 'bourgeois' character of Imperial culture. That this social class may be so exactly defined is a consequence of the tendency – with its roots in the reforms of Augustus and steadily growing stronger during the Imperial age – towards a legal fixing of the borderlines between the social classes. This had been unknown to the Roman Republic and, despite its extreme social contrasts, also to the Hellenistic East. In the Empire, for example, there were explicit instructions for a different application of the penal code to *honestiores* and *humiliores* and, towards the end of the Classical age, all professions which were of any importance in fiscal terms had been made hereditary by law.

The upper-class burghers, whose economic power could be based on the possession of agricultural land, trading or banking, the production or the transport of goods, usually sent their representatives to the municipal council, which in turn elected the holders of administrative, juridical, and religious offices from its midst. Even though a hierarchy of stages of appeal for difficult cases existed, leading via the provincial governor to the central Imperial administration in Rome, and in spite of the fact that occasionally the state sent commissaries whose main task was to investigate faults in the financial administration of a city, the legal powers of an independent municipal administration were far reaching. Thus the members of the upper classes found ample opportunity to use their talents in public life and to satisfy their social ambitions.

It was not only the holders of municipal office who could gain social prestige: this was also possible through, above all, donations for public enterprises such as building, organising festivals, or improving education. Institutions founded on private generosity found ample recognition for which countless inscriptions in honour of benefactors stand as evidence. At the same time such institutions also increased the municipal pride of the mass of free citizens, small-scale craftsmen, tradesmen, workers, and farmers, who did not have a share in the administration. For as in Rome, so in the Empire: Augustus had initiated a development which in due course replaced the democratic elements of the Republican constitution by oligarchic-aristocratic ones, such as the election of the one-year officials by the Senate instead of the popular assembly in the so-called Comitia; and, similarly, the last remains of a democratic order vanished in the dependent territories.

Still, the responsibility of the upper classes for the welfare of their cities was even more far reaching. The Roman Republic, lacking until its end an administrative apparatus able to provide an orderly government for the mass of dependent territories it had acquired, had met the problem of taxation by resorting to a means called tax lease. This meant that bankers or investment companies could, by paying the sum expected as tax return into the public treasury, lease the right to collect the predominantly indirect taxes and duties within a certain area. This procedure opened the door to all kinds of abuse, blackmail, and money-grabbing, especially if the tax collector lent an insolvent debtor the money he owed, at an extortionate interest rate.

It is hardly surprising that the long-suffering inhabitants of the Greek cities of Asia Minor massacred thousands of the hated Romano-Italic tax collectors, money-lenders, and profiteers during the temporary expulsion of the Romans by King Mithridates of Pontus at the beginning of the first century BC. On the whole, the reforms of Augustus had improved the situation here, even if the lease of certain taxes, most notably road and bridge tolls as well as customs duties, was retained. 'Publicans and sinners' are well known from the New Testament which portrays the situation in Palestine during the early days of the Empire. But in the cities it was common for an official to take over the liability for taxes owed to the treasury so that the collection of taxes could then be arranged internally by an independent administration. This procedure had a long tradition, especially in the Greek world where in Classic times wealthy citizens had been taxed directly only in exceptional cases. Generally they were asked, individually or in groups, to finance precisely defined public projects by a so-called liturgy; this could be for a festival, or for the equipment of a warship.

During the Empire a complicated system of such contributions or *munera* to the state or the local community took shape in East and West alike, the lower classes invariably being asked for physical labour, while the requirement from the upper classes, particularly the elected holders of offices, was for financial dues. This mechanism of financing public projects worked well while the Empire enjoyed a certain wealth. But in the economic crisis of the third century AD, the Emperors introduced the collective liability of entire municipal councils, and forced payments of tax debts so ruthlessly that the members of this group kept trying to abandon their legal status, and to move into the ranks of the lesser bourgeois, who were under less pressure. As a privilege the complete exemption from such demands could be expressly granted. Such immunity was given, for example, to professors, physicians, or priests; but occasionally also as a reward for excellence in political or administrative service.

In spite of the fixed borders between social classes, there were plenty of possibilities for upward mobility, at least in the Early and the High Empire, and always within a municipal framework. One approach was through service in the army and the Imperial administration, whose posts were mostly filled by officers and non-commissioned officers on temporary leave. The legions were recruited among holders of citizenship. Whoever had made it to the rank of a senior NCO or a junior officer after twenty years of service, was entitled to the status of a Decurion when returning to civilian life, either to his home city or to a colony of veterans. Such a man was considered to be qualified because of his knowledge of the world and his insight into administrative matters, as well as his command of two languages; his offspring had no harder task to perform than to maintain their social status. In the so-called auxiliary troops non-citizens served twenty-five years and were given Roman citizenship on discharge. Thus their sons were able to enter service in the legions, and consequently start the path of social climbing described above.

The other way was by winning one's freedom. The status of the unfree population was fairly varied: there were hereditary leaseholders who were not legally slaves but were still not allowed to leave their places on the land; their freedom was curbed legally to the same extent that other leaseholders or farmers were restrained by economic necessity. Then there were slaves who lived in barracks, working in mines and on large agricultural estates; those hardly had any chance of rising above their status. But the mass of slaves in the cities belonged to the household – called *familia* or *oikos* – of their owners, and it was not unusual for such slaves to occupy an important position with some responsibility for their masters' affairs, the education of their children, or the management of the household. Some had a shop or a workshop of their own and many of them were allowed to keep the profits of their labour. In such a milieu the liberation of a slave was a frequent occurrence, enacted during the master's lifetime or in his will; and liberation entailed citizenship. It is evident that there were plenty of chances for promotion for a liberated slave from a house of some reputation, and especially for one from the huge household of the Emperor.

It is, of course, important to make a distinction between Roman citizenship and that of a Greek city in the East. Only the former entailed those many privileges which were valid in the whole of the Empire. Awards of Roman citizenship, to individuals or to communities, were pretty frequent. All free inhabitants of Italy had already been made Roman citizens in the later days of the Republic, at the end of the so-called Social War, and the same thing happened to the rapidly Latinised Celts in what today is northern Italy, under Pompey and Caesar. Similarly, it had been a habit in the Empire since the time of Augustus to give Roman citizenship *en bloc* to the chieftains or the nobility of Gallic tribes as well as to the dignitaries of Greek cities; but individual awards, as a consequence of personal relations with high-ranking officials of the Roman state, for instance, could also easily reach ordinary people or members of dynasties outside the Empire's boundaries. Two cases in point are the Cheruscan chieftain Arminius who had served in the Roman army and even belonged to the Roman knighthood; he was as much a Roman citizen as the apostle Paul who came from a family of Jewish craftsmen in the city of Tarsus in south-eastern Asia Minor.

It can safely be assumed that already during the early days of the Empire, all members of the upper classes in the Greek cities of the East had Roman citizenship in addition to their own local ones, and were on an equal footing with the Roman knighthood. In the year 212 AD, incidentally, this development culminated in the award of Roman citizenship to all free inhabitants of the Empire. These circumstances also helped to ensure the continual regeneration of the capital's Senatorial nobility, the highest class in the social hierarchy of the Empire, through the influx of successful dignitaries from the Latin and also the Greek provinces. On the other hand the underprivileged status of the rural population was thus made evident, even where people did not live in bondage. The claim to a share in civilisation which was documented by citizenship was of no real practical importance outside the cities and if a rural person wanted to rise in society the only way was to join the army. Here were the roots of social conflict between city and country, a conflict which could become dangerous at a time when the army, mainly recruited among the rural population, intervened in public life which was ruled by the urban upper classes.

Any discussion of the issue of citizenship is bound to highlight two other important features of the Empire's culture. The Empire was, according to a staunchly Roman tradition, the rule of law. It was this very feature which made it different from many earlier and later structures which are otherwise comparable. Without exception, the Romans respected those laws which were already in force among the inhabitants of dependent countries; beyond that, they merely used the penal code to curb certain customs which were insufferable for a civilised state. Thus, for instance, they abolished the religious sacrifice of human lives in Gaul and north Africa, in the same way as the British in India left the legal codes of the Muslims and Hindus intact but brought criminal charges against those who practised the traditional burning of widows.

Thus the inhabitants of the Empire lived according to very different laws. But the many awards of Roman citizenship, the intensive trade across all regions of the Empire, and the freedom of movement for its inhabitants soon brought about the problem of clashes between legal systems. Cases where this occurred had to be decided by the Roman provincial administration, and at the last stage of appeal by an edict or rescript issued by the Emperor; for this reason the Imperial offices came to educate specialists in the different legal systems. Especially in the case of Egypt this process can be seen very clearly, for in the Egyptian sand thousands of legal documents of different sorts were preserved on sheets of papyrus. These indicate the superimposition of Greek-Ptolemaean and Roman law on native Egyptian law and the developments that eventually led to an Imperial law which bore the stamp of Rome.

Roman jurisprudence, arguably the most precious heritage which the Romans left to the latter-day world, had already emerged towards the end of the Republic, even if it was the changes brought about by the Empire which gave it a considerably greater and legally recognised importance. It is telling that the last flowering of jurisprudence came about in the Greek East of the Empire, at the legal school of Berytus (modern-day Beirut) where, however, people taught and studied in Latin. The development of the law towards a progressively greater uniformity was maybe the major factor which strengthened the consciousness in East and West of belonging to the one Empire.

At the centre of the world empire was Italy, its heartland, with its capital Rome. Italy enjoyed a privileged status, for all of its free inhabitants had

Roman citizenship and the country was not included in the provincial administration. This was an advantage with regard to taxation, and on top of this, the economy of Italy was shielded by protectionist measures, as its wool could not compete with that of Asia Minor, nor its grain with that of Egypt and north Africa, or its oil with that of Greece and Spain. Also, on the whole the industry of craftsmen and the commercial skill of tradesmen had developed over a longer time and to a higher degree in the Greek cities of the East. This caused the Latin West to use its political dominance as a weapon in economic competition.

At the beginning of the Empire Italy provided the majority of soldiers in the legions, and its municipal nobility most of the officials and officers in the Emperor's service. But above all Italy was the home of the highest class in the Empire, the Senatorial nobility. It is true that when Augustus created the new order many of the proud Senatorial families whose ambition and experience had made Rome great had already become extinct during the bloody chaos of the last civil wars. They were replaced by new families from the knighthood, from the municipal nobility of Italy and also beyond, a class many of whose members had been promoted because of the Emperor's gratitude for services rendered during the civil war, or in the administration and in the army. But these new Senators became Romans very quickly and they and their families adopted the old traditions of their new peers. One reason for this was that they could assume their responsibilities in Rome alone; responsibilities meaning participation in the meetings of the Senate and the holding of elected offices according to the old Republican order as a means of qualification for high positions in the army and the administration.

However, there was also a set of rules dating from Republican times which barred Senators from any commercial activity, as opposed to the knighthood who were the real 'entrepreneurial class' of the Empire. Consequently the Senator who wanted to invest his fortune had to do so in real estate; but a certain part of the land he owned had to be in Italy. Thus throughout the age of the Emperors more and more families from more and more distant corners of the Empire were integrated into the Senatorial class, with its entirely Roman tradition.

This tradition held some dangers for its upholders, particularly at the beginning and, for different reasons, at the end of the epoch dealt with here. It is a fact that the Emperor Augustus could already manipulate the Senate almost at will: he named the new members, he could also exclude Senators from the group, and it was only at his suggestion that the people's assembly (and from Augustus' successor Tiberius onwards, the Senate) elected the holders of one-year offices from its midst, and thus decided their careers. But, nominally, the Emperor was only the 'first' or *princeps senatus* among his peers; and, potentially, every Senator was entitled to stand for those special offices which theoretically had a Republican legitimation, but functioned as the base of the Emperor's power. These were the *imperium* or unlimited command of the army and all territories where it was stationed; the permanent authority of the former people's tribunes, which included the right to call meetings of the Senate, to initiate legislation, to veto any law, and to enjoy special legal protection of one's own person; and finally, the office of *censor*, controlling social stratification, and public morals. All these were functions taken over from the Republican order, while the real fullness of power which the Emperor possessed was a result of his personal authority, his wealth, his charisma, and the number of his followers.

This power could not but ask for its continuation in a dynasty; but passing it on to the Emperor's heirs had no constitutional legitimacy, even if the majority of the population, especially in the Greek East, supported such a step. After all, Augustus had attained the position of sole ruler by his cold-blooded brutality in waging a murderous civil war, which was only just over. By securing internal and external peace, he was able to make the mass of the population forget this fact. But the careful proclamation of his new political order as the restoration of the Republic could not deceive those whom the very principles of the Republican order made his equals, and who were now unable to realise this claim. The tradition for which the Senate stood took the values of the Republican past as a yardstick. Among them, the most important one was *libertas* or liberty, which above all guaranteed freedom of political activity for those qualified by rank and *dignitas* or merit, through the award of constitutional offices.

This concept of the state led to a struggle for power among the members of the Senatorial nobility in the Republic, which certainly did not correspond to the modern ideal of a well-ordered society. There was a constant confusion between personal loyalty or *amicitia* and legality; legal institutions were unscrupulously used as political weapons; public offices were used for the accumulation of wealth, to be spent on buying votes at the next election, or for paying followers for their services. All this gave rise to some contemporary disapproval too when this practice, which had made the political life of Rome so immensely dynamic, failed to function in the face of the administrative, social, and economic problems of a world empire, and had consequently degenerated in the last century of the Republic into the civil war which kept flaring up again and again.

However, the more orderly conditions created by Augustus had the features of an authoritarian, bureaucratic state, and not of a republic. Social stratification was made stricter by law, and although it secured for the Senators uncontested primacy, this was no adequate compensation to the politically active and the talented among them for those political opportunities which they had lost, and hence for the loss of liberty or *libertas*. Thus tension was created between the Senate and the Emperor, a tension which frequently led to open conflict, particularly in the Early Empire.

Considering the distribution of power the outcome of such conflicts was always a foregone conclusion, but the effect was the incessant creation of martyrs for the Republican tradition.

When Augustus came to power, Rome had been a cosmopolitan city for a long time, a place which attracted merchants, bankers, and ambassadors from all the countries of the world, and where physicians, gladiators, actors, cooks, and dancing-girls found the same opportunities to exercise their talents as architects and poets, philosophers and teachers. The immense wealth which was concentrated in the city through tributes from dependent states, the spoils of war, and the profits of financial transactions can be explained only by political gravitation, and not at all by any kind of particular productivity of the city and its environs. On the contrary, Italy had become an extremely unproductive country during the second and first centuries BC.

Whole regions had come to lie waste because a large number of soldiers who had been recruited from the rural population were sent to the faraway battlefields of Spain or Asia Minor and often remained absent for several years. If they returned they were more likely to prefer living in Rome with their families – either off their spoils or off their former generals' alimentation – than to take up a rural existence again under more difficult conditions than before. Their estates were bought by the landowning families from the knighthood or the Senatorial class, who ran their purchases extensively – for example, as pasture – with slave labour.

There were repeated attempts to maintain and strengthen the peasant class by introducing agricultural laws which provided for the distribution of land to war veterans; but without success. The reason was that the capital had another, even greater attraction. The conquests in the East, from which the Roman commanders used to return as men of immense fortune, had enabled them to use vast sums of money to help their political careers. Hence it became a habit among them to try and win the voters' favour by handing out food or money, or organising splendid games with wild animals or gladiators, during an electoral campaign. The same means were used to organise mass rallies to intimidate political opponents; for instance, on the occasion of a court hearing. Yet those who were entitled to vote in the Comitia of the people's assembly were *de facto* only those Roman citizens who were resident in Rome, and not the inhabitants of veterans' colonies in Campania or Spain, nor the free inhabitants of the countryside, although they were officially registered on the list of a *tribus*, one of the municipal voting districts of Rome.

In this manner, the working of internal Roman politics of the later Republican years was financed by the exploitation of conquered territories to feed and entertain the broad mass of the urban proletariat who had neither to work nor to take on political responsibility; they did not even have to do military service, as the long foreign campaigns since the turn of the second and first centuries BC had made it necessary to change the Roman army from a force in which conscripted citizens formed the majority, to a fully professional one. Neither Augustus nor any one of his successors undertook the task of putting an end to the parasitical existence of an idle urban *plebs* in Rome, supplied with 'bread and games' – this goes to show that, in spite of its pretty ideological cover, the Empire had arisen from a state of civil war, with all its corrupting elements.

Not only was there no attempt to end the practice: on the contrary, a law was introduced to establish the right of each resident citizen of Rome to receive basic foodstuffs free of charge, and Emperor and officials vied in their efforts to make the life of the urban population more pleasant by providing more and more splendid gladiators' games, more and more luxurious baths, and more and more generous financial gifts. This was another reason why securing the import of grain from Egypt was of such vital importance in Imperial politics. Economic activity in the capital, at least as far as crafts and small-scale trade were concerned, came to be largely the domain of foreign incomers – Greeks, Syrians, Jews, and Egyptians, all conversing in Greek. Thus the urban *plebs* of Rome, deeply and lastingly demoralised, became one of the most unpleasant phenomena in the history of the Empire. Still, the idea that the inhabitants of the capital were entitled to be maintained from the resources of the world empire took such a firm hold that the Emperor Constantine created a carbon copy of the Roman system on the Bosphorus when he founded Constantinople, the second Rome.

In spite of the less appealing features of its social life, it must be taken for granted that the atmosphere of the cosmopolitan city which attracted all the world was stimulating in more ways than one. There was, for a start, the fascinating consciousness of being in the centre of the civilised world when in Rome and finding evidence of this fact in many everyday experiences. Then there was the outward splendour of the metropolis, steadily growing among the general prosperity of the Early and the High Empire. The incomparable status of Rome corresponded to the incomparable status of the Emperor. Augustus had been very cautious in the outward expression of his monarchic position, with a special regard to Romano-Italic traditions; but the peace, wealth, and legal security which the Empire provided made the people increasingly accustomed to the idea that there was a good reason for the global state to have one head, just as the universe was ruled by one supreme God. This opinion remained unshattered even when individual emperors proved to be morally incapable of handling the fullness of their power, which led to abuses caused by the frequently cited 'Caesarean madness'. Still, even the resulting chaos, including, in a few cases, the violent removal of such emperors, could never again pose a serious threat to the existence of the monarchy.

At first, the strongest supporters of Imperial power were the wealthy bourgeoisie of the countless cities in East and West. They found ideal conditions for their economic activities, their educational interests, and their political concern as local patriots, while the Imperial peace lasted. From their ranks came most of the officials in the Emperor's service, and the loyalty to Emperor and Empire which developed in this milieu was one of the most important influences on public morale. Even prominence achieved in political debate was no longer a criterion for social distinction, when compared to devotion to one's duties, and industriousness in regular service in the administration or in the army.

The social class which was the foundation of this state was marked by a strong educational tradition. The written word was of such importance in the economy and administration that only a peasant could survive as an illiterate, while this was impossible even for a small-scale tradesman or a subaltern in public service. For those who belonged to the upper bourgeoisie, an essential condition for success in life was a higher education with a linguistic, literary, and philosophical orientation. This made the educational system so important; and the issue will be raised again in what follows because of the importance of this fact for an understanding of the literature of the period. As regards the general atmosphere to be found in the public and private life of the epoch, the most striking feature is the high degree to which the principles of tolerance and moderation as well as humanitarian ideas are in evidence, thanks to the dominance of an educated class. Yet, although philosophy had a wide influence, there was a limit to general philanthropy; not surprisingly so if one considers the contrast between rich and poor, slaves and freemen, city and country, Barbarian foreigners and citizens of the Empire. All the same, this period left us an astonishing number of documents, only rarely paralleled in history, giving evidence of humane thinking not only in philosophy and literature, but also particularly in legislation and jurisdiction, administration and social politics; and, indeed, in private life.

Still, it must be taken into account that this society lacked one reason for intolerance, an attitude which might have been aroused by any religion or ideology laying claim to absolute truth. Romans and Greeks took for granted that there was a large number of deities appertaining to individual places, countries, or groups of people; deities whom an educated person could interpret as the manifestations of one supreme divine world ruler, or as powers subordinate to the highest God, mediating between him and human beings. Even a philosopher following a specific doctrine based on dogmatic atheism could see traditional forms of religion as worship of nature and its powers, and so justify them. This was a reason why people did not perceive a problem in participating in several different forms of worship: for instance, in practising a secret cult imported from Egypt in addition to the traditional rituals in the temple of one's home community.

People believed in intermediate levels between man and God, and in a certain mobility between them, for they reckoned on the existence of many gods of a lesser rank, and they were convinced that great talent or extraordinary achievement could elevate a man to a near-divine state. The dead and the heroes were honoured by worship as well as the gods. Thus deification of the dead ruler and worship of the living one, which already had a long history in the East, entered the religious consciousness of the period quite easily. Augustus' reluctance to introduce this in the West was more politically motivated than a result of religious considerations. But all people of this epoch shared the belief that there had to be harmony between the order of state and society on the one hand, and the natural cosmic order, whose existence created the conditions for the physical existence of man, on the other. The worship of deities was the means of creating and preserving this harmony since the gods, however they were individually perceived and worshipped, were the guardians of the universe. This meant that political community was by Classical standards always, and above all, religious community. Integrating the Imperial world ruler into the circle of those gods who gave men the fundamentals of existence presented no theological problems, and in worshipping him the inhabitants of all parts of the Empire, however different their religious traditions, found a convincing means of expressing their loyalty and their sense of community.

Nevertheless, there was one thing which Romans as well as Greeks found blasphemous and intolerable: the claim to have one god who was the only true God. No one within the cultural world of Greece and Rome was likely to take offence if a group of people claimed that their god was stronger than others. But whoever denied other countries' and other people's gods their divinity, who was not even ready to accept them as dimly recognised manifestations of a divine world ruler or as subordinate powers, was denying the divinity of the cosmic and the political order, and hence threatening the basis for human co-existence.

At the time when their country came under the domination of Rome, the Jews were advocating such a kind of exclusive religion. Because of this, they had left the Seleucidan Empire with its strong Greek features after a bloody revolt, in resistance against those tendencies towards Hellenisation which finally would have brought even the worship of Jehovah into line with the basic views which were shared by the other inhabitants of the Classical world. The Jews had to bow to the superior power of Rome; the Romans, however, were clever enough to tolerate their exclusive monotheistic religion in spite of its alien outlook, probably because their own basic resentment was checked by the legal argument that the Jews had their religion long before the entry of the Romans into the Eastern world, and that Judaism thus had a claim to priority. But the arrangement remained unstable and after two bloody uprisings in 70 and 135 AD, the existence of a distinct Jewish community within the Roman Empire came to an end. However, there was another inevitable conflict when a new religion, consciously detaching itself from the Jewish faith, proclaimed the same kind of exclusive monotheism, and thus robbed the order which the Roman Empire had given to the civilised world of its cosmic legitimacy, and of its sacred character. Try as they might to avoid an outward clash between their lifestyle and the laws of the state, the Christians were unable to avoid confrontation. But more of that later.

First, a few remarks about the educational system of this culture, which created the most important condition for the existence of a literary life. During the second and first centuries BC, the immigration – sometimes also through deportation – of Greek intellectuals had made the educational system of Rome largely similar to the Greek one; the one important difference, however, being that education in the East was always education in the medium of the Greek language exclusively, while members of the upper classes in the West enjoyed a bilingual education in Latin and Greek. The system had three basic divisions, similar to those of today. It began with elementary instruction in the arts of reading, writing, and arithmetic. Then came guided reading and interpretation of certain canonised pieces of poetry and prose; and the importance of the selection of authors for the school curriculum can hardly be overrated, as it largely determined which parts of Greek and Roman literature would survive until today. A certain training in music and sports also took place at this second educational stage, while that which later became the standard curriculum for instruction in the so-called Seven Liberal Arts, the *enkyklios paideia* or *artes liberales*, belonged to the highest stage of education during the Empire, as a preparation for studies in philosophy.

In this third phase, instruction in rhetoric was of the greatest importance. In the Athenian democracy of the fifth and fourth centuries BC, forensic eloquence had developed into a highly differentiated art of oratory, with a multitude of rules. In that community the ability to convince had doubtless been the most important instrument of politics, especially in the legal field, as there were only juries composed of laymen and no professional courts. In this context, rhetoric meant above all the art of constructing an argument, with the linguistic presentation being of secondary importance.

That this art could become the very essence of higher education was due to the merit of Isocrates, the Athenian teacher of oratory. His view was that of a Skeptic, who considers it impossible to have secure knowledge of anything but minor matters; consequently he rejected science and philosophy, in the sense of a search for demonstrable truth, as a means of educating young people. On the other hand Isocrates was convinced that, basically, men are naturally aware of the facts they need to know in their lives and are especially able to make the distinction between good and evil; albeit that they are constantly thrown into the greatest difficulties in communication by the ever-changing situations they encounter during their existence. This was the reason for regarding the refinement of linguistic expression as the cornerstone of all education, particularly one in preparation for a life in the political community.

Isocrates' educational programme was a great and lasting success. One of his notions which is still influential today was that an education designed to give people the ability to perform important tasks in the community must first and foremost concentrate on linguistic ability, on the art of producing and understanding refined and elaborate speech. This premise meant that the method of instruction was by reading and stylistic exercises, improving linguistic competence by analysing and imitating texts of exemplary quality, especially prose. Pupils had to summarise poems in prose, write eulogies and fictitious letters, memorise and recite, practise the construction of arguments, and much more. Understood like this, rhetorical education could emancipate itself from the conditions imposed by the democratic state, where practical eloquence was instrumental to political success, and instead apply itself to all forms of political and social interaction. Already Philip of Macedonia as well as Alexander and his successors preferred among their office staff people who could express themselves in the elegant Attic of the traditional Isocratic school; and the public documents of Hellenistic times which have survived in the form of inscriptions bear witness to the importance of such a rhetorical education in public life.

One of the greatest proofs of excellence which anyone could give during his education – and this was the case throughout the Classical age – was a perfectly worded and recited plea in a fictitious court case; correspondingly, the speeches of the great Attic orators of the Classic period were regarded as the genre which represented the greatest literary achievement in prose. The reason for this was that in didactic theory the form of a speech in court had been most precisely analysed and described. During the Hellenistic epoch the methods and the systematics of rhetorical education underwent ever-new refinements, and where literature was a means of education it came to be regarded exclusively from a rhetorical perspective.

From the second century BC, this established literary-rhetorical curriculum began to take hold in Rome as well; naturally in Greek. At the time of Cicero a cultured Roman would consult one of the famous teachers of rhetoric in the cities of western Asia Minor for ultimate refinement. But Rome differed from the Hellenistic East in that practical eloquence in court and in the Senate gave a Roman of later Republican times political power of the first order. As in Classic Athens, speeches decided issues of historic importance in Rome, and eloquence was a means of gaining a reputation and a position in political life. This made the application of the Greek theory of rhetoric to Latin, in order to help people to achieve perfection in practical oratory, a necessary development. In the last decades of the Republic the result was a short heyday of Roman eloquence, recalled by the names of Hortensius, Cicero, Caesar, and Calvus. But at the same time there was the development of a Latin rhetorical school curriculum parallel to the Greek one; and, like its Greek model, this Latin curriculum long outlived the practical political importance of rhetoric and gave rise to very similar concepts of literature and education, both with a rhetorical basis.

As an educational force, rhetoric was from the beginning in keen competition with philosophy. The fronts became clear in Plato's *Gorgias*: there can be nothing more detrimental to the education of the young than teaching them to make something seem probable even if it is not true, to persuade instead of testing and proving. Rhetoric is a fake art. The only way to acquire moral and political virtues is through the lifelong, never-ending, methodically controlled, imperturbable search for truth; an activity which one must be taught. A moral existence in a community with others is not achieved by knowledge and ability but by constant, honest searching, testing, and questioning.

The drive towards this completely different kind of education, emanating from Plato's teacher Socrates, remained alive in a number of philosophical schools. But the formation of several clearly separated school traditions led to a precedence of positive doctrine, specific methods of research, categorical and didactic elaboration of many fields of knowledge, and finally the systematisation and detailed vindication of certain views of the world and of life, as opposed to the free, questioning philosophy of the Socratic type. Still, the impressive development of philosophy from Plato and Aristotle to the threshold of the Augustan age had a lasting influence on science and education, on political life and moral ideas. Many members of the educated classes found philosophy to be a source of ideological and moral security, and quite a few young ones spent one or more years in Athens or another centre of philosophical studies to round off their education in a philosophical school. From the second century BC onwards, professional philosophers from different schools also found employment in the households of the Roman nobility as teachers, advisors, or confessors; and young Roman aristocrats went to the classes which philosophical schools held in Athens, Rhodes, or Pergamum.

Plato had found a pointed expression for the contrast between philosophical and rhetorical ideas of education, but even he had used milder words later on, and as time passed, the distinction became less sharp. One reason was that many educated people demanded both rhetorical and philosophical-scientific education, as both had a proven importance in public and private life. Also, oratory and rhetoric themselves could be made the objects of philosophical enquiry. As a sub-discipline of linguistic philosophy and of logic, rhetoric was finally fully accommodated in the Hellenistic schools of philosophy, each of them intent on giving its followers an ethical foundation in a doctrine that presented a complete system of nature in physics, and of the functioning of human thought, judgment, and speech, in dialectics or logic. In turn, rhetorical schools discovered philosophical argument as an important type of elaborate linguistic expression, and acknowledged many philosophical texts as models of Classic prose. The export of philosophy and rhetoric to Rome, and their translation into Latin, meant that a synthesis was achieved there too. Cicero, the first to write philosophical texts in Latin, proclaimed with great insistence the ideal of the orator with a philosophical education. He was convinced that his philosophical view of the world, acquired in the school of Plato which had been restored in his own time, was able to provide an adequate foundation for the development of the art of oratory.

In spite of the basic differences between Academics and Stoics, Peripatetics and Epicureans, Cynics and Skeptics, they all had the common intention of teaching an attitude to life which could be understood rationally, and justified logically. To all of them, the scientific study of nature, combined with the ability to form correct judgments and pronouncements, was what enabled man to recognise his proper place in nature and the resulting moral obligations. Of course the conflicting opinions of the various schools, and the discussions arising from them were a permanent reminder of the fact that this aim could not be achieved all that easily. But the constant endeavour to formulate rationally understandable criteria for judging the morality of human behaviour, an endeavour which was essentially the true content of all philosophical trends, influenced contemporary thought in many ways.

The commonly recognised ultimate unit of reference which was to be grasped intellectually was the natural order of the universe. Hence people had a greater respect for nature than in Christian Europe, for they did not know of any creator of the world with whom human beings could communicate directly, without reference to natural creation. The Elder Pliny, in many ways a typical representative of intellectual life in the High Empire, declared that even a god cannot let two and two be five as this would go against nature. The exalted state of the world ruler worshipped by philosophical religion was a consequence of the total rationality of his being and his works, a rationality most clearly expressed in the laws of nature, in the regular movement of heavenly bodies, and not in the manifestations of an all-powerful will. It was the task of humans to rise morally by unceasing efforts to recognise and understand divine works.

The many aspects of religion which meet the observer's eye in documents of Imperial civilisation, whose sources lie far apart geographically and historically, range from the crudest forms of magic to sublime speculations of philosophical theology. But religious thinking always focused on nature, on the cosmic order; even for those followers of Plato who looked for the true laws of the universe beyond that reality which was accessible to the senses. Alien to the Classical world was the idea, first developed by

Augustine, to see the interrelatedness of God and the soul, the nucleus of individual personality, as the only fact of ultimate importance. This idea marks the discovery of subjectivity, which is the significant factor in more recent thought; and the victory of this concept meant the end of Classical culture.

In this survey of the culture of the Empire in its many manifestations I have surely presented sufficient justification for the attempt to portray the Greek and the Latin literature of the period together. A further reason, however, may be found in the after-effects of this literature, in the history of its reception.

Imperial civilisation had a Classicist basis. This means that all of the upholders of the educational tradition during the Imperial age tried to find moral and aesthetic criteria for their existence in the products of a certain period in Greek or early Roman history. Moral life and achievement were thus seen as the result of an attempt to come to a proper understanding of exemplary documents of past morality, and to give this understanding shape in one's own actions. Of course reference was made to different periods of 'Classic' reputation: on the Greek side it was the Athenian culture of the fifth and fourth centuries BC, which was considered as a model in an aesthetic or literary sense as well as with regard to political morality. Roman classicism took the authors from Cicero to Virgil as models in the whole field of literature, but Roman society of the second Punic war as exemplary with regard to political and moral values. Another difference was that in the Greek world this attitude came to dominate as early as the second half of the first century BC, but on the Latin side not until the first century AD; and while Roman references to Classic Greece are in evidence at a very early stage, explicit references to Roman examples in the East can only be found from the turn of the first to the second century AD onwards.

The reasons for the first difference named will be discussed in detail later. For the moment it is enough to remember that on the Greek side the reason for the growing consciousness of a common Graeco-Roman heritage in the Imperial age was the irresistible shift of cultural, economic, and political power from West to East. This trend continued throughout the Empire, received a kind of official approval when Christianity – an Eastern faith – was made the state religion, and finally led to a political and cultural continuity in the East which outlasted that in the West by a thousand years. But the inhabitants of the Byzantine Empire, which survived until 1453, were called Romans in their own Greek language as well as in the speech of their Oriental neighbours. In the religious and political world of eastern Europe a Roman tradition with a Greek stamp was continued after the fall of Constantinople until the present day.

The Latin tradition of Rome, on the other hand, was eventually continued by the western church centred on Rome itself. This came after the agony and the fall of the western Empire, before it arose again, after an interval of a few centuries, with the coronation of Charlemagne. Today this tradition lives on mainly in the civilisation which is shared by the nations of western and central Europe, in spite of their different languages. This civilisation must be seen as a continuation of the Latin culture of the Middle Ages in all important aspects.

So, throughout the Middle Ages, the culture of the Roman Empire survived in the Latin medium in the West, and exclusively in Greek in the East, influencing the development of cultural variants in different languages. While this remained on the whole the case in eastern Europe during the early Modern age the rest of Europe saw a rediscovery of Greek language, art, and literature in several separate steps between the Italian Humanism of the fourteenth and fifteenth centuries, and the Classicism of the eighteenth and early nineteenth centuries. To be sure, this rediscovery meant at first the loss of that naivety with which until then the almost exclusively Latin heritage from Classical times had been kept alive and influential. Direct access to the Greek elements in the dominant tradition was likely to qualify the view of many of the other components' importance. Natural continuity in the medium of an idiom which lived and changed in everyday use gave way to a conscious, premeditated recourse to 'real' Classical times which, in a linguistic sense, meant long-dead 'Classical' Greek and 'Classical' Latin.

This loss of innocence in dealing with the Classical heritage paved the way, in those parts of Europe with a Latin tradition, for a comprehensive stock-taking and analysis resulting in an overwhelming mass of inspiration in philosophy, poetry, science, art, and many other areas. The price to pay was the steadily growing awareness of historical distance between the then and the now, a distance which no longer permitted the direct communication with the past which the Middle Ages had seemed to take for granted. The repeated efforts by the Classicist movements of the Modern age to represent the Classical age as the time of man's general supra-historical self-fulfilment were attempts to bridge that very historical gap which had not been perceived as such in the Middle Ages.

Modern Classicism, first in evidence during the age of the Renaissance, was in many ways similar to that of the Roman Empire both on the Greek and on the Latin side. Both knew the conscious recourse to the heritage of a certain epoch, and the attempt to approach this period through study and reflection until a stage when one was able to create a conscious reproduction of it, and to revive the validity of its aesthetic and moral values. The fundamental loss of faith in the naive preservation of tradition implied on both sides that linguistic and literary life demanded a well-defined education of both producers and consumers. This education could not be had without laborious studies; hence it led to a sphere which was separated from life as lived in the medium of the everyday language.

Still, modern Classicism coincided with the flowering of science and philosophy in entirely new ways; and likewise, the extremely diverse developments of national literatures in different languages – something which was not entirely unconnected with Classicism, but largely independent of it in its results. In contrast to that, the Classicism of the Empire dominated all aspects of intellectual life, so that even Christianity could not escape its influence once it had taken root among the educated classes. Modern Classicism, referring to Classical Greece and Rome, became the instigator of radical changes in intellectual and social life, because one could invoke its name to challenge living traditions, even if they were sanctified by religion. By contrast, the Classicism of the Empire merely had the function of conservation. To it we owe the preservation and handing down of a major share of those works which it had canonised. But canonisation all too often prevented contemporaries from thinking independently and correcting inherited knowledge according to their own observations and critical opinions. Nevertheless, a great treasure trove of human experience was preserved for posterity in this manner.

2 THE ROOTS OF LATIN CLASSICISM

Eloquence and philosophy

Even the bloody turmoil of the civil wars from which the new order emerged had not prevented the extension and consolidation of Roman rule around the entire Mediterranean Sea. Neither had they hindered the development of Latin literature to a Classic perfection, generally accepted as a model as early as the first century AD.

Latin prose reached such a peak with the generation of Cicero and Caesar. The upward development had set in during the second century BC, that is during Republican times, when forensic eloquence had been encouraged. An orator who was successful in court, above all in those important criminal trials which were politically motivated, gained the necessary support both of the plebeian electorate in the capital, and the politically active families and other groupings whose quarrels constituted the internal politics of Rome. Successful speeches in the meetings of the Senate or the legislative Comitia of the people's assembly were no less decisive for the fortune of the state than military achievement, or administrative action in the provinces. In comparison, the quasi-professional jurisprudence which had steadily spread since the second century BC was of lesser importance. It was a means of gaining status in the public eye, but as the legal experts were counsellors rather than decision-makers their knowledge did not make their political careers;

although there were quite a few politically successful members of the nobility who also had a reputation as men who knew the legal ropes.

Such was the situation in the second century BC when rhetorical theory was first taught in Rome in the Greek language. This led Latin orators to try to imitate the forms and devices defined in the Greek theory of rhetoric, and it helped to sharpen aesthetic judgment in a field which had been totally geared to political effect.

Greek could serve as a model quite easily when it came to the imitation of figures of speech, metaphors, or rhythms, but it could not equally well provide a norm for the correct or 'pretty' use of Latin. In this respect Greek instructors could turn to the great Attic prose of the fourth century BC as something to be emulated, while up to Cicero's time, the only way to judge the purity and correctness of Latin usage was via grammatical theory. Whether a word or a phrase was good Latin could only be discussed in terms of whether it was old or new, common or uncommon, regular or irregular, technical or popular; whereas a Greek contemporary would simply quote the prose of an author who was regarded as exemplary.

'When we were young, we had no stylistic models in Latin' says Cicero in the *Brutus* dialogue which contains a history of Roman eloquence from its beginnings to Cicero's own time. Similarly Suetonius remarks around 130 AD that the 'old grammarians' in Rome – evidently in contrast to more recent times – had all taught rhetoric as well. This is an important clue indicating that rhetorical instruction in Greek had nothing whatsoever to do with grammar. There was only a secondary relationship between the two disciplines, if a philosophical system approached both with regard to questions of linguistic philosophy and of logic.

Thus in Rome the tradition of a linguistic standard for elevated prose took shape, from its very beginnings, under the influence of a grammatical approach to language. The earliest evidence of this dates from the second century BC; the heyday of such efforts was the era of Cicero, when a group of orators and rhetorical theorists attempted to impose a particularly strict set of rules on rhetorical usage. The leader of this group was C. Licinius Calvus who, in spite of his early death, achieved poetic fame as well. Great Caesar himself also wrote about the subject, insisting on the avoidance of all unusual vocabulary, whether poetic or archaic words, slang words or neologisms. As the only criterion for the correctness of an expression, Caesar established analogy, the regulator of linguistic structure.

Cicero himself was no such purist. His major dialogue *De oratore*, written in 55 BC, indicated his belief that a talented, trained, and, most importantly, philosophically educated speaker needed no other foundation for his art than that tradition of good linguistic usage which he himself had found in existence. Only the confrontation with Roman Atticists forced Cicero to consider grammatical questions in the context of rhetorical instruction. In fact the survey of orators from older periods which he offers in *Brutus* proves the claim that by Cicero's lifetime the tradition of good linguistic usage in public speech had already attained a remarkable degree of refinement and differentiation.

This is connected with the boom in grammatical studies in Rome, first in Greek, then in Latin. The first person to be mentioned here is Cicero's contemporary M. Terentius Varro, possibly the most versatile scholar Rome ever produced, with works ranging from geography to linguistic theory, and from agriculture to chronology. Following Q. Aelius Stilo, who had taught both Cicero and himself, Varro acquainted the Roman public with the different grammatical theories of contemporary Hellenistic thinkers whose ideas he applied to Latin. Not that there were no Greek grammarians in Rome at the time, offering first-hand information on those discussions and theories. One of them was Philoxenus, from the school of the great Alexandrian philologist Aristarchus. Among other works, he produced a thesis in which he tried to prove that Latin was a dialect of Greek; he also wrote an extremely ingenious treatise on the genesis of language, using strictly analogical deductions from monosyllabic verb roots.

It took Cicero's linguistic genius to use the elements of the linguistic tradition, in a milieu offering much competition and much inspiration, to create the vast corpus of legal and political speeches which posterity – even the following generation – came to regard as unsurpassable examples of the highest form of prose literature, the oration. His vocabulary and syntax were particularly admired. But Cicero was not the only one who had a reputation for excellence in this field: it seems that to his contemporaries, his rival and older friend Hortensius appeared as an equally exemplary master of rhetorical art, and the same goes for the somewhat younger purists Caesar and Calvus.

Cicero's merit, however, may not be judged exclusively from those documents showing his practical eloquence; documents which were meticulously edited prior to publication. Of equal importance is the fact that he created the necessary range of expression in Latin to deal with the two essential disciplines in traditional Greek education, that is, rhetoric and philosophy.

Since the early first century BC there had been rhetorical instruction in Latin, and one extant Latin textbook from that period which deals with a part of systematic rhetoric is very similar indeed to a rhetorical treatise by the young Cicero. Both authors had quite simply paraphrased Greek manuals, but Cicero then proceeded to follow his study of rhetorical technique with the study of philosophy. Antiochus of Ascalon, the reformer of dogmatic Platonism who had taught both Cicero and Varro, showed Cicero a treatment of rhetoric as part of an all-inclusive, scientific-philosophical training. This gave Cicero the conviction that a truly great orator and statesman had to have a thorough general education with a philosophical basis. Thus he began a reform of rhetorical theory and didactics directed at the needs of Roman practice, taking special care to include the time-honoured values of the Roman tradition.

In the mid-fifties of the century, when he was approaching old age, Cicero wrote his monumental work *De oratore*. Its subject matter is divided into the usual five sections of rhetorical handbooks: *inventio* or investigation of the legal nature of the case and of the possible lines of argumentation; *dispositio* or ordering of arguments; *elocutio* or linguistic and stylistic expression; *memoria* or memorising; and *actio* or delivery. But Cicero's presentation takes the form of an extremely lively dialogue with a specific historical setting, the speakers being the most prominent orators of the generation before him. There are many digressions about state and law, history and literature, Roman and Greek tradition, and other specialised issues. Above all, the work is constructed as a fundamental dispute between a merely practical and a philosophically orientated art of oratory. Following a long line of dry textbooks, Cicero's work not only translated into Latin all the technical terms and all the means of expression of Greek rhetoric, but completed this potentially tedious task in a manner that created a literary work of art of the highest category. His *Rhetorica*, written in the previous decade, may be of equal interest from the point of view of content; but for the history of literary Latin, this work does not have the importance of his major dialogue.

Cicero also made a remarkable contribution to the language of philosophy. Within a very short time, he wrote a number of treatises on topics dealt with by contemporary school philosophy; most of those treatises were also in dialogue form, set in a historical or in a contemporary situation. Without any doubt, this was motivated by his own experience of philosophy which, like many educated Romans of his time, he had learned to perceive and to practise as the art of proper living.

His philosophical writings show that Cicero wanted to give the Romans their own philosophical literature: like Plato, he wrote a treatise about the state, complemented by another one about the law. Nevertheless, he appears to have regarded his own contribution to philosophy as neither original nor productive, although he tried time and again to apply philosophical ideas to Roman tradition. He himself saw his philosophical writing as paraphrasing. 'All I need for it is words, and of them I have plenty', he wrote in a letter, meaning his own writing and not the translation of Plato's *Timaeus*. This explains his endeavour to give a voice in his dialogues to all the major philosophical schools of his time, debating their doctrines which were more often than not in complete contradiction. At the same time, Cicero never tried to hide his personal decision in favour of the Platonic school.

Cicero was not the only Roman in his time to write philosophical tracts in Latin. His aforementioned friend Varro, too, wrote dialogues about philosophical issues, among other works. But in this respect also, it was Cicero who came to be remembered; and again, it is due to the perfect artistic form of his *Philosophica* that most of the numerous technical terms of the discipline have entered the Western linguistic tradition in the Ciceronian translation from the Greek. The *Philosophica* were read and imitated as works of art even by people who did not have a specific interest in their philosophical content. But because of their formal excellence the *Philosophica* came to preserve the content of Hellenistic philosophical writings, many of which did not endure because of their lack of form. Thus, there were good reasons to canonise the language of Cicero and his contemporaries, for it is hardly possible to overestimate their achievement – and especially Cicero's own – of making of Latin a truly cultivated language.

Still, one fact must not be overlooked. Cicero's generation, and to a certain extent even their predecessors during the preceding sixty to seventy years, saw the Latin language subjected to a process of severe disciplining which greatly impoverished it. By banning, more or less categorically, vulgarisms, neologisms, archaisms, and many other unusual expressions from all kinds of prose with literary aspirations, the literary language eliminated countless words and expressions of especially emotional appeal. But thus it acquired that objectivity, monumentality, and regularity which today is considered as typical of Latin in general. However, it only takes a brief look at Latin poetry, or at texts which are archaic, closer to colloquial speech, or written in technical jargon, to show that living, spoken Latin always had an abundance of words and expressions which had emotional overtones, apparent irregularities, and so many nuances as to appear vague. It was this Latin, and not the Ciceronian variety with its limited vocabulary, which became the mother of the Romance languages. As the language of an educational tradition, however, so-called Classical Latin can nowhere be matched for succinctness and disciplined force. This was already recognised by Cicero's immediate successors.

Poetry

Just like other nations the Romans also had their traditional children's songs and work songs, their prayers, charms, and proverbs, in metric form. But literary Roman poetry in the proper sense of the word began with a translation of the *Odyssey* – which soon became a school text like the original – and of Greek drama for an Italic audience in the third century BC. From these beginnings, made by the freed Greek slave Livius Andronicus and the Roman knight Naevius, the formation of a repertoire of poetic forms took place under the constant influence of Greek models, and of Greek theories. The prologues of the earliest surviving comedies by Plautus and Terence contain explicit references, meant for the audience, to the underlying originals, and to the manner of their adaptation. While the earliest epics, including that of Naevius about the first Punic War, were written in a native metre, modified only slightly under Greek influence, the translations or adaptations of drama preserved the Greek metres, with slight modifications to suit the Latin language. Early in the second century BC, the Greek hexameter in its Latin adaptation became the metre of the Roman epic too. This was brought about by the versatile Ennius, well-versed in Greek poetry, whose major epic about Roman history, the *Annals*, very soon replaced the old translation of the *Odyssey* as a textbook for schools.

It is clear that under such circumstances the linguistic conventions for the various genres of poetry, such as the rules for the use of metaphors, epithets, or rhetorical figures, were formed in conscious reference to Greek models. The studies of Greek grammar and philology which began in Rome in the second century BC had a close connection not only with the art of rhetoric, but with that of poetry also. The fragments of the so-called *Satires* of Lucilius – hexametric poetry of loose form and varied, mostly topical, content – contain discussions of grammatical problems and poetic theory, topics that were current among the well-educated nobility of Rome, with their interest in Greek literature and philosophy. Characteristically this poetic form, especially suited for the treatment of theoretical problems in the shape of educated, but unsystematic conversation, was a Roman addition to the family of literary genres.

Thus, the proverb 'Minerva's owl flies in the evening' does not apply to Roman poetry which does not show the historical succession which can be observed in many national literatures; the transition from great poetry to poetic theory, and finally to epigonal-scholarly poetry influenced by theory. It was in conscious imitation of Greek models that Roman poetry grew, at a time when Greek poetry had long reached its late theoretical and scholarly phase. From its beginnings Roman poetry was created by people with a keen perception, sharpened by theoretical knowledge. To a certain extent this may explain the exceptional formal perfection achieved by Roman poets in the first century BC, and the especially dense network of references and allusions to Latin as well as Greek material, in which their poetic tradition grew from generation to generation.

The high degree of consciousness in the creative process is evident not only on the formal side of poetic art, in metre, composition, or choice of words, but also in the selection of subject matter. Greek poetry had grown with and alongside the immensely rich mythological tradition, and even when myth ceased to function as an interpretative pattern for life in general – that is in the fourth and fifth centuries BC – it remained the subject matter and thus the vehicle of expression for most poetic genres. The mythical imagination of the Romans was underdeveloped: this is why characters, scenes, and images from Greek mythology entered Roman art and poetry, partly via the Etruscans and other Italic nations, and partly directly. Consequently many Greek myths, especially those of which numerous artistic representations existed, became at an early stage part of a common Graeco-Roman, or rather Graeco-Italic, heritage. Lower Italy and Sicily had long been part of the world of Greek civilisation and as forms of worship, political institutions, or cultural achievements of Greek origin found their way into the Italic world, so did mythical characters.

This, however, is only one side of the coin. The highly developed consciousness which may be taken for granted in the creation of even the earliest Roman poetry necessarily revealed the lack of an indigenous Roman mythology. The gap was filled by material from the history of the Roman state, although historical memory became rather vague as it receded into remote, legendary times. But the focal role which the entirely conservative Roman mentality gave to the state, to its values and demands, and to people and events past and present who influenced its fate, led to a peculiar process during which those historical memories which had been handed down in the form of political institutions gained mythical status; that is an exemplary and interpretative quality.

Early cases in point are Naevius who wrote an epic about a period as difficult as it was glorious in very recent Roman history; and Ennius made the bold attempt to tell the whole history of Rome in poetic form. It cannot be denied that it was the Hellenistic historical epic which served as a model, and it is true that the author virtually invented mythological tales in the Greek fashion to embellish the account of early Roman times. But in doing so Ennius was motivated neither by delight in playing with pieces of mythical narrative, nor by a merely antiquarian interest in a slice of life from the past. On the contrary, the intention was to take stock of the Roman past, in as much as its events and its personalities had set standards for the solution of those problems which the Roman state faced at the time of writing. Ennius was well respected as an author until the first century BC; this shows, for example, in Cicero's many references to him. Apart from his indisputable achievement as a poetic craftsman, he deserved this respect because of his representation of a valid political morality, in presenting the tradition which told of the destiny of Rome.

There were works of considerable quality in several genres of Roman poetry around the middle of the first century BC, but any Roman with a bilingual education would have had to admit that there was a vast difference in merit between Homer and Ennius, Euripides and Accius or Pacuvius. Caesar called Terence, an author of comedies who came especially close to his own feeling for style and language, a 'Menander cut in half', and this was meant as a compliment! The same sentiment had been expressed in Cicero's *Brutus* in the comparison of those works of Roman and Greek eloquence from which the young author had to choose his stylistic models. In this situation a poetic movement was born which looked back to the scholarly poetry of Early Hellenism, written for a small audience of connoisseurs. This movement, which proclaimed the goal of ultimate formal perfection in metre and choice of expression, can be seen as an equivalent to the extreme purist tendencies in contemporary rhetoric, the so-called Atticism against which Cicero had to make a stand. Both movements could only exist in closest connection with grammatical and philosophical theory; both tried to avoid, in form as well as content, anything grand, solemn, or pompous; both favoured concise, simple, and pointed statements. The Atticist Licinius Calvus was also one of the so-called Neoteric poets, the innovators, whose influence can now only be felt in the one extant collection of poems by the Veronese Catullus.

In many respects Catullus may be seen as representative of the aims of the Neoteric poets. His work shows the effort to achieve perfection in metrical and grammatical form, conciseness and elegance; it has all the traits of scholarly poetry which, with its many references and allusions, yields its sense only to the literary connoisseur. In his rejection of all grand poetic forms Catullus as well as other Neoterics followed the most famous of the Hellenistic poets, Callimachus, some of whose poems Catullus translated into Latin.

The most important kinds of Neoteric poetry are short narrative poems in an elegiac metre, short epics, and above all, short poems of a personal content, addressed to the beloved, to friends or to enemies and written either as epigrams or in one of the Hellenistic short stanza types. But there are also experiments with difficult forms of lyrical verse, taken from poetry that was sung; and the archaic poetry of the island of Lesbos was first brought to the attention of Rome's creative poets through the Latin recreation, which became famous in its own right, of a poem by Sappho. On the whole, richness as well as strictness of form are the qualities that make Catullus a representative of the Neoteric poets; but he had one very individual characteristic which sets him apart from the movement. This was his passionate temper which led him to make statements of an emotional intensity alien to Neoteric poetry.

The Neoteric movement was by no means unopposed in the later days of the Roman Republic. Cicero, for example, had little time for it. In his own poetic attempts, an epic about his Consulate and a translation of Aratus' didactic poem about astronomy from the third century BC, Cicero followed the tradition established by 'Father Ennius'. The same applies to the one other great poet of that generation, T. Lucretius Carus, who undertook the task of composing a didactic poem that described in detail the materialistic philosophy of Epicurus. To Lucretius that doctrine, which had a sizeable following among the mighty of Rome, had become the means of liberation and salvation. He succeeded in living up to his self-set literary task without the help of those means which Neoteric poetry had at its command, relying solely on what the Ennian tradition had to offer, and thus giving the didactic epic a secure place in Roman literature.

In the aggregate, Roman poetry at the time of Caesar and Cicero had reached a considerable standard, with plenty of highly developed genres and individual works. It did not match the achievement of Roman rhetoric which through Cicero's lifelong effort had equalled its Greek model, but at least Roman poetry had made recognisable progress in that direction. What it lacked was a kind of writing that could, in a sense, mediate between the archaic gravity of the Ennian tradition in epic and drama, and the formal virtuosity of Neoteric poetry, emulating the brilliance of later Greek art. What may well be called the miracle of the Augustan age is that works of such a kind were indeed created in the tense atmosphere of those years which preceded Augustus' final victory, and in very close correlation with political events in the first years of his undisputed reign when new, rich ground was opened up for the development of Latin poetry.

The first author to be mentioned here is of course Virgil. P. Vergilius Maro came from a distinguished family in Mantua and thus, like Catullus, from the periphery of Italy which had not been Latinised for long. He received the kind of education which was the preparation for a career in public life, an education culminating in a period of rhetorical instruction in Rome. He did not follow this path any further, however: but this was not primarily because of his poetic inclinations, documented by two extant short poems in the Neoteric style. More important was his early connection with a circle of friends in Naples, a group of followers of Epicurus who saw a withdrawal from public life as a condition for cultivating individual morality.

After the Battle of Philippi in 42 BC, when the Triumvirate vanquished the murderers of Caesar, the landowners around Mantua were dispossessed in favour of veterans from the victorious army. Virgil, who had lost the basis of his livelihood, gained the support of some people close to the later Emperor Octavian, men with a literary interest whom Octavian employed in the military and administrative restructuring of the Empire which he was beginning at that time. Among them were the legal expert P. Alfenus Varus from Cremona, Consul in the year 39 BC; C. Asinius Pollio, a tried and tested Caesarean, Consul in 40 BC and afterwards a prominent historian; Cornelius Gallus who for several years had the important task of directing the administration of Egypt; and, slightly later, but most importantly, C. Maecenas, Augustus' closest confidant in Rome and himself a creative writer.

Like other poets, Virgil enjoyed the patronage of Maecenas, resulting in the restoration of his financial independence which allowed him to become at once an involved and a distant partisan of Augustus; distant in so far as he could keep well clear of the bloodshed and other morally depressing events in those days of political and social revolution, and involved because his poetry gave a dimension of historical and moral profundity to the Emperor's declared aim of a renewal of Rome, and to his reign over the civilised world. Thus Virgil became the Classic Roman poet *par excellence*, and moreover 'the poet of the Western world', as he has been called because of his undeniable influence over two thousand years.

Virgil's rise to such an eminence happened in three stages, the first one being marked by the writing of the *Eclogues* during the years 42 to 39 BC. Those hexametric poems are in the tradition of the Hellenistic poet Theocritus, who ostensibly wrote of the natural life of herdsmen, their worries about sheep and goats, their happy or unhappy loves, their singing and their flute-playing. Beneath the surface, however, we find allusions to literary life in the cultural centres of the period. In Virgil's Latin adaptation the scenery remains more or less the same but the significance of the indirect statement changes radically. There are references to literary life in Virgil's work too; but more important is the image of a life-giving, innocent, natural world threatened, but not destroyed, by political and historical events in which human beings are destined to be agents as well as sufferers.

Because he gave a new meaning to bucolic poetry, Virgil was able to include in his collection, planned and published as a whole, one poem which transcended bucolic convention. In the form of a Sibylline prophecy, this fourth eclogue sang of the dawn of a new era, repeating the golden age of prehistory. For more than a thousand years this came to be interpreted as a reference to the birth of Christ and Virgil was consequently grouped alongside the prophets of the Old Testament. In terms of literary tradition his pastoral poetry had a seminal influence which outlived Roman literary history, affecting all national literatures of the Renaissance and the Baroque.

Between 37 and 29 BC Virgil wrote a long didactic poem about agriculture. In this genre he could also follow Hellenistic examples such as the poet Nicander's didactic epic from the second century BC on the same subject; there was also the aforementioned poem by Lucretius. That Virgil's epic became a classic of Roman didactic poetry was due to the fact that he went beyond the Hellenistic aim to make dry subject matter attractive for the literary connoisseur through artistic virtuosity. However much he owed to Hellenistic and Neoteric poetry in a technical sense, Virgil managed to present agriculture, but differently in every detail: as the one activity in which humans show themselves as natural and cultural beings at the same time. In doing so, he showed that human life as he portrayed it needed to be embedded in a political order which was in harmony with that of the universe.

Thus didactic poetry acquired a new depth, in form as well as content, as the technical structuring of the subject matter acquired a cosmological and anthropological significance. We know that Virgil read the complete epic to Octavian in 29 BC prior to publication. This gives special weight to another fact on record, namely, the Emperor's frequently repeated wish that his own deeds and the rebirth of the Roman state should be celebrated by Virgil in a major epic.

In his later years, until his death at the age of fifty-one in 19 BC, Virgil worked on the one piece of writing which brought him more fame than the others even if it remained unfinished, and even if the friends who saw to its posthumous publication acted against the express wish of the poet. The *Aeneid* is an account in twelve books of Aeneas' flight from conquered Troy, of his wanderings and his ultimate landing in Italy, and of the large-scale war which he and his followers had to wage in order to secure their new homeland Latium and to make the foundation of Rome possible. Thus in his epic Virgil unites the contents of a Roman *Odyssey* and a Roman *Iliad*, in obvious competition with Homer.

The particular achievement of Virgil, however, is not the elaboration of an older, fairly patchy tradition which connected Aeneas, a hero of the Trojan War, with different places in Italy. The author being a true Roman, Virgil's power of mythological creation was poor in comparison with the strong, inexhaustible flow of Greek myth. What was novel, and deeply moving, was the context in which Virgil placed the action, told as myth, and as events linked to Greek mythology, by making outspoken comments about his own contemporary reality. The heroic career of Aeneas has only one goal, about which the protagonist himself is instructed in a magnificent scene set in the underworld: to initiate the foundation of Rome and its rise to global rule as preordained by divine universal powers. Thus the myth is only the beginning of a vast, cosmologically founded historical construct, and its hero is only the executor of a divine universal plan which did not become visible until Virgil's own lifetime.

Homer's narrative also presents events that 'fulfil the decree of Zeus'. But those heroes whose struggles bring this about appear as human beings with a marked will of their own, suffering the purposeful actions of the gods because they themselves direct their heroic activity – more often than not unsuccessfully – at other aims, and different ones in each case. Compared with them Aeneas is a model of obedience, dutifully performing his heroic as well as his everyday actions according to divine orders. He is not in the least a tragic character and this is why he leaves the reader cold. Still, the epic did have an emotional impact at all times, for which there are a number of reasons. On the one hand there are minor characters such as Turnus or Dido, whose fate calls for immediate sympathy. Then there are many individual scenes endowed with much pathos, often using psychagogical devices of contemporary rhetoric. Finally, and this may be the decisive factor, the poet succeeds in making each episode, each constellation – however unexpected – of the complicated plot remind the contemporary reader of the fact that he is following a chain of great events, divinely directed and hence meaningful; events whose fruits had become ripe in that reader's own lifetime.

Looking at this characteristic feature, one is inclined to ask whether Virgil's epic is a continuation of the Greek mythological tradition, or the Roman historical one. The answer has to be a 'yes' to both propositions since the author used fictional stories from mythical prehistory to interpret the course of Roman history up to the Augustan age. This is, however, not true in the superficial sense favoured by typological interpreters of Virgil, who maintain that all the characters and the events of the *Aeneid* have a parallel in more recent Roman history. It is certainly possible to see some intentional parallelisms of this sort but on the whole the relationship between past and present is something of a more fundamental nature to Virgil: they explain one another, as the original and the final stages of the realisation of a divine universal plan, with Rome in the focal role. Thus myth is changed into history, and history remythified.

Of course the *Aeneid* is the work of a thoroughly educated, even scholarly poet. In every detail we can feel that the author is familiar with the philosophical and rhetorical knowledge of his age; his use of poetic forms and his mastery of metre, as well as allusions and explicit references, show how complete a command he had of the traditional skills of the poetic craft, and how well he knew a large canon of Graeco-Latin literature and its grammatical, antiquarian, and poetological interpretation. Hence Virgil's writing is the exact opposite of naive poetry. All the same, throughout the centuries it has never lost its direct appeal to the reader, an appeal independent of scholarly understanding; and this is due to the solemn earnestness with which this poet pronounced his message of Rome's mission and Rome's greatness.

Very quickly, the *Aeneid* replaced Ennius' *Annals* in the canon of school curricula, and became the national epic of Rome – 'greater than the *Iliad*', as Propertius had claimed even before its publication. It is said to have been Qu. Caecilius Epirota, a freed slave and schoolmaster of Greek origin, who first introduced Virgil's writing into grammatical instruction. Virgil's influence went beyond the history of the epic form; as far as this genre is concerned, it can be said that any subsequent epic in Roman or post-Roman literature was written with reference to Virgil. Moreover, Virgil became to the Classical Latin world and to the Latin culture of the Middle Ages the archetype of the poet whose work, reinterpreted ever afresh, set standards for poetry in general.

There are some parallels between Virgil and a man five years his junior, Qu. Horatius Flaccus, born in 65 BC as the son of a freed slave from Venusia in southern Italy. His experience of life was also greatly influenced by the last civil war, and the birth of the Augustan order. In Athens where he had gone to study philosophy Horace, like many other intellectuals, came to support the cause of Caesar's assassins; and at the Battle of Philippi he fought on the losing side. Virgil's intercession gained him access to the house of Maecenas in 38 BC; Maecenas gave the young man a small patch of land to provide him with a basic income and he encouraged his writing by showing a benevolent interest, without limiting the poet's external or mental independence.

Horace commented on the battles of the civil war, the victory at Actium over Antony and Cleopatra, and the great reformatory work of Augustus, in poems expressing anxiety, triumph, and enthusiastic agreement respectively. He received the order to compose a song of praise for the *ludi saeculares* held at the command of Augustus in 17 BC, in order to give a religious testimonial of the beginning of a new, better age. But Horace never became a court-poet, and all attempts to bind him more closely to the Emperor's person met with resistance that was as polite as it was determined; some extant private documents illustrate this in a very impressive manner.

One has to be extremely cautious in using works such as those of Augustan poets to draw conclusions about the character and the biography of the poet; still, Horatian poetry is commonly taken to bear the stamp of a man who, as much as he supported the newly founded order, was not in the least blind to the deep shadows in the picture which the new rulers presented of their characters, and their actions. He also saw the demoralising effect of the new concentration of power, and realised that only distance from the centre of power could preserve the independence and the integrity of a poet's life, in close communion with faithful friends.

The small body of poetry which Horace left us is of a remarkable diversity and of the highest artistic perfection. With incomparable delicacy, he succeeded in his self-set task of rendering the forms and devices of archaic Greek poetry in Latin and thus opening up new ground for Roman poetry. The necessity of scholarly and artistic reference to older poetry places the task and its attempted completion in the Hellenistic-Neoteric tradition. The same applies to the transformation of poetry that was sung, and thus had a firm place in social life, into literature meant for a reading public. What is new is a wider range of subject matter in Horace's works, ranging from drinking songs or love songs, or congratulations on a friend's birthday, to political-ideological manifestos, and philosophical maxims for living. This lively diversity of subjects is matched by a multitude of different metres, taken from the old iambic and epic poetry of the Ionic period as well as from Lesbian lyric. The vivacity of such older poetry in form and content was thus regained through scholarly-artistic reanimation. This is the vital step with which Horace transcended the Hellenistic-Neoteric tradition in the composition of odes and epodes. Still, without having been trained in this tradition, he would not have been able to show such dexterity in adapting complex metres to the needs of Latin, and selecting precisely those words and phrases which suited the poetic register selected in each case.

At least from a formal point of view, the other half of Horace's poetic output belongs to a specifically Roman tradition. His satires and epistles are hexametric poems of varied length, discussing questions of philosophy or the theory of art, describing funny scenes from everyday life or events in the life of the poet or of his friends, or mocking at human weaknesses. Their tone is light and conversational, their construction unsystematic, and their metre loose. But the poet lets his reader know that this looseness is not the result of ineptitude – as with Lucilius, the founder of the genre – but should be seen as *negligentia diligens*, the product of the greatest artistry and of perfect urbanity.

Horace's satires found some imitators, whereas his odes, which soon achieved classic fame, proved to be inimitable in their combination of extreme linguistic and metrical perfection which could be shown as an objective fact and, on the other hand, an expressive power that was highly individual. Thus the odes established a tradition which was, on the whole, very modest, even if they acquired great importance as models which made their mark on poetic taste. In this respect, Horace's poetological works, especially the *Ars poetica*, were of similar significance.

Another great achievement of Augustan poetry is connected with the names of several poets. In archaic-Greek times, the elegiac metre, composed of couplets containing a hexameter and a dactylic pentameter, had become the form of an early kind of propaganda, as easily memorable slogans expressing political or moral opinions. Hellenism knew the same form in short verse narratives, outside epic contexts. Moreover, the epigram – consisting of one or more elegiac couplets – had at an early stage become the favourite form of poetic inscriptions. Since the fourth century BC it had served authors of short, pointed statements of a polemical, erotic, descriptive, or fictitiously funereal kind. Thus they could carry messages of a very personal sort, including the erotic, as can be seen in some of the Latin epigrams of Catullus. But, even at that time, formal criteria did not suffice to make a distinction between a short elegy and a long epigram.

In this situation, it was Virgil's friend Cornelius Gallus who raised the status of the elegy to the canonical form of subjective erotic statements. The close connection of this new poetry with the scholarly investigation of Greek heroic tales is shown in a short treatise on erotic tales by a Greek man of letters called Parthenius who dedicated it to his patron Gallus. From Gallus, unfortunately, we have no writings apart from some verses which were recently found on a piece of papyrus. The reason for this is that as governor of Egypt, Gallus incurred the displeasure of Augustus, and his memory was forcibly deleted. Still, he found successors in T. Albius Tibullus and Sextus Propertius in whose hands the new genre of Roman literature took different shapes.

Both these authors came from distinguished families; because of the impact of the civil war, both avoided the political-military career which their birth suggested; both found security and space for development in friendly conjunction with great men of their time who were literary enthusiasts. Propertius belonged to the group around Maecenas, and Tibullus to the circle of M. Valerius Messala Corvinus. The latter, who like Horace had first taken the side of Caesar's assassins, later became a follower of Augustus whom he served faithfully in the army and the administration. He was a major orator and a literary patron very much in his own right and of his own taste, attracting a considerable number of authors. Sadly, Tibullus is the only one of them to whose work we have access today.

In their elegies, Tibullus and Propertius, with their very different temperaments and correspondingly different linguistic means, created the means of illuminating and explaining the panoramic aspect of the soul of a man who is entangled in a longstanding amorous relationship, happy or unhappy, but always painful. The intensity of psychological reflection and the highly differentiated manner of expression in their works should not lead the reader to any rash conclusions regarding the authors' biographies. The characters and the situations reported in these poems are largely fictitious and shaped according to literary convention. The experience of love's joy and sufferings which the poets express in such an eloquent and emotionally appealing way cannot be traced down to historically verifiable events. These statements operate on a much deeper level as fundamental insights into what human beings are capable of doing, and of suffering.

Like the other Augustans, Tibullus and Propertius were scholarly poets. Hence their work contains a dense network of references to ancient and contemporary literature, a network of a kind which can only be created or perceived by someone with a specialised knowledge. Motifs borrowed from myth or literary tradition were also used in their thematically new poetic context, in many different ways. But at the same time – and here again, the contrast to Hellenistic-Neoteric poetry becomes evident – the poetry of Tibullus and Propertius presents a mirror-image of the artists' own times, with their demands on art and on life which the poet accepted or rejected, with their greatness of which he was proud and with their dangers which he recognised. The social impact of this eventful period in history can thus even be felt in an artistic genre which may seem entirely personal, and of no more than individual relevance. The experience of distress during the civil war, and of the hard struggle for the new order, made their mark on all those Augustan poets discussed so far; and as far as we can tell also on the many others of the same generation whose names we know but of whose works we have only a shadowy notion.

In contrast to all of those, the last major poet among the Augustans, P. Ovidius Naso, grew up at a time when the new state had already attained a new stability. Nowhere in his abundant writings, continuing the rich poetic output of his older contemporaries whose work he brought to a certain conclusion, do we get the impression that the author Ovid perceived the relationship between his own art and life in the reformed state as an existential problem. The state secured peace and order, and at the same time put an end to the moral power inherent in the civil liberty which ancient Rome had known. Now there was no longer any need for special moral justification for a poet who lived as a private individual.

Like the two great elegiac poets Ovid, born in 43 BC, belonged to the knighthood; and after the rhetorical education which was normal for members of his class, he even took the first steps in a career in public service. But his fairly substantial fortune enabled him to abandon this course and to dedicate his life solely to poetry. From about 20 BC he found inspiration and personal contact with the literary circles of the capital in the house of Messala, which became the most important centre of literary life after the death of Maecenas. Ovid's outstanding talent and his prodigious output ensured his rapid success: within a short time he became the most celebrated poet in the metropolitan milieu. But in 2 AD he was banished by an Imperial decree, which came as a total surprise. In some way or other, he must have become linked with a scandal caused mainly by the immoral behaviour of members of the Emperor's family. Until his death in 18 AD the spoiled, sophisticated, urban poet had to live in a Barbarian environment on the farthest border of the Empire – in Tomis, near the mouth of the Danube – because the decree was not revoked by Augustus' successor.

Ovid's first works were a continuation of the elegiac poetry of Tibullus and Propertius, but without the sensibility of the one, and without the pathos of the other. Ovid treated the motifs of their erotic poetry, which to him were already traditional, from a distanced point of view, in a manner that was ironical and witty. His next work was a tragedy, an adaptation of the Medea myth which stood in a line with many other writings referring to the drama by Euripides best known at the time. It did not take long until Ovid's drama was recognised as a classic among Roman tragedies; unfortunately it was lost, and can only be guessed at from what seem to be its reflections in the works of other writers, such as Seneca. A similar loss was the *Thyestes* by L. Varius Rufus, a tragedy which was performed in 29 BC as part of the belated victory celebrations after the Battle of Actium.

That we possess hardly any of the dramatic writings of the period is particularly regrettable because we know that, at the time, tragedies were written not only for the stage but also for a reading public; and moreover, there were also performances of individual scenes from popular plays. This shows that the art of dramatic writing must have been especially rich in variety.

Medea remained Ovid's only attempt at drama; in his early writings he kept his preference for poetry of an erotic content. An important addition to the genre were the *Heroides*, fictitious letters in the elegiac metre from famous heroines to their husbands or lovers in which Ovid found new ways to analyse and portray the heartfelt thoughts of women in love. Finally, three didactic poems mark Ovid's move to an elegant-frivolous treatment of erotic subjects, no longer hampered by any concern for true emotion: *Of the Care of the Female Face*, *Of the Art of Loving*, *Of the Art of Liberating Oneself from Amorous Passion*. The second of these epics is the longest. At first it was published in two books for the instruction of men; the third book, directed at women, was later added in a second edition. Wit and elegant diction, metrical virtuosity, playful treatment of various levels of epic style, graphic description of settings, and an inexhaustible flow of new ideas: all these qualities ensured that Ovid's curious epics became classics of erotic literature. To Augustus, they provided convenient material for the official explanation of his decree which banished the author.

When Ovid had to leave Rome his major work which more than all others earned him fame beyond his death had already been completed, even if it was not published until later. The fifteen books of the *Metamorphoses* contain versions of a large number of traditional tales, such as the story of Niobe whose grief made her turn into a rock, or that of the nymph Daphne, pursued by the amorous Apollo and finally turned into a laurel tree which is now consecrated to that god. Most of these tales are versions based on adaptations in scholarly Hellenistic literature; but there are also some Romano-Italic episodes, and a prologue about the creation of the world as well as an epilogue about the deification of the Emperor were the poet's means of giving his whole composition a cosmological-political framework. Thus the kaleidoscopic narrative whose components hardly hang together at all appears to illustrate, nevertheless, a cosmic regularity which is still at work. Besides, there are many compositional devices, some of them of great artistic refinement, which serve to bind the dispersive subject matter together.

Ovid was the great narrator among the Roman poets. He had the skill of giving graphic descriptions of funny, exciting, or sad events, all with the same ease. Apparently neither metrical restrictions nor the strict rules governing the epic use of language created any difficulties for him. The amused, ironical distance from which he lets his readers experience events does not at all preclude an exact, sympathetic description of what happens in his characters' minds. Like no other work, the *Metamorphoses* turned a large part of the wealth of Greek myth into Roman property; not as a contribution to the explanation of the world but as the inexhaustible subject matter of an autonomous art. Nevertheless, it was mainly Ovid's *Metamorphoses* which made Greek mythology known to poets and artists from the Middle Ages until the Early Modern age.

There was a second work of a narrative kind which Ovid did not complete until after his banishment. Its content is purely Roman but its form purely Hellenistic, closely modelled on the major work by Callimachus. That Greek author had written a long sequence of elegies, collected in several books, which contained marginal legends explaining the origin of all kinds of different customs, rituals, or cults. Ovid applied the same pattern to the Roman calendar of festivals, revised shortly before by the most prominent of contemporary scholars, Verrius Flaccus, who at the Emperor's request had undertaken some scientific-antiquarian research. Consequently the result was a work that was specifically Roman, attuned to the religious and moral reforms introduced by the Emperor, and yet again making a specifically Greek genre part of Roman literature.

The final years in Ovid's life were a cheerless time for the poet; but they saw the creation of a group of writings only equalled by Cicero's letters, as documents which show in a very personal way how individual human beings thought and felt in the Classical age. They are poetic epistles in the elegiac metre, printed in two collections with the titles *Tristia* and *Letters from Pontus*. Here the poet talks of his life and his art, his longing for life in the capital, and the unbearable nature of his own existence at the time. All those statements have only one aim: to win sympathy and support for his endeavour to get himself recalled to Rome. It is the poet who talks, without the help of poetic fiction, and purely on his own behalf. This is why these works, similar in perfection to the other creations by Ovid, belong to the very few writings from the Classical age in which a poet's intention and emotion find a truly direct expression.

With the exception of those late writings, the poetic work of Ovid seems to be devoid of the terrestrial heaviness which can be perceived in the creations of other major Augustan poets, a quality which is due to their different experiences of, and their attitudes towards, those events which moved the people of their epoch. The literary reflection of all this is undoubtedly an integral part of what constitutes the classic nature of Augustan writing. One could say that even where charm and elegance are aimed for, playfulness is never permitted. Ovid, on the contrary, had crossed the borderline into a realm of pure, unfettered poetry. This liberation was possible because of the changes which brought political and social stability and because of the achievements of his older contemporaries who had mastered the use of the forms and the shades of poetic expression. The gravity and sadness which dominate the poetry of Ovid's final years do not signify the return of art to political and social ties: they can be explained only by the author's own personal misfortune.

Ovid's *oeuvre* added several genres to Latin poetry, and it seems that it completed the inventory of poetic possibilities inherent in the Latin language, rounding off a system which made sense in itself. Any writing during the following centuries of Roman literary history was explicitly tied to the creations of the Augustan age, even if those were not always regarded as superior.

Of course there were other poets beside the major writers of the Augustan age, and some of their names are known. But of the countless poems by minor writers, only a few have been preserved because they came to bear the name of one of the great authors. There are enough cases in point to throw proper light on classic works by comparison and to illustrate the surprisingly wide spreading of the poetic craft, which is also documented in many verse inscriptions. It was mainly the great authors, however, who made an impact on the poetic tradition.

Historiography and science

As in eloquence and poetry, the Late Roman Republic and the age of Augustus saw achievements in historiography which rounded off earlier efforts and created new traditions.

The beginnings of Roman historiography date back to the third century BC when members of the Senatorial nobility would sometimes become authors after a long career in public life. They wrote in Greek, for their own class as well as for a Hellenistic public far more receptive to literary products, with which Rome sought ever-closer ties at that time. The aim was to make the politics which they and their supporters stood for palatable by a correspondingly biased portrayal of current and recent events. In the Greek world this kind of historiography had a long tradition already. There, too, kings and statesmen had published their memoirs and autobiographies as early as the fourth century BC, and this tradition was likewise continued by the Roman nobility until the Imperial age. A case in point are the famous descriptions Caesar gave of his military campaigns, accounts that do not try to pose as literary historiography.

Latin historiography proper was begun with a curious work by Cato the Elder in the early second century BC. Of it we have only fragments, but they are sufficient to give us an idea of the whole. Cato lived at a time when the process of Romanisation of all Italy had set in, a process which led to the loss of linguistic, political, and cultural individuality of cities and regions. Cato, whose own family was not from Rome, attempted to create an encyclopaedic work in the tradition of Greek antiquarian writing, recording the historical heritage of Rome as well as that of Italy as a whole. Contrary to Greek conventions, he put the emphasis on the achievements of nations, tribes, and institutions, and not on the deeds of individuals. Thus, for instance, he avoided all proper names, and merely spoke of individuals as 'the Consul' or 'the general'. But his work would have been unimaginable without the example of Greek literary historiography, and this shows in other features which are in accordance with Greek convention, such as the interpolation of speeches and addresses explaining the opinions and intentions of the protagonists.

Around the middle of the second century BC Roman historiography received another strong impulse through Greek influence. Among the major families of the nobility it became fashionable to employ rhetorically educated intellectuals whose job it was to rewrite recent, but also especially ancient, Roman history according to the tradition and the political actions of the family who paid them. Being less concerned with historical facts and their objective documentation than with the glorification of the commissioning family, this kind of literature, rhetorically ornate in the Greek manner, produced countless stories about the heroes of the Early Roman Republic, stories which more often than not ended in an anecdotal punch line. Whereas family archives and public records frequently featured the names, the birth and death dates, and the political functions of such men, the events which were to show the greatness of those ancient Romans had to be invented by the writers.

In a work whose writing was clearly influenced by the dawning of the new Augustan age, all this traditional material of literary origin was remoulded into one monumental presentation of Roman history from its beginnings until the author's lifetime. Another important source for this work were Greek accounts of specific periods in Roman history. Among the Greek authors of such writings, one of the most eminent was Polybius, who had lived in Rome for a considerable length of time in the second century BC. He had socialised with many of the most influential people of the capital, and recognised and described the reasons for the Roman state's potential on the grounds of his own political-military experience, with an accuracy that defied comparison.

The author of a gigantic work of Roman historiography in the Augustan period was T. Livius from Patavium, modern-day Padua; during the first century BC, incidentally, Roman literature was enriched by many other talented writers from that region. All told, Livy produced 142 books or volumes on standard-sized papyrus scrolls; thirty-five of these are extant, filling four to five volumes in modern print. Of the books that were lost we have descriptions of the content from the Classical age.

Livy had received a thorough training in rhetoric, and he regarded Cicero, who was about forty years his elder, as the supreme authority on all questions of style. The historical work whose writing kept him busy for forty years is not the result of methodical historical research but an achievement which must be appreciated according to purely literary categories. None the less, it was written to express a certain notion about the nature and meaning of Roman history, and it employed a method of counting the years from the foundation of Rome. This innovation by the learned Varro had recently supplemented the official marking of each year by the names of the two acting Consuls.

Livy was full of admiration for the grandeur of ancient Rome, and of the conviction that the world as well as the Roman state were subjected to the inevitable progress of decadence. It is impossible to say what his opinions were on individual aspects of Augustus' policy of restoration, as those parts of his writing which dealt with contemporary events in particular were lost. Livy's heart, however, belonged to the Republican tradition, and as he himself confessed, he found consolation in the greatness of the past for the inner decay which he perceived in the present.

Livy's work was the main source from which people got an image of Rome's past throughout the Imperial age. Hence it contributed to the survival of a substantial part of Republican ideology, which remained alive and influential in the thoughts and values of an educated class which was getting ever more accustomed to the monarchic state, and a corresponding social hierarchy. This Republican ideology was sanctified by the most venerable traditions in the Roman heritage, and was therefore indestructible in a culture which defined itself entirely in relation to a glorious past.

Even before the literary production of Livy, however, that form of historiography which could be called a continuation of politics by other means had found its Classic-Roman form. C. Sallustius Crispius, a fervent follower of Caesar, had failed in his political ambitions in the 30s of the first century BC and then turned to historiography; a step which he himself justified as the attempt to contribute to a cure for the state, which he saw as fundamentally corrupt.

It was above all in the philosophical circles of Greece that historiography was seen as a means of political and moral education through the description of examples. The great Stoic scholar Posidonius, who was friendly with Cicero and Pompey, had obviously had this aim in mind when he wrote his historical work which continued the *oeuvre* of Polybius. Sallust himself first selected two episodes from the recent past which he portrayed in two short historical monographs: the military expedition against the Numidian King Jugurtha towards the end of the second century BC and the plot of Catilina of 64 to 62 BC which was discovered and suppressed by Cicero during his Consulate. Those events served Sallust as examples for the nature of a state which has been corrupted; and also as occasions for demonstrating how this institutional decline is caused by the moral deficiency of individuals, and how the good, the bad, and the average citizens behave in such a milieu.

According to Sallust it was the political and economic rise of Rome which in itself condemned Rome to inner decay. This pattern, which is hinted at in the prologues to the two monographs, pervades the *Histories*, a continuous presentation of a period from Roman history in the first half of the first century BC. Unfortunately we have only fragments of this work.

For the analysis of human behaviour in clearly outlined historical situations, the historical work of Thucydides was a good example. This is why the Greek, whom contemporary stylists saw as a representative of archaic-rough diction, served Sallust as a stylistic model, even if Sallust imitated him in a particularly Roman way. As Cicero confirmed, no one at that time even considered in earnest the possibility of taking an older Latin author as a stylistic model; for until the age of Cicero and the other great writers mentioned so far each generation of Romans was convinced of having surpassed the previous one in its mastery of the language. Sallust was the first to include, consciously and with great dexterity, elements from the diction of older Latin authors, especially Cato the Elder, in his own linguistic usage. Those elements, which would have seemed misshapen to contemporary readers, were moreover part of a syntax which appeared as irregular and random. The reason was that the richness of ideas which characterised Thucydides' Greek writing would have left the very same impression on a reader with a rhetorical education.

In the Early Empire, others began to imitate Sallust with regard to his notion of the significance and the purpose of historiography as well as to his method of archaising, even if archaism did not become a common stylistic principle until the second century AD. The Sallustian style as a historiographical method became a constant factor in the history of stylistics during the Empire. But as the chronicler of the inner decay of a political community, Sallust had a successor who excelled him; that man was Tacitus.

The Augustan age also produced great, representative works of scholarly literature. The versatile M. Verrius Flaccus, for some time a teacher of the Emperor's sons, wrote a large number of tracts on grammar, linguistic theory, religious law, and antiquarian issues. Among them there is a gigantic work called *Of the Meanings of Words* in which countless words, names, and phrases from ancient Latin tradition found a linguistic as well as an antiquarian explanation. We have access to a partly preserved excerpt made in the second century AD, while a shorter version of this excerpt made in the eighth century AD is completely extant.

Verrius' antiquarian research on the Roman calendar of festivals is documented in an inscription in the city of Praeneste, while his studies of the system of Roman orthography or of the language of Cato the Elder can only be perceived in occasional reflections in later writings. Those indicate that scholarly investigation of the Latin language had surpassed the level reached in the preceding generation by Varro, and had attained the full methodical certainty of Greek science.

There were other productive scholars besides Verrius Flaccus, but we know about them only from mentions of their names or from occasional references to their works. The only writing of technical-scientific content from the Augustan age which has survived is a manual of architecture written by an architect called Vitruvius. He had initially served as an engineer in Caesar's army, and later took part in the construction of Rome's water-supply system which was built under the auspices of Agrippa, a close collaborator of Augustus. The division of the book illustrates the attempt to give architecture a place in the framework of a philosophically structured and founded general education; and the sources drawn upon are mainly Greek. Still, the work also contains the detailed description of a public building erected by the author himself, the basilica, or market and court hall, in the city of Fanum, modern-day Fano. The author was unaffected by the linguistic refinement of his age, so that his manual stands as one of the few extant examples of a technical language largely exempt from literary influence.

Conclusions

The brief survey which I have given here of the course of Roman literary history until the establishment of Imperial power should have made one thing quite clear: in nearly all literary genres, urban-Roman or Italic authors writing in Latin had by the second half of the first century BC created works which equalled their Greek prototypes, or even excelled them. But this came about in a tradition which had begun with simple translations from Greek and had kept a close relationship with the Greek tradition at every single stage of its development. The ever-renewed, conscious reference to Greek culture was for centuries a matter of course in each domain of intellectual life in Italy and Rome, in architecture and poetry, in philosophy and fine art, in legislation, and much else besides.

Classical civilisation on Italian soil was either genuinely Greek, as in the many Greek colonies between Naples and Taranto, or it developed under the dominant influence of Greek prototypes wherever urban centres were formed. Thus it is well justified to talk of an all-Italic Hellenism which may have had different features among the Etruscans and Oscans, Latins, or Picentians; the orientation towards Greek models, however, was always obvious. Even when certain specifically Roman forms of literary creation had no immediate prototypes in Greek – for instance, the satire or the classic elegy – the elaboration of such forms to ones with a claim to artistic merit happened, as can be seen in many details, in each case with reference to similar phenomena and achievements in Greek literature.

What has been called the originality of Roman literature can be perceived in the fact that Greek prototypes found Latin parallels which contemporary and later judgment saw as equivalent or even as superior if measured with the same yardstick as the models. It is clear beyond any doubt that the Romans began as pupils of the Greeks and were happy to remain so for centuries; but equally clear is that from the beginning the pupils' efforts were not exclusively directed at simple imitation. On the contrary, the process should be perceived differently: being in the role of pupils for centuries, the Romans learned to make forms, ideas, or values from the

Greek tradition entirely their own and to adapt them so as to make them means of expressing their own experiences and their own ideas in their own language, in a manner which gave them validity beyond the historical situation to which they belonged.

Nevertheless, one has to consider this achievement of the Romans as part of a larger context (i.e. Italic Hellenism) and thus of a culture that had been created by an intermingling of native and Greek elements over several centuries. This culture existed in a large number of distinct varieties in different regions of Italy. Sadly we can only judge those from the material remains which they left behind; for as to verbal evidence there is a complete blank due to the absolute dominance of the language of Rome whose literature marginalised and superseded all others.

Consequently there is a certain historical logic in the fact that the literary works of that short epoch in which standards set in the Greek tradition were met or even surpassed in nearly all genres of Roman literature, should have been immediately recognised by the Romans as exemplary or, as they were called later, Classic. They included the prose of the Ciceronian period, the poetry of the Augustan age, and the scholarly writing of the Ciceronian-Augustan era; in other words, of the short timespan of just over half a century. Afterwards there was not a single author of Latin prose with literary aspirations who did not refer in some way – positively or negatively – to the norms of Ciceronian Latin; there was not a single epic composed in Latin whose author did not choose his specific place among the successors of Virgil. The canonisation of Late Republican and Augustan literature happened in the Augustan age itself. It proved to be irreversible, and even those authors who later subscribed to anti-Classicist doctrines found that their vehement opposition served to cement rather than to undermine the status quo.

In the eyes of their contemporaries the prose writers and poets of the Ciceronian-Augustan era became master craftsmen in their own right after a long apprenticeship in the literary workshop of the Greeks, where they had certainly been turning out plenty of good and even excellent pieces of work through independent effort even before their graduation. Neither did the promotion to master craftsmen mean a departure from the Greek tradition. On the contrary, what came to pass in the Ciceronian-Augustan era was the complete absorption of Greek traditional elements into Latin thought and speech. Hence being naturally bilingual must have meant something other to the educated Romans of the Early and High Empire than it had done to those of the third and second centuries BC. A knowledge of Greek was no longer the only path to participation in higher intellectual life, but rather one of two lanes of the same road between which one could change backwards and forwards without altering one's direction or one's goal.

It is telling that this Graeco-Latin bilingualism never became a general feature of the educated classes in the eastern half of the Empire. An absorption of the vital elements of a specifically Latin tradition into Greek education had simply not taken place. This is not contradicted by the interest which, quite understandably, Greek intellectuals took in the rise of Roman power. The great historical work by Polybius from the second century BC has Rome as the focus of attention. Theophanes of Mytilene gave an account of contemporary events in the first century BC from the perspective of one of the chief protagonists, his patron Pompey; and, during the reign of Augustus, Dionysius of Halicarnassus wrote a detailed presentation of the early history of Rome, the city in which he was living. But those writings had parallels in the many works written on Parthian, Celtic, Ethiopian, or Indian history. Each instance shows an unflagging interest in valuable knowledge, but never a desire to adopt anything foreign. Only in matters of state and Empire did the East grow similar to the West; and it was surprising how quickly the Greek world came to identify with the Roman Empire, and to accept it as its own political order. This is why in their own and in the languages of their Eastern neighbours, Greeks from the Late Classical to the Early Modern age were called 'Rhomaeans'; their thought and speech, however, remained Greek throughout the Empire, the Late Classical age, and the Middle Ages.

The transposition of the Greek educational tradition into Latin had far-reaching consequences. There were various causes for the alienation between Greek East and Latin West which set in during the last centuries of the Classical age, and continued throughout the Middle Ages. Command of the Greek language became more of a rarity among the Latin educated classes from the fourth century AD onwards, even if then as throughout the Middle Ages there were always individuals who used Greek for practical purposes as merchants, diplomats, or soldiers. But as an educational factor, Greek disappeared from Western, Latin civilisation. Still, the 'Hellenisation' of Latin as an educational and literary language which had been brought about mostly in the first century BC made it possible for large parts of the Greek heritage in philosophy and theology, in literature and science, and in rhetoric and poetry, to survive in the medium of Latin, and to remain productive during the entire Middle Ages. Without this important element in Latin mediaeval culture, the Italian Renaissance, which directly reintegrated the Greek language into the world of education, could not have brought about the modern revolution in European culture with such vehemence.

In the aggregate, the role of the language and the literature of the Ciceronian-Augustan era as parameters of Latin Classicism from the Early Empire until the present day may be explained by historical events and conditions of a very specific kind. Another circumstance, however, remains a puzzle: the fact that those genuinely Roman ideas and values which had from the start been linked with the Latin educational tradition were not made to connect in any way with the historical period in which Cicero, Sallust, and Horace had written. To the educated, the periods in which one saw specifically Roman values realised were the early years of the Roman Republic, which were documented mainly in a semi-legendary way, and the time of the Punic Wars, when ancient Rome had been put to its severest test.

In contrast, the age of Cicero was viewed as a time when those moral and political qualities which had given Rome its glory were lost. Thus the great works of literature on which the Classicising tradition was founded were not regarded as the products of an epoch equally exemplary for its political-moral attitudes. This is remarkable because the exemplary character of Cicero's or Virgil's works was not at all limited to the formal or aesthetic side but at least equally well founded on those values which these works expressed. For Classicists in the Greek world the situation was different: they regarded Sophocles and Demosthenes also as exemplary representatives of Classic Athens, and thus of a political-historical reality which could serve, if correctly interpreted, as a model.

Of course this specific trait of Roman Classicism is largely due to the content of the texts it canonised: Cicero's works abound with praise of ancient Rome whose moral greatness he sets against the inner decay of the present. In as far as they treated political subjects, the image presented by the Augustan poets is also not that of an already stabilised, benevolent order; rather their works conjure up the contrast between a dreary recent past witnessed by the writer himself and a recently and gloriously begun future. But even present and future are not exempt from shadows in Augustan literature. This is evident in a passage from the major historical work which Livy wrote during the reign of Augustus: in the preface, Livy says that there is no greater consolation than looking at the good old days if you live in a bleak present. Even more extreme are Sallust's visions of inescapable and proven decadence. If Attic literature of the fifth and fourth centuries BC is also full of praise for a past which makes the authors' present seem deficient, this literature was nevertheless claimed as the documentation of a period in Greek history which was glorious both in a physical and a spiritual sense, and was hence exemplary as a whole.

There may be an explanation for the curious division in the Classicist tradition in Rome of intellectual-literary and moral-political models between two separate historical periods. I would suggest that the reasons lie in some very specific events and processes during the last stage of the civil wars and during the Augustan reform period. Those events and processes, in turn, must be understood as consequences of a conservatism which was deeply rooted in Roman thought.

The century of the civil wars had given rise to symptoms of political degeneration which made a comparison with a better state of affairs in older times well justified. But the extreme conservatism in Roman political life which kept many institutions alive, even when they had become non-functional or anachronistic in the course of historical change, was likely to make any alteration in political-moral behaviour at first appear as a reprehensible departure from time-honoured custom. Albeit that new economic, social, military, or administrative tasks called for correspondingly new measures or institutions, even useful innovations could easily be discredited as offences against a tried and tested order. To boot, the misuse of ancient institutions which had long lost their practical justifications became a popular manoeuvre in political competition, a trick with which everybody was familiar.

All this proves that a Roman with a political interest or with political ambition would be inclined, to an extent that we can hardly imagine, to see innovations primarily as degeneration or abuse and not as tokens of the new order which heralded the future. The Roman Republic perished because of its inability to enforce radical reforms which responded to the major social and economic changes; and this was largely due to the aforementioned fact. The Imperial reconstruction under Augustus sprang from a real revolution, in the course of which a social elite was almost exterminated, law and custom were violated in the highest imaginable degree, the social hierarchy was changed, institutions were modified, and political power was redistributed. All the same, Augustus succeeded in making his new construction appear as the rebuilding of an old framework and thus managed to fulfil a vital need which was part of Romano-Italic mentality.

Almost without exception, and with great determination, Augustus completed all the innovations that his adoptive father had begun with less bloodshed, but with the explicit purpose of an internal reform of the Empire. This is why no group in Roman society which possessed any degree of political awareness could be mistaken about the largely non-traditional character of the new state. But on the whole, the Emperor's claim to be the restorer of ancient Rome did meet with approval. It also found its way into the educational tradition through the works of Augustan poets. All this was not too surprising because, in trying to appear as the recreator of the Republic, Augustus had to pay his respect to the values and ideas of the very individuals and groups whom he had to fight as Caesar's heir and executor of Caesar's will. Plutarch reports that the Emperor once found one of his grandchildren reading Cicero: that Augustus took the scroll from him, read for a good while, and gave it back with the words: 'He was a great orator and a great patriot'. This anecdote with its expression of admiration for a man for whose horrible death Augustus himself was largely to blame, represents exactly the spiritual intention of Augustan reform. The new political framework, un-Roman and un-Republican as it was, was to accommodate the reborn ancient Rome which had been the ideal of the Republic's defenders.

In spite of its revolutionary origin, Augustus still tried his best to legitimise his power by claiming a link with Republican tradition, the bearers of which were the Senatorial nobility. This situation changed with later monarchs: as the political order displayed its monarchic character in a more and more blatant manner, the Republican tradition which the Senatorial nobility represented even if they fully recognised the status quo, became the ideology of a potential opposition. This interlinkage sealed the fate of many of the Senatorial aristocracy, because not all emperors made due efforts to emphasise, in explicit reference to Augustus' behaviour, the pseudo-Republican character of the Imperial state and their own role as a member of the Senate.

The Senatorial nobility came to consist more and more of educated bourgeois from outside Italy, and from the second century AD onwards also of Greeks; but the tradition which linked this class with ancient Rome proved to be so strong that after two or three generations all those families had become dyed-in-the-wool Romans. This is why the Senatorial nobility remained wholeheartedly dedicated to Roman educational ideals until the final centuries of the Classical age. From the third century AD the emperors and those men whom they invested with practical power in the army and administration were likely to come from less educated classes; the tradition of Roman Classicism with its emphasis on the literature of the first century BC, and on the moral-political values of the ancient Roman Republic, could survive nearly undisturbed among the urban upper classes of Rome and also in their country seats. The consciousness of tradition which the Senatorial nobility possessed was, especially during the last centuries of the Classical age, the basis for an affectionate cultivation of Classic-Roman literature, and an important reason for its preservation. Hence the image of ancient Rome which the literature of the Ciceronian-Augustan age had created remained influential down to the present day.

3 GREEK CLASSICISM

Atticism

Literary life in the Greek half of the Empire was dominated by a Classicism which became, from generation to generation, increasingly similar to its Roman counterpart, although it had entirely different roots.

Even in the evaluation of contemporaries, the unique blossoming of poetry in the fifth century and of rhetoric and philosophy in the fourth century BC, for which Athens had provided the setting, stood out as something out of the ordinary. In his *Frogs* Aristophanes laments the end of Greek tragedy with the deaths of Euripides and Sophocles: and from our point of view we have to admit that he was right, in spite of the numerous later writings in this genre. The influence of Isocrates on Greek literary language as a whole is as palpable as that of the great philosophers of the fourth century BC, of Attic origin or at least resident in Athens, on the entire intellectual life of later generations.

It is true that in the following centuries the many cities of the Hellenistic world saw an immense quantitative growth in poetry, prose literature, philosophy, and science; each of these disciplines with its modernist tendencies whose advocates saw their own achievements as superior to those of the past. But without a doubt, most people who played an active or passive part in the intellectual life of the period would have been conscious of their task as custodians and propagators of a vast and admirable heritage. An important reason for the formation of this attitude was that, in the Greek world, major centres in which economic and political power accumulated were situated in the colonies; like many centres of cultural and literary activity, they lay in regions with a lower class which spoke a foreign language. It is reasonable to assume that under these conditions Greeks who inhabited and ruled those parts of the world would form a much earlier, and much more extreme, awareness of the civilisation which distinguished them from their neighbours than they would have done on the cultural soil of ancient Greece.

As a foundation of the first Ptolemy Alexandria on the Nile delta saw the creation of the Museum, a famous centre of scholarly research which gave the most prominent among the learned men of the period the means to perform all kinds of work, and especially to pursue the ceaseless effort of editing and interpreting all that had been preserved of older Greek literature. In the third century BC most of the scholars of Alexandria had made a name for themselves as poets, in addition to their varied scientific work. This can be said of Callimachus, of Apollonius of Rhodes, or of the universal scholar Eratosthenes. The latter was the first to call himself a philologist, thereby emphasising his love of ancient poetry, and in the same breath modestly renouncing the philosopher's claim to worldly wisdom. The term also reflected the fact that, like other Alexandrians, he had at the same time a scholarly and an artistic interest in ancient poetry.

The development of ever stricter methods for the philological treatment of texts during the third and second centuries BC made a union of the two approaches more of a rarity; however, the institutional and methodical cultivation of literary tradition spread over the entire Hellenistic world where numerous libraries were founded in emulation of the one in Alexandria. Great philologists such as Zenodotus, Aristophanes of Byzantium, and Aristarchus, all of them in Alexandria, or Crates of Mallos in Pergamum and Apollodorus in Athens, developed methods for critical editing, and grammatical, historical-antiquarian, and aesthetic interpretation. Beyond that, they sought to live up to the highest task of a literary scholar, that is critical evaluation.

In the process these men succeeded in establishing critical editions of purified texts of older Greek writings, often handed down in a careless and imperfect form. Their commentaries, or specialised works of an antiquarian, grammatical, or biographical nature, helped the understanding of those texts. Of course there was no printing at the time and so there were only a few copies of each of the major scientific works of this kind, to which only fellow specialists had access. But there were selections and anthologies of older literature for schools and domestic reading in educated circles. In their presentation of texts these followed the example of scholarly editions, and the existence of a vast number of schools throughout the Hellenistic world ensured a wide circulation. All that we possess of Greek literature comes from such anthologies for schools and domestic reading from which mediaeval manuscript copies were made. The dry sand of Egypt has preserved a considerable number of fragments of the original papyrus scrolls; this was the common format for books in Hellenistic-Roman times.

The choice from the vast treasure of Greek literature, a selection which determined the tastes of the educated classes because of its use in schools, was ultimately made according to the judgment of literary critics who were thought to perform the highest and most important scholarly task. It did not take long until the philologists of the Alexandrian Museum had arrived at a canon which contained fixed numbers of lyric, tragic, epic, and comic poets respectively. In doing so, they had used and refined the categories of a literary criticism which had sprung up in the fifth century BC and was developed and practised by Aristotle, as well as by philosophers from his or other schools. The corresponding canonisation of certain prose writers, especially of major Attic orators, was also the work of the philologists and grammarians; but in this case the demand for models to imitate in higher rhetorical education played an important part. At that time the major centres of rhetorical education which influenced linguistic tastes, not only in reading but also in the writing of texts which called for a language other than colloquial, lay in western Asia Minor. Cities such as Smyrna, Ephesus, or Miletus, which lay on ancient Greek cultural soil and did not have a foreign lower class, were richer and larger by far than the cities of Greece itself, where only Athens retained its supra-regional reputation as the main seat of philosophical scholarship.

The cultivation of the literary tradition during the last three centuries before the birth of Christ had its effect on linguistic taste which remained under the influence of prototypes from the past, while in many other aspects this period was characterised by a conscious modernity or progressiveness, as evident, for example, in science, technology, economy, or administration. Linguistic models for non-poetic written language, that is to say for the type of usage that was most important in general education, could only be sought and found in the great Attic prose of the fourth century BC, above all in oratory.

The strong influence of such models is perhaps best illustrated by the case of Hegesias of Magnesia. This man was one of the famous teachers of rhetoric in Asia Minor during the third century BC; and to the Classicists of the Empire his style was the epitome of baroque eccentricity. Hegesias himself, however, saw his own use of language as an imitation of Lysias, the strictest and plainest writer among the Attic orators.

Of course there were also linguistic or stylistic fashions which sought a conscious detachment from the traditional forms of fourth-century Attic prose. But it is important to note that 'un-Classic' phenomena could even result from the deliberate imitation of Classic patterns. This may be compared to the impression which we get from copies of older Greek sculpture made in Pergamum during the second century BC: namely, that to us, the copies seem have more of the stylistic features belonging to the period when they were made, than resemblances to the original models.

It is a fact that during the entire Hellenistic age there was a basic 'Classicising' mood, looking back to older Greek literature. But in linguistic-literary practice modern forms kept superseding older ones, in spite of the desired closeness to exemplary, revered ancients. A logical explanation for this lies in the life of a civilisation which was spread over a large area, the existence of a society with a high degree of mobility, and the effect of rapid political and economic change. The language of Hellenistic prose literature documents this: its basis is the Attic of the fourth century BC but its vocabulary and range of forms, its syntax and style show the deep and pervasive influence of the new age.

When Roman politics began to affect Greece directly at the beginning of the second century BC, this led to the dissolution of the system of Hellenistic states and their piecemeal absorption into the Roman Empire, a process which was completed by the incorporation of Egypt after the Battle of Actium in 31 BC. The transition was accompanied by bloody wars and a steady decline in an economic as well as in a cultural sense. The Greek world, which had still produced numerous achievements of the highest order in many fields of intellectual life during the third and even the second century BC, now had almost nothing to show, with the exception of philosophy. The people in the countries surrounding the eastern Mediterranean had become deeply depressed, mainly because of economic exploitation by the victorious Romans. Quite understandably, relief and enthusiastic approval were the Eastern reactions to Augustus' final victory, and to the establishment of a global monarchy with a well-ordered administration.

The dawning of the Augustan age was perceived throughout the East as the beginning of an entirely different, better era. But because of this, the period also saw an astonishing degree of reanimation and intensification of the Classicist tendencies in Hellenistic civilisation. The good new times were to be like the good old times, and those good old times were those of the glorious ancestors who had defended Greece against the overwhelming might of the Persian Empire; who had created a political community of free citizens in Athens; and who had been the contemporaries of the great names in the literary tradition, of Sophocles, Plato, or Demosthenes. The uncontested greatness of literary achievements in Athens in the fifth and fourth centuries BC was, more often than before, seen in connection with Athens' political distinction, and its moral force. Thus a moral dimension was added to the literary-linguistic imitation which was firmly established as a method of higher education.

The movement which brought about a more categorical affirmation of the ancient authors' authority than ever before bore the name of Atticism. It was a major influence on literary life and on the development of the Greek language, and this influence has lasted until the present day.

Of course the choice of one or more authors of a certain epoch as prototypes of an intended style was nothing unusual. But such imitation had always been limited to those elements belonging to the highest stylistic level, such as rhythmic organisation, periodic construction, and the use of figures of speech. The Atticism which was proclaimed towards the end of the first century BC added a new demand: its advocates maintained that the ancient Athenian authors should be imitated even on the most basic linguistic level. For instance, ancient Greek possessed a third mode for the conjugation of verbs, besides indicative and subjunctive. That optative mode had disappeared from the spoken language during the last three pre-Christian centuries. In the written language, it had survived only in a few well-established phrases. An Attic author around the mid-fourth century BC would use the optative mode about seven times as frequently as, for example, the learned historian Polybius who wrote about two hundred years later.

There was a common written language known as Koine which came to be used in the entire Greek world between the third and the first century BC, replacing the numerous, highly varied dialects of the ancient heartland of Greek civilisation. The Koine was largely based on the Attic language, which had become an important vehicle of supra-regional commercial and literary communication during the fifth and fourth centuries BC. But there were also many words and forms from other dialects which had entered the Koine; and moreover, the change of living conditions had given rise to a new range of expressions in colloquial usage, many of which found their way into the written and literary language.

The Atticists saw those without exception as symptoms of decay, following the loss of liberty which the Greek city-states had suffered at the hands of Alexander and his successors. The literary language which was created at a time of intermingling of tribes and nations, languages and dialects, in the urban centres of the Hellenistic states, was contemptuously called 'Asian' by the Atticists, because at that time, the most important rhetorical schools were indeed on Asian soil. The Atticists demanded no less than a return to the vocabulary and to the range of sounds and forms of the Attic language of three to four hundred years earlier in written-literary usage, which was to be entirely different from the oral variety. If anyone insisted today that an educated German should use only Middle High German in writing this would be no more radical than Atticist demands in their day. However, those demands were not only taken seriously, but actually complied with by subsequent generations, and therefore shaped the history of the Greek language until the present day. For this there are several different reasons which are worth discussing in some detail.

To begin with, the convention of writing literary prose in a language which differed greatly from colloquial, everyday usage, and which had to be acquired through specific efforts, was merely the conscious application of a principle which had influenced Greek literature from the beginning. Of old, each genre of Greek poetry had its own dialect, and those dialects were often as different from one another as, for example, the Romance languages. But none of those artificial dialects was identical with any of the spoken varieties of the language. All of them were composed of elements taken from different spoken dialects; and occasionally the composition makes it possible to deduce the early history of the genre concerned, in the absence of records of early texts.

Initially, the rule which prescribed the distinction of genres through language applied to prose as well. The earliest pieces of Greek prose writing were produced where people spoke the Ionic dialect; and for a while Ionic remained the language of literary prose, used even by authors whose mother tongue was Doric, like Herodotus or the physicians of the Hippocratic school. Naturally this Ionic changed in literary use, and gradually moved farther away from spoken local dialects. From the beginning of the fourth century BC Ionic was more and more frequently replaced by Attic as the idiom of literary prose for reasons that lay within as well as without the realm of literature; and it was from this Attic that the literary Koine of the Hellenistic age arose in the aforesaid manner.

The use of writing became more widespread in the Hellenistic age as a consequence of the epoch's 'modernity' which I have already mentioned, bringing an unprecedented increase in scientific research and technological know-how, in planned economic activity and rationalised public administration. Everywhere and in all kinds of situations people wrote texts whose linguistic forms varied between all kinds of shades representing intermediate stages between purely literary prose and everyday spoken language, according to the different purposes of a banker's order, the minutes of a court case, an agricultural manual, a petition addressed to the administration, or a letter of condolence. This ensured a strong and varied link between literary, artistic prose and colloquial language, via a multitude of intermediary elements. This had not been the case with the artificial dialects of older literature: and hence the permanent flow of new words and forms from various walks of life into the language of literature and education, even among those who had the intention of following examples from older writing. The purists of the Atticist movement, however, could see the organic growth of the language of Hellenistic education as nothing other than the degeneration of an ancient prototype of traditional literary language in need of purification in order to bring it back to a level corresponding to the particular idioms of poetic genres.

Between the end of the first century BC and the mid-second century AD, the efforts of the Atticists to subject literary and educational language to a process of re-pristinisation were thoroughly successful. At the end of the Hellenistic epoch the optative had disappeared almost completely from the non-literary papyrus scrolls of Egypt; that is, from tax receipts, private letters, IOUs, land registers, or letters to and from the administration. In the same kinds of texts, the frequency of the optative was on the increase during the entire first and second centuries AD, even if colloquial mediaeval and modern Greek give no indication of its return to the spoken language. This fact must be regarded as a consequence of elementary education in schools, where apparently the demand for instruction in the old Attic language, so different from the colloquial form, had been realised.

The rapid success of a programme which had been designed for literary prose and rhetorical instruction, a success which reached beyond those targets to affect all written language, can also be explained by the existence of abundant means for the implementation of the programme. The grammatical-philological studies of the Hellenistic period had provided comprehensive and methodical keys to the artificial literary dialects, some of which were fairly obscure. Such keys existed also for Attic, the language of the ten canonised orators of the fourth century BC as well as Old Comedy. Fourth-century oratory contained many political and legal expressions that had been current in ancient Athens but had become obsolete since. Without explanation a reader of the Hellenistic age would likewise have been unable to understand countless words and phrases from Athenian everyday life which occurred in comedy.

Around 200 BC one of the most important philologists at the Alexandrian Museum, Aristophanes of Byzantium, wrote a dictionary of words and phrases that were 'Attic contrary to appearance' – of course without the intention of providing a norm for the language of literary prose. Grammatical-philological books of this kind were used immediately by those teachers of rhetoric who had subscribed to the Atticist reform programme. In the Augustan age one of the earliest theorists of Atticism, the Hellenised Jew Caecilius from Sicily, wrote a bilingual dictionary in which 'Greek' words, word forms, and meanings, were juxtaposed with 'Attic' ones. Throughout the Imperial age, many more such dictionaries were written for use in linguistic-rhetorical education.

What certainly also helped the efforts of the Atticists from the start was the dominance of Athens in the literary tradition since the fifth century BC, which made Hellenistic grammarians and philologists take Attic for 'normal' Greek. This was the reason for Aristonicus, a major Alexandrian scholar of the first century BC, to go so far as to claim Athenian origin for Homer, undoubtedly the most important poet in Greek culture. The same ideas also inspired linguistic theories which people sought to deduce from the wealth of philologically ordered linguistic material. Philoxenus was a Greek grammarian teaching in Rome at the time when the Atticist movement took shape; among other works, he produced a cleverly argued theory concerning the genesis of language, which did not follow philosophy in seeing the names of objects as the first words but claimed precedence for monosyllabic verb roots (i.e. the names of actions). He also tried to prove that Latin was a dialect of Greek; within the Greek language, he took the Attic dialect forms to be the primary ones.

It is true that grammatical instruction was only of minor importance in the system of Greek rhetorical education. It was through imitating exemplary texts, and not through observing rules which one had learned, that correct utterances were to be formed. But of course the 'grammatical Atticism' of which I have just given some examples belonged to the background of a programme of rhetorical training which aimed at restoring the Attic literary prose of the fourth century.

Without a doubt, however, it was the general mood of the period which was the most important reason for the success of the Atticist movement. This becomes clear from remarks made by the leading Atticist of the first generation, Dionysius of Halicarnassus in Asia Minor; especially from statements in the preface to a treatise in which he parades the orators of ancient Athens before the reader, pointing out all their qualities. As Rome had recently given peace and order back to the world after a long period of decline, so should education – its primary parameter being the use of language (i.e. eloquence) – return to the healthy purity of ancient Athens after the degeneration which it had suffered in Asian cities in the past.

The wealthy, educated bourgeoisie was the dominant social class in the Roman Empire. It was the same class which had most readily co-operated with the Romans earlier on, when Rome was extending its power to the Greek East. The political values of this class stemmed from the image of the *polis* as an independent urban community in pre-Hellenistic times, while in reality Greek cities on the territory of Hellenistic monarchies may have had largely independent administrations and were often nominally sovereign, but remained *de facto* under a king's power. To secure the goodwill of the bourgeois upper class the Romans repeatedly proclaimed the restoration of liberty to the Greek cities as part of the propaganda campaign which accompanied their subjugation of the Greek East. This policy was sometimes successful, for the fact is that resistance to, or insurrections against, Roman power always sprang from loyal supporters of the old dynasties, while economic and social reasons made the urban upper class more inclined to take the Romans' side.

Thus Atticism as an educational programme focusing on the image of an ancient, free Athens, suited the traditional policy of the Romans towards the Greek upper class and made Rome appear as supporting a return to the best cultural traditions of the Greeks. It is certainly no coincidence that famous theorists of Atticism such as Dionysius of Halicarnassus and Caecilius, both of whom I have mentioned previously, were influential primarily in the capital, Rome. In any case, Rome was a centre of Greek intellectual life during the Augustan age. Many Greek teachers of oratory, scholars, and philosophers had arrived in Rome as prisoners of war or slaves, even as late as the first half of the first century BC. Some of them, such as the learned Alexander Polyhistor, had been set free and had risen to the bourgeois class. Now men such as the historiographer Timagenes or the grammarian Philoxenus, who had freely chosen to work in Rome, belonged to the typical representatives of metropolitan intellectual life. Rome, then, became the first centre of the Atticist movement; but it was the subsequent generation which saw Atticism also take a firm hold in the rhetorical schools of Asia.

The ever-increasing influence of Atticism in the period from the reign of Augustus until that of the Antonines had three important consequences. One was the loss of most Hellenistic prose literature because of the new overall orientation of linguistic-literary-rhetorical instruction. Dionysius already names a number of great prose writers of the third and second centuries BC as authors not to be read or even imitated because in his opinion they had a bad style and wrote in degenerate Greek. This attitude remained predominant among the educators and, as the Hellenistic prose writers were rejected as stylistic models, only those of their works where the subject matter was of particular interest were still copied and read; for instance, some specialised scholarly books, the historical work of Polybius which portrayed the most glorious period in Roman history, and parts of Jewish-Hellenistic literature which interested the Christians. But all we have from most prose writers of the Hellenistic period is in the form of chance quotes in grammatical or historical works of later origin, or of occasional partial summaries given by other authors.

The second consequence of the victory of Atticism was Greek bilingualism which has survived until the present day. Since the time of the Roman Empire any Greek who wanted to write in his language had first to learn a linguistic variety whose systems of grammatical forms and whose vocabulary were quite different from those in spoken Greek. The ramifications for the educational system and for literary life as a whole are evident. For centuries, the dichotomy between pure and popular language dominated Greek history. Even if there were folk songs and folk tales in all epochs, a palpably literary poetry in popular language did not develop until the Middle Ages, after the Crusades had brought closer contacts with the West. The Germanic and Romance nations had developed a literature in popular language at a much earlier stage to supplement educated writing where Latin dominated. In Greece an Emperor's daughter in the twelfth century might well get away with the claim that she was unable to understand the words of a funny popular song about her father: this was Anna Comnena, who referred to a ditty sung by soldiers about the Emperor Alexius, of whose reign she wrote a historical account in perfect literary Greek. Even today there is a big difference in nearly every single lexical item between, for example, information printed in a hotel brochure and a corresponding reservation transmitted orally to the receptionist, in spite of the identical content of the two.

Of course, the degree of perfection in the imitation of fourth-century Attic varied considerably over the entire Roman-Byzantine era depending on the level of education which individual authors had reached. To the modern philologist, it is obvious that none of those authors wrote in the language which they spoke, for no work from this epoch is entirely without violations of the rules of Classic Attic. Still some writers, most notably in the second century AD, attained a remarkable virtuosity in their command of the language and the style of ancient Attic literary prose.

There has been plenty of arguing about the benefits and the disadvantages of this bilingualism. On the one hand it undoubtedly contained the risk of stagnation in literary life, which had lost the possibility of regeneration through contact with everyday reality, expressed in colloquial language. On the other hand the continuity of a tradition which gave educated people free access to the sources of their culture contributed to the impressive persistence of Greek religious and cultural identity in the bitter centuries under foreign, Turkish rule.

In this context, a third consequence of Atticist influence is also important; and that is the entirely Classicist nature of literature in the Imperial age. 'Classicist', in this case, means more than the fact that literary creation followed some ancient or traditional prototypes according to which literary taste was formed. It was in fact a very specific and clearly defined section of the literary tradition which became the measure of all linguistic-literary activity. For the first time in literary history, there was a canon of Classics, selected from a larger body of writings through aesthetic evaluation. The term 'Classic', however, was not yet common at the time.

Those authors whose works were recognised as Classics, primarily because of literary-aesthetic evaluation, possessed an authority that was not confined to language and literature, for they were seen as representatives of an epoch that was perceived as glorious and 'Classic' in all respects. This caused something like an irresistible urge to regard them as models also in a moral and intellectual sense. There are passages from Imperial literature which judge the documentary value of the report of a fact by an older writer according to whether the author counted as one of the ancient Classics or not. To an educated person in the Empire literary Classics had such a supreme status that the possibly much wider knowledge of a younger, possibly even a contemporary author with many more sources of information at his command, did not count for anything in comparison. Neither, occasionally, did evidence which was before one's very eyes.

In the work of the geographer Strabo, who wrote in the Augustan-Tiberian era, there are two references to a piece of information concerning events in central Asia, as reported by the Greek historian Apollodorus from the Greek city of Artemita. At the time this city was in the Parthian Empire, being situated near today's border between Iraq and Iran. Naturally this author was especially well informed on matters concerning Iranian and Indian history. In one instance Strabo questions the accuracy of a passage in Apollodorus' book about India with the perfunctory remark that the Greek – to wit, one who wrote around 100 BC – was contradicting the recognised standard works on India: that is the accounts of Alexander's campaigns, and the report by the envoy Megasthenes from around 300 BC. In his book about central Asia, however, Strabo quotes the same account uncritically: the absence of doubt in this case can be put down to the lack of standard works about that part of the world in older Greek literature.

Literary-linguistic Atticism was only one branch – if undoubtedly the most important and consequential – of Classicism, as formed and generally accepted in the Empire after the bad historical experiences of the Late Hellenistic epoch. A comparable tendency showed in sculpture, and in some cases also architecture, where the Augustans would occasionally imitate models from the fifth and fourth centuries BC. The independent municipal administrations of Greek cities also went back to 'Classic' traditions: for instance, by using long-dead local dialects in the writing of official decrees, as in the remote past. But the earliest manifestations of Classicism were to be felt in philosophy.

Philosophy

During the three centuries of the Hellenistic age philosophy developed in different schools, most of which tried to establish a complete and systematic doctrine incorporating most, if not all, branches of scholarship and forming the basis for a system of ethics which was practicable and scientifically well-founded at the same time. Philosophical investigation and further development of doctrine took place in the continuous debate among the schools. However, some of them – including for two centuries also the school of Plato – explicitly renounced the aim of establishing a comprehensive doctrine. Moreover, with regard to its ethical purpose, they saw philosophy in the Socratic tradition, as a lifelong, methodical questioning and testing of one's own opinions as well as of those of others. But there was general agreement as to the goal of philosophy, namely, to teach the art of living properly, and in harmony with nature. This is why the community established by a school was always understood as one that bound people's whole lives together.

In the first decades of the first century BC the Platonic Academy returned to dogmatic philosophy, and thus to the aims of those who had first succeeded the school's founder. But their new Academian dogmatics was not constructed from elements of pure Platonic philosophy exclusively, but also included – as did some recent Stoic writing – complete didactic pieces from the traditions of other schools, especially of the Peripatetics, the Aristotelian school, and of the Stoics. This philosophical syncretism was the first hint of a method which is characteristic of all kinds of Classicism: that is the selection of particular elements from a tradition which is no longer continued naturally and independently, but eclectically and derivatively.

More important for philosophical Classicism were the contemporary beginnings of efforts at collecting, editing, and commenting on the writings of the school founders, not only out of respect for the dead or out of philological interest but as a means of philosophical investigation. The underlying idea must have been the assumption that all the important philosophical questions had already been answered in the writings of the school founders, and the only remaining task was to find and understand those answers by a close reading of their books. To a growing extent philosophy came to be understood as the gathering of information, of truths which had already been put down in writing, and not as individual questioning and investigation guided by the ideas of the founder of a school.

Around 70 BC such was the motivation for the first edition of Aristotle's lectures, which were never intended for publication but which have survived until the present day, while those books which Aristotle did publish for a large readership during his lifetime were lost. The tradition of commentaries on Aristotle began a little later and, for all we know, the early edition of Plato's complete works which introduced the still common division into parts composed of four dialogues each belongs to the same period. That edition was a result of philosophical interest: in contrast, Aristophanes of Byzantium, the great philologist of the period around 200 BC who placed Plato among the great prose writers of Greek literature and hence alongside Attic orators, had preferred a slightly different order in his edition of Plato's works.

Lastly, that return of school philosophy to the 'ancients' which preceded the rise of Atticism by one generation, but which was entirely congenial to it, may be perceived in the rising interest in so-called doxography, the discipline which dealt with the history of doctrines. It remained alive throughout the Imperial age and is particularly well documented for the reign of Augustus.

The Empire had an educational system which was dominated by Classicism from its very beginnings and thus was not likely to encourage originality, spontaneity, or creativity. The literature of the Empire is therefore not very rich in works of freshness, originality, and immediacy. On the other hand a literary tradition with such fixed parameters would discipline and refine the tastes of authors and readers to an extent which we can hardly imagine. It created the conditions for an ever-tighter network of allusions and references linking literary works with one another. In such a manner, the communicative potential which literature possesses is multiplied for those who share the tradition.

Certainly, any all-powerful Classicist tradition does condemn generations of creative writers to thinking that they are, after all, no more than epigonal. But at the same time it sharpens the awareness of the task of conserving a rich heritage respectfully and responsibly, and of keeping it accessible. Without those periods in which this task was taken seriously there would have been a far greater loss of cultural assets and a far lesser chance of moral continuity during the course of history. It is not only historical catastrophes which destroy cultural assets and put an end to educational traditions. In times of great intellectual activity, great wealth, and self-avowed progressiveness, the leading individuals of a society may often unintentionally destroy that of which posterity may at some stage be badly in need. By looking back again and again to nothing but the past, the educational tradition of the Empire was able to conserve a rich heritage from the most creative periods of Graeco-Roman culture so well that this heritage remained alive and accessible in the Middle Ages and in the Modern age.

2

THE JULIO-CLAUDIAN ERA

1 GENERAL REMARKS

The change of government after the death of Augustus in 14 AD was accompanied by some rather sinister events, as reported a century later by Tacitus. In the first part of his *Annals*, Tacitus gives a very detailed account of happenings which could not have failed to make a deep impression on the court and the Senators. But with a view to the vast Empire as a whole, the beginning of Tiberius' reign appears as a smooth transition. During the almost fifty years under Augustus, the *orbis Romanus* had become accustomed to the reign of a monarch at the head of a strong army, and of an efficient administration. Hence the failure of the new Emperor's initial attempt to change the governmental practice of his predecessor and father-in-law, for whom he had very little liking. The Senators mistrusted Tiberius' efforts to enlarge the scope of the Senate's legislative powers; that shift of emphasis towards the traditional Republican features of the political order merely earned the new monarch the reputation of a sly hypocrite.

Well intentioned as they might have been, any token gestures of self-restraint on the part of the Emperor were doomed to be regarded as insincere in view of the Imperial power actually accumulated by Augustus, a power which had come to be seen as vital to the preservation of peace and order in a huge Empire. The members of the highest class, many among whom qualified for the Imperial succession according to contemporary law, were condemned either to the role of undignified yes-men, or to an oppositional stance which was as dangerous as it was fruitless. The only way in which the Senate could demonstrate its dislike of a monarch to the public in a lasting manner was after his death, by denying him inclusion among the number of officially recognised gods about which it had to decide. A monarchic-dynastic order left no space for *libertas*, the free competition of those made eligible by birth and ability for the position at the head of the state. That concept of political life, however, was deeply rooted in the tradition of the highest social class; and this is why denunciations and trials for high treason within the Senate could be observed during the entire first century of the Empire. The first spate of such events came already during the second half of Tiberius' reign.

The subsequent fates of the Julio-Claudian dynasty make for a highly bizarre story, illustrating the disintegration of one of the last remaining families of Rome's high nobility as a consequence of almost unlimited power. Tiberius' successor Gaius, known as Caligula, was killed after a short reign: long enough, however, to show the pathological features of his mind beyond any doubt. Gaius' murderers were members of the Praetorians, the Imperial guard, the only troops stationed in Italy. They put Gaius' uncle Claudius on the throne, a succession which was subsequently rubber-stamped by the powerless Senate.

Claudius was a wise and well-educated man, well meaning but inept, and entirely without charisma. He introduced some fairly sensible governmental measures, but his skills were utterly inadequate when it came to coping with the intrigues at court, and he was finally murdered by his own wife. By poisoning her husband, she cleared the path to the throne for her son Nero, a highly talented and cultured young man who took the hearts of the people by storm, especially in the Greek half of the Empire. Nero's reign had a promising beginning, but soon afterwards he rid himself of his counsellors, who had become too troublesome; he ruthlessly eliminated very close relatives who annoyed him; he gratified his passion for public building and official splendour with blatant disregard for state finances; and he led an eccentric life without any self-restraint. The insurrection of an army commander put an end to Nero's reign and drove him to suicide. For a year afterwards, four claimants to the throne waged war on one another, until the general with the most disciplined troops emerged victorious.

It is an astonishing fact that, all told, public order and administrative continuity in the Empire were not disrupted during the five decades when all these events took place, in spite of the deplorable image presented by the successive holders of supreme power. Even during the worst days of Nero's reign, the Roman army achieved some glorious victories against the Parthians on the eastern border, and the other frontiers of the Empire remained secure under the protection of loyal troops. The succession was not seriously disputed until after the death of Nero, who did not leave a legitimate heir. In East and West alike, people had grown accustomed to the monarchic order, loyally supported by the educated and wealthy bourgeois class which was the cornerstone of society. From their ranks, holders of higher offices in the army as well as in Imperial and municipal administration were recruited, and their loyalty was not affected even when a monarch proved to be unworthy. On the whole, it was only the members of the Senatorial class who felt morally obliged to oppose the Emperor, being confronted with him in person in Rome, and not having any power of their own to set against the fullness of his authority.

2 RHETORIC

Latin rhetoric

The literary life of this period provides an accurate reflection of the circumstances described above. This will be shown in detail in the following sections, beginning with an outline of contemporary rhetoric.

The extant *Controversiae* and *Suasoriae* by Seneca the Elder provide us with priceless evidence of rhetorical instruction as practised at the time. Their author came from the Roman civic colony of Cordoba in Spain. He lived between about 50 BC and 40 AD and spent some years of his working life in Rome as an advocate, civil servant, and teacher of rhetoric. His works are a collection of so-called declamations, that is speeches written as exemplary exercises for fictitious legal cases, or for situations either from a historical or a mythical past. According to Seneca himself, those speeches were written down from memory in his old age, and copiously annotated: the original sources were the classes of famous teachers of oratory in which he had participated.

Beside instruction in systematic rhetorical theory chapter by chapter, the writing and the delivery of exemplary speeches was an obvious method in the teaching of rhetoric, as documented from the fifth century BC onwards. The importance attached to scholarly eloquence grew after the death of great political oratory, brought about by the decline of forensic activity concerning external affairs in the Greek *polis*. The exemplary speech came to be recognised as a literary achievement in its own right, a fact which can be seen in a choice of topics which moved farther and farther away from reality.

On account of this, rhetorical instruction was sometimes criticised even at an early stage; for centuries, however, it was generally esteemed to be an adequate preparation for every kind of public function, and lectures by well-known teachers of rhetoric found large audiences. Seneca not only lets those famous people speak, but also characterises their appearance and their effect on the public. He seems to be well aware of the difference between a classroom situation and speeches in real life, such as pleas in a court of law. In one of the *Suasoriae* the banished Cicero considers burning his speeches against Antony, and imploring the mercy of the Triumvirate (*Suas.* 6): Seneca is at pains to make the reader aware of the fictitious nature of such a rhetorical exercise by the juxtaposition of a number of excerpts from historical accounts of Cicero's end.

Among the exemplary speeches of a legal kind (*Contr.* 2, 2, 8ff.), there is one ascribed to the poet Ovid; a text which illustrates very well the extent to which poetic narrative was influenced by the art of argumentation learned in rhetorical schools.

At that time literature, including poetry, in the East as well as in the West had long been rhetoricised through a transfer of those argumentative, linguistic-rhythmical, and phonetic devices which had been invented for the purpose of persuasion in lawcourts to literary texts in general. Thus the theory of eloquence along with its categories and terminology which had been progressively refined between the fifth and first centuries BC provided the most important tools of all literary criticism. Rhetorical training not only procured access to public life: it was also the gateway to acceptance among a group whose common property was a predominantly formal education, measured mainly by the ability to appreciate and to produce elaborate speech.

It is true that philology, known as grammar in Classical terminology, had produced its own methods for the evaluation and the interpretation of poetry. In educational practice, however, the rhetorical approach was dominant, even for the understanding of poetry. People were busily searching for passages of particular rhetorical merit in the works of Homer or Virgil, the most prominent authors in Classical schools; and in the case of Virgil, this was not altogether inappropriate, for his poetry as well as that of Ovid already belonged fully to that tradition of rhetorical education which was essential for the appreciation of the poet's art (see my remarks on Lucan, p. 113).

Apart from Livy, Seneca the Elder gives us the earliest testimony of the Classic status of Cicero's language (*Contr.* 1 praef. 6f.; Livy in Quintil. inst. 2, 5, 20). Seneca clearly perceived the disappearance of opportunities for great political eloquence, a development caused by the vanishing of the Republican order and the disintegration of its institutions. Consequently he modified the image which Cicero (*De orat.* 1, 80–95) had given of the significance and the purpose of rhetorical instruction (*Contr.* 3, praef. 1–7). Unfortunately the historical work which Seneca is said to have written (Suet. *Tib.* 73, 2) was lost. It featured the first known comparison of the phases in a nation's history with the different ages of man (in *Lact.* inst. div. 7, 15), a popular parallel until the present day.

Another work that illustrates the nature of rhetorical education in the same period is the collection of *exempla* by a certain Valerius Maximus, otherwise unknown to us. This work, dedicated to the Emperor Tiberius, was written between 27 and 33 AD. It consists of nine books or papyrus scrolls containing short narratives, often ending in a memorable aphorism, illustrating topics such as filial love, steadfastness, faithfulness in matrimony, women's pleas in court, greed, recklessness, or bizarre deaths. For his rich collection of anecdotes and apophthegmata, Valerius used all kinds of sources, mostly historiographical; but he certainly also borrowed from earlier anthologies of a similar sort. The purpose was to provide material for authors who wanted to add attractive embellishments to a speech, or to some other work with a claim to literary merit.

To the modern reader, Valerius' collection provides a wealth of historical detail which is otherwise not documented. But it is frequently impossible to track down the primary source of the information, and thus to form an adequate assessment of its validity. However, there is another aspect which is far more interesting, and which I will discuss in the following.

Aristotle had already pointed out that a successful orator had to have a good understanding of psychology, paying particular heed to the moral reactions of his audience. In the didactic programme of Isocrates the perfection of ways and means of reaching a consensus about things generally held to be just and true by all men formed an important part of the education of a good citizen and statesman. This tradition clearly shows that instruction in what could be called formalised popular ethics formed an integral part of rhetorical training, contrary to the polemical accusations brought against rhetoric in Plato's *Gorgias*. Cato the Elder's definition of the orator, *vir bonus dicendi peritus* ('a good man who knows how to speak'), is certainly in keeping with Greek tradition, like so many other statements by this representative of ancient Rome.

The Romans were originally an agricultural nation, and for centuries their thinking was characterised by a rural mistrust of anything fabricated, any intellectual construction, anything which had not grown organically and which was not backed up by tradition. Roman law is the best example of this, with its pervading deep aversion to fixed legal codes, and its preference for traditional rules and terms, however obsolete, or for the use of legal precedents as the means of solving a case. Hence the most important source of guidance in Roman society was the *exemplum* – the exemplary action of an ancestor, of a predecessor in office, or of any other model character from the past. For hundreds of years, such *exempla* had shaped the historical consciousness of the Romans. As Greek influences became ever more powerful in all aspects of Roman social life, and as thoughtful Romans such as Cicero asked how all the new things from the East could be adequately incorporated into Roman civilisation, his contemporary Cornelius Nepos wrote a major work containing literary portraits of great Greeks and Romans. Those parts of it which we know consist of character sketches rather than biographies, written with the intention of showing how Themistocles or Epaminondas belonged to the same line as the exemplary personalities of the Roman tradition.

The importance of the example in Roman thought has to be borne in mind by anyone who studies the collection by Valerius Maximus: such an approach makes the text yield an astonishingly deep insight into the Roman mentality, however trivial the content of individual pericopes may have appeared at first sight.

Greek rhetoric

Greek rhetoric of the period is known to us almost exclusively through intermediate sources, not from the original works. We hear of two schools which were at odds with one another, the Apollodoreans and the Theodoreans. Apollodorus of Pergamum was the teacher of Augustus, and his rhetorical textbook was translated into Latin by C. Valgius Rufus, a man of Consular rank. Theodorus of Gadara in Syria was the teacher of Tiberius. Both schools seem to have existed throughout the first century AD, but the scanty evidence from a much later period (Spengel, *Rhet. Graec.* I, 2nd edn, 352ff.) gives us no clue as to what the points of contention between them were. Neither do we have a clear image of any of the other teachers of rhetoric during this period of whose existence we know (Dio *Pr. or.* 18, 12). All we can be sure of is that they would all have subscribed to the Atticist programme which came to prevail during the reign of Augustus, and that they consequently agreed with the canonisation of Classic-Attic prose.

This also applies to the especially versatile rhetor Aelius Theon of Alexandria. When exactly he lived is not clear; the name Aelius, which indicates that he was a Roman citizen, became fairly common in the East during the reign of Hadrian, but the promotion of a Consul named Sex. Aelius Catus in 4 AD proves that there had been representatives of the *gens Aelia* much earlier on, and thus Theon may have inherited rather than acquired Roman citizenship. Besides, several passages in the major textbook which Quintilian wrote at the turn of the first and second centuries AD indicate that Theon's work had already been published by then.

We know of several commentaries which Theon wrote on Attic orators through a Byzantine encyclopaedia called *Suda*, which contains long biographical essays compiled from older grammatical writings. It also mentions essays on linguistic theory and a *technē rhetorikē*, a rhetorical manual giving a systematic account of the orator's work, the structure of speeches, the levels of style, the forms of argumentation, and more. A work by Theon which is extant, if only in a mutilated version, is entitled *Progymnasmata*. This is a systematic survey of different major and minor genres of literary prose, such as sententia, encomium (eulogy), *chriē* (treatise), and fable. These are defined, characterised according to their special demands on choice of expression and syntax, and documented by examples from Classic-Attic prose literature as well as from poetic texts. Although all similar ones we know of date from later periods between the second and the fifth centuries AD, Theon tells us that even in his own time his work was not a new type of textbook but that he had indeed introduced some new criteria in his definitions.

His polemical remarks about the 'Asians' and his choice of model authors prove that Theon was a staunch Atticist. Still, it is worth noting that he, like Cicero, demands that an orator should also receive a philosophical education. It is true that at the time rhetoric, as part of logic or dialectics, was part of the systematic curriculum in most philosophical schools, particularly the Peripatos and the Stoa. But Theon seems to have been entirely unaffected by their doctrines. By philosophical education, he can thus only mean acquiring the art of proper living, the ideological-moral instruction which was regarded as the essential task of philosophy in those days. However, it must be said that the competition between philosophy and rhetoric for the monopoly or at least the priority in the education of the young, first in evidence in the writings of Plato and Isocrates, flared up again and again in spite of many attempted compromises. I will come back to this issue in a later section.

There is one work from the first half of the first century AD which must be classed as rhetorical writing, even if it goes far beyond the narrow limits of rhetorical instruction. This is the treatise *Of the Sublime*, written by an unknown author, one of the best and most original pieces of Classical literary criticism. In the absence of any biographical information, only the content of the work allows us to date it. It is addressed to someone called Postumius Terentianus, probably a high-ranking Roman; but that, again, is merely surmise.

Even early rhetorical theory had already been concerned with the question of stylistic levels, and a distinction between three different styles had come to be generally accepted. These were the plain style, suitable for reports and pleas in lawcourts; the intermediate style, in which plain and more elaborate passages alternate, suitable for convincing an audience of the speaker's opinion by occasionally evoking delight in formal beauty; and finally the sublime, grand style, suitable for ceremonial addresses in praise of a god or ancestors, showing the full range of the speaker's rhetorical skills.

One target of the Atticist movement was the bombast and extravagance of Hellenistic eloquence; and quite a few of the early theorists of Atticism seem to have set up Lysias, by far the plainest orator in ancient Athens, as a stylistic example. However, this was a rather blinkered view, and Cicero already felt obliged to point out that good Attic style could not be equated with total simplicity of diction as the Attic Classics such as Demosthenes had been equally at home with all three stylistic levels.

There were, of course, fairly precise definitions of the characteristics of the sublime style as shown, for instance, in Cicero's summaries of Greek theory. Those definitions had to be of a formal nature, referring to the use of certain words, rhetorical figures, and syntactic structures. The author we are concerned with at present takes part in the debate on the sublime by taking a stand against the aforementioned Caecilius (see p. 55). Caecilius' work on the same subject is no longer extant.

Entirely in the tradition of rhetorical theory is our anonymous author's attempt to provide a new definition of the sublime style, inevitably according to formal features. In this context, he mentions figures such as the asyndeton (the unconnected succession of identical grammatical units); the rhetorical question, or the hyperbaton (a deviation from the normal word order); and he also includes the criteria for the choice of vocabulary. There are likewise definitions of the psychological effect of sublime diction, as, for example, the vivid visualisation of objects and actions described.

Especially original, however, is the one chapter (cap. 9) which follows the inventory of the features of sublime diction. Here the author explains that the first and most important condition for the use of the sublime style is the ability to think great thoughts, rather than the mastery of stylistic devices. To illustrate this, he gives an example from the beginning of the Book of Genesis: 'God said, let there be light; and there was light'. The author's comment is that the 'giver of Jewish law' has understood divine power and found an adequate expression for it. We know for sure that Caecilius was a Jew; and, in view of the reference to the Old Testament, this may well be true of our anonymous author too. The Old Testament had long been translated into Greek, but at that time even those men of letters in the Greek world who otherwise showed an interest in the Jews and their way of life tended to ignore that text.

As for the rest of the examples from poetry and prose which illustrate the theoretical argument in the treatise *Of the Sublime*, they indicate that the author respects the Classicist or Atticist canon, an impression borne out by plenty of disparaging remarks about Hellenistic writers. It is from this source that we know the Greek text of that poem by Sappho which the poet Catullus reproduced in Latin. However, our author shows himself uninhibited by the Classicist prejudices of his period. Contrary to the demand for the imitation of great examples – something which all Classicising traditions must encourage – he gives the express warning that imitation is no guarantee for success in attempts at sublime diction. As I have said before, he regards the individual capacity for sublime thought and emotion as the true source of the sublime style.

Homer is, of course, especially prominent among the examples chosen. In discussing quotes from Homer's poetry, the author shows himself both as a scholar and as a man of unfailing sensibility in his assessment of the appropriateness of linguistic expression with regard to narrative content, or to the qualities and emotions of the characters described. The author is quite obviously an exponent of the long tradition of meticulous interpretations of Homer's works. His choice of subject explains why he should pay particular attention to the *Iliad*: to him, the *Odyssey* is a late work that shows Homer's declining poetic powers which bring him down to the level of a common teller of tales. This conclusion may not be altogether justified, for there are other qualities of the *Odyssey* which it does not take into account; however, nobody else in the Classical age has so clearly identified the tragic-dramatic character of the story in the *Iliad*.

The treatise *Of the Sublime* has an appendix, styled as a record (put down on the following day) of a conversation between the author and a philosopher. This discussion features a conundrum which had appeared already in the works of Seneca the Elder, and reoccurred in the writings of Quintilian and Tacitus: Whence the decline of eloquence? The author extends the question to literature in general; his counterpart provides the same answer which we find later in Tacitus: that it is the loss of political liberty in the monarchic state which leaves but few occasions for public eloquence and which inhibits all literary activity. The author, on the other hand, maintains that it is the struggle for material wealth as the only means to achieve status and power, which saps all the energies of human beings and gives rise to no other than base, morally reprehensible ideas which cannot serve as the foundation for great literature. Even if men were generally inclined to put the past above the present, he would agree with Plato in saying that his contemporaries were more concerned with the mortal part of their beings than with the immortal part.

This appendix clearly shows how closely related questions of literary criticism and of morality were in the eyes of people at that time, and how easily the rhetor could assume the role of philosopher. This is all the more remarkable because there is virtually no indication of any contact on the part of the author with the literary theories of particular philosophical schools, such as the Stoa or the Peripatos. A completely different case is that of another, equally important work of literary theory, which some philologists have dated very close to the treatise *Of the Sublime*, but which rather seems to belong to the Late Hellenistic period. This is the treatise *Of Style* by an otherwise unknown Demetrius, who gives us a survey of Peripatetic stylistic doctrine (i.e. that of the school of Aristotle). This treatise not only features many examples, but also refers to other works on literary theory in its description of syntactic structures, rhetorical figures, and stylistic qualities as parts of elaborate speech. In the process it defines the stylistic features which are specific to individual literary genres.

Through a French translation made by Boileau in 1647, the treatise *Of the Sublime* had a great impact on discussions about literary theory in the eighteenth century, above all in France and England. There is no evidence of a similarly wide reception in the Classical age. However, this work must certainly be ranked alongside Aristotle's *Poetics* and Horace's *Ars poetica* as one of the best and most original products of Classical literary theory.

3 PHILOSOPHY

General remarks

I have already talked about the new orientation in philosophical thought during the first century BC. Naturally, this is most evident in the teachings of the major schools, and less so in texts which document a broader impact of philosophy outside the narrow confines of the systematic doctrine of one of those great schools.

The example set by Socrates had established a basic principle recognised in all the different philosophical traditions: that philosophy had to be first and foremost *ars vitae*, the art of living. But at first it was only the school of Epicurus and the Stoa, both of which had sprung up during the Early Hellenistic era, that had come to the conclusion that the intellectual education which should lead to philosophical living had to consist of the communication of a secure, systematic fundamental knowledge of the world, and of human life. In contrast to this, the school of Plato had for a long time put its emphasis on individual searching and questioning, while in the Peripatos, the school of Aristotle, the main activity was the scientific investigation, divided into a large number of disciplines, of all aspects of the world and of human life.

During the first century BC philosophy had come to be dominated by a general movement towards systematisation and dogmatisation. This had several consequences and side-effects. To begin with there was the founding of a new major school beside the four existing ones. The Skeptics took up the tradition of several forerunners from the period around 300 BC as well as the Socratic one of the art of ignorance, seeing their task in challenging any kind of rigid, dogmatic doctrine with the weapons of logic and dialectics. In this way, they claimed, they were able to teach people how to be independent and thus to enable them to lead a philosophical life.

For Aristotelians and Platonics, the turn towards dogmatism meant a return to the works of the school founders as the only possible source of authentic elements of fundamental dogma in the school tradition. Hence the first complete edition of Aristotle's didactic works around 70 BC; prior to this, there had only been books for a broader public with a literary interest. The first century BC also saw the publication of that edition of Plato's works which has remained the standard one until today, in spite of another edition published in the first century AD by a certain Thrasyllus, court physician to the Emperor Tiberius. A parallel development was a spate of commentaries on Plato and Aristotle which continued throughout the remaining centuries of the Classical age.

Studying the school founders' works was to provide the basis for valid dogma in the tradition of the respective schools. As evidence of the result of such efforts, we have outlines or chapter headings of two systematic surveys of Academic ethics; one written by the Platonic Philo of Larissa, one of Cicero's teachers of philosophy, and the other by the Alexandrian Eudorus, who lived between about 35 BC and 35 AD.

Syncretism

The conclusion drawn from the reassessment of the works of Plato and Aristotle was that there were more areas of agreement than differences of opinion in the teachings of those two. This was undoubtedly true with regard to the assumption of a dichotomy between the spiritual and the material which both had proclaimed as vital to an understanding of the world, while Epicurus and Zeno had subscribed to a monistic-materialistic view. It also turned out that Aristotelian logic could serve to interpret some of the difficult and frequently obscure statements by Plato on logical and epistemological problems, and even to illuminate certain aspects of his central doctrine, the so-called theory of ideas. Although the Academy and the Peripatos survived for a long time as separate schools, and some of their exponents would still draw attention to the differences between them, the notion that there was a unity between Platonic and Aristotelian philosophy came to prevail at last.

The amalgamation of the doctrines of individual schools went even farther. During the Hellenistic era heated debate between philosophical schools had been the main reason for the elaboration of very sophisticated doctrines. A particular case in point was the argument between the dogmatically orientated Stoa and the basically anti-dogmatic Academy before the first century BC. This explains why the first Academic who led his school back towards a comprehensive systematic doctrine – Antiochus of Ascalon, one of Cicero's contemporaries – would exploit the Stoa's insights and terminological distinctions in psychology and ethics, and incorporate them into the dogmatics of the Academy.

Shortly before that, a similar development had occurred within the Stoa. The Stoics were materialists, to whom all processes of thought and consciousness were based on material movements. What the Stoics referred to here, however, was an extremely fine kind of matter which had to be conceived of as existing everywhere within coarser substance, endowing it with form, life, or consciousness, according to its degree of concentration. The function of this fine substance, the *pneuma*, was not too different from that of the immaterial spirit in Platonic-Aristotelian ontology; and there was one famous and learned Stoic in the first century BC, Posidonius of Apamaea in Syria, who was not at all loath to admit the existence of this parallel between the doctrine of his school and that of the Platonic-Aristotelian ones. He also made no bones about other points of agreement, and least of all about his admiration for the great philosophers of the

Classic period, especially for Aristotle, whom he regarded as a kindred spirit mainly because of his scientific interests.

Thus, the tendency to synthesise individual doctrines of different origins in a dogmatic system caught on among Academics, Peripatetics, and Stoics alike. Besides, they all began to show an interest in the remnants of the Pythagorean tradition, which had survived during the entire Hellenistic age.

Pythagorean traditions

Until the fourth century BC the Pythagoreans had formed secret societies in the Greek cities of southern Italy, in all cases presumably with the intention of supporting an aristocratic regime. Their basic doctrines combined highly archaic taboos with the most diverse speculative elements. Plato had used two notions from the Pythagorean tradition in the construction of his own doctrine: first, the notion of the transmigration of souls, based on the concept of an immortal, immaterial human soul which enters successive bodies to receive rewards or punishment for its actions in previous lives on earth; and second, the conviction that fixed numerical relations are the basis of all being, determining the structure of the visible and the invisible world, and the processes of life and of consciousness. A consequence of this axiom was the demand that geometry, arithmetic, and musical theory should be the foundation of all philosophy, including also ethics.

While Plato's first successors placed particular emphasis on such Pythagorean notions, their importance declined greatly during the non-dogmatic phase of the Academy. However, they experienced a kind of resurrection in the course of a general return to Academic dogmatics in the first century BC.

The intellectual climate of Early and Middle Hellenism was marked by a fundamental rationalism, one of whose effects was the blossoming of the exact and empirical sciences. Philosophers were bound to caution in speculations about transcendental matters, about the Absolute which is beyond all discursive thought, and which is yet the prime cause of all. During this period the Pythagorean tradition as such seems to have survived largely within sectarian conventicles of ill repute, beyond the pale of professional philosophy. We have a number of Pythagorean treatises, some of them written in the Hellenistic age, on topics ranging from ethical questions concerning state and family to cosmology. Among the issues raised were the social position of women as well as the sacred status of monarchs, the latter subject being very topical at that time. All of the authors used pseudonyms, taking the names of male or female disciples of Pythagoras, the philosopher from the sixth century BC who had long been a legendary figure. Their treatises are even written in an artificial dialect, erroneously assumed to have been the language of southern Italy and Sicily in Pythagoras' lifetime.

Hellenistic school philosophy completely ignored these writings; where their authors touch on philosophical issues, there is a mere regurgitation of various Peripatetic tenets, without any inner coherence. Presumably the reason for this was that it had been disciples of Aristotle who had studied the beginnings of Pythagorean thought because of their interest in the history of philosophy. Another plausible explanation would be the hope of Pythagorean circles to move closer to the status of respectable school philosophy by claiming well-known doctrines as pieces of ancient Pythagorean wisdom.

The resurrection of the Pythagorean tradition is a sign of an increasing interest in transcendental matters, an interest in things which are inaccessible to the senses, but which can give people faith in life after physical death, and in compensation for injustices they have inevitably suffered. At that time, the Greek word *sōtēriā*, originally signifying the preservation of the physical integrity of human beings, came to mean 'immortality' in philosophical and religious usage, as referring to an immaterial core of human life.

From the aforementioned facts, it should be evident why Platonism, with its outstanding interest in the transcendental and in the destiny of men's souls, should have dominated the course of philosophical thought during the entire Imperial age. Plato's school incorporated Stoic ideas into its ethics and Peripatetic notions into its logic and epistemology; this led to a growing belief in the unity of all serious philosophy. However, notwithstanding the survival of their school, the Epicureans remained excluded.

Epicureans

The school of Epicurus had preserved the founder's doctrine in a much purer form than other philosophical schools had done. Epicurus' thought, however, was based on axioms which could not be accommodated by the unified philosophy of the Imperial age as described above.

According to Epicurean doctrine the world, including all processes of perception and thought, is constituted by the accidental accumulation and separation of atoms in the void. Cosmic-natural processes follow no laws which could serve as models for human behaviour. The only messages from nature which man receives are his own feelings of pleasure and displeasure, with him being at liberty to act accordingly, or – to his own detriment – against nature's commands. In social relationships, too, people are to follow the course which promises increased pleasure; this pleasure, however, can be expected to grow as individuals assume social responsibilities, and thus avoid conflict.

In contrast to those views, the other philosophies based their potential of faith needed for a good and happy life on insight into the irreversible and benevolent order of nature. It did not matter whether this order became palpable in sensual experience, as the Stoics believed, or if one had to penetrate to a higher level of existence through intellectual effort, as the Platonics thought. In any case, the world order was regarded as reasonable, and thus as accessible to human cognition.

The Stoics had even developed a doctrine concerning the irrefutable, optimal determination of all events, the *heimarmenē* or fate, which was not to be influenced by human actions. Man's only hope was to comprehend it as a rational being, and to incorporate it into his own will. Wise men would do so and bear it freely and without coercion, whereas fools would be compelled by fate against their will. Neither wise men nor fools were responsible for the exterior shape of events, but merely for the state of their consciousness. On the basis of this notion which was to lead to unlimited trust in the order of the universe, the Stoics were also able to accommodate as part of their doctrine mathematical astrology, which had sprung up in the second century BC. Astrology confirmed their concept of a close and meaningful relationship existing between all parts of the universe.

The doctrine of *heimarmenē* or *pronoia* (i.e. providence) could very well be combined with the concept of a supreme God who orders and directs the world even in its remotest corners, through a multitude of lesser divine beings. The idea of the one universal God was part of Platonic-Aristotelian tradition from its very beginnings; however, that God was not thought of as the sovereign ruler of the world, like the divine creator of the Bible. On the contrary, he remained bound by the order of nature which he himself had established, and which he guaranteed. The notion of subordinate divine beings could be related to the many gods of popular religion. Whether they followed the Peripatos, the Academy, or the Stoa, all those who were educated in philosophy thus knew that they were one in their belief in a supreme universal God, and the belief in providence inherent in a meaningful universal order. They were likewise able to justify their participation in the many different forms of worship in their environment by reference to their philosophical understanding of the true nature of the gods who were thus revered. Participating in the worship of the community was the most important condition for active political involvement; thus such a philosophical position did nothing to prevent educated people from becoming active in Imperial, regional, or municipal administration.

All this did not apply to the Epicurean. To him, the gods were beings who lived in a blissful state in another world. Taking care of this world and the welfare of men would have meant an insufferable detraction from their perfection. For an Epicurean, piety was the unceasing attempt at imitating the serenity and the bliss of the gods in one's own life by avoiding all displeasure. All other philosophers saw the exemplary nature of divine existence in the intellectual or the practical-charitable activity of the gods. To them, philosophical involvement in the community could be a legitimate task for the philosopher, while the consequence of the Epicurean ideal of mental peace as the goal of moral endeavour was to discourage political action and to recommend the 'life in hiding'.

During the chaotic dying years of the Republic Epicurean thought had become very attractive to many members of the Roman upper classes. The didactic poem by the Roman Lucretius is the most vivid representation of the Epicurean doctrine of salvation from the period. A philosophy which encouraged trust in a meaningful and beneficial universal order, and which called on people to take a share in the effort to realise such an order on earth, was much better suited to the Imperial age with its growing stability. In spite of that, the tradition of the Epicurean school survived for two more centuries, even if the Epicurean became a less and less respectable figure. He was regarded as a blasphemous denier of divine existence; as a parasite unwilling to make a contribution to the welfare of the community; and worst of all, as a hedonist who lived for nothing else than for his sensual gratification. This last accusation was particularly unjust, for Epicurus had taught that the highest goal was a state of permanent intellectual and mental pleasure, and according to him, nothing could jeopardise this more than unrestrained physical desire. In the last instance the Epicureans recognised only individual perfection and not communal welfare as the aim of moral endeavour; this, however, did not contradict the ethics of the other philosophical schools, even if those tended to put a greater emphasis on the fulfilment of social obligations as a condition for individual perfection.

Doxography

The incipient unification of philosophy and the growing interest in the writings of the school founders gave rise to an entire new philosophical discipline – doxography, the study of philosophical doctrines. The habit of starting the discussion of a problem with a comprehensive survey of existing opinions was nothing novel: Aristotle himself had always been at pains to do so before setting out his own reflections. Until the present day this procedure forms a vital part of the presentation of the results of philosophical and scientific research. Doxography, on the other hand, was limited to giving accurate accounts of older doctrines as reference material which could be drawn on by anyone who was undertaking the construction of a new doctrine of his own. There is one example from the Augustan age in a Late Classical anthology – the survey of Peripatetic ethics from a major doxographical work by the Stoic Arius Didymus of Alexandria. This survey illustrates the development of Peripatetic doctrine in post-

Aristotelian times; most other doxographical writings, however, date from a later period.

Part of doxography in a wider sense was a motif which dates back to the fourth century BC, but which acquired a new topicality in the period discussed here. Philosophy was to provide an insight into the natural order, and thus to enable people consciously to do right in accordance with nature. Aristotle had already claimed that primitive man had been able to do so, but that mankind had lost this ability through catastrophes, or through unnatural social constraints. However, this primeval knowledge which Greek philosophy tried to regain was thought to have been preserved in the time-honoured wisdom of exotic peoples such as those traditions kept alive by the Egyptian priests or the Indian Brahmins.

This popular notion of a 'Barbarian philosophy' encouraged interest in the exotic world with which the Roman Empire was connected by a multitude of trade links. On the other hand the idea favoured the habit of giving credibility to new doctrines by passing them off as pieces of ancient Egyptian or Chaldaean wisdom. This motif could be found even in school philosophy: it played an important part in the philosophical debate about Judaism and Christianity, as well as in the spreading of semi-philosophical doctrines of salvation, which abounded in the High and the Late Empire.

School philosophy

There are very few original texts which provide evidence of philosophical instruction and research in schools in the first century AD. As to the doctrines of individual school philosophers most of what we know is from references and excerpts in later philosophical writings.

As before, Athens was the most prominent location for traditional school philosophy; however, an interesting development during the period discussed here was the increasing importance of Alexandria. During the Hellenistic era Alexandria had been unrivalled as a centre of scientific research: nevertheless, it had contributed little to the development of philosophy. The aforementioned Stoic Arius Didymus worked in Alexandria, and likewise Eudorus, the leading Academic of his generation, whom I have also mentioned earlier. His influence is documented in references and excerpts in later writings as well as in the works of a younger contemporary, the Jew Philo, who also lived in Alexandria. Philo came from a distinguished family which belonged to the large Jewish community among the population of the metropolis on the Nile. Like presumably all Jews outside Palestine, Syria, and Mesopotamia, those Jews had Greek as their first language. It is fairly certain that Philon spoke neither Hebrew – then still common in religious and scholarly usage – nor Aramaic which was the vernacular of his fellow believers in Palestine.

Philo is one of the many representatives of a rich Jewish literature in the Greek language which sought to interpret the traditions of Israel with the means and within the forms of Greek literature. Such writing was partly directed at a Jewish readership, and partly also at an audience of Gentiles, with apologetical or propagandistic intent. This subject will be discussed at length in a later section. Philo had received a comprehensive philosophical education, which certainly contributed to his high social standing. This is documented by the fact that his fellow citizens made him one of the delegates whom they sent to the court of the Emperor Gaius on the occasion of one of the many quarrels between the Jewish and the Greek communities in Alexandria.

In his numerous writings Philo uses Stoic, Peripatetic, and above all Platonic terms and concepts in explaining the texts of the Old Testament to the philosophically educated reader. Occasionally we find ideas which definitely stem from the school of Plato, even if they are not documented in school texts until a later date. An obvious explanation would be that Philo was using notions originally conceived by Eudorus. There is, for instance, the concept of a *theologia negativa*, the description of the Supreme, the One, the Absolute, of that which is to be sought beyond all being and thus beyond all that is speakable, by means of negation: God cannot be delineated spatially or temporally, his existence is without a cause, he can not be described by a single concept, and so on. This method of verbalising speculation about the Absolute has remained influential up to the present day.

Cynics

The literary heritage of school philosophy as such is far less rich (and this is not a quantitative judgment) than those texts which show the broader influence of philosophy. There are particularly many literary traces left by those philosophers who, once again following one of the many possible interpretations of the Socratic example, refused to offer their disciples a systematic doctrine. Their education in proper living was founded on the example set by the teacher in communal life with his pupils, to whom he would offer advice whenever an essential problem arose.

This method was followed by the Cynics who first appeared in the fourth century BC, temporarily vanishing from our view during the age of Hellenism, and resurfacing during the Empire. The Cynics were migrant teachers or preachers of proper, natural living. Their aim was to liberate men from the imaginary needs of civilised life and from social conventions. Casting aside the *typhos*, the 'haze', of demands and prejudices, they sought to educate the common man and help him with his everyday problems. Like stray dogs – hence the nickname Kyon for their hero Diogenes who became a legend in his own lifetime – they had no sense of shame and no respect for popular opinion, for the reputation of dignitaries, or for the erudition of philosophers. The example of their free, undemanding life was enough to show the absurdity of all social pretensions. When Alexander the Great invited Diogenes to ask him a favour the philosopher replied, 'Move out of my sun'; when Diogenes saw a child drinking spring water from its hands he threw away the cup which had so far been part of his travelling kit alongside the rucksack and the stick. Angrily he asked himself why he had not parted much earlier with that superfluous gadget from civilised life.

In an authoritarian state with well-defined social classes, the Cynics were a constant challenge and a source of perpetual unrest, all the more so because they had a very precise notion of government: only the best should be allowed to rule, those who like Hercules had risen to a superhuman state through their efforts and their merits. In a more moderate form, other philosophers supported this notion, which could not be reconciled with the idea that Imperial rule was justified by the Emperor's and his dynasty's charismatic qualities, which placed them closer to the gods than other human beings. The charismatic status of the monarch, which made him a 'living law' exempt from the laws of the state which he governed, had always been vital to the official ideology of Hellenistic monarchies and also of the Empire; its most obvious expression was the religious worship of the ruler.

Alexander the Great, a man whose historic influence can hardly be overestimated, served as an example for such superhuman charisma. It is significant, though, that those philosophers who applied the same standard of natural morality to all men drew a very negative picture of the great Macedonian's character, referring to the typical vices of a tyrant: pride, cruelty, lack of self-control, and greed. This criticism was not directed against monarchy in general, for the rule of one man over the others was the legitimate reflection of the rule of the supreme God over the universe. Still, according to this opinion the only proof of legitimacy was evidence of the fact that a ruler was the best and most capable individual according to those moral standards applicable to all men; he could not claim to be naturally superhuman, and could thus not treat the people he governed as if they were his personal property.

The Cynics were the most uncompromising advocates of this philosophical definition of the ruler, a definition which did not at all suit official ideology. This is why it did not take them long to become notorious to the authorities as subversive elements. But other philosophers also became ideologically opposed to the Imperial state, whenever an emperor massively violated the basic laws of philosophical morality. This applied above all to the Stoics, who were closely related to the Cynics in their radical moral demands; the school founder had previously been a Cynic for quite some time. The opposition among the Senators which upheld the ideal of Republican liberty found a natural ally in Stoic philosophy, promising individual independence as well as encouraging political activity. The complex system of Stoic philosophy tended to provide intellectual ammunition for oppositional thinking among the educated; while Cynic philosophy, with its contempt for studying, scholarly erudition, and systematic doctrine, had more of an impact among the masses.

Literary forms of popular philosophy: anecdote, letter, sententia

In the works of Seneca (see p. 88ff.) there is frequent reference to a Cynic called Demetrius, who seems to have had a great influence on a small circle of disciples as well as on a wider public, through his way of life, his counsels, and his teachings. He was banished several times, and there are numerous anecdotes illustrating his asceticism and his intrepidity in the face of the Emperor or of high-ranking officials. Similar anecdotes exist about early Cynics of the fourth century BC, and the perpetual retelling of such stories created a literary genre typical of the Cynic tradition. Frequently such anecdotes would travel widely, being spread by all kinds of different representatives of Cynicism including, of course, Diogenes. This process in turn provided authors with a motivation for collecting or inventing entire cycles of such stories, attributing them either to a historical person or to a fictional character from the past. The attempt to legitimise contemporary ideals by transposing them into the past is yet another expression of the Classicising nature of Imperial culture.

Beside or within anecdotes, letters play an important part; that is, letters ostensibly written by the heroes of a continued or newly created literary tradition, addressing friends, disciples, tyrants, or generals. One example is the collection of letters ascribed to a certain Chion of Heraclea, reputed to have lived in Late Archaic times, when he dauntlessly resisted the tyrant of his native city. Those letters were probably written during the reign of Nero; like the collection of Diogenes' letters, they are of Cynic origin, glorifying the pride of the philosopher who, conscious of his mental independence, refuses to bow to the mighty.

The literary motif 'manly pride before princely thrones' was certainly topical in the Empire. There are a number of curious texts found on papyrus scrolls which are known as Acts of the Pagan Martyrs. Those are the records of interrogations of Alexandrian citizens, conducted by high-ranking officials of the Roman administration or even by the Emperor himself, because of denunciations or internal quarrels between the city's different ethnic groups. The individuals examined are obviously members of the upper classes, whose speeches express their pride in the civil liberty of the metropolis, and in the unassailability of the philosophically educated man.

The letter had been a literary form since the fourth century BC, used for communicating philosophical ideas, political proposals, or historical information. The epistolary literature of the Cynics is only part of a rich production, especially from the first century BC onwards, comprising fictitious letters from almost all the great personalities of the past, from Hippocrates to Alexander. Particularly popular choices were those philosophers who had left little or no writing to posterity; later authors would invent voluminous correspondences, or choose to illustrate the relationship between two famous personalities of the past through a corpus of letters. There is, for instance, a fictitious exchange between Alexander the Great and Aristotle about the wonders of India. Sometimes such series of letters constitute entire novels, with the correspondence giving a complete account of the chosen person's life. This applies to the aforementioned letters of Chion, but presumably also to the text which was the predecessor of the so-called Alexander novel. This work, probably produced in the late first century AD, has not been preserved; we can only guess at its characteristics from the numerous extant later versions and translations into many languages of the legendary story about Alexander the Great and his conquests (see p. 367).

Cynic letters and anecdotes often culminate in a sententia, a wise saw from the mouth of the hero. The tradition of such proverbial statements is extremely ancient, dating far back into pre-literary times. Naturally, it became particularly important wherever philosophical living was taught without dogmatic instruction, as in the case of Socrates and those philosophers who followed his example in building no systematic doctrines, and leaving no writings behind. Thus, for instance, numerous sayings or apophthegmata of the aforementioned Cynic Demetrius were widely known (for example, Sen. *De prov.* 3, 3; Epict. *diss.* 1, 25, 22).

According to Socrates' disciple Phaedon of Elis, as quoted by Seneca (*ep.* 94, 41), such sayings were supposed to have the effect of an insect's bite, hardly noticeable at first but itching violently after a while. A comparable didactic impact can be made by coining an easily memorable formula, achieving perfect congruence between content and form. To achieve this congruence was, of course, one of the main goals of rhetoric. Earlier on, authors had tried to attain such memorability by writing sententias in verse. However, the form thus imposed on the statement was likely to clash with its semantic and syntactic structure. The perfect prose sententia, as attempted again and again in the post-Isocratic rhetorical tradition, proved to be superior to its poetic counterpart in matching formal, phonetic-rhythmic structure with the semantic-grammatical.

Sententias were collected in very early times already. The didactic poem by Hesiod from about 700 BC contains many in verse form; nearly as old, presumably, is a hexametric poem entitled *Teachings of Cheiron*. Cheiron was the wise Centaur who had educated Achilles, and the poem seems to have consisted exclusively of maxims for proper living. From the school of Isocrates comes the so-called *Address to Demonicus*, a collection of prose sententias with connecting passages. Philosophers, too, were interested in the gnomic tradition. They saw the possibility of finding remains of prehistoric wisdom; and another reason for their interest was that the relationship between form and content was an issue which touched on the core of a philosophic discipline: dialectics or, as it was later called, logic. This was reason enough for philosophers to pay attention to certain aspects of rhetoric.

We know that the Stoic Chrysippus compiled a large collection of sententias. From the Imperial age, we have another compilation which was highly esteemed even by Jews and Christians. It was ascribed to Sextus, a philosopher who lived in Rome in the first century AD, who did not take part in philosophical research or debate but merely taught an attitude to life which was based on Stoic and Pythagorean ideas. There were excerpts of sententias from the comedies of Menander and the writings of Epicurus, and there was a collection in Latin which bore the name of Cato the Elder. Finally, Pythagorean circles of the first or second century AD created a didactic poem whose argument was almost exclusively made up of sententias. This *Golden Poem* was widely read and frequently commented on (see p. 489).

Many of the extant collections bear the mark of gradual compilation, which means that they are really extensions of older collections. This is true of the aforementioned sayings of Sextus or Sextius, finally edited around 200 AD, but containing a lot of much older material. During the entire Hellenistic-Roman age, there were countless oral and written sources and traditions which could be drawn upon to supplement existing collections of sententias; thus it is possible that such collections contain a few of the sayings of the Cynic Demetrius, even if we can no longer identify them as such.

The so-called diatribe

The Cynics of the fourth century BC, above all Crates of Thebes who was the true founder of their tradition, were gifted and witty men of letters, well able to parody demanding genres such as tragedy, even if in their teaching they used artless, blunt, and sometimes even downright vulgar language. Some writers who sympathised with the Cynics, most prominently Bion of Borysthenes on the Black Sea who lived in the third century BC, had developed a literary form out of this informal method of instruction. This literary form has come to be called, rather unfittingly, 'Cynic-Stoic diatribe'; unfittingly, because the term diatribe means something like occupation or study and cannot really be applied to a didactic speech or its form. In any case, the genre is an adaptation of the unsystematic, easily intelligible lecture or didactic dialogue about moral issues such as wealth and poverty, luxury and asceticism, the family, or fashion. It could contain questions from the audience, jokes, anecdotes, sententias, and even pieces of poetry. Since the early Hellenistic period, this form had been extremely popular, and there are Latin examples from the first century BC onwards. Not only the Cynics themselves used the diatribe, but also philosophers and literary men of all shades and colours who wanted to discuss moral questions of general relevance without following the doctrine of a specific school. The resulting products were frequently very elaborate, as the rhetorical education of a large part of the reading public could lead authors to the assumption that their artful, deliberate artlessness would be appreciated.

Most works we know of this genre were written by authors who used the form merely as a stylistic device as, for example, the philosopher Seneca did in many of his writings, which will be discussed in a subsequent section. On the other hand we have some more or less authentic transcripts of oral instruction, recorded by the teacher himself or by a member of the audience. A Late Classical collection contains lengthy remnants of the lectures of C. Musonius Rufus, a Stoic from an equestrian family in the ancient Etruscan town of Volsinii. His long life which ended around 100 AD was exclusively dedicated to the teaching of Stoic philosophy; he used no other language than Greek, although he did not live in a Greek-speaking area except during the times of his banishment. Like other philosophers, he was banished on several occasions, as a potential enemy of the Emperor.

Among Musonius' disciples there were many famous philosophers and literary men of the following two generations. The extant texts provide an insight into an instruction tending to take the basic tenets of Stoic philosophy for granted, rather than discussing them and explaining them to the pupils. Instead, Musonius tried to give Stoic answers to manifold questions concerning practical aspects of living, from the wearing of beards to family planning, or the handling of money. This illustrates the philosopher's role, which could be similar to that of a confessor or spiritual advisor in Christian settings. The one or more years which they spent in one of the smaller or larger centres of philosophical instruction were for many young men from the wealthy bourgeoisie the final stage of their education, providing them with an attitude to living and to the world in general which was to be put to the test in moral decisions in private and public life. The scholarly, scientific aspect of philosophy became thus rather insignificant, and some philosophers would go so far as to declare that intellectual-scientific education was superfluous; some, like the Cynics, even disapproved of philosophical research.

Education and edification

One of the best illustrations of the philosophical background of literary production in the Empire is provided by a number of prose works in which certain doctrines and methods of school philosophy are applied to subjects belonging to general knowledge. One particularly fine specimen is the treatise *Of the Cosmos*, dedicated to a certain Alexander who may be Tiberius Julius Alexander, a man from a distinguished Jewish family of Alexandria, who became prefect of Egypt under Nero. Contemporaries believed that the dedication referred to Alexander the Great; this is why the treatise was ascribed to the latter's teacher Aristotle, and preserved among Aristotle's collected works.

In bold language, the anonymous author draws a comprehensive picture – albeit with very little detail – of the universe with its manifold phenomena of inorganic and organic nature. Wherever there are specific theories explaining natural phenomena, these are drawn from Peripatetic philosophy, emphasising the rational and meaningful character of natural processes. However, the author seems to be less interested in communicating specific scientific information; his aim is to present an edifying account of a perfect, meaningful universal order shaped and directed by one supreme God, an order in which mankind is well provided for. In this context, he repeatedly compares the universal God governing the world through servants and messengers of lesser divine status, to the High King of Persia, one of the predecessors of the Roman Emperor as a monarch who governs indirectly through vassals, ministers, officials, and messengers.

There is hardly a better illustration of the world view and of the political-social attitude of educated people in the Empire than this comparison: the source of legitimacy for political power is its imitation of the eternal, irrefutable order of the universe. This universe, however, lives and exists according to immutable laws, unaffected by its supreme ruler. It is not, like creation according to the Old Testament, completely at the mercy of its creator, whose thoughts and plans are inaccessible to human reasoning. In this sense, according to philosophical opinion the supreme God and world ruler is not a transcendent being, but a part of the universe; notwithstanding the fact that human reason may never achieve more than a partial understanding of his regime.

The faith of the ancient Greeks and Romans was not given in a unique revelation, but it had grown organically from numerous local and regional forms of worship. Those had always been directed at the establishment of friendly relations with the superior powers, on whose benevolence depended the fertility of humans and animals, protection from natural catastrophes and diseases, and the welfare of the group, constituted by the family, the coevals, or the political community. Those superior powers could be perceived as persons, that is as gods, as dead ancestors, as semi-divine natural beings, or as abstract forces. In any case, men's relationships with them were limited to performing the rituals which would satisfy their demands. Moral demands made by such gods could only concern the proper performance of ritual, and what one thought during the performance – or to put it in Christian terms, what faith one had – was entirely irrelevant. This explains the much-debated religious tolerance of the ancients, to whom participation in the most diverse rituals was a matter of course. Any violation of the rules of ritual, however, met with extreme intolerance, as it was likely to disrupt the communication with the gods which was vital to the survival of the community, exposing the worshippers to the wrath of the offended power.

The Greeks with their fertile imagination had always embellished those traditions on which worship was founded, with a plethora of stories. Ancient literature thus came to be populated with numerous divine personages of well-defined character, who provided material for the imagination independently of forms of worship, which were always limited to certain regions. The practically-minded Romans, on the other hand, were satisfied with the exact performance of ritual, and with the creation of a religious law which defined the proper forms of worship appropriate to all kinds of different political situations. It was Greek mythology, which gave the gods the characteristics of individuals, that provided a medium for religious influence on moral thought, as the relationships between the gods had to be conceived of as similar to those within human society.

Since the fifth century BC philosophical speculation had included the issue of divine existence; and none of the philosophical systems which were developed in subsequent centuries was without a chapter on theological doctrine. All philosophical theologies had three basic axioms in common: the first being the notion that it is first and foremost the universe in its entirety which is divine, and that gods are only powers at work within the universe. Second, there was the idea that the meaningful order of nature can only be explained on the basis of the assumption that there is ultimately only one ordainer of events. Last, there was the belief that it is the divine benevolence and providence revealed in nature which establishes the gods' moral authority over human beings; and hence literary tales which made gods act just as immorally as humans were blasphemous nonsense. These basic views explain why Classical philosophy regarded theology as part of physics, the study of nature.

The trial of Socrates in 399 BC shows how easily philosophers could be accused of blasphemy, as philosophical theology contradicted many of the notions expressed in traditional rituals and tales. Still, popular opinion and philosophy agreed in claiming that any political community had to be primarily a cultic community. This is why blasphemy was a particularly grave accusation. After all, Herodotus had already said that it was Homer and Hesiod who had given the Greeks their gods. This was certainly true, and remained so as long as Homer remained the teacher of his nation, as the most prominent author on the school curriculum. But as Xenophanes had criticised in the fifth century BC, Homer in particular kept going on about divine theft, adultery, and treachery: and this is why Plato wanted to exclude all poets from the educational system of his ideal state.

In the second century BC the Stoic doctrine of a *theologia tripartita* came as a compromise between philosophical and traditional religion. It distinguished between three different manners of honouring the gods: a philosophical one, directed at the properly recognised powers in nature; a poetical one, expressed in myth; and a political one, expressed in ritual, and binding communities together. The Stoics still claimed that philosophers alone knew the true nature of the gods and thus alone knew true worship; they acknowledged, however, that there were other forms of expressing vague ideas of divine nature and influence. Philosophers were thus not to be reluctant to participate in the religious life of their environment, in full knowledge of its deeper significance which the uneducated person, depending on stories and images, could merely guess at.

There was a particular need for interpretation of those poetic narratives about the gods which were common knowledge, confusing as they were in their contradictory diversity. In fact, the Stoics taught, the stories told by poets and especially by the sage Homer are representations of cosmic processes; their gods are natural forces and elements. Poetry should thus seen be as allegory. Even before the fifth century BC the allegorical method had occasionally been applied to parts of Homeric poetry; such interpretations can be put down to the existence of explicitly allegorical poetry in the seventh and sixth centuries BC when, for instance, the dangerous situation of a community would be described through the image of a ship in a storm. Theagenes of Rhegium is commonly regarded as the true inventor of the allegorical interpretation of Homer. Theagenes' example, set in the fifth century BC, was also followed by philosophers, even if Plato explicitly disapproved of the method (*Phaedr.* 229E). In the second century BC, in the context of a debate about the relationship between tradition and philosophy, allegorical interpretation became a sophisticated tool, used above all by Stoics to gain philosophical insights from tales of gods and heroes. Other philosophers such as Academics and Epicureans remained hostile to this approach, which nevertheless came to strengthen the authority of Homer as the supreme instructor of the Greek nation.

L. Annaeus Cornutus from the Roman civic colony of Leptis in North Africa was the author of a Greek manual of Stoic allegoresis. His work, which is fully extant, is a kind of catalogue, listing interpretations of individual gods and narrative episodes with reference to natural or moral philosophy. Many characters and motifs are ambiguous, for this interpretative technique had a long history during which plenty of new devices and readings were developed; new interpretations, however, did not always displace older ones. The battle between the gods and the Titans, for instance, could be read as the physical confrontation between the elements, or as the moral contest between virtues and vices. Frequently, allegorical readings of the names of gods followed etymology. A case in point is the goddess Rhea, whose name was taken to refer to the earth. This somewhat far-fetched explanation was based on the fact that the earth is where we find running water, which is called *rhei* in Greek.

Cornutus was a famous exponent of Stoic philosophy, who counted the poets Persius and Lucan among his disciples. A parallel to his manual exists in the roughly contemporary work of an otherwise unknown Heraclitus. It is entitled *Homeric Problems*, and contains allegorical readings of difficult passages from Homer's poetry. Thus, for instance, Classical philologists studying Homer had quite rightly noticed that Dionysus is not featured among the gods in heaven. His appearance in Book 6 of the *Iliad* is in the role of a fugitive pursued by the Thracian King Lycurgus, escaping narrowly only because of the intervention of Thetis. Did Homer not recognise Dionysus, worshipped by all Greeks, as a god? Heraclitus' allegorical explanation maintains that the story is merely an allegorical representation of grape picking and wine-making: thus, according to him, the name of the god stands for nothing more than wine!

Heraclitus appears to belong to the grammatical tradition, and to have had little contact with the Stoa. Many of the fragments of Classical interpretations of Homer featured in the Byzantine scholia commentaries contain individual allegorical readings; but this does not mean that the authors, Greek grammarians from Hellenistic and Roman times, could all be identified as Stoics. The method of allegorical interpretation was also extremely popular with many grammarians, if mostly in places such as Pergamum where grammatical studies were conducted under the influence of Stoic linguistic philosophy. There were also Jewish and Christian adaptations of the allegorical method of interpretation; those efforts at Biblical exegesis will be discussed at a later stage.

The habit of distilling philosophical insights from ancient poetry through allegorical reading was likely to suggest the reversal of the process: the communication of philosophical ideas in the shape of allegorical narrative. Of this, we also find an example in the period dealt with here. It is a dialogue – a popular form for expressing philosophical ideas since the days of Socrates' disciples – in which an old man explains to a stranger a huge painting in a shrine sacred to Kronos. The rather cryptic picture shows many human figures: there is a twin circular wall with two gates, a large crowd outside, and a number of women within. The old man claims that the image represents the paths leading to proper philosophical education and to counterfeit education respectively; it is, he says, a votive gift from a Pythagorean who once visited the town.

The interpretation is clearly based on Stoic philosophy; the reference to

Pythagorean thought, however, indicates the rising popularity of that tradition in the Early Empire, even if the anonymous author presumably knew very little about it. But it is only in this period that we find Stoics with Pythagorean leanings such as Sotio, one of Seneca's teachers of philosophy. Later on, the Stoics came to be more and more hostile to Pythagorean notions, which influenced above all the school of Plato. The mention of the old Pythagorean was presumably the reason for ascribing this curious piece of writing to Cebes of Thebes, who is the speaker supporting the Pythagorean doctrine of the nature of the soul in the Platonic dialogue *Phaedo*. It is not clear whether Cebes' name was added later, or used as a pseudonym by the author himself.

Several facts should have become clear in this survey of literary phenomena illustrating the role of the two major educational forces, rhetoric and philosophy, in the first half of the first century AD. One is that the linguistic boundary between Latin and Greek had very little impact on literature and education. Second, that we can take for granted that many among the reading public of the urban bourgeoisie were quite familiar with the linguistic techniques of rhetoric in reading and writing, as well as acquainted with the basic views of different philosophical schools. This is in keeping with the importance of writing in administration and economy, and the existence of a large number of schools for the young.

But perhaps the best illustration of the influence of the two educational forces mentioned is to be found in the writings of L. Annaeus Seneca. His life and his literary work, which was to have a lasting impact, made him an especially typical representative of his era.

4 SENECA

Life

L. Annaeus Seneca was one of the three sons of the aforementioned teacher of rhetoric with the same name. He came from a distinguished family in a Roman civic colony in Spain; one of those families from whom higher officials in local administration were recruited, and who were legally equal to the knighthood of Rome and Italy. Seneca received his rhetorical and philosophical education in Rome, and after a fairly long sojourn in Egypt, the patronage of a noble lady secured him election to the lowest of the ancient Republican yearly offices in the Senate, and thus the rise to the highest class in Roman society under the Emperor Caligula. During the reign of Claudius Seneca was involved in a public scandal, and banished to Corsica; at the instigation of the Empress, however, he was recalled to Rome as tutor to the heir, who was eleven years old at the time.

The succession of Nero brought the zenith of his teacher's career. Seneca was Consul in 55 and 56 AD and for five years, together with the Praetorian prefect Burrus, he practically controlled Imperial politics, with considerable success in internal and external affairs. As the Emperor showed more and more of the pathological side of his character – for example, when he ordered the assassination of his mother in 59 AD – teacher and pupil became alienated from one another. Seneca offered to resign, and to hand back the colossal gifts which Nero had heaped upon him.

Nero never officially accepted the resignation; yet Seneca retired to his estates in Campania, concentrating entirely on literary work until 65 AD, the year of an unsuccessful plot by members of the Senatorial nobility. Seneca was accused of being an accessory and was forced by Nero to commit suicide. If Tacitus' report is to be trusted, Seneca staged his own death after the manner of Socrates' departure from life, as reported in Plato's *Phaedo*. Seneca was sixty-one years old at the time of his death.

Philosophical writings

Large parts of Seneca's prodigious literary output have been preserved. Some works can be precisely dated; from those, we can infer that the others cover all the stages of his eventful life with its many high points. Irrevocably lost, though, is that part of his literary creation which was most admired by his contemporaries and which contributed largely to his rise in society: that is his speeches as an advocate in court.

Seneca's works can be easily divided into groups according to form and content. It is not so easy, however, to put them in an order which reflects the development of specific features in the author's thought and style. On the contrary, the world of ideas expressed in all of Seneca's writings is astonishingly unified.

The seven books of the *Naturales quaestiones* contain a discussion of all kinds of natural phenomena, such as comets, earthquakes, thunderstorms, or winds. One entire book deals with the floods in the Nile Valley, with explanations that follow orthodox Stoic physics. Seneca does not include any original observations or reflections, a fact which indicates that his work is not aimed at a specialist readership. But neither is it designed to introduce laymen to research in the natural sciences. It is rather meant to communicate basic doctrines about nature, doctrines which in the philosophical tradition formed the foundation of rationally comprehensible, natural ethics. Consequently Seneca tries to use all his literary-stylistic art to make the text palatable and memorable for the reader. Moreover, he points out the significance of each piece of information about natural processes, as a guideline for morally correct behaviour.

As could be expected the constraint of a rigid philosophical system as a framework for presenting fundamental knowledge about the universe in general resulted in some fairly premature conclusions, and some of the theories explaining natural phenomena may well seem rather adventurous to the modern reader. We should not forget, however, that they are without exception attempts at a rational explanation of the world, and that Seneca was serious in trying to provide people with reliable information helping them to understand their natural environment. If scientific research in the Empire did not attain the same standard as in Early Hellenism, it still produced remarkable results in astronomy, geography, and medicine. This was largely due to the persistent philosophical interest in natural structures, which stimulated scientific development and supplied new issues for discussion.

There is a large number of mediaeval manuscripts of the *Naturales quaestiones*, whereas our knowledge of Seneca's so-called *Dialogi* is based on only one extant version. The title of the latter is presumably from the Classical age; it is misleading, though, because the work does not contain any dialogues at all, but shorter treatises on moral philosophy, mostly in the manner of the previously discussed 'diatribe'. There are also some consolatory addresses, examples of a genre which had a long tradition in philosophical literature, as the best proof of the validity of a philosophical world view was the comfort which it could give to someone who had lost a close friend or relative.

The treatises in the *Dialogi* were written at very different stages during Seneca's life. They deal with issues of moral philosophy, in the manner of the Stoics; the subjects include providence, steadfastness, peace of mind, or the brevity of life. The discussions focus on practical issues concerning everyday living. For instance, Seneca compares the room which should be given to public, economic, and philosophical activity respectively during the short span of a man's life; he reflects on the compatibility of wealth and philosophical living, which was evidently a very personal problem for him; and he tries to outline the practical consequences of the belief in an irrefutable, but at the same time optimal, predetermination of all events. Basic Stoic doctrines are taken for granted and referred to only briefly, with just a few exceptions where more background detail is given.

One of the longer passages of theoretical discussion occurs in the more extensive treatise about anger, where Stoic authorities are quoted in a moral assessment of this emotion, of its psychological basis, and its therapeutic treatment. In contrast to Peripatetics and Academics, the Stoics did not believe that emotions arise independently in the irrational part of the soul. They maintained that each incitement to action is based on rational judgment concerning a sensual impression received by the individual. In the case of a misguided response inadequate to the circumstances, the reason should not be sought in an emotion arising without rational control, but in the erroneous nature of the underlying rational process. This is the justification for the Stoic ideal of apathy, the complete lack of emotions, which is a sign of flawless rationality.

This interpretation was particularly problematic when applied to anger as the most obvious emotion of all which, as 'righteous' anger, often arises from a moral judgment that is morally and intellectually correct. This consideration had led the aforementioned Posidonius and his teacher Panaetius to modify the doctrine of their school concerning the emotions, agreeing with Plato and Aristotle in the assumption that there were independent irrational forces at work in the human soul. In the Empire, the Stoa was returning to earlier orthodox positions, and it is in the context of this development that Seneca's contribution belongs.

It was not until fairly recently that Seneca's writings on applied ethics came to be appreciated as an elaborate system of rules and devices for spiritual guidance, comparable to those developed by Plutarch and Epictetus (see pp. 193, 200). With the help of a teacher or through independent effort, their followers would meditate on moral laws and different situations, and systematically practise their judgment of good and bad in everyday life by the standards of philosophical morality. The aim was to achieve mental liberty, and to be immune to all kinds of blows dealt by fate, being in control of one's behaviour under any circumstances. The goals of this psychagogical and meditative practice, which was common in all philosophical schools, influenced the structure of Seneca's treatises far more than systematic ethical theory did. Even where the devices of rhetorical art shape the linguistic form, rhetorical persuasion and manipulation are merely a means towards that end.

We have two separate longer treatises by Seneca, of very different content. *De clementia* (*Of Mercy*) was dedicated to the Emperor Nero in 56 AD. It is a 'mirror for princes' in which the virtues and the duties of the ideal monarch are defined. Such a monarch must first and foremost possess four virtues: in spite of his exalted position, he should behave as a man among men, and not be unapproachable; he should perform acts of generosity to show that the means at his disposal are used not for his own benefit but for the welfare of his subjects; he should be moderate, resisting the temptation to abuse his power in immoral and unjust acts; and above all, he should exercise the virtue of *clementia*, of mildness, mercy, and forbearance, which proves him to be the perennial benefactor of the people. This canon of princely virtues, to which numerous others could be added if required, had been established by the theorists of Hellenistic monarchies, and adopted by the Roman one. Caesar's ostentatious use of *clementia* in treating his conquered opponents nourished the suspicion that he was trying to become a monarch of the Eastern type.

These ideas about monarchy survived in the society of the Empire, being quoted again and again in proclamations, legal preambles, and edicts of the Imperial administration. The visualisation of social values as divine beings was part of the Roman tradition: a case in point is the goddess Venus, who was not modelled on Aphrodite, in spite of the later identification.

From the beginning, the personified qualities of the reigning Emperor were treated with religious reverence, something that can be seen on Roman coins, which for several centuries carried representations of the Emperor's *Aequitas* (i.e. Justice), or *Liberalitas* (i.e. Generosity).

One problem, however, remained unsolved: the question whether those qualities were part of the Emperor's superhuman nature, or to be regarded as the results of the conscious observation of ethical principles – in other words, whether the monarch's legitimacy was derived from his charisma, or whether in the last instance, he was subject to those moral demands according to whose fulfilment praise or blame are given to any human being.

As a philosopher, Seneca naturally emphasises the general-ethical character of princely virtues, stressing the importance of proper education and permanent self-scrutiny on the part of the ruler. But the idea of the monarch's charismatic nature is not alien to him, and he mentions it approvingly without discussing the resulting problem, that is the relationship between premeditated action subject to moral judgment, and spontaneous action resulting from natural properties, and hence exempt from moral laws. Any potential contradictions in Seneca's work are covered up by the use of themes and motifs from the rich literary tradition of 'mirrors for princes', dating back to the fourth century BC and providing more than enough material for this purpose. Seneca is quite frank in the statements directed at his Imperial pupil: however, in no way does he refer to the Senatorial ideology of political liberty which in those days was frequently linked with the Stoic idea of inner freedom and independence, and thus could justify opposing an unworthy holder of supreme power. This documents the fact that Seneca was new to the Senatorial class, as a social climber whose rise had taken place within the framework of an undisputed monarchic order.

The seven books of the treatise *De beneficiis* or *Of Good Deeds* come closest to the specialist writings produced by school philosophy. The subject was a common one in the Stoa: Seneca gives a detailed explanation of morally correct behaviour defined as mutual benefaction. In this work, written during the final years of his life, he quotes a large number of authorities, above all the Stoic Hecaton, a contemporary of Posidonius from the first century BC.

Stoic doctrine assessed all objects and all creatures according to the degree to which they were endowed with *pneuma*, the finest, invisible matter which gives form, life, and consciousness. The high concentration of *pneuma* in man enables him to understand the rational order of the universe which is likewise caused by the *pneuma*, and thus it gives him the power to act rationally. The *hēgemonikon*, which governs the human soul, is entirely pneumatic, like those divine beings who direct the course of the world and the lives of men in the context of a universal providence.

By doing good to other men, man follows the example of the highest rational beings, helping to preserve the cosmic order which is based on reason. Thus the true form of worship is recognising divine power and divine order, and imitating the perennial good deeds of the gods. Hence in the Stoic system theology and ethics converge in the definition of benefaction; and it is precisely this idea which dominates above all the fourth book of Seneca's treatise, at the exact centre of the work.

Seneca's best-known prose work consists of his 124 letters to Lucilius. Early quotations prove that originally there were even more of those epistles, which are written in the same style as the *Dialogi*. Many of the letters are ostensibly answers to questions posed orally or in writing by the addressee, Seneca's younger friend. The length of individual pieces, which varies between one and twenty-five pages, also helps to create the impression of a genuine correspondence. But a look at content and diction as well as comparisons with other of Seneca's writings show that the epistolary form has been superimposed on these shorter or longer essays, as suitable to the manner in which the author liked to discuss philosophical, scientific, or literary questions.

The subjects included in this collection are much more numerous and much more varied than those of the other treatises. There are topics concerning everyday life, such as the handling of money, the need for rest, the dangers of luxury, the best use of one's time, social obligations, or attitudes towards political power. Besides, above all the second half of the collection contains longer pieces dealing with theoretical problems which belong to the domain of school philosophy, such as the relationship between philosophy and science, or theories concerning the origin of culture, differing doctrines about the division of philosophy into individual disciplines, as well as the importance of fundamental doctrines and individual rules in philosophical-ethical instruction. Some topics outside the realm of philosophy are also touched upon, such as stylistic theory or historiography.

In his longer letters, Seneca deals with a voluminous specialised literature, of which he has preserved numerous fragments by way of quotation. The books and authors are not exclusively of Stoic origin. Seneca was a man of the world, and far from merely repeating the doctrine of his own school. He also shows a liking for Epicurus, whom he quotes frequently and more often than not approvingly; and among the Stoics he prefers the learned Posidonius, even if that man's opinions were often regarded as unorthodox by Stoics of the first century AD.

It is only natural to compare the philosophical writings of Seneca and those of Cicero, for in both cases the authors reproduced Greek philosophy in Latin, endeavouring to clothe philosophical ideas in an appealing literary form. However, there are differences which become apparent in such a comparison, and those do not only concern style, an aspect which will be discussed in a separate chapter. Most importantly, those differences document the entirely different roles which Greek philosophy had among the upper classes of Rome in the age of Cicero and in the mid-first century AD respectively.

Cicero had tried to popularise philosophy in Rome, in Latin apparel. This is why his dialogues are works of art satisfying the high literary standards of his contemporaries and peers; they steer clear of all scholarly nit-picking, while yet giving a comprehensive insight into those philosophical disciplines touched upon, and above all while featuring the differing opinions of individual schools. Thus Cicero's philosophical writings all present a well-rounded picture of the complex subject matter they deal with, even if their author appears as a great writer with a philosophical interest rather than as a professional philosopher.

Seneca was no professional philosopher either, but in the meantime, Greek philosophy had won a secure place in the educational system of the Latin world. There was still an audience with a literary education, a public which demanded an elaborate and appealing presentation of philosophical ideas; but it no longer required an introduction to the nature and the significance of philosophy. An author like Seneca could take for granted that his readers possessed a possibly undifferentiated, but not necessarily mistaken, idea of philosophical doctrines. Their expectations of a writer with a philosophical interest would thus rather be directed at information concerning the meaning or the application of individual philosophical problems or teachings. Such changed circumstances explain why Seneca should frequently neglect clarity and comprehensiveness of explanations even in his more scholarly letters, and instead employ his art in using linguistic-literary devices all the more effectively for psychagogical purposes. It seems that he was more afraid of tiring the reader than of becoming incomprehensible because of the unexpected arrangement of the material, or of gaps in the argument. He was counting on a substantial amount of a priori knowledge which would enable the reader to pick up all sorts of subtle references.

Both rhetorical and philosophical education were directed more at forming an ability rather than at establishing a knowledge: the aims were to enable the pupils to formulate good texts, and to lead a proper life. It is true, however, that both goals presupposed a considerable amount of specialised information. Rhetorical education included familiarisation with many works of poetry and prose, collections of exempla, proverbs, and anecdotes, as well as texts from the historiographical and mythographical tradition. Philosophy, if it was not reduced – as by the Cynics – to guidance for practical living, included a substantial knowledge of the world and of man, a knowledge leading directly into the discussions of scientific disciplines. Seneca's letters indicate the close relationship between philosophy and science, even if he repeatedly points out that knowledge and erudition are worth far less than a philosophical attitude to life. He attacks those philosophers who 'turn philosophy into philology' by making their profession a merely scholarly pursuit. In Graeco-Latin usage, the term philologist meant a person who seeks knowledge from books, no matter in which area of learning; the word acquired the connotations of pedantry and ivory towers already at a very early stage.

Seneca did not contribute any more to the development of philosophical thought than Cicero had done. Still, especially in his letters, we find detailed discussions of motifs which had a merely marginal place in school philosophy, but which helped him to tone down the dogmatic character of school doctrines by referring to his own experience of the world, and of human beings. Thus we find (*ep.* 23 *et al.*) a fairly clear definition of conscience which is akin to our modern understanding: this is something which gets no more than a cursory mention in Stoic and Epicurean philosophy. The exclusive intellectualism of the Stoics could see the phenomenon of conscience only as a result of self-scrutiny and self-recognition in the absence of psychological categories for naming a spontaneous twinge of remorse which is entirely independent of intellectual endeavour. Another case in point is the use of the Latin words for the verb 'want', indicating the idea of a will existing independently of instinct and cognition. This notion was entirely alien to psychological definitions in Greek philosophy, which knew a moral evaluation of human will only in so far as this will was the result of man's cognitive efforts.

Seneca's philosophical writing was much more voluminous than those parts of it which we have today. Quotations and references document the previous existence of further letters; of numerous tracts comparable to the *Dialogi* on particular problems of moral philosophy; and of several works on natural science and geography, including treatises about India and Egypt. The latter were certainly not intended as contributions to a specialist debate, but as literary communications of general knowledge.

Prose style

Without any doubt, it was their high stylistic-literary quality which ensured the great influence of Seneca's prose works. Seneca occupies an eminent position in the history of Latin prose style; his striking use of language which may often seem extravagant to the modern reader marks an important stage in stylistic development.

Cicero and the orators of his generation had managed to Latinise that form of the syntactic period which Greek oratory had developed, thereby setting a standard for all later literary prose. In Classical stylistic theory, the period was a syntactic structure expressing at least two interrelated central ideas. Ideally those as well as the potentially numerous subordinate statements were to be phrased in a manner which results in *isokōlia*, that is, roughly the same length for all corresponding syntactic parts or *kōla*; and *parisōsis*, that is the same order of syntactic units within each *kola*. This consistent parallelism of the *kōla*, which can also include clusters of more than two, is underlined by the occasional use of end rhyme or *homolioteleuton*, but above all by the rhythmic regularisation of *kōla* endings according to fixed metres, differing from those used in common verse forms.

It is evident that great linguistic skill is needed to achieve exact congruence between such a complex phonetic-rhythmic construction and a correspondingly complicated syntactic structure as demanded by the content, with main and subordinate clauses, and further subordinate syntactic units. In spite of the length of such constructions, the listener should have no problems in following, for the strict regularity and the numerous phonetic-rhythmic signals always indicate which part of the text he is hearing at any given moment. It is true, though, that this periodic style does not permit any particular surprise effects, because each constituent part must be followed by another one of the same structure, in a corresponding position. This principle of a progressive completion or rounding-off of a statement was the reason for the name 'period', or 'circular path'. The term was coined by the rhetor Gorgias, who developed the principles of the periodic style in the fifth century BC, demonstrating his art in a humorous defence of Helena, who had been the cause of the Trojan War. The following passage should give an impression of Gorgias' writing, even if the translation can not convey the rhythmic-phonetic effects of the original text:

> If she was forcibly stolen
> and unlawfully coerced
> and unjustly hurt
> it is evident
> that the stealer breaking the law did wrong,
> the stolen one suffering wrong was plunged into misery.

Just as in the age of Hellenism 'anti-Classicist' writers had developed a different style as an alternative to the art of periodic syntax, Seneca's own style must be seen as a deliberate departure from Ciceronian tradition. Instead of long, rounded-off sentences he uses utterances of varied length, but mostly short, and even seemingly disjointed. Strict parallelism is replaced by surprise turns which make the progress of the argument appear erratic. If syntax is thus simplified, the rhythmic pattern is not; for Seneca applies the technique of using metrical clauses to shorter units or *kommata*, which produces an even greater proportion of metrical language in the text as a whole.

The result is speech which moves at an irregular pace, but on the whole very fast, while the listener has to be prepared for surprises at any moment. This style is particularly well suited for the frequent inclusion of striking sententias, as quotes, or as demonstrations of the author's own brilliance. On the other hand such a mode of writing can hardly be used in longer systematic discussions where clarity of content and continuity of argument are needed, and where the periodic style is the more appropriate vehicle of expression. The latter went with strict rules for the choice of vocabulary, banning poetic and vulgar expressions as well as neologisms or archaisms. From the possible alternatives, an author using the periodic style had to select the words which conveyed the idea he wanted to communicate in the most objective manner, without any of the emotional connotations of vernacular or poetic language. The kommatic style, on the other hand, includes expressions with emotional connotations to add to the appeal of the speech.

No modern reader can miss the distinction between these two stylistic modes, even if they did not always appear in their purest forms. In the Classical age, however, when reading aloud was the norm, their distinctive qualities would have appeared even more clearly, with the full effect of phonetic and rhythmic patterns not only being realised in the actual delivery of an oration.

The pointed style of Seneca's philosophical writings with its many surprise turns of phrase answers the demands of a readership with a high degree of literary education and philosophical knowledge; the author's intention is to influence those readers by an emphatic assertion of the importance of philosophical living. The combination of great erudition and sincere pastoral concern is expressed in the many literary quotations – most of the poetical ones from Latin, most of the philosophical ones from Greek sources – as well as in unforgettable, poignant phrases coined by Seneca himself. Even a modern reader could not fail to be impressed by sentences such as *Errat qui putat deos nocere nolle – non possunt* ('A fool is he who believes the gods do not want to harm us – they cannot'); as well as *Quaeris quid profecerim? Amicus mihi esse coepi* ('You ask where I have progressed? I have begun to be a friend to myself'). Such formulas show Seneca's exhaustive use of those possibilities which the Latin language offers for the most concise and hence memorable expression of ideas.

Seneca himself discusses problems from stylistic theory in letters 114 and 115. It is telling that as a starting point, he should use a question which touches on ethics and psychology: does linguistic style reflect moral character? Seneca answers in the affirmative for to him elaborate speech is the vehicle and the result of moral education: *oratio cultus animi*. Linguistic virtues as well as moral ones have to be learned and rehearsed side by side, and in the same manner.

The examples which Seneca mentions in this context show that he regarded his own uneven style, which avoided all smoothness or roundedness, as not at all extravagant or even decadent. This view is not altogether unjustified. Seneca quotes stylistic *faux pas* from the speeches of Maecenas, putting them down to that man's eccentric lifestyle which oscillated between unrestrained indulgence and feverish work. These quotations prove that alternative and very idiosyncratic forms of literary prose could be sought and found even at a time when the Ciceronian style prevailed as a model.

Seneca makes it clear, however, that his own preference for a diction which unfolds in short and frequently unconnected sentences, making the progress of the argument appear erratic, is not to be seen as a return to the harsh and clumsy prose of Old Latin. Such an archaising tendency could be observed above all in historiography, beginning with Sallust who had imitated the vocabulary and the syntax of Cato the Elder, and deliberately avoided the smooth and rounded style of his older contemporaries, in order to make his presentation of historical events even more poignant. Seneca mocks the curtailed sentences and the archaic use of words preferred by his contemporary L. Arruntius, the author of a history of the Punic Wars, and an imitator of Sallust. Indeed Seneca himself never does violate the rules of contemporary linguistic usage, or employ obsolete grammatical constructions. His reaction against the smoothness and the long-windedness of the Ciceronian style was a conscious expression of a marked modernity; something which could only be appreciated by those who were familiar with the Ciceronian tradition.

Posthumous influence

The influence of Seneca's prose works was exceptionally wide ranging and lasting. The texts document the combination of philosophical commitment, highest literary art, and extreme urbaneness; another factor which helped to keep readers fascinated was what they knew of the fate of this philosopher beside the throne. The Stoic rigorism of numerous passages appealed to Christians who saw a parallel with Christian ethics – hence, for instance, the fictitious correspondence between Seneca and the apostle Paul which was written in the fourth century AD. Seneca remained in high esteem in the Middle Ages and during the Renaissance, but his work probably had the greatest impact in seventeenth- and eighteenth-century France, which rediscovered the ideal of a philosopher who is a well-educated man of the world and not a scholarly pedant, a man who has worked hard to gain an insight into the nature of man, and is thus able to preserve his moral independence in the hustle and bustle of society, and in the vicinity of the mighty.

Apocolocyntosis

One shorter work by Seneca has so far received only little attention; as the author remained unidentified for a very long time it did not contribute anything to Seneca's posthumous reputation. This work is the *Apocolocyntosis*, the *Pumpkinification* of the Emperor Claudius.

If a Roman Emperor had not fallen out with the Senate, he was posthumously included among the officially recognised gods as *Divus*, after the example set in the case of the dictator Caesar, in a ceremonial Senate meeting. Claudius was thus honoured after his wife had killed him by poison; and it was Seneca, the tutor and closest confidant of Claudius' successor Nero, who eulogised the dead man on this occasion. From the common public, especially in the East, as well as from literary circles, there was an enthusiastic welcome to the exceptionally gifted, multi-talented younger man who replaced the awkward stutterer Claudius, well meaning and reasonable though he had been. As people celebrated the dawning of a new era, Seneca wrote an earthy satire about the dead Emperor, a book whose effect has the subtlety of a donkey's kick. In it, the new god is received by the other gods with unconcealed astonishment and disgust: Claudius is put on trial for various offences, and finally, after a long debate about the appropriate punishment, he is given to the deified Caesar as a slave.

This minor work is not exceptionally witty, but yet of interest to the literary historian as a surviving example of so-called Menippean satire. This genre had been developed by the Cynic Menippus of Gadara in the third century BC for the presentation of Cynic ideas in a humorous form, to an audience with high literary standards. It consists of short prose passages with a mixture of narrative and paraenetic elements, made even more varied by verse interludes, an element which Seneca used as well. The first Latin adaptation of this formula of creating a *spoudaiogeloion*, a hotchpotch of the serious and the humorous, was by Varro, Cicero's learned friend.

The title *Apocolocyntosis* is without any doubt a parody of the term apotheosis, or deification. But as Claudius is not shown as turning into a pumpkin during the course of the events described, we must infer that the word chosen for the title was used somewhat like the German verb for taking the mickey, '*veräppeln*', literally, 'applify'.

Tragedies

From the point of view of their influence on literary history, Seneca's tragedies must be seen at least as equal in importance to his philosophical writings. They are the only examples we have of Roman tragic art, and before the philological opening up of Attic tragedy, they were the only

Classical tragedies which could influence dramatic theory and dramatic writing in sixteenth- and seventeenth-century Europe.

Two voluminous mediaeval manuscript collections feature altogether ten tragedies as written by Seneca. One of them is certainly not genuine: a so-called *fabula praetexta*, a tragedy dealing with an episode from Roman history. This play is entitled *Octavia* and deals with the fate of the Emperor Nero's first wife who was banished in 62 AD. Seneca himself is one of the major dramatis personae, but that does not necessarily mean that he could not be the author as well. However, there is mention of events during Nero's reign which happened after Seneca's death, and besides, the plot follows exactly the historical account given by Tacitus, so that this play could not have been written before the second century AD. All the other nine dramas are based on material from Greek mythology; but there is one more which is most probably not from Seneca's hand, entitled *Hercules Oetaeus*, which presents the story of Hercules' self-incineration.

The formal structure of those nine plays follows the structure of Classic-Athenian tragedy, as developed during the fifth century BC in the works of the three major tragedians, and fixed in writings on poetic theory from the fourth century BC onwards: there had to be a chorus and three actors, a division into five acts, and a prologue giving the audience advance information. The influence of Classic or more recent Greek examples can be perceived in almost every detail; but as far as we can judge without knowing any of the older Roman tragedies, Seneca did not copy any Latin authors.

Phaedra follows the first Hippolytus drama by Euripides, a text which we can reconstruct from fragments and from the sequel, which has been preserved in a complete form. *Thyestes*, dealing with the most gruesome episode from the story of the Atrides, may have been modelled on a Greek tragedy from post-Classic times. *Troades*, *Phoenissae*, and *Medea* follow Euripides' plays with the same names; *Oedipus* is modelled on Sophocles' *Oedipus rex*; and *Agamemnon* on the first part of Aeschylus' *Oresteia*, which bears the same title.

The dramatic plots were largely dictated by traditional myths. The only scope for individual variation on the part of the poet concerned minor nuances in the story, new evaluations of major characters, or the introduction or elimination of minor ones, in contrast to one or more previous dramatisations of the subject matter.

A comparison of Seneca's tragedies with their Greek models shows that the Roman makes his characters more crass in words and actions, going to extremes of pathos throughout his plays. Those gruesome episodes which abound in myth are presented in full detail, through dialogue as well as through action, whereas in Greek tragedy such things would mostly be reported by a messenger on stage. Seneca seems to have taken a particular delight in great graphic gruesome detail, and this is something that very strongly influenced European drama from the sixteenth to the eighteenth century.

Characterisation and evaluation of the dramatis personae are marked by Stoic psychology and ethics. Fateful events are caused above all by passionate emotion, and it is the struggle between passion and reason which separates the good from the bad characters. The suffering hero proves his victory over passion by showing persistence in acting according to reason. Such evaluations of dramatic action are frequently given through the chorus, which is not involved in the plot itself. Most of the songs performed by the chorus do not follow the strophic pattern of the songs in Greek tragedy; they are poems with a succession of identical verses which are modelled on types from sung Greek lyrics, but which were in Seneca's plays quite obviously meant to be spoken, as in the poems of Catullus or Horace. Seneca's dramatic dialogue is also in verse in a form that was an adaptation of Greek models to the conditions of the Latin language, a form which had long been common on the Roman stage.

The language of the tragedies reflects contemporary rhetorical taste. The author gives his characters long speeches and long clever argumentations, including all those elaborate rhetorical devices which we would rather expect to find in prose. This, of course, was also a means of achieving high pathos.

Comparing the structure of any of Seneca's tragedies with that of a Greek one will show that the Roman author paid little heed to the unity of action with a beginning, a climax, an end, and with recurring motifs binding all the parts together. Unlike the Greeks, Seneca focused on the artistic elaboration and the forceful effect of individual scenes. He seems to have intended each scene to create a distinct impression, rather than wanting it to appear primarily as part of a unified, dramatically convincing plot. This assumption is also borne out by the frequent changes of setting; the Greeks had rarely used such shifts, and most often observed the unity of place.

Critics have commented on Seneca's disregard for unity, on the violent nature of individual scenes which makes it difficult to imagine how they would have been staged with the technical means of Classical theatre, and on passages in which characters on stage give lengthy descriptions of the actions which they are just in the middle of performing. This has led some people to the conclusion that Seneca's tragedies were texts meant to be read, and not intended for performance at all.

Others have argued that there is plenty of evidence of tragic performances in the Imperial age, in the Greek East as well as in the Latin West, and that Cicero and Horace already mocked the technical extravagance and the glamorous style of such performances in Rome. Thus, there was a highly developed stage technology which would have permitted the presentation of even the most drastic actions; and finally, the concentration on detail seems to be a phenomenon common to many Latin-Roman adaptations of Greek literary forms as, for instance, comedy and epic. This critical argument has not yet been settled, and any possible conclusion must take into account all that we know about theatrical practice in the Graeco-Roman world of the Early Empire.

Theatre in the Empire

In Classic Athens tragedies were performed only twice a year, as part of religious festivals officially dedicated to the worship of Dionysus. Each occasion required the writing of three complete new tetralogies, consisting of three tragedies and one satyr play each, to be entered in a competition. This institution survived well into the Imperial age, even if the achievements of the three great tragedians were honoured by a modification of the rules, allowing entries which were new productions of one of their three hundred or so plays.

From the close of the fifth century BC such dramatic performances became common in the entire Greek world. This was made possible by book editions of the major tragedies, the building of theatres, and above all the rise of professional acting. Actors had to try to meet the increasing musical demands posed by the increasingly popular arias, whereas the chorus parts, originally the centre-pieces of tragic compositions, became mere interludes between acts. A typical phenomenon in the Greek world during the Hellenistic-Roman age were actors' associations, which had the legal status of international organisations. Many of their members were specialists in comedy or tragedy, modern or Classic drama, female roles or the parts of messengers. They kept moving from place to place, for each one of the hundreds of Greek cities between Sicily and Afghanistan had its theatre, even if that building was also used for other occasions such as public lectures or assemblies; each city also had its own calendar of festivals, setting apart some days of each year for theatrical performances. An inscription from the second century BC states that one actor had taken part in ninety-two such productions to date, and had in most cases given more than one performance.

This was roughly the form in which Greek theatre became known in Rome, from the third century BC onwards. The actors were professionals, the performances linked to *ludi* or games such as gladiator fights, or the release of wild beasts in the arena. Other occasions were large-scale funerals, or rallies organised by victorious generals or successful politicians. As the prologues of Old Latin comedies show, the plays which were performed were openly advertised as imitations of Greek originals. The heyday of Roman tragedy was the second century BC with the authors Ennius, Accius, and Pacuvius; later centuries were less productive in this genre.

The professionalisation and the spreading of theatre was matched by the extent to which drama featured in literary criticism and in education. In his comprehensive theory of drama, Aristotle speaks of tragedies which were exclusively meant for reading; and it is this aspect of dramatic writing which must be kept in mind in the study of Roman drama's origin as literary translation.

As regards theatrical practice, another factor must be taken into account: many of the smaller and poorer cities which had a theatre for dramatic performances could hardly have had the financial means or the refined audience needed for the production of an entire tragedy. This is why inscriptions or documents from the Hellenistic-Roman age often report that individual actors or companies arrived in a town in order to perform particular showpieces such as arias or messengers' reports, or to enact scenes from famous tragedies. The same applies to Rome and the Latin world. Cicero describes a huge theatrical show which the director Sp. Maccius Tarpa produced for the opening of the theatre founded by Pompey: a great spectacle garnished with well-known tragic scenes. According to his biographer Suetonius, the Emperor Nero contributed a dramatic one-man show, including some dancing and some singing, with highlights from Classic and from self-penned plays.

Naturally there were still also complete performances of tragedies in Greek as well as in Latin. One example is the aforementioned *Thyestes* by L. Varius Rufus (see p. 37), produced as part of the victory celebrations after the Battle of Actium. But the co-existence of dramatic texts for readers with performances of dramatic highlights is typical for the entire Hellenistic-Roman age, if only with regard to tragedy. Both Greek and Latin tragedy were based on Greek myth, which was no longer of religious significance, but still central to all general education with a literary emphasis. A broad public would have been acquainted with the plots of countless tragedies; thus, Medea's lamentation, Oedipus' curse on his sons, or the argument between Eteocles and Polyneices could be performed out of context. The public would not only know those characters from school or from private reading, but would also recognise them from the numerous pictorial representations surrounding the inhabitant of any Greek or Roman city. This, however, does not apply to comedy which did not have prefabricated mythological plots. This is why our sources do not mention any enactments of individual scenes from comedies, or isolated performances of comic songs.

All this suggests that Seneca might well have intended his tragedies mainly for non-scenic recitals, which were extremely popular in Rome at the time. Pliny the Younger's correspondence and Tacitus' *Dialogus de oratoribus* prove that many members of the Roman upper classes with literary aspirations in the second century AD were extremely fond of writing tragedies in Greek and Latin which they read to their friends, whom more often than not they bored intensely. If those plays or parts of them were also enacted, this fact obviously merited a special mention: Tacitus reports an example concerning Seneca's contemporary and friend, the ex-Consul P. Pomponius Secundus. Thus we cannot exclude the possibility that parts of Seneca's tragedies were in fact performed and written with that purpose in mind. The great attention to detail coupled with disregard of dramatic unity suggests this very strongly. Still, Tacitus says that Seneca showed great self-restraint in writing for the stage, in order to avoid a jealous reaction on the part of the conceited Emperor, who also used to perform scenes from self-penned plays.

This controversy is a good example of how the discussion of a problem which is perhaps ultimately insoluble on the strength of our known sources can yet lead to the discovery of a whole new field of study. The debate about the purpose of Seneca's tragic writing has opened up a whole area which would have gone unnoticed, had the interpretation of Seneca's plays been limited to purely literary aspects. It was only natural, though, that those European dramatists and theorists between the sixteenth and eighteenth centuries who were influenced by Seneca should have regarded his tragedies only as plays for the stage.

In the Graeco-Latin educational tradition of the Empire, both tragedy and comedy belonged to the highest forms of literature, and this applied especially to those plays which were exclusively intended for reading. Ovid's *Medea* ranked as a Classic.

Still, most of the theatrical productions in places such as Seville, Carthage, Smyrna, or Antioch, were of subliterary texts belonging to the *mimus*, comparable to operatic libretti or film scripts. Our knowledge of such texts, written and performed until well into the Late Classical age, is almost entirely based on examples from the East, numerous fragments having been found on Egyptian papyrus scrolls. From the West, we have mostly epigraphical evidence, concerning actors specialising in this genre who performed in the capital as well as in the camps of the Roman army's legions. The Empress Theodora, the wife of Justinian, began her professional career as a mimic actress as late as in the sixth century AD.

The *mimus* did not respect the conventions of tragic and comic theatre where female roles were enacted by men, as in Japanese Noh and Kabuki plays, and where masks were obligatory. The texts of the *mimus* were extremely varied: we have poems written for solo singing complemented by mimic dancing; there are also scenes in simple prose with a large number of characters, asking for many more actors than the canonic triad of traditional tragedy. The plots are parodies of myth, adventure stories in historical or exotic settings, love stories, and tales of everyday life; this corresponds roughly to the repertoire of dramatic subjects in modern-day film and television. There were many realistic features, and some Indologists even claim to have found corrupted words from a Dravidian language on a papyrus fragment which contains a dramatic account of the adventures of two lovers at the court of an Indian Rajah. A parallel to this exists in the Punic fragments of a comedy which Plautus based on a Greek original; and the trade relations between Carthage and the Graeco-Roman world in the Hellenistic era may well be likened to the trade between southern India and Greek Egypt in the Imperial age.

As our own modern subliterary entertainment keeps going back to forms tried and tested in literary tradition, the Graeco-Roman *mimus* used to borrow in form and content not only from tragedy and comedy, but also from the novel. Beside all the art forms that used words there was also the non-verbal *pantomimus* or mime. This kind of performance, however, also frequently took plots from literature and above all from myth, presenting them through mimic dance. The *pantomimus*, incidentally, completes a full circle in the historical reception of Greek drama. The historian Livy tells us that in the last decade of the fourth century BC, and thus long before the first performance of any Latin play, Etruscan actors performed the first drama in Rome. The Etruscan influence on the Roman theatre is documented by the origin of several Latin theatrical terms, such as the word for actor which seems to have a genuine Etruscan root, or the one for mask or role, which the Romans acquired in its Etruscan form, and hence via the Etruscans from the Greek. According to Livy, those Etruscan performers he talks about acted mimically, without any dialogue. Considering the omnipresence of Greek myth in Etruscan art, it may well be possible that the dramatic plots thus represented were based on Greek sources.

5 POETRY

General comments

Seneca's diverse writings prove the outstanding importance of Rome, capital of the civilised world, for the growth of literature; they also document the high prestige of literary productivity in social life. This circumstance was already enough to favour Latin literature in competition with its Greek counterpart.

Moreover, the Romans had their Classic models in the not-too-distant past, and reference to them could be established without giving them an artificial topicality. Greek Classicism, on the other hand, looked back to the fifth and fourth centuries BC, that is to say to political and social conditions which could hardly be visualised any longer without recourse to mythology. The struggle of free Greek city-states to preserve their independence against the Persian Empire or the Macedonian monarchy belonged to a dimly remembered past, whereas the highest social class in the Empire preserved a vivid memory of what life had been like before the global Roman monarchy; of a time when members of a proud nobility waged bloody wars on one another for political power, while nevertheless the frontiers of the realm were pushed continuously wider. The Romans were also aware of the fact that the greatest literary works in Latin had been written in the final years of that very epoch. From a Greek point of view, the decline of morality and of literature which was lamented in the society of the Empire as in many other cultures, had a much longer history than it did for the Romans. It was also true that the Greek part of the realm took longer to recover from the century of devastating civil wars than Italy, which was privileged in the economic and political order of the Roman state.

The greater literary productivity of the Latin West shows most clearly in poetry. Here, the Greek side was particularly disadvantaged. The very early flowering of many poetic genres had created an incomparable wealth of poetic tradition and had endowed many writers with a thorough command of poetic techniques. But poetic innovation had suffered from the impressive development of philosophical and of literary prose. Those two forms of the literary visualisation of reality asked more for analytical reasoning than for imaginative power. It was only the scholarly study of ancient writings, and the influence of poetic theory, which permitted a second, brief flowering of poetry in the Early Hellenistic period.

In comparison, Roman poetry was still young and fresh, even though the continuous influence of Greek models and Greek literary theory was crucial to its first attainment of Classic maturity. We know of no naive poetry in Latin: that is of no poetic writing which precedes all understanding of reality through discursive thought. But the topicality enjoyed by Roman poetic achievements continued well into the first decades of the second century AD. There were authors who produced remarkable works, creatively developing given conventions, for more than a century after the Augustan Classics, when poetic writing still attracted talented men and independent thinkers as a rewarding pursuit.

Bucolica

With the exception of drama, all Latin poetic writing of the Early Empire is marked by the influence of the Augustan Classics. One case in point is a collection of poetry of various genres which has been handed down under the name of Virgil. It features a didactic poem about volcanic activity, entitled *Aetna*; *Dirae*, the poetic curse by a dispossessed landowner; and *Moretum*, the hexametric description of a herb dish. *Ciris* is a short, pathetic epic narrating an episode from Greek mythology; in *Copa*, a landlady gives encouragement to her customers in the elegiac metre; and *Culex* tells the sentimental epic tale of a shepherd who kills the gnat that bit him in his sleep, only to find that the insect's bite had saved him from that of a snake, a realisation which prompts him to erect a monument in honour of the gnat's memory. Finally, there is the *Catalepton*, a collection of short occasional poems in different metres.

Only two poems in this collection are demonstrably Virgil's own early poetic efforts; all other pieces in the so-called *Appendix vergiliana* are difficult to date. Some of them are close imitations of Hellenistic models in the Neoteric tradition, after the manner of Catullus. Examples are *Culex* and the *Catalepton*, including those poems genuinely written by Virgil; and also *Copa*. Others such as *Ciris*, *Dirae*, and *Aetna* belong to the Neoteric tradition, too, but they also show the influence of Virgil; just as *Ibis*, ascribed to Ovid (see p. 37) shows Virgil's impact on later authors.

Virgil's example was also crucial to the survival of bucolic poetry. A number of mediaeval manuscript collections feature Latin pieces of varied origin and quality; I shall come back to those compilations on more than one occasion. They contain epigrams, hexametric and elegiac poetry, but also so-called *centos*, plays for reading patched together from verses by Virgil and other Classic authors.

One manuscript of this sort from the monastery of Einsiedeln has preserved two bucolic poems which closely follow Virgil's example in style and in content. Virgil was the first poet to express the distress and the hopes arising from contemporary political experience, through dialogue between simple shepherds. In the established order of the Empire, bucolic poetry became a vehicle for panegyrics on the Emperor; for this, too, Virgil had set a precedent in his fourth eclogue, a Sibylline prophecy that talks of the birth of a new world ruler who would restore the perpetual peace of the Golden Age.

The Einsiedeln manuscript does not give an author's name for the two poems, of which the first one is probably incomplete. Efforts to identify the author have so far been unsuccessful, though we may assume that the poems were written during Nero's reign. Their structure follows the Virgilian pattern: an introductory conversation between two shepherds leads into a longer verse sequence in praise of the monarch. He is compared to the gods Apollo and Jupiter, and his restoration of the golden age is described in exactly those terms and formulas developed by Virgil and other Augustan poets: the establishment of peace in nature and among men, the return of justice on earth, and the end of all acts which violate nature, with the result that people once again feed on nature's bounty without tilling the soil, just as they used to do in blissful prehistoric times.

The poems not only convey an impression of the continuity of a highly developed poetic tradition, but also offer an insight into the official monarchic ideology of the court. To be monarch of a global Empire is to play a role of cosmic dimension, or at least it justifies the claim to such a role: thus the Emperor may without any hesitation be placed alongside the highest gods, or even be identified with them. Sculptors of the period have grafted likenesses of the living monarchs' heads on to statues of Jupiter:

there could be no better proof of the aforementioned fact. Imperial power derived its legitimacy from its destiny which was to achieve perfect harmony between natural order and human society, putting an end to discord, injustice, and want in both. Evidently a monarch who could bring this about must be superhuman by nature; and therein lay the potential for conflict with those who upheld the philosophical definition of monarchy, demanding that the holder of supreme power should prove that he was the best man according to those moral standards which are valid for all men alike.

There is another strand of manuscript tradition which has preserved four bucolic poems by the known author Nemesianus from the fourth century AD, and seven pieces of bucolic poetry from a T. Calpurnius Siculus about whose identity we are still in the dark. Like Virgil's eclogues, these poems were originally published as a book, in a well-defined order set by the author himself, with pieces in bucolic dialogue alternating with monologues with or without a dialogic introduction. The first, fourth and seventh are panegyrics on the Emperor like those in the Einsiedeln manuscript; the others focus on the musical-artistic and the erotic themes of bucolic poetry. As in the case of Virgil's shepherds, the shift from traditional subjects to the higher plane of Imperial eulogy - not really a suitable subject for discourse among the shepherds of the poetic milieu – is explicitly justified by the experience of the characters who speak. This clearly shows that the authors were consciously using the new functions which Virgil had given to bucolic poetry.

The panegyrics of Calpurnius show the reader exactly the same elements of official monarchic ideology as the poems in the Einsiedeln manuscript, texts which likewise belong to a courtly milieu. It is probably no coincidence that we have those and other examples (see p. 117) of Imperial ideology from the reign of Nero, but also some particularly vivid evidence of philosophical-political opposition against the same monarch. There was hardly any other Emperor whose accession was greeted with so much hope and approval, and who was then despised and hated so intensely by so many.

Manilius

The tradition of Greek didactic poetry dates back to a time long before the creation of literary prose, a time when poetic language and verse form were the only means in oral and, later, in written epic to give its statements a formal meaning beyond the vernacular level. Some philosophers of the fifth century BC still regarded the language of Homer as a better vehicle for discursive thought than Ionic prose, which had as yet little flexibility at that time. Attic, first refined in political and economic usage and then also in linguistic-rhetorical education, did not emerge as the language of philosophy, of science, and of historiography until the fifth and fourth centuries BC; but once it had done so, any attempt to use the language of the epic tradition in any other than purely poetical contexts was bound to seem obsolete.

This situation changed during the age of Hellenism: then poetic creation was often inspired by the scholarly study of older poetry, highlighting the artistic quality of poetic writing. This led to a revival of the tradition of didactic poetry, with works written in order to demonstrate erudition and complete mastery of poetic devices to an audience of connoisseurs. Hence, we have several didactic poems from this period, and we know of even more. A good example is the epic by Aratus of Soli in Cilicia, a text presenting the astronomical world view and the meteorological knowledge of Early Hellenism in epic form. This work was widely read, frequently commented on, and translated into several languages. A slightly younger author than Aratus was Nicander of Colophon, whose didactic poems about poisons and antidotes have been preserved, while others dealing with hunting, agriculture, or bee-keeping, were lost.

The writing of didactic poetry continued well into the Imperial age. From long quotations which the famous physician Galen included in two of his treatises in the second century AD we know a didactic poem which his fellow physician Andromachus dedicated to the Emperor Nero. It was written in elegiac distichs composed of hexameter and pentameter, and dealt with animal and vegetable poisons. An anonymous fragment of a hexametric epic about the flora of Egypt, preserved on a papyrus from the second century AD, may likewise have been written in the first century AD; so too the didactic poem on astronomy by Dorotheus of Sidon, of which we have some fragments, a prose paraphrase, and a translation into Arabic. This text was frequently used by Islamic astronomers.

The popularity of this genre in the Imperial age is also documented by the fact that Germanicus, the nephew of the Emperor Tiberius who showed the most outstanding military talent in the Emperor's family, translated Aratus' poem into Latin, as Cicero had tried to do before him. The Imperial prince's 725 verses show an astonishing mastery of poetic language and of the techniques of versification, which proves that a large number of people at that time were able to write hexametric poetry, and to give expert judgment of its quality. Germanicus' brother, the Emperor Claudius, appears to have been a serious scholar and thus, like Seneca, the Emperor's family is another good example for the link between education and social status which is not at all uncharacteristic of the first two Imperial centuries.

Still, it was not the continued interest in Greek didactic epic which kept this genre alive in Rome. The Roman adaptation of didactic poetry in the works of Lucretius and Virgil had created a genuine Latin tradition which outshone the Greek model. Lucretius, still entirely within the tradition of Old Latin poetry, was a fervent advocate of Epicurean philosophy, and used his great poetic talent to preach its doctrine of salvation, so that his comprehensive presentation of a complex philosophical system became a poetic manifesto.

Virgil wrote an epic about agriculture, one of the traditional subjects of Greek didactic epic, demonstrating the full range of his knowledge and of his poetic skills in that manner of Hellenistic poetry which had been introduced in Rome by the Neoterics of the preceding generation. But in Virgil's hands, the didactic epic became much more than a token of poetic virtuosity: the experience of living in a period of historic change helped him to provide an anthropological framework for the presentation of technical processes, as demanded by the genre's tradition. Thus his poetic treatise on farming was an interpretation of human existence in that characteristic form which had evolved during the history of the Roman state.

Such were the Roman models which Latin didactic epic had to emulate; one of the authors who took up this challenge was the poet Manilius who dedicated a poem on astrology in five books to the Emperor in the early years of Tiberius' reign. We have no biographical information about Manilius, and we do not even know his full name.

The first book of Manilius' epic contains essentially descriptive astronomy, while the other four deal with different astrological topics, such as the signs of the zodiac and their significance for horoscopes; the doctrine of the *decani*; or the problem of geographical astrology, concerning the influence of the stars on the common characteristics and the common fate of an entire region's population.

Manilius' writing is not easy to comprehend for it was not only contemporary astronomy which was a highly refined science. Astrology – and it must be remembered that our terminological distinction between astronomy and astrology was not yet known in the Classical age – was also a complex technique, developed around the second century BC among the Greeks of Egypt, on the basis of a thoroughly mathematical astronomy. It was its strictly systematic character which ensured the continued popularity of astrology among educated people; and the Stoics explicitly included astrology in their doctrine of nature. The anti-astrological polemics from the other philosophical schools did not deny the scientific nature of its methods, but referred to basic assumptions which were improbable as well as non-verifiable, and to morally questionable consequences which such axioms could lead to. Those professional scientists who studied the stars without belonging to any one of the philosophical schools generally approved of astrology, as did the Emperor Tiberius himself, one of whose closest confidants was the physician and astrologer Thrasyllus.

There was, of course, also a vulgar astrology whose exponents had no scientific education; one could consult them on street corners about one's horoscope, or about the most auspicious time for a business transaction. As evidence of popular astrology, we have magic papyri, amulets, or vernacular expressions; moreover, certain religious cults like the Mithraic Mysteries incorporated astrological ideas, such as the significance ascribed to the signs of the zodiac. The great influence of astrology on all levels of intellectual and religious life may be explained by the fact that it catered for the ancients' urge to see man and his fate in close connection with the cosmos, with universal nature. The notion of an immaterial soul with an independent fate which outlasts the body, an idea which had become more and more widespread since the age of Hellenism, could find a cosmological interpretation which located the home of the soul among the stars; that concept was also in keeping with astrology. The fact that astrology was taken seriously is likewise proved by frequent references in our sources to the persecution and the banishment of astrologers. The explanation for this is that their calculations and resulting predictions of political events, especially as to the impending demise of monarchs, could be seen as threats to public order and security.

In writing his epic Manilius used not only previous poetic and hence necessarily simplified accounts of the complex subject matter, such as the *Phaenomena* by Aratus, but also astronomical-astrological literature of a highly specialised and demanding nature. Thus only a reader with a good deal of knowledge about astronomy would be able to follow and comprehend Manilius' argument at length. His linguistic artistry in dealing with a subject matter which is on the whole rather dry is astonishing; at the same time, it illuminates the pioneering role of Virgil who adapted the language of Latin poetry for such uses. On the one hand we perceive the canonisation of a poetic vocabulary distinct from that of literary prose as well as from that of the vernacular, and in addition to this there were many well-established constructions enabling poets to avoid – or sometimes to emphasise – the clash between the metrical constraints and the syntax dictated by content.

The subject matter of didactic poetry, however, would often force the poet to coin new expressions which did not feature in the basic vocabulary of poetic genres. In such cases, proof of the poet's linguistic skill was through the creation of neologisms of a stylistic level and with connotations that were in keeping with the poetic style. The rise of this particular problem and the beginning of continuous attempts to solve it is of course best shown in the works of Lucretius, the pioneer of the genre on Roman soil. Lucretius himself occasionally lamented the *egestas*, the poorness of his own language. In the foreword to the third book of his epic, Manilius discusses at length the difficulty of transforming scientific terminology into poetic diction. However, he could refer to much better model solutions than the ones Lucretius had been able to draw on.

One characteristic feature in Manilius' work can be appreciated entirely without knowledge of astronomy. The first four books of his work are prefaced by prooemia of varied length; the one in Book 3 has already been referred to. Those prefaces contain some very conventional exordial motifs: the dedication to the Emperor; the invocation of an inspirational deity, in this case the Greek Hermes, and not the Roman Mercury; and the statement concerning the difficulty, the unprecedented character, and the originality of the chosen task. But there are some entirely different aspects besides these.

Thus, in the second half of the prooemium to Book 1, the poet places the origin of astrology in the very earliest period of human culture, presumably following the detailed doctrine concerning the origin of culture developed by the Stoic Posidonius, a man whom Manilius also quotes as an authority on special aspects of astronomy. The preface to Book 2 contains the poet's solemn declaration of faith which shows a pantheistic piety of the Stoic kind, based on the beauty, grandeur, and order of the universe. The long prooemium to Book 4 teaches and justifies the view that the entire history of mankind and its division into nations of different character and with different customs can be put down to the influence of the stars.

Just as Virgil uses prooemia and digressions to put his account of agriculture into a moral and historical framework, Manilius likewise makes his poetry more than a mere collection of technical information. His prooemia place astrology in the context of the poet's personal view of the world based on Stoic philosophy, linking it with human morality as the result of historical change, and with the knowledge of a universal order governing all events in the world of men. These parts of the epic contain some of the most beautiful and most poetic passages; and this is certainly not only due to the absence of any necessity for using complex specialist terminology, or to the common practice of devoting particular attention to style in the beginning of a literary work. In the Greek didactic epic, we find no parallel to this enrichment of a traditional genre.

Slightly younger than Manilius was the versatile poet Caesius Bassus, who died at a very old age in the eruption of Vesuvius in 79 AD. Of his rich output, praised by his friend Persius (see the section on that poet), we only have a fragment of a didactic poem about the nature and origin of different verse forms, a passage incorporated in a much later prose treatise on the same subject. Caesius Bassus' theory of the development of metre is of Greek origin; it claims that all different metres are derived from hexameter and iambic trimeter. Such theories were of particular importance for poetic writing at that time, as scholars have tried to prove with reference to the metre used in the chorus songs of Seneca's tragedies. In any case, all poetry of this period was scholarly poetry in the sense that its writing and its appreciation were dependent on familiarity with long-established, mostly Graeco-Latin, genre traditions. This is also true of an extant didactic poem about a specialised aspect of grammatical research.

Lucan

Virgil's grand plan to give the Roman people an *Iliad* and an *Odyssey* at one and the same time had been recognised as something extraordinary by well-informed contemporaries even during the composition of the *Aeneid*. Propertius had said: 'Something greater than the Iliad is being created – step aside, you Greek and Roman poets'. What had actually been written by the time of Virgil's death did not find the approval of the author himself, who dictated in his will that the unfinished *Aeneid* should be burned; nor was the text exempt from criticism in literary circles, especially because of the ambitious nature of the plan. But those *obtrectatores Vergilii* mentioned by scholarly biographers of the poet, critics against whom a grammarian pamphlet was still levelled as late as at the end of the first century AD, could not sway public opinion even in the first generation of the Imperial age. This was largely due to the interest which Emperor and court took in the new national epic, a text which like no other literary work before or after expressed the moral and historical justification for Roman rule over the civilised world.

The *Aeneid* quickly replaced Ennius' *Annals* as an obligatory school text, and thus came to occupy that position which Homer's works held on the Greek side. A Greek slave liberated by Cicero's friend T. Pomponius Atticus, a man called Q. Caecilius Epirota, is reported to have been the first who thus honoured the *Aeneid*. Virgilian manuscripts on tablets and papyri have been found as far apart as in the vicinity of a military camp on the Scottish borders, and in the sands of Egypt. Seneca's writings are full of quotes from the *Aeneid*, but frequently Seneca would also complete verses which Virgil had left unfinished. The resulting uncertainty about the original text soon gave rise to a Virgilian philology, beginning at the close of the first century AD, and continuing well into the Late Classical age. Its results are featured above all in extensive commentaries by Servius and Donatus from the fourth and fifth centuries AD. At that time adherents to the ancient religion sought in Virgil's works proof for their philosophical and cosmological monotheism; while from Constantine onwards Christians would place Virgil alongside the prophets of the Old Testament, on account of his Sibylline prophecy in the fourth eclogue, claiming that like the prophets of old, Virgil had predicted the coming of the universal saviour. With that reading, Virgil's role as the so-called 'father of the Western world' was firmly established.

In view of the profound and immediate impact of the *Aeneid*, it is not surprising that all subsequent efforts to produce a great Latin epic had to refer to the tradition established by Virgil, as readers would necessarily base their judgment on categories derived from their knowledge of the *Aeneid*. Of course, such reference could also be made by writing a 'counter-*Aeneid*', a kind of Virgilian writing turned upside down. One example for such a work is the *Pharsalia* by the poet M. Annaeus Lucanus.

Lucan was a nephew of Seneca and like him he was influenced by an education in the medium of Stoic philosophy; his tutor was the aforementioned Cornutus (see p. 86). Lucan became known in literary circles of the capital as a gifted orator and also as a writer of poetry; this is how Nero came to involve him in a circle of close friends of similar inclinations, and to secure his rise to the Senatorial class by making him a Quaestor and by giving him the priestly office of the Augurate. Lucan also won a prize in the Neroniana, a musical-artistic competition in the Greek fashion, established by Nero.

It is not clear how in 60 AD Lucan incurred the Emperor's disfavour and the prohibition against publishing any more poetry. In any case, he veered more and more towards the Senatorial opposition with its Stoic background, and he finally took part in the Piso conspiracy. After the discovery of that plot, Lucan was forced to commit suicide, like his uncle Seneca. Lucan's great epic, or those parts of it which he managed to finish, saw posthumous publication in ten books; all the rest of his writings, including a Medea tragedy, were lost. We know quite a lot about Lucan's life and work because, on the one hand, Tacitus mentions his part in the plot of Piso, and also because the *Pharsalia* soon became the object of grammatical – or as we would say, philological – studies, whose results have been partly preserved in two Late Classical commentaries, and in one short biography.

Lucan's epic deals with the civil war between Caesar and Pompey, which according to the poet sealed the fate of the Republic. Four books treat of events between Caesar's crossing of the Rubicon, the border between the so-called Cisalpine Gaul – modern-day upper Italy – and Classical Italy, and his arrival in Greece. The next four books tell of the battles fought in Epirus between Caesar's army and Pompey's Senatorial troops, of the decisive encounter at Pharsalus on the Thessalian plains, and of the flight of Pompey, who was murdered in an attempt to seek refuge in Ptolemaean Egypt. Book 9 deals almost exclusively with the march of the remaining Senatorial troops through the Libyan desert; a story designed to glorify Cato the Younger as the true Republican hero. The tenth book finally tells of Caesar's military exploits in Egypt. In all likelihood, the original plan foresaw twelve books as in the *Aeneid*, taking the account up to Cato's suicide in the Punic town of Utica.

Such a historical subject was not an unusual choice. In the absence of a genuinely Roman mythology, Roman epic had been historical from its beginnings in Naevius' account of the first Punic War, and in Ennius' *Annals*. There were also influences of the historical epic of Hellenism which had, however, always been of minor importance beside the rich tradition of Greek myth. For the treatment of recent events, a parallel could be found in Cicero's epic about the year of his Consulate; and the last decades of the civil wars were a favourite topic of Early Imperial historiography. Thus, for instance, the historical work by Seneca the Elder deals with the period from the civil wars up to the author's own lifetime.

Neither was it uncommon for authors to sympathise with the Republican cause, and to glorify Cato the Younger. When Augustus launched the ideology of the Principate he took due care to suppress the memory of his adoptive father and of that man's ambitions, which had been too blatantly directed at establishing a monarchy of the Eastern type. Instead, Augustus gave a quite honourable place in his gallery of ancestors of the new political order to the champions of the Republic such as Pompey or Cato; the latter had already been described as a hero not long after his death, in a treatise by Cicero. Augustus paid his respect to such Republican gallants in spite of the fact that in the last civil war, Cicero and Pompey's sons had taken a stand against the forces of Augustus and Antony, and had paid for that with their lives.

One unusual feature of Lucan's epic is the refutation of Virgil's Imperial ideology. The artificial myth of the origins of Rome, largely invented by Virgil on the basis of the Homeric model, lacked the legitimising power of deep-rooted tradition, a power which makes genuine myth a means of interpreting the present. Virgil had provided such a reading himself by presenting the entire complex of Aeneas' story as foreshadowing the global role of the Imperial state and the destiny of the Roman people as foreseen in the divine universal order. It is above all Book 6 with Aeneas' visit to the underworld where this interpretation, giving a meaning and a goal to Roman history as a whole, is expressed in all explicitness. An ideal basis for this procedure was a convention of narrative technique in ancient epic, a convention which had corresponded to religious belief in Homer's age, but which had become a mere artistic device in Hellenism. The convention dictated that all epic narrative had to describe events on two planes: the divine and the human. What was proposed on the upper level was to be enacted by the agents on the lower level in spite of their own intentions; only occasionally were they allowed a glimpse of the divine plan. The gods, also individuals with their own preferences and dislikes, often intervened directly; they could not change the plan completely, but they were able to cause some major disruptions.

Virgil adopted the two-tiered structure, invented for the interpretation of a traditional plot which the narrative poet had to follow, using it in the presentation of a story which he had invented himself. It suited the Platonic world view of an educated man, a view which was based on the notion of a duality consisting of a material, imperfect world and of a divine-spiritual one which is the source of all order. The passivity of the main hero Aeneas, which cannot but appear strange to the reader of a heroic tale, may be explained by this function of Virgilian myth: Aeneas follows the commands of divine providence in an absolutely flawless manner, so perfect that it sometimes even makes his moral character appear in a less than advantageous light. It is this very fact which allows Virgil to make his artificial tale of ancient Rome convincing in its presentation of the city's glory and its global power, which had become a reality in the poet's own lifetime, as the result of divine preordination which had directed the course of events from the very first beginnings.

Lucan scorned the 'divine apparatus' of the epic technique. As a Stoic he was convinced that there was only one level to the world and that all its creatures were ephemeral, just like the universe itself. He saw the death of the Republic as a process of inevitable destruction, which lies in the nature of all things. To the Stoic, decline and death are inevitably decreed by fate, but not in the eminently teleological sense which sees this as a condition for the creation of something higher and better, giving death a meaning which points to something beyond. Good and bad things in this world are alike doomed to die, regardless of the fact that the forces of good call for our sympathy, and their representatives prove to be morally superior human beings. They must nevertheless perish with the cause they support; proof of their moral status is only given by the fact that they preserve their independence, their morally founded liberty even in their downfall.

In the *Pharsalia* fateful events are realised by human actions. Caesar, the epic's anti-hero, is portrayed as a man possessed by the urge to act, and thus appears as the exact opposite to Virgil's Aeneas. But human action which looks like the product of a law of nature must appear demonic in its baffling successes, its intensity, and its unscrupulousness.

To Lucan, Pompey is a tragic character: first he belongs to the violent men of the Late Republic such as Sulla, Marius, or Crassus – men whose lust for power leads them to destroy the order which can alone preserve liberty, and who thus pave the way for monarchy. In the final instance Pompey realises the higher worth of the dying cause, becomes its champion, and pays with his life. The positive hero Cato, on the other hand, is non-tragic: he has opted for the better cause from the start, and merely holds his position in the knowledge of inevitable defeat, never for even a moment letting the course of political events rather than his moral convictions direct his actions. This is how he remains free and sovereign in the sense of Stoic ethics, and this is how his suicide of 46 BC had come to be interpreted long before Lucan.

One famous passage in the foreword to Book 1 contains a statement by Lucan on the issue of good and evil in the events he describes (1, 126f.): 'We do not know which party took up arms for the better reason. Each side can support its claim with a weighty judgment; for the victorious cause found the favour of the gods, but the losing one that of Cato'. As we have seen, the gods were no longer important to the epic poet Lucan, but all the more so the authority of a perfect sage, who according to all philosophical doctrines during the age of Hellenism provided the yardstick for measuring what was right and moral.

Without any doubt, Lucan's view of history was diametrically opposed to that of Virgil; and Lucan's intention was to portray the death of the Republic as inevitable, but nevertheless as lamentable, and not as justified through the creation of values of a higher order. His parody of Virgil is evident in structural parallels down to minute details, as well as in countless direct quotes and allusions. It is all the more astonishing that in the prooemium to Book 1, Lucan's epic should be dedicated to the Emperor Nero who is, moreover, evoked as the inspirational deity, the role traditionally reserved for the Muse. On top of that, about thirty lines of this preface contain a eulogy on the Emperor, a passage presenting him entirely in the terms of official ideology, as a universal ruler with a cosmic legitimation, whose reign justifies even the past terrors of civil war.

This praise of Nero has caused much bewilderment; it has been seen as ironic, or as a cover to protect the poet who had chosen such a risky subject. W. D. Lebek seems to have been first to point out that not a single line of the first three books published by the author himself is in open contradiction to the Nero prooemium. It is true that the negative image drawn of the dictator Caesar concerns the predecessor, and by adoption even the ancestor of the reigning Princeps, recipient of the dedication. But in the long run Augustus' efforts to make the monarchic order which he had established appear as restorative, and above all as his own work rather than as a realisation of his adoptive father's plans, had been successful. Thus in the popular view of the period the line of Emperors began with Augustus and not with Caesar. Seneca's work *De clementia*, the 'mirror of princes' addressed to Nero, does not mention Caesar at all, although none had exercised that particular princely virtue as lavishly as he had.

In the later books of the epic, published after Lucan's death, passages which cannot be reconciled with any kind of positive judgment of Nero's reign occur with increasing frequency. Thus in Book 7 (455ff.; 550ff.), liberty is mentioned as a value essential to the Republican order, and irretrievably lost in the civil war between Caesar and Pompey. Furthermore, it is said that not one in the line of successive Emperors differed from Caesar, who had been guilty of major crimes. Above all in Book 9, we find passages expressing the irreconcilable moral conflict between the champions of liberty led by Cato and the successors of Caesar (88ff.; 190ff.; 293ff.). Thus the basic contradiction can only be interpreted by reference to Lucan's biography; and all that we know about his life from sources other than his own works seems to justify this assumption.

The linguistic and poetic art of Lucan is a continuation of that of Virgil. The versification is equally brilliant and equally musical. In his diction, however, Lucan amplifies the rhetorical element which we find in Virgil, taking it to an extreme that is hardly bearable. Quintilian says in his rhetorical textbook which was published about forty years later than the *Pharsalia* that reading Lucan would do more good to an aspiring orator than to an aspiring poet (10, 1, 90). Lucan indulges in the graphic description of hardly credible or horrifying events; he takes great pleasure in lengthy descriptions of peculiar landscapes or situations; and he gives his characters pathetic, over-subtle, or laconic speeches, according to his view of their respective characters: all this corresponds to rhetorical rules for the writing of effective and vivid speeches in prose. A parallel to the rhetorical ornamentation as a modernistic feature of the poetic style is his show of erudition. Lucan loves imparting scholarly knowledge in individual episodes, or in digressions inserted for no other purpose than to impress his reader.

The model of the *Odyssey* had established a scene set in the underworld as part of the repertoire of great epic art. Lucan does not send his hero to the world of the dead – as happens in Book 6 of the *Aeneid* – because that could not have been done without bringing in divine characters, or at least ones with a divine legitimation. Instead, Lucan presents a *necromantia*, an invocation of the dead by a witch (6, 413ff.) as it would certainly have been practised at the time, in spite of its prohibition by Imperial law. This innovation of Lucan's has parallels in other parts of his epic; for instance, wherever astrology is mentioned. His link with the rhetorical tradition is shown in certain striking formulas, of which Lucan has produced more than any other Roman poet. The first examples are found in the outline of the argument, in phrases such as *bella plus quam civilia* ('more than civil wars'); and *iusque datum sceleri* ('legitimacy given to crime'). Many of Lucan's phrases, like the one of the *furor Teutonicus* (1, 256) have become part of the tradition of world literature.

The art of rhetoric created many novel means of expression in its application to the epic style. But at the same time it introduced an element alien to the epic tradition, through the unprecedented intensification of the psychagogical effect on the reader or listener. Traditional epic art was based on the commonly recognised greatness and dignity of its subject matter, which because of its own weight had the greatest effect if expressed in an objective and generally acceptable way. Virgil's artificial mythological inventions needed psychagogical devices to hold the listener's attention, and that is even more true of Lucan's thoroughly negative portrayal of history. It was only natural that such devices should have been borrowed from rhetoric, that art being well-established in the educational system of the period. The dominance of rhetorical categories in the basic aesthetical concepts of the readership was also expressed in the demand for ever-new stylistic fashions and variants; and it is this demand which is catered for by Lucan's epic art which we would be inclined to call baroque. Lucan's contemporaries evidently loved art that was bizarre, shocking, or exaggerated, seeing this as the best way to escape the compulsion to produce and consume progressively refined imitations of canonised models. In the case of Lucan the escape turned into an open rejection of tradition; in the process his changes in both form and content may well have grown more extreme through mutual interaction, making Lucan's departure from traditional patterns more and more radical as his work progressed.

Not only later generations, but also Lucan's contemporaries, perceived him as an anti-Virgil in the formal sense as well as with regard to content and basic concepts. This is shown in a most peculiar document, a verse interlude in Petronius' great novel which I shall discuss at a later stage. Those three hundred or so lines are the beginning of an epic about the civil war between Caesar and Pompey: they are quite obviously meant as a correction of Lucan's *Pharsalia* in the sense of a return to the Virgilian tradition. There is a lengthy narration telling how the gods prepared and began the civil war, with the divine action including a division of the Olympians into two parties, as in the case of the Trojan War. Those few verses which describe events in the world of men tell of Caesar's crossing of the Alps, and of Pompey's reaction on receiving news of that move. The description of many natural phenomena which accompany the events again emphasises the two-layered nature of the plot.

The whole piece is certainly an ironic parody, presented as an improvisation within the action of the novel. There is a comic effect in the inflation of the number of gods by various personifications; the genesis of the war appears as a ridiculously complicated process. Nevertheless, the critique of Lucan's concept of an epic without gods is evident. It corresponds to the opinion of a grammarian, expressed in a Late Classical commentary on Virgil (Serv. on *Aen.* 1, 382): because the *res divinae*, the theological dimension of the narrated events, is excluded by Lucan, that man should be classed as a historian rather than as an epic poet.

Persius

Satura tota nostra est – 'satire is all our own': this is what Quintilian says in a survey of masterpieces of Greek and Roman literature, texts which he as a teacher of rhetoric recommends as reading matter for the aspiring orator. Indeed, there was no Greek model for satire in the style of Lucilius who wrote in the second century BC, or in that of Horace. The term satire is also of Latin origin, derived from the word *satura*, the name for a dish concocted from very different ingredients. It was above all Horace, with his satires and epistles, who set the standards for a tradition of hexametric poetry dealing with varied topics from everyday morality to literary criticism in a loose, unsystematic, and often mockingly humorous manner. With inimitable tact, Horace had succeeded in reproducing the tone of the everyday language of educated people in syntax and diction. At the same time he reduced the metrical constraints of the hexameter to such an extent that the metre of high, pathetic epic became the vehicle of charming chat.

Thus, those very violations of the rules of high poetic art, which the educated reader could not fail to notice, became an essential part of a kind of educated conversation in which everyday events were described in an epic, but not in a heroic-epic, manner. In the Greek language, the epic style could be used like that only in isolated formulas, in epigrammatic poetry, for example. For the Greeks, there was a nexus between the hexameter and an artificial dialect differing from any spoken form of Greek not only in the selection of words according to stylistic level, but also in structural aspects such as phonology, inflection, and word formation. Thus it was impossible to give a credible imitation of a lengthy piece of educated conversation in Homeric language and Homeric verse. In Latin, on the other hand, there was a strictly prescribed selection of vocabulary for individual types of literature, but beyond that, there was no structural difference between the languages of different genres.

None of Horace's successors achieved the same lightness of touch that he showed in the presentation of serious as well as humorous subjects, an effect which was achieved through the combination of educated everyday language and modified epic verse.

To us, the genre tradition in the Julio-Claudian period is represented by a contemporary of Seneca, Aulus Persius Flaccus, who came from an ancient Etruscan family of equestrian rank. Persius arrived in Rome in 46 AD at the age of twelve. He was educated by famous men of learning, above all the Stoic Cornutus; and very soon, he became known in the literary circles of the capital, including the group around Lucan and Seneca. This in turn brought him into contact with members of the Senatorial opposition who had an interest in literature and philosophy. Persius wrote several poems about the mother-in-law of Thrasea Paetus, one of the victims of the failed conspiracy of Piso. After Persius' death in 62 AD his tutor Cornutus destroyed those poems because of their obviously dangerous political content; he did the same with a *fabula praetexta*, a tragedy about an episode from Roman history.

No more than six satires with a short introductory poem in so-called limping iambs were edited by Cornutus after Persius' early death and published by a friend, the poet and grammarian Caesius Bassus. Most contemporaries were somewhat taken aback by those satires, but the next generation already regarded them as exemplary specimens of the genre. This may be due to the fact that the texts were in the hands of grammarians or philologists from the beginning and thus became the object of scholarly exegesis very early on. It is this circumstance which also explains the existence of an exceptionally large amount of information about Persius' short life, as well as the existence of fragments from Classical interpretations of his poetry.

Unlike Horace's, Persius' satires deal exclusively with themes from practical philosophy; the reason for this choice is given in the first poem of the publication, which contains a condemnation of contemporary literary life. The topics include the question of man's inner freedom, as well as the relationship between knowledge and action, between wealth and poverty, or between men and gods. Questions and answers follow Stoic philosophy: and yet not in the light conversational tone preferred by Horace, but with strong pathos. Persius is often sarcastic in his descriptions of human behaviour; he lacks that light-hearted humour with which Horace pronounced the truth, however disagreeable or shameful it might be.

Persius' poems are among the most difficult of Latin writings. One reason for this is his endeavour to catch the reader's attention and to make him think by using uncommon expressions and unusual syntax. But also – and this is a relatively recent insight based upon extensive philological studies of Persius' work – the gist of Persius' pointed formulas can only be understood by readers who are familiar with a philosophical and literary tradition to whose motifs and phrasings the poet refers less frequently in direct quotations than in often obscure allusions. He shows a great deal of wit in doing so, but the pathetic-declamatory diction as well as the sheer weight of scholarly information featured make his writing appear far removed from the charm of Horatian satire, in which the author's philosophical-literary knowledge and his linguistic virtuosity were hidden behind a *neglegentia diligens*, or methodical casualness. Still, Persius' satires are invaluable evidence of contemporary literary standards, and of the philosophical interests of literary circles.

Epigrammatics

If verse satire belonged exclusively to the Latin language, the opposite is true of the tradition of the literary epigram. This goes back to the eighth century BC, the time immediately after the invention of the Greek alphabet, which was based on the Phoenician one. Among the Greeks of that period, it had become a habit to use verse in inscriptions on graves and on buildings consecrated to gods, but also in those marking the origin or the destination of diverse kinds of man-made objects. Above the level of the many different dialects of contemporary vernacular, the only available linguistic form for such verses was that of the epic tradition, at that time still an oral one. That literary language knew only slight regional variations, and was thus understood in the entire Greek world.

Hence epic language became the norm in verse inscriptions, with only occasional intrusions of local dialect. This remained unchanged even when from the seventh century BC onwards the elegiac distich – composed of hexameter and pentameter – began to replace successive hexameters in standard verse inscriptions. The pentameter, which could be seen as composed of the first halves of two hexameters, likewise lent itself best to the use of the traditional formulas of epic verse narrative. The very occasional occurrence of inscriptions in different metres, mostly iambic, did not affect the existing linguistic convention either.

The Greek world of the sixth and fifth centuries BC was abounding with verse inscriptions; naturally people would distinguish between the good and the less successful ones and would often – rightly or wrongly – ascribe the former to famous poets. Thus there seem to have been early collections of verse inscriptions from the fifth century BC published under the name of the poet Simonides. One epigram featured in such a collection was the famous inscription about the dead of the Battle of Thermopylae in 480 BC, a piece which Cicero translated into Latin, and Schiller into German.

The next step towards the establishment of a literary genre was taken in the fourth century BC, when fictitious funereal or consecrational inscriptions were written for a reading public: that is, when the form of the epigram was used for a purely literary purpose. We have one specimen from a poet named Theocritus, a man not to be confused with the author of bucolic poetry. That text was ostensibly inscribed 'by the numskull Aristotle, on the empty grave' of his friend Hermias of Atarneus. Here, the form of the fictitious funereal epigram is used as the vehicle for personal polemics.

The necessary conciseness of an inscription had made the writers of epigrams early masters of the art of concise, pointed form. In the 3rd century BC, one could already use the term *epigramma* for a 'humorous point', a meaning which was adopted along with the word in several European languages. The ability to express oneself in a short, precise, and at the same time eloquent way, was held in particular esteem in the scholarly poetry of Hellenism. The Hellenistic age brought the first heyday of epigrammatic poetry; we have epigrams from nearly all the major poets of Hellenism, and some of them even wrote exclusively in the epigrammatic form.

The production of literary epigrams remained linked to the writing of epigrams for practical use, that is for engraving on stone. Among the extant hundreds of epigrammatic inscriptions from the Hellenistic and the Imperial age we find many pieces of high quality, and some which have also been handed down in literary sources. On the other hand literary epigrammatics gradually moved farther away from the traditional forms of votive and funereal epigrams, extending the range of subject matter beyond that covered by the two most popular kinds of verse inscription. Hence, epigrams came to be written on erotic, sympotic, or literary subjects; they could be descriptions of existing or imaginary works of art, personal invective, atmospheric sketches, or retellings of jokes.

The diversity and the widespread popularity of epigrammatic poetry led to the formation of different schools in the Hellenistic age, and there were also attempts to introduce different dialects. The spoken dialects of Greek had gradually become extinct in the age of Hellenism, being replaced by the Koine which was fairly unified, in spite of certain regional variations. The love for the past brought a new interest in the ancient dialects, linguistic forms which could only be regained by the scholarly interpretation of literary texts and epigrammatic inscriptions. The attempts at a revival were not altogether unsuccessful, as ancient dialects did in fact reappear in epigrammatic poetry. From a later period we have epigrams by the poetess Balbilla, pieces written in the old dialect of the island of Lesbos, as it had been used by Sappho and Alcaeus. Balbilla accompanied the wife of the Emperor Hadrian on her voyage to Egypt; the lady-in-waiting composed a verse inscription to immortalise the court's visit to the so-called Memnon Colossus.

No other literary genre ever had such a long and unbroken tradition as that of the epigram; on the Greek side, that tradition included the entire Byzantine era. As early as 70 BC the epigrammatic poet Meleager from Gadara in Syria put together a large collection of older and contemporary epigrams in alphabetical order, including of course his own works. Around 40 AD the poet Philippus of Thessalonica adopted this collection, adding some more recent specimens. The collection edited by Agathias around 500 AD had a similar genesis but it grouped the epigrams according to subject matter; that collection was in turn adopted and enlarged around 900 AD by Constantinus Cephalas. The latter collection, complemented by an anthology of non-epigrammatic poetry from the Late Classical and the Early Byzantine ages, is presumably what we have in the famous *Anthologia Palatina*, a codex from the tenth century, one half of which is kept in Heidelberg, and the other half in Paris. One later compilation, though largely identical in content, was written by Maximus Planudes around 1300 AD; his collection features an appendix with four hundred poems which are missing in the *Anthologia Palatina*.

Beside the numerous specimens handed down in Classical and Byzantine manuscripts and the countless verse inscriptions which have been discovered, even more epigrams from all periods of Greek literary history survived in the form of quotations in the works of many authors. This is true of the Classic era, but even more so of later centuries; for from the Hellenistic age onwards inscriptions were systematically collected as source material for historical-antiquarian research and thus preserved as literary material too.

Like the Greeks, the Romans also developed the early habit of composing and engraving verse inscriptions above all on tombs, but also sometimes on sacred buildings. In older times they used the native Italic Saturnian metre, which was also that of the first Roman epics. The hexameter and the elegiac distich came to be used in inscriptions after the introduction of the hexameter in Roman epic poetry. As on the Greek side, there were also some Roman inscriptions in metres known from dramatic dialogue; those were likewise adaptations of Greek models to the peculiar features of the Latin language.

Thus we also have hundreds of Roman verse inscriptions of very different quality preserved on stone, specimens dating from the first century BC to the Late Classical age. Roman literary epigrams are not as well documented as on the Greek side, because of the lack of comparably rich collections. There is only one slightly mutilated codex from the seventh century AD, the *Codex Salmasianus* in Paris, which contains short poems from different genres, periods, and places of origin; among them are also numerous epigrams. As the most recent authors featured belong to Vandalic North Africa, this collection must have been put together there, in the late fifth century AD. In the manuscript, many epigrams are ascribed to famous writers such as Virgil, Ovid, Lucan, Germanicus, or Seneca; such indications of authorship are frequently – but not always – correct. Of some of those poets, there are also epigrams in Greek. Strangely enough, there is one prominent name which is missing among the authors quoted in the *Codex Salmasianus*: it is that of Catullus, who was arguably the most brilliant epigrammatist the Romans ever had.

All of the aforementioned collections as well as other anthologies of shorter poems preserved in mediaeval manuscripts were published around 1900, together with those verse inscriptions known at that time, in the several volumes of an edition entitled *Anthologia Latina*. The combination of its material is well justified, especially with regard to epigrams. The *Anthologia Latina* contains particularly good evidence for the fluency with which people in the Latin West also wrote such poems on all kinds of occasions, closely or loosely following traditional epigrammatic formats. As the great poets – especially Virgil – were read in schools, a large public would be familiar with the formulas and the other linguistic-metrical conventions of hexametric poetry, and would understand allusions in content or form, to passages from high literary art. The extensive and intensive study of Classic Latin poetry in Humanistic circles from the fourteenth century onwards resulted in a similarly fluent and effortless production of epigrams of the most diverse content. However, the truly Classic author of the Latin epigram, Martial, belongs to the end of the first century AD.

The first names to mention on the Greek side are those of Philip of Thessalonica, who compiled the second major collection of epigrams, and of his slightly older contemporary Antiphilus of Byzantium. The *Anthologia Palatina* contains about eighty epigrams by Philip, and about fifty by Antiphilus. Both prefer topics which lend themselves to paying homage to the court, to the Emperor's family, and to his reign. Philip seems to have lived in Rome: he describes a swarm of bees which built its hive on the monument commemorating the Battle of Actium, choosing those parts which represent ships' prows. This he sees as an emblem of law and peace secured under Imperial rule (6, 236). A baffled Antiphilus asks if the new gigantic jetty of the port of Puteoli is perhaps the work of Cyclops, as it alters the face of the earth in such a drastic manner. The answer points to Rome, the centre of the world, for which even such a harbour is hardly sufficient, though it can shelter the merchant fleets of all seafaring nations (7, 379). This epigram pays homage to the great engineering and building feats of Augustus' confidant and son-in-law Agrippa. Another, trimetric poem (16, 52) contains similar hyperboles and allusions to myth; it celebrates the strength of a pancratiast, a sportsman competing in a discipline which combined boxing and wrestling.

Both Philip and Antiphilus represent an epigrammatic style which is less distinguished by especially artful versification – for instance, in the regular distribution of word endings to specific places within the verse – than by its use of verbal mannerisms. In their works we find obscure expressions alien to the genre tradition, daring metaphors, or phrases referring with great pathos to ordinary objects, or to everyday events. An early model for this style was Leonidas of Tarentum, a poet from the Early Hellenistic age, who had a preference for pathetic-emotional expressions and made use of a large vocabulary, including technical and vulgar terms. A different style was represented by Callimachus who wrote a little later than Leonidas. Callimachus composed his humorous or serious epigrams without recourse to rare expressions, and with extreme conciseness of diction.

Part of the baroque or mannerist tradition was the fashion of writing dialogical epigrams. For that, there was a precedent in the old convention of formulating inscriptions on tombstones as messages from the dead to passers-by. In literary epigrammatic poetry, this was extended to full dialogue; and a favourite device in that tradition was the epigrammatic conversation with alternating short questions and answers exchanged between a living person and the deceased about, for instance, the dead person's impressions of the underworld. Such a dialogue form was also used for other kinds of inscriptions: there is one in two distichs engraved on the base of a statue dating from the year 49 AD, in which the athlete honoured by its erection answers questions concerning his name, his home, and his victories (Inscr. of Olympia, 225).

Entirely different from the mannerist tradition is the epigrammatic art of Lukillios, who lived in Rome during Nero's reign, and from whom we have about a hundred specimens of the genre. Lukillios dedicated a collection of epigrams to the Emperor; the introductory poem of that collection has been preserved in the *Anthologia Palatina*.

Lukillios wrote some of the most amusing epigrammatic poems in Greek; our sources indicate that he wrote almost exclusively mocking verses. His satire is directed at different phenomena and characters from city life, but above all at the world of sport. In the Greek as well as the Latin world of the period, each major city had specific dates set aside in its calendar for sports festivals or *agones*. Most of the competitors were professional sportsmen who moved from city to city, enjoyed great popularity, and often amassed considerable fortunes. One of the main duties of the municipal aristocracy was the organisation and the sponsorship of those events. From the members of the aristocracy, the top officials of independent municipal administrations were recruited and a successful career in sports could occasionally provide access to the ranks of this class. Our knowledge of sport in those days is mainly based on inscriptions honouring successful athletes, commissioned by or in their native towns. There are also inscriptions commissioned by such athletes themselves, accompanying votive gifts donated as tokens of gratitude for athletic successes.

Lukillios used the formulas of dedicatory, honorific, and also funerary inscriptions as means to deride the sports business, just as he would censure bad table manners or vices peculiar to certain professions. One epigram in three distichs ostensibly honours a boxer in the conventional poetic terms for describing victory in a competition; however, from this text we learn that the recipient of the praise had in three respective fights lost an ear, lost an eyelid, and been carried from the ring unconscious (11, 81). Another epigram of an anecdotal kind tells of a boxer who was mutilated to such an extent that his brother refused to give him his share in their paternal inheritance, claiming that the sportsman no longer fitted in with the family image (11, 75). Another, shorter one (11, 50) parodies an inscription in which a sports club honours a member: he is given a statue because he never hurt anyone – meaning that he cannot have been a serious competitor.

Among the targets of these mocking epigrams, there are physicians and astrologers as well as sportsmen. They are all given proper names but we cannot know whether those names refer to real persons or to characters created through literary fiction. In any case, Lukillios' satire is not personal invective, but rather aimed at social or human conditions and behaviour. His language is plain and devoid of manneristic frills; his versification is extremely smooth and correct.

6 NARRATIVE PROSE

Petronius

Unfortunately we have no more than fragments of that major novel written by Petronius which is certainly the most original literary work in the history of Roman prose. Its originality makes it extremely hard to give this work a proper place in the history of genres; still, there is ultimately reason enough for labelling it as a novel, in spite of the fact that it contains elements which are entirely alien to the Greek novelistic tradition.

There are no known references to Petronius' narrative before about 200 AD. At the end of the first century AD both Pliny the Elder and Plutarch mention a T. Petronius; a little later, Tacitus talks of a C. Petronius as one of the closest friends of the Emperor Nero. We learn that this man was Consul in 60 AD; that he was regarded as an *arbiter elegantiarum*, an authority on all aspects of refined, luxurious lifestyle; and that like Seneca he was forced to put an end to his own life in 65 AD in the aftermath of the conspiracy of Piso. But neither Tacitus nor the two earlier sources link the name Petronius with literary authorship, and the difference between the first names Gaius and Titus makes an identification even more problematic. Still, we have good grounds for the assumption that Pliny and Plutarch as well as Tacitus meant the same person, the author of the *Satyrica*, whom the manuscripts quote as Petronius Arbiter, or C. Petronius Arbiter.

There is a problem also with the title *Satyrica* or *Satyricon libri*, the latter featuring the Greek genitive form. *Satyrica* recalls, for instance, Virgil's *Georgica*. The title chosen by Virgil was an adoption into Latin of a Greek adjective in the plural form; as the name of the book it meant something like 'agricultural issues'. Titles of this kind were popular in Greek literature, above all in narrative writing. Names like Indica, Parthica, Babyloniaca, Phoenicica, or Milesiaca were given to historiographical and geographical works, but also to novels and erotic novella cycles.

As Plutarch noted around 100 AD the word *satyrikos* was a common epithet used to describe a man who led the life of a libertine, occupied only with the pursuit of sensual pleasure, just like a satyr or nature demon in the train of the wine god Dionysus. That seems to be the meaning which Petronius had in mind when he selected the title for his book which tells of the adventures of two men of this type who have a homosexual relationship with one another. However, we may assume that a connection between the word *satura* or *satira* and what we associate with the word satirical in the modern sense had already been established through the *saturae* of Lucilius and Horace, and through the genre called *satura menippea* (see p. 99), which mixed poetry and prose, humour and seriousness, in the manner of Cynic moral instruction. Thus it seems likely that Petronius' choice of title is a pun linking the satyr to satire; for his book brims over with lasciviousness as well as with mockery.

The original narrative presumably comprised twenty or even twenty-four books. Extant are only a number of shorter excerpts and one longer one, giving us altogether no more than a fraction of the plot and hence only a rough idea of its outline. The story was about the wanderings of a couple of friends called Encolpius and Giton who were haunted by the wrath of Priapus just as Ulysses had been pursued by the angry Poseidon. Priapus was a rural god of fertility, all but unrelated to the major deities of urban and state cults. His entry into literature was only through erotic associations; a case in point is an extant small corpus – difficult to date –

of erotic poems which focus on Priapus who was invariably represented in ithyphallic form in the visual arts.

During their 'odyssey', Encolpius and Giton are confronted with many different characters, some of whom join the travellers for a part of their way, creating jealousy and causing quarrels. Among them are the teacher of rhetoric Agamemnon, the poet Eumolpus, the sea-captain Lichas, and the libertine Ascyltus who is Giton's second lover; plus diverse witches, priestesses of Priapus, and *hetairai*, or newly-rich freedmen. Most of the adventures related are of an erotic nature, but there are also tales of shipwreck, trade with stolen goods, witchcraft, legacy-hunts, or culinary orgies.

Petronius chose a contemporary setting; most of the action, narrated by the chief protagonist Encolpius, takes place in the cities of southern Italy. Even those few excerpts which we know give us an exceedingly rich image of the social reality of the period. Through the medium of first-person narration the author derides business malpractices and misguided religious ideas, bad amatorial habits and abuses common in educational institutions, extravagant literary fashions and the culinary ostentation of rich upstarts trying to imitate the style of the court. Further targets include superstition and astrology, the disparaging and humiliating treatment of slaves, and much more.

One surprising fact which runs counter to all known Classical conventions is the precision with which the linguistic spectrum of Petronius' novel reflects its broad social canvas. It is true that the existing fragments do not feature the portrait of any member of the upper classes in the narrower sense. However, the main protagonists in particular are educated people who are well equipped for conversing with the poets and teachers of rhetoric whom they meet on their travels, but whose wanderings equally bring them into contact with people who are socially and educationally far below them.

Petronius' language expresses all those distinctions. The best example for this is the one longer excerpt, handed down separately from the others, in which the narrator Encolpius tells us about a feast at which he was a guest. The host is a newly rich liberated slave, indulging in excessive luxury which reveals his lack of taste. The narrator speaks an informal, but educated colloquial language, which deviates only slightly from written usage in phonetical and grammatical forms, as well as in vocabulary. In contrast to him, the ostentatious host and his friends converse in an idiom which is our only textual evidence of Latin as it was spoken by ordinary people in the first century AD, apart from graffiti in the ruins of Pompeii that were buried by the ashes of Vesuvius in 79 AD. Trimalchio, the rich host, occasionally has a go at elevated diction, improvising or quoting verse. But his language is vulgar throughout and his vocabulary together with the grammatical forms he uses show the modern reader how close the spoken Latin of that period was in many ways to the later Romance languages. Yet the author shows remarkable tact in his total avoidance of all obscene words, in spite of the largely erotic character of the narrative, and in spite of his portrayal of many extremely ill-educated people.

As the language of the simple Trimalchio occasionally rises to a higher plane, so do people of a higher social class sometimes switch to a more elevated register as, for instance, when the conversation turns to a literary topic. In such cases Petronius uses the clause structure which characterised all educated language, that is the rhythmic regularisation of clause endings according to quantitative patterns dictating the distribution of long and short syllables.

The differences between the characters in Petronius' novel are reflected not only in their use of language, but also in corresponding behaviour and attitudes. From Trimalchio's utterances the reader learns that in his circles neither the gods of traditional religion nor the concept of a life after death are of any importance. Instead, there are superstitious beliefs which make people perform all kinds of ritual actions and pronouncements in order to secure material wealth, the only recognised goal in life. Trimalchio, for example, has one of his slaves see to it that each one of his guests puts the right foot forward when entering the dining room; another slave is entrusted with the keeping of his astrological diary. Part of the grotesque luxuries which the upstart offers to his guests is the anointing of their feet, also performed by slaves. That habit was generally seen by Petronius' contemporaries as being typical of inappropriate pleasure-seeking in the Oriental style. We know, however, that the custom was introduced at Nero's court exactly at the time when Petronius wrote his novel.

In the book Trimalchio shows that even he has heard of popular philosophical doctrines, mainly of the Stoic kind, concerning the moral – if not social – emancipation of slaves, and their masters' duty to treat them as fellow humans, something which is repeatedly preached by Seneca. Trimalchio echoes such opinions but his actions give his words the lie: thus, for example, he uses the hair of a young slave to dry his hands after washing them. In a similar manner Petronius also characterises other personages, such as boozy old priestesses, shameless scroungers, or conceited literary authors. But Petronius never comes across as an outraged moralist; rather as an amused, ironic observer.

His novel includes lengthy verse passages in various metres. The extant parts open with a scene in which Agamemnon, the teacher of oratory, sums up a preceding debate about the decline of eloquence and the futility of rhetorical instruction. This summary is given in a poem which Agamemnon announces as a satire in the plain style of Lucilius from the second century BC; however, as his profession suggests, his product turns out to be rather more on the bombastic side. By looking at a painting by the famous artist Apelles, the poet Eumolpus, who accompanies the narrator for some time, is inspired to give a poetical description of the conquest of Troy in the iambic senarius, the prevalent metre of tragedy. This verse interlude is undoubtedly a parody on two passages of identical content from the tragedies of Seneca. I have already mentioned another piece of poetry likewise spoken by Eumolpus, the three hundred opening lines of an epic which constitute a correction of Lucan's *Pharsalia* (see p. 119).

Besides these and other, shorter verse interludes, the action is also interrupted by the embedding of entire stories. Some of those are popular tales of horror about witches and werewolves, while others are concisely narrated novellas, such as that about the widow of Ephesus, a story which has become famous. It tells of a woman who is sitting in the family vault lamenting her husband's death during the night after his funeral. Her moans are heard by a soldier guarding the corpse of a crucified criminal at the nearby place of execution. This soldier comes to console the bereaved, comforting her so successfully and for such a long time that meanwhile, the crucified man's family manages to take the dead body off the cross. Then the widow gives her new lover the corpse of her husband to hang on the cross in order to help him to avoid punishment!

Petronius' monumental work is full of allusions to older and contemporary literature, from Homer to the tragedies of Seneca; but all the same, it is impossible to assign the *Satyrica* a proper place in the literary tradition. Petronius' influence seems to show in the picaresque novel which originated in sixteenth-century Spain, and which was later imitated in other countries; examples of the genre are *Lazarillo de Tormes* or *Gil Blas*. Like Petronius, their authors tried to make the adventures of an amoral hero give a moral portrayal of an entire society, especially with its faults and vices, in a manner that avoided moralising pathos. Still, the fashion of writing picaresque novels began long before the literary discovery of Petronius which did not come about until the seventeenth century, although the scholarly study of Petronius' work had started a couple of centuries earlier.

Anyone who looks for models for Petronius' writing would first have to consider the Greek novel, a genre well known in Rome at that time, as Persius asserts (1, 134). The most popular type of plot featured a couple of lovers, outstandingly beautiful and virtuous, who were separated by a hostile fate. Each one had to pass through the most trying adventures before both were finally reunited, having preserved their chastity and proved their faithfulness.

The similarity to the plot of Petronius' novel is obvious, and furthermore the resemblance to the plot of the *Odyssey* which served as a model in both cases. But there are just as many differences between the *Satyrica* and the type of Greek novel I have just described. Petronius' realism and his satirical-ironical tone are quite distinct from the moral solemnity and the idealising or typifying presentation of milieu and character in Greek novels.

Some of the latter also feature verse interludes, but those are quotations from Homer or from other poets, designed to heighten the pathos at climactic points of the plot; they are not at all like the showpieces in which the author Petronius himself comments in an ironical or polemical way on contemporary literary issues.

Petronius' specific mixture of poetry and prose, as well as his extensive portrayal of human weaknesses and bad habits, must definitely be seen as related to the example set by Menippean satire. However, Petronius uses the devices and motifs of that genre not at all in order to exert a moral-pedagogical influence on the readers, but instead to entertain them with a kaleidoscope of human stupidity and depravity.

One excerpt, from the last part of the novel, tells of how the two friends Encolpius and Giton set out to obtain a large inheritance by fraud, hiding their true identities: in the text this is compared to the stage production of a *mimus*. Many of the novel's motifs are indeed familiar from comedy and *mimus*; those two genres of dramatic writing also knew the characterisation of individual dramatis personae by giving them linguistic peculiarities. But Petronius' use of this device aims at the indication of social class, whereas on stage linguistic oddities merely marked characters out as foreigners or strangers. Petronius' typical and consistent adaptation of dialogue to the different speakers' social status and to the given circumstances, a technique which produces a large variety of linguistic nuances, is without a parallel in Classical literature.

Beside the many obvious literary allusions in the text, we thus also have other evidence proving that Petronius used elements of a large number of literary as well as of popular subliterary traditions in the writing of his gigantic work without fully embracing any of those traditions. It is chiefly this which makes his novel, even in its fragmentary form, one of the most fascinating pieces we have of Graeco-Roman literature. The author's originality must largely be seen in his sovereign use of the most diverse possibilities existing in given literary traditions.

The Greek novel

Like other nations, the Greeks had what is now called prose fiction from a very early time in their history, in the oral forms of fairy tales, animal fables, humorous stories, and other kinds of folk tales. Where those types of narrative prose found a written literary form, they were mostly embedded in larger works with entirely different themes and intentions, such as Herodotus' major historiographical account from the fifth century BC. In such a larger context a folk tale or a traveller's tale would quite often be presented in the shape of an artfully composed novella. From the fourth century BC onwards we find literary authors narrating longer pieces from the mythological or historical tradition; likewise with a purpose that goes beyond the stories as such. Thus Xenophon used historical information in writing a novel which tells the story of Cyrus, founder of the Persian Empire, with the aim of drawing a picture of an ideal monarch. Antisthenes, a contemporary of Socrates, retold the story of Hercules as an example of the moral ascent of man.

It was not until about 100 BC that Greek literature began to feature novellas and novels where the only interest ultimately lay in the question: Will the hero and the heroine get married? Around that time a certain Aristides published the *Milesiaca*, a collection of erotic novellas into which, for instance, Petronius' story of the widow of Ephesus would have fitted quite well. The first longer novels were written shortly after the *Milesiaca*; fragments of those texts have only recently been discovered on papyrus scrolls. A text which originated in roughly the same period as the latter is the novel by Chariton, the oldest among the extant novels handed down to us through mediaeval manuscripts. I have already mentioned the typical plot of such narratives, which all deal with the fate of a couple of lovers (see p. 130). The full range of the authors' imagination is reflected in the invention of trials and adventures through which those lovers have to pass: there are instances of shipwreck and suspended animation; they are sold as slaves or forced to live with kidnappers; or they are amorously pursued by other men or women. All that, and much more, is often transposed into exotic settings, in order to heighten the stories' appeal to the reader.

In the beginning there was a good deal of uncertainty about the literary evaluation of the novelistic genre. This is proved by the fact that the earliest novels we know of wrap their plots around situations or characters described by Greek historians of the Classic or the Hellenistic era. Cases in point are the *Sesonchosis* and *Ninos* novels, set in an Egyptian and Babylonian milieu respectively; and the *Parthenope*, *Calligone*, and *Chione* texts which borrow mainly from Herodotus. All of those novels are known to us only from papyrus fragments. They cannot be dated with any precision but we may assume that they belong to either the first century BC or the first century AD. Linguistic features indicate that Chariton's *Callirhoe* novel was written in the first century BC; this book, mentioned by Persius in his first satire, was extremely popular in the Classical age, and is extant in a complete form. Its action is set in Syracuse after the defeat of the Athenian army which had laid siege to the city, as reported by Thucydides. The plot of the novel is composed with great diligence and strict logic, and the sufferings of the separated lovers do not seem too exaggerated. Those novels which were written in the second century AD, the true floruit of the genre, often go well over the top in the invention and description of adversities and agonies, and are thus likely to strike the modern reader as fairly unpalatable.

The structural framework of the *Callirhoe* novel consists of straightforward third-person narration of the story's events, which are partly set in Persian surroundings. But even in this early specimen of the genre, the characters' speeches are already quite prominent. Together with the high dramatic tension in many of the situations described, this emphasis on dialogue gives certain episodes of the book the character of dramatic scenes. The part where the lovers recognise each other at their final reunion was particularly likely to remind readers of what was a common stage motif, occurring in a scene which marked the climax and the conclusion of the dramatic plot. Among the great authors of Greek theatre, Euripides had been the one most fond of using this constellation as a central part of the action; and the same motif was recreated time and again in New Comedy. All this shows the closeness of the Greek novel to drama; but the *Callirhoe* text is also in keeping with the rhetorical quality of most post-Classic Greek prose literature, in that the speeches of those characters directly involved in the action are often of a declamatory character. This is a feature which is bound to strike a modern reader as particularly strange in a novelistic context.

The novel by Antonius Diogenes, of which we have an excerpt made by the Patriarch Photius of Constantinople in the ninth century, was presumably written in the late first century AD. This monumental work in twenty-four books told the story of two lovers from the Phoenician city of Tyre who are pursued all over the world by an Egyptian magician. The setting for their most terrifying adventures was the far North, the lands on the other side of the legendary island of Thule, which is why the title was *Miraculous Things beyond Thule*. The fantastic quality of that novel gave rise to a parody in Lucian's *True Stories*, written in the second century AD. But the most peculiar feature of Antonius Diogenes' narrative, whose complex structure was made up of reports from different characters involved in the action, is the use of motifs from the Pythagorean doctrine concerning the transmigration of souls. Thus, for instance, the hero and the heroine are for a long time condemned to live only by night, and to be dead during the day.

From the extant excerpt we get only a rough idea of the plot which combines the motif of the fleeing and temporarily separated lovers – already a well-established constituent of the novel by that time – with motifs from two other literary traditions. They were the description of the wonders of exotic countries; and the reporting of incredible events in the manner of those writings known as *paradoxa*. The first of these two traditions had evolved alongside historiography and geography. As the horizon of those disciplines widened, more and more authors were tempted to write fictitious reports about the wonders which were to be found in distant lands. Literary *paradoxa* originated in the context of natural science as pursued, for example, in the Aristotelian school where philosophers recorded and explained natural phenomena. Again it was natural that other writers should recognise the entertainment value of such reports and consequently compose miraculous tales based on their own invention, or on popular oral traditions. From the Late Hellenistic age, we have the famous cock-and-bull stories by Antiphanes of Berge, featuring the motif of the frozen sounds which we know from the German tales of Baron Münchhausen. All extant collections of paradoxography are from much later periods; but quite a few episodes in the novel by Antonius Diogenes – whose name indicates that he held Roman citizenship – as well as in subsequent productions in the same genre prove that authors of Greek prose fiction at that time had access to such material, and made extensive use of it.

7 HISTORIOGRAPHY

Romans

The historian Tacitus began writing his last major work in the third decade of the second century AD, looking back at the history of the Early Empire since the death of Augustus. Tacitus' account starts with a review of the historiography of that period, which the author could not avoid using as a source of information. He does not name any individual writers, but he maintains that historiography had generally declined under the conditions established by the monarchy, in spite of the fact that the historiographical tradition had initially been continued by major authors. Another statement to the same effect comes from the Senator Cassius Dio, who wrote a voluminous history of the world in Greek in the early third century AD, and who used the same source material as Tacitus in his chapter on the Early Empire. A similar idea is articulated also in the only extant fragment of the biography which the philosopher Seneca wrote of his father, the teacher of rhetoric. This reference to Seneca the Elder's historical writings expresses another version of the aforementioned sentiment, as does an isolated mention of the Emperor Claudius' attempts at historiographical writing.

All these sources indicate that the actual or supposed decline of historiography was a much-discussed topic in the Early Empire. The reasons which are suggested for the decline of the genre could be summed up in an argument which runs like this:

> Before, in the Republic, historical truth could be assessed in spite of the biases of historiographers; for they were either active politicians from the great families of the nobility, or clients of those houses. Hence, the judgment on historical events was as open to debate as were political decisions, and each reader of historiography could make his mind up for himself. Now, under the monarchy, the only remaining forms of bias are flattery directed at the reigning Emperor,

secret resentment against the living monarch, and open hatred against the dead ruler. Political decisions used to be taken after controversial public debate in the Senate and the people's assembly; now such business is transacted behind the closed doors of the Imperial cabinet. Even war, formerly the one occasion most likely to make citizens aware of being part of a community, is now merely the Emperor's private concern, for the army consists of professional soldiers whose loyalty belongs to him alone. He is the only one who decides about the deployment of troops; and in any case, military engagements can only be expected on the Empire's borders or in colonial wars: for within the realm which unites all civilised humanity there is that peace which can only be guaranteed by the monarchy, and which nobody would seriously want to jeopardise.

It is unfortunately no longer possible to examine continuous historical narrative from and about the Early Empire in the light of such reflections. All those works which continued the annalistic tradition of the Republic were lost – as for example, that by Cremutius Cordus. At the instigation of Sejanus, the man who for some time held nearly absolute power as counsellor to the Emperor Tiberius, Cordus was charged in the Senate with labelling Caesar's assassins Brutus and Cassius in his historical work as 'the last Romans'. The accused starved himself to death rather than wait for the verdict. His historical writing was confiscated and burned; his daughter, however, saved one copy of the work, and published it during the reign of Tiberius' successor Caligula. Of the Consular Thrasea Paetus, one of those who participated in the conspiracy of Piso in 66 AD, we know only that he followed Stoic philosophy and that his historical work hence praised Cato the Younger as the last champion of Republican liberty, as Lucan's epic had done.

These facts indicate that representatives of the Senatorial opposition among the historiographers were inclined to air their views through the description of the last civil wars, rather than in the portrayal of current events. In doing so they could refer to the example set by historians contemporary with Augustus. Those men, such as Virgil's first patron Asinius Pollio, had provided important services to the future monarch, but regarded his rise to absolute power with Republican misgivings.

Among the historiographers of the Early Empire, there were also two prominent figures who seem to have had little sympathy for the opposition. These two men, who were held in high esteem at least during the second century AD, were M. Servilius Nonianus and Aufidius Bassus; the first, who died in 59 AD, was one of the most reputable Senators, a close friend of the Emperor Claudius, and famous above all for his elegant literary style. Aufidius Bassus did not belong to the Senatorial class, and as a staunch Epicurean, he would have kept his distance from the world of politics. In his thirtieth letter, written not long after 60 AD, Seneca tells of a visit to the aged Aufidius, saying that the old man's philosophical stance had helped him preserve his peace of mind and his intellectual vivacity in spite of the severe frailty of his condition.

A textual fragment describing the killing of Cicero shows that Aufidius' historical work included the final decades of the civil wars. A chronological survey from the Late Classical age indicates that his writing covered the death of Tiberius, and possibly even later events: for Pliny the Elder's account of recent history, dedicated to the Emperor Vespasian, is a direct continuation of Aufidius' work.

It is regrettable that we know so little about the lost literary production by the Emperor Claudius who, according to his biographer Suetonius, wrote historiography before as well as after his accession to the throne. One historical work in Latin began its account with the assassination of Caesar; but the author seems to have abandoned this delicate subject after being cautioned by his mother and his grandmother. When he started to write again Claudius took the safer option of commencing the narrative with the establishment of Imperial peace in 31 BC. His second work, which dealt with current history, ran to as many as forty-one books or papyrus scrolls. It is not known whether Claudius included much material of historical interest in his autobiography; what is certain, though, is that his historiographical efforts in Greek were of an antiquarian nature and included a history of the Etruscans as well as one of Carthage.

We have only indirect evidence or minute fragments of those historiographical works I have referred to in the present chapter. But what we do have is enough to prove that the Early Empire with its as yet undigested recent past could offer no more than an insecure foundation for the continuation of Roman historiography, a genre dominated by aristocratic traditions.

Of this fact, however, we find no indication in the one historical work from the period which has been preserved, if only with a number of gaps. Its author was C. Velleius Paterculus, a man of equestrian rank who went through a long military career during the reign of Augustus, and who rose to the Senatorial class as a Praetor under Tiberius. Velleius' work is dedicated to M. Vinicius, the son of his first military superior, on the occasion of Vinicius' Consulate in 30 AD. Velleius was presumably between fifty and sixty years old at that time. His two books give a survey of Roman history from its beginnings to the author's own lifetime. The first book also deals with the mythical early history of Greece, with the succession of the great world empires, with Greek and Roman literary history, and with the founding of Roman colonies. The second book includes a survey on Roman provinces.

The relative brevity of the whole account explains the sketchiness in the author's portrayal of historical events belonging to the more remote past.

In the writing of those parts of his work, he made use of historical compendia, a kind of source which had been available for quite some time. The division of the narrative into two books is marked by the year 146 BC which makes the destruction of Carthage stand out as signifying the end of an epoch. This assessment goes back to Sallust who had put the inner decay of Roman society down to the annihilation of Rome's last serious rival. Velleius' account becomes more detailed in the second book and in the description of Tiberius' reign it attains the depth of genuine contemporary history. Here the author could largely draw on his own experiences: he had been a high-ranking military commander in campaigns led by Tiberius before his accession to the throne, along the Rhine and the Danube. It is likely that Velleius occasionally also used archive material.

Velleius' portrayal of Tiberius' military and political achievements is full of unqualified praise, and thus contrasts strangely with the sombre image drawn by Tacitus from the material which Early Imperial sources offered. However, the suggestion that Velleius was prone to flattery as a successful careerist is too facile. The knighthood, especially those of its members who were of a municipal origin, was bound to perceive the monarchic order and its representatives in a light that differed greatly from that in which it appeared to the Senatorial families, who cherished Republican traditions. The latter's prime concern was the Emperor's relationship with the Senate; to the former, it was administrative efficiency as a necessary condition for economic prosperity. Moreover, many opportunities for distinction and promotion were open to the educated equestrian bourgeoisie through service in the Imperial army and administration where most offices were reserved for the members of this class. All told, the knighthood had come to constitute a very special part of the framework supporting the state; and in Velleius' writing, we hear the voice of a typical exponent of an equestrian way of thinking. Velleius' loyalty to Tiberius is that of an officer to his general; and it is that individual loyalty to the person at the head of the state which ensured the survival of the Roman Empire's global order over the centuries. This order would hardly have lasted as long as it did without the work of countless individual officials, sharing a marked sense of personal duty.

In his assessment of the transition to the monarchic Principate, Velleius differed radically from the historiographers in the Senatorial tradition, who perceived a break in the continuity of Roman history. To Velleius there was none (2, 89): and this proves that in the circles which he represented, the Augustan ideology which saw Octavian's final victory as the restoration of the Old Roman order had been completely accepted, only one human lifespan after its initial propagation. Velleius shared this view of recent Roman history; and he would certainly have expressed it even more clearly if he had been able to realise his plan to write a separate detailed account of the events between Caesar's civil war and his own lifetime.

Velleius' work thus introduced a new element into Roman historiography; and it was not his only innovation. The old Roman-Republican tradition had cherished the memories of great men because they stood for virtues which were regarded as specifically Roman, and which had guided their political actions. As individuals, those men were regarded as being of little interest; and this is why Cato the Elder had been able to write a history of Rome and Italy which did not feature any proper names at all, calling the actors by their official titles only. The dominant concern with exemplary rather than individual actions in the historical process is also documented in Livy's major work, a comprehensive collection of traditional historiography.

This concept of history had been practically refuted by the great and brutal men of the Late Republic, like Sulla, Marius, Caesar, Antony, or Octavian; men whose actions were without precedents. By giving the monarch an exalted position, the new order effectively provided the legitimation for a kind of historiography that focused on the unique achievement of individuals. Velleius was a historian with a biographical interest; and significantly enough, the first evidence of this interest can be found in his account of events during the final years of the Republic. The biographical focus is then fully developed in his portrayal of Tiberius' reign, which reads like a life of the Emperor. A century later than Velleius, Tacitus used a similar approach in the first six books of his *Annals*. Tacitus' aim was, however, to present the biography of a tyrant sinking to ever-lower depths, with the author expressing his regret for the fact that Imperial Rome no longer produced any material which was really worthy of the historiographer's attention. Unlike Velleius, Tacitus after all saw himself as belonging to the Republican tradition.

The introduction and the digressions in Velleius' history show that the author is keen to present historiography as a part of general education, including the knowledge of non-Roman traditions, and of the geography and particularly the literature of the Greek as well as the Latin world. This is likewise characteristic of the author's social class, as is his endeavour to maintain a refined style. Velleius was an old soldier and not a scholar or a rhetorically trained man of letters: for those roles, his talent may not have sufficed anyway. His style, for instance, shows that he knew the pattern of Ciceronian periods but that he never mastered it. Nevertheless, any member of his class who became an author would have had to prove his education in form as well as content.

Since the days of Isocrates historiography had been classed as high literary art; and thus nearly all Greek and Roman authors in the genre would follow the changing rules of rhetorical stylistics. Only a few, such as Polybius, were content with collecting historical facts and presenting them in an objectively ordered form. Accounts like his were called *hypomnēmata*, or *commentarii* in Latin; and quite a few of them were also published beside historiography proper. The most famous examples are Caesar's reports about his military campaigns. In this case the choice of form was dictated by his propagandistic intentions: what Caesar tried to create in those writings was the impression of immediacy and objectivity, of facts unimpaired by any literary art.

We know of quite a few *commentarii* written in the Early Empire, by authors like the Emperor Tiberius, the Empress Agrippina, mother of Nero, or Cn. Domitius Corbulo, a famous and successful general under Claudius and Nero. Unfortunately, our sources feature only isolated pieces of information taken from such works; we have no indication of the plan and the style of any of those writings.

Greeks

We have much less evidence of Greek than of Roman historiography from the Early Empire; and this fact is consistent with the generally richer literary production in the West at that time. The Late Republic already saw a growing number of Greek historians working in Rome, or at least keeping close relations with great men there. Thus Theophanes of Mytilene was the historiographer of Pompey; and Nicolaus of Damascus initially lived at the court of Herod the Great and later wrote a biography of Augustus. Dionysius of Halicarnassus, an advocate of the new Atticist stylistic programme by whom we have a history of Early Rome, presumably spent most of his life in Augustan Rome; likewise Timagenes, who came to Rome as a prisoner of war and became for some time one of Augustus' favourites. King Juba of Mauritania, who had grown up at the court of Augustus and was a faithful vassal of the Romans, proved to be a versatile scholar. Like Dionysius, he published a work about the early history of Rome, a 'Roman archaeology'; his work, however, is no longer extant.

Strabo of Amasea, whose geographical writings will be discussed in one of the following sections of my book (see p. 148), was another of those Greek historians closely connected with Rome. He lived between about 50 BC and 25 AD, visited many of the Mediterranean countries, and also took part in an expedition into the Sudan which was led by Aelius Gallus, Prefect of Egypt, and one of Strabo's personal friends. Strabo's literary legacy contains a major historical collection, continuing the histories of Polybius, which deals with events between 145 BC and the end of the civil wars. There were about forty books of which only a few fragments have survived, but Strabo's geographical writings also give us an idea of where his historical interests lay. There we find countless marginal remarks and digressions with a historical reference; largely to ancient history, although they also include a detailed account of an unsuccessful military campaign led by the aforementioned Aelius Gallus, who failed to achieve the conquest of that region which we now know as the Yemen. Strabo himself asserts that during his numerous voyages he was also an avid collector of historical information. Nevertheless, his major historical work seems to have been mainly a compilation of material from diverse literary sources and thus similar to the slightly older universal history by Diodorus of Sicily, of which large parts have been preserved. The latter work belongs to the reign of Augustus but did not become popular until the Byzantine era. Through it, we have access to at least the content, if not the precise wording, of much of Late Classical and Hellenistic historiography. In the Classical age, Strabo's work seems to have found only few readers, because of its obvious lack of literary merit and because of its language which was as yet uninfluenced by Atticism.

8 SPECIALIST LITERATURE

There are several reasons why most authors of the Modern age who deal with Greek and Roman literary history should also include so-called specialist literature: that is to say books about medicine, about phonetics, or about horse breeding. To begin with, that class of writings does contain numerous works with an aesthetic-literary appeal, directed at a broader public rather than at specialist readers. Second, what we have today is no more than a minute fraction of the so-called fine literature or the *belles-lettres* of the Graeco-Roman Classical age. It is the small number of those works and their isolated status that make their language and their content hard to understand. Thus insights gained in reading specialist writings are an indispensable help for modern-day scholars in this field. Finally, we also have to take into account that the interpretation of literary works within a living linguistic-cultural tradition is greatly facilitated by those cultural experiences, documented in language, which are shared by the authors and the readers. It is only this circumstance which makes the interpretation of literary works of art in isolation possible and meaningful. In the case of Graeco-Roman literature of the Classical age, the interpretation of the literary legacy must be accompanied by the study of the culture in general because both belong entirely to the past.

Grammar

Even within the conditions created by a general decline of intellectual life during the Hellenistic age, there was no serious disruption of grammatical research in Greek centres of learning such as Alexandria or Pergamum, where Greek literature, language, and poetic art were analysed and interpreted from many different points of view. We know particularly many names of grammarians from the reign of Augustus, but the productivity of grammarian scholarship remained at a high level throughout the Early

Empire. I have already mentioned those works of linguistic theory and lexicography which were used in the drafting of the Atticist programme (see p. 53); likewise, I have talked about efforts at applying the results of grammatical or, in modern terminology, of philological research, to issues concerning literary criticism and literary aesthetics.

There are only very few treatises by grammarians of this period which have been preserved in their entirety. We have an excerpt from one by a certain Lesbonax, who wrote a catalogue of *schemata*: that is of recurrent syntactic-stylistic peculiarities in the works of certain poets or prose authors. But most of our knowledge is based on isolated references in so-called scholia commentaries. Such commentaries were added to the editions of Classic texts in many Byzantine manuscripts; they feature explanatory remarks on individual passages of the text by scholars from different periods who are quite frequently named. Further information about grammarians of the Early Empire can be gathered from Byzantine anthologies and encyclopaedias.

In the context of the Early Empire the name of one man may stand as an example for many of his contemporaries: this is Ptolemy of Ascalon, a particularly versatile scholar who lived in Rome for at least part of his life, like numerous other people of that period who had an interest in science. Ptolemy wrote extensively about the laws governing the pronunciation of Homeric language; about criteria for assessing the correctness of linguistic utterances; about metre; about the textual criticism of the great Aristarchus from the second century BC; and about the Pergamum school of Homeric exegesis which had also produced a general doctrine about the correct use of language. In the variety of his chosen topics, Ptolemy was no exception among those scholars known as grammarians in the Classical age, who dealt with an extremely wide range of subject matter. King Juba of Mauritania, for instance, who was also a distinguished historian and geographer (see p. 139), wrote treatises on the degeneration of linguistic usage, on painters and paintings, and on the history of the theatre. The latter work included aspects such as the development of stage technology, and the making of musical instruments.

From the second century BC onwards the methods and topics of Greek grammar had also taken hold in Rome. The Ciceronian-Augustan era saw the first heyday of grammatical-antiquarian achievements, with Varro and Verrius Flaccus as the most prominent exponents. In the Early Empire, there was the learned Q. Remmius Palaemon, tutor to the poet Persius (see p. 120) and to the rhetorician Quintilian. Remmius wrote an *ars grammatica*, or school grammar of Latin, for which he adopted the categories from the Greek *technē grammatikē* by Dionysius Thrax, a pupil of the aforementioned Aristarchus of Samothrace. Remmius' grammar has not been preserved, but we know that it served as a model for some extant Late Classical grammars which were used throughout the Middle Ages.

This explains why we are still using grammatical terms which are translations from the Greek, such as accusative, object, or pronoun. Such terms were frequently coined under the influence of Stoic linguistic philosophy; but it must be said that some of their translations into Latin tended to make them sound much more ambiguous than they had been in their original Greek context.

I have already mentioned Persius' friend Caesius Bassus as the author of a didactic poem on the origin of different verse forms. Caesius Bassus was not the only grammarian who tried his hand at poetry: Remmius Palaemon produced some poetic efforts, too, as M. Terentius Varro had done before both of these men. Thus we perceive a Roman parallel to a phenomenon belonging to Early Hellenism, when learned grammarians such as Callimachus or Eratosthenes would write as well as study poetry. Among the Greeks this habit died out with the growing specialisation of scholarly research during the second century BC. In Rome the same happened in the late first century AD and we do not find a return to such a state of affairs until the age of Italian Humanism.

The grammarians fully deserve pride of place in any discussion of Graeco-Roman specialist literature: for it was only due to their tireless efforts that we have any pieces of Classical poetry and literary prose at all in any comprehensible form, in spite of all the vicissitudes of history, and lacking as they did the perpetuation of the wording of texts in print. In the late twentieth century, the existence of printed and hence essentially fixed texts has become so normal to us that we are prone to forget what the first and foremost task of philology is: the conservation, the re-establishing, or at least the approximation of that wording originally given to a text by the author.

Medicine

The educational system of the Classical world had arrived at a very early canonisation of general knowledge, after the manner underlying the later order of the so-called Seven Liberal Arts. Linguistic-literary education in grammar, rhetoric, and dialectics came to be complemented by basic mathematical-scientific instruction in geometry, arithmetic, astronomy, and musical theory. Of course a truly well-educated person had also to be acquainted with other areas of knowledge which were investigated by scientific or philosophical disciplines; and among those, medicine was the most important. Hence the tradition of medical literature written for a general public from the fifth century BC onwards. That phenomenon appears as complementary to an understanding which scholars in the field of medicine had developed much earlier than those in other scientific disciplines: an awareness concerning the demarcation of their subject matter as well as the particular nature of their methods.

In the first century AD medical science was dominated by three competing schools which had formed during the previous century. The Empiricists claimed that there was no need for physiological theories as the basis of medical diagnosis and therapy; they saw medicine as a science where knowledge is gained exclusively from experience. This indicates the existence of links with the philosophical school of Skepticism, which had experienced a revival during the first century BC. The Skeptics denied the existence of verifiable knowledge, and consequently combated any kind of dogmatism with a weaponry produced through an extreme refinement of dialectics. To them, science was only acceptable as an ordering of complex experience.

The Methodist school traced its tradition back to the physician Asclepiades and his pupil Themison. The followers of this school developed a medical-physiological theory about the causes of illnesses; but they scorned the corresponding doctrines of the philosophical schools, believing that medical theory should evolve independently. One of the exponents of the Methodist school was Thessalus of Tralles in Asia Minor, of whom we have a letter addressed to Nero. Thessalus claimed to have a simple method of medical instruction which allowed him to make a physician of any pupil at all within six months. An extant treatise which bears his name deals with the affinities between certain medicinal herbs and stellar constellations; however, that document of astrological medicine belongs to a much later period.

Most of our knowledge about the writings of the early Empiricists and Methodists comes from the works of the famous physician Galen from the second century AD. The only primary sources extant belong to the many treatises produced by the Methodist Soranus of Ephesus who practised in Rome around 100 AD. We gain an excellent impression of the level of his medical knowledge and expertise from his surviving works, which include books about bone fractures and bandaging; a manual of gynaecology; and the Latin translation from the fifth century AD of a treatise on acute and chronic illnesses. There are fragments of other books, but unfortunately none of a work entitled *The Physician's Friend*, presumably written as a kind of advertisement directed at a broader public. Soranus' book on psychology was used by the Christian Tertullian in what is the earliest known draft of a theological doctrine about the soul.

The Pneumatist school based its physiological theory on Stoic physics, and on the Stoic doctrine of the *pneuma* (see p. 72). Its founder, Athenaeus of Attaleia, was a pupil of the great Posidonius. We know quite a lot about the doctrines of this school from the extant work about chronic and acute diseases by Aretaeus of Cappadocia. A remarkable feature of that book, published in the first century AD, is its use of the Ionic dialect. Ionic had been the language of all medical literature in the days of Hippocrates; but as in other kinds of prose writing Attic came to replace it in the fourth century BC. Aretaeus' use of Ionic is a case of Imperial Classicism turned archaism. Hippocrates was the Classic author on medicine; all medical schools, as Galen asserts, quoted him as an authority; and his works remained in use in medical instruction even if they were written in a pre-Classic idiom like the historical writings of Herodotus.

There are references to other Pneumatists such as Agathinus, a friend of the Stoic Cornutus, and Agathinus' pupil Archigenes. But Rufus of Ephesus, who was a famous physician around 100 AD, seems to have belonged to none of the contemporary medical schools. Rufus wrote a work about kidney and bladder complaints as well as an extremely interesting treatise on basic aspects of medical diagnosis, particularly the technique of recording a patient's medical history. His treatises prove that the high standard of medical skills and medical ethics in the Greek world remained constant for centuries.

Dioscurides, a military doctor during the reign of Nero, wrote a book which was translated into many different languages, and used by physicians and pharmacists until well into the Middle Ages. *Of Medicinal Materials* is a voluminous and fundamental work, dealing with all the plants, animals, minerals, and foodstuffs which were used in the production of drugs. Many of the numerous extant manuscripts of this book are copiously illustrated; that tradition also dates back to the Classical age.

We also have two specimens of medical literature in Latin from the first century AD. During the reign of Tiberius, an otherwise unknown Celsus wrote eight books on medicine as part of an encylopaedic work; we know nothing more about its scope and structure than that it covered all the disciplines of science, of philosophy, and of rhetoric. Celsus' general outline of medicine shows such a great deal of knowledge, erudition, and circumspection that scholars have repeatedly expressed their belief that the author himself must have been a physician. Celsus gives a brief but comprehensive survey of internal and external diseases, as well as of injuries, surgery, pharmaceutics, and dietetics, a particularly important discipline in Classical medicine that dealt not merely with nutrition but with lifestyle in general. All recent researchers have refuted the old allegation that Celsus' work was based on no more than one Greek source. To scholars of today, it is evident that the author knew and used a large amount of specialist literature, naturally mostly in Greek, without subscribing to any of the existing school doctrines. In the writing of his work Celsus seems to have attached little importance to linguistic-stylistic elaboration, in spite of the fact that as part of an encyclopaedia his text was meant to be read by a wider public.

Another interesting piece of writing is a short book of prescriptions, written by the physician Scribonius Largus during the reign of the Emperor Claudius. Its preface asserts the independence of Roman medicine from the Greeks as a fact which the rest of the book is intended to demonstrate.

The exact sciences

Like the work of grammarians, Greek studies in the exact sciences such as mathematics, astronomy, optics, or mechanics were not disrupted during the transition from Hellenism to the Imperial age. There was a high degree of continuity; but nevertheless, the scientific achievements of Early and Middle Hellenism, represented by names such as Eratosthenes, Hipparchus, Archimedes, Euclid, or Apollonius of Perga remained unsurpassed, and even unequalled.

The extant writings in this wide field are not always easy to date. Some pieces bear the names of less prominent authors who were largely ignored in specialist debate, so that no mentions in other sources can help us to determine when their works were written. Frequently such treatises would also be ascribed to very famous writers as time went by; and in many cases it is not possible to verify or to disprove such claims about authorship. Scientific literature does not give us many linguistic clues either: in the conservative tradition of specialist jargon, we cannot notice any sea-change like that which the rise of the Atticist movement brought about in what we would call literary prose in the narrower sense. In the novel, for example, we can easily distinguish Hellenistic from post-Hellenistic works on the basis of linguistic criteria.

Under the name of Heron of Alexandria, we find several treatises and fragments featured by later authors in works of very varied content and quality. The Neo-Platonist Proclus quotes passages from a Greek commentary on Euclid's *Elements*; a mediaeval mathematician features some such pieces in an Arabic translation; and a Byzantine anthology contains definitions of mathematical terminology which partly stem from Heron. We have a complete *Art of Mensuration* in three books, containing mathematical formulas for calculating plane and curved areas and the volumes of differently shaped bodies, as well as giving instructions for the division of areas and volumes. A later Byzantine work about rules for architectural calculations seems to be partly based on Heron. One extant specialist treatise describes the making and the use of a geodetical apparatus, and of an odometer, a 'distance counter'.

Heron's most famous work is his *Mechanics* of which the only completely extant version is an Arabic translation; beside that, we have fragments of the original as quoted by later Greek mathematicians. The book deals with fundamental aspects of mechanical theory in its discussion of devices such as levers, screws, and cogwheels; but it also gives practical instructions – on the making of cranes or winches, for example. Of the book Heron wrote on the construction of vaults, there is no other trace left than one reference to it in the Late Imperial period. In contrast, we do have a completely extant *Catoptrics* including the discussion of convex and concave mirrors, which seems to be Heron's work although it was ascribed to Ptolemy. Heron was also the author of a book about catapults; this writing belongs to the old tradition of Hellenistic artillery whose efficiency remained unrivalled until about the eighteenth century, in any case long after the invention of gunpowder. A further work, entitled *Pneumatica*, deals with the pressure and suction effects of air and water, and their technological applications. Another treatise in two books discusses the construction of automata.

Heron's *oeuvre* illustrates a high refinement of theoretical mechanics and gives us many examples of advanced mathematical approaches to problems of mechanics, optics, and mensuration. However, it is remarkable that the practical applications discussed rarely go beyond the facilitation of heavy manual labour, through the use of devices such as pulleys or cranes. Most importantly, there is no trace of any idea for the mechanisation of production processes. The most useful inventions mentioned concern the construction of catapults, and of automata as exhibition pieces.

The most recent author quoted by Heron is Archimedes, who died in 212 BC; the earliest author who quotes Heron is a mathematician by the name of Pappus who lived around 300 AD. This leaves a gap of five centuries and consequently different scholars came to suggest very different dates for Heron's life. The debate was practically closed by Neugebauer who proved that a lunar eclipse mentioned by Heron in his treatise on the theodolite could only have been that of 13 March, 62 AD. Heron had based a calculation of the distance between Rome and Alexandria on observations of the duration of the eclipse in both cities. Thus we may conclude that he lived around the middle or in the later decades of the first century AD; this assumption tallies with what we know about the progress of mathematical and optical discoveries.

In my discussion of the didactic epic by Manilius I have already referred to the diffusion of astronomical knowledge, a process not least due to the great influence of astrology. As a scientific document from presumably the late first century AD we have a treatise by an otherwise unknown Cleomedes, *Of the Circular Motion of Heavenly Bodies*. The title is rather misleading as to the scope of the work, for in spite of its brevity, this treatise contains a concise but complete description of the cosmos as seen by Stoic physics, with plenty of polemical remarks about the world view of the Epicureans. Cleomedes' account falls somewhat short of the high standard which specialist astronomy had reached in the mathematical explanation of phenomena. Yet the author seems to have had a different intention, and rather tries to give as plain and as concrete as possible a notion of the size of the sun, the limits of the cosmos, the motion of the stars, the shape of the earth, or the distance of the moon from the earth's surface;

all according to Stoic ideas. The attempt to be plain quite frequently leads to faults in Cleomedes' argumentation.

The author's favourite authority seems to have been the Stoic Posidonius; yet Cleomedes' work remains on a much lower scientific level than that of his predecessor. That Cleomedes' treatise really belongs to the first century AD rather than to the second is not quite certain. Nevertheless, some scholars have discovered a clue in parallels with the writing of the astronomer Geminus, a man with better scientific credentials than Cleomedes who also quotes Posidonius as an authority. Geminus definitely lived in the later decades of the first century BC, and hence the assumption that Cleomedes likewise belongs to the Early Empire.

It is unlikely that Cleomedes' work accurately reflects the state of contemporary astronomical research, but what it does do is to illustrate the debate on astronomical problems carried on between the philosophical schools. The object of such debate was not so much the advancement of scientific knowledge as rather the development of a clear image of the universe which could be upheld in discussion. Through such a plan philosophy was to show man his proper place in the cosmos and would thus enable him to act correctly, that is naturally. It is evident that such a grand design could not be achieved without taking into account the insights gained by specialised scientific disciplines. This explains the close links between scientists and philosophers, even if the latter never regarded science as anything more than propaedeutics, or *ancilla philosophiae*.

Geography

From the Classical age onwards, there was a distinction between the domains of geography and chorography. Geography was concerned with the exact locations of all known points on the earth's surface, to be ascertained by astronomical-mathematical means. Chorography described individual countries, their topographical features, inhabitants, traditions, and peculiarities. The terminological distinction between the two was not always strictly kept, but the distinction of subject matter was. It is true that a few major mathematical geographers, such as Eratosthenes or Posidonius, also proved to be dab hands at the description of countries and peoples. But in any case, geography was regarded as a pure science, and chorography as a literary genre, with corresponding demands on language and style.

That genre had a long tradition which dated back to the Ionic ethnographers of the sixth and fifth centuries BC; at that time it was not yet separated from historiography. Herodotus' *Account of his Discoveries* (*Historia*) still united both. This is why throughout the Classical age historiographers, as writers of high literature, had to give an exact description of the setting for the events they were going to narrate, most properly in an introduction or in a lengthy digression. Mathematical geography did not become a fully fledged scientific discipline until the Early Hellenistic age. The conditions which led to its promotion were a widening of geographical horizons following Alexander's campaign; a growing interest in foreign countries which arose in the spacious world of Hellenistic states with its freedom of individual movement; a resulting debate about the size of the earth and of its habitable parts; and lastly, a boom in the exact sciences.

Plato, Eudoxus and Aristotle had assumed and proved that the earth was round: that notion had since become an accepted fact among educated people, and it provided the foundation for mathematical geography. This discipline saw a first major achievement in the third century BC when the versatile scholar Eratosthenes calculated the circumference of the earth. His method is described in the book by Cleomedes which I have already mentioned. Eratosthenes based his work on that knowledge of foreign countries which had accumulated by the mid-third century BC through military campaigns, and the voyages of merchants and explorers. On this basis, he drew up a mathematical-geographical plan of the inhabited parts of the globe, including the three continents of Europe, Asia, and Libya, or Africa. In the second century BC Hipparchus introduced some major amendments to this map on the basis of more exact calculations; and in the first century BC the results of recent voyages of discovery caused Posidonius to modify it even more. Both of those scholars, however, adhered to the basic features of Eratosthenes' plan.

Posidonius was also the man who produced the greatest achievements in descriptive geography. His many voyages acquainted him above all with the countries of the West; he became familiar with the topography and with the character of the different inhabitants of Spain, Gaul, and north Africa. Posidonius' interest was caught by the Atlantic tides as well as the possibility of circumnavigating the African continent, and even the drinking habits of uncivilised Gallic tribes. As a Stoic, he was able to see all those different phenomena as integral parts of one universal order, because of the doctrine of the divine *pneuma*: the substance present throughout the world in different concentrations which endowed all objects and creatures with varied degrees of form, life, and consciousness. As a highly talented writer Posidonius was moreover capable of expressing this world view in a convincing form.

I have already mentioned Strabo of Amaseia as a historiographer (see p. 139); but he also features in the same tradition as Posidonius on account of an extant geographical work in seventeen books. Like Posidonius, Strabo travelled widely, formed close relationships with several great Romans, and was also influenced by the Stoic view of the world.

The first book of Strabo's work contains a definition of geography as part of philosophy. This is a contribution to a long-standing debate about the relationship between the sciences and philosophy as the art of living. Strabo also acquaints his reader with the older geographers, especially

Eratosthenes. Furthermore, he undertakes to prove that Homer must be seen as the inventor of geography, in keeping with the idea that Homer's works were the ultimate source of all knowledge. This notion was upheld in educational practice, where Homeric epics provided the basis for so-called grammatical instruction; and also in philosophy, which saw in Homer's works a wisdom that predated philosophical inquiry, and provided instruction in practical living as well as an allegorical portrayal of physical events (see p. 86).

The second book of Strabo's work contains an introduction to mathematical geography and a cartographical representation of the earth's inhabited parts, with special references to Eratosthenes and Posidonius. Strabo's background in mathematics did not sufficiently equip him for a discussion of this subject matter on that high level of mathematical knowledge which his scientific contemporaries had attained. Still, his account is of great interest to us, as a source of valuable information about the history of the geographical world view.

Descriptive geography sets in with Book 3, beginning in the West with Spain; this is followed in Book 4 by Gaul, Britain, and the Alpine countries. Books 5 and 6 deal with Italy and Sicily; Book 7, unfortunately incomplete in parts, is about central, northern, and eastern Europe. Macedonia and Greece, including Crete and other islands, are featured in Books 8 to 10; Asia Minor with the islands off its western coast as well as with the eastern land of Armenia in Books 11 to 14. Book 15 describes the Iranian countries and India with Ceylon; Book 16 Mesopotamia, Syria, Palestine, and Arabia. Finally, Book 17 covers Egypt and Ethiopia, that is to say the Sudan, as well as the Mediterranean coast of north Africa.

It goes without saying that most of these descriptions are based on literary sources and that the length of Strabo's chapters was determined by the availability of source material, rather than by the relative size of the countries he described. The same circumstance explains the vast differences in the quality and the vividness of description. There are parts of the work in which the author reports what he himself has seen; sometimes he does so for an entire pericope, as where he describes Nubia in Book 17, drawing on his experience as part of Aelius Gallus' expedition. There are also occasional isolated remarks which refer to impressions gathered on his journeys, thus giving us valuable clues as to the author's biography. We learn, for instance, that in 20 BC in Alexandria he saw the python which an Indian delegation carried to Samos as a gift for Augustus. Strabo also mentions the death of King Juba of Mauritania, a fact from which we can infer that his geographical work was not finished until after 23 AD.

Strabo appears as a true child of his times, that is as a staunch Classicist, in the selection and evaluation of sources. There were evidently some very important scholars among the geographers and historians of the second century BC; examples are Artemidorus of Ephesus, Apollodorus of Artemita, or Agatharchides, of whom we have a description of the Red Sea coasts. Yet Strabo only refers to such sources in cases where there are no older authorities. Thus Polybius and Posidonius are his informants about the geography of Spain and Gaul as there were no detailed reports about those countries from Classic writers. On the other hand Strabo completely ignores Apollodorus of Artemita, who came from a Greek city that had belonged to the Parthian Kingdom from the second century BC onwards. Apollodorus wrote a Parthian history which also included the fates of the Greek city states in Bactria, that is modern-day Afghanistan, and India. But instead of this author, Strabo prefers the historians of Alexander's campaign, and ambassadorial reports from the early Hellenistic age, dating back to around 300 BC. This was as much of an anachronism as it would be for a late twentieth-century author to describe today's United States of America as the country of Daniel Boone. However, it was Strabo's deliberate policy to quote the oldest and hence canonised literary sources, and not the newest and most up-to-date ones.

One of Strabo's marginal references to his own experience tells us that in his day, 120 ships per year would set out for India with the monsoon from the southern end of the Red Sea, and that many of them went as far as the mouth of the River Ganges. But Strabo explicitly refuses to base any geographical conclusions on information gleaned from ill-educated sea-captains. This shows that Strabo had a literary and not a scientific mind; for the scientists of the Early Empire were certainly neither unwilling nor unable to process information from extra-literary sources. In any case, Strabo's work has preserved a great deal of descriptive geography, including that of the Late Hellenistic age. But newer sources are only admitted because there were simply no other authorities on some of the regions dealt with; and it is telling that Strabo is particularly inclined to make polemical remarks about more recent authors, especially Posidonius.

That orientation towards the past which is so obvious in Strabo's work led him to ignore some sources of information but at the same time to draw extensively on some others, including a group of texts which were nearly all lost afterwards. Those belonged to the tremendous wealth of writings by local historians, publications which first appeared in Athens in the fourth century BC, and then in almost every single *polis* all over the Greek world. Strabo's work features countless pieces of information from such accounts, which were often based on extra-literary sources such as archives, inscriptions, traditions linked to festivals, or local mythology. Naturally Strabo uses such material mainly in his books about Greece and Asia Minor thus giving his report a depth which is in keeping with the importance traditionally given to ethnography in descriptive geography.

All told, we may safely say that Strabo left us a work that illustrates very well what kind of an image an educated contemporary would form of the earth on the basis of scientific as well as of literary tradition.

Because those authors who provided the necessary facts were canonised or disqualified on purely literary grounds, this geographical view of the world proved to be fairly resistant to corrections resulting from the extension of global trade, and from scientific progress.

We have no more than fragments of the Greek works written by King Juba of Mauritania who grew up at the court of Augustus and proved to be a faithful vassal of Rome. He wrote mainly about African geography, but also about Arabia and Syria; his books seem to have been widely used.

A representative of mathematical rather than descriptive geography is a certain Isidorus of Charax, modern-day Basra, a Greek city within the Parthian Kingdom. He seems to have lived in the first half of the first century AD, but we know very little about him. Apart from fragments of a treatise on the relative sizes of parts of the *oikumenē*, the inhabited world, we have a short work listing distances on the road network in the Parthian kingdom, between the Rivers Euphrates and Indus. From Early Hellenism onwards such lists provided the basis for all cartography which could use them in drawing maps after one or more locations had been related to an astronomically determined position.

Sadly enough, we have no detailed information about the world map which Augustus' advisor, admiral, and later son-in-law Agrippa had installed at the Forum Romanum. Agrippa himself wrote a treatise explaining the map's features; there is, however, no reference to that in the extant work by Pomponius Mela. Mela was one of the many Romans from civic colonies in Spain who played important roles in the intellectual and political life of the period. He wrote a short descriptive survey of the entire inhabited earth during the reign of Claudius, whose British campaign in 43–4 AD he mentions. Mela's image of the world corresponds to that of Strabo; but naturally his work lacks the extensive descriptions and the wealth of historical detail which Strabo features. In Mela's treatise, there are only isolated references to the present and to mythological characters, which occur among the lists of place names, and the short characterisations of individual countries, mountains, or rivers.

Technical literature

From the fifth century BC onwards Greece witnessed a rich production of technical writings on topics such as architecture, painting, hunting, military strategy, horse riding, and agriculture. It is certainly no coincidence that the earliest known didactic treatise in Latin, written by Cato the Elder around 200 BC in emulation of a Greek model, was about the latter subject. The Roman tradition of agricultural treatises is particularly well represented, with the extant texts including a piece by the learned Varro, Cicero's contemporary, and, of course, Virgil's *Georgica*. Both of these are closely related to specialist literature in Greek.

It is yet another Spaniard who represents this tradition in the Early Empire: Seneca's contemporary L. Junius Moderatus Columella. His extant work on agriculture now comprises twelve books but Book 3 in the manuscript tradition, which deals with the growing of fruit trees, actually belongs to an earlier treatise by the same author. The first book of the voluminous work begins with the discussion of general questions, mainly concerning the moral and social importance of agriculture; it then treats of farming, viticulture, tree growing, animal breeding, and horticulture. The tenth book on gardening is written in hexameters; according to the author it was to be the final one. Nevertheless he added another book dealing with the same subject in prose, and then even another volume describing the duties of an estate manager's wife.

Columella was an extremely elegant stylist, but obviously also an experienced farmer. In writing his work, composed with great taste and in a plain and clear language, he certainly did not rely on literary sources only. Of the many available publications on the subject in both Greek and Latin, as shown by the long list of authors given in Book 1, Columella himself used only a few; most importantly the five books on agriculture from C. Cornelius Celsus' encyclopaedia, of which the medical section is extant (see p. 144). Columella seems to have had a genuine love for farming, and the reader learns that the author held agricultural land in Italy. The moral praise of rural life and labour was already an ancient motif at that time as an almost inevitable consequence of the urban milieu's cultural domination. The call for a return to nature was thus one of the common exordial topoi of agricultural literature. However, it gained added importance in view of the extravagant luxuries at Nero's court, as reported, for instance, in Seneca's letters.

One remarkable feature of Columella's treatise is the choice of a poetic form for the first of the two books about horticulture. In its prose prooemium the author gives a reason for this choice, claiming that he wants to fill a gap which Virgil has left in his *Georgica* through the omission of gardening. This is yet another proof of the fact that educated people of that period perceived a close connection between literary and technical- or scientific-didactic activity.

We may presume that an even greater percentage of Classical technical literature was lost than of writings with a purely literary intention; and we can count ourselves lucky to have any technical works at all. A particularly fortunate fact is the survival of the architectural treatise by Vitruvius, who practised the profession under Caesar and Augustus. The long bibliography which Vitruvius' writing contains gives us a good impression of how many publications have not been handed down to us; Vitruvius' own work had a great influence on Renaissance architecture.

From the end of the first century AD we have an equally interesting treatise whose author was also an eminent expert on his chosen subject.

This work about the water mains system of the city of Rome was written by Sex. Julius Frontinus, head of the water board as Curator Aquarum; later on, he was promoted to the Consulate. Frontinus' work describes the layout, length, and diameters of the pipes, as well as the distribution system, and other details of the capital's magnificent water installations. Moreover, Frontinus deals with legal questions concerning water consumption, water conduction, and the maintenance of the conduits.

Sex. Julius Frontinus is later mentioned by Tacitus and other writers as the author of two treatises on military subjects. One of those is extant; on the basis of mostly literary sources it describes martial ruses, or *stratagēmata*, and military manoeuvres, or *strategica*. It is unlikely that the lost treatise, apparently a manual of warfare, was exclusively based on literary material, for Frontinus' career would have enabled him to gain some practical knowledge of military issues. A Late Classical author who quotes Frontinus among his sources is Vegetius (see p. 501), who deals with the same subject matter. Vegetius gives a lot of detail about topics such as weapons, tactics, military organisation, or drill; yet his facts do not refer to the troops of his own lifetime, but to the Roman army serving under Augustus' first successors.

Another treatise by Frontinus which was unfortunately also lost dealt with land surveying. It began a specifically Roman tradition of technical literature which we can appreciate only from later documents. In technical literature, the form was considered to be less important, and thus new works often replaced older ones whose contents they incorporated, with the result that the later texts were usually the ones which survived.

Military literature had first developed in the fourth century BC when the first mercenary soldiers appeared, and when warfare became an affair for professionals. We have some early writings dating from that period, which deal with cavalry tactics and siegecraft; and the tradition thus established continued until the Late Classical age. The earliest extant Latin mention of it tells us that Celsus' encyclopaedia also contained a section on military matters.

The treatise by Onasander about the tasks and duties of a general is dedicated to a high-born Roman who was Consul in 49 AD. We learn from other sources that the author of this tract was a professional philosopher, and that he also wrote a commentary on Plato's *Republic*. The treatise itself gives no indication of philosophical expertise, and neither is there any evidence of a closer acquaintance with military matters. In the most general manner possible, Onasander's book deals with a variety of general topics: the proper treatment of soldiers and officers; the management of relations with allies, with conquered enemies, or with prisoners of war; correct behaviour in dangerous situations or in camp; different means of encouraging demoralised troops; or possible ways to punish a traitor or a spy. There is not a single word about the specific conditions in the Roman army of the first century AD. Where he does touch on concrete situations, the author has the phalanx of a bygone age in mind. We cannot but ask ourselves how an experienced trooper like the addressee of the dedication would have received this piece of writing, composed in good ivory-towered Attic. In spite of all that, the book had a lasting influence: it was avidly read in the Byzantine age, and translated into nearly all the European languages from the fifteenth century onwards.

9 JEWISH LITERATURE

General remarks

Numerous Jewish communities existed not only in the Syrian territories adjacent to Palestine, but also scattered all over the vast Roman Empire. Jewish individuals and groups could be found in Asia Minor and Greece, in Rome and other Italian cities, in Sicily and north Africa, and in southern Gaul or Spain. Egypt and the neighbouring territory of Cyrenaica seem to have had the largest share of Jews among their population. In Alexandria, the world's second city, the strong Jewish community even enjoyed a certain extent of self-government.

In Judaea, the religious heartland of the Jews with the Temple of Jerusalem as its centre, people spoke a dialect of Aramaic, which was the language of all the vast Syrian-Mesopotamian region. Greek was the mother tongue of all Jews who lived elsewhere, including Rome and the western provinces. For quite some time the use of Hebrew had been restricted to worship and religious scholarship. Consequently there was a demand among the Jews of Palestine and of Parthian Mesopotamia for having the words of Holy Scripture explained to them in their Aramaic tongue; correspondingly there were Greek translations of the Bible for other Jews. In Egypt Greek versions of Jewish Holy Scripture appeared as early as the third century BC. One most peculiar piece of writing which seems to date from the second century BC, the epistle of Aristeas, contains a legend concerning a translation of the Pentateuch, commissioned by King Ptolemy II. It is said that the monarch wanted to have a copy of the book in the great library of Alexandria, and thus invited seventy-two scriptural scholars from Jerusalem. Each one translated the text locked in a room by himself: and lo and behold, all the translations were identical down to every single detail. The legend was quite obviously designed to authorise one specific Greek translation of the Bible, also for cultic practice; it gave rise to the name Septuagint for the definitive Greek version of the Old Testament.

Greek translations of the Bible were not the only Jewish contribution to intellectual life. On the one hand several sources indicate that from the age of Hellenism onwards educated Greeks would show an interest in Jewish religion and the Jewish social order, because they perceived a parallel to their own monotheism. On the other hand some members of Jewish families rose to the very highest positions in the Imperial administration and during the reign of Augustus a Sicilian Jew even played an important role in the incipient Atticist movement. This illustrates how fully the upper classes of the Jewish Diaspora were integrated into Greek intellectual life, having found their appropriate place in society.

The linguistic and cultural Hellenisation of Judaea, a development which had followed the establishment of Seleucid rule, came to an end when a Jewish state was formed after the Maccabean uprising in the second century BC. This explains why Palestine remained a trouble spot after its integration into the Roman Empire; for under the given circumstances hopes for a restoration of the Jewish state had to go hand in hand with resentment against Greek civilisation as the culture of the foreign masters. As a faithful vassal of Augustus, Herod the Great attempted to bring his country into closer communion with the Graeco-Roman world; but his efforts had no lasting success. Soon after the Romans established direct Imperial administration of the unruly country, including Jerusalem with its Temple, the holiest shrine of all Judaism. The fact that the cult of Jerusalem was more ancient than Greek or Roman rule over Judaea was reason enough for the Romans to tolerate Jewish monotheism, even if its exclusive character was an alien element in the Classical world, and could not be reconciled with the religious notions of educated Greeks.

In spite of such conditions in Palestine, Roman rule did not affect the continuity of a rich Jewish intellectual life in many parts of the Diaspora and above all in Egypt, a life which had developed solely in the medium of Greek during the Hellenistic age. The years between the second century BC and the second century AD saw the publication of a vast number of Jewish literary works in Greek; partly for a Jewish public, and partly for Gentile readers as a means of improving the image of Judaism in the outside world. This explains why Jewish ideas and Jewish thought were frequently expressed in the traditional forms of Greek literature.

Thus an otherwise unknown Ezekiel wrote an artfully composed tragedy about the exodus of the Israelites from Egypt; large parts of the play are extant as quotations in the work of a Christian author. A hexametric poem of Jewish origin, which sums up rules for day-to-day living, has been handed down under the name of the poet Phocylides, who lived in the seventh or sixth century BC. Jewish authors also ascribed their works to other famous authors from Greek literary history, such as Heraclitus or Aeschylus. The first two Maccabean books of the Greek Bible give largely parallel accounts of the Jewish uprising against the Seleucid Antiochus Epiphanes; they allow us to make a comparison between a historical work of Hebraic origin in a Greek translation and – even if we have only an abbreviated form – one that was originally written in Greek, in the tradition of dramatic-pathetic historiography. It is almost self-evident that with the choice of Greek forms Greek ideas would also enter the intellectual world of Judaism.

This process did cause some tension though. Confronted with the overpowering force of Greek civilisation and encouraged by the success of the Maccabean uprising, the Jews came to entertain a renewed hope for the restoration of David's great kingdom; a hope which they had in fact never fully abandoned since the deportation of their upper classes into Babylonian exile. Eastern speculations – especially of Persian origin – about the dawn of a new era, and comparable Egyptian expectations concerning an end to centuries of alien rule, put the envisaged revival of a Jewish kingdom in a larger historical context of global-cosmic dimensions. It was assumed that after four or more successive global empires, cosmic catastrophes would herald the day of divine judgment for all mankind, followed by a restoration of David's kingdom as the guarantor of eternal peace. The Book of Daniel, written in Hebrew and Aramaic during the Maccabean Wars, is the earliest literary illustration of this concept.

As such religious-political prophecies were based on a comprehensive interpretation of history, they could be reapplied time and again to ever-new political constellations. This phenomenon can be seen in the so-called apocalyptic literature of the Jews, and later of the Christians. Another example is the so-called Potter's Oracle, a prophecy about the restoration of the Pharaonic Kingdom; of this text, there are different successive versions which were found on papyrus scrolls. It goes without saying that prophecies of this kind were regarded as extremely dangerous by the Romans who claimed that their Empire was that very order which would realise law and peace among all civilised mankind, and hence had a cosmic legitimacy. Even a small local insurrection could cause enormous damage, if the rebels managed to present of themselves convincingly as those who were destined to usher in an ultimate empire of peace.

In the Roman Empire the Jews produced an apocalyptic literature which was as rich in volume as it was in variety. There were detailed accounts of the coming of the age of salvation, of the preceding battles and catastrophes, and of the final establishment of perpetual peace. Some of the books were written in Greek, and some in the sacred Hebrew or the vernacular Aramaic of the Palestinian-Mesopotamian Jews; but there were countless translations from one language to another which gave the genre a unity that transcended linguistic borders. The forms in which the revelations were clothed – for instance, the journey to heaven, or the visionary's last will – came from Jewish-Oriental as well as Greek tradition. In order to give them greater authority the visions were often ascribed to a major figure from the Old Testament, such as Enoch, Moses, Ezra, or Job.

There were also some Jewish authors who took the chronology suggested by apocalyptic speculation as the basis for a rearrangement of all the canonised texts in the Biblical tradition. The so-called Book of Jubilees divides the content of the Books of Genesis and Exodus into units of forty-nine years each, according to an eschatological timetable. Of this work, presumably written in the first century BC, there are complete Greek and Ethiopian translations, as well as fragments of a Latin version and of the Hebrew original. This state of affairs is quite typical, for during that phase of Jewish history which began in the second century AD, apocalyptic literature became less important to the Jews, but not to the Christians. This is why we quite frequently find Greek translations of the lost Hebrew or Aramaic originals. Such translations were presumably still destined for a Jewish readership; they were in turn translated into the different idioms of early Christian literature, such as Armenian, Syriac, Ethiopian, Old Slavic, and also Latin.

The most comprehensive Hellenisation of apocalyptic ideas is found in the corpus of the so-called Sibylline prophecies. The word *sibylla* is presumably not of Greek origin; initially it seems to have been used to denote the type of migrant female prophet that emerged in the Greek world during the seventh or sixth century BC. Not long after their appearance, many of those women would settle down at the sites of ancient oracles, a fact that altered their mantic practices. It seems that the term Sibyl was used as a generic noun, but it was also understood to be the proper name of the first such prophet. This explains why we have evidence of several Sibyllae, linked with well-known oracles such as Delphi, Erythrae, or Cyme, from the fourth century BC onwards.

The tale of Numa Pompilius and the Sibylline books as parts of the state cult, but also Book 6 of Virgil's *Aeneid*, prove that the complex of apocalyptic ideas also became known in Rome. Such Roman documents are particularly good illustrations of the importance of oracle collections, which are in evidence from the sixth century BC onwards. Virgil's fourth eclogue cites a Sibylline prophecy which announces the birth of a future world ruler. Lucan also refers to such prophecies, and numerous Sibylline or other oracles are quoted elsewhere in Graeco-Roman literature. Presumably in the second century BC a poet called Lycophron wrote a long poem in iambic trimeters, as his rendering of a prophecy uttered by Priamus' daughter Cassandra. In cryptic oracular language, it predicts the Trojan War, the Persian Wars, Alexander's expedition, and the global rule of the Romans, the descendants of the Trojan Aeneas. In the process the history of the world is divided into periods, in a manner similar to that found in the Book of Daniel.

The corpus of the Sibylline prophecies, written in the language and metre of Greek epic, belongs to this tradition of Greek oracle literature. The collection consisted of fourteen books, twelve of which are extant. They contain heathen, Jewish, and Christian sections, compiled and edited at different times during the period between the second or first century BC and the fifth or sixth century AD. The Jewish parts are propaganda for

Jewish monotheism: one of the Sibyllae who speaks the prophecies is even introduced as a daughter-in-law of the patriarch Noah from the Old Testament (3, 26). Here we find threats meant to intimidate enemies and persecutors of the Jews and descriptions of the impending age of salvation, as well as of the preceding battles against those who oppose the Messiah and his people.

All those prophecies originated in specific historical circumstances, and thus there are plenty of references to contemporary history which allow us to date some of them fairly precisely. There is mention of Ptolemy VII who ruled in the second century BC; but also of the second Triumvirate of 43 BC when Augustus, Antony, and Lepidus shared supreme power. We find a reference to the expected return of Nero as the awaited Messiah's enemy: this could obviously not have been written until after Nero's death in 68 AD. A passage in Book 5 even alludes to successors of Hadrian, the Emperor during whose reign the Bar Kochba uprising was suppressed; thus that part was not written any earlier than the second century AD. In spite of many editorial changes shown in the extant texts, the style of the collection is very consistent. This reflects the strength of a poetical tradition in which Greeks and Jews had an equal share for several centuries.

The Jewish sections of the Sibylline prophecies are a particularly impressive example of the complete adoption of a Greek literary form. Other Jewish writings reflect the result of a process which was something like an inevitable consequence of the many efforts at translation: the recreation of genuinely Biblical and hence Semitic literary forms, in the medium of Greek. An example is the Greek text of the Apocalypse of Baruch, describing how the man mentioned in the Book of Jeremiah as that prophet's companion is carried through the seven heavens on an angelic vehicle. In spite of later Christian editing, this may be taken as a specimen of Jewish apocalyptic literature which was not translated into Greek, but originally written in that language: this accounts for the fact that it contains motifs from Greek mythology.

A similarly interesting co-existence of Jewish texts in Greek translation with others written in Greek is found in the so-called literature of wisdom. In the ancient Orient, the collection of wise saws as sources of advice and explanation already had a long tradition, including also the canonical Books of Proverbs and Ecclesiastes or Koheleth, the 'book of the preacher'. Their equivalents on the Greek side are some older gnomic collections in verse form, and compilations of prose sententias written and collected in the post-Isocratic rhetorical tradition.

In that version of Ecclesiasticus which is the only completely extant Greek text of the Book of Sirach, we find an explicit reference to the process of translation. The translator names the year when he arrived in Egypt, which was in 132 BC according to our reckoning. He also refers to the years after 117 BC as the time when he translated his grandfather's

Hebrew writing into Greek, for his Egyptian fellow Jews. Large parts of the original, which was never included in the Hebrew Biblical canon, are known from later discoveries of manuscripts.

It is important to note that the Book of Sirach is not merely a compilation of isolated wise saws of religious or moral content. As in older collections, these are often integrated into a rhythmic pattern following the laws of Hebrew metrics creating pairs of corresponding statements – whether complementary or contradictory – which form one single saying with strictly parallel constituents, or a *parallelismus membrorum*. The book also contains some longer poems, such as a song in praise of those men who never cease in their endeavour to attain divine wisdom (14, 20ff.), or another one glorifying the beauty and perfection of God's creations (42, 15ff.).

It is this formal development of the literature of wisdom which is used in a text written in Greek, the Book of Wisdom, ascribed like the Books of Koheleth and Proverbs to the sage King Solomon. This most peculiar work combines prose sections and poetic parts, where the aforementioned principle of Hebrew metrics is imitated in the Greek language. The book describes how the pious sage is superior to the ungodly fool; it praises in a highly poetic part that sapience which is to be sought above all by kings; and finally it describes divine wisdom, as revealed in the creation of the world, and in the history of the Israelites until their arrival in Canaan.

There have been many different guesses as to where and when the Book of Wisdom was written; however, Atticist elements in its language show that it could not have been produced any earlier than the first century AD, most likely in Egypt. The choice of form follows Biblical tradition, but individual phrasings express quite a number of ideas which are distinctly Greek, and entirely alien to Biblical thinking. In the final part, for instance, wisdom or *sophia* appears as a distinct hypostasis, an intermediate being used by God in his creation and his ruling of the world. There is also a mention of the four cardinal virtues, which had been firmly anchored in philosophical ethics since the age of Plato. Like the Platonics, the book teaches that the soul exists prior to the body which is a burden and an impairment to the soul as well as its temporary habitat. This view clashes with the image of man expressed in the Old Testament; and so does a passage which questions the value of human fecundity.

It is hard to decide whether this work was written primarily for Jewish or for Gentile readers. In any case, it contains a long digression condemning idolatry and polytheism, and contrasts the immorality of the ungodly – that is, the heathens – with the purity of pious Jews. The aim is to prove the superiority of the Jewish faith, and to this end, the author also uses means from Greek speculative thought, with which he was obviously familiar.

Part of religious propaganda and apologetics since time immemorial were reports about miracles worked by the god of one's canvassed religion and by its followers, and in particular stories about the latters' miraculous steadfastness under persecution. The attitude of the Jews to their Graeco-Roman environment was ambivalent, and so were attitudes towards them. There is evidence of fervent hatred of the Jews among uneducated as well as educated people; but there are also facts which indicate that Jewish propaganda had a certain success, and that some people were genuinely interested in Jewish traditions. The emperors and their counsellors were also inconsistent in their behaviour towards the Jews, oscillating between acts of favour and of suppression.

It is only from Greek versions that we know the miraculous stories about the adventures of the pious Tobias and the courageous Judith. Those Greek texts seem to have been written in the Hellenistic age under the conditions described above. Nevertheless, the originals were in a Semitic language and thus aimed at Jewish readers, setting the action in a distant past. Two pieces of writing which form the third and the fourth Maccabean books in the Greek Bible are likewise miracle-stories; but they were composed in Greek, with all the rhetorical devices of that language. Both seem to date from the first century AD and may have been intended for Jews as well as for Gentiles.

The so-called third Book of the Maccabees narrates a legend about a cruel persecution of the Jews of Alexandria, instigated by Ptolemy IV after his victory at Raphia in 217 BC. He orders those Jews who refuse to perform sacrifices to the Graeco-Egyptian gods to be rounded up in an arena where they are to be crushed to death by elephants. A miraculous divine punishment prevents Ptolemy from carrying out his plan and later the Jews of Alexandria commemorate each anniversary of the event with a joyous celebration. There is an obvious parallel in the Book of Esther, describing the legendary origin of the Purim holiday which is still observed by Jews today. The text of Book 3 of the Maccabees is ornamented with many quotations from Aeschylus' tragedies, a fact which proves that it was written for readers with a Greek education, who could be Jews or Gentiles.

The fourth Maccabean book tells in great gruesome detail about the death of the priest Eleazar, killed with his seven sons by the henchmen of King Antiochus IV, during whose reign the Maccabean uprising broke out. The author tells his readers how the eight men die as martyrs for their religion, because they refuse to break Mosaic law by eating pork. But he also makes it plain that the aim of his account is to illustrate the mind's control of the affections, as put to the test in such extreme circumstances. Thus he proves that Jews who remain faithful to their religion to the point of martyrdom reach the professed goal of philosophical-ethical endeavour. There was a difference between the Stoic ideal of apathy or lack of affections, and the Academic-Peripatetic one of metriopathy, or moderation of affections; but both implied the supremacy of reason as a condition for proper behaviour. The author was familiar with all aspects of this issue and his discussion shows a sovereign command of the relevant specialist terminology. His narrative, therefore, could serve to admonish Jews who had a Greek education, as well as to appeal to educated Greeks for sympathy.

The survey of Graeco-Jewish literature given in this chapter is by no means complete, even if I have included some of the many works which predate the Roman Empire. Nevertheless, what I have said should provide the necessary background for the following discussion of Philo and Josephus, two authors whose voluminous *oeuvres* are largely extant.

Philo

Philo came from a distinguished Alexandrian family, which had connections with the dynasty of Herod; some of its members even rose to high positions in Imperial service. Philo himself became the leader of a delegation of Alexandrian Jews, sent to Caligula's court in 40 AD in order to protest against the harassment of Jews by Greek citizens and the Imperial Prefect. One of his writings is a report about this journey. Philo's education was one hundred per cent Greek, and his works are full of quotations from Greek poetry. He never acquired a command of Hebrew, although he was a pious Jew who once went to Jerusalem on a pilgrimage. Philo's profound knowledge of Holy Scripture was, of course, derived from Greek texts.

Unfortunately our knowledge of Philo's life is based on no other sources than some passing remarks in his own writings. Nevertheless, we can be sure of the fact that he acquired a thorough philosophical education, in close contact with the Platonic school in his native city. Platonic philosophy was in vogue at that time, and the Alexandrian school was flourishing, making a crucial contribution to the development of so-called Middle Platonism.

This phase in the history of Platonic philosophy is inseparably linked with the names of Antiochus of Ascalon and Eudorus of Alexandria, the two main recreators of Academic dogmatics. Eudorus was about twenty years older than Philo. We can achieve no more than a fragmentary reconstruction of his doctrines which seem to have incorporated numerous elements from the Peripatetic, Pythagorean, and Stoic traditions; the latter were included above all in Eudorus' ethical teachings. In Philo's large *oeuvre*, we find quite a number of references to individual doctrines from this philosophical milieu, a long time before they appear in any texts belonging to the Platonic school. Thus, for instance, Philo gives an early mention of the method of the so-called *theologia negativa* which sources from the second century AD present as an obligatory part of Academic dogmatics (see p. 78). On the whole, Philo's literary legacy is the richest contemporary source of information about that period in the history of philosophy. What he definitely had in common with the Middle Platonists was a familiarity with elements and terminologies from very different philosophical traditions.

Philo's greatest achievement, however, was the application of philosophical terms and methods to the interpretation of his religion's sacred texts, a process which led to the deduction of specific theological doctrines and terms. Thus, we may call Philo the earliest known Biblical theologian; or at least, we may say so if theology is not defined in a general sense as the result of any reflection on a complex of religious notions, but more narrowly as the analysis of the meaning of religious statements and ideas, with the help of terms developed by a distinct, disciplined philosophy. In the latter sense, Philo was a forerunner of that Christian theology which developed from the second century AD onwards.

Among Philo's writings different forms of Biblical commentaries constitute a part that is as large as it is important. There are running commentaries on longer segments from the Bible, such as his *Allegorical Explanation of the Law*, of which the extant text has several gaps. Then we find lengthy isolated commentaries on selected short pericopes as, for instance, his treatise on the confusion of languages. We cannot always tell whether the extant commentaries of the latter kind initially stood as parts of larger works, and were then handed down to us as individual treatises. Finally, Philo wrote short commentaries dealing briefly with difficulties arising in the exegesis of entire books of the Bible, as for instance the *Problems of Genesis*. All those types of exegetical literature which Philo produced had been traditional forms used in the interpretation of Classic poetry and prose from the third century BC onwards, first by Greek and then by Latin grammarians.

As did the forms, so did the methods of Biblical exegesis of the philosophical kind stem from Greek tradition. Greek grammarians had developed highly elaborate procedures for analysing obscure and cryptic texts; for solving problems with specific passages on the basis of the author's general linguistic usage; and finally for using mythological and historical knowledge as aids to textual interpretation. Besides, rhetoric had worked out categories for the aesthetic evaluation of texts; and lastly, there was the method of allegorical interpretation which dated back to the fifth century BC and had been refined above all by literary critics influenced by Stoicism. By means of allegorical reading, the plain narration of events in a text could be explained as a coded representation of moral value judgments, or of cosmic-natural processes. Thus each ancient poet, and especially Homer, could be recruited as a supporter of one's own philosophical world view.

In his works, Philo shows himself as one who is familiar with all of these methods of interpretation. He is ready to discuss the ambiguous syntax of a Biblical passage (*agr.* 99); to reflect on different uses of the word 'God' with and without article (*somn.* 1, 229); or to weigh the merits of several alternative readings of a Biblical text (*qu. deus s. immut.* 141). But his pet choice is clearly the allegorical method, as the one enabling him to show that Biblical characters and events are images of spiritual-intelligible truths, expressed in a form suited to the limited capacities of human understanding.

Thus, for example, the departure of Abraham from Ur and his journey to Canaan stand for the way which every man is meant to take to get closer to God, on a path leading from the sensual to the spiritual world. The many strange individual commands found in Jewish law are also without exception symbols of truths which can only be understood spiritually; nevertheless, Jews should keep obeying them in faithful adherence to their fathers' creed. The priestly garment described in Leviticus or the third Book of Moses is an image of the cosmos, and as such embodies the 'physics' of Jewish philosophy: for it is as philosophy that Philo wants the teachings of his religion to be understood. To him, the Jews are 'philosophising' when they attend the Sabbath service in the synagogue (*vit. mos.* 2, 216; 117ff.; *spec. leg.* 2, 61 *et al.*).

In Philo's reading, each one of the patriarchal characters in the Old Testament is the concrete illustration of a certain virtue or force. In arguing this view, he also exploits the art of etymology, a discipline developed predominantly by the Stoics who believed in the existence of an ontologically describable connection between the phonetic form of each and every word, and the thing signified. Thus Philo links the Greek word *theos* or god with the verb *tithenai* or put, deducing that *theos* means the creator (*conf. ling.* 137). In the word *anthrōpos* or man, he recognises the adjective *arthroumenos* or well structured; he also perceives a reference to *anō trophai* or nourishment from above, and hence sees man's name as an expression of his origin and his natural allegiance (*det.* 22; 85). In a similar manner, Philo interprets Hebrew proper names (for example, in *de Ios.* 28) about whose meanings there was already a traditional lore among Greek-speaking Jews. Philo gives his own readings whenever he wants to present the bearer of such a name, and what the Bible said about him, as exemplifying an ideal realisation of a philosophically defined lifestyle, or a perfect way of attaining consummate virtue.

Modern readers would be inclined to see such a compulsive search for meaning as greatly exaggerated; a view that is supported by those critical voices raised against the allegorical method of interpretation even in the Classical age. But it is only fair to consider that any art of interpretation which claims to operate on a higher plane will necessarily aim at grasping ideas of which the wording of a text does not constitute a plain and obvious one-to-one expression. Ultimately, even any single metaphor can already be described as an allegory *in nuce*; and as metaphor is one of those means of expression which are characteristic of poetic language, there is a certain case for the allegorical reading of poetry.

Because of their spatial distance from the Temple in Jerusalem, the only officially recognised shrine of their religion, Greek-speaking Jews were much quicker in developing a bookish form of religion than their fellow believers in Palestine. It was only after the destruction of the Temple that Judaism in Palestine experienced the same reorientation. Being exposed to the manifest influence of a rich foreign civilisation with a particular emphasis on literature, Palestinian Jews were naturally led towards conducting the inevitably resulting argument as the comparative interpretation of two literary traditions. But those traditions were very different in character, and thus the given goal of harmonisation meant that it was necessary to call in all interpretatorial means available.

Many of Philo's statements indicate that even those Jews who spoke Greek and thought in Greek never denied their awareness of belonging to a nation chosen by their God in preference to all others. This is why Philo has one and the same explanation for all parallels, whether discovered or artfully created by himself, between the Bible and Greek philosophy: that Greek philosophers and legislators had learned from Moses. But this claim, in turn, corresponds exactly to a view cherished among Academics, Peripatetics, and Stoics. There philosophy was frequently defined as an attempt to regain a primeval knowledge which civilised mankind had lost through historical catastrophes while fragments had survived in the traditions of other peoples in a form described as 'barbarian philosophy'.

Some of Philo's numerous treatises are lost completely, while we have others only in Latin or Armenian translations. The thirty or so extant original texts cover a great variety of topics; they abound with references to selected Biblical passages, which are more often than not explained in an allegorical manner. This characteristic feature exists more or less in all of Philo's treatises, regardless of the subject matter. The topics can be purely philosophical, as in the discussions of different virtues, of the relationship between liberty and virtue, or of the problem of predestination; the treatises can also be based on pieces of Biblical tradition which Philo relates to philosophical doctrines in a comprehensive fashion as, for instance, the story of the sacrifices performed by Abel and Cain, or that of Noah's efforts at viticulture. Another group among Philo's treatises are the portraits of Biblical characters, such as Moses. Those writings combine several pieces from Biblical tradition and point to the exemplary status of their respective protagonist using the categories of philosophical ethics. Of all the extant treatises of Philo, it is only a small number of the purely philosophical ones, such as the tract about the eternal nature of the world which contain relatively few references to the Bible. It has been said that those few must be early works, written not long after Philo received his philosophical education. However, there are no other convincing reasons for this assumption beyond the one which I have just given.

It is not at all difficult to list a great number of individual philosophical and theological teachings formulated by Philo; but it is hard or even impossible to construct a unified systematic doctrine from those elements. There are three reasons for this. First, the fact that Philo keeps reinterpreting a large number of different passages from the Bible, always with a great deal of imagination, but taking little care to avoid contradictions. Moreover, he applies philosophical terms and categories in a very eclectic fashion, a manner even more extreme than the syncretism of contemporary Platonic philosophy. And finally, Philo was fighting an uphill battle in his attempts to correlate Biblical statements with theological concepts based on philosophy's entirely incompatible views of God, man, and the world. Consequently his theology was often forced to overstep the boundaries of philosophy, and thus it remained immune to all systematics.

I have already discussed specimens of Philo's varied readings of Biblical texts. To illustrate his eclecticism, the best example is his treatise on providence, a work of which we have only a Latin version. The Biblical view of the world and of man contained at the same time the idea of an all-embracing, divine providence governing the world down to the smallest detail, as well as the appeal to man's own responsibility to choose freely what is right. The theoretical contradiction between divine providence and human freedom of choice remained unresolved in the Old Testament. Philosophical schools offered different solutions for this problem. Nevertheless, the relevant doctrines proposed by Epicureans and Peripatetics were of no use at all to Biblical theologians as both of those schools ascribed a causal role to coincidence, albeit in varied degrees.

The Platonics followed a famous passage in Plato's *Republic* in claiming that man as a rational being always has the freedom of choice, but that he nevertheless remains bound by all the consequences of his decisions, including the unintended ones. In cases of aberrations caused by human error, the Platonics believed that supreme divine reason would come in to redirect the course of events into the path foreseen by providence, and that men would perceive this as retribution for their actions. The Stoics, on the other hand, held that all events in the world correspond exactly to the design of providence, and that men are free if they freely decide to do what the *heimarmenē* or fate has decreed; decisions taken merely because those men have understood the world order, and thus without any form of coercion. Philo does not hesitate to combine Platonic and Stoic doctrines, because the Bible forbids him to question either God's all-embracing providence, or the human freedom of choice which alone justifies reward or punishment.

Philo agrees with the philosophers in seeing man primarily as a spiritual being whose errors arise from affections to which he is susceptible because of his material existence but which he should control or even eliminate with the help of reason, the better part of his being. God himself, according to Philo, is pure spirit and hence without affections: if the Bible talks of God's wrath, that is only for pedagogical reasons and the statement is not literally true. Like the philosophers, Philo also regards the order of the visible as well as of the invisible world as rational and he sees an all-pervading harmony which binds both realms together. To him, the world is eternal even if it has been created because – and this is again a Platonic notion – the creator's kindness would not allow him to replace perfection by imperfection.

Ultimately such a picture leaves no room for any other law-giving force within man and within the cosmos than reason alone. How is it then to be reconciled with Biblical statements concerning the inexplicable revelations of God's self and of his will, as direct communications from God who asks man for his obedience in a way which completely bypasses the universal order? Philo's attempt to answer this question starts with the first known outline of a theological doctrine of grace, a notion which does not fit into any philosophical concept. The idea of divine grace implies that God himself, out of his friendliness and sympathy, decides to approach the ones he has chosen. In the prophets he completely replaces natural reason with his own spirit, so that they become children of his own will, of which a little bit is part of every man. Describing a man's reason as his divine protector and lifetime companion was a common motif in philosophical paraenesis: but when Philo talks of such a companion in the human soul, he means something existing beside reason, a being which can turn man's attention directly to God's commandments. In this way, Philo develops an early doctrine of conscience, which was a concept altogether unheard of in philosophy.

An ancient philosophical doctrine, going back to Plato's description of the Eros, claimed that human reason is unable to grasp the rational order of the universe in its entirety, but that man's own share in it gives him an unquenchable thirst for knowledge. This justifies seeing the meaning of life in the search for truth, on the understanding that the world order is basically accessible to man's rational cognition in every detail, and ideally also *in toto*. Philo, however, attaches greater importance to Biblical statements about the unfathomable nature of God. Thus he adapts the aforementioned philosophical doctrine by amplifying the motif of duration in the search for knowledge, a search which – as in the case of Moses – is successfully concluded only when the searcher has fully recognised God as unknowable.

Philo's world of ideas is extremely rich and there is hardly a single issue raised in contemporary school philosophy which he does not mention at some point or other – whether it be the relationship between science, philosophy, and general education; the theory of dreams; or the structure and origin of the world. But the verve of his highly figurative language emanates primarily from a deep piety which appears as firmly rooted in his nation's traditions, as well as showing many elements borrowed from the spirituality of contemporary philosophical religiousness. Philo once says that even proper prayer has to be a purely spiritual act. In spite of his great, if not always well-ordered, show of erudition, there is a paraenetical strain in all his treatises; and paraenesis or persuasion is the purpose for which many of his impressive phrasings are either borrowed or invented (*ebr.* 198). Hence it should not seem odd that comments on political, moral, and social issues of the day should feature also in other works than the report about his mission to Rome, and the pamphlet against the Prefect Flaccus. Whenever Philo makes such comments, he shows himself as a loyal citizen of the Roman world Empire, and as a fervent advocate of that civilisation which supported its worldwide rule.

Josephus

Josephus came from a family which belonged to the priestly nobility of Palestine. He spent some time in Rome as a well-connected young man before he joined the great Jewish uprising that began in 65 AD, ending five years later with the destruction of the Temple. Josephus was taken to Rome as a prisoner in 66 AD; there he was set free, and managed to establish personal relations with the new dynasty whose first Emperor, Vespasian, had been elevated to his new dignity in a military camp outside the city gates of the besieged Jerusalem. Josephus continued to live in Rome until after the turn of the century, enjoying the benefits of citizenship as well as a state pension, and producing all of his literary works there.

First of all, Josephus wrote a history of the Jewish uprising in his Aramaic mother tongue. This work, which is no longer extant, was presumably intended for an eastern Jewish readership inside as well as outside the Roman Empire. An extant text on the same topic is apparently a later and lengthier treatment of the same subject matter, put together by Josephus and a few helpers between 75 and 79 AD. This extant account of the great uprising is very detailed, and goes far back in its explanation of the roots of the revolt. We may assume that the author used different literary sources as well as eyewitness accounts, and also his own notes, taken while he was a participant in the events described. In contrast to the first version, this text is meant for a Graeco-Roman audience. Its purpose is to exonerate the Jewish upper classes, who had been open to Greek cultural influences for centuries, from any responsibility for the outbreak of the war, for which Josephus puts the blame exclusively on uneducated religious fanatics. But in fact it had only been the support of the aristocracy which had converted the local gang warfare of the so-called Zealots into a major popular uprising in 65 AD. Yet in spite of Josephus' bias and his many genuflections to the Flavian dynasty, his work is an invaluable historical source; its linguistic-literary merits, however, are fairly negligible.

Another historical work which Josephus wrote – apparently with the aid of some assistants – in the last two decades of the first century AD, is called *Jewish Archaeology.* The title recalls the *Roman Archaeology* of Dionysius of Halicarnassus; Josephus' twenty books sum up the history of the Jews from the creation of the world until the year 66 AD. The account follows first the canonised books of the Bible, and then authorities from the age of Hellenism, Jews but also Gentiles such as Polybius or Strabo. Books 1 to 10 are interesting examples of how the novelistic and psychological techniques of a certain branch of Hellenistic historiography could be applied to the retelling and the elaboration of Biblical stories. This, as well as the extensive use of non-Jewish sources, indicates that the work was aimed at a Gentile readership. In the precarious situation after the Jewish War Josephus wanted to give them a favourable image of true Judaism, its time-honoured traditions, and its institutionalised wisdom.

Those Jewish sects such as Sadducees, Pharisees, and Essenes, about which we have recently received additional information from the Qumran scrolls, are presented by Josephus as philosophical schools, with different cosmological and ethical doctrines just like their Greek counterparts. In Early Hellenism Egyptian and Babylonian priests had used a similar approach in introducing a Greek public to their own peoples' traditions; and Josephus repeatedly quotes their writings beside his other sources. There is, however, good reason to doubt whether his work had the intended effect on the readers whom he and his helpers were appealing to in view of the fact that the text they produced would have often fallen short of the audience's stylistic demands.

After his *Archaeology* Josephus wrote his apologetical book against Apion, a grammarian from Alexandria whom the Greeks of his native city had sent to Rome in 40 AD, as the leader of an anti-Jewish delegation. Apion was a highly prolific author, who had published works about subjects such as the Latin language, Homeric vocabulary, and the study of ancient Egypt. But he had also written an anti-Jewish tract whose criticism focused especially on doubts concerning the age, the genuineness, and the originality of Jewish tradition. That tract was yet another manifestation of the particularly strong anti-Jewish feeling in Alexandria, which repeatedly saw cruel pogroms such as those in 38 and 39 AD. One reason for this was the co-existence of two equally large and equally influential communities, Greek and Jewish, within that city. Also, Alexandria was for a long time the only autonomous Greek *polis* on Egyptian soil, whereas other Hellenistic states had several such centres. Hence Alexandria's inhabitants had a particularly marked sense of civic pride which led to numerous confrontations with central Imperial power. In such cases that power was inclined to favour either the Greeks or the Jews, and thus to keep the conflict within its local boundaries. The sending of the two delegations in 40 AD marks a typical instance of such a constellation.

In this context I must mention a strange kind of propaganda literature which recent papyrus finds have brought to light. This literature consists of fictitious transcripts ostensibly made at interrogations of members of the Greek upper classes in Alexandria, conducted by the Emperor himself or by high-ranking Roman officials. The detainees courageously profess their support for civic liberty; among the informers, we occasionally find some Jewish characters. As evidence of anti-Imperial feelings, such documents can be compared to sources which tell us about the Senatorial opposition in Rome. Their form recalls the early Acts of the Christian Martyrs which are likewise styled as the records of interrogations.

When Josephus wrote his pamphlet against Apion, the latter had already been dead for a long time. This indicates that Josephus' work was meant to contribute to a broader challenge to contemporary anti-Jewish tendencies, and it is by far the best source concerning those. Another valuable feature of Josephus' tract is the many quotations from literary works that were lost afterwards, especially ones dealing with Egypt. Anti-Jewish polemics kept referring to the report about the Israelites' captivity in Egypt from which they deduced that all Jewish tradition was a plagiarism of far older and far more venerable Egyptian models. To Josephus, such accusations deserve much more attention than the horror stories which had been spread about the Jews, the tales of ritual murders and the worship of donkeys. He counters Apion's contentions with a portrayal of Jewish religion and morality which appeals to those values cherished by educated Greek readers.

After the turn of the century, not long before his death, Josephus also wrote something like an autobiography. This work is not a full account of his life but rather a self-defence which refers only to certain episodes of his career. By the time he produced this piece of writing other accounts of the Jewish War had been published, such as that by the Jew Justus of Tiberias who presented the event in a totally different light. Many fellow believers thought of Josephus as a traitor, on account of his early success in fraternising with the victorious powers after his imprisonment. Such Jews would think little of Josephus' endeavours to bring about a belated mediation between the Jews and the Roman state. The pursuit of this goal makes his autobiography a slightly disjointed narrative, whose composition is not dictated by a coherent curriculum vitae, but by various apologetical motifs. The value of the work lies in individual pieces of information given; Josephus' late work, however, often contradicts that account of the Jewish War with which he had made his literary debut.

The fate of Jewish literature in Greek

Josephus' writings belong to the Flavian era, which followed the Julio-Claudian. I have dealt with them in the present section of the book because of the general fate of Graeco-Jewish literature which I will now outline.

The war that ended with the destruction of the Temple was not the last one waged between the Jews and the Roman state they lived in. The reign of Trajan saw the outbreak of a major Jewish rebellion, put down with great military effort, in Egypt and Cyrenaica; under Hadrian the Romans fought the Messianic movement of Bar Kochba in Palestine, during a span of three years. The result of those conflicts was the establishment of the civic colony Aelia Capitolina in lieu of Jerusalem; Jews were banned from this new colony on pain of death. The Jews of Judaea were evacuated and circumcision was prohibited by a law which thus prevented any conversion to the Jewish faith. As before, many Jews would be going about their daily business in all parts of the Empire, but Judaism had ceased to be accepted as a partner which could debate intellectually and compete socially with Graeco-Roman civilisation.

Such catastrophic events made the Jews turn back to their roots. Scriptural scholarship, which had remained unaffected by Greek tradition, found a new stronghold in Parthian Mesopotamia; soon after that a centre was also established at Tiberias in Palestine. Judaism came to be dominated by the beliefs of the Pharisees, who demanded a stricter separation from the Gentiles, and the preservation of cultic purity in Jewish life even among those who could not hope to participate in cultic worship proper. The rich heritage of Jewish literature in Greek was neglected by the Jews of the so-called Rabbinical tradition which was growing stronger at that time, in the wake of an increasing alienation of Judaism from Graeco-Roman civilisation.

Being regarded as a Jewish sect the first Christian community in Jerusalem had fallen victim to the aftermath of the Jewish War in 70 AD. But the Christians remained exempt from those catastrophes which befell the Jews in the Roman Empire under Trajan and Hadrian because by then they were generally perceived as distinct from the Jewish communities. Like the Jews, the earliest Christians in the Roman Empire regarded the Greek Old Testament, which circulated in numerous different versions, as their sacred book. When the church detached itself from the synagogue, Jews would first demand new and more precise translations; later on, as they moved farther and farther away from the Greek tradition, there was a general return to the Hebrew Bible which superseded all translations.

In this situation the survival of large parts of Graeco-Jewish literature was only due to the efforts of Christians. Christians kept reading such texts in addition to the Greek Bible and sometimes edited them in a Christian sense, thus giving practical proof of the continuity between

Christianity and its Jewish roots. Philo's work is another case in point. We cannot tell whether his writing, with its very comprehensive reflection of Greek philosophy, was really as exceptional as it certainly appears in the context of extant Graeco-Jewish literature. It is not unthinkable that the milieu of Late Hellenistic or Early Imperial Alexandria bred other theologians of Philo's kind: but if it did, their works have been lost for ever. Philo's writings, however, received much attention during the growth of Christian theology, for he had shown the way towards a synthesis of Biblical and philosophical thought: a path which Christian theologians between the third and the fifth centuries AD followed to a logical conclusion.

Disowned by Jews as the product of a traitor, Josephus' work remained largely unknown until its rediscovery in the Middle Ages. Then it was also read with great interest by Christians, especially because his historical accounts include the lifetime of Jesus. Yet Josephus does not mention Jesus at all, in spite of the fact that he refers to several other self-proclaimed Messiahs. Hence an early Christian translator of Josephus felt the need to add some remarks which could be construed as evidence of Jesus' life.

Josephus was certainly not the last Jewish author to write in Greek; but after the destruction of the Temple, and particularly after the end of the Bar Kochba uprising in 135 AD, Graeco-Jewish literature became more sparse, ceased to represent the imaginative powers of the Jewish world, and finally disappeared altogether.

3

THE FLAVIAN ERA

1 GENERAL REMARKS

Nero's fall in 68 AD was followed by armed confrontation between four contenders for supreme power, each one backed by a different part of the army. Their battles did not constitute civil warfare in the full sense of the term because only one claimant managed to enlist the support of a section of Italy's civilian population, beside that of his military camp followers. Thus the impact of this war can in no way be compared to that of any phase during the century of civil wars.

After a few ephemeral reigns, the final victor was T. Flavius Vespasianus, commander of those Roman troops engaged in the Jewish War, who was able to use the same military might against his domestic rivals. His accession to the throne in 69 AD marked the beginning of a new era, as the last descendant of an ancient family of Roman nobles was replaced by a man from a rather minor section of the Italic municipal aristocracy. Instead of a multi-talented monarch with a taste for music and art, there was now a sober, thrifty administrator; and instead of a Philhellene, a fervent advocate of Italian supremacy. Vespasian put the administration back on a sound financial footing after the havoc which Nero's extravagance had wrought, and proved to be a capable ruler in every administrative and military measure that he took. On that plot of land where Nero had built his Golden House as a symbol of Imperial splendour and supreme individual luxury, Vespasian ordered the construction of the Colosseum for the entertainment of the metropolitan masses.

Numerous anecdotes which have been handed down to us prove the grassroots popularity of Vespasian; but on the other hand his openly declared intention to found a new dynasty was resented by the philosophers, who had a great influence on public opinion, and likewise by tradition-conscious Senatorial circles. Vespasian was the first Emperor who took to banishing troublesome philosophers; he also ordered the banishment and then presumably the murder of the Senator Helvidius Priscus, a distinguished man with a sound philosophical education.

Such tensions abated slightly between 79 and 81 AD, during the short and very humane reign of Vespasian's older son Titus who had been commissioned by his newly enthroned father to put an end to the Jewish War. However, when Titus was succeeded by his younger brother Domitian the opposition became more vehement than ever before. Domitian was another capable, responsible monarch, but even more inclined than his father had been to see himself as a holder of absolute power. Domitian was the first Emperor who demanded the official address of 'dominus', traditionally the title with which a slave had to greet his master. He was relentless in his persecution of any real or imagined opposition in Senatorial or philosophical circles, and even more so after the discovery of several conspiracies, when many of those involved died at the hand of the executioner. But it is also true that Domitian gave generous patronage to intellectual life, and likewise did his best to further Senatorial careers whenever he found men who were willing to suffer his manner of government.

Domitian was killed after fifteen years on the throne, with his own wife among those who plotted his death. When he died, men like the historian Tacitus, that is to say members of the highest social class who had risen to important offices and built their reputations during Domitian's reign, were left with the feeling that they had been the cowardly collaborators of a tyrant. Like those of Nero, Domitian's Senatorial victims were commemorated in biographies praising them as martyrs who had died for political liberty, and for a philosophical attitude to life. Yet it must be said that in the ranks of the military and in the equestrian class there had been no comparable animosity towards Domitian during his reign.

2 GREEK ELOQUENCE

A characteristic of the Flavian era were measures taken to protect Italy's economic and political supremacy, in reaction to a marked strengthening of the East seen by the first two generations who lived in Imperial peace. As regards intellectual life, there had been a flowering of rhetoric in the cultural and economic centres of western Anatolia since the reign of Nero. This phenomenon came to be known as the beginning of the Second Sophistic movement, a term first featured in a literary document from the early third century AD, which consists of biographies of the main characters involved (see p. 340).

The name sophist, which Plato had used in a pejorative sense, was commonly given to teachers of rhetoric, that is to instructors in tertiary, higher education. But the epithet was likewise applied to practical orators whose skills made them eligible to act as official speakers on the major holidays celebrated by autonomous cities; to be spokesmen for delegations handing petitions or donations to the Emperor or to high-ranking Imperial officials; or to give public lectures on moral, patriotic, or literary issues to interested audiences. This so-called epideictic eloquence was deemed to be the most prestigious, even if the ability to deliver pleas in lawcourts still remained important to would-be social climbers. The sophists, who began to appear in the first century AD, were generally held in extremely high regard. Especially in the second century AD, quite a number of them attained high positions in independent municipal administrations as well as in Imperial service, where some even rose to the Consulate. Finally, success as a sophist was often also the key to the accumulation of a large fortune.

In spite of the fact that the Second Sophistic movement was in full swing at that time, we have only a few names of sophists from the Flavian era, such as Nicetas of Smyrna, Scopelianus of Clazomenae, and Lollianus of Ephesus. The latter was also known as the author of treatises on rhetorical theory. The earliest sophists and rhetors whose achievements are documented in extant texts belong to the second century AD; nevertheless, the revival of a representative Greek art of oratory appears as an essential feature of the literary scene during the Flavian era (see p. 228).

3 ROMAN POETRY

Before the renaissance of poetic writing in the fourth century AD, the Flavian era was the last in which Roman poetry could be described as productive in the full sense of the word. Among the remarkable achievements during that period, the most impressive ones belong to the last heyday of the epic genre. The major epic authors of the Flavian era were without exception members of the upper classes, a fact which proves that serious poetic efforts had at last become socially acceptable in those circles.

Valerius Flaccus

C. Valerius Flaccus Sentinus Balbus was a high-ranking Roman priest, who wrote an epic retelling of the Argonaut story. On the Greek side the Early Hellenistic poet Apollonius of Rhodes had produced that epic version in which this tale became known to posterity. It seems that Valerius Flaccus spent quite a long time on his own epic poem, whose prooemium was almost certainly written during the early years of Vespasian's reign. We have evidence of the fact that Valerius Flaccus died in the early 90s of the first century AD; what he left behind was an unfinished epic narrative, which had not progressed beyond Book 8.

While ancient epic had focused on action, Apollonius' version of the old tale had already given plenty of room to psychological description. Through his rendering of the tale, Apollonius had established Jason and Medea as one of the Classic loving couples. It was Virgil who made the

Greek poet's style of presentation with its psychological slant a common element also of Roman epic. Valerius Flaccus took it to such an extreme that ultimately even the logic of his plot suffered; he also took the liberty of adding other ornamentations, such as intimate or idyllic scenes, or passages elaborating on the personal relationships between epic characters and their divine protectors.

To a modern reader without a specialist background, an epic like that which Valerius wrote is bound to seem weird. At first sight the work appears to be all too artificial in its far-fetched and stilted diction, in its often declamatory rather than narrative quality, and in the sheer weight of scholarly-mythological erudition which it is made to carry. Indeed Valerius' work can only be understood in the way which the author intended by a reader who is able to spot its countless allusions to the entire epic tradition. Flaccus does a lot more than just evoke or vary, in the most diverse contexts, motifs and phrases from the *Aeneid*, as the Classic-Roman epic. The anti-Virgil Lucan can also be identified as the model for many of Valerius' passages; and the same can be said for writers of didactic epics, from Virgil and his *Georgica* to Germanicus and his translation of Aratus. It goes without saying that Valerius' reader is also expected to be familiar with his Greek model, Apollonius' *Argonautica*.

All this is crucial to an understanding of Valerius Flaccus' artistic intention. The author belongs to an age when there was only a thin line separating the ability properly to comprehend poetical works which presupposed so much knowledge from the urge to produce such poetry oneself. The common requirement for both achievements was a thorough familiarity with an extremely rich literary tradition.

Valerius Flaccus' prooemium, addressed to Vespasian, alludes to the epic which the later Emperor Domitian wrote about those heroic feats which his father and his brother had performed in the Jewish War. This reference is meant to justify the poet's choice of a mythological subject rather than of one which lends itself to the glorification of the Emperor. However, Valerius' poem does not contain so much as a single indication of an oppositional stance against the Emperor or his family.

Silius Italicus

If Lucan was an anti-Virgil he in turn was followed by an anti-Lucan in T. Catius Asconius Silius Italicus. We have several pieces of biographical information concerning this man who held the Consulate in 68 AD, governed the province of Asia in 77 AD, and died around 100 AD. There is a parallel between Lucan and Silius in that both produced an historical epic, for which the latter chose the second Punic War as a subject from Rome's heroic past. But whereas Lucan's sardonic portrayal of the civil war between Caesar and Pompey can only be understood as an expression of the poet's deep distaste for contemporary politics, Silius' work contains no recognisable allusions to events or conditions during the author's own lifetime. The prooemium even lacks the reverential address to the Emperor as featured, for example, in Valerius Flaccus' epic poem. The only part in Silius' work which refers to the achievements of the Flavian dynasty, in particular to the conquest of Scotland under Domitian, is a divine prophecy of Rome's future greatness, a speech embedded in the narrative of Book 3.

Silius' account spans events between the Siege of Saguntum and the Battle of Zama, in seventeen books which closely follow the report given by Livy. Silius uses the entire arsenal of traditional epic art including, for instance, parables, duels, descriptions of shields, underworld scenes, and battles between gods. Each passage harbours references to older epics from Homer to Lucan, with variations or exaggerations of the originals. We find individual phrases in which the reader is to recognise allusions to older texts as well as whole new characters that recall models from earlier epic art. The details given in Silius' narrative and description produce a fairly crude effect; but the most interesting feature of his epic is not artistic merit but the underlying ideology. This ideology can in turn be seen as continuing an epic tradition, and it makes Silius' work a historical document in spite of the lack of references to contemporary affairs.

In Virgil's epic, the author had expressed a philosophical belief in destiny through the construction of the plot, whose hero was obliged to carry out a precise divine plan and thus, without any intention of his own, lay the foundations for that future greatness of Rome to which the poet himself was a witness. Lucan turned this constellation upside-down, using the Stoic doctrine of fate in his reading of that epoch in Roman history which determined his own contemporary reality as a preordained period of destruction. This is why Lucan eliminated the gods from his narrative, where according to the epic tradition they would have featured as helpful or benevolent influences; and why he made his necessarily negative hero a man of action, with superhuman energy and success. In such circumstances a positive hero would have been able to do no more than prove his moral superiority through the manner of his downfall.

Silius was a Stoic, too: or at least, he was influenced by Stoic thinking. He adopted Virgil's basic concept of seeing in the second Punic War a fateful step on the road to Rome's future greatness, preordained and hence supported by the majority of the gods. In his epic, however, Silius goes further than Virgil had done in trying to illustrate how the actions of the great Romans of the period – such as Marcellus or Scipio – reveal that harmony between divine-natural predestination and human choice which was demanded by Stoic philosophy. This is manifest in the fact that those Romans remain loyal to the ancient values of their nation, which are unknown to the antagonist Hannibal. Silius shows both Scipio and

Hannibal as trying to emulate Heracles, that Greek hero whom Stoics and Cynics had presented as the archetype of a man whose unceasing endeavour and striving make him able to attain perfection through his own efforts. The Roman Hercules was, moreover, an important figure in popular religion and in Flavian Imperial ideology. In Silius' epic only one of the two claimants is Hercules' legitimate successor: Scipio whose individual striving for perfection is subordinate to serving Rome, and thus in harmony with the universal order in which Rome has its divinely given place.

By using the Stoic doctrine of fate to explain the tradition of Rome's heroic past with its many Republican memories the epic poet Silius tried to establish a meaningful connection between that tradition and the Imperial state which he himself lived in. Silius' aim was to prove that a Classicising frame of mind with its orientation towards the past could lead to an affirmation, instead of a rejection, of contemporary reality.

Statius

P. Papinius Statius was born in Naples as the son of a teacher of rhetoric who belonged to an equestrian family. Statius moved to Rome at a fairly early age; and there, like Martial, he gained access to the circle of poets with whom Domitian surrounded himself. He also won several prizes in the poetry competitions instituted by the Emperor; and he probably died around the time of Domitian's murder. There are some mentions of Statius' name in contemporary documents, and further information about his biography can be gained from his own occasional poetry.

Statius' major work was the *Thebais*, an epic in twelve books like Virgil's *Aeneid*, about the War of the Seven against Thebes. The poem was written in the 80s of the first century AD; the prooemium pays homage to the Emperor, announcing Statius' intention to produce an epic account of the monarch's deeds. This promise is repeated in the prooemium to Statius' second epic, an unfinished *Achilleis*; and thus it appears as an instance of a common exordial motif, an expression of humility which the poet has inserted as a refusal to sing the praises of the Emperor's prowess at present, or at any stage.

Statius takes for granted that his readers are familiar with the motifs and formulas of the epic tradition; and in the *Thebais*, he goes to the greatest imaginable extremes in his effort to come up with yet another set of variations. The battle descriptions abound with unbearable horrors; the characters' speeches are incredibly long and brimming over with pathos; and the individual scenes are so extensively theatrical that they obscure the coherence of the narrative.

The author even attempts to augment the horrors in the traditional story about the fight for Thebes, which is a sombre enough tale to begin with. The plot, culminating in the death of two hostile brothers in a duel, comes from a piece of ancient myth which provided the material for several Attic tragedies. Like those, Statius' poem portrays the events as resulting from men's guilt in the eyes of fellow humans and of gods. This is why, especially in the underworld scenes, the divine powers of his epic apparatus intervene to punish and to destroy, rather than to help.

In Statius' unfinished epic about Achilles, the narrative stops in the middle of Book 2. So all we have is the author's account of the hero's youth, which gives us no certain evidence as to how Statius interpreted the story he set out to retell. What we have as proof of his poetic versatility are the five books of the *Silvae* or *Collections of Poetic Material*, a title of a kind which became popular at the time for all manner of different compilations. Each book of the *Silvae* presents a sequence of occasional poems, with a prose introduction dedicating it to a patron or a friend. The volumes were published separately as well as in the full set.

Form and content of the poems are extremely varied. Among the topics there are, for instance, congratulations on weddings or birthdays; poetic expressions of mourning and condolence; descriptions of works of art or of buildings; or verses about animals such as a parrot or a tame lion. The forms are of a similar diversity. Most poems are written in hexameters but we also find some that consist of those lines of eleven syllables which the Neoterics had introduced into Latin poetry, as well as two odes in the Alcaic and Sapphic metres which Horace had used.

In the *Thebais* Statius applied his gift for formal elegance and his comprehensive mastery of poetic devices in order to create an epic style which was far removed from the genuine qualities of epic narrative. The poet's linguistic skills were put to much better use in the *Silvae* with its wide range of topics, including serious as well as humorous, or at least more light-weight, subjects. For example, in a consolatory poem addressed to the poet Lucan's widow on the occasion of the dead man's birthday, Statius manages to find a tone that conveys respect as well as genuine sympathy; and there is a credible expression of heart-felt grief in the poem on the death of his own son. On the other hand we find a highly successful evocation of comic pathos, with all the means which epic language had to offer, in a hexametric poem about hair that was cut from a handsome boy's head. On the whole, the poems of the *Silvae* are an excellent illustration of those forms of poetic communication which were fashionable in the literary circles of courtly-metropolitan society.

Martial

Of all the poets of the Flavian era the one who was most famous and most widely read by subsequent generations was M. Valerius Martialis, a Spaniard who came to Rome as a protégé of Seneca's family, likewise of Spanish origin. Martial's poetic talent brought him into contact with the courts of Titus and Domitian; the latter finally knighted him and gave him the 'third-child privilege' which Augustus had introduced to encourage childbearing among the Italic upper classes. Notwithstanding his success, there was one thing which Martial never managed to achieve: he could not attain financial independence, in spite of the fact that his Imperial eulogies were ultimately written with precisely this goal in mind. Thus, Martial remained a late specimen of the poet-client, a type that had been the norm in former times.

Martial became the Classic writer of Roman epigrams. It seems that he published his poetry in several shorter collections, of which a few are extant. We have the so-called *Liber spectaculorum* with thirty-three epigrams of different length written in 80 AD, about the presentations on show at the opening of the Colosseum. Another twelve books contain epigrams of varied length and content. Those are mostly composed in elegiac distichs, but we also find eleven-syllable lines, limping iambs, pure iambs, hexameters, and so-called sotadees, a metre originally intended for poetry that was sung. Finally, two extant books contain epigrams consisting of one distich each, conceived as inscriptions on gift labels. The length of Martial's epigrams varies between two and thirty lines; his range of subjects is similarly broad covering serious as well as humorous topics. These include poetic expressions of condolence and of congratulation, Imperial homages, satirical portrayals of human behaviour, and literary polemics, as well as pointed descriptions of remarkable events and objects.

In the previous section of my book, I have dealt with Greek epigrammatic poetry, which also existed in Rome during the period in question. In Martial's work we can detect occasional references to poems by the slightly older Lukillios; and a comparison between these two is a good way to highlight the distinctive features of Martial's writing. What we find is that the Roman poet puts a greater emphasis on the surprising punchline which his poems lead into, and thus Martial's wit becomes more aggressive than that of his Greek predecessor, in spite of a certain impersonal quality that exists even in his satirical-polemical epigrams. Most of the names which Martial cites belong to fictitious characters, and the poet gives away very little of himself, of his feelings, or of his wishes. Catullus, another important author in the tradition of Roman epigrammatic poetry, wrote in an entirely different manner. Unfortunately we can make no similar comparison between Martial and the most famous poet of the Augustan era, Domitius Marsus, whom Martial certainly knew but whose works are no longer extant.

The most astonishing feature of Martial's writing is its wide range of linguistic expression. There are poems in high epic diction, beside others whose verses include vulgar or even obscene words. Martial also makes frequent use of those Greek expressions which writers of high poetic language were normally at great pains to avoid. They would still allow no other Greek words than proper names from mythology in poetic diction, while the colloquial language of educated people had been full of Greek words and phrases since the age of Cicero.

It is well known that witty and pointed phrases always come more easily to someone who wants to criticise than to someone who wants to praise, no matter at what time in history, or in what language. It is not surprising, then, that Martial's most impressive epigrams are of a satirical-polemical nature, and this in turn explains a certain image which he had even among his contemporaries. As Pliny the Younger put it, 'he was ingenious, astute, and aggressive; and his manner of writing did not reveal only salt and gall, but also sincerity'. Those qualities are indeed the most obvious ones in Martial's radical exposure of the vices of his age. But occasionally the poet was also not incapable of a touch of humorous mockery, as in this amusing epigram which is about Lucan's epic:

> Some say that I am actually not a true poet,
> But the man who hawks my stuff, the
> Bookseller, he believes it!

4 PLINY THE ELDER

In literary history we find only very rare instances where the *oeuvre* of an individual author represents the intellectual life of a whole epoch as completely as it does in the case of C. Plinius Secundus. Although the only extant one of his works is the *Naturalis historia*, we have a letter by the Younger Pliny which contains an annotated list of his uncle's writings, and thus gives us a fairly accurate idea of Pliny the Elder's literary production as a whole. In addition to that, we find reflections of the Elder Pliny's writing in many texts by other authors; and in his natural history, Pliny himself occasionally also refers to his other publications.

Pliny came from an equestrian family resident in that city which is nowadays known as Como. He was educated in Rome, and entered military service under Nero's great general Corbulo. As an officer in the 40s and 50s of the first century AD he got to know the frontier along the River Rhine; then during the Jewish War he was posted to Palestine, where he made the acquaintance of Vespasian and became friends with Vespasian's son Titus. His career finally took off properly when Vespasian succeeded the Emperor Nero, a man whom Pliny despised. Gaul, north Africa, Spain, and once again Gaul were the geographical stages in Pliny's rise to a high office in the Imperial administration, and finally to one of the three highest positions open to men of equestrian rank: commander of the Roman war fleet, which had its base at Misenum, on the Gulf of Naples.

It was there that Pliny the Elder died of a heart attack in 79 AD at the age of fifty-six, while trying to organise the evacuation of those urban areas which were threatened by the eruption of Vesuvius. We have a very detailed account of these events in two more letters written by Pliny's nephew, epistles which are addressed to the historian Tacitus. Pliny was the typical representative of a social class that served the Flavian dynasty most loyally, because they saw the rule of the Flavians as the best possible guarantor of moral and political order in the world Empire. Given that so much of Pliny's life was taken up with the fulfilment of military and administrative duties, it seems almost miraculous that he also found time to produce a substantial literary *oeuvre*.

Pliny's earliest work, written in 47 AD, was a short military treatise about the use of the spear as a distance weapon by mounted troops. This work was based on his experiences as a cavalry officer in many encounters with Germanic tribes on the right bank of the Rhine. Next came the life of Pomponius Secundus, a biography presumably written in 57 AD – the year of Pomponius' death – or shortly afterwards. Pomponius, one of Seneca's friends, had distinguished himself not only in administrative and military service, but also as an author of tragedies; from this we can infer that Pliny's account of his life would certainly also have included literary aspects. This piece of writing was followed by a history of the wars between the Romans and the Germans. In the aforementioned list of Pliny's writings his nephew states that his uncle began his first historical work after Drusus, the brother of the Emperor Tiberius, appeared to him in a dream. Drusus had achieved fame through his victories over the Germanic tribes; he had died in a riding accident on the banks of the River Elbe. We may assume that the Younger Pliny got his information from the preface to his uncle's history, a book which Tacitus used as a source, but which scholars in the fourth century AD were already unable to track down.

Pliny the Elder's next publication was a rhetorical textbook which was greeted with very little enthusiasm by specialists in the field. The work may have been written during the final years of Nero's reign when Pliny had retired from state service. A grammatical treatise in eight books, which belonged to the same period in his life, was a compilation of unusual word forms from older Latin literature, with a morphological and orthographical analysis. Here, Pliny criticised the normative tendencies expressed in Remmius Palaemon's *ars grammatica* (see pp. 141–2): his own approach to grammar was empirical, based on actual linguistic usage. Pliny's work became a major source of material for later grammarians who dealt with the same kind of problems, and this very fact explains why Pliny's text is no longer extant: the material he had collected was later presented in the context of systematic grammatical treatises.

Pliny's interest in grammatical issues is well documented, even if there is no proof for the assumption that he had a close personal acquaintance with the celebrated grammarian Valerius Probus. Nevertheless, Pliny the Elder's rhetorical-grammatical publications were followed by another historical work, which continued the historiography of Aufidius Bassus (see p. 135) with an account that covered the period from 47 AD to the first years of Vespasian's reign. The Younger Pliny praises the wealth of detail in this writing of his uncle, while to Tacitus, who subscribed to the Republican-Senatorial tradition of historiography, the Elder Pliny was one of those authors of the Flavian era whose exaggerated devotion to the ruling dynasty made them somewhat less than impartial. In spite of that, it is certain that Tacitus used Pliny's historical account as a source.

As I have said before, the only extant work by Pliny is his *magnum opus*, the *Naturalis historia*. Its thirty-seven books were published in 77 AD, with a comprehensive dedication to the Emperor Titus. However, we may assume that the gathering of the material by Pliny himself or by assistants began more than one decade before that date.

The *Naturalis historia* has a systematic structure, with a long preface in which the author tells us about his library, about the volume of his collection of excerpts, and about the goal and the method of his account. Its first book contains a long list of Greek and Latin source material. Book 2 deals with astronomy and meteorology, and Books 3 to 6 with geography. Biology comes next, with Book 7 on man, Books 8 to 11 on animals, and Books 12 to 19 on plants, including agriculture. Books 20 to 32 are a comprehensive pharmacology, and Books 33 to 37 a mineralogy, divided into sections on metals and rocks. As he features agriculture in his botanical books, so does Pliny incorporate historical surveys on bronze and marble sculpture in the relevant volumes. There is also a historical account of painting, featured in the part of his work which deals with mineral colours; this report has preserved at least some fragments of the largely lost genre of Classical writings on art.

Pliny did not contribute much to the advancement of science or research but he was motivated by an exceptional thirst for knowledge. This is clearly evident in the description which his nephew's letter gives of Pliny's final hours during the great natural catastrophe of 79 AD. The wealth of information which Pliny gathered from books is always mixed with references to things he himself has seen or experienced. He also includes pieces of contemporary knowledge which were presumably not yet on literary record at the time.

One of the aspects in which Pliny's natural history appears as non-scientific is its organisation as the information is conveyed in consecutive summaries of different sources. The author does not even vary his approach in those cases where the synthesising of pieces of information would seem an obvious necessity. Thus, for instance, there is a survey of the geography of India, based on the book which Megasthenes wrote around 300 BC; this is followed by more recent or even contemporary reports about Ceylon, about regular monsoon navigation between the southern exit of the Red Sea and the Malabar coast, and about the coastline between the deltas of the Ganges and the Indus. The new information is presented without any attempt to correct Megasthenes' geographical account which was based on far fewer facts.

We have a contemporary parallel text for precisely these chapters of Pliny's geography, in the Greek *Periplus of the Red Sea*. This small treatise, written without any literary aspirations, is a description from the point of view of an experienced sailor. It deals with the course of the monsoon passage and the adjacent harbours, with political conditions at the ports, and above all with the many different goods exported and imported in the numerous trading centres between the Red Sea and the Gulf of Bengal. This little book is one of the most important documents concerning the history of trade in the first century AD and there are several parallels with the content of the corresponding chapters in the *Naturalis historia*. It is telling, however, that Pliny's account should also include facts from the history of monsoon shipping: a subject of no interest at all to the anonymous author of the periplus, who appears as a man concerned with practical issues only.

Naturally there are plenty of occasions where misunderstanding and confusion occur in Pliny's long summaries, whose order does not always tally with the list given in Book 1. In any case, we may well assume that only a limited number of Pliny's excerpts were based on original works by the many authors cited in his long survey of source material. There is also none of that systematic criticism of sources which one would expect in any scientific work. Instead Pliny displays a very subjective skepticism concerning certain pieces of literary information, or of traditional lore. In most cases this skepticism reflects the author's astute intelligence, but it never leads into a methodical-critical discussion.

Another non-scientific feature in Pliny's writing stems from his desire to present a complete account of all accessible information. Consequently, in spite of his basic rejection of magical concepts and practices, Pliny's pharmacology also lists those drugs which were believed to have a magical effect. It is the same encyclopaedic urge which occasionally also makes the author lose his way in ever-new digressions and sub-digressions. It is true that in the context of Pliny's basically anthropocentric view of nature, it makes sense to talk about jewellery in a chapter on precious stones, and about the technical history of writing in a chapter on the papyrus plant. But Pliny does not stop there: in the section on metals, for instance, he comes to talk about the wearing of finger rings, beginning with some references to sources from early Greek history, and suddenly branching out into a lengthy digression on the Roman knighthood, its history and its privileges, up to the most recent past. The only justification for all this is that beside the small purple stripe on the *toga*, the finger ring was one of the insignia of the equestrian class! Still, it must be said that modern readers often find Pliny's text interesting especially because of digressions of this kind.

What Pliny says in the long prooemium indicates that his major work is supposed to be seen as an encyclopaedia of general knowledge, with a focus on nature. To the author, the natural order is the ultimate source of legitimacy for all norms and values. In one passage Pliny says that not even a god can decree that two times two make five, because that would be against nature. This is in keeping with the common philosophical concept which defined the divine as part of nature and recognised no opposition between nature and the lives or the history of men, or human society. Pliny apparently did not subscribe to the doctrines of any philosophical school, and thus his statement is evidence of the fact that this principle was one accepted by all educated people. Pliny was driven by the urge to know and tell as much as possible about the life-giving power of nature and all of its effects on men. The root of this zeal is a reverential trust in nature, an attitude which is religious in character, and presumably represents the essential content of those religious notions which were held by educated people of that period.

The linguistic-stylistic form of the *Naturalis historia* also indicates that it was meant to communicate general knowledge, and not to contribute to scientific debate. Pliny's style has been much maligned; and indeed those often antithetical phrases with which he describes phenomena like the style of a statue or the shapes of sea-shells, are frequently artificial, sonorous, and imprecise to boot. On the other hand in his endeavour to avoid the dull tone of specialist literature, the author tries to keep varying his vocabulary and his syntax all the time, even in the long enumerations of distances in his geographical books. The result is that Pliny's text is sometimes hard to follow.

All the same we should not forget that Pliny faced the difficult task of finding literary expressions for information which most of his sources would have given in plain, non-rhetorical diction. From literary language, however, only vulgar vocabulary was as strictly banned as that specialist terminology which scientific disciplines had developed for the sake of precision. The many oddities in Pliny's style may be explained by this dilemma: he had to try to avoid ambiguity in transmitting information, but at the same time he was forced to shun specialist jargon and stick to the vocabulary of literary language, which admitted exceptions only when it came to naming people, places, or objects.

It was thus only in his long and elaborately written prooemium that Pliny was free to show all of his stylistic skill. The resulting text is a good example of a common prose style of that epoch, a manner of writing which had obviously been developed as a contrast to the regularity of Ciceronian periods. Pliny's diction is not as pointed as Seneca's, nor is it as full of surprising shifts and turns in content and syntax. But Pliny also shows a preference for the asymmetric and hence the unexpected, rather than the use of strictly regular syntactic structures. In short, he may be called the exponent of an anti-Ciceronian literary prose. We have too few parallel texts to judge whether this phenomenon was typical of the literature of the Flavian era in general, or whether it was just one stylistic trend among others. Nevertheless, the first assumption seems more likely if one considers the great influentiality of Seneca as well as the vociferous demand for a return to the Ciceronian style which was heard towards the end of the Flavian epoch. From these facts we may infer that the departure from the Ciceronian style set in during the reign of Nero and continued as the dominant fashion during the Flavian era.

Pliny's natural history was very widely read. We have evidence for the high regard in which it was held during the second century AD; and in the third century AD C. Julius Solinus wrote an encyclopaedia which was largely based on Pliny. The *Naturalis historia* was used as a textbook and as a reference work until well into the Renaissance, and it is due to this popularity that we have more than two hundred mediaeval manuscript copies.

5 QUINTILIAN

Like so many other outstanding personalities in Roman intellectual life of the Early Empire, M. Fabius Quintilianus was of Spanish origin. He received his grammatical and rhetorical education in Rome where he was taught by the most eminent scholars in the two respective disciplines, Remmius Palaemon and Cn. Domitius Afer. Quintilian then went back to Spain from where he returned to Rome in 68 AD in the train of Galba, the first of the short-lived Emperors after Nero. This time Quintilian stayed and became the most distinguished teacher of rhetoric in the capital. Vespasian gave him the first ever chair of rhetoric which was endowed with a state salary; Domitian made Quintilian the tutor of his adopted sons, and he also decorated him with the *ornamenta consularia*, which signified Consular status without the duties of the Consular office. Most of these biographical data are known from Quintilian's own writings; as for the author's death, we may assume a date around the turn of the century.

Under the name of Quintilian there are two extant collections of declamations, that is of exemplary speeches or rhetorical exercises. Those may belong to the context of his teaching but it is very unlikely that they are Quintilian's own productions. Some legal pleas which he published were lost, whereas we have the full twelve books of Quintilian's *Institutio oratoria*, the most comprehensive Classical account of rhetorical theory known to us. This work is based on Quintilian's rich experience as a teacher, which explains why it contains no new or original systematic plan, but rather a meticulous inventory of the traditional curriculum of rhetoric, as well as of all the related disciplines. The author also discusses fundamental aspects and different theories of general education, a fact which led to his modern-day reputation as a Classic author of pedagogical literature.

Book 1 of the *Institutio oratoria* deals with grammar, musical theory, and geometry, as propaedeutics to rhetorical instruction. Book 2 treats of the preconditions and the potential achievements of systematic rhetorical teaching; Book 3 contains a general introduction to rhetorical systematics. The systematic survey as such, divided according to the different parts of speech, forms the content of Books 4 to 6, with additional chapters on the ancient doctrine of ethos and pathos as well as on the theory of the joke which Cicero had already dealt with in a longer treatise. Book 7 contains the doctrine of *status*, a theory developed in the Hellenistic age in order to provide exact categories for the classification of a case, as tools to facilitate the *inventio*, the planning of a speech. Books 8 to 11 feature lengthy discourses on aspects of style. In this context Book 10 gives the reader a list of Greek and Latin authors whom an orator should read to improve his stylistic skills: and here as in the theoretical discussions Quintilian shows that he is equally familiar with the Greek and the Latin side. Book 11 contains rules for the memorising and for the delivery of a speech. Finally, Book 12 discusses the intellectual and moral qualities, as well as the extent of general knowledge, which an orator should possess. In this section of his work, Quintilian echoes Isocrates' claim that rhetoric should play the central role in general education.

The structure of this broad survey follows the traditional schemata of the parts of speech, the tasks of the orator, and the three levels of style; but Quintilian does not stick to those in any pedantic manner. Like Cicero, he demands that the orator should be well versed in philosophy, in literature or grammar, and in law: hence an orator should simply be the ideal educated person as such. But to Quintilian, the educational function of the other disciplines mentioned is limited to their being part – or rather the material – of rhetoric. He is particularly adamant in denying the claim that philosophy is important in its own right. In Quintilian's view, the subject of philosophy belongs to the scope of rhetoric and rhetorical instruction, because it is the latter which produces the morally outstanding orator or, in the Elder Cato's words which Quintilian quotes repeatedly, the 'good man who also knows how to speak'. Consequently Quintilian explicitly rejects the opinion that rhetoric is only aimed at persuasion, regardless of truth; this view had first been expressed in Plato's *Gorgias* and was then taken up again and again as philosophers and rhetors fought for the supremacy of their respective discipline in the education of the young.

Quintilian agrees with the contention that the art of oratory had been in decline ever after the age of Cicero; this had been stated first by the rhetor Seneca and then by numerous other writers including Petronius and the unidentified author who wrote the treatise *Of the Sublime*. Quintilian even goes so far as to make critical remarks about the writing of fictitious speeches, a method which he himself employed in his teaching. What he suggests as a cure for the corruption of eloquence is a return to the Ciceronian style. In Book 10 the author makes a very oblique comment on the style of Seneca, a manner of writing which Quintilian could have seen as nothing else than a result of the general degeneration. On the one hand Quintilian pays verbal homage to his famous fellow author, but in the same breath he deplores the fact – as he knows from practical experience – that young people refuse to imitate any stylistic model other than Seneca. Quintilian says that because of that blinkered attitude he would not allow his own pupils to choose Seneca in preference to other, better examples. This confession is followed by a scathing judgment of Seneca's sententious diction, which splits a statement up into minute *kola*. That ultimate verdict is only slightly qualified by a subsequent remark saying that beginners should be wary of imitating Seneca, but that mature rhetors may be permitted to admire the virtuosity of that versatile writer.

At the end of the first century AD, when the ageing Quintilian wrote his *Institutio*, there were certainly some good reasons why one should ask for a return to the Ciceronian style, as well as for a reversion to those views concerning the nature of oratory and the character of the orator which Cicero had expressed in his rhetorical treatises. On the one hand as Quintilian himself makes quite clear, this demand was a reaction to the developments in prose style between the reign of Tiberius and the Neronian-Flavian epoch. But another circumstance which favoured the creation of a 'back-to-Cicero' programme was the great progress made in the grammatical and historical study of older Latin literature, especially during the Flavian era.

We have parts of a major commentary on Cicero's speeches, which was written by the extremely learned and meticulous grammarian Asconius Pedianus. Asconius' aim was above all to illuminate the texts in the light of those historical circumstances in which the speeches had been produced. His commentary is the work of a scholar who had acquired a number of diverse skills, and certainly knew how to use archive material. Like Livy, Asconius – who died not long before 80 AD – came from Padua. He also produced writings on Horace and Virgil; in the latter case he defended the poet against disparaging critics.

The most famous grammarian in the second half of the first century AD was M. Valerius Probus from the Roman civic colony of Berytus, modern-day Beirut. Probus pursued grammatical studies in Rome after a fairly unsuccessful career in the army. He wrote very little, and only about very specialised subjects such as the Greek genitive, or the system of abbreviations in legal documents; but he was held in such high esteem by contemporaries and subsequent generations that numerous grammatical works of the Late Classical age were published under his name. Probus' influential role among his contemporaries is documented in a reference by Martial. Today, we can hardly arrive at an accurate assessment of the extent to which Probus' marginal remarks and insertions of punctuation in copies of older literature allegedly altered the shape of those texts as they were handed down to us. But it is certain that the work of this distinguished man increased the interest of the literary public in Republican and Augustan authors. This very fact was another precondition for the revival of Ciceronianism, a phenomenon which paved the way for the even more extreme archaism of the second century AD, with its return to pre-Classic Latin.

6 PLUTARCH

Biographies

The figure of Plutarch, who came from the minor Boeotian city of Chaeronea, personifies a large share of the intellectual life of the Flavian era. In this Plutarch is comparable to Pliny who was about twenty years his senior, albeit that Pliny represented the epoch in quite a dissimilar manner. A further difference between the two men is that Plutarch lived well into the subsequent period, the age of the Antonines; he died around 120 AD.

Plutarch came from one of the distinguished families of his native city, where he himself held a number of municipal offices. In addition he served for many years as a priest of Apollo in nearby Delphi. In the 60s of the first century AD Plutarch studied in Athens; among those teachers from whom he received his comprehensive education in philosophy the most influential was Ammonius, head of the Platonic school at that time. Plutarch travelled widely in the Aegean and Asia Minor, as well as in Italy.

In the capital he formed close acquaintances with several Roman nobles, and he adopted the name of one of those men – Mestrius, a friend of the Emperor Vespasian – when he became a Roman citizen. But the person closest to Plutarch seems to have been Q. Sosius Senecio, an intimate confidant of the Emperor Trajan, who held the Consulate several times, and also achieved fame as a general. But in spite of his Roman ties, Plutarch spent most of his life in his home city surrounded by a varying circle of friends and disciples among whom there were members of the local upper classes, as well as great Romans and itinerant professional philosophers from very different schools, who stopped at Chaeronea on their travels. Plutarch was a voracious reader, and his remarkable powers of memory – possibly assisted by copious notes – enabled him to turn out a vast number of works, seemingly with the greatest facility. His writings dealt with the most diverse subjects which he nevertheless always related to the entire spectrum of philosophical and literary tradition. Besides his memory, another factor which helped Plutarch to achieve this was his temperament, more suited to an affectionate lingering over the treasures of traditional education than it was to assiduous research or scientific debate. Consequently to communicate the learning he had acquired meant more to him than any endeavour to shine as an elegant stylist, and thus to endear himself to the many contemporary readers who looked for stylistic brilliance.

Plutarch's extant writings, including some works by other authors that were attributed to him, fill more than a dozen large volumes. About twice the number of today's extant titles is cited in a list of Plutarch's publications in a Byzantine manuscript, where it is alleged that the inventory was compiled by Lamprias, one of Plutarch's sons. However, the most likely source of those data is some Late Classical library catalogue. As for the content, this is borne out by many references in the works of other authors to writings by Plutarch which we no longer have today. What there is now of his *oeuvre* was collected and edited by Byzantine scholars in the thirteenth century: Plutarch was a particularly popular author in mediaeval Byzantium. In the ninth century AD the learned Patriarch Photius still had access to some of his works that were lost afterwards. There is also a short poem from the eleventh century by the metropolitan Bishop John Mauropus, a text in which Christ is asked to exempt Plato and Plutarch from the sojourn in hell, to which they would have been condemned just like all other heathens. The reason given is that whatever their religion, both had none the less lived and taught in a manner that was in keeping with God's commandments.

I have chosen to start my survey of Plutarch's *oeuvre* with the biographies, in spite of the fact that the extant specimens were written fairly late in his life. The reason is that they have only a loose connection with the philosophical writings which will be discussed later on; moreover, Plutarch's biographies are the first completely extant examples of a literary genre whose history reaches far back into the past.

Of his *Parallel Lives*, we have twenty-two pairs and we know of one more that was lost. From a large number of single biographies that included lives of poets, philosophers, and ancient heroes, the two extant ones deal with Aratus of Sicyon and the Persian King Artaxerxes II, men who lived during the third century BC and around 400 BC respectively. Out of a complete set of Roman Imperial biographies, continued up to the beginning of Vespasian's reign, there are two about monarchs who belonged to the group of ephemeral rulers of 68 and 69 AD.

Each set of the parallel biographies combines the lives of two remarkable personalities from Greek and Roman history respectively, whose characters, achievements, and circumstances suggest a comparison. Thus we find Alexander the Great matched with Caesar; Cicero with Demosthenes; Dion, Plato's friend and victim of a tyrant's despotism, with Brutus, who killed a tyrant because of his philosophical beliefs. Theseus, the legendary hero of ancient Athens, is paired off with Romulus, the founder of Rome; and Agis and Cleomenes, who unsuccessfully attempted the social reformation of Sparta in the third century BC, stand beside Tib. and C. Gracchus, the Roman reformers at the beginning of the century of civil wars.

This selection should be sufficient to illustrate that Plutarch chose to describe characters that were historical or regarded as such, from any time between mythical prehistory and the beginning of the Imperial age. Hence his account is of necessity almost entirely based on historiographical sources, whose reports Plutarch actually retells to a large extent. Thus he preserved – if not in the original wording – many pieces of Hellenistic historiography which would otherwise have been lost just like most of the rest.

Considering this fact it may appear strange that Plutarch should time and again tell his readers that he is no historiographer and that history and biography are altogether unrelated anyway. In the second century BC the historian Polybius had already pointed out the difference between the two genres. In his preface to the life of Aemilius Paullus, the great Philhellene and conqueror of the Macedonian monarchy, Plutarch says that a biographer invites his heroes into his own house in order to get to know them; just as Priamus and Achilles got to know each other over a meal according to Homer's report in the last book of the *Iliad*. This image is in keeping with a passage from Plutarch's life of Alexander, in which the reader is warned not to expect a complete enumeration of all the King's great deeds. Plutarch maintains that minor habits in a man's table manners, or such seemingly insignificant details in his behaviour towards his closest friends as would be reported in anecdotes, are more revealing to a biographer than the same person's comportment on occasions of state, or his most celebrated feats. According to Plutarch, the writer of a biography should draw a picture of his hero's life and character which is commensurate with the reader's own experience regardless of all historical or social differences; a picture which can thus serve the reader as a positive or as a negative example in his own striving for moral perfection.

That negative examples may also help to further such endeavours is what Plutarch declares in the preface to the parallel biographies of Demetrius Poliorcetes, a violent genius of a type which we find among the monarchs of early Hellenism, and the Triumvir Antony, the last rival of Augustus. However, in the preface to his life of the Emperor Galba the author qualifies this statement by saying that such an effect can only be achieved if the biographer selects only those among the available facts which clearly illustrate the moral physiognomy of the character described.

Classic Greek historiography had sought to interpret historical events less as the creation of great individuals than as the result of supra-individual forces, whose working follows universal laws. A more and more personal kind of historiographical writing had come in with the appearance of the great monarchic figures such as Philip II, Alexander, or Alexander's successors, the Diadochi. In the new brand of historiography, biographical information was taken into account in so far as it served to explain or to connect historical events. Words to that effect can be found in programmatic definitions of historiographical writing by Polybius and Cicero, in the second and first centuries BC respectively. According to such views biography is the exact inversion of historiography: in the latter selected biographical information serves to make the succession of historical actions or events seem more understandable, while in the former selected historical events illustrate the character of a person.

Biography was based on the assumption that by describing a man's actions, one can reveal his character: or his ways of behaviour, as it was commonly put in Greek and Latin, with the first noun always in the plural form. The same principle had long been used in the writing of encomia, that is speeches in praise of individual human beings. This genre had arrived at a well-defined form as early as the fourth century BC and was hence incorporated in rhetorical theory as we can see in the works of Aristotle. Biography, however, went further than the encomium in its attempt to present the course of a person's life as an organic whole, if not in all known detail.

The interest in such a holistic view of human lives had a philosophical basis. Socrates had taught that a proper life can only be a life of perpetual reckoning. Hence philosophy is the art of living, an art in which one has to train oneself throughout one's life: and therefore only the final assessment can show whether a person has missed or achieved his life's goal. Considering all this, it seems as no coincidence that the first mentions of biographical writing emanate from philosophical circles, especially the Aristotelian school from the end of the fourth century BC onwards. It was the Peripatetics who had devoted particular attention to the classification of human lives as belonging to different types or forms.

The terms and categories Plutarch uses in his endeavour to describe the formation and the development of a moral personality are closely related to the basic concepts of Peripatetic anthropology as worked out above all in Aristotle's writings on ethics. In his attempt to give an answer to the much-debated question of whether virtue can be taught Aristotle had emphasised one central point: moral virtue is neither a natural gift, for in that case nobody could claim any personal credit for it: nor is it something that can be learned first and put into practice later. To Aristotle, a man eventually becomes righteous if – on the basis of his natural disposition and with the help of his reason – he consciously keeps on directing his actions towards the goal of righteous behaviour.

It is consistent with this point of view that in all of Plutarch's biographies the early chapters on the hero's childhood and adolescence tell the reader a lot about the family background, the innate characteristics, and the early education of the men he portrays. Thus the reader gets to know the hero's nature, which merges with education in forming the basis for his moral development. The main or middle parts of Plutarch's lives are often of a very loose composition, as the author is less concerned with the chronology of personal fates and more with the formation of his hero's individual characteristics and manners of behaviour as moral, and hence not natural, features. Most of the final sections which describe the last years of a person's life and the circumstances of his death are fairly long and detailed accounts: for it is here that the author feels able to arrive at a final, irrefutable assessment of a life as a moral entity.

All that Plutarch himself says about the aim of his biographies, as well as everything else that we can find out about his methods, suggests that biographical writing had to follow the formal rules derived from that definition of human life in moral philosophy which I have just described in order to be recognised as part of an established literary genre by Classical readers. The numerous extant short biographies from the post-Classic Antiquity were certainly not written or read as part of literature in the narrower sense. They look more like biographical articles in reference books, in which industrious scholars gather data about the life of a poet or a philosopher which can help people to understand that man's works; or facts about the life of a king or general which are to be learned as a part of general education. It is quite fitting, then, that many of those short biographies were handed down to us in Byzantine encyclopaedias; and there are plenty of Greek and Latin examples for this manner of catering for the demand for biographical facts. Biography as written by Plutarch was as distinct from such efforts as it was from the encomium and from historiography; even if subsequent generations would often read Plutarch as a historian.

As I have shown, each one of Plutarch's *Parallel Lives* aimed to assimilate the image of a historical character to that complex of moral ideas which educated contemporary readers would entertain in their private lives; a set of notions which focused entirely on the individual. But we can also recognise a political intention on the part of the author if we look at the corpus of parallel biographies as a whole. We have a dedication to Sosius Senecio but no detailed programmatic introduction: the reason for this is presumably that such a preface was lost with what must have been the first pair of lives, dealing with Scipio and with Epaminondas, the most famous man from Plutarch's native region of Boeotia. But there can be no doubt as to Plutarch's intention to show the Greeks that the Romans were no barbarians, and that they were able to look back on a past which could very well be compared with Greek history. To the other side he wanted to prove that Greece had to offer other things beside what it had been giving to Rome's labour-market for centuries: a ready supply of philosophers, professors, physicians, cooks, or female dancers, who found it easy enough to make a living among the Romans. Plutarch's aim was to remind the latter that Greek pride could likewise refer to a long line of great generals and statesmen.

These targets reflect the social and intellectual self-confidence the Greek world had regained in the second half of the first century AD in the wake of its economic recovery. Plutarch, the person who spoke on behalf of the Greeks, was a man whom great Romans treated as an equal and who thus had no occasion to show such a resentment as is often exhibited by people who feel culturally superior, but socially inferior. Nero's Philhellenism – one of the reasons why that Emperor's memory was much less tainted in the East than in Italy – had given such great encouragement to the Greek world that the Flavians already saw a necessity for new laws to protect Italy's privileged status. However, it was no longer possible to halt the shift of power towards the East which possessed much greater potential, or to stop the corresponding infiltration of more and more Greeks into high, and even the highest, administrative and military positions: a development which culminated in the second century AD. In this context Plutarch's *Parallel Lives* illustrate how the Greek intellectual world cast off those reservations concerning Roman Imperialism which they had cherished for centuries – and for good reasons too. Now though, Greek intellectuals began to identify with the Empire and its legal order and ultimately became its most loyal supporters.

Moralia

Plutarch's reputation and influence extended to much of Early Modern Europe, as documented in the works of authors from Shakespeare to Schiller. Those writers knew Plutarch mainly as the author of the *Biographies*, of which the excellent French translation by Amyot appeared in 1559; in the Classical age, Plutarch was more famous as the man who wrote the so-called *Moralia*. This collective title is slightly misleading as only some of the treatises featured under it deal with issues of moral philosophy, even if aspects of that discipline obviously provided an important factor in the choice of the other topics.

Within the *Moralia* as well as the *Parallel Lives*, clues to the relative chronology of the individual parts can be found in a fair amount of backward and forward references. But the chronological order reveals hardly any significant development in Plutarch's world of ideas, so that a discussion of the *Moralia* may just as well be divided according to different subjects. The various spuria which have also been handed down to us among the heading of *Moralia* seem to have been included because they deal with related themes and express similar sentiments; moreover, most of them belong to a period which was not far removed from Plutarch's life.

We know of about sixty treatises in which Plutarch dealt with aspects of practical living, of education, and of pastoral care: always from the point of view of a philosopher if not in the jargon of school philosophy, but in a style suited to the comprehension of the general reader. About thirty such writings are extant under Plutarch's name, including a number that were not actually written by him. They include rules for matrimonial life; advice on the use of poetical texts in the education of children; and discussions of certain types of good or bad behaviour, such as talkativeness or parental love. There are consolatory treatises and instructions for auto-therapy as a means of finding mental peace, and we also find more theoretical discourses: for instance, on the question of whether moral depravity in itself can cause human misery; or about the problem of deciding on systematic categories for virtues and vices. The non-genuine treatises are on topics such as the relationship between fate and free will, or the upbringing of children, and hence in keeping with the rest with regard to subject matter: they also fit in because of parallels in the basic philosophical convictions expressed, and in the manner of presentation.

The different groups of writings within the *Moralia* illustrate very well the various aspects of an issue which was of paramount importance to educated people of that period: the question of how guidelines for practical living can be deduced from philosophical principles. Whether there is a question about the correct treatment of friends, the proper use of money, or the right way to be truthful; whether the subject is how to deal with shyness, over-activeness, or vanity; or whether it is a problem concerning education, health care, or family relationships the philosophical speaker in Plutarch's treatises acts as an advisor who is not only able to analyse a problem and give a theoretical description of the way to its solution, but who also has concrete psychagogical and meditative methods to offer to people trying to cope with anger, grief, or restlessness.

Unlike the Christian Occident which succeeded it, the Classical world knew no god whose will reveals itself in commandments directing human interaction down to specific detail. Traditional Graeco-Roman religion was exclusively founded on cultic practice; from this, ethical rules could only be deducted as the particular demands of individual deities, or as the very general conviction that a certain deity was the guarantor of moral order as a whole. Most of the speculative energies invested in philosophy and science were thus concentrated on ethical issues, and it was exactly this which gave philosophy a permanent influence on private and public life.

A topic closely connected with ethics was politics, about which Plutarch wrote eleven treatises. Only five of them are extant, and some of those merely in a fragmented form. Plutarch certainly had a serious attitude towards his functions in the independent municipal administration of his small home community; and he also recognised the importance of giving a sound education and philosophical advice to the bearers of supreme power in the civilised world. It is true that his writings which have a bearing on politics – for instance, the *Political Counsels* – often follow philosophical sources which refer to entirely different political conditions than those existing in Plutarch's own lifetime. But his relevant works are particularly good evidence of the fact that however authoritarian the constitution of the Roman Empire there was a political dimension to the life of any one among its educated citizens.

Plutarch was a fully qualified professional and school philosopher, as is evident from a large number of scientific-philosophical tracts. This group of his writings is difficult to delineate, mainly because many of the sciences were regarded either as propaedeutics for philosophy, or as parts of it. Another problem lies in the fact that we can make out a clear practical-paraenetical purpose in some of those theoretical treatises on ethics which Plutarch wrote in the manner of school philosophy. If we take a broader view of the latter category, we know of no less than sixty-six tracts, even if only fourteen of them are extant. Some of these are polemical attacks levelled at Stoics and Epicureans by the Academic Plutarch pointing his finger at contradictions in their systems, at the implausibility of some of their axioms, or at the general uselessness of their doctrines to those who seek a moral basis for directing their lives towards the goal of a fulfilled and happy existence. Beside such polemics, there are or were treatises on aspects of doxography or the history of philosophy; this explains why a later doxographical work about the different philosophers' doctrines on physics was handed down under Plutarch's name.

Other writings in this group interpret specific statements made by Classic philosophers, or deal with isolated problems in Platonic and Peripatetic philosophy, which Plutarch basically sees as one. Particularly important in this category are his philosophical writings on natural science such as, for example, the one on animal psychology. This was a much-discussed topic, with the central question being whether animals have reason to an extent that makes them comparable to human beings. The Stoics denied this saying that only adult humans and gods can be described as rational beings in the full sense of the term. The Platonics, who believed in the transmigration of souls, had no choice but to take the opposite view; and those who were influenced by Pythagorean ideas consequently demanded that people should abstain from eating any kind of meat. Plutarch's writings on the issue give us an impression of the rich empirical material which had been collected in the course of this controversy and which was available to him in the form of literary sources.

Other works by Plutarch on natural science deal with issues concerning cosmology, astronomy, or physics, such as the facial features on the moon's surface, or the origin of coldness. In his scientific explanation of natural phenomena Plutarch always focuses on the relation between nature and human beings and the treatise on the face of the moon is a good case in point. It contains some fairly original astronomical-meteorological theories which give this peculiar phenomenon on the surface of the earth's satellite a place in a large cosmological context; but he also propounds a doctrine about the immaterial part of the human soul as coming from a region beyond the sidereal sphere, and about the moon as the place where souls gather before their entry into earthly bodies. This doctrine is clothed in the form of a myth, and the whole treatise is a vivid, carefully styled dialogue in the Platonic manner.

Among the extant scientific writings by Plutarch we have two collections: one of explanations for the most diverse natural phenomena, and the other of *Table Talks* or *Discussions of Problems at the Symposium.* In the latter work Plutarch uses a form which had been a well-established literary convention since the days of Plato: that is the presentation of philosophical and scientific discussion as conversation at a dinner party. In Plutarch's work different hosts and guests debate countless aspects of natural science, literature, or history; and sometimes they also converse about mere curiosities. The topics include the farsightedness that comes with old age; the art of dancing; the reasons why old and young should have different levels of resistance to alcohol; or the question of whether the bird or the egg was there first. The settings for the dialogue scenes appertain to very different stages of Plutarch's life, and there are corresponding changes in the sets of participants in the discussion. All of them, however, are vividly portrayed in their individual characters as young or old men who are, for example, Peripatetic or Epicurean philosophers, physicians, or military officers. Thus this work, as well as other writings of Plutarch which are styled as dialogues, gives us a fair amount of valuable information about the changing circle of friends and disciples who surrounded the author during a large part of his life.

Plutarch was a pious man who felt very strongly about his priestly office at Delphi. In Plutarch's lifetime an educated person was someone accustomed to basing his orientation in the world on rationally developed theories. Such people were likely to have a very spiritualised, philosophical notion of the divine; but in their religious ideas there was also room for sentiments of a quite different kind. This shows in Plutarch's anti-Epicurean treatise in which he argues that Epicurean philosophy is not a suitable basis for proper living. In this context Plutarch also discusses the Epicurean doctrine of the divine, which saw the gods as necessarily existing in complete separation from the world of men; for any attempt to take care of humans would spoil the perfect bliss of those exemplary beings. In a tone of heartfelt pity, Plutarch says that the poor Epicureans can never know the happiness brought by participation in communal worship, and especially in a sacrificial meal: the joy of experiencing true communion with the deity.

Of Plutarch's fifteen known theological treatises, seven are extant. In these writings, the elementary piety which I have just described as arising from traditional religion, permeates a theology which philosophical systematics saw as a branch of physics, the explanation of nature. Plutarch's tracts deal with topics such as oracles in the past and present; the interpretation of the *daimōnion* which Socrates had felt as part of himself; the essential definition of superstition and ungodliness; or the question of how people should imagine the manner of divine reward or punishment of human actions. The most interesting one of these writings, however, is the major treatise on Isis and Osiris. In the Graeco-Roman world the complex of Egyptian legends about Isis had become known – albeit with certain adaptations – from the second century BC onwards, along with the Isis cult, a mystery religion that admitted none but the initiated. Plutarch gives a comprehensive allegorical reading of those tales which were still perceived as weird and exotic by his Greek contemporaries; and thus the author provides us with a deep insight into the nature of religious syncretism in the later centuries of the Classical age when Greek and Oriental elements were amalgamated and the mixture made palatable for educated people by an added speculative-theological interpretation.

Like most of his educated contemporaries, Plutarch derived his moral and aesthetic standards from the image of a great Greek past. This fact is reflected, for instance, in his fondness for antiquarian collecting, an inclination which led to the production of about a dozen writings. Extant examples are a collection of sayings by famous Spartans, and one of reports of heroic deeds performed by women. It is evident that in the tradition, this group of Plutarch's writings was particularly open to the intrusion of similar compilations of sayings and anecdotes from other authors. However, one particularly characteristic feature of Plutarch's genuine collections is that like his other writings they do not leave out Roman traditions. Plutarch compiled one collection each of Greek and Roman *aitia*, that is mythological or historical derivations of names, festivals, or customs. In these two texts, he preserved some very valuable information which is of interest above all to the religious historian. There is also a collection of episodes that illustrate parallels or similarities between Greek and Roman history. A sad loss is that of Plutarch's treatise about the Roman system of proper names with its *tria nomina*, which was a unique phenomenon in the Classical age.

Plutarch's lifelong, tireless reading led him almost inevitably to the discussion of literary theory and exegesis. In such writings he showed a clear bias for authors from his native region of Boeotia, such as Hesiod, Pindar, or Crates; or for discourses on writers such as Herodotus who had spoken disparagingly of the former. A commentary on Hesiod was unfortunately lost, but we do have a treatise on the malice of Herodotus whose pro-Athenian bias, according to Plutarch, made him glorify their authors at the expense of Boeotians and other Greeks. In his comparative study of Aristophanes' and Menander's comedies, Plutarch comes across as a spokesman not for a region but for the literary taste of his period in general. His verdict is clearly in favour of Menander on account of that author's discreet use of language and his humane attitude, which Plutarch regarded as preferable to the coarse humour and the impetuous political commitment shown by the greatest exponent of Old Comedy.

We know of several other treatises about aspects of Homeric philology, Hellenistic epic, and Attic tragedy, which were all ascribed to Plutarch. None of them was really from his hand, but all the same this group contains some valuable tracts. Cases in point are the ones about the ten canonical Attic orators, about the life of Homer and about the history of music. The latter focused on the relationship between music and poetry and on music's educational and ethical role. Up to a certain point, the loss of so many genuinely Plutarchian texts on such topics is compensated by those parts of the *Table Talks* which deal with literary history and exegesis.

A similar statement can be made about Plutarch's treatises on rhetorical theory, of which, however, none is extant. Nevertheless, we do have four genuine declamations by Plutarch which may be taken as typical for the epideictic eloquence of his epoch: these are entitled *About the Luck of the Romans*, *About the Luck and the Virtue of Alexander the Great*, *Have the Athenians Distinguished Themselves More through Martial or through Intellectual Achievements?*, and *Which is of Greater Use: Water or Fire?* It is evident why Plutarch had no particularly marked interest in rhetoric; and consequently those texts which reflect his familiarity with that element of education impress the reader more on account of their richness of content and the references to many different sources rather than through any special show of stylistic or argumentative virtuosity which was the primary object in such exercises.

Prose style

Many passages in the extant works of Plutarch prove not only his erudition, but also a remarkable refinement of taste. Moreover, the extent of his *oeuvre* shows that he wrote with great ease; but all the same, he was not really a great literary artist. He neither sought the perfection of form and the elegance which was the aim of rhetorical training nor did he try to achieve the precision and the clear argumentation of good scientific prose. He used various different forms in his many writings, and always opted for one that was suited to the chosen subject matter.

Plutarch was particularly successful in his use of dialogue to illuminate scientific or philosophical problems. The reason for this is that the form did not demand a strict framework for the progression of thought and argument but only a credible representation of diverging opinions and of the zest for debate shared by participants in the discussion who otherwise were very different from one another in terms of temperament and knowledge. This indicates that with the exception of mere collections of material Plutarch's writing was a direct reflection of the discourse which was the medium of instruction and exchange of ideas at his 'private Academy'. This in turn explains why not even Plutarch's scientific-philosophical texts give us a complete picture of Academic school philosophy as it stood around 100 AD. What they do provide are insights into the then current state of debate on numerous individual problems. This information is given on a consistently high level, and more often than not with regard to the history of the problem's discussion within the philosophical tradition.

Naturally those of Plutarch's works which have a more systematic structure than others include the biographies, whose compositional principles I have already outlined (see pp. 189–91). These principles guided Plutarch's selection of material from the available sources and in the process he left us some particularly good evidence of his literary taste. The biographies feature many gripping scenes: for instance, when the author describes a battle or the state of mind of a person involved in the action. All of those are based on the reports of major historiographers, whose texts Plutarch adapted and incorporated into his account with great discrimination and skill.

Plutarch's use of language corresponds to his use of literary forms. He shuns the construction of artfully balanced sentences and clauses, as well as the strict limitation of vocabulary according to old Attic norms. His syntax is loose, agglutinating, and not very concise. Sometimes this results in syntactic constructs which are so long and complex that the modern reader finds them difficult to understand without first-hand aural experience of the living language behind this style, the language used in animated but entirely relaxed conversation among educated people of that period.

Of course Plutarch's diction is not simply a rendering of the spoken word, let alone of the vernacular. It follows – if not in a slavish manner – the rules of written Attic in forming sentences of a literary character, which presuppose a reader who is able to grasp complex progressions of thought in educated oral discourse. This is why Plutarch's language could hardly be called artless. We must remember that the most important criterion for assessing which of the works ascribed to Plutarch are not genuine was based on the fact that unlike the other anonymous authors, Plutarch himself stringently followed the rule which banned the creation of a hiatus, a clash of sounds caused by placing a word that begins with a vowel immediately after a word that ends in one. This was an ancient rule in poetry, and had also been accepted in literary prose, as always in competition with poetry, from the fourth century BC onwards.

In Plutarch's diction we can clearly perceive all those qualities which made him so extremely influential among European intellectuals between the sixteenth and the eighteenth centuries. The biographer Plutarch taught how to judge characters from Graeco-Roman history according to the norms of a humanitarian morality; the author of the *Moralia* showed how great knowledge and erudition could be made to serve the goals of unpedantic moral education and practical counselling. No reader, regardless of historical circumstances, could ever fail to be affected by Plutarch's attitude – based on general benevolence – as that of a man who rejected neither time-honoured traditions nor efforts to find rational answers to essential questions about human life.

7 EPICTETUS

Like Plutarch, Epictetus was a philosopher who devoted his whole life to education, instruction, and practical counselling. All the same, Epictetus' biography looks entirely different from that of Plutarch. Epictetus began his career in bondage to Nero's friend Epaphroditus, who had himself been an Imperial slave before he became an influential and wealthy freedman. Epaphroditus allowed Epictetus to be taught by the Stoic Musonius (see p. 83); soon after that Epictetus was set free and became a Roman teacher of philosophy himself. After Domitian's decree of 89 AD Epictetus had to leave Italy like all the other philosophers. He settled down to teach in the coastal city of Nicopolis in north-west Greece, where he continued his work well into the 2nd century AD.

Epictetus was an orthodox Stoic who seems never to have departed from the grounds of Stoic school philosophy, in which he had been thoroughly instructed. Nevertheless, his teaching was not meant to introduce future philosophers or scholars to this school doctrine. Epictetus' pupils were laymen from the upper classes in East and West, and quite a few among them became holders of high state offices.

This is why in Epictetus' teachings, logic and physics are only of marginal importance. The emphasis is on ethics, and within this discipline, on issues concerning practical living. Epictetus repeatedly reminds his disciples that science and scholarly erudition – which he calls philology, in keeping with contemporary linguistic usage – cannot be the goal of his teaching aimed only at forming a general attitude to life with a secure foundation in philosophy. Thus Epictetus saw philosophy as an activity, inseparably linked with practical living as a whole. According to him, the only way in which man may succeed in doing right is by understanding and trusting the comprehensive divine-natural world order which has given man as well as all other beings a fixed place in the cosmos. This understanding enables man to judge the extent to which a specific set of circumstances gives him scope to act; he can then decide whether the task, the temptation, or the danger which he encounters require his independent and responsible action: or, in other words, whether he is concerned. In such a situation, says Epictetus, everything depends on using one's freedom of choice in a manner that does not contradict the natural order. It is only by choosing the path thus indicated that some men can escape those affections, errors, and confusions to which others fall prey because of their failure to understand.

In Stoic school dogma, the idea of a natural order which provides for all in the best possible manner was combined with a materialistic world view. The charitable order of nature was seen as emanating from that finest matter which gives structure, life and consciousness to the entire cosmos, where it is present in different concentrations. In the mind of Epictetus this notion was condensed in a religious trust in the deity, perhaps not thought of in a personalised form, but still as a counterpart and a partner for man. The stupendous moral impact of Epictetus' doctrines stems entirely from this natural piety, which is at once elementary and sublimated.

The practical issues which Epictetus' teachings deal with include virtually anything that could ever have occurred to his pupils and their environment. He talks about questions concerning bodily hygiene, matrimonial life, the upbringing of children, or the chances of leading a natural lifestyle in a highly civilised world which is dominated by many social restrictions and prejudices. He also talks about the problem of slavery and the demand for the equality of all men; about the cultivation of friendships; or about what is involved in assuming a position of public responsibility. Epictetus' admonitions to his pupils to be modest, to love their fellow men, to be content with little, to be frank, and to trust in the benevolence of divine rule, have frequently and also quite rightly been compared to New Testament paraenetics. Indeed there are marked parallels in the advice which Epictetus and New Testament authors give to people for use in their everyday lives. In both cases the aim is to endow human beings, regardless of their status and their function in society, with that freedom of thought and action which comes from the awareness of complete and final security in a divine order. However, there is an important difference concerning the source of this awareness which in Epictetus' view emerges from recognising the natural order of the universe, while the teaching of the New Testament regards it as the result of divine revelation.

The founder of the Stoa had for quite some time been a follower of Cynic philosophy, a movement which scorned all theory and understood philosophy as practical, natural living, independent of all conventions and ties. The Stoa had been neglecting its Cynic origins, mainly because the Cynics' hostility to science was an embarrassment to a school which was just about to launch itself into the intellectual debates of the Hellenistic age. Its revival in the Empire produced a more moderate version of Cynic philosophy even if – as Seneca or Lucian tell us – all of its exponents were men who led a vagrant life, whose appearance showed that they had renounced the comforts of civilisation, and who had no regard for school philosophy and literary erudition. Instead Cynics tried to assist people in leading their everyday lives, by showing them what was good and just.

His pupils often asked Epictetus about the goals and values of the Cynic lifestyle; and in his own teachings, there are obvious links with Cynic philosophy. Epictetus respected its aims, but he emphasised his view that it is not a beard and a shabby coat, nor ostentatious disregard for good manners in the name of natural behaviour, which make a man a philosopher. That, Epictetus says, is just another form of conceitedness which comes from the pride in philosophy itself rather than from any social prejudices. According to Epictetus a true Cynic must first recognise the one truth which ultimately removes all possible obstacles standing between men and proper living: that providence has cast him in a certain role, like a director does with an actor. No matter what this part may be, all a man can do is to play it well, to act as part of a larger order out of his own free will.

It is thanks to the efforts of one of his disciples that we know so much of Epictetus' teaching. This pupil was Flavius Arrianus who came from a noble family resident in Bithynia in north-western Asia Minor; his name indicates that he held Roman citizenship. Arrian rose to the very highest military and administrative offices, and finally became Consul in 130 AD. He wrote eight books which recorded the didactic conversations and lectures of his teacher; four of those books are completely extant, but we have no more than fragments of the others. Arrian's transcripts keep the authentic style of informal, vivid exposition, including reactions to actual or anticipated interjections from the ranks of the audience. Arrian also recorded many short conversations which followed questions put to the lecturer. In spite of all their authenticity, however, Arrian's records contain only very rare indications of the vernacular which Epictetus would certainly have used. For the most part, Arrian wrote in literary language, even if he did not aim at any rhetorical elaboration.

The many practical issues which Epictetus dealt with in his teachings make Arrian's records a source of great value to the social historian. They contain much detailed information on aspects of private and public life, social attitudes and prejudices, and many seemingly insignificant details of everyday living. However, Epictetus' main influence on later authors was not itself based on Arrian's records but on yet another intermediate text, the *Encheiridion*, literally *Dagger* or *Handy Weapon*, which is a systematic excerpt of nuclear sentences from Arrian, arranged according to different topics. This text, of which we have numerous manuscript copies, became the subject of a commentary written in the sixth century AD by the Neo-Platonist Simplicius. The author was one of the last members of Plato's school, closed in 529 AD.

The banishment which Domitian decreed also concerned one man whose major works will be discussed in a subsequent section. Like Epictetus, Dion Coccianus from the Bithynian city of Prusa was taught by the Stoic Musonius, after a rhetorical education which had first refined his great stylistic talent. Being banned from Italy, Dion was forced to wander about for a number of years during which he got as far as the borders of the Greek world in what is now southern Russia. In later writings Dion describes the life he led during the period as that of a Cynic philosopher. The fall of Domitian opened the door for his return to Rome where he made the acquaintance of the Emperors Nerva and Trajan and where, as a celebrated orator, he acted as spokesman for the new ideology of the Antonines. But all philosophical motifs in his speeches come from the doctrine of the Imperial Stoa, as represented by Musonius and Epictetus: a philosophy with an entirely practical orientation and with a recognisable amount of Cynic elements.

In this context I must also mention another, very peculiar figure from the Flavian era, even if his literary legacy consists only of a few not very informative letters. The character and the life of Apollonius of Tyana in Asia Minor are known exclusively through a biography written by Philostratus at the beginning of the third century AD and hence nearly one-and-a-half centuries later. Much of this account seems to be legendary; what we may take for granted, however, is that Apollonius did indeed lead the life of a migrant miracle-worker. He is said to have possessed supernatural gifts like second sight and powers of healing which we can recognise as attributes of his Pythagorean lifestyle and teaching. Apollonius travelled widely, perhaps even as far as India; and when he eventually became one of those individuals banished from Italy after Domitian's decree, he grew into a very outspoken opponent of Flavian rule during its final phase. In the second century AD, Platonic school philosophy absorbed more and more Pythagorean motifs; and what we know about Apollonius indicates that Pythagoreanism flourished also outside school philosophy. In the eyes of the general public, miracle-workers lent considerable authority to instructions for an ascetic life according to fundamental Pythagorean doctrines. In this Apollonius was by no means unique: from the second century AD there are also many reports about other philosophers with miraculous powers.

8 CHRISTIAN LITERATURE

Letters

The Neronian-Flavian epoch saw the very first beginnings of a Christian literature which could initially be regarded as part of Jewish writing in as much as Christian groups formed and developed entirely within the framework of Judaism. Their intense missionary activity, soon differentiated to suit different languages and traditions, concentrated exclusively on those Jewish communities which were scattered all over the Empire: for the new creed proclaimed the fulfilment of what the old religion had promised. Even where the new faith made non-Jewish converts this was merely as a by-product of missionary work among the Jews. The Jews themselves knew two different forms of converts to their own religion; apart from those who embraced the Jewish faith and Jewish lifestyle in full, there were also the so-called 'God-fearing ones', who subscribed to Old Testament monotheism without becoming part of the Jewish legal and cultic community. Thus it was not necessary to see anything new in a practice which the Christians developed early on, if not without internal debate: that is to exempt converted heathens from Jewish ritual law. The only real novelty was that those converts were nevertheless to be regarded as the Biblical God's chosen property, equal to other Christians.

The greatest and most important exponent of such early Christian missionising was also the first author of a nascent Christian literature which, over the following four or five centuries, spread its forms and its messages in many different languages throughout and beyond the Roman Empire. As my survey is hardly the right context for assessing the apostle Paul's significance in the history of the Christian religion, my discussion will limit itself to the question of where Paul's letters stand in relation to the literary traditions of the Greek world, with regard to form, style, and function.

Paul was born in Tarsus, on the border between Syria and Asia Minor. His family was Jewish, but held Roman citizenship, and was most probably bilingual. We know from a number of sources that this was quite a common phenomenon in that region, and Paul's many years of work in Palestine are a fact that seems to support the assumption. All of his letters are written in Greek, the language of his addressees, in which he expressed himself without any apparent effort. This distinguished him from the circle of Jesus' first and closest followers, and from the so-called first congregation in Jerusalem which developed from those roots. It was quite natural that this group's rootedness in the Palestinian-Jewish tradition remained a dominant factor, which means that Aramaic would have been their only language in everyday as well as sacred use.

Paul's letters are addressed to well-established Christian groups who already had their own forms of communal worship and who all traced their special status within their Jewish and heathen environments back to a specific apostle as the man who had brought them the new faith. Links between such groups were established and maintained by many wandering teachers and apostles, and thus it is not surprising that not all congregations that received letters from Paul had been founded by himself in the course of his extensive missionary work; one case in point is his Epistle to the Romans. His letters contain passages which are meant to retain or to recall the memory of central elements of the new creed. They answer questions aimed at a better understanding of the faith; they comment on instances of worry, fear, doubt, and distress which occurred in a specific community; they seek to allay quarrels and clear up misunderstandings; they take a stand against opponents or rivals; and they communicate numerous moral-paraenetical messages. There are also plenty of personal elements in the epistles, in references to the author's own experience, or in the mention of friends and collaborators. Theology in the narrower sense, as the definition of the new faith's content, features only in a much-abbreviated form. One exception is the Epistle to the Romans, with its long outline of the doctrine of God-given justice. But most of Paul's epistles are full of isolated formulas and entire passages which can be understood only as blessings, prayers, or praises in the practical context of communal worship.

We may assume that the letters were meant to be read out to Christian congregations and thus we may regard them as evidence of continuing or incipient preaching and pastoral care over a distance. The only exception is the Epistle to Philemon, which was to be handed to him by a runaway slave whom Paul sent back to his Christian master. The other genuine letters – Romans, Corinthians 1 and 2, Galatians, Philippians, and Thessalonians 1 and 2 – all seem to fit my very general description, even if Paul wrote them under very different circumstances.

In the rich and varied epistolary tradition in Classical literature, there is nothing which constitutes an exact parallel to Paul's letters. But Paul's epistles in turn established a specifically Christian tradition of epistolography during the following two or three generations, whose products found a secure place in the Christian cult. Letters which monarchs or officials addressed to whole communities had been known since the Early Hellenistic age, as a means of announcing important political or religious measures and directives to the public concerned. Most of those letters are known because they were published in the form of inscriptions. There were also genuine and imputed epistles from philosophers to whole groups of followers rather than to individuals, explaining details of the author's teaching, or arguing against opponents or rivals. One good example of this phenomenon is the corpus of Plato's letters. But in all earlier epistolography we find no model for that which characterises Paul's epistles: the synthesis of instruction, pastoral care, and personal communication on the basis of a bond of common worship between the sender and the addressees. It is hardly surprising that scholars have also long recognised other unique features of Paul's letters in some ostensibly insignificant formal detail, such as the initial and final greeting, or the different linguistic forms of direct address.

Some scholars have pointed out another possible link of Paul's letters with Greek literary convention, claiming that their diction and manner of argumentation may have been influenced by the so-called diatribe (see

p. 82). This form was used mainly by Cynic philosophers; its style was deliberately artless, with plenty of interjections and exclamations, and a general lack of systematic organisation. It is true that Paul's writing also features elements such as odd jumps in the argument, exclamations and interpolated questions which create a resemblance to oral discussion, or intense appeals to the reader formulated without any rhetorical polish. Even before reading diatribes, Paul may very well have heard a Cynic philosopher speak in the streets of Tarsus; and yet we should be wary of any rash conclusions. Among all of those terms and phrases from popular moral philosophy used by Paul, there is not a single one which had not long been incorporated into the vernacular vocabulary by the first century AD. It is even more significant that in turn all those expressions belonging to Paul's own specific terminology – as far as we may call it thus in spite of a lack of consistence in its application – have no parallels in the diction of popular philosophy. So, for instance, a Greek had no choice but to understand the word *sarx* or flesh, which Paul uses quite frequently, as referring to a morally or anthropologically defined dichotomy between body and soul, or between the material and the spiritual. Paul does sometimes use the term in this Greek sense; but more often than not, he applies it in describing man as a whole, including his spiritual side, wherever he talks of attempts to escape from dependence on the creator. Correspondingly Paul uses the parallel term *pneuma* not for the mind or for spirituality in general, but only to mean the active power of the divine spirit.

Given all these and more peculiar features of Paul's diction it seems highly unlikely that the style of his letters was influenced by a specific formal tradition shaped by philosophy. Whatever is unsystematic, erratic, and immediate in his writings – hence those features which have been seen as linked with the so-called diatribal style – is most probably accidental rather than intentional, as the product of Paul's exceptional wealth of ideas and his strong temperament, unfettered by that rhetorical and philosophical schooling which any educated Greek would have gone through. Paul's notions about God, the world, and man, were based on a heritage entirely incommensurate with the Greek educational tradition, which had shaped the very language he was using. This explains why like no other Christian author for many years to come, Paul recognised the clash between Classical and Biblical views of the world and of man, even if he had major difficulties in finding the right terms to express his perception.

Semitisms have been identified in Paul's diction, but most of those are indirect influences which reflect the language used in Greek Biblical translations: after all, the Septuagint was the definitive Bible to the first Christians, who had as yet no New Testament. Paul's manner of argumentation has been likened to that of Jewish scriptural scholarship which was of great importance among the Pharisees, of whom Paul was one before his conversion. In all these aspects Paul appears as distinct from his contemporary Philo whose ways of thinking and writing were so truly Greek that his efforts to interpret his people's traditions led to an essential Hellenisation. Paul, on the other hand, managed to express the very essentials of the Biblical faith in an idiom which was highly resistant to the intrusion of non-Greek ideas.

The further development of Christianity in the Roman Empire over the following centuries was characterised by the progressive Hellenisation of a theology which used Greek philosophy as a tool. Thus the peculiar characteristics of Paul's theological doctrine went unnoticed for a long time, until their rediscovery in the fourth century AD. Since then, however, virtually every new approach to ecclesiastical history has gone hand in hand with some kind of reassessment of Paul's letters. To one who studies Classical literature nowadays, Paul's texts are difficult, but none the less largely admirable products of an entirely unique personality, whose urge to convey a message found totally unconventional, and hence doubly impressive, means of expression.

There were many contemporary and later Christian authors who emulated the example set by Paul's letters. Some of their works were ascribed to him, and some to other apostles; this production continued well into the second century AD. All of its authors are anonymous, and can only be distinguished because of differences in the doctrines which they express. That they should have laid claim to apostolical authority cannot simply be condemned as literary forgery, just as this term can not be applied to the letters which were published under Plato's name. Choosing the name of an apostle signified no more than the author's public declaration that he was advocating the pure, true faith; and it was this very criterion which later caused church authorities to canonise some of the non-genuine letters in the second part of Holy Scripture.

Gospels

Oral tradition was the means by which the first Christians kept alive the memory of their master: his words, his deeds, his sufferings, and his rising from the dead. Their thinking was deeply rooted in the Jewish tradition and they saw little need for writing things down, believing that the appearance of Jesus had fulfilled the prophecies of the Jewish religion and that the end of the world was imminent. Paul's letters, for instance, do not indicate any call for written records of Jesus' life. Christian oral tradition was at first passed on in the medium of Aramaic, the language of Jesus himself, of his first followers, and of the first congregation in Jerusalem led by Jacob, known as the Lord's brother. Greek was not used until later when missionary activity began to spread to Greek-speaking areas. Paul's letters, which contain, for instance, the ritual formula of the Eucharist in its earliest known version, prove that the transition from Aramaic began during the stage of oral tradition.

Where and when the first written records appeared is uncertain. We know neither what language such texts were in, nor what form; whether, for example, they were collections of Jesus' sayings, of his parables, or of reports about his miracles. Equally uncertain is the chief motive that led their authors to secure oral tradition in a written form. Possible factors are the deaths of Peter and of Paul during the first wave of anti-Christian persecutions in Rome; the destruction of Jerusalem; or the pressure of competition with Judaism, from which the Christians gradually detached themselves. However, we can only guess at the main reason for the new literary production, of which our earliest evidence is generally dated around 70 AD. This is the Evangelium or Gospel of Mark, who, according to a piece of very ancient oral lore, accompanied Peter on his travels, and acted as his interpreter.

Mark's work can be likened to Paul's letters, in that it stands at the beginning of a literary tradition for which no real precedent can be found in Greek or Jewish writing. In spite of the fact that it is composed mostly from pre-shaped pieces of oral tradition, Mark's narrative has all the characteristics of an account deliberately styled by one single author. It draws a picture not of Jesus' biography but of his key role in the history of man's redemption. There are very detailed descriptions of the beginning, with the baptism by John and the desert sojourn; and likewise of the end, with Jesus' sufferings, his crucifixion, and the witnessing of his empty grave. The account of these events keeps referring to the Old Testament, claiming that Jesus' life fulfilled promises expressed not only in the Books of the Prophets. Thus Psalm 22 is referred to as predicting the sufferings of Jesus; and a prophetic precedent for his sojourn in the wilderness is seen in the march of the Israelites through the desert. The middle part of Mark's text contains reports on various sayings, parable speeches, miracles, and other events from Jesus' life, without any recognisable logical or chronological order. It is evident why this main part should contain references to contemporary history; but likewise, it provided the author with occasions to insert rules for practical living, wise saws, or miracle-stories of an entirely different origin, or of his own invention.

The name evangelium, which in English was replaced by the Anglo-Saxon word gospel, means something like good news; and hence Mark's work bears the title 'The good news, as told by Mark'. Paul uses the term evangelium in a similar manner, indicating that it generally meant news of salvation through the coming of Jesus of Nazareth, a message which could be given in quite different wordings or degrees of elaborateness. From such a point of view, it cannot be said that Mark wrote an evangelium, but merely that he passed the evangelium on through his writing.

Its title alone indicates that a work like Mark's Gospel is no biography, and cannot even be called the literary production of an author in the narrower sense as, for instance, the first five books of the Bible were attributed to Moses. This assumption is substantiated by a fact concerning the manner in which evangelia were handed down. Like the Torah which is still used in Jewish ritual, the Classical book was a scroll which the reader would open with one hand and close with the other as he went through the text. The book as we know it, with folded and bound leaves to be turned over in succession, was originally used only for non-literary texts in the Classical age. Thus it seems significant that the earliest papyri containing parts of the evangelia – documents which date back as far as the early second century AD – should have the format of modern books. At that time this format, known as the so-called codex, would normally have been that of notebooks only: it was only in the very last centuries of the Classical age that it superseded the scroll as a vehicle for carrying literary texts.

Those pieces of information from which evangelical literature was first composed served the purpose of reassuring Christians of the fundamental elements of their faith. Their messages could only be fully understood in connection with the Bible, which was the common possession of Jews and Christians. It was only from the second century AD onwards that a second part of Holy Scripture began to take shape as a recognised canon for use in communal worship, selected from a sizeable production of gospels and letters. This, however, happened largely at a time when the Greek version of the Old Testament was the exclusive property of the Christians, who would not follow Judaism in its return to the Hebrew-Aramaic tradition.

Mark's Greek usage is largely correct, if different from Atticist written language: the closest existing parallels can be found in specialist literature, or in official and private records. This is why his text contains elements that belong to spoken language, or at least show an oral influence. Mark's Gospel is without any stylistic elaboration in the manner of school rhetoric. The many Semitisms in the text can partly be explained – as in the case of Paul – as borrowings from the Greek translation of the Bible. In other instances, though, it is evident that the vocabulary and syntax of Mark's Greek text were influenced by pieces of oral tradition in Aramaic. This applies especially to many of Jesus' sayings; and it is in keeping with the fact that Jesus' parables mention numerous features of everyday life among the rural people of Galilee. It is widely known that the Christian church has preserved certain Aramaic formulas and quotations from the Hebrew Bible throughout the centuries, as well as a few isolated Aramaic words which are still part of Christian liturgy.

As regards Mark's Gospel, those passages whose language has a particularly strong Semitic colouring lend added weight to the question of which literary sources and which pieces of oral tradition were used by the author. In such cases, we can never exclude the possibility that the full meaning of a part of the text may only be discovered through a successful retranslation into Aramaic: for the risk of misunderstanding is present in each and every translation from one language into another.

After the work of Mark had broken new ground, there were several distinct possibilities as to how other authors could develop the genre of Christian evangelical literature. One was by including more pieces of oral tradition, or by expanding and embroidering the ones which Mark had used. Writers who went for this option would often focus on incidents or sayings which appeared to confirm predictions made in the Old Testament. The search for this so-called scriptural proof (see p. 207) provided an important motive for authors who elaborated on reports about the life of Jesus; for after all, this was the most obvious way to find arguments for the controversy with Judaism about the proper interpretation of the Bible.

Of course the very plainness of Mark's account was in itself sufficient to encourage efforts at elaboration and particularly at giving a more complete picture of Jesus' biography. It is thanks to such endeavours that we have stories about the birth and the childhood of Jesus, as told by Matthew and Luke. The addition of a genealogy was meant to justify Jesus' claim that he was the expected Messiah from the family of King David, the one who was destined to restore David's Kingdom. This is yet another instance of scriptural proof, a method based on the assumption that every detail in traditional reports about Jesus' life had a parallel in some passage of the Old Testament. As I have said before, such prophetic statements were sought and found not only in the Books of the Prophets, but also in other parts of the Biblical canon.

New gospels kept appearing until well into the third century AD and the later ones tended to pad out especially the description of Jesus' childhood with more and more miracle-stories. While the oldest version in Mark's evangelium closes its account with the discovery of the empty grave, all other evangelists feature reports about Jesus' rising from the dead and his appearances afterwards. Paul's letters confirm that such reports did have a foundation in pieces of oral tradition; but the latest evangelists enlarged on those to such an extent that they quoted long discourses allegedly given by the risen Jesus, communicating the quintessential parts of his message only after his death.

From the point of view of theology, the most important form of reproduction and elaboration of oral traditions was that which implied a statement concerning the debate about the true faith; in other words, that kind of narrative which was a vehicle of theological argument. In Matthew's Gospel, for instance, the author is concerned with a question put by a pious Jew, as to the proper way of living according to God's law. The evangelist asserts that only those who follow Jesus can do so, and consequently, he opens his account of Jesus' works with the Sermon on the Mount. In this sermon, Jesus gives detailed rules for human behaviour as a second set of divine commandments which at once confirm and transcend the laws given on Mount Sinai. In John's Gospel, the retelling and elaboration of traditional lore leads to a doctrine about Jesus as the human incarnation of the pre-existing divine *logos*. This concept seems to have arisen around 100 AD within a Christian community which had already detached itself completely from Judaism. Expressions of individual doctrine or of a specific theology in the form of an evangelical account became a particularly important motif among the Christian Gnostics as well as among their opponents in the second century AD. The reason behind this is clear: as the authority of Jesus was often claimed for tried and tested maxims for everyday living, it could also add weight to one's own theological opinions.

Another exponent of the evangelical genre was Luke who belonged to the sphere of Christianity established by Paul. Luke tried to bridge the gap which separated Christian writing from Greek literary conventions, as well as from the general knowledge communicated in Greek education. His account is largely based on the same pieces of oral tradition as the Gospels of Mark and Matthew. However, it has an introduction in the style of Greek historiography, in which his book is dedicated to a presumably distinguished and educated man called Theophilus. Entirely in keeping with the topoi of Greek prefaces, Luke refers to the existing precedents for his project. He establishes a chronological and causal link between the birth of Jesus in King David's city of Bethlehem, and an administrative measure taken by the Roman Emperor which concerned the entire civilised world, while Matthew dates Christ's birth only with reference to the reign of King Herod. Luke's account acknowledges an entirely new context for an event which in the light of previous tradition concerned the Israelites alone, and whose significance in global history was exclusively seen from their perspective. Luke suggests that the birth of the Messiah as part of the history of redemption should be seen within the framework of the Roman Empire; and ever after, Christian historical philosophy was greatly influenced by the conviction that there was a providential coincidence between the birth of the universal saviour, and the unification of the world through Augustus. A good illustration of this belief is the Christian interpretation of Virgil's fourth eclogue (see p. 31).

Luke's historiographical *oeuvre* consists of the evangelium plus a report about the works of the apostles, whose missionary activity proves that global union under the Roman Emperor's sceptre served the divine plan for the spreading of God's message of salvation. It is justified to call Luke's writing historiography because his new perspective brought his evangelical account within the scope of comprehension of the Greek cultural world. What Luke tells the reader about the birth of the Christian community and the missionary work of the apostles, and in particular of Paul, is composed from some very different pieces of traditional lore: some of them came to him already complete with legendary ornamentations, while he found others in quite a credible form. To Luke, the events of apostolic history are a logical continuation of Jesus' life on earth, and part of the visible attempt to establish the Kingdom of God all over the world.

Of all the evangelists, it is only Luke who writes in a style that comes close to the language of educated Greeks; in his prefaces, he even tries to achieve a certain stylistic elegance. But even so, we cannot claim that Luke managed to establish a genuine connection between Christian writing and the world of Classical education.

While evangelical literature is a specifically Christian phenomenon, there are two other early pieces of Christian writing which definitely belong to the Jewish tradition. The first is the Apocalypse of John, written under the influence of anti-Christian and anti-Jewish measures taken by the Emperor Domitian. The circles among which this work originated had no connections at all with the groups among which John's Gospel was produced. John's Apocalypse is a Christian adoption of a form which had long been common in Judaism, a visionary description of events expected to accompany the end of the world. The *Didache*, presumably written around the beginning of the second century AD, is the first extant constitution of a Christian parish, defining its structure, organisation, offices, ritual practices, and moral laws. Isolated facts of this kind about Christian communities can also be found in certain passages in the non-genuine texts among Paul's letters. The *Didache* was obviously based on Jewish models; examples are the so-called Brotherhood scroll and the Damascus scroll, which were found in the literary legacy of the Qumran sect.

4

THE SECOND CENTURY

1 GENERAL REMARKS

The men who were behind the murder of Domitian also directed the selection of his successor. This was M. Cocceius Nerva, an insignificant old man and hence one who had no real enemies anywhere. He called back those who had been banished, but took very little action against informers or against people who had otherwise profited from Domitian's reign of terror. When a potentially dangerous opposition against Nerva began to form among the Praetorian guard the Emperor decided to adopt a son and make him joint ruler. The person thus honoured was governing the province of upper Germany at that time, and was the most gifted general the army possessed.

This promotion of M. Ulpius Trajanus, a man from a Spanish family of Consular rank, led to a fundamental change of attitude among the upper classes in the Empire: a development which proved to be crucial for the history of the entire second century AD. The Emperor's choice found the approval of the Senate which thereby became involved in deciding the succession. The succession of monarchs in turn lost its odious dynastic aspect and could no longer make the Empire appear like mere family property to be passed on from father to son as a matter of course. The new method of adopting a successor made it possible to fulfil the philosophers' demand that the best man should hold the highest office. The first case in point was, of course, Trajan who enjoyed an excellent reputation in military and administrative circles when he became sole ruler upon Nerva's death in 98 AD, only one year after the adoption.

The age of the Antonines, which lasted until 180 AD, can thus be characterised as a time of reconciliation between the Senatorial nobility and Imperial power. Nevertheless, the actual distribution and the mechanisms of power remained almost unaffected. Outside Senatorial circles, and especially in the East, it was in any case administrative efficiency and continuity which people were interested in first and foremost, and not so much the monarch's attitude towards Roman-Republican tradition.

No observer can fail to be impressed by the competence and the sense of duty shown by the Emperors of this age. The changes in political ideology meant that Trajan was free to present himself openly as a monarch in the tradition of Caesar and Alexander. The Empire was once again considerably enlarged during his reign, through the conquest of Dacia, modern-day Rumania, of Mesopotamia up to the Persian Gulf, and parts of Arabia. Though Trajan's successor Hadrian gave Mesopotamia up again, he worked hard and successfully at improving Imperial administration, military discipline, and security on the Empire's borders. In addition to that, Hadrian managed to make the existing intellectual and emotional ties which bound the Greek world to the Roman one even stronger than before.

The reign of Hadrian's successor Antoninus Pius is remembered not so much for any spectacular events as for a style of government which was both solid and humane. The subsequent years present a slightly darker picture, for Marcus Aurelius, the philosopher on the throne, had to cope with a major epidemic as well as with dangerous intrusions of barbarian tribes into northern regions of the Empire. Still, although Marcus Aurelius' nature was not at all that of a military man, he took decisive and successful action against the raiders. Under his successor Commodus, who ruled from 180 to 192 AD, the course of events mirrored those under Nero. Commodus was another gifted emperor, educated with the greatest possible care, whom the lack of any institutionalised control of supreme power allowed to lapse into all sorts of eccentricities. Both emperors indulged in a kind of behaviour whose harmful consequences for the state could only be temporarily averted by competent officials. Ultimately, there was a spate of diverse failures and insurrections and a wave of opposition among the Senatorial nobility causing both emperors to react with persecutions and executions. With Commodus as with Nero, the end of the story came when one of the many conspiracies was successful and the Empire was left in a state of general confusion after the killing of the monarch.

In the second century AD the nations who lived together under Roman rule saw the zenith of prosperity, of legal security, and of global civilisation. There was an immense amount of architectural activity, whose remains can still be seen today, spread out from Spain to Syria, and from England to Algeria. The literary production of the period was comparably rich, albeit that its most impressive feature was its bulk, and not its originality. People came to feel that the world had grown old. The cultural and economic centre had now quite definitely moved to the East: its inhabitants became Romans who based their sense of worth on the achievements of their Greek ancestors. More and more members of the Greek upper classes found their way into the Senatorial ranks. Administration and jurisdiction became increasingly humane or humanistic: any man who aspired to a military or an administrative office or to any kind of social standing had to prove a considerable degree of general education. The general spirit of the period is epitomised by the fact that in 143 AD, the Consulate was held jointly by M. Cornelius Fronto and Herodes Atticus, the two most renowned men of letters from the Latin and the Greek side respectively.

2 TACITUS, PLINY THE YOUNGER, AND FLORUS

Tacitus

The works of Tacitus, arguably the greatest of all Roman prose authors, contain the most convincing literary evidence we have of that change of mood in the highest social class which set in with the age of the Antonines. But unlike many of his contemporaries, Tacitus also recognised the persistence of those social and moral factors which had permitted developments like those during the reign of Nero or Domitian.

P. Cornelius Tacitus came from an equestrian family, which was presumably resident in Gallia Narbonensis, that is southern France, or northern Italy, known as Gallia Cisalpina. During his rhetorical education in Rome Tacitus showed such exceptional talent that he very soon became the most celebrated orator in the capital. This success was most probably what triggered off his Senatorial career, initiated by Vespasian and leading up to the Praetorship – the second highest of the honorary offices established in ancient Republican times – during Domitian's reign. As holder of this position in 88 AD Tacitus was involved in the preparations for a splendid secular celebration with which Domitian wanted to give his reign a particular significance. Ten years earlier Tacitus had married the daughter of Cn. Julius Agricola, one of the outstanding generals under Domitian.

Up to this point, Tacitus' biography can be described as a typical example of the rise of a man from the municipal nobility to the ranks of the highest class in Roman society. There is nothing substantial to indicate that he perceived any conflict between his loyalty to the emperors to whom he owed his rise, and his allegiance to the ideology of his new class. There is only very scanty evidence in support of the claim that there was a clash of loyalties at that early stage of Tacitus' life. Tacitus' self-avowed shunning of the capital for several years after his Praetorship does not seem too significant; rather more weight could be attached to the fact that he held the Consulate in the year after Nerva's accession to the throne, and that he was chosen to speak at the funeral of L. Virginius Rufus. Rufus was the most prominent Senator at the time: a man who had never compromised the dignity of his class by concessions to Imperial power, and who had thus several times spoiled his chances of becoming Emperor himself. Some years later, as a public prosecutor, Tacitus was involved in the trials of people who had profited from Domitian's tyranny. As a Proconsul in 112 and 113 AD, Tacitus governed the province of Asia, which was that region which is today known as western Anatolia. We do not know what happened to him after that: it seems certain, however, that his last and greatest piece of writing was not produced before the reign of Hadrian. There are no writings to document Tacitus' activities as an orator; his career as an author began with a biography of his father-in-law.

There was a whole literary genre devoted to the memory of those martyrs of liberty who had fallen victim to the conflict between Imperial power and the Stoically-minded Senatorial opposition at the time when the quarrel came to a head under Nero and Domitian. The readers of such works were likely to be left with the impression that any philosopher or Senator who maintained his moral integrity during Domitian's tyrannic reign would have invariably paid for this with his life. Tacitus himself describes the difference between the past and the years after 96 AD in a passage of the prooemium to his histories, saying that now people were free to feel as they pleased, and to say what they felt. In the life of Agricola the knowledge of having crossed the threshold of a new age is expressed in the claim that those who had lived through Domitian's reign of terror felt like 'survivors of their own selves'. Tacitus explains that this perception arose from an awareness of shared guilt on the part of those who had watched the persecution, the banishment, and the killing of fellow members of their class without trying to prevent it.

Nevertheless, Tacitus' life of Agricola criticises the glorification of the martyrs by Stoa-orientated authors such as Arulenus Rusticus or Herennius Senecio. Tacitus claims that in the last instance the fate of the victims was merely the result of a fruitless gesture which helped them preserve their moral integrity, but which did not in the least serve the public interest. Against such fruitless martyrdom Tacitus sets the example of his father-in-law to illustrate that even under Domitian there had been virtuous men who refused to compromise themselves morally in spite of the fact that they served under a tyrant: men whose great achievements for the good of the state highlighted ancient Roman virtues.

Unlike a martyr's biography, intended to demonstrate the hero's moral perfection as an individual guided by philosophical standards, Tacitus' life of Agricola is a political biography in as much as it explains the impact of an individual life on the community. Such an attempt at coming to terms with the past thus involved historical-political as well as moral aspects: and this meant that Tacitus modified the intention given for the biographical genre, as described in my section on Plutarch, in a way that could not but affect the structure of his writing.

In fact only the introduction and conclusion of the life of Agricola follow the conventions of biography. The middle part, containing the account of the major war Agricola waged in Britain, contains all those elements of the high art of historiography which were alien to the formal tradition of the biographical genre. Hence we find features such as the obligatory geographical digression; the strict division of a chronological account according to successive years; the description of a decisive battle in a form that puts dramatic effect above factual accuracy; and the addresses of the two hostile generals to their troops. The resulting mixture of formal elements from two very different genres must have seemed a fairly strange hotchpotch to any Classical reader. However, this could come as no surprise to those who took a close look at the preface, where Tacitus on the one hand introduces the account of his father-in-law's life in terms that promise nothing else but a conventional biography, but where on the other hand he calls his work a kind of an advance deposit on histories to be written later.

There are more details which prove the historiographical intention of this biography. The major speech of the Britannic chief Calgacus presents a mercilessly scathing view of Roman Imperialism and its motives. Towards the end of the book, Tacitus speaks of his hero Agricola's stay in Rome, where he led a quiet life and tried with great prudence not to provoke the ever-suspicious Domitian. Not so much by conveying facts as by presenting rumours and suggestions, those passages portray the oppressive atmosphere of anxiety and fear which prevailed in Rome during the last years of Domitian's reign. This atmospheric description is the first in a series of comparable historical sketches, which count among the most impressive parts of Tacitus' major historiographical writings.

Presumably because of its formal oddity the life of Agricola was read only by few people and imitated by none after its appearance in 98 AD. In the same year, however, Tacitus also produced his monograph about Germany. The description of nations and countries had a long tradition going back to the fifth century BC, and all writers in this genre had also discussed the relationship between a country's natural features and the character of its inhabitants. Naturally enough, this issue became even more important to geographers and ethnographers who operated within the framework set by Hellenistic philosophy, where the core area was the doctrine of natural ethics. In this context, I must once more mention the Stoic and versatile scholar Posidonius (see p. 42).

Tacitus' description of Germany and its peoples is part of this tradition. The tract deals with the physical features of the country as well as with the characteristics, manners, customs, and institutions of its inhabitants. The work is based on different ethnographical sources, and thus contains many of the typical elements that were commonly found in descriptions of exotic nations. Besides older ethnography, we may assume that Tacitus was also able to use more up-to-date material, taken from Pliny the Elder's account of the German wars.

What is innovative in Tacitus' tract is certainly not that he presents an idealised image of a nation as yet free from the corruptions of civilisation, and thus invites his contemporaries in the Graeco-Roman world to take a good look at themselves in comparison. The novel element which Tacitus introduces is the historical perspective, from which the difference between the respective moral levels appears as the main reason why the Empire and its civilisation were being seriously threatened by the unspent force of the Germanic tribes. According to Tacitus, the only reason why matters had not yet come to a head was the Germans' natural tendency to quarrel among themselves.

The third and last of the shorter treatises which predate Tacitus' major historical works is the dialogue *On Orators*, which seems to have been written some years after the other two. The recipient of the dedication is Q. Fabius Justus, who was Consul in 102 AD. The central issue is the decline of eloquence, a much-debated topic since the Early Empire: Quintilian, for example, had devoted a whole treatise to the same problem not long before Tacitus did so (see p. 185). Tacitus, however, widens the issue by putting an advocate for modernism into the debate; by making another participant in the discussion weigh the relative merits of oratory and poetry as pursuits for a man of noble rank who wants to play an active role in intellectual life; and lastly, by making his characters discuss in a very unbiased manner the question of which historical conditions give rise to great eloquence. The whole piece is styled as a conversation that Tacitus had ostensibly listened to as a young man: the speakers in the fictitious literary dialogue bear the name of leading Roman intellectuals from the Flavian era. The extant text unfortunately has quite a large gap in the middle.

Nevertheless, this short work by Tacitus stands as one of the most perfect creations in Roman prose literature. The dialogue is written in Ciceronian Latin, with an elegance that makes it anything but a pedantic imitation. There is enough stylistic variation to permit an excellent portrayal of the individual speakers' characters and tastes, in a manner far more animated than that found in any Ciceronian writings of the same kind. Seemingly casual side remarks add up to present the reader with a vivid image of the mood prevalent among intellectual circles in Flavian Rome, which was already part of past history when Tacitus wrote his treatise. The tone of the conversation is delightfully urbane, although there are great differences of opinion between the participants.

The work begins with an introductory talk between M. Aper, Tacitus' teacher of rhetoric, and the orator and poet Curiatius Maternus who has just written a tragedy. The two men argue about the relative merits of rhetoric and poetry, after which the others join them in a debate on the difference between past and present states of the rhetorical art. Only Aper sees the latter as superior, while Maternus, Vipstanus Messala, and Julius Secundus find contemporary oratory degenerate. Messala puts this down to a decline in the educational system; the gap in the text prevents us from knowing the argument with which Secundus backed up his view. Maternus closes the debate with a lengthy explanation of why he finally opted for the poetic medium. In this part we can once again perceive the voice of the historian Tacitus, who has learned to form a suitably balanced view of those positive and negative features which determine the image of a historical epoch in the eyes of posterity.

According to Maternus, great eloquence can only exist where political life takes the form of a fight between different forces. Hence great oratory is a product of social and political disorder, even if that disorder may be positively defined as a situation where political agents are at liberty. In the rigid order of a monarchic state, where everything is done according to set rules, there is no longer any room for political infighting, and thus neither for great political eloquence. This, Maternus says, may well be regretted as causing the decay of a great art form, and the loss of a way of achieving individual fame: however, nobody should forget that such is the price that has been paid in exchange for the chance to live safely under the protection of a political order which guarantees legal security. Through Maternus' argument, Tacitus concisely and convincingly exposes the blinkeredness and the ephemeral character of a cliché which dominated the historical notions of an entire epoch. In this respect, this part of the dialogue *On Orators* stands out not only in Tacitus' work, but in historical writing as a whole, where it is extremely rare to find any author who proves to be as independent as Tacitus from the prejudices of his own age.

Tacitus' two major historical works, the *Histories* and the *Annals*, are both extant in parts. The different titles are not matched by any difference in structure or intention; and it is very likely that they were chosen by somebody other than the author himself. The works belong to the context of that major historiographical plan which Tacitus outlines in the two famous prefaces: this plan, however, changed substantially over the years. Both prefaces deal with the particular difficulties facing the historiographer under the Principate. Older literary parallels show that this was a much-discussed topic even in the Early Empire, where authors already complained that in a state where decisions were made behind the closed doors of the Emperor's cabinet, and not in Senate debates, the historiographer was no longer able to look into the causes of political events. It was also hard to preserve the frankness and the truthfulness of traditional Republican historiography in an atmosphere where people were either busy flattering or slandering the living Princeps, and showing their hatred or their gratitude towards his dead predecessor. Before he describes the events which he witnessed himself, Tacitus thus feels compelled to state that his account will be influenced by neither love nor hate, in spite of the fact that his career was furthered by the Flavian emperors. In the preface to his history of the Early Empire, his contention that he writes *sine ira et studio* is backed by the argument that he could not have had any personal connection with any of the Emperors of that period.

This illustrates the fact that the source of all the problems in Imperial historiography was ultimately its one-sidedness, in relating each reported event to the Emperor's person. Tacitus more than once expresses his belief in the necessity of concentrating all power in one individual, in order to safeguard peace and stability in the global Empire. Nevertheless, he regards this concentration as a result of the exhaustion of the Roman state, and there is a passage in his work in which he shoots down the Republican pretensions of the Augustan order in his inimitable style, with one pointed statement (*Ann.* 1, 1, 1).

The *Histories* deal with the time between the fall of Nero and the fall of Domitian. It seems that there were originally fourteen books, of which we have only the first four, and parts of Book 5. The intended sequel to the *Histories* was a work about the reigns of Nerva and Trajan and thus, in Tacitus' own words, one on a richer and more agreeable subject matter. Instead of realising this plan, however, he ended up writing the *Annals* whose sixteen books describe events between the end of Augustus' reign and the accession of Nero to the throne: hence the period prior to that dealt with in the *Histories*. Of the *Annals*, we have the complete Books 1 to 4 and 12 to 16, together with parts of Books 5, 6, and 11. That some manuscripts feature Book 1 of the *Histories* as Book 17 of the *Annals* indicates that both publications came to be largely regarded as parts of a whole, even if the existence of separate prefaces actually refutes this view. Nevertheless, it is undoubtedly legitimate to emphasise the great similarity in scope, structure, and intention between the *Histories* and the *Annals*, even if the later work clearly reflects the increasing radicalisation of the author's political principles, and the growing individuality of his style.

Tacitus saw himself as a spokesman for the time-honoured traditions of the Roman Senate; he tried to live up to the dignity of these traditions by aiming for the stylistic level that was suited to great historiography. Hence Tacitus' works contain specimens of each and every device or convention which was thought of as essential to this literary art form. Although we may presume that the author laboured most diligently to gather facts from archives and libraries, Tacitus' perfectly formed literary account is purged of all references to such menial groundwork.

According to Tacitus his task of meeting the high literary standard set in the long tradition of this genre was made difficult by the lamentably inadequate subject matter. In Book 4 of the *Annals*, we find the complaint: 'My toils are performed in a narrow field, and I harvest no glory'. He can report no victories of the Roman nation, no captures of hostile kings, no conquests of enemy cities, nor any great rhetorical battles in the Senate or in the Forum. Instead, he must tell of cruel decrees issued by the Emperor, of denunciations, accusations, and betrayals among friends – all of them in such uniform repetition that the reader might confuse the past with the present. In the Imperial peace, however, which reigns within the borders of the Empire and has made the city of Rome as quiet as a graveyard, even seemingly insignificant happenings can cause great commotion, and must thus be reported.

Tacitus' contemptuous-melancholy outlook on contemporary reality sometimes reaches the level of downright nausea. This is expressed in often grandiosely drawn atmospheric sketches whose writing suited the author's temperament much better than giving exact summaries of administrative procedures, let alone of military action. When Tacitus reports a battle, the mood among the troops and the generals is most often more vividly portrayed than the actual happenings on the battlefield.

The lament about a lack of that kind of material which would vindicate an impressive manner of presentation is louder in the *Annals* than in the *Histories*; the introductory chapters of the latter even emphasise the particular eventfulness of the Flavian era. But even there Tacitus' account is meant to prove that the history of the Roman people had ended with the arrival of the Emperors as the sole subjects of Imperial Roman history. In Book 1 of the *Histories*, Tacitus recounts with grim irony how the populace reacted to the increased forebodings of warfare on Italian soil between Otho and Vitellius, two of the Emperors of 68 and 69 AD. Tacitus says that the Roman people were incapable of seeing this situation as a test of their community spirit, because ever since the reign of Augustus they had experienced war only from afar, and thought of it as a source of individual concern or glory for only one person: namely, the Emperor himself. This is the precise description of a situation where the entire civilised world knew border or colonial warfare only. In the circumstances of 68 and 69 AD, the public's reactions were thus governed by fear or frivolousness, and not by any consideration for the needs of the state, from which people had become so thoroughly alienated. There were no more than a few level-headed men who appreciated the precious benefits of that peace which was being jeopardised.

According to Tacitus, a historian had no choice but to devote all his attention to the person of the ruler, on whose qualities and intentions all events depended. Consequently the first books of the *Annals* read like a biography of Tiberius. Tacitus is trying to show how the Emperor, whose personal sympathy lay with the Republican tradition, reluctantly inherited monarchic power from his ill-beloved stepfather; and how he was then contaminated by the servility and treachery of all those he encountered as the holder of supreme power, being led to dissimulation, despotism, and misanthropy, and ending up as a cruel, ruthless tyrant. It is doubtful whether this psychogram really does Tiberius justice: what it certainly does is to show that Tacitus understood the corrupting influence of absolute power on the person who holds it, as well as on those subjected to it.

Tacitus' historiography is full of accounts of individual lives, and this is one of the features which make for exceedingly captivating reading. The author does not state his anthropological and political insights as abstract general laws, exemplified by historical events: he rather chooses to express them implicitly in the description of human interaction. His approach towards historical events focuses on individual human beings; and this is evident not only in the dominant role he ascribes to the Emperors, or in the biographical obituaries which, as was common in traditional Classical historiography, he appended to reports about the deaths of eminent men. Even more significant is the fact that when Tacitus tells of the actions and the sufferings of countless individuals, he rarely does so without adding – mostly in an explicit manner, but occasionally also implicitly – a psychological explanation and a moral evaluation of the behaviour he describes.

Tacitus takes two things for granted: that monarchy is an inevitable necessity, and that it has fateful consequences for the people living within the monarchic order. Whether such a nexus is due to a general and fatal predetermination or to chance, or whether responsible and free actions of human beings have some say in this as well, is a question which he ponders in a famous chapter in Book 6 of the *Annals*: he does not, however, arrive at any conclusion. Earlier on, in the respective prefaces to his life of Agricola and to the *Histories*, he had exempted the new system of the Antonines from his negative judgment. The beginning of the *Histories* even presents the Emperor Galba as delivering a speech that sounds very much like the manifesto of a new order, one which reconciles monarchy and liberty. In the later *Annals*, there is nothing of the kind. As some scholars have pointed out, there is even good reason to assume that when Tacitus reports the sinister events which accompanied the succession of Tiberius, he is deliberately alluding to happenings around the beginning of Hadrian's reign, with a particular emphasis on the respective roles played by Augustus' widow Livia, and Trajan's widow Plotina. In any case, the panoramic view of the Early Empire which Tacitus gives in his *Annals* can hardly warrant the assumption that the work was written by a man who still believed it possible to see a monarchy which would not corrupt the people within its sphere of power.

Tacitus was a thoroughly educated man who had studied his sources diligently. Even though he was at pains to avoid any kind of technical-philosophical terminology, his reflections show that he was also well-versed in philosophy. But first and foremost, he was a trained orator, with a unique linguistic sensibility, and great powers of expression.

In rhetorical systematics historiography had been classed under the heading of epideictic eloquence, which meant that among the three recognised stylistic levels it belonged to the category of the sublime. This had several different consequences, beginning with the fact that historiographers were free to transcend the narrow limitations of the vocabulary assigned to the elegant style, and to use archaic and poetic words for emotional effect, or as a means of evoking the atmosphere of times past. Following this trend, which naturally ran counter to the purist notions of that Classic Ciceronianism which had left its mark also on historiography, Sallust had developed his own archaic style. He was regarded as an outsider (see p. 42), but still some authors came to imitate him (see p. 43). Sallust's choice of words was matched by a syntax that avoided any kind of smoothness or symmetry. He went for surprising, seemingly incomplete and unconnected phrases, which merely hinted at the intended meaning, and left the reader with the task of completing it.

As his dialogue proves, Tacitus was capable of showing great virtuosity in writing Classic-Ciceronian prose in a style which had shortly before his lifetime attained a new eminence through the influence of Quintilian. However, in his historical works Tacitus rather chose to follow Sallust, whom he once called the most outstanding figure among all Roman historiographers. Tacitus emulated not only Sallust's style, but likewise adopted the stance of a moral judge from which Sallust had described people and events, and which the use of archaic Roman diction had served to underline. Tacitus came to surpass his model by far, for as the most distinguished orator of the period his own range of expressions was much greater. With the utmost sophistication, Tacitus used words and word forms which were alien to the language of prose, and which to an educated reader must have had a wealth of connotations which we can hardly assess today. In syntax and in the choice of individual phrases, Tacitus' writing tends to insinuate the authorial judgment rather than to objectify it, especially when it comes to conveying important information, or to drawing conclusions. This is exactly why the author so often succeeds in conveying an impression of the inscrutable, enigmatic, and threatening nature of life under the rule of one man without any institutionalised control. The reader is bound to feel that in such a situation everything ultimately depends on psychological factors which can hardly be grasped.

Tacitus maintained the elevated style of traditional historiography by avoiding any kind of trivial, let alone vulgar expression. In certain passages – for instance, addresses of generals to their troops or final authorial evaluations – he creates pathos by stylistic means such as the rhythmic parallelism of clause endings. Another means of making the language of his account differ from everyday usage is the frequent featuring of one-liners or striking, extremely concise and memorable sententias, such as he had been taught to compose during his rhetorical training. It was especially this quality which fascinated those who read Tacitus after his rediscovery by the Humanists, and in particular during the seventeenth and eighteenth centuries. There is hardly any other Classical author who achieved the same perfection in not only describing, but also judging facts in a minimal number of words.

A particularly good example of this is found in Book 1 of the *Histories* which contains an obituary of Galba, the first ruler in the Year of the Three Emperors. Tacitus talks about Galba's administrative and military achievements and his moral integrity, but also about his total lack of political instinct or charisma. The passage ends with the words *omnium consensu capax imperii nisi imperasset* ('generally deemed fit to rule, had he not ruled'). And in the preface to the *Annals* where the whole of Roman history is summed up in one sentence, Tacitus describes Augustus' assumption of power with the formula *qui cuncta discordiis civilibus fessa nomine principis sub imperium accepit* ('he who under the name of Princeps assumed supreme command over a community exhausted by the civil war').

The peculiar features of Tacitus' style are stronger in the *Annals* than in the *Histories*; but in the last book of the *Annals* this state of affairs is reversed, and we find a slightly more polished, and thus often a more readily comprehensible diction. A possible explanation for this fact is that those parts of the work may not have been subjected to a final editing on the part of the author before publication.

It was not until the late flowering of Latin literature during the fourth and fifth centuries AD that later generations began to read and imitate Tacitus. The oldest manuscript versions of Tacitus' works, discovered and copied by Humanists of the fifteenth century, had been produced in Frankish monasteries of the Carolinian period. However, the most significant impact of this great, but not too easily readable, author came only with the flowering of political theory from the seventeenth century onwards.

Pliny

The literary legacy of Tacitus' friend Pliny the Younger makes for much easier reading than Tacitus' world of ideas expressed in his obscure, highly artificial language. C. Plinius Caecilius Secundus grew up in the house of his uncle, the author of the *Naturalis historia*. When Pliny the Elder died during the eruption of Vesuvius in 79 AD, his nephew, then eighteen years of age, was present. By his will, his uncle made him an adopted son. Pliny the Younger received his rhetorical education in Rome, where the celebrated Quintilian was among his teachers. Pliny then worked for some time as a lawyer; and in 88 AD, after holding some lesser provincial offices, he was first appointed to one of the honorary Republican offices as a Quaestor, nominated – like all other candidates for such posts – by the Emperor. This career led as far as the Consulate in 100 AD and made Pliny also eligible for a number of different administrative functions. From 110 AD onwards he was the Imperial emissary in Bithynia, where for some years he supervised the autonomous Greek cities, and where he presumably remained until his death.

Apart from Pliny's known activity as an orator and legal practitioner, a largely autobiographical letter tells us that he also tried his hand at poetry, and even managed to get some of his efforts published. An extant text, featured in a collection that otherwise contains only specimens of Late Classical oratory, is a eulogy in which Pliny expresses his gratitude to the Emperor Trajan, on the occasion of the author's promotion to the Consulate. Throughout this speech, published shortly after its delivery, Domitian's tyrannic actions are portrayed as a foil for the proven or expected princely virtues of Trajan, a feature which makes the text an important illustration of the 'reformed' monarchic ideology of the second century AD. The image of the monarch which Pliny draws does not reflect any doubt on his part about the exalted position of the Emperor above his subjects, but nevertheless Pliny demands that of his own free choice the monarch should make himself a part of that legal framework which he himself guarantees. The charismatic nature of the Emperor is acknowledged, but this is tied to the demand that a monarch should first and foremost have the moral qualifications to be the first among the citizens, and thus be judged as the best man according to those standards valid for each and every individual alike.

Pliny's panegyric illustrates very well what Tacitus meant when, in his life of Agricola, he spoke of a union between *libertas* and *principatus* under the new adopted emperors. One could also describe this as a synthesis between the charismatic image of the monarch expressed in the Imperial cult and the ethical image upheld in philosophy. But we should also remember that Roman jurisprudence, which I shall discuss at length in a later section, had in any case never accepted the belief that a monarch was exempt from the laws of the state.

The style of Pliny's speech is Ciceronian, a fact which reflects the influence of his teacher Quintilian. In Pliny's many letters we find an educated literary language that is also largely Ciceronian. These letters were definitely written with a view to publication, and indeed published by the author himself; nevertheless, they are genuine communications addressed to persons whose existence is in most cases historically verifiable. Thus Pliny's epistles provide us with invaluable information about the literary, social, and political life of the capital, as seen by a member of the upper classes. One important feature are the many recollections of the bad years under Domitian, and the references to the later treatment of those who had compromised themselves at that time. There are reports of Senate debates which are not always taken seriously; of judicial hearings; or of the roles which philosophers had as domestic chaplains and confessors in noble families. Pliny talks of the treatment of slaves, of sojourns in the country, of occult events, of the causes of political rivalry, and above all of literary ambitions. He explains that it would be thought impolite to refuse the invitation of a friend to a reading of his latest tragedy, even if one dreads the inevitable boredom of the occasion. Nevertheless, Pliny asserts that people are particularly inclined to recommend a young man for a post in business or administration if that person has already produced some Greek and Latin plays.

Pliny's letters portray a social life in which it is possible to maintain humane attitudes at the same time as conforming to the legal and political order. Literary interests play an important part, but likewise the handling of inheritances and financial management. A particularly strange fact which emerges from these epistles is that serving the Emperor and the Empire appears to be regarded as no more important than gratifying one's minor vanities in the large amount of leisure time available.

Among Pliny's published epistles, there are also 121 letters to and from the Emperor or the Emperor's secretaries, from the years when Pliny was working in Bithynia. They discuss matters relating to law, finance, or public building, and give quite a good illustration of the mechanisms of Imperial administration, especially in its relationship with autonomous municipal bodies. For a high-ranking emissary authorised by Emperor and Senate Pliny shows an astonishing lack of independence, asking for instructions from Rome even in trivial matters. The style of the letters is concise and official, even if it allows for polite and personal addresses to the Emperor or his legate.

In one of the epistles Pliny asks what should be done with people accused of being Christians. The Emperor's rescript, which for a long time provided the legal basis for the official treatment of the growing Christian religion, demanded a procedure that was highly questionable from a legal point of view, but that was, on the other hand, pragmatic and humane. No Graeco-Roman community could tolerate in its midst any group whose exclusive monotheism was incompatible with the worship of those deities seen as having provided indispensable protection to that community since its beginnings. The Romans had come upon the Jewish religion when they extended the Empire to the East and hence, like the gods of other conquered nations, the Jewish God could be seen as one of the deities protecting the global Empire. This was not so with the God of the Christians whose followers made no bones about the fact that their faith had sprung up and detached itself from Judaism under Roman rule. Hence belonging to a Christian community could be perceived as nothing else than a criminal offence. This was Trajan's view too: yet Trajan insisted that in any trial the accused should have the opportunity of renouncing the Christian faith, and that past membership of a Christian community was not punishable. Trajan also explicitly prohibited any operations aimed at hunting down the Christians, presumably because of Pliny's report which describes them as harmless. That was inconsistent with the view that being a Christian was a crime, but it shows the humane nature of Trajan's government. This is borne out also by the final statement of the Emperor's instructions, ordering that the authorities should not act upon any anonymous denunciations, as such a procedure would set a very bad example, inconsistent with the spirit of the period.

In two long letters, Pliny describes how he experienced the eruption of Vesuvius in 79 AD. The addressee is Tacitus, who was to use Pliny's information in his *Histories*. At the beginning of his account, Pliny tells the reader that his uncle came into the room where he was sitting, and asked his nephew to step outside and join him in watching this unique natural spectacle. The young man, however, preferred to stay indoors, and to go on with making an excerpt from a book by Livy. There is hardly any better illustration of Imperial Classicism: people expected to find more interesting things in old books than in contemporary reality.

Florus

A case in point for the usefulness of such excerpts is a short work written by P. Annius Florus. The author is presumably identical with the Florus who wrote a dialogue on the question whether Virgil was to be seen primarily as an orator, or first and foremost as a poet. This dialogue is no longer extant, apart from a preface which includes some autobiographical information. From it, we learn that Florus came from the province of Africa, modern-day Tunisia. In 88 AD he took part in a poetry competition in Rome and looked certain to win until the Emperor himself intervened. Around 100 AD the author of the dialogue on Virgil lived in the Spanish city of Tarraco, modern-day Tarragon.

Florus' epitome from Livy gives a survey of Roman history, seen as a sequence of wars fought by the Roman people. In the preface the author divides the events into periods corresponding to the different ages of man. As far as we know, this motif was first used by Seneca the Elder (see p. 90), even if Seneca himself may have borrowed it from Varro. Florus saw the era of the Roman Kings as the childhood of Rome, the period up to the complete conquest of Italy as belligerent adolescence, and the age of global conquest up to the reign of Augustus as mature manhood. Consequently, the Imperial age could be nothing but the sere and yellow, and this classification is explicitly underlined by the author who cites the military inactivity of the Emperors as proof. When Florus wrote his epitome the Empire had not been enlarged any further for a very long time; but shortly afterwards, Trajan's campaigns would have forced the author to contemplate talking about a return of Rome to full manhood.

Florus' epitome was widely read, especially in the fourth and fifth centuries AD when Biblical-Christian speculations about historical periods suggested comparisons with the relatively few Graeco-Roman classifications of this kind. Any consistent periodisation of history is necessarily based on a teleology independent of nature: and this was unacceptable to the Greeks who saw rationally recognisable laws at work in nature alone.

Hence the few extant Classical attempts at such speculative history are exclusively of Roman origin.

3 GREEK EDUCATIONAL LITERATURE

Orators

In the previous section, I have already mentioned the revival of a representative art of oratory which began in the major economic and cultural centres of western Asia Minor, and which was soon labelled Second Sophistic Art by contemporaries. This development was firmly rooted in the educational system; its heyday was in the mid-second century AD, and it had a far-reaching influence on the genesis and the rise of a richly varied prose literature.

In the educational consciousness of the period, the rhetor occupied an important place both as a teacher of rhetoric and as a 'concert orator'. This very apt term has been coined to describe those who wrote and delivered public speeches on the occasion of a festival, as spokesman for a delegation, or simply for the edification of an audience. As I have said before, such activity could be a source of great social as well as political prestige. Competition in the business pushed rhetors to attain ever higher levels of virtuosity in instruction and practice, and this in turn set the standards for all kinds of prose literature, which experienced a mushroom growth amid the conditions of general prosperity. As far as the products of the genre are not obviously of a scientific nature, their form – without any exception, if to varying degrees – was dictated by the linguistic and stylistic norms of rhetoric, regardless of the diversity of subject matter. This explains why such large parts of the prose literature of the second century AD have survived: the perfect imitation of Classic Attic made readers of the Late Classical age and the Middle Ages regard this Classicising literature as Classic itself, according to those norms of written Attic which remained valid in written Greek until well into the Modern age.

The first rhetor I must mention in this context is Dion of Prusa who has already been referred to in a previous section (see p. 189). Because of the purity of his Attic, posterity gave him the name of Chrysostomus or 'Goldmouth'. Dion was the most celebrated orator during Trajan's reign, having used his art to proclaim the new brand of Imperial and monarchic ideology ever since Nerva came to power. Some of his speeches given in eastern locations such as Alexandria, Rhodes, and Tarsus, take quarrels within those cities as occasion to describe the notion of a concord based on two factors: the amicable collaboration of free, autonomous civic communities, combined with the protection of that Imperial power which governs the whole civilised world. This constellation is to preserve harmony on a global as well as on a municipal scale. Dion also produced a number of speeches about the role of the monarch; these appear to be meant for private reading rather than public delivery, although they contain all the rhetorical devices of oratory. In the aggregate, they constitute a complete theory of monarchy, which starts from the stage which the centuries-old philosophical discussion on this topic had reached. With a lot of verve, Dion presents his central notion of monarchy: it possesses cosmic-divine legitimacy, because it mirrors the rule of the one universal God over the world and is a means of reflecting the rational order of the entire universe in the form of justice among men.

Throughout his splendid career as a rhetor Dion never forgot his philosophical background. He kept dealing with philosophical issues, especially topics related to Cynic doctrine, which had provided the guidelines for his own life during the time of his banishment. It is Dion to whom we owe many of the existing anecdotes about Diogenes, the hero of the Cynic tradition. In two of his speeches Dion also talks of his own experiences during his travelling life: he describes them from the point of view of a Cynic critic of civilisation, even if the style he uses is elegant and ornate.

Thus Dion tells us of his visit to Borysthenes or Olbia, modern-day Odessa on the Dnepr. There he found a strong Greek *polis*, able to hold its own in spite of its isolation in the wide Scythian lands, and hence unaffected by the effeminate character of urban life in the Roman Empire. That city, says Dion, had truly preserved the spirit of ancient Hellas through the ages. A similarly romantic image of bygone better times emerges also from his account of a journey to the island of Euboea, where Dion, or rather the man whom he is quoting, discovered a remote village which had had no contact at all with urban culture, and where people did not even know the use of money. In this way, Dion holds, they had preserved the moral purity, the sincerity, and the strength which characterise those who lead a natural life. This story, told in a very appealing style, presents an ideal image which illustrates the deep resentment an educated person of the period was bound to feel against his own culture, as having a one-sided bias in favour of the urban lifestyle. It cannot be denied that the rural population was disadvantaged in the social order of the Empire, and the resulting tension led to open conflict as early as in the third century AD, with deep and lasting damage to the Empire's social framework. Nevertheless, the entirely individualistic approach which was the norm among educated people of the Hellenistic-Imperial age prevented them from seeing the social dimension of such problems and made them look only to the past whenever they sought cures against contemporary evils.

Some other topics which Dion writes about are likewise related to philosophy: thus, for instance, he talks about the proper selection of reading matter for educational purposes, or about the recognition of the divine through contemplation of the cosmos. In spite of its elegance, Dion's language is fairly plain, and without specific background knowledge, a modern reader may well get the misleading impression that this idiom could not have been all that remote from contemporary everyday usage. Dion remained an extremely famous author among later generations, until well into the Late Classical age.

Among the eighty extant speeches bearing the name of Dion two were actually written by his pupil Favorinus of Arelate, modern-day Arles in Provence, a Greek city of the far West. Favorinus was presumably educated in nearby Massilia, or Marseille, as we know it today. He travelled extensively; among his friends were Plutarch and Herodes Atticus, but also Gellius and Fronto, the two most eminent literary figures in Rome. Favorinus seems to have been equally at home in both Greek and Latin literature. He gained access to the court and was banished under Hadrian, but was recalled later on, and died in Rome as a highly renowned equestrian man of letters.

What we have today is only a very small part of Favorinus' rich and diverse literary output. Apart from the two speeches mentioned above, substantial fragments of his tract on banishment have been discovered on papyrus. The issue was a very popular topic among philosophers, for it was in enforced exile that a philosophically educated man had to prove his moral-spiritual independence. Like his teacher, Favorinus maintained his philosophical interests during his career as a rhetor, even if he himself preferred the Platonic approach to the Stoic-Cynic one. But he also wrote extensively in a kind of genre which we would be inclined to call literary journalism: a kind of writing produced by people who were willing to take on any subject that seemed interesting or worth knowing about, and who produced aesthetically pleasing texts without any scientific ambition. Of two major encyclopaedic compilations by Favorinus, which comprised nearly thirty books in all, we have countless fragments as quoted by the most diverse authors. These remnants show that Favorinus' work contained a motley mixture of grammar, history, antiquarian matter, curiosities, biography, and much more.

The importance of the sophist or rhetor in Imperial culture gave rise to a good deal of professional vanity among this group, a vanity which could in turn lead to fierce rivalries. In the case of Favorinus, we know the colleague who was his pet enemy, the sophist Antonius Polemon from Laodicaea in Asia Minor, slightly older than Favorinus, but equally well known. He also performed all over the entire Graeco-Roman world; and once when both men happened to meet in Ephesus, there was a public row, after which the two master orators referred to each other only in the most scathing terms. Like Favorinus, Polemon also found his way into the court; Hadrian commissioned him to speak at the inauguration of the

Olympieum in Athens, a building whose completion Hadrian had taken care of himself, at great personal expense.

Polemon's fame was founded on his many speeches in courts of law, as a member of delegations, and on the occasion of festivals. None of those speeches is extant, but we do have plenty of anecdotes and witticisms, featured above all in Philostratus' lives of the sophists (see p. 340). There is also a Latin translation of a work in which Polemon showed his talents as a journalist, a man who could write about anything under the sun for an educated readership without a true scientific interest. This work is a book on physiognomy, the art of reading a person's character in his facial features and body postures.

The most famous sophist was undoubtedly Herodes Atticus: not because of his exceptional ability, but because of his situation. He came from a noble Athenian family; his full name was Tib. Claudius Atticus Herodes, which indicated that his ancestors had become Roman citizens in the first half of the first century AD under the Claudian dynasty. Herodes lived from 101 to 177 AD, was acquainted with Polemon and Favorinus as well as with Gellius and Fronto, and held many public offices. This is partly documented by inscriptions, as in the cases of the two orators discussed above. Herodes had close ties with the court, and the Emperor Antoninus Pius made him a Consul in 143 AD, together with Fronto, tutor of the later Emperor Marcus Aurelius.

What made Herodes so famous was his immense fortune which he owed to the fact that his father had discovered a hidden treasure. Herodes spent the money lavishly on public building in his native city as well as in Alexandria, Corinth, the famous religious centres of Delphi and Olympia, and also in some less prominent locations. Modern readers can still go and hear a concert in the rebuilt theatre of Herodes Atticus at the foot of Athens's Acropolis.

Intellectuals all over the Empire were engaged in animated communication with each other, regardless of language boundaries, and it is owing to this that we have numerous more or less random pieces of information about Herodes' life, as well as summaries of his speeches and reports on his character and his views. Here as in other cases Philostratus features as an important source. According to him Herodes' oratory was by no means universally acclaimed, and his high social rank as well as his wealth were the cause of his involvement in many legal quarrels. However, none of the speeches he made on such occasions is extant, and neither are the ones he delivered at festivals. Thus, we can not tell whether his philosophical education at the hands of the Platonic Taurus had any lasting influence on him. The only extant text by Herodes is a rather lacklustre declamation, a fictitious speech based on political facts from the fifth century BC.

That virtuosity which was the object of such exercises is most impressively displayed in the *oeuvre* of Ailios or Aelius Aristides. He came from a distinguished family in Asia Minor and lived from about 115 to 185 AD. We may assume that the extant texts under his name include his complete published works. However, the fifty-five speeches and two theoretical-rhetorical tracts include quite a number of writings by other authors who imitated Aristides' style. As a stylist, Aristides was widely thought to be on a par with Demosthenes and thus he was soon recognised as one of the Classic authors.

Aristides suffered from neurasthenia. He was taught by Herodes in Athens, and spent some years travelling to Egypt, Rome, and several other places. After that, he developed an illness which showed in the most diverse symptoms, and which remained with him for the rest of his life. In his search for a cure, he repeatedly underwent treatment at the shrine of Asclepius, the god of healing, in his native city of Pergamum. To patients sleeping within the sacred area, the god was believed to appear in dreams, giving them detailed instructions for all aspects of day-to-day living. In the six so-called *Sacred Tales*, written in the final years of Aristides' life, the author gives a detailed description of this therapy which he followed for a very long time. Further evidence exists in the form of consecrational inscriptions and words of thanks on a large number of shrines sacred to Asclepius. Aristides' speeches are a vivid illustration of the religious ideas common to educated people of the period. But at the same time they reflect an unstable personality, and the virtually insufferable egocentricity of a man who expects his reader to be interested in even his most minor personal complaints.

Aristides' ill health as well as his hypochondria prevented him from entering public service. He performed no other work beside that of a teacher and an orator, even if that could also be in the public interest. A case in point is a speech he gave before the Emperor Marcus, asking for aid for the city of Smyrna which had suffered heavily during the major earthquake of 178 AD.

Except for the autobiographical *Sacred Tales*, Aristides' orations deal with three kinds of topics in particular. The first is the splendour and the glory of ancient Greece as the source of the Greek nation's contemporary self-confidence; then he talks about the global civilisation and the political order of the Roman Empire as securing peace and prosperity for Greeks and Romans alike; and finally he speaks in defence of rhetoric as the basis of all education.

The first of these topics is exemplified in the *Panathenaikos*, a speech on the occasion of the Panathenaic festival which subsequent generations came to regard as Aristides' masterpiece. An example for the second category of subject matter is a eulogy on the city of Rome, a work valued above all by modern-day scholars as a source of information about the political and social attitudes of educated Greeks in the second century AD.

Even if we make allowances for the euphoric tone which was a normal feature of such panegyrics, this oration must be regarded as a very impressive portrayal of a legal and social order regarded by the class that upheld it as being primarily based on civilisation: a culture which united people of very different origin, and distinguished them from the uncivilised humanity outside the Empire. The author emphasises the spaciousness of the Graeco-Roman world and the freedom of movement within its borders. Aristides sees these factors as crucial preconditions for the steady growth of prosperity which he perceives in the Empire, as well as for the development of a common political and cultural consciousness among its citizens. No historian can deny that at the time when Aristides lived the creative forces in the Graeco-Roman world were no longer at their former height. At the same time, however, we must agree with the speaker's claim that the spreading and the rooting of Graeco-Roman culture in the many countries around the Mediterranean was a considerable achievement in its own right, and ultimately ensured the lasting influence of Classical culture.

Unlike Dion or Favorinus, Aristides showed no interest in philosophy. He went back to the old controversy between the schools of Plato and Isocrates, and hence between philosophy and rhetoric as vying for precedence in the education of the young. Aristides was particularly keen to reject the opinion which Plato had expressed in his *Gorgias*, where he denied the usefulness of rhetoric as an educational medium. There is, however, good reason to doubt the topicality of this ancient dispute during Aristides' lifetime, when most trained orators would use their art to propagate and to popularise specific philosophical doctrines about ethics. Cases in point are Dion, Favorinus, and Maximus of Tyre (see p. 279). That Aristides still took up the debate and singled Plato out as his enemy proves yet again how seriously people living in the Classicist culture of the Empire could take problems belonging to a distant past. The reason was that the ancient texts which discussed such matters were thought to have an immediate, unadulterated bearing on contemporary reality.

Aristides was an astonishingly erudite man. The extent of his reading enabled him to reproduce the style of Classic-Attic prose of the fourth century BC so accurately and successfully that he came to be regarded as a Classic prose author himself. People of our own modern times are liable to find it strange that such great educational value should have been attached to mere imitation. However, we should acknowledge that this concentration on a literary-linguistic canon made education especially functional, as providing the means of communication between members of the upper classes who lived scattered over a vast area. It is this peculiar feature of post-Classic education which to a large extent explains the survival of Graeco-Roman culture against all odds.

'Miscellanists'

In the preceding chapters I have mentioned more than once that the rules of rhetorical art were applied to many different literary genres outside oratory itself. The literary legacy of the second century AD, in particular, contains many instances of this phenomenon, which already had a long history, and which could naturally produce varied levels of artistic achievement. As readers of such texts we have to imagine people with a broad general knowledge, whose education had made them sensitive to differences in stylistic quality, and had also given them a desire to accumulate factual information concerning the diverse subjects which 'literary journalists' dealt with.

Among those there was a certain Claudius Aelianus, born in the city of Praeneste in Latium, and hence a native speaker of Latin. He was instructed in the literary language of Atticism by the sophist Pausanias (see p. 254), and attained such perfection that he could produce a rich *oeuvre* in Greek. From a multitude of literary sources, he compiled two collections of short tales retold in his own wording. One collection contains accounts of peculiar events involving animals, and the other features reports on natural curiosities as well as anecdotes, mostly about famous characters from history. The tenor of all of these stories is moralistic. Aelian also wrote a number of fictional erotic letters, a genre that was particularly popular among the so-called sophist writers of the second century AD.

Aelian or Ailianos, as he used to call himself as a Greek writer, belongs to the end of that century, while the 'Classic' author of such letters was the slightly older Alciphron. His 124 extant epistles from farmers, fishermen, and *hetairai* contain motifs and phrases found in scenes from Attic comedy. Being of exclusively Attic origin, this genre was frequently imitated by writers of the Empire who sought specimens of pure Attic language, and found especially many expressions from everyday usage in comic dialogue. The letter had been a recognised form of prose literature since the fourth century BC, with its own set of rhetorical rules.

One of the most versatile of the so-called 'miscellanists' was Ptolemaeus of Alexandria, known by the strange epithet Chennos or 'Quail', whose life largely belongs to the late first century AD. Ptolemaeus wrote a mythological novel entitled *Sphinx*, as well as an epic in which he presented himself as an anti-Homer. From a work called *New History* dedicated to a Roman lady, the learned Byzantine Patriarch Photius made an excerpt in the ninth century AD. It contained all sorts of curiosities, such as obscure versions of myths or anecdotes.

Completely extant is a book on dreams, written by Artemidorus of Daldis in Asia Minor. This features a theory of dream interpretation, as well as a collection of reports about dreams which came true. Artemidorus' writings on palmistry and the reading of bird-flight were lost; but we may assume that like the extant book, those were also written in good Atticising style and thus declared themselves as educational rather than specialist literature. Around the same time another writer called Ailianos produced an extant military manual, describing in faultless literary style not any contemporary phenomena, but the tactics of Classic-Hellenistic Greek hoplites.

Anyone who read Classical poetry had to have a profound knowledge of Greek mythology which had long become a possession of the Romans likewise and a source of plots and motifs for Roman poets. From the mid-second century AD we have a collection of tales about supernatural transformations, stories taken from older poetry and retold in Atticist prose. The author Antonius Liberalis was presumably yet another writer whose native language was Latin. A much less carefully written mythographical manual from the same period bears the title *Bibliotheca*, and was handed down under the name of the great scholar Apollodorus of Athens from the second century BC. It contains short versions of Greek tales, mostly in that form which had been given to them by writers of Attic tragedy. Books of this kind demonstrate quite clearly that efforts were needed to maintain the public's familiarity with mythological material which kept providing the motifs for literature as well as for fine art.

The *Library* of the pseudo-Apollodorus has an exact equivalent in Latin, which dates from about the same period. This is also the work of an unknown author: his collection features short retellings of mostly Greek, but sometimes also Latin, mythical tales in their epic and dramatic versions. It was handed down under the name of Hyginus, a freed slave of the Emperor Augustus who became a distinguished grammarian.

From the end of the second century AD we have another work written in good Atticising Greek, although it also contains many allusions to older Ionic literature. This is the *Voyage through the Bosporus* by Dionysius of Byzantium. The description of coasts was the oldest form of geographical literature, dating back to the voyages of Greek sea-farers in the sixth century BC. Dionysius used this form purely as a literary convention, with a view to a readership that wanted to be entertained as well as to enlarge their general knowledge. At that time, scientific geography had for several centuries been presenting its results in entirely different forms of writing (see p. 147). Yet similar accounts of shipping routes along a coastline still existed as merely practical guides, written without any literary ambitions. I have already mentioned the *Periplus of the Red Sea* (see p. 183), describing the monsoon passage between Arabia and India, and produced about a hundred years before Dionysius' book. When Dionysius wrote his work, some people were also collecting and editing older *periploi*, like those ascribed to Scylax, a famous navigator from the sixth century BC. This book describes the coasts of all three continents known at that time,

Europe, Asia, and Libya or Africa. The extant version is based on texts that were all produced before 300 BC.

4 GREEK ENTERTAINMENT LITERATURE

Novels and short fiction

In Chapter 2 of my account, I have already dealt with the beginnings of the Classical novel. This genre became increasingly popular in the second century AD, and the boom continued in the third and fourth centuries. Judging by the extant examples, the dominant type seems to have been that represented by Chariton's novel, with a plot focusing on a couple of lovers separated at the beginning, sorely tried in long wanderings and sufferings, and finally reunited. Writings that belong to this category are the novels by Xenophon of Ephesus, of which we have an abridged version; that by Achilles Tatius and that by Iamblichus, of which we have excerpts; and finally, the one by Heliodorus, which is the latest and arguably the most valuable text in this group.

As the history of the genre progressed authors of such novels came to invent ever more fantastic events and adventures for their couples, and to choose more and more exotic settings. To make the story interesting, writers brought in accounts of suspended animation and ritual murder, torture and magic, mistaken identity and slavery, life among bands of robbers, and courtly intrigues. Achilles Tatius preferred the Egyptian milieu, while the Syrian Iamblichus, whose mother tongue was Aramaic, had a penchant for Babylonian scenery. Of course the works do to some extent reflect the authors' own everyday lives: but most references to such contemporary local reality are certainly unintentional, as, on the whole, the authors meant to transport their readers into a fantasy world. It is not easy to date their novels, for all of them are composed in literary Atticising language, with modifications that are mostly due to the varied degree of linguistic competence among the writers, and tell us little about when their books were created. The one by Heliodorus, which we may assume to be the latest known work in this category, has been placed in the third as well as in the fourth century AD by scholars who claim to have discovered allusions to historical events which happened then. I will come back to this novel in a later chapter (see p. 365).

Beside the love stories of the type described above, there were also other kinds of novels. We have a long papyrus fragment of the *Phoenician Stories* by a certain Lollianus, presumably also from the second century AD. It contains a particularly revolting scene, with an account of a killing that is clearly part of some ritual, and leads on to acts of cannibalism. Beyond that, the existing fragment does not tell us anything about the structure of the work. The *Story of an Ass* by Lucius of Patrae, a book reporting the adventures of a man who had been turned into an ass, is known to us from a long retelling of the story by Apuleius (see p. 267), and an excerpt which ended up among the works of Lucian. Of the novel about Apollonius, the King of Tyre, the only extant version is a Late Classical Latin translation (see p. 368). The story, however, contains some of the oldest novella motifs, such as a prince who falls in love with his beautiful stepmother, and a king who benefits from the wisdom of his court physician. Longus' pastoral novel *Daphnis and Chloé* became enormously popular in the literary world of the Baroque, and later Goethe also found words of praise for this book. In it, we find the traditional motifs of the lovers' separation and reunion in a much-condensed form; the space thus liberated is taken up by a lengthy account of how the two lovers are initiated into the mysteries of love, at an age when they are hardly more than children. The setting for this tale is a romanticised pastoral milieu of the type that was portrayed in bucolic poetry. The novelist's evocation of a natural-naive world, which made a deep impression on Goethe, is in fact accomplished by means of a highly artificial literary diction, and the emotions of Longus' shepherds are anything but naive.

The Alexander Romance is a category which deserves a special mention. The oldest completely extant text dates from the third century AD, and will be discussed in a later section (see p. 366). However, papyrus finds indicate that there was an earlier version of Alexander's story in the form of an epistolary novel, written for a more select kind of readership. The basic structural idea was that of a correspondence between the global conqueror and his teacher, the universal scholar Aristotle, to whom the pupil gives an account of the wonders he has seen in distant lands, particularly in India. This set-up explains the inclusion of motifs from popular philosophy: the Brahmins and Yogis were regarded as teaching that art of perfect natural living which was identical with the Cynic ideal. Hence it was only proper for the world ruler to talk to such men and to learn from them. We know that under Alexander and his successors there were indeed encounters between Greeks and Indian ascetes, whom the former called gymnosophists. These meetings were bound to be of particular interest to the Cynics who projected their ideal picture of Hercules on to the image of the ideal monarch. This is why the lore about Indian sages had such lasting repercussions in Graeco-Roman literature, even outside the context of Alexander's story. Cases in point are the abovementioned novel by Heliodorus, or the account of the travels of Apollonius of Tyana (see p. 203).

Of the Alexander Romance, we have several very different Greek versions which were written at different points during a period which reaches far into the Byzantine age. Until well into the High Middle Ages, the story was, moreover, retold again and again in Latin as well as in numerous other European and Oriental languages. The extant specimens are not copies or translations of a fixed text, but – as is common in folk literature – they present ever-new reworkings of the same traditional material.

We have only very few examples of short narrative texts from this period. The corpus of animal fables ascribed to Aesop, who is said to have lived in the sixth century BC, must have existed in constantly changing form throughout the Classical age after the fifth century BC. Poetic versions of the tales were written in Latin by Phaedrus, a freedman of Greek origin who lived in Rome under Augustus and Tiberius; and in Greek by Babrius, who came from Italy but lived in the East. The latter author presumably belongs to the second century AD. Such literary-artistic versions of old fables would sometimes give them a moral meaning which had not necessarily been present in the original. The authors thus engaged were, moreover, likely to augment the existing corpus of traditional tales by products of their own invention.

Phlegon of Tralles in Asia Minor, a freed slave of the Emperor Hadrian, produced a number of antiquarian-historical writings which I shall discuss in a later section. The same author also compiled a collection of stories about curious facts of history and the natural world, from reports which he had found in older literature. Such so-called paradoxographical writing was a fairly important branch of philosophical-scientific as well as of entertainment literature. One collection, for instance, has been handed down under the name of Aristotle. In Phlegon's book we see that the author worked with great diligence to perfect his retelling of stories about, for example, the return of people from the grave, or the birth of deformed creatures. He names his literary source in every instance and some parts of his book read like well-formed novellas.

Lucian

Taken as a whole, the many writings of Lucian constitute something like a large mirror reflecting all the facets of literary life in the second century AD. The mirror image, however, is one distorted by the uneven glass of satire.

A fairly complete chronology of the satirist Lucian can be constructed from the considerable number of autobiographical references in his numerous works. Lucian came from Samosata, modern-day Homs in Syria. An uncle first tried to teach the young man the art of sculpture but if we may believe Lucian's own account this effort had only a very limited success. Lucian then went to western Asia Minor, where he learned the Greek language. It is not known under which teacher he acquired his comprehensive knowledge of literature, and his perfect mastery of contemporary rhetorical art. In any case, his wanderings as a successful travelling orator took him to many different parts of the Empire, including Gaul and Italy. In Antioch in Syria Lucian met the Emperor Verus, then joint ruler with

Marcus Aurelius. In Athens, where Lucian seems to have stayed for a longer period of time, he became closely acquainted with the heads of the philosophical schools. Influential patrons then secured Lucian a clerical post on the staff of the Prefect of Egypt. He must have been over fifty years old when he took up this job but even so he does not seem to have stayed on until his death. One of the events which Lucian lived to witness in his old age was the death of the Emperor Marcus Aurelius in 180 AD.

With the exception of two lost works whose titles are mentioned occasionally, the extant corpus seems to include the texts of all of Lucian's published works. Besides, there are also quite a number of writings by other authors which were ascribed to him; this, however, is not always easy to determine as Lucian liked to use a great variety of different styles. But even among the definitely non-genuine pieces, there are some very interesting works, such as the aforementioned short version of the *Ass*, and a treatise on the weird cult of the Syrian goddess. The latter is not only an important source for the religious historian, but also interesting from a linguistic point of view: it is written in old Ionic as used by Herodotus, and thus documents the rise of archaistic tendencies going beyond the demands of Attic Classicism.

Lucian ridiculed each and every characteristic feature of contemporary intellectual life. In a series of short tracts such as *The Trial of the Vowels*, he derides purist hair-splitting and points out the factual misconceptions held to be true by dogmatic Atticists. Elsewhere he makes fun of the tricks of rhetorical technique, as in a set of mock instructions for the successful orator. Particularly amusing also is his *True History*, a parody on the novel of travel and adventure in which Lucian describes a voyage to the moon, found to consist of white cheese. Lucian's treatises about religious personalities of the period are complete biographies. One of them exposes Alexander of Abonuteichos, of whose role as founder of an oracle cult there is also archaeological-epigraphical evidence, as a ne'er-do-well and a liar. Lucian also lays open some compromising facts in his life of Peregrinus Proteus, a wandering philosopher and miracle-worker who had committed suicide by fire at Olympia in 165 AD during the Games which Lucian attended. The author reveals that Peregrinus temporarily joined a Christian community and deliberately got himself arrested so that he could spend some time in prison where he would live it up for some time on the good food provided in abundance by his fellow believers. A report by Gellius (see p. 265) shows that Peregrinus could also be seen in an entirely different light.

Many of Lucian's writings are styled as dialogues. Among them is the autobiographical piece *Doubly Accused*, in which the author finds himself attacked simultaneously by rhetoric and philosophy for turning his back on the one, and making fun of the other. In the form of talks between gods and dead men, Lucian mocks the implausibility of philosophical doctrines about the world, the gods, freedom, and fate; he demonstrates the absurdity of the Homeric-literary portrayal of the deities; or he denounces the superstitions cherished by ostensibly enlightened philosophers. Only the Epicureans and the Skeptics are exempted from Lucian's scathing wit, and a portrayal of the Cynic Demonax even expresses genuine respect.

One treatise by Lucian is dedicated rather ambiguously to the Platonist Nigrinus: the work presents Nigrinus' critique of contemporary culture and his glorification of the simplicity of ancient Athens, with an ironic twist that makes Nigrinus' views sound somewhat less than convincing. The style of some of Lucian's tracts resembles that of Menippean satires (see p. 99) in features such as the inclusion of poetic interludes. Others read as though they could have been performed as *mimus* pieces as, for instance, the delightful *Auction of Lifestyles* in which the founders of different philosophies are offered for sale at a slave-market. Their outward appearances mark each one of them as a caricature of what his philosophy teaches as the art of proper living. In his *Eunuch*, Lucian derides professional philosophers like those he had met in Greece, presenting them as in the main greedy, vain, and quarrelsome.

There seems to have been virtually nothing which did not qualify as a target for Lucian's satire: the only exception being the state, its institutions and officials, and above all the Emperor. We may well surmise that Lucian was purposefully avoiding any risks by avoiding the subject. The pride he took in his independence seems to have co-existed with at least a certain amount of caution, and did ultimately not prevent Lucian from accepting his appointment in the bureaucracy.

Not all of Lucian's writings are satirical or polemical. From the time when he worked as a professional orator, we have declamations and descriptions which are sometimes humorous but which lack the mocking tone of satire: one good case in point is Lucian's eulogy of the fly. When the Emperor Verus was preparing a campaign against the Parthians Lucian made a fairly disparaging remark about a spate of new history books as the dreaded result of this event; but the treatise which he himself wrote on this occasion is a very serious theoretical discussion of historiography, and thus a valuable piece of Classical literary theory.

Lucian was a versatile writer as regards form as well as content. His great erudition is proved in countless traces of the influence of comedy, tragedy, historiography, philosophical dialogue, Menippean satire, epistolography, and other literary genres. That a Syrian of lowly birth was able to acquire all this knowledge when he was already an adult, and that he managed to perfect his literary skills to such a high degree, is on the one hand certainly proof of his exceptional talent. Yet it also goes to show that in Imperial culture, the vast wealth of educational knowledge had been well systematised and made easily accessible to learners.

5 HISTORIOGRAPHERS AND ANTIQUARIANS

In the hierarchy of high prose literature historiography followed immediately after the three traditional types of eloquence and was often even classed as a part of epideictic oratory. Consequently the historiographer's task was primarily to meet a literary standard. Only a few historians such as Polybius explicitly refused to comply with this demand, claiming that attention to literary form cannot but detract from the factual precision of the account, and makes it difficult to produce convincing explanations of causal connections between individual facts. To Polybius, these two aspects of content were indispensable if historical knowledge was to have any political-moral application; and hence they had to take precedence over formal considerations. To many historians, however, perfection in form and precision in content did not seem mutually exclusive. Hence they would often engage in the most diligent study not only of literary sources, but also of archive material, monumental evidence, or chronological calculations: but they would not let the results of their scholarly research interfere with the stylistic unity of their presentation. There was a rich scholarly literature presenting the results of epigraphical, chronological, or antiquarian research, as well as of studies on genealogical traditions, or on political and religious institutions. This genre, however, remained completely separate from historiography because of its entirely non-artistic manner of presentation.

Historiographers

As is the case with other genres, a relatively large share of historiographical writings from the second century has been preserved until the present day, even if this share still constitutes only a fraction of the entire production of the period. The first writer I must mention in this context is Flavius Arrianus or Arrianos whose case is one of many examples that show a growing difficulty in maintaining a consistent distinction between Latin and Greek in the spelling of proper names from this epoch. I have already talked about Arrian as a pupil of Epictetus, and as the man to whom we owe the written records of Epictetus' teaching. He held high military and administrative posts in many different parts of the Empire, and his career finally took him as far as the Consulate. Throughout his professional life, but above all during his stay in Athens after retirement, he was busy producing a large literary *oeuvre* which is at least partly extant.

One of his works is a description of the Black Sea coasts, based on a report on military measures taken to contain belligerent tribes of horsemen in the steppes of southern Russia, an operation which was directed by Arrian himself. What is unfortunately no longer extant is a monograph about one of those Iranian tribes, the Alans. An extant short book about the breeding and the training of dogs for hunting shows the author's particular passion for that sport, and the existing parts of a manual of military tactics include reflections of his personal experiences in the army.

The bulk of Arrian's writing, however, was historiographical. Among the lost works was a detailed history of his native country Bithynia in the north-western corner of Asia Minor; of this we have only a few quotations. Likewise lost were a history of the Parthian Empire, especially of the Parthian-Roman War under Trajan, and a book about the successors of Alexander the Great. Extant is the *Anabasis*, an account of Alexander's campaign, complemented by a description of India. The latter work includes an account of the voyage of Nearchus, the admiral of the great Macedonian King, who followed the advance of the army on a parallel sea-route along the southern coast of Iran from the mouth of the Indus to that of the Euphrates.

Alexander's short life had been long enough to change the face of the world, and there were many contemporary and later biographers who wrote about him. Among them, however, there had not been a single one whose literary achievement was in any way proportionate to the impact of Alexander's conquests on global history. Even contemporary accounts, including those by men who had taken part in the campaign, were already distorted by courtly flattery, philosophical criticism of the King's character and lifestyle, political opposition from the point of view of subjugated Greece, or legendary ornamentation. It seems that neither Alexander's personality nor his deeds provided the kind of subject matter suited to the objective approach of the historian, as someone who is interested in nothing but the facts and their causal connections.

Written nearly four hundred years after the events, Arrian's book is nevertheless by far the most reliable and useful account of Alexander's history. With the keen eye of a seasoned officer and administrator, Arrian managed to select the most reliable sources and to evaluate these mainly in relation to his own experience, rather than by reference to any philosophical-anthropological, panegyrical, or araetalogical categories. Thus, for instance, he would occasionally use information taken from a document written without any literary ambitions, the personal records of Ptolemaeus, who had been a general in the campaign, and later became the first Macedonian King of Egypt as Ptolemy I. In relating those extraordinary happenings which were frequent in Alexander's life and which gave rise to a profusion of legends, Arrian also told his reader about later critical comments made by men such as the great scholar Eratosthenes from the third century BC.

Arrian's account is vivid, clearly structured, and composed in a very pure and correct kind of written Attic. However, the author abstains completely from ornamenting his language with those artistic devices of the sublime style which were used by historiographers whenever they wanted to create a strong emotional effect on the reader through linguistic pathos. Of course Arrian's selection of subject matter as well as of idiom illustrates his rootedness in the all-pervading Classicism of the period, when people would quite naturally choose to highlight an epoch from the past as a means of defining general moral and aesthetical norms. Moreover, shortly before Arrian wrote his work the conquests of Trajan had given a new topicality to the history of Alexander and his achievements.

Arrian's Classicist outlook is reflected in several different ways in his book on India, explicitly declared to be a complement to the history of Alexander. Its second part, based largely on Nearchus' report, does indeed deal with an episode from the great campaign which was particularly interesting from a geographical point of view. However, the first part with the general description of India is certainly not confined to that part of the subcontinent which Alexander conquered: the land along the Indus, the river from which the Greek name for the country was derived, and along its tributaries. Arrian's account covers the entire Ganges plain, a region that Alexander never entered. The explanation for this is that at the time the most authoritative source on India was the book by Megasthenes who shortly after Alexander's death spent many years as envoy of Seleucus I at the court of Paliputra on the Ganges plain. Like most of the many authors writing on India, Arrian chose to follow the account of Megasthenes, even if that man had never been to southern India, the area with which the strongest trade links existed during Arrian's lifetime. But the canonisation of a specific author meant that Arrian would not be guided by the knowledge gathered by those who had accompanied Alexander, and neither would he give priority to contemporary information. This backward orientation in time is also evident in the linguistic form of the book on India. The choice of Ionic, a literary idiom which preceded Classic Attic, links Arrian's book with the ethnographical parts of Herodotus' work, as well as with the writings of the ancient Ionic authors of the fifth century BC.

There is plenty of similar evidence for the rise of archaism from the reign of Hadrian onwards. Arrian's contemporary Cephalion also used the old Ionic dialect in writing a history of the Greeks up to the reign of Alexander: the limitation of subject matter to the archaic-Classic period is likewise significant in this context. Like the corresponding work by Herodotus, Cephalion's history was divided into nine books, each named after one of the nine Muses. Identical titles had been given to Herodotus' books not long before Cephalion wrote his history, and they were also used by an otherwise unknown historian called Bion, of whose work we have only a short excerpt containing facts about the history of the ancient Orient. Lucian ridiculed such fashions in his treatise *How to Write History* (see p. 240), but nevertheless fads of this kind survived well into the following century. Even the pseudo-Lucian who wrote the treatise on the strange cult of the Syrian goddess did so in the Ionic idiom of Herodotus.

Arrian's life and literary legacy document in a very impressive way how naturally members of the upper classes would combine education guided by philosophical ethics, and literary erudition, with conscientious, efficient work in public service. It was this synthesis which for centuries made the Roman Empire not only the guarantor of a legal order, but also the protector of a culture whose influence outlived the Empire itself.

Arrian's historiographical work covers a number of different sub-genres: there are national or regional histories, histories of specific periods, particularly from the recent past, and historical monographs about series of events dominated in each case by one central personality. What can be seen of the theory of Classical historiography in the works of Polybius, Cicero, and Lucian (see p. 240) indicates that writers were well aware of individual sets of rules governing each one of these forms. For each sub-genre, we know of numerous examples from the second century AD through quotations or references to authors and titles; however, only very few of the works thus identified are extant.

In regional history books dealing with exotic peoples and countries occupied a special place. Long fragments of the Phoenician history by Philo of Byblus, a contemporary of Arrian, are quoted in the work of a Christian author, who was naturally interested in the relative chronology of early Greek and Biblical-Oriental history. Philo's account of the mythological tradition of Syria and Phoenicia was earlier written off as pure invention because authors in the second and third centuries AD were often inclined to disguise their own doctrines as ancient Oriental wisdom. Nevertheless, recent research on local sources has proved that Philo did in fact know a lot about traditional lore. Among his works was also a history of the Emperor Hadrian's reign; of this, however, nothing at all has survived.

Of a very different nature is the partly extant *oeuvre* of the Alexandrian Appian who lived first in Rome as a rhetorically trained lawyer and then worked in Egypt as an official in the Imperial financial administration until around 165 AD. This appointment was secured for Appian by his friend Fronto, the tutor of the Emperor Marcus Aurelius; Appian and Fronto corresponded in the Greek language. Appian's major literary work, likewise written in Greek, was a *Roman History* in twenty-four books. Eighteen of those are extant but some of them only in the form of excerpts made by Byzantine authors. But we do have the preface to the whole work, which tells us quite a lot about the overall structure and the author's intentions.

Appian's account covers the entire history of Rome beginning with the legendary story of Aeneas. From then on, though, the main divisions follow geographical lines: all the countries around the Mediterranean are dealt with one by one, in the same order in which they came under Roman rule, generally through some kind of warfare. It is this process of military extension of the Empire which is the focus of attention in Arrian's narrative. The chosen structure frequently leads to a strange distribution of the subject matter: thus, for instance, the Punic Wars are dealt with in several different books, as their battles were fought in such diverse locations as Sicily, Africa, Spain, Gaul, and Italy. As Italy was already fully Roman at that time, the geographical aspect does not influence this part of the report about Hannibal's campaign. The last books of Appian's history were unfortunately lost; they contained a brief survey of the few conquests made by Trajan's predecessors, followed by a longer account of Trajan's exploits in Dacia, Parthia, and Arabia. The final book featured an inventory of the Empire's provinces and their revenues, corresponding to the listing of countries under Roman rule and their borders in the preface. The tenor of this enumeration is panegyrical since Appian puts the establishment of the global Empire down to the virtues of the Romans, properly highlighted by comparing their achievements with those of Assyrians, Medes, and Macedonians. Thus the author's view of history gains a certain depth. Appian himself took great personal pride in being a citizen of the global state and having attained high honours by serving its Emperor in Greek Egypt, his native country.

Appian was a literary rather than a scholarly author. This explains why his historical work consists of a mere retelling of numerous sources without any critical scrutiny of traditional lore in the light of scientific research, or in the light of his own political and military experience. Consequently the great differences in style, factual accuracy, and manner of presentation between the various parts of his history can be explained as a reflection of the difference between the sources he used. In the preface Appian tells the reader that his material included both Greek and Latin texts, and there is no reason at all to doubt this assertion. But he was writing for Greek readers who would have known very little Latin: this is indicated by the fact that Appian thought it necessary to include a short explanation of the distinctions between Greek and Latin proper names.

Of particular value to us are those books in which Appian deals with the century of the civil wars. These parts constitute the only extant complete portrayal of a period which proved to be decisive for the course of Roman history, and of which we also have much first-hand evidence in the letters and speeches of Cicero, as well as in Caesar's *Commentarii.* However, the only other extant historiographical works proper which cover the events of the civil wars are Sallust's monographs on selected short episodes. There are different theories as to what sources Appian actually drew on for this particular part of his narrative. One of them may well have been the major work by Asinius Pollio, first patron of the poet Virgil, who had maintained a certain degree of independence from Augustus throughout his life. But Appian's books on the civil wars also contain many dramatic scenes and pathetic descriptions, written with much emphasis on rhetorical devices. This would seem to indicate the use of a kind of Greek historiography in which the authors tried for the same effect as the writers of tragedy: namely, to move the reader to pity and fear. Several long passages in the famous *Roman History* by Theodor Mommsen consist of a retelling of Appian's account.

I have already talked about the short survey of Roman history from its beginnings which Florus distilled from Livy (see p. 227). Another epitome from the same author was made by Granius Licinianus. Long fragments of it were discovered on a palimpsest, a parchment manuscript on which a second layer of writing was superimposed during the Middle Ages. Roughly contemporary with Licinianus' work is another excerpt which attempted a similar kind of summary of a long and complex historical process. Around the end of the first century BC a freed slave of the Triumvir Pompey, a Gaul called Trogus Pompeius, had written a universal history in Latin. This work in forty-four books began with ancient Assyrian and Egyptian history and finished with the end of the civil wars, covering also the history of all the Oriental nations known to the Greeks and Romans. The structure of the work is documented by the extant prologues to all the books; an excerpt from it was taken by an otherwise unknown M. Junianus Justinus, who did not try to summarise the historical-geographical facts it contained, but rather picked out memorable events, sayings, or anecdotes, which he retold with only slight alterations to the original wording and in an order that followed the author's division into books. Only the transitional passages between those retellings are genuine summaries. This epitome remained greatly popular until well into the Middle Ages; the existence of more than two hundred manuscript versions explains why the original text was lost. Especially in school instruction, the emphasis was on exempla more than on facts, and as a result of this the distinction between exempla collections such as those by Valerius Maximus (see p. 65) and short versions of historiographical works became all but obliterated.

The interest in the exemplary is also evident in Polyaenus' collection of *Strategica* or *Stratagems*, dedicated to the Emperor Marcus Aurelius and his co-regent L. Verus at the outbreak of the Parthian War in 162 AD. Polyaenus was a rhetorically trained lawyer practising in Rome; his eight books feature reports on military ruses and heroic deeds, which he gathered from Greek historiographers. The work does not indicate whether its author understood Latin. In the first five books he narrates events from Greek history; Books 6 and 7 contain reports about exotic nations; and Book 8 deals with Roman history, as well as with women who played some important part in warfare. The episodes are not retold in the manner of the sources, but in Polyaenus' own style, using a diction that is plain but correct according to the rules of Atticism.

The only known Latin version of Alexander's history was presumably written around the same time. Nothing is known about the biography of the author, Q. Curtius Rufus, although his work was widely read, and consequently handed down to us in many manuscript versions. Curtius Rufus' account was based on a selection from the many existing books on Alexander. However, the author professes to have attached but little importance to historical criticism, so that occasional references to specific authorities reflect his conforming to a historical convention rather than any genuine weighing of contradictory information. The author's primary goal was to produce a richly ornate account. The speeches are particular showpieces and occasionally the report of the great Macedonian's deeds takes a novelistic form. Arrian's history of Alexander had pointed the way back to the oldest and most reliable sources in view of the fact that more and more fantastic additions had distorted the account of events which were not far short of miraculous to begin with. Though he may well have read Arrian's work, Curtius was exclusively interested in literary effect: this is why his book became extremely popular, and even influenced the tradition of the Alexander Romance. We also know the names of many other historiographers from the second century AD but most of their works exist only in the form of fragments quoted by other authors.

Antiquarians

I have already mentioned P. Aelius Phlegon of Tralles in Asia Minor as one of the so-called paradoxographers (see p. 238). He was a freed slave of the Emperor Hadrian, at whose court he presumably continued to live as a scholar. Phlegon wrote a major chronographical work which was frequently used in subsequent generations and which also had an influence on Christian chronography.

The problems of chronology were of special importance in the Classical age, because of the lack of a universally accepted way of counting the years. Each municipal community would identify a year by one or more eponymous officials; in Rome, it was the Consuls who gave their name to the year in which they held office. As every municipal community also had its own calendar with its own date for the beginning of a year, historiographers faced major difficulties in the relative dating of events. This explains, for instance, why Thucydides dated only the beginning of the Peloponnesian War according to the eponymous officials of various cities, but went on to count only the successive war years in the rest of his account without any further external points of reference, thus steering clear of possible ambiguities.

Historiographers had realised fairly early on that a consistent numbering of years was crucial to all practice of their art. In the fifth century BC chronology was based on a list that enumerated those who had won the stadium race at the four-yearly Olympic Games, going back to a fairly distant past. This list of Olympic champions was continuously re-edited and complemented by information about the important historical events of each year. Phlegon used it as a source for the sixteen books of his chronicle that covered the time up to the death of Hadrian. He added further chronological references to events from Greek and Roman history, using the products of a long tradition of scholarly chronography, in particular the works of Eratosthenes and Apollodorus from the third and second century BC respectively.

A Byzantine encyclopaedia tells us that Phlegon also wrote a description of Sicily, a book about Roman festivals, and another one on the topography of the city of Rome. This shows that antiquarian-regional research experienced an impressive second flowering in the second century AD, having seen its first heyday in the age of Hellenism when methods for the study of archive materials, inscriptions, monuments, and institutions were developed. It also underlines the fact that Rome remained an important centre of Greek intellectual life in Phlegon's lifetime.

It was the second century BC which also saw the composition of the most important document of Classical antiquarian scholarship which is completely extant: the perihegesis of Pausanias. We have very little information about the author and do not even know his place of origin. Occasional clues in his work indicate that he lived between 110 and 180 AD. In addition to his Greek homeland, he had also seen Italy, Egypt, and Syria, and he was particularly well acquainted with Asia Minor.

Pausanias' work bears the title *Journey through Greece*. Its ten books give a detailed description of landscapes and cities in mainland Greece and in some of the islands, while the Greek cities in Asia Minor are only mentioned in a digression. The account follows an itinerary from Athens to Argolis, Laconia, southern Arcadia and Messenia, then via Elis and Achaia to northern Arcadia, and finally to Boeotia and Phocis. The routes are mostly by land but sometimes also by sea, and all are detailed with great precision. At the end of his description of the Peloponnese Pausanias even gives a survey of the entire road network in that region.

The bulk of his work consists of the description of temples, shrines, tombs, and other municipal or rural buildings, so that those passages dealing with places such as Athens, Delphi, or Olympia are the most lengthy ones. The topographical and architectural observations are so detailed and accurate that they provided many archaeologists from the nineteenth century onwards with important help in choosing the sites for their excavations, and in labelling their finds. In quite a number of cases buildings or remains of statues in Olympia or the Athenian Acropolis could not have been correctly identified at all if it had not been for information given by Pausanias. He also made it possible to come up with fairly exact recreations of lost works of art, such as Phidias' statue of Zeus in Olympia, or the famous chest of the tyrant Cypselus of Corinth, an object whose relief carvings and inscriptions Pausanias describes down to the smallest detail.

Apart from pure description, however, Pausanias' work contains a large number of historical or mythological accounts concerning the places, buildings, tombs, or religious sites he is dealing with. In many cases he tells the reader the exact wording of inscriptions which documented the consecration of a site, and thus gives valuable clues to historians. Especially because so many poetical and historical works were lost, Pausanias' perihegesis stands as a first-rate historical source which has saved from oblivion a large number of facts concerning the history of religion, politics, and mythology.

It goes without saying that Pausanias' work is part of a time-honoured genre tradition. In archaic times a favourite form for geographical reports had been the periplus, the description of a sea-voyage along a coast, with corresponding information about the hinterland. In the post-Classic age this method was applied to the description of regions which were of particular interest to readers, as being the settings for mythical or historical events. The most famous author of such perihegeses was Polemon of Ilium who worked in Alexandria around 200 BC. He wrote four books about the Acropolis of Athens alone; he also produced numerous descriptions of different regions, and he was a systematic collector of inscriptions. There were also many specialist treatises about cults, festivals or temples. This has led some scholars to assume that Pausanias' perihegesis was not the fruit of his own travels but was concocted at a desk with the help of a good library. What is certain is that Pausanias did use a fair number of literary sources, especially for his long reports on history and mythology, which were definitely not based only on information gathered on site. But his countless precise descriptions of topography can only be accounted for as the result of the author's own keen perception. The same goes also for what Pausanias wrote about his travels in other countries. As readers, however, he seems to have envisaged people with a literary education, interested in books rather than in travelling, and thus his perihegesis is no Classical prototype of a Baedeker. Still, we may assume that the interest of the reading public in such a book does indicate the existence of a certain amount of tourism within the Greek heartland.

Greece at that time did not really have any major economic importance for the Roman Empire. With regard to wealth, productivity, population, and density of traffic, the country could not compare with Anatolia, Egypt, or Spain. But Athens was still the centre of philosophical studies which it had been, and the great festivals of Olympia or Delphi attracted pilgrims, spectators, and professional sportsmen from all over the known world. Hence many foreigners got to see that country of whose contribution to their own civilisation and values at least all educated individuals had a very clear idea.

Consequently Pausanias could expect his readers to share his reverence for the glory of ancient Greece. His writing shows a marked awareness of the distinction between Classic and post-Classic Hellas, and only the former is an object of admiration and a source of inspiration for his affectionate descriptions of historic sites, as well as for his detailed accounts of historical and mythological traditions. Nevertheless, Pausanias proves an astute critical sense in the selection and evaluation of his sources, being always ready to incorporate contemporary information as well. Therefore, for instance, he is the first Classical author who expresses a correct notion about how the imported Chinese silk was made. That material had been known then for about two hundred years but the method of its production was initially a total mystery to Europeans who only came to know about it after Alexandrian merchants had travelled to China.

Pausanias was no art historian in the narrower sense of the term, although his precise descriptions of ancient works of art express his appreciation and his antiquarian-historical interest as well as his admiration for the people who created those objects. But he never talks about aesthetics or the theory of art, topics which we find, for example, in the relevant chapters of Pliny the Elder's *Natural History*. But on the whole, Pausanias' perihegesis is an invaluable document in several different respects: to the archaeologist because of the many clues as to the sites of ancient monuments; to the historian because of the many otherwise undocumented pieces of traditional lore; and to the literary historian as evidence of a Classicism without which the knowledge of the greatest period in Greek history, and of the works of art that were created at that time, would most probably have vanished for ever.

6 GRAMMAR AND RHETORIC

For a long time, the relationship between grammar and rhetoric had been of a different nature in East and West respectively. In the East instruction in exemplary forms of language and style could be limited to the imitation of works from a rich prose literature, without any need to refer to grammatical theory. In the West, which at first lacked a comparable canon, the distinction between good and bad use of Latin could then only be made with the help of theoretical points of reference. This situation changed during the Imperial age. As Atticism came to prevail at all levels of writing, people who wanted to master the Attic idiom of the past had to rely more and more on the results of grammatical studies of ancient texts. And on the Latin side, as the period of the Ciceronian-Augustan Classics became increasingly distant, their works were also subjected to grammatical interpretation. Ultimately instruction in rhetoric, which aimed to teach the mastery of Classic linguistic norms, could no longer ignore the scholarly efforts of grammarians to make Classic texts accessible to contemporary readers. Thus the state of affairs in East and West began to look increasingly similar.

Greek grammarians

The so-called scholia commentaries, which accompany many texts of Classic poetry or prose in Byzantine manuscripts, have preserved explanatory remarks from different epochs of the Classical age. Sometimes they also cite the names of the authors who provided such explanations, and thus we know of several Greek grammarians or philologists from the second century AD who were engaged in interpretative or editorial work. Such activities had been going on without any serious disruption ever since the heyday of Alexandrian scholarship in the third and second centuries BC.

In the High Empire, however, literary interpretation and scholarly editing produced fewer remarkable achievements than descriptive grammar and linguistic theory. The man who must be mentioned first of all the exponents of those latter disciplines is Apollonius of Alexandria, also known as Dyskolos or 'Grumpy'. He worked in Rome as well as in his native city, and produced a large number of writings. We know of more than twenty titles; the extant texts are monographs on pronouns, adverbs, and conjunctions, as well as the four books of a major treatise on syntax. Among the lost works were studies of individual Greek dialects which were no longer spoken at the time but still used in literature. Apollonius' work continued a long tradition of research on grammar and linguistic theory: this had arisen from philosophical reflections on language, but then led to the constitution of a strictly systematic discipline with its own methods for dealing with a vast amount of evidence, partly literary, but partly also from oral usage. Within this branch of scholarship there were naturally also different schools with diverging opinions, for example, as to how far a grammatical paradigm can be said to set norms for the system of a language, and consequently, as to whether correct usage is to be judged by empirical evidence, or by analogies in word formation or inflexion. The scientific discipline dealing with such issues had largely detached itself from older philosophical theories of language and their central concern, the relationship between signifier and signified.

A more influential scholar than Apollonius was his son Herodianus, whose *oeuvre* had a considerable impact on Late Classical grammar. Herodian taught first in Alexandria, and later in Rome. His major work, extant in Byzantine editions and excerpts, was dedicated to the Emperor Marcus Aurelius; its twenty books give a comprehensive account of the accentual and the quantitative system in the Greek language. This was a very topical issue at the time, when that major linguistic change whose results can be perceived in Modern Greek was well under way.

Old Greek had known a clear distinction between long and short syllables or vowels; a syllable was emphasised by raising the pitch and not by increasing air pressure in the vocal channel, as done in German or English. This is why ancient Greek metrics differed from its German or English equivalent in regulating only the succession of short and long syllables, without any regard to word stress. From the second century AD onwards, however, papyri and inscriptions tend to feature occasional spelling mistakes and irregularities in scansion, a fact which proves that authors or speakers were no longer instinctively aware of the short/long distinction, and that the musical emphasis was turning into a respiratory or dynamic one. Of course this process went on gradually over several centuries; but it appears that in the fourth century AD the situation was already such that the quantitative distinctions which characterised ancient Greek verse could only be recognised in writing, and no longer be aurally perceived when a poem was recited. Consequently the systematic distinction between high, low, and shifting accents lost its meaning, as the only difference in pronunciation came to be a dynamic one between stressed and unstressed syllables.

Herodian's comprehensive study on accent thus perpetuated a system which was on the brink of disappearing from the spoken language. His work provided the basis for the Byzantine convention of adding a mark for one of the three accents to each written word, even if such indicators no longer had any influence on pronunciation. Virtually at the last moment Herodian had thus defined the 'proper' accentuation according to the original pronunciation in Old Greek. Formerly, nobody had perceived any need to indicate the accents in writing, except in literary texts using dialects whose accentual patterns deviated from the general norm as, for example, the form of Aeolic spoken on the island of Lesbos. The regular marking of accents in all written texts was introduced only when people had become aware of the difference between the old and new pronunciations, and sought to retain the knowledge of the former in writing.

Herodian divided his nineteen books on accent according to word classes: that is to say he dealt separately with the accentuation of nouns, verbs, and other word groups. The last book was about the special case of the so-called dichrona. While with the letters omega/omicron, epsilon/ēta, and the diphthongs, the long/short distinction was evident from the written characters, the letters alpha, iota and upsilon could represent either long or short vowels. Consequently special rules were needed here for a correct definition of those quantitative values which were no longer audible in contemporary spoken Greek so that one could avoid errors in the writing or the reciting of poetry, and occasionally also in accentuation.

Beside his *General Prosody*, Herodian produced many other specialist treatises on subjects such as orthography, defective verbs, or the prosody of Homeric language. All our information about those works comes from Late Classical and Byzantine grammarians who used them. The only extant original text is a treatise on words which have an exceptional status in Greek because of their composition or inflexion.

The changes in the living language over the centuries also gave added weight to another branch of grammatical scholarship. This was the study of metrics, especially of the complex metres found in ancient poetry and in the chorus songs from Classic-Attic drama, whose form reflected the airs to which the words were sung. A form of musical notation had been known ever since the Classic period, but none the less only very few of the melodies that went with great archaic and Classic poetry survived until post-Classic times. One reason for this was that the final epoch of the Classic period had seen a fundamental change in the technique of musical composition, and consequently also of musical taste. Hence most of the old airs were forgotten, and the scholars of the Hellenistic age already encountered exactly the same problems with the metres of ancient lyrics which modern-day philologists have to contend with. Parallel to the aforementioned change the characteristic metres of ancient lyrics, which were always sung, likewise became divorced from their musical contexts in the age of Hellenism; their transfer to spoken poetry involved a strict standardisation. It is exactly the same transformation which we find applied to Latin lyrics in Horace's odes.

The scholia commentaries handed down to us alongside Pindar's poems reflect the considerable efforts which grammarians of the Hellenistic and the Imperial ages made at identifying and analysing ancient metres. With the original musical design lost, those scholars would tend to split a poem into lines, identify the dominant structure of the verse, and catalogue all possible variations. From such material they would construct metrical systems in which the complex forms were seen as derived from simpler ones, and hence the entire art of versification appeared to be based on a small number of archetypes.

The only extant manual describing such a system comes from the grammarian Hephaestion of Alexandria, who is said to have taught the Emperor Verus, Marcus Aurelius' co-regent. Hephaestion's manual is an abridged version, presumably produced by the author himself, of a work that originally consisted of forty-eight books. The short version was widely used in schools, and it is the source of almost all that terminology which we still use today in talking about Classical metres. It has also been the means of preserving exemplary quotations from many poems otherwise lost. Moreover, the extant text contains a number of additions which are definitely not from the author's own hand, and whose inclusion appears as a result of the frequent use of the book in Byzantine schools.

The sheer bulk of Greek literature, together with the large number of dialects and specialist jargons that appeared in writing, posed various considerable problems for a post-Classic reader. To begin with, his own vocabulary would amount to no more than a mere fraction of that used in the vast amount of existing literary works in Greek. This made access to lexicographical information a particularly important precondition for the study of ancient texts, and consequently the relevant branch of grammatical scholarship kept turning out ever-new compilations until well into the Byzantine era.

In the first century AD a medical practitioner and grammarian called Erotian wrote a dictionary dedicated to the Emperor Nero's court physician. This book contained the vocabulary of the Hippocratic writings which were particularly difficult to read on account of the old-fashioned Ionic idiom they used, as well as because of the many technical-medical expressions featured. Likewise from the first century AD is the Homeric dictionary by Apollonius Sophistes. In the second century AD, around the time of Hadrian's reign, Diogenianus of Heraclea on the Black Sea compiled a dictionary of the Greek language in five books; this work was based on the much more comprehensive dictionary by Zopyrion and Pamphilus. Diogenianus' dictionary was meant to help readers of Classic poetry and prose, and not to reflect contemporary spoken Greek. Being user-friendly and concise, this work remained in vogue until well into the Byzantine era and provided the lexicographical foundation for the largest and most valuable Classical dictionary extant, which Hesychius of Alexandria wrote in the sixth century AD. A common feature of all the dictionaries I have named here is that they list their words in alphabetical order, just like their modern counterparts. The main difference between them lies in the extent to which – if at all – the authors cite exemplary evidence for their semantic descriptions.

The dictionaries I have listed so far were meant as aids for readers and students of literature; but there were also others designed to help people write correct literary Attic. Those works also incorporated the results of grammatical scholarship, as shown in the extant fragments of the dictionaries by Aelius Dionysius and by Pausanias. The latter is not identical with the author of the perihegesis.

The grammarian Phrynichus, whom Byzantine authors call either an Arab or a Bithynian, wrote a *Selection of Attic Verbs and Nouns* in which he juxtaposed the correct word forms or idioms found in Classic Attic sources with corresponding vernacular expressions not permitted in writing. Phrynichus was extremely rigid in his judgment, which shows him as one opposed to a different trend evident in second-century grammar; for example, in a dictionary by an anonymous author known only by the name of Antiatticistes. What he tried to show was that many of the words and word forms scorned by strict Atticists could in fact be found in the good Attic of the Classics. His examples are largely taken from a collection published by the great Alexandrian philologist Aristophanes of Byzantium around 200 BC, long before the stylistic programme of Atticism took shape.

The great orators of the fifth and fourth centuries BC were generally regarded as providing the best examples of pure Attic. The Alexandrian grammarians had canonised ten of them and had produced critical editions of their speeches. For this canon, the grammarian Harpocration wrote a lexicographical aid, listing linguistic facts as well as other background information to facilitate the reading of the stylistic model texts.

Yet another type of dictionary is represented by the major work by Polydeukes, known as Pollux in Latin and English, who dedicated his book to the Emperor Commodus. The author came from the ancient Greek city of Naucratis in the Nile Delta. He applied for the professorship in Athens which was endowed with an Imperial salary, and he was appointed in preference to Phrynichus. Pollux compiled a large Attic vocabulary in ten books divided according to different semantic fields. His sources were mainly existing lexicographical works, but also excerpts made by himself. His dictionary has become a valuable source for the cultural historian since it lists words appertaining to such fields as medicine, agriculture, or children's games, and it also includes plenty of synonyms. In featuring even very marginal topics and disciplines Pollux found himself compelled to violate the strict rules of Atticism, as in many instances he could not avoid the inclusion of dialect words. This became a major issue in the controversy between him and the much more dogmatic Phrynichus.

The most primitive among the extant Atticist dictionaries was written by an otherwise unknown Moiris at the very end of the second century AD. Its vocabulary is compiled exclusively from other dictionaries, with no more than a simple juxtaposition of Attic and vernacular expressions. Moiris grouped them alphabetically, but he did not take into account any more letters than the first one of each word.

Greek rhetoric

The Atticist dictionaries mark an area of overlap between rhetoric as the theory and didactics of good, high linguistic usage, and grammar as what we would call linguistics and literary studies. The most common form of the rhetorical-didactic treatise which gave a survey of the system of linguistic art was the *ars rhetorica*, or *technē rhetorikē*. Within the group so designated the individual writings were, however, often very different in terms of structure. Among the works of Dionysius of Halicarnassus we have a didactic treatise from the second century AD which begins with some remarks about the different types of epideictic eloquence, such as funeral speeches or eulogies. This part is followed by two long essays on rhetorical figures, with most of the examples taken from poetry, in particular that of Homer and Euripides. As the reading of poetry in rhetorical instruction was mainly intended to help the development of stylistic skills, rhetorical categories could be used freely in all kinds of literary criticism. The last two chapters in this work deal with mistakes which must be avoided in the writing and the delivery of any non-improvised speeches, as well as with stylistic categories and stylistic judgment.

The genuine author of this *technē rhetorikē* is not known, nor is there any real justification for linking him with the man who was arguably the most famous teacher of rhetoric in the early second century AD, Alexander, the son of Numenius. Alexander ingratiated himself to the Emperor Hadrian by writing a speech of condolence for him after Hadrian's favourite Antinous had drowned in the Nile. From the author's many works, we have only one short treatise on figures of thought and speech, a work that shows Alexander's great didactic skill.

A definite step forward in the development of rhetorical theory in the second century AD was made by the introduction of the so-called doctrine of ideas which is most commonly associated with the name of Hermogenes of Tarsus. This man lived well into the next century and while he seems to have exerted only a moderate amount of influence initially he came to be held in very high esteem from the fourth and fifth centuries AD onwards. His works, especially the treatise on ideas, were then widely read, copied, and enlarged, and became the subject of several commentaries. An anonymous rhetorical treatise handed down under the name of Aristides features a draft of the doctrine of ideas which seems to be a development of the model put forward by Hermogenes.

The categorisation and the qualitative assessment of style is undoubtedly one of the most difficult tasks in literary criticism since it involves the ordering of largely subjective impressions according to objective criteria. Ancient rhetoric, to some extent even before Aristotle, had developed different theories distinguishing between two, three, or four stylistic levels. Among those models the tripartite division into sublime, middle, and plain style emerged as the most popular one. There was also a theory which named four principal virtues of linguistic expression, a model which was canonised by Aristotle's disciple Theophrastus and occasionally enlarged later. The theory of the four *aretai* or *virtutes* – purity of diction, clarity, aptness, and decorum – had one major disadvantage. This is evident in the fact that its advocates frequently failed to clarify whether their categories referred only to the form of a text, as did the theory of stylistic levels, or whether they included the aspect of content, the report or message itself, by introducing such criteria as clarity or intelligibility. Any consideration of content was of course bound to make the exact definition of stylistic features as such a very difficult task.

Dionysius of Halicarnassus, the influential rhetor and literary critic who lived during the reign of Augustus, had already tried to solve this problem by introducing his own set of 'virtues of the report'. Moreover, Dionysius had brought a greater amount of differentiation to the theory of the virtues of expression, by combining it with the theory of stylistic levels, and applying it to selected texts by Classic orators. This procedure allowed him to come up with much more subtle categorical distinctions for the description of style.

The most recent studies in this still largely unexplored field have shown quite clearly that Hermogenes was a direct successor to Dionysius. But in addition to what he borrowed from his predecessor, Hermogenes also adopted the terminology of literary theory which had been developed in philosophical schools, particularly the Peripatos and the Stoa. By linking the terms from different systems in ever-new permutations, he arrived at a number of seven stylistic qualities, some of them with subdivisions, which he called ideas or forms, and which he tried to define as precisely as possible by selecting examples from the rich corpus of Classic oratory. In the process, he maintained a clear distinction between purely formal criteria and aspects that involved the progress of the argument. Nevertheless, Hermogenes acknowledged that both form and content had to be taken into account in the discussion of any given text. The labels he gave to the ideas were often metaphorical, such as sweetness, bitterness, roundness, or swelling. But in spite of these flowery names, his theory of ideas permits a quite exceptional degree of exactness in the definition of stylistic peculiarities.

The aforementioned treatise by Ps. Aristides lists twelve different ideas and also introduces some new terms; it does not, however, surpass the precision of Hermogenes' system. Some of the works ascribed to the latter were certainly not written by him, but such use of his name shows his unchallenged position of authority in the Late Classical and the Byzantine age. A genuine work by Hermogenes is the treatise on the so-called theory of *stasis* or status, belonging to a branch of rhetorical theory that dealt with finding the right categories for a legal case before writing a plea, so as to find the appropriate arguments and to put them in the correct order. In this work Hermogenes takes a very traditionalist stance, adopting with only minor changes the system of Hermagoras of Temnos, which had been widely accepted since the age of Hellenism, and which Cicero had also followed in his *De inventione*.

Latin rhetoric

Hermogenes' literary legacy is a very vivid illustration of a key feature of Imperial culture. His writings reflect the great amount of intellectual energy, and indeed of original thought, which was invested in an education that aimed exclusively at the refinement of linguistic performance, and of literary taste. That the didactic methods used in such education were miles away from practical reality was a fact already recognised and criticised by a significant number of Hermogenes' contemporaries. This remoteness from everyday life can be seen fairly clearly in, for instance, the extant Latin declamations from that period. One such corpus of fictitious legal and political speeches from the second century AD has been handed down to us under the name of the older author Quintilian. We also have a collection of declamations by C. Calpurnius Flaccus, whose choice of subject matter shows a particularly strong penchant for the bizarre. In spite of all valid criticism, however, the prominence of the declamation in rhetorical instruction remained undiminished throughout the Imperial age, in West and East alike.

Latin grammarians

As in the East, there was a second flowering of grammatical scholarship also in the Latin West of the second century AD. During the reign of Hadrian, the grammarian Velius Longus produced a number of works of which only a treatise on Latin orthography is extant, while a commentary on Virgil, a treatise on the distinctive features of Old Latin, and another one on adjectives derived from proper names were lost. Longus' choice of topics shows the close parallels between Greek and Latin grammatical studies of the period.

The most famous grammarian in the first half of the second century AD was Q. Terentius Scaurus. His *Ars grammatica* was widely quoted, but finally came to be superseded by Late Classical surveys of Latin grammar. Scaurus also wrote a tract on orthography. This work is partly extant, while a commentary on Horace was lost like some other treatises, including one dealing exclusively with the misconceptions held by his colleague Caesellius. Apparently slightly younger than Scaurus was Sex. Pompeius Festus, who published an excerpt in twenty books of Verrius Flaccus' gigantic opus *De verborum significatu* (see p. 43). This work contains a wealth of information about the vocabulary of older Latin texts, explained with reference to the history of language and culture as well as to antiquarian, mythological, and literary facts. We have about 40 per cent of Festus' excerpt, which came to replace the original; as for the rest, we rely on the excerpt which Paul Diaconus made in turn from Festus' excerpt in the ninth century AD. Like the comparable works by Florus and Justinus, Festus' epitome illustrates that among the educated classes of the Empire, there was a considerable demand for short compendia providing easy access to an already vast knowledge which was growing vaster and vaster with the steady progress of scholarship. That the existence of their compendia often doomed the original works to oblivion was a side-effect certainly not intended by the authors.

The most interesting personality among the scholars of the second century AD was undoubtedly C. Suetonius Tranquillus from the Roman civic colony of Hippo Regius in modern-day Tunisia, a man whose biography is fairly well documented. Suetonius was the son of an officer, and thus of equestrian rank; he received a rhetorical education in Rome, and afterwards worked there as a lawyer. He found an influential patron in the Younger Pliny who helped Suetonius invest his modest fortune in a rural estate, and who persuaded the Emperor Trajan to grant him the *ius trium liberorum*, the set of privileges which the law reserved for the fathers of three children. From an inscription in Suetonius' native city we know that he was employed in the central Imperial administration under Trajan, holding the successive offices of *a studiis* and *a bibliothecis*. Hadrian even appointed Suetonius to the important office of *ab epistulis* which involved the responsibility for dispatching the Emperor's rescripts in response to enquiries from the provinces. According to the *Historia Augusta* Suetonius was finally dismissed because of a *faux pas* which offended the Empress and he died in Rome as a private scholar. Still, his biography indicates that for many years he had free access to the Imperial libraries and archives, and this was presumably what enabled him to produce a quite astonishing amount of scholarly writings.

In Greek, Suetonius wrote books on children's games, Roman festivals, and critical symbols used in scholarly editions of older texts. He likewise wrote about Cicero, about swear words, words for shoes and items of clothing, about Roman customs, and about the genealogies of famous Romans, including the Emperors from Caesar to Domitian. Fragments from these writings have been preserved in the form of quotations in the works of other authors, and those quotations show that beside his antiquarian preoccupation, Suetonius was above all interested in aspects of language. What we know of his work moreover documents the fact that educated people in the East, who mostly spoke very little Latin or none at all, wanted to be informed about that Roman world to which they felt they belonged. A substantial part of Plutarch's Roman writings also deals with subjects fairly similar to those chosen by Suetonius.

Most of Suetonius' *oeuvre*, however, was written in Latin. The first work I must mention here is the *Prata*, literally translated as *Meadows*. Titles of this kind were commonly given in the Greek and Latin literature of this time to unsystematic collections of varied content: other examples are *Carpets*, *Tapestries*, or *Building Materials*. The existing fragments indicate that the *Prata* were structured like a dictionary, with an alphabetical listing of linguistic or historical-antiquarian explanations of word forms, words, or idioms. Suetonius' main source of information were the writings of Remmius Palaemon from the previous century.

Parts of another major Latin work by Suetonius have been preserved in several different ways. *De viris illustribus* was a collection of short biographies of famous Romans; its individual sections dealt separately with orators, grammarians, philosophers, poets, and other groups of distinguished intellectuals. Suetonius' intention was not to produce literary accounts of lives and characters, but to provide precise biographical and bibliographical data. Instead of going for literary effect, he aimed for accuracy and completeness: and that he lived up to this goal is proved by the fully extant parts from the books about rhetors and grammarians, where we find a vast amount of very detailed and often also very interesting facts concerning their lives and achievements. Numerous isolated pieces of information from Suetonius' work have been preserved by the church father Hieronymus, who found Suetonius' exact datings a great help in the writing of his own world chronicle. Similar use of Suetonius' work was made by authors of Late Classical commentaries on Latin poets, and in short biographies that introduced the editions of individual poetical *oeuvres*.

The most influential work by Suetonius, however, was one that seems to have had no precedent in older literature. In spite of its complete chronological coverage, his collection of lives of the emperors from Caesar to Domitian is unique in being neither historiography nor biography as defined by Plutarch. For historiography, the *res gestae*, the political-military events, are mentioned far too briefly, if at all. Caesar's war in Gaul, for instance, is summed up in half a sentence, and there is not a single word about the glorious campaigns of Nero's distinguished general, Corbulo. But neither are Suetonius' lives biographies of the Plutarchian kind, for although Suetonius includes a wealth of detail about the lifestyles and the characters of the emperors, he does not do so only for the one purpose which Plutarch had in mind: to create a unified image of a life that had formed or developed a moral personality, with all its good and bad sides. But beyond this negative definition, it is hard to say what did motivate Suetonius to record such a mass of facts. His entirely artless and tiresome style makes it even more difficult to assess his intention; and the preface, which might have enlightened contemporary readers about it, was unfortunately lost.

In spite of major differences in the respective amount of detail included, all the chapters about individual emperors follow more or less the same plan. Facts related to family background, birth, education, and the years prior to accession to the throne are narrated in strictly chronological order. The same goes for information about the last days of the monarch's life, his death, and his funeral. The account in between, as far as it concerns the Emperor himself, is largely divided according to different topics, such as jurisdiction, public building, dietary habits, famous sayings, or travels. A further division is introduced where the reign of a monarch clearly divides into different periods, because of a radical change in individual behaviour and governmental practice as, for example, during the reign of Tiberius or Nero. But besides giving plenty of information about the Emperors' comportment in private and public life – including, of course, also plenty of gossip – Suetonius' Imperial lives also feature many facts that are of interest to the social or economic historian. Thus he talks about innovations in the capital's circuses, the significance of public building, or customs observed in the awarding of military decorations, as well as about aspects of literary and religious life.

It is true that such information is frequently connected with the Emperor's person, for Suetonius tends to focus on innovations introduced by the monarch himself. But what he proceeds to tell the reader in such cases goes much farther than a merely biographical interest would have warranted, and provides insights into many different features of political and social life in Rome as well as in the provinces. In many different ways Suetonius shows that he wants to know and tell what life was really like under the different emperors; and it is as a description of situations rather than events that his *Caesares* are a fully valid historical source. Thus Suetonius appears to belong to that tradition of scholarly literature which had been distinct from historiography ever since the early writings about Attic political institutions. With his works on Roman religion, institutions, manners, and customs, the learned Varro had been the first representative of this genre in Rome.

From this point of view, Suetonius' detailed account and his excellent documentation of facts make him appear as a worthy representative of a tradition which today we would probably subsume under the heading of cultural history. The only novel element which Suetonius introduced to this tradition was that he presented the results of his research in the form of Imperial biographies. His books about grammarians, rhetors, or poets, written with similar diligence and with a similar abstention from literary-stylistic elaboration, certainly also contain much information whose relevance goes beyond the purely biographical. But the life of an emperor had quite simply a greater impact on the world than that of a poet, and any facts belonging in the context of an Imperial biography would actually concern the public as well as the private lives of all the individuals over whom this monarch ruled. Consequently any chronological series of Imperial lives would quite naturally turn into a history of the Empire, or into at least a mirror of successive stages in the development of Imperial society. The events, the *res gestae*, required a presentation according to more rigid formal conventions, and hence remained the property of literary historiography.

I have already mentioned that Tacitus, the author who showed the greatest keenness to continue the high art of literary historiography, complained that the Empire did not supply him with adequate material for doing so (see p. 220). What he identified as the only subject matter left for historians is exactly that which Suetonius actually features in the *Caesares*. In this context, it is of no importance that Tacitus' works frequently give the lie to his own assertion: but this assertion does explain why

Suetonius' *Caesares* soon came to be regarded as historiography. In the third century AD Suetonius was held up as a model author for a new literary genre in which history was now deliberately and explicitly written as the history of the Emperors, their behaviour, their achievements, and their sufferings. Such a development was a logical consequence of the fact which Tacitus had observed, and which was certainly recognised by the general public too: that since the reign of Augustus each and every event depended on the monarch alone. But the traditional sublime historiography still had its advocates, and from the fourth century AD we hear of a quarrel between them and those who championed the new kind of historical writing, focusing on the Emperor alone. In this quarrel the latter party referred to Suetonius in their claim to greater factual accuracy, if not to better style.

This shows that Suetonius enjoyed a lasting reputation as a great scholar, which he undoubtedly was. However, there is good reason to assume that he had no intention at all of becoming the founder of a whole new tradition in historiography, a genre whose way of describing an entire epoch through one person's biography is still a popular method today. But the *Caesares* did show others how biography could be used as a vehicle of historiography, even if their author certainly never meant his work to be historiographical in the sense of that tradition with which he was familiar. This assumption is borne out by one seemingly insignificant detail, in which Suetonius' work deviates from a time-honoured historiographical convention which is still valid today. Writers of historiography who cover a period that includes their own lifetime usually feature a growing amount of detail as their chronological account progresses. With Suetonius the opposite is the case: his most detailed biographies are those of the early emperors, while the Flavian monarchs, who had reigned not too long before Suetonius produced his *Caesares*, do not receive any more space than just a few pages. Finally, it must also be said that Suetonius' literary talent would quite obviously not have sufficed to meet the high literary demands of the traditional historiographical genre.

Latin archaism

As befits an antiquarian, Suetonius preferred the past to the present. His portrayal of the Emperor Augustus clearly depicts this monarch as exemplary, and that is exactly how Augustus was to be generally perceived during the following centuries, being placed alongside Trajan, the first 'good' exponent of a reformed monarchy, and a ruler who had once again enlarged the Empire. Tacitus' writings prove that especially among the metropolitan aristocracy, there were still admirers of the discipline, the simplicity, and the glory of ancient Rome. But any thinking person had to realise that the transition to monarchy was irreversible, and that there was a need to locate valid ideals within that order. If finally the reign of Augustus was chosen as a political model, this corresponded to the tenets of literary Classicism. Around the turn of the first and the second centuries AD, the Classicist view with its emphasis on Augustan-Ciceronian models had come to dominate literary tastes, and there is good visual evidence of the fact that parallel developments also took place in the fine arts.

When Classicism triumphed, however, learned grammarians had for a long time also been studying the language and literature of ancient Rome, and had made them accessible to the understanding of an educated readership. I have already mentioned such efforts several times (see, e.g., p. 258). In a situation where all literary production in any case consisted of the competitive imitation – the *imitatio* or *aemulatio* – of canonised models, it was only logical to go back beyond the Augustan-Ciceronian period, to Old Latin literature. This must have seemed even more natural to people who kept reading the Ciceronian-Augustan Classics, and thus found themselves involved in the perpetual recreation of a romantic image of ancient Roman grandeur. A further factor which favoured the growth of archaism was that the technique of imitation used in the training of rhetors or authors made them potentially capable of adopting virtually any kind of style.

A tradition of archaism, that is of conscious imitation of pre-Classic language, did already exist in historiography. It dated back to Sallust who used the language of Cato the Elder with its peculiar roughness as a vehicle for his scathing critique of the political-moral degeneracy of his own epoch. Moreover, above all in its presentation of exemplary characters and events from ages past, Roman historiography had always had a certain linguistic affinity with high poetic art, and particularly with the epic, in whose range of expressions archaic words and word forms were firmly established. Several instances of this can be found in Livy's account of early Roman history, even if on the whole this author tended to use the much more limited vocabulary of Cicero and his contemporaries. One of Seneca's letters ridicules L. Arruntius, an author who like Sallust wrote a historical work in the language and style of Cato the Elder, from 200 BC; and in his particular attempt to do justice to the grandiose and sublime manner of traditional historiography, Tacitus created a very subtle mixture of archaic, poetic, and modernistic elements, likewise with explicit reference to Sallust.

Around the middle of the second century AD archaism also began to infect other genres of literary prose; and this development was yet another one that took place simultaneously in East and West. However, on the Greek side we have no texts which explain the rhetorical-literary theory behind the use of ancient Ionic, such as in Arrian's book on India. The programme of Latin archaism, however, can be reconstructed from the lengthy extant parts of the works of two eminent teachers of rhetoric.

One of them was M. Cornelius Fronto, born in Cirta in modern-day

Algeria. After a sound philosophical and rhetorical education, he became the most famous lawyer and rhetorical instructor in the capital during the final years of Hadrian's reign. His reputation was reason enough for Hadrian's successor Antoninus Pius to make Fronto the tutor of his adopted sons and designated successors, the later Emperor Marcus Aurelius and his co-regent L. Verus. Although Marcus Aurelius disappointed his teacher by turning from rhetoric to philosophy, the friendship between the two men endured. In 143 AD Fronto held the Consulate, together with Herodes Atticus, the most eminent figure among the Greek sophists. After Fronto's death in 175 AD, the Emperor honoured him with the erection of a statue.

Nothing at all is extant of Fronto's speeches which included, for instance, legal orations as well as addresses thanking the Emperor on behalf of municipal communities. This seems particularly regrettable in view of the praise heaped upon Fronto's oratory in plenty of historiographical and grammatical writings. However, at least many of his letters were discovered in the nineteenth century on a palimpsest, that is a codex with the original text deleted, and a second one superimposed. Most of the epistles are addressed to the Emperors or princes Antoninus Pius, Marcus Aurelius, and L. Verus, and contain communications of a personal-private nature. The same goes for some letters to Fronto from Marcus Aurelius, which have been preserved with those that went in the opposite direction. Some of Fronto's epistles, especially those to Antoninus Pius and to members of the metropolitan aristocracy, deal with public affairs, and contain such messages as recommendations for the appointment of officials.

Such letters are mainly of interest to the social historian, as giving some insights into the life of a man who was highly esteemed but also very touchy, and who had a marked sense of his own importance. Moreover, these epistles illustrate the nature of social life among the élite of the capital. More significant from the point of view of literary history are those of Fronto's letters which should rather be called epistolary treatises. Among them we have genuine declamations, such as *The Praise of Dust and Smoke*, an example of the choice of highly bizarre topics in order to demonstrate all one's skills in argumentation and persuasion. There are also essays on the theory of historiography, discussions of different aspects of literary style, and a eulogy of Verus, a draft introduction to a historical work covering Verus' Parthian campaign. From these largely didactic letters, we can distil something like a full programme of archaism: Plautus and Cato are the sources for the most apt expressions, while Cicero is of very limited use as a model, and the modernist Seneca of no use at all. Among all the authors of the Augustan-Ciceronian period, Sallust stands out because of his borrowings from Old Latin.

In the long history of philosophy's and rhetoric's struggle for primacy in education, Fronto occupies a very special position. The second century

AD saw plenty of attempts to effect a reconciliation between the two educational forces; this is documented, for example, in the writings of Dion of Prusa or Maximus of Tyre. Fronto, however, was totally against philosophy. His key argument was mainly directed at the Stoics: he claimed that by being far too problem-conscious any philosopher was bound to get caught up in progressively more fruitless questions and would thus lose the ability to express himself clearly.

Some of Fronto's epistles are in Greek: they include a love letter that should be read as a declamation or rhetorical exercise, as well as two epistles to the Empress, and an entire correspondence between Fronto and the historian Appian, whom Fronto had recommended for a post in the administration of Egypt. These letters prove that Fronto's preference for archaism had no effect on his use of Greek.

While the extant Latin works of Fronto illuminate the programmatic side of archaism, the *Attic Nights* by his contemporary A. Gellius illustrate the educational background for such a return to pre-Classic roots. Gellius was presumably born in the city of Rome, where he received his grammatical and rhetorical education in both Latin and Greek. In talking about this, Gellius expresses particular admiration for Favorinus (see p. 230). Of Gellius' role in public life we know nothing more than that he was a Roman civil law judge. This meant that he would be called upon by the Praetor to preside over the second stage of a case between private individuals, after the first stage of court proceedings had clarified the legal position, but not yet assessed the factual justification for both parties' claims. We may assume that the social prestige going with this position was very high indeed.

At the age of thirty Gellius spent a year in Athens where he came into contact with philosophers such as the Platonic Calvisius Taurus or the Cynic Peregrinus Proteus who died in 165 AD. Gellius also met sophists or rhetors such as the famous Herodes Atticus. It is his Athenian experiences to which Gellius refers in his title *Attic Nights*.

The twenty books of this work, all extant apart from Book 8, are a collection of short treatises on very different subjects, pieces variously styled as dialogues, didactic tracts, or commentaries on specific quotations. The topics range from religion to antiquarian matters, grammar, and rhetoric. Many discussions of problems and suggested solutions are clearly taken from older Latin and Greek literature, although the sources are not always acknowledged. The *Attic Nights* contain a wealth of facts and quotes from largely lost texts, including original works by poets, philosophers, historiographers, or lawyers, but also from the rich scholarly literature produced by grammarians. Gellius' collection also demonstrates how educated people of the period handled the mass of knowledge that was accessible to them. Gellius tried to find a simple, but nevertheless linguistically appealing form for each one of his treatises, and thus went against the convention according to which the results of grammatical scholarship were to be presented in an artless manner. Gellius' texts are recognisably the fruit of scholarly research on literary sources; but still the author includes references to his own student days and to discussions in which he had participated, to such an extent that we may also take his *Attic Nights* as evidence of the manner of oral communication between educated people of the period.

Like Fronto, Gellius admired the past. He preserved countless fragments of Old Latin literature as well as of legal documents, drawing partly on his own reading of the original sources, and partly on his study of grammatical treatises that were lost afterwards. Because of the vast amount of information featured, Gellius' work was widely read, summarised, and used as a source by scholars of the Late Classical age.

7 APULEIUS OF MADAURA

Apuleius, whose full name is not known, came from the Numidian city of Madaura in modern-day Algeria. He received his schooling and further education in Carthage, the major centre of Roman north Africa, during the years around 140 AD. Later Apuleius spent some years in Athens and on extensive travels, which according to the author himself depleted his inherited fortune considerably. Apuleius then worked in Rome as a lawyer, but after a short while he seems to have returned to north Africa, where he first lived in the minor city of Oea and then in Carthage. He did not hold any administrative office there, but he did join the provincial priesthood of the Imperial cult. Thus his birth as well as his rank mark Apuleius as a member of the municipal aristocracy; visible evidence of his fame is a statue which the city of Carthage erected in his honour.

Apuleius is the only writer of the second century AD whose forensic eloquence is documented well enough to permit an individual assessment. In Oea Apuleius had married a rich widow; this match gave rise to accusations of sorcery, for rumour had it that he had used magic in winning the wealthy lady's favour. His speech in his own defence was published after the trial, and can still be read in a complete form. The plea demonstrates the author's brilliant wit and logic, and it also gives us many clues about judicial practice in a provincial city of the period. Moreover, Apuleius' defence reflects the great importance that people of that epoch attached to magic, a fact that is also underlined by the occasional appearance of the occult in the letters of Pliny the Younger.

More evidence of Apuleius' oratorical powers is to be found in the collection *Florida* or *Garland*, which is a selection of twenty-three particularly impressive passages from his declamations and epideictic speeches. The latter category includes the oration in which he thanked the city of Carthage for the statue with which he had been honoured, as well as an address about the use of philosophy, likewise delivered before an audience in Carthage.

The philosophy of Plato was the topic which the rhetor Apuleius loved best. Three major extant works by Apuleius deal with philosophical issues, in a manner that would have appealed to a lay public with high literary standards. In his treatise *De genio Socratis* we find an outline of Platonic doctrine about the gods. The tract *De mundo* is a Latin version of the pseudo-Aristotelian treatise on the universe, a work which was about a hundred years old at that time, and which had already been ascribed to either Aristotle or Theophrastus. The tract *De Platone et eius dogmate* contains a systematic but easily comprehensible survey of official Academic doctrine as it was recognised in Apuleius' lifetime; this work is thus an important source for the history of philosophy. Of its three books mentioned in the preface, however, the only extant texts are the one on ethics and the one on physics, or the doctrine of nature. In the manuscript tradition, Apuleius' book on logic or dialectics came to be replaced by a work that was written much later.

That Apuleius was no original philosopher is manifest in the total absence of any independent reflections on philosophical issues from his writings. Nevertheless, the author made a very sincere attempt to acquire a philosophically based world view, and to communicate it to others. Subsequent generations showed their appreciation of his efforts by ascribing to him a number of semi-philosophical works. But strangely enough, especially when one considers his successful defence against the accusation of sorcery, Apuleius also acquired the reputation of a miracle-worker and magician of the kind represented by Apollonius of Tyana. The enemies of Christianity even held up Apuleius as a counter-example to Jesus and his miracles.

Apuleius' most important literary work is the *Metamorphoses*, a version in eleven books of the Greek *Story of the Ass*, of which we have extracts in the work of Lucian as well as in the *Bibliothek* by the Patriarch Photius. In his account Apuleius pads out the adventures of poor Lucius, the protagonist who was turned into an ass by a witch, with new episodes of his own creation. The volume of the tale is further inflated by the embedding of entire self-contained narratives such as the famous tale of Amor and Psyche, as well as of other stories about ghosts and robbers, and several erotic anecdotes. On top of this, the author adds a new edifying ending to the plot. In Apuleius' version, the ass regains human shape after an intervention by the Egyptian goddess Isis, who gives instructions as to how a retransformation can be effected during her festival. Thereafter Lucius is to lead his life in accordance with the rules of religious and moral purity, to which he is bound after his initiation to the mysteries of the goddess. Through this ending, Book 11 of the *Metamorphoses* has become one of the few extant documents reflecting the kind of piety that was associated with the mystery cults of the Empire. We know quite a lot about the practices of those secret religions but only very little about the ideas of the people who followed them.

From the perspective established by the last book of the novel, the adventures and wanderings of the hero, as one deprived of his human existence, appear as portraying the trials and errors each man has to undergo until he is blessed with divine grace. In Apuleius' version, a spiritual interpretation is likewise suggested by the embedded allegorical tale of Amor and Psyche, a story which has inspired countless painters and sculptors. But for us modern-day readers, it is hard to reconcile the idea that the author intended such a message, with the material which forms the bulk of Apuleius' narrative. What we find here is a mixture of burlesque and horror, of obscenities and realistic scenes from everyday life: and very often the only recognisable aim of the author seems to make his readers laugh at the vices, the nastiness, the weakness, and the stupidity of human beings, as perceived by a maltreated ass.

However, what cannot be denied is Apuleius' virtuosity in finding the proper and apt linguistic expression for each one of the very different situations and moods through which the novel moves. The author's stylistic canvas is broad, with a differentiation of shades and colours almost as rich as that produced by Petronius. However, there is one fundamental difference between Petronius and Apuleius in that the latter never uses more than just an occasional word from the many levels of non-literary spoken Latin. In spite of his large stylistic scope and his many fine nuances, Apuleius remains entirely within the traditional framework of written usage.

As far as we know, Apuleius was the first author who managed to achieve lasting fame as a major prose writer by working almost exclusively in a provincial environment. To him, Rome was no more than a station that he passed through, and that did not leave much of a mark on his education or his literary career. All of the other Spaniards, Gauls, or Africans whom I have so far mentioned as prose authors made the grade in the capital. In view of this, it has been suggested that the exceptional linguistic variety and versatility which characterises not only the *Metamorphoses* but also Apuleius' other writings may be due to the very fact that he did not work in Rome; and efforts have even been made to find traces of a specifically African form of Latinness in his work. This seems all the more apt because many of the leading writers of Latin prose literature after Apuleius also lived and worked in Africa: but still, I do not think that the hypothesis is justified. There were indeed regional variants of spoken Latin in the second century AD, mainly among the uneducated people, but those variants did not exert any influence on literary usage until much later when the foundations for different national literatures in the Romance languages were laid. The educational system of the Empire, a system based on the imitation of literary models, preserved the unity of traditional literary language in spite of the vastness of the Latin world. We should also remember that in their long years of service, all high and subaltern functionaries in administration and army would get to see large parts of the Empire, and this bureaucratic apparatus, which had to conduct a great deal of its business in writing, was another factor vital to the long-lived unity of the Latin language.

However, what Apuleius' stylistic versatility may very well be taken to document is the fact that rhetorical training encouraged the most talented people in particular to master a range of different styles and to choose from them as the situation required. Under the conditions given in the Empire, we must put a big question mark behind the assertion that linguistic style is invariably an expression of the writer's personality, as claimed by Buffon, and long before him by Seneca. In his penchant for literary role-playing, Apuleius seems to be an especially typical representative of Imperial Latin prose.

8 GREEK AND LATIN POETRY

No more really great poetry was written in the Empire during the second and third centuries AD, in spite of the fact that more poems than ever before seem to have been turned out on the Greek as well as on the Latin side. Countless consecrational and funeral epigrams have been preserved on stone in the East as well as in the West, and frequently these texts show a quite astonishing degree of mastery of metre and poetic diction. From Pliny's letters and Tacitus' *Dialogus*, we know that many educated people would compose Greek or Latin tragedies, and bore their friends with play readings. On Egyptian papyri, we have at least many fragments of second-century poetry. There are parts of didactic poems and poetic encomia in hexameters; many religious hymns in hexameters or anapaests; and short hexametrical or elegiac poems of a convivial nature, to be recited at banquets, with a flute accompaniment. There are also parts of mythological epics about topics such as the god Dionysus and his wanderings through the world of men, or legendary stories concerning the foundation of famous cities. Such papyri also give us a fairly good idea of the poems produced by the sophist Aristides, which are occasionally mentioned in his extant other writings.

Some poetry from the second century AD is also featured in mediaeval manuscripts. Among this, there is a didactic poem by Dionysius in the traditional format of the periplus (see p. 235), a very elegantly written description of the earth, which gives us valuable information about the history of geography. In the first half of the century the physician Marcellus of Side wrote a major didactic poem about the animals, plants, and minerals used in the production of drugs; from this work, the section on fishes is extant. Didactic poems on fishing, hunting, and hunted animals were written by two poets both called Oppian, one of whom was a contemporary of the Emperor Marcus Aurelius, while the other belonged to the following generation. The older author was a skilled versifier, while the younger one seems to have had problems with traditional epic diction.

The epic written by Nestor of Laranda in Asia Minor must have been quite a curiosity. It was a retelling of the *Iliad* in twenty-four books like the original; in each of those books in turn, one successive letter of the alphabet was absent. Rather more interesting than this work are the surviving pieces of Orphic poetry from the second to the fourth century AD. The Orphic sect, which taught a semi-philosophical, semi-mythological cosmology as well as a doctrine about the transmigration of souls, experienced a second flowering in the Empire. From Orphic circles, we have a collection of hymns to the gods, a didactic poem on the magical powers of certain stones, and an epic retelling of the story of the Argonauts, interpreted according to Orphic doctrine. For a long time, these poems were counted among the oldest pieces of Orphic tradition, until the great philologist Gottfried Hermann, a friend of Goethe's, proved through metrical analysis that they were written a lot later than had been assumed.

Lyrical poetry was also still being written. A *hymnus* on Rome, a text written in the Sapphic metre but in the dialect of ancient chorus lyrics, was accidentally preserved in the great *Florilegium* compiled by John Stobaeus, Bishop of Stoboi in modern-day Bulgaria, a man who lived in the fifth century AD. The poem was presumably written for the festival of Roma, a goddess worshipped in many eastern cities.

From the reign of Hadrian, we have the collection of lyrical poems by Mesomedes, who even recorded some of their melodies in an easily decipherable musical notation. Incidentally, some of the hymns preserved on papyrus have a musical notation as well, albeit in a different system. Mesomedes' poems are in stichic, radically simplified versions of old lyric metres. The collection features hymns to different gods, as well as descriptions of objects such as a water clock or a sponge. There are humorous verses about a mosquito or a swan which are comparable to rhetorical school declamations, but also to similar showpieces in Hellenistic poetry.

I have already mentioned the survival of epigrammatic poetry well into the Byzantine age (see p. 123). The same goes for the production of short poems in the anacreontic metre. A collection handed down to us together with the epigrams of the *Anthologia Palatina* contains pieces dating from the second to the sixth or seventh century AD. In these poems the versification is of very varied quality, and the same can be said with regard to poetic originality. The content is similarly diverse, ranging from erotic and sympotic jests to philosophical reflections. This poetry was frequently imitated in later European literature, above all in the eighteenth century.

Finally, I must also mention the poetic evidence which reflects the changing pronunciation and accentuation of the Greek languages. Most of this poetry is of the more popular kind, and of not too high a literary standard. Its distinctive features are the regular distribution of word accents to certain fixed syllables within the verse, and the replacement of long syllables prescribed by the metre with short syllables which carry a word accent. This phenomenon occurs more and more frequently in texts dating from the late second century AD onwards, such as the poetic fables by Babrius, the verse interludes of the Alexander Romance, some of Lucian's writings, and above all popular songs preserved on papyri. It is significant that in the transition to a new metrics where rhythm was created by a regular spacing of word accents, the Christians were the pioneers (see p. 570). Traditional Classic versification survived well into the Byzantine age, although its rhythms could then only be perceived in writing, or, because normal pronunciation no longer distinguished between short and long syllables (see p. 252), be realised in a scanning that stressed the long syllables of the verse regardless of the distribution of word accents.

On the Latin side things look slightly different. For a start, we lack the evidence of 'everyday poetry' which we find in the Greek papyri. Moreover, the West saw yet another attempt to put poetry on a new basis, while in the East the poetic tradition was neither enriched nor modified.

The last major exponent of that specifically Roman genre, satire, lived around 100 AD. D. Junius Juvenalis came from Campania, and as we can infer from an allusion in a poem by his friend Martial, he worked as a rhetor. Juvenal's poems initially met with very little interest, which explains why information about his life is scarce and inconclusive. His sixteen long satires belong to the tradition represented by Horace and Persius, and were presumably written during the reigns of Trajan and Hadrian. They contain extremely crude invective against the vices of urban Roman society, and they quite obviously try to evoke an image of what life was like under the previous Emperor Domitian.

Whereas Horace had treated the faults and weaknesses of his fellow humans with good-natured irony, Juvenal followed the example of Persius by preaching morality with all the pathos of righteous indignation, denouncing social vices which he was all the same ready to describe in great detail. But unlike Persius, Juvenal avoided the kind of artificial diction which was unintelligible to any but those with a literary education. As Horace had done, he incorporated a good deal of non-poetic vocabulary in his satires. Juvenal's zealous pathos, which differs radically from the light conversational tone of Horatian satire, is created through his graphic description of vices, and particularly also through the use of tropes and other rhetorical figures.

Juvenal's writings are of limited value as sources for the cultural historian, for they contain too much that seems to belong to the conventional moralistic topoi of popular philosophy. However, the author does express the spirit of the epoch in borrowing the positive counter-images for his scathing indictments from the idealised picture of Republican Rome. Roman Classicism commonly referred to this era in its historical vision, while it sought its few literary models in the Ciceronian-Augustan period. The curious fact that Juvenal's satires were extremely popular in the Late Classical age and in the Middle Ages may be due to their apparent confirmation of the view that Imperial Rome was in a state of moral decay prior to Christianisation. It is because of this interest that we have so many manuscripts of Juvenal's satires, with detailed commentaries on selected passages.

In the reign of Hadrian, there was a poetic movement whose followers called themselves *poetae novelli* or Moderns, a name which proclaimed a link with the Neoterics of Caesar's times, and thus indirectly with Hellenistic poetry. The Moderns preferred polished short forms; they produced pointed, witty poems written as verse epistles and salutary addresses, as humorous and mocking comments, but also as expressions of serious reflections. The Emperor counted himself among the members of this group, and in the *Historia augusta*, a Late Classical history, we find the results of some of the monarch's poetic efforts. One anacreontic poem is an answer to a text written in the same metre by a certain Annius Florus, who had expressed pity for the Emperor as a man who was always busy with something or other. The author of that piece is presumably identical with the historiographer who wrote the epitome from Livy.

Through the Late Classical grammarian Charisius, we know also of a correspondence between Hadrian and Florus. The *Codex Salmasianus*, one of the mediaeval manuscripts featuring short poems of various origin (see p. 595), includes some under Florus' name. These texts, written in hexameters and trochaic tetrameters, give us a fairly good idea of Modern poetry from the second century AD. Written in iambic dimeters are the verses of a certain Alfius Avitus, lines quoted by grammarians from the second to the fifth century AD either as examples of this rare metre, or because of the peculiarities in their diction. They belong to poems narrating events from early Roman history, on the basis of Livy's account: a very extraordinary context for the use of such a metre, which may well indicate that the *poetae novelli* were prone to formal experiments.

The most attractive piece of Latin poetry from the second century AD is undoubtedly the *Pervigilium Veneris*, a work frequently ascribed to Florus. It consists of ninety-five iambic trimeters, with a recurring refrain that establishes a quasi-stanzaic pattern, with subsections of different lengths. The imaginary setting is on the eve of a Venus festival, when the verses are sung during a procession. They begin with the praise of spring, the season in which people celebrate the festival of the goddess of love; then the poem looks forward to the euphoric mood of the celebration itself. This is followed by a praise of the goddess, whose power is reflected in nature as well as in Roman history, beginning with her son Aeneas, the forefather of the first Imperial dynasty. The ending is a departure from the joyful mood which pervades the rest of the poem, with the poetic speaker now lamenting the waning of his artistic inspiration.

This poem is a minor masterpiece in its description of the anticipated joy of the festival, but also in its effortless linking of images of the coming celebration with an entire Venus theology, and its political-patriotic implications. The six lines in which the goddess herself sums up Roman history have been read as a deliberate allusion to personalities and events from the third, fourth, and fifth centuries AD. This is most certainly incorrect, for the poem was most probably written during the reign of Hadrian, when in 128 AD the big temple of the Forum Romanum was built and consecrated to both Venus and Roma. The text does, however, contain allusions to passages from Augustan poetry, and was undoubtedly meant for an educated audience which was familiar with its Classics.

9 PHILOSOPHY

It was in the second century that philosophy arguably had its widest impact ever, even if there were only a few original thinkers among the many professional philosophers. Philosophy itself and its exponents were held in high esteem, and received official support. Since the reign of Hadrian a growing number of philosophers in the four major Athens schools had been getting state salaries, as did some professors of rhetoric. Like physicians, sophists and grammarians, they also enjoyed considerable tax privileges (see p. 7). The old debate as to whether rhetoric or philosophy should have the monopoly in higher, tertiary education was no longer conducted with the same fierceness as before. Many people would study both, and among literary authors we find plenty of rhetors with an interest in philosophy, or philosophers who took an interest in rhetoric (see p. 228). Much more problematic was the relationship between philosophy and the sciences. Natural science as an independent discipline serving only the accumulation of knowledge had no place at all in that hierarchy of intellectual activities which was taught by philosophy: its only right to exist was as a preparation for philosophical studies concerned with the art of living.

Aristotle had maintained that all sciences which in any way made parts of reality accessible to rational understanding belonged to philosophy. During the age of Hellenism, therefore, the exponents of all scientific disciplines were given the title of philosopher, and the many scholars working at the Alexandrian Museum had retained this official appellation well into the Imperial age. But with the establishment of fixed dogmas in the major philosophical schools of Hellenism, philosophy had ultimately become that specialised discipline which studied the art of proper living.

As this art was to be founded on a rationally intelligible, and hence scientifically founded view of man and the world, scientific disciplines provided valuable help to philosophy, which in turn supplied them with ideas, with questions, and with terminological categories. Hence quite a few innovative scientists were also ardent and trained followers of some philosophical school. But all philosophers, and not only the Cynics and Epicureans who rejected any kind of science, agreed that scientific research could not be an end in itself, and that the human search for knowledge needed a moral justification. The only intellectual activity which possessed such a justification intrinsically was the one directed at the art of living.

Throughout the centuries, there were nevertheless always individuals who found meaning as well as satisfaction in a life dedicated to one of the sciences. Those men often tried to define their work as philosophising, or to establish at least a close link with philosophy. Thus Strabo would describe geography as part of philosophy, and Galen defined the physician as a philosopher on account of an exact structural parallel which he saw in the two disciplines. Mathematicians and astronomers showed the least hesitation in claiming the name of philosophy for their sciences, referring to Plato's dictum that geometry was the one discipline which came nearest to the immaterial primal forms of the world. These many attempts to claim philosophical status for science, and thus to define the latter as providing a meaningful goal for human life, are probably the best possible proof of the high prestige which philosophy enjoyed at the time. Where the claim that science was philosophy could not be backed with sufficiently convincing arguments, scholars at least sought to establish a philosophical basis for their science as, for instance, Heron did in his systematic introduction to mechanics.

School traditions

Among the school traditions in the second century AD, the dominant one was that of the Academy. The second century AD saw the dogmatic completion of so-called Middle Platonism, which had been emerging since the first century BC. We know its system from summaries in catechistic form featured in the biographical work by Diogenes Laertius (see p. 324), in the writings of Apuleius (see p. 266), and in the introductory treatise by Albinus. It is only of the latter author, who taught in Smyrna around the middle of the century, that we have complete treatises from the Platonic school of the second century AD. Beside his aforementioned *Didaskalikos*, there is also a *Prologos*, an introduction to the study of Plato. We may assume that the essential parts of the doctrine Albinus expounds stem from his teacher Gaius, a philosopher of a much greater calibre than himself, whose systematic treatises and commentaries on Plato were frequently quoted by Neo-Platonists of the fourth and fifth centuries AD.

There were some differences of opinion between Platonic philosophers of the second century AD, even if they all shared the aim of formulating a doctrine which was based on an authentic interpretation of the school founder's writings. In this effort, they would also use the methods and terminology developed by other schools. Aristotelian logic was adopted *en bloc*, as well as the Stoic classification of the emotions. On the other hand, though, the Stoic ideal of apathy or freedom from affection was rejected, because Platonic philosophy supported the Aristotelian view that the irrational parts of the human soul had a value of their own. Nevertheless, Platonic dogmatics also incorporated the Stoic opinion that the unity of virtue lay in the indissoluble synthesis of all individual virtues.

With the help of the Stoic doctrine of the *heimarmenē*, that is, of providence and predestination, Middle Platonists interpreted a doctrine which Plato had expressed in the form of a myth: it implied that as a rational being man was always free to choose between right and wrong, but that humans still remained irrevocably bound to the consequences of their actions. In Middle Platonism, this general tenet resulted in the specific doctrine of a providence that works on different levels. Middle Platonists held that the dichotomy between freedom and necessity did not exist in the purely rational order of immaterial being. However, in the relative disorder of the sensual world with its mixture of the spiritual and the material, free choices of men would often have irrational consequences, and thus divine retaliation was necessary to restore universal order.

The core of Middle Platonic doctrine was theology, which also defined the goal of moral living as 'assimilation to God'. The deity was seen as pure, active spirit, having brought the world into being by forming it from matter, after immaterial primal images which it carries within itself as ideas. Man's task is to draw near to the deity by the constant exercise of his capability for rational cognition. In his lifestyle, man should thus minimise the influence of his material nature, so that the immaterial part of his soul may rise to a higher plane of existence in the next life.

The doctrine of the transmigration of souls also played an important part in the Platonic system. But a still more important issue was the nature of the Supreme Being, the one that gives the world form, life, and consciousness, and that man can approach through reason. There was a major problem here, for the Platonic pyramid image of the hierarchy of being in the world was based on a time-honoured postulate by Parmenides who had said that all being must be thinkable, and hence only that which can be thought is part of being. But if the Supreme Being is transcendental in the sense that as the source of all being it is higher than all being, can it still be understood by thinking, by the exercising of reason? This was a question which occupied the followers of Plato right through to the end of the Classical age.

The Platonic and the Aristotelian schools were closely linked by a common axiom which the Stoics and Epicureans rejected, namely that the world must be explained by means of the distinction between spiritual and material. The consensus between the school of Plato and that of Aristotle could be widened by using the Aristotelian doctrine of potentiality and actuality as levels of being, to interpret the Platonic tenet that matter as such has no being at all. In the Aristotelian reading, matter thus appears as pure potentiality, a possibility turned into a reality only through the power of the spirit. This and other links between Platonic and Aristotelian ideas were perceived as so fundamental that most Middle Platonists would not acknowledge the existence of any basic contradiction between Plato and Aristotle.

This view, however, was not entirely unopposed within the Platonic school, as we can see in the writings of Atticus, a Platonic philosopher from the second half of the century. Extant fragments of his work show that he combated specific Aristotelian doctrines above all with theological arguments. Thus Atticus claimed that the Peripatetic explanation of the world was marred by the omission of divine providence; and he denied the Aristotelian axiom that anything created must also perish, referring to Plato's dictum that the benevolence of the universal God could give eternal being even to something created. We know of similar anti-Aristotelian polemics by the Platonic Nicostratus. His contemporary Severus, on the other hand, wrote a much-quoted *Timaeus* commentary in which he tried to prove that there was even wider agreement between Plato and Aristotle in previously unacknowledged areas. A case in point was the Platonic concept of the parts of the soul, which Severus interpreted according to the Aristotelian doctrine of the soul's powers.

A considerable knowledge of the history of philosophy was of course needed to make such multiple connections between individual philosophical doctrines of different origin. This knowledge was gathered and handed down in a special genre of philosophical literature known as doxography (see p. 76). In the second century AD an otherwise unknown Aëtius wrote a work of this kind which came to be used with particular frequency. His book *Philosophers' Opinions in their Teachings on Nature* was based on earlier sources; excerpts from Aetius' tract were preserved among the writings of Plutarch, and in the works of later Christian authors. In the second half of the second century AD the physician Galen used it in the writing of his own history of philosophy.

About other Platonic philosophers from the second century AD we have no more than occasional pieces of information. There was, for instance, Calvisius Taurus, the head of the Athenian Academy, and the teacher of Gellius (see p. 231); or Nigrinus, a man highly esteemed by Lucian, as one who tried to combine Platonic philosophy with a Cynic lifestyle. More evidence concerning the school of Plato exists in anonymous treatises discovered on papyrus scrolls, such as a commentary on Plato's *Theaetetus*.

Its author, who was a pupil of Gaius, makes a very interesting attempt to construct a Platonic doctrine of virtue by means of the Stoic notion of *oikeiōsis*, that is, of man's coming to terms with his own human nature. The Middle Platonist doctrine of fate is the subject of an entire treatise preserved among the works of Plutarch. Handed down under Plato's name was a collection of definitions for philosophical terms, a motley mixture of Academic, Stoic, and Peripatetic elements which shows the syncretistic character of Middle Platonist philosophy.

I will deal with the flowering of Pythagorism and its influence on the Platonic school at length in a later section (see p. 281). It is evident already from Plato's own writings that one of the important affinities between Platonic and Pythagorean philosophy was their common regard for mathematics. To the Platonic, mathematics made non-material phenomena visible, and thus prepared him for dialectics, which in turn provided access to the highest level of pure spiritual being, detached from every sensual perception. This explains the words above the entrance to the Academy in Athens, an inscription which allegedly barred all those from entering who knew nothing of geometry.

In keeping with the Platonic programme, the mathematician Theon of Smyrna wrote a manual which gives a systematic survey of the mathematical disciplines geometry, arithmetic, musical theory, and astronomy, with the explicit intention of preparing the reader for the study of Plato's philosophy. Theon seems to have lived in the first half of the second century AD according to the known mathematical works which he does or does not quote. Other authors occasionally mention two lost treatises by Theon on Plato; a fact which proves that this mathematician may equally well be classed as a philosopher.

Some second-century commentaries, such as the partly extant one by Aspasius on Aristotle's *Nicomachean Ethics*, come from the Peripatetic school. Adrastus of Aphrodisias wrote commentaries on works by Aristotle and Theophrastus, as well as on Plato's *Timaeus*; Herminus commented on Plato's writings on logic, and Aristotle's on physics. Aristocles of Messene, who like Herminus taught Alexander of Aphrodisias, the most famous Peripatetic of the Imperial age, wrote a history of philosophy in ten books, frequently used and quoted by later generations. All these facts document the continued interest in scientific-philosophical research, an interest that was especially marked in the Peripatos.

From the inner circle of the Stoic school, there are no extant writings from the second century AD; but we do have such textual evidence from the school of Epicurus, although its reputation had declined in the Imperial age. None the less, the school survived with Athens as its centre, and for some time it even found the favour of the Empress Plotina. But in general Epicurean philosophy attracted few followers in the Empire, and this was mainly because of its doctrine concerning the gods. People were becoming more and more religious, and hence less sympathetic to a philosophy which saw the gods as beings leading a blissful life in a world apart, not rewarding or punishing men, but quite simply paying no heed at all to human beings. Hence the followers of Epicurus were often branded as godless men, and this indictment was more serious than the unwarranted accusation of extreme hedonism.

Presumably in the late second century AD a certain Diogenes commissioned an inscription in the minor city of Oenoanda in Anatolia, with a message advertising Epicurus' doctrine of salvation to his fellow citizens as a means of eliminating the fear of the gods, as well as the fear of dying. Most of this inscription has been preserved; it explains Epicurean doctrine very accurately, and in great detail. The text even contains polemical references to the opinions of other philosophies, such as the doctrine of fate and the theory of language taught by the Stoics, or Democritus' doctrine of the atoms, which differed from the Epicurean tenets on the same subject. The author of the inscription was evidently a philosopher with a sound education and an up-to-date knowledge of current debate, and one who believed that his readership had a genuine interest in real school philosophy.

Another Epicurean who appears to belong to the second century AD is Diogenianus, who wrote a treatise criticising the Stoic doctrine of fate, and the resulting vindication of mantics and astrology. The Christian Eusebius quotes large parts of this tract: for while Christians were inclined to join in with the general polemics against the 'godless' Epicureans, they were still quite ready to use Epicurean texts in their search for arguments against traditional religion or astrology.

The dominance of the Platonic school in the extant writings is not coincidental: it bears witness to the fact that Platonism became the dominant type of philosophy in the second century AD, if not earlier. Likewise, it may also be more than a coincidence that a Platonic philosopher called Celsus wrote the first pamphlet that was a serious attack on the new Christian religion. I will deal with his polemics in a later chapter on Christian literature; in this context, however, I can already divulge that Celsus saw himself as advocating a doctrine that was explicitly in agreement with the global civilisation protected by the Roman Empire. His main accusation against the Christians was that their religion undermined the political and moral foundations of the civilised world.

Philosophical literature outside the schools

I have already discussed Cynic philosophy as a school of thought which propounded no elaborate system, but contented itself with giving practical guidance for proper living (see p. 78); and I have also mentioned the links between Cynicism and certain literary genres. Cynics could be found throughout the second century AD, and one of them, Oenomaus of Gadara in Syria, seems to have been a prolific writer. He published works on the Cynic lifestyle and on Homer as the father of philosophy, but like Crates, the founder of the Cynic tradition in the fourth century BC, Oenomaus also wrote tragedies. These were presumably of a parodistic-satirical nature, denouncing the follies of men. As in the aforementioned case of Diogenianus, it is the Christian Eusebius who quotes at length from Oenomaus' work.

Close to the school of Plato were two philosophically orientated authors who wrote treatises on different aspects of practical living, but without really discussing any of the finer points of school philosophy. Of Juncus' tract on old age, a longer passage is featured in the so-called *Florilegium* by John Stobaeus, a collection which I have cited before. Completely extant are the edifying speeches or sermons by Maximus of Tyre in Phoenicia. Maximus deals with issues such as the goal of philosophy, friendship, prayer, the worship of idols, or poetic and philosophical views of the divine. Other topics include the use of science, the moral significance of physical and mental illness, or the question of whether it is permissible or not to retaliate for injustice suffered. All these subjects are dealt with from the point of view of Middle Platonist teachings, but without any detailed reference to internal school discussion. Maximus' diction is relatively plain, but the speeches are written with great attention to style, and in a language which indicates that the author had a sound philosophical education. It is hard to say whether they were originally meant to be delivered before an audience or read in private; but to us, that would constitute a far greater difference than to Maximus' contemporaries, who would mostly read aloud anyway.

The treatises of Hierocles, once mentioned by Gellius as a contemporary (see p. 265), were written from a Stoic point of view, and in an artless language. The aforementioned John Stobaeus has preserved large parts of a major work in which Hierocles gives moral instructions, dealing in separate chapters with the different kinds of duties which a man has towards his parents, his spouse, his fatherland, or his friends. A papyrus find has also brought to light fragments of a systematic introduction to the basic tenets of Stoic ethics.

There is no other Classical text which illustrates the impact of philosophy on the individual and on public life as vividly as the book which the Emperor Marcus Aurelius entitled *To Himself*, and presumably never intended for publication. The monarch recorded these reflections at different times, separated by long intervals, during the years 172 to 180 AD which were a time of great unrest within and without the Empire. Some notes were taken in camp, during the hard-fought defensive war against Quadi and Marcomanni invaders. Marcus Aurelius had received a thorough rhetorical education as a pupil of the famous Fronto, with whom he formed a lifelong friendship. In 146 AD, fifteen years prior to his accession to the throne, the future Emperor became a convert to Stoic philosophy, to which he remained faithful until his death. In a long letter preserved among Fronto's correspondence (see p. 264), Marcus Aurelius explains the reason for his apostasy to his deeply disappointed teacher.

The so-called *Meditations* give us a good impression of those philosophical convictions which gave the Emperor inner strength through most of his life. The work is written in an entirely artless Greek; however, it is not a diary, but rather a written record of a series of meditations, in which the author recalls again and again the fundamental doctrines and insights of his philosophy. Book 1 is an exception in that it evokes the memory of all those people to whom the Emperor feels indebted: parents, teachers, tutors, and friends are mentioned, with specific reference to what Marcus Aurelius learned from each of them. The philosophical reflections as such begin with Book 2; they are unsystematic, recalling individual doctrines more often than not in connection with an impression from everyday life, or a passing thought.

The kind of Stoicism represented by the Emperor was actually already out of fashion at that time. He does not mention those questions which contemporary philosophers were most concerned with, about transcendency, the immortality of the soul, or how to draw near to the Supreme Being. Neither does his work reflect the many salutary doctrines of a semi-religious and semi-philosophical kind which were spreading at that time, and which promised to show men the right path by means of some supernatural knowledge. Marcus Aurelius also ignores astrology and its promise to steel man against all blows dealt by fate, through a revelation of what is preordained. On the contrary, Marcus Aurelius bases his ideas on the knowledge that man is one with nature by virtue of his rational being. Nature gives man life for a limited period, puts him in a specific place, and gives him abilities adequate to his role in the great universal plan. Hence it is man's task to perform faithfully his duty each and every day, and only in so doing can he achieve inner freedom and the consciousness of a fulfilled life. However, the knowledge of living in an order that is entirely good and just must also be borne out by a general benevolence extended to all living creatures. It is not right to be angered by their behaviour, even if it is strange or offensive, for they are all part of the same cosmos which gives them their lives and their specific tasks, and thus they are all related and interdependent.

The Emperor's meditations can easily be linked with well-documented Stoic school doctrines, and sometimes even with their specific interpreters. The ostensibly random compilation produces an overall impression of supreme peace and serenity. The philanthropy and self-discipline, the sense of duty and the readiness to make sacrifices which are expressed in this work do not result from any overflowing emotion, and likewise not from the belief in received divine grace, nor from high hopes of leaving this world for a better one. Their only source is a firm trust in the natural order in which everything must serve a beneficial purpose. At one stage the Emperor says that one should die 'falling like a ripe apple, grateful to the tree that bore it'.

Pythagoreanism

At a very early stage in its development, Pythagorean doctrine already combined traditional lore about Pythagoras the miracle-worker and his supernatural message of salvation, with subtle mathematical speculation. A Pythagorean tradition survived the entire Classic epoch and the age of Hellenism. Plato, Aristotle, and their first successors had shown a great interest in Pythagoreanism, unlike Hellenistic philosophy, which had formed a close symbiosis with an entirely rationalistic science. The Empire, however, saw a renaissance of Pythagorean thought. I have already mentioned one of its exponents, the miracle-worker Apollonius of Tyana from the Flavian era (see p. 203). Apollonius regarded himself as a successor to Pythagoras, and like the Cynics, he preached a particular lifestyle different from the common norm. But whereas the Cynics derived this only from the general principle of a life in accordance with nature, Pythagorean rules were based on specific doctrines. That they were to abstain from eating meat, for instance, was a consequence of their belief in the transmigration of souls.

Since the first century BC the school of Plato had once again turned its attention to the elaboration of a comprehensive dogmatic system, based on the writings of Plato himself and his first disciples. Such efforts invariably led to the rediscovery of Pythagorean elements in the school tradition of the Academy. Platonic and Pythagorean thought converged in their esteem for mathematics, as can already be seen in Plato's own writings. The Academy, however, never went as far as Pythagoreanism: Platonics would agree that the structure of the world can be perceived as based on numerical relationships, whereas Pythagorean thinkers declared the numbers themselves to be the substantial components of matter, and hence equated mathematics with philosophy. This seems to have been the gist of a treatise by Moderatus of Gades, modern-day Cadiz, a work which has been quoted by several Neo-Platonists. The author lived around the turn of the first and second centuries AD shortly before Nicomachus from Gerasa in Syria. Several of Nicomachus' treatises are extant, including one similar to the work by Theon which I have mentioned (see p. 277). Nicomachus' introduction to mathematics as philosophical propaedeutics includes a survey of the Pythagorean theory of music, as well as a classification of mathematical disciplines, which is an interesting piece of scientific theory. A lost writing entitled *Arithmetical Theology* was presumably about Pythagorean numerical-cosmological speculations.

The most influential Pythagorean of the second century AD was Numenius of Apamea, another Greek city in Syria. What we have of his philosophical writings illustrates his attempt to prove that all philosophy was one until the time of Plato. As evidence, the author points out the parallels between Platonic and Pythagorean thought and 'barbarian philosophy', that is the time-honoured traditions of exotic peoples such as the Indians or Egyptians. This is why Numenius calls Plato an 'Attic-speaking Moses'. According to Numenius, it was not until the development of post-Platonic philosophy that the differences between individual schools arose, in a departure from true philosophy which was the common property of all men. Consequently Numenius' book about the hidden truths in Plato's writings was meant to enable the reader to understand Plato's works in the sense of the old, unified philosophy, and not from the point of view of those misguided school traditions which followed after.

Numenius' own doctrine is very peculiar. It is completely dominated by the question as to the relationship between the transcendental supreme God, and the world which emanated from him. The being which Numenius calls the 'first god' is entirely transcendental, without any link with matter. This link is established by subordinate second and third gods, whose existence makes the creation of our cosmos possible. The extant fragments of Numenius' work do not indicate how he imagined these processes in detail. All we can say with any certainty is that his concept of the doctrine of the three gods was inspired by Gnosticism (see p. 299). The Neo-Platonists' answer to the question of how the sensual world emerged from a transcendental, intelligible Supreme Being was fairly similar to that of Numenius, even if they used a much more elaborate system of ontological categories. However, they too tried to solve the problem by assuming a hierarchy of several divine beings at the top of the world order. This explains why Numenius, who is always introduced as a Pythagorean in the older texts, came to be labelled as a Platonic philosopher by all the later Neo-Platonists, from Iamblichus onwards.

Philosophical-religious literature

The teachings of Numenius can already be counted among those messages of salvation which appeared in ever-increasing numbers from the second century AD onwards. All of them combined pieces of the most varied dogmas from school philosophy, explained in philosophical terms and by philosophical methods. As self-contained doctrines they all claimed to be revealing a supernatural knowledge with a divine legitimacy. Thus, the recipients of the message were asked to accept it unconditionally at first, as its truth was guaranteed by an authority that transcends human reasoning. Only the convert or believer was called upon to use his reason, in order to deepen his understanding or to arrive at a better interpretation of the received truth. As such messages of salvation were clothed in popular philosophical language they were obviously aimed at an educated public, and hence we may assume that the appeal to converts to exercise their rational faculties in the aforesaid manner was not made in vain.

Two of those elaborately formulated doctrines of salvation are the Gnostic systems of Basilides and Valentinus, which were created in the first half of the century, and which I will deal with in the context of Christian literature (see p. 299). A comparable phenomenon are the treatises ascribed to Hermes Trismegistus, a name that points to an Egyptian connection. The oldest one of these pieces dates from the second century AD. They are revelatory speeches, using Middle Platonic and Stoic philosophemes to develop a doctrine which tells men about the origin of their souls and which promises that this knowledge is the key to attaining immortality in an immaterial existence. The creation of this *Corpus hermeticum* seems to have taken place over a long timespan; the congregations for which the treatises were written appear to have consisted of educated people only, who never performed missionary work in the manner of the major world religions. The texts indicate that within these circles, there were great differences in doctrine. But all the treatises, written in elevated language and containing hymnic parts which may well pertain to religious ritual, have one feature in common: the endeavour to endow the message with the authority of ancient Oriental wisdom, especially of Egyptian provenance. Consequently we can at least not exclude the possibility that the doctrines themselves occasionally contain elements of a non-Greek origin. One example may be the strict dualism equating mind and matter with good and evil respectively; this could well have infiltrated from Iranian regions.

The extant fragments of the so-called Chaldaean oracles represent another text of the same kind, which Neo-Platonists interpreted as a sort of Holy Scripture. The author was supposed to be the Chaldaean Julian or his son, who both lived around the end of the second century AD. The adjective Chaldaean may point to the eastern, Babylonian origin of this piece of wisdom; another plausible reading is suggested by the fact that at that time professional astrological soothsayers had also come to be called by the same name.

Like the Sibylline prophecies, the Chaldaean oracles are written in hexameters. They preach a theology which is very similar to that of Numenius, featuring many philosophical terms and categories, and dominated by the idea of a trinity of supreme beings. The first God is the father, the being at rest within itself, from which the second god *Nous* or Reason emerges, whose task is to create an ordered world. The third divine being is female: this is the force of power which creates life and motion. In addition to these three, the theology and cosmology of the oracles named an entire system of subordinate gods, and taught men about the origin and the destiny of their souls. Also featured were rules for everyday living, with great emphasis on asceticism as liberating the soul from the body, as well as instructions for so-called theurgy, the use of magical practices in communicating with the divine. As in the *Hermetica*, the goal of the teaching was to help the reader free himself from the fatal constraint of the material cosmos, in order to attain immortality in a purely spiritual existence. The Chaldaean doctrine of the trinity was taken up by the Neo-Platonist Porphyry, who used it in his ontology. Through his mediation, it also came to affect the Christian trinitarian doctrine, as is first in evidence in the writings of Marius Victorinus (see p. 379).

Gnostic, Hermetic, and Chaldaean teachings were levelled at an educated public exclusively. However, we find expressions of often very similar notions in the lengthy magical texts which have been preserved on papyrus, even if the magical practices for which they provide instructions are mostly directed at very profane goals. There are formulas and charms in a kind of gibberish composed of all sorts of linguistic fragments. None the less, we also find hymnic passages which reveal a whole world of religious ideas: a world in which the notions of liberating the true self by separating the immaterial soul from the body, of escaping from the causality of nature, and of attaining immortality, were alive in the very same manner documented by the aforementioned semi-philosophical texts.

10 SCIENCES

The most illustrious scientific achievements in the Graeco-Roman world date back to the periods of Early and Middle Hellenism, that is the third and second centuries BC. The flourishing of science at that time was made possible by a historical constellation in which very different factors combined. One was that Alexander's campaign had led to an extremely sudden extension of that world where a Greek could attain wealth and status through his own efforts in any location. The new opportunities opening up for individuals as well as for groups encouraged the use of reason without any traditional constraints. The rulers of the states that succeeded Alexander's empire were ready to lend generous support to scientific research, for cultural-political reasons, but also because of utilitarian considerations. The most famous example of such munificence was the establishment of the Museum in Alexandria. Well-funded and permanent institutions of this kind gave an entirely unprecedented continuity to scientific research, and an equally new prestige to its patrons.

Another important factor was that philosophy had taken a hold on nearly all areas of knowledge, first in the Academy, and then predominantly in the Aristotelian school. The effect of this was that when individual scientific disciplines began to detach themselves from philosophy around the turn of the fourth and third centuries BC; they took the road towards specialisation carrying the valuable dowry of a well-developed consciousness of methods and problems, an awareness formed while scientific efforts had taken place within the context of philosophy. Thus conditions were extremely favourable for the advancement of diverse and successful scientific research in many different specialist disciplines; and the great scholars of the age of Hellenism knew how to make the best of such favourable circumstances.

The Empire saw only a very few individual achievements which can be compared with the scientific feats of Hellenism. But still, we should not underestimate the overall productivity of the Empire's scientists in several disciplines. The continuity of scientific work remained guaranteed through institutional continuity, and the results of previous research remained accessible as a basis for further work, even if there was a palpable decline of interest among educated people in the genuine progress of knowledge as such, and hence for new and original scientific discoveries. Neither rhetorically- nor philosophically-based education encouraged people to venture into the unknown as both derived their ideals from the past and aimed at no more than a proper understanding or imitation of time-honoured models. If scientific research nevertheless continued, this was largely due to a factor noted already by Aristotle: man's natural thirst for knowledge.

Geography

In the second century AD there were a number of impressive achievements in geography. Geographical writings from this period belong to one or other of two groups, between which we must distinguish quite clearly. One contains descriptions of countries and their inhabitants, works that were written with a literary intention, and were thus to be judged mainly according to stylistic criteria. This explains why the aforesaid Dionysius (see p. 269) should have chosen the verse form for a description of the earth which was nevertheless meant to communicate geographical knowledge; and there are plenty of similar examples from subsequent centuries. Scientific geography was exclusively concerned with the ascertaining of positions by astronomical-mathematical means, as the basis for cartography. In the latter area, the major figure was the versatile Alexandrian scholar Ptolemaeus or Ptolemy, whose epoch-making work around the mid-second century AD took in the entire known world.

Compared with that factual knowledge shown in the writings of Strabo from the beginning of the first century AD, the geographical horizon of the inhabitants of the Mediterranean world had been considerably broadened. During the first century AD military campaigns in Germany and Britain provided new information about northern Europe, and other isolated military operations penetrated deep into the Sudan, the Sahara, and southern Arabia. Agents of Greek merchants in the commercial centres of Syria reached the central Asian cities along the silk route, and captains from Greek Egypt sailed along the east coast of Africa, as far as those regions which we now know as Mozambique. Around 100 AD the sea-farer Alexandros managed to pass through the barrier formed by the Malay peninsula and the islands of Sumatra and Java; he got as far as modern-day Vietnam, and made direct contact with Chinese navigators. China's imperial annals for the year 166 AD record the presence of emissaries, probably merchants, from the Roman Empire in the capital Lo-Yang. Those had reached China from the south, that is by sea, and they complained about the fact that the land route was blocked by the Parthians.

All the information gained from such military and commercial ventures was used to develop scientific geography's picture of the earth. The literary description of countries, on the other hand, was based on texts canonised in the literary tradition, and if the genre developed at all it was towards the use of progressively older sources. Most authors of such accounts thus stuck to a level of knowledge which had long been made obsolete by practical experience.

Methods for the calculation of geographical positions and distances had existed since the age of Hellenism, and the system of latitudinal and longitudinal degrees which we still use today was well known in the second century AD. For the countries around the Mediterranean, a fairly dense network of established positions had been developed over the years, and thus the map of this part of the world came pretty close to an accurate representation of reality. The situation was more problematic with places outside the Roman Empire for there the only existing information was to be found in journals describing the routes taken by ships or caravans. The latitude and longitude of ports of call along the route of a ship could only be estimated and even a small mistake in the indicated course could lead to grotesque errors where long distances were concerned. More reliable maps existed only for those areas covered by a tight web of trade routes, where the position of each geographical location was ascertained on the basis of several available data. One of those regions was southern India, a part of the world much frequented by Graeco-Roman traders. Incidentally, Alexander the Great had already tried to measure the Asian countries which he conquered by an exact logging of the distances his army was covering. There were also the so-called *stadiasmoi*, books listing the distances for routes in certain areas.

Divided according to the three known continents, Ptolemy collected many hundreds of geographical calculations for the positions of cities, mountains, and rivers. On the basis of these data, which were naturally of very varied value, he drew up a map of the world from the Sudan to Scandinavia, and from Ireland to China. When it came to the old question whether the continent of Libya – modern-day Africa – was surrounded by water or connected to Asia by a southern land bridge around the

Indian Ocean, Ptolemy's disbelief in existing reports about the successful circumnavigation of Africa led him to opt for the latter theory.

In the first book of his major work Ptolemy deals with fundamental questions concerning his science and quotes a number of authorities on whose accounts he bases his estimates for distances in the more remote regions. He also discusses the achievements of a predecessor, the slightly older Marinus of Tyre, who must likewise have been famous as a geographer. From Book 2 onwards, Ptolemy's work consists almost exclusively of place names and figures; and it is with the latter that there is especially ample scope for errors in the making of manuscript copies. The text was originally accompanied by a map of the world, but sadly enough, the maps we find in mediaeval manuscripts differ considerably from one another, and none of them really tallies with the data given in the text itself. Thus it seems that Ptolemy's image of the world will never be reconstructed with the precision which it deserves, being the result of rigorous scientific endeavours.

Ptolemy and astronomy

Ptolemy's scientific writing was prolific. Of his five books on optics, we have only a Latin translation, itself based on an Arabic one. The work is a systematic account of phenomena belonging to two-eyed vision, and of the reflection and deflection of light in different media. Most of Ptolemy's text is based on experimental data, and the laws derived from those are invariably expressed in mathematical formulas. The validity of his calculations for the reflection and deflection of light was unaffected by Ptolemy's adherence to a theory which was dominant, if not unchallenged, until the Middle Ages: namely, that the process of seeing was caused by a ray emanating from the eye, and grasping the object.

Through a commentary on Euclid's *Elements* by the Neo-Platonist Proclus, we know of a treatise by Ptolemy on Euclid's postulate concerning parallel lines. This work was lost, whereas a theory of music in three books has been preserved in an almost complete form. Also extant is a short philosophical treatise on the theory of cognition. Its first part deals with the respective roles of perception, thought, and language in the perception of truth. Part 2 gives an answer to the question of where the guiding organ of the human soul is located.

In the eyes of posterity, however, Ptolemy was first and foremost a famous astronomer. His numerous works on this subject are partly extant in the original Greek, and partly also in Arabic and Latin translations. There are writings on the rising and setting of a number of fixed stars; tables for calculating the movements of planets; instructions for the making of astronomical instruments; a treatise explaining planetary motion; and another one describing the projection of the firmament onto the plane of the celestial equator.

Ptolemy's major astronomical work is the *Mathematical Manual* that was later called the Great or the Greatest: the Greek 'megistē syntaxis' became *Almagest* in Arabic. This book is the Classic account of the geocentric world view; it remained the standard text in its field for centuries, and numerous commentaries on it appeared throughout the Classical age. In the book Ptolemy gives very detailed reasons for his decision in favour of the geocentric view. In the past, the importance of this piece of writing was often seen as a summing up of such astronomical knowledge as had been accessible since the second century BC when the great astronomer Hipparchus drew up a plan of which we can trace no more than a rough outline. Today, however, scholars are inclined to rate Ptolemy's own contributions to astronomical research and observation much higher than before. In keeping with this revised estimate is the fact that in his treatise on the planets, Ptolemy corrected the theoretical plan of the *Almagest* on the basis of new observations.

In some of these strictly scientific treatises on astronomy, Ptolemy also deals with questions that go beyond mathematically verifiable insights. Like all Platonics and Stoics, he thought of the stars as beings which have a capacity for individual motion. He also embraced a theory inherited from Plato, who claimed that the revolving of the firmament's seven strata within the all-embracing sphere of the fixed stars produces musical tones corresponding to the notes of the seven-stringed lyre. From such ideas, it was but a small step to astrology, for the regularity of stellar motion suggested that the stars were more thoroughly rational beings than humans are; that they should be revered as divine; and that their motions could be read as describing the destiny of the entire universe. The fascinating feature of Greek astrology, which developed in the second century BC, lay in the strictly mathematical nature of its calculations, which it had adopted from contemporary astronomy. Although astrological texts would often claim the authority of ancient Oriental wisdom, and although Egyptian priests or Chaldaean sages were also known as astrologers, there can be no doubt about the fact that astrology in that form in which it has come to interest people in many cultures since the Imperial age, is a genuinely Greek product.

Ptolemy also wrote a manual of astrology entitled *Tetrabiblos*. This work became extremely popular and was translated into many different languages. Apart from the doctrine of individual horoscopes, the four books also contain a theory of geographical astrology, concerning the effect of specific stellar constellations on the inhabitants of entire countries.

Ptolemy's *Tetrabiblos* clearly shows that it was written by an expert astronomer. This is less so in the case of another astrological manual, whose featured horoscopes indicate that it was written between 152 and

162 AD, and thus likewise during Ptolemy's lifetime. Its author Vettius Valens was widely known as a great astrologer; consequently his work was frequently used and all kinds of different additions were made to the text. Many later works were also ascribed to Vettius Valens whose nine genuine books deal with fundamental astrological doctrines and terms in no recognisable order. The work also contains many specific instructions, as well as plenty of examples. Its language is remarkably unpolished in comparison with the norms generally accepted for written Greek in the second century AD. The most interesting passages are those which tell us something about the reasons why so many people turned to astrology at that time. Vettius Valens promises those who follow his teachings that they will become 'soldiers of destiny'. People are to gain courage and confidence from learning about the great causal link connecting each individual life to cosmic happenings. As the course of all events is preordained, a person educated in astrology may contemplate the future without fear or hope, and hence have all the more energy for coping with the tasks of the present.

Mathematics and technology

I have already dealt with the development of natural sciences such as mechanics or optics (see pp. 165 and 287). Mathematics was a very different case, as there were plenty of innovative thinkers in this discipline throughout as well as after the second century AD. The mathematical writings by Theon and Nicomachus have been mentioned in a previous section (see p. 281); they demonstrate the place of mathematical studies in the context of philosophy. The major representative of mathematics as an independent discipline in the second century AD was Menelaus of Alexandria, an older contemporary of Ptolemy's. His extant major work in three books deals with spherics, and especially spherical trigonometry; but Menelaus also wrote on astronomy and physics. Alexandria remained a major centre for research in the exact sciences until the Late Classical age, and another scholar who worked there in the second century AD was the mathematician Sporus. Parts of his writings have been preserved in the excerpts made by Eutocius, yet another Alexandrian, in the sixth century AD (see p. 502).

The technological application of mathematical methods and physical-mechanical knowledge is best illustrated by the work of Apollodorus of Damascus, the most famous engineer and architect the Empire ever had. During Trajan's Dacian campaign, he had a stone bridge built across the Danube at Debreczen; and he designed the grandiose Forum of Trajan, as well as many other buildings in Rome. Some extant excerpts from one of his writings on the construction of catapults and siege engines show that ballistic technology had reached a remarkably high standard.

Medicine

Medical science saw its last Classical flowering during the age of the Antonines, the most prominent figure being Galenus of Pergamum in Asia Minor. To contemporaries, this man was known as the most famous physician in the entire Roman Empire; to posterity, he was the prime communicator of a rich legacy of medical knowledge to the Latin Occident and the Byzantine East as well as to the Islamic world, where some of his books were preserved in Arabic translations. Until well into the Modern age, Galen's writings retained their undisputed status as authoritative textbooks on the medical art.

We have plenty of information on Galen's life because of the many autobiographical references in his vast literary output, even if that is only partly extant. Galen was born in 129 AD to a father who was an architect and mathematician. From the age of thirteen onwards, Galen studied philosophy and mathematics in his native city; at sixteen he began his medical training in Alexandria. About ten years later he started work as a sports doctor, as we would call it today, first for a troupe of gladiators in Pergamum, and then for one in Rome. During this first sojourn in Rome he produced his first literary works. He also managed to become a fashionable doctor among the highest ranks of metropolitan society, and thus he enjoyed the patronage of several influential people. When the plague broke out in Rome in 166 AD Galen returned to Pergamum – a move not much to his credit as a physician. But at the end of the same decade he was recalled to Rome by the Emperors Marcus Aurelius and Verus, to work at court and as their personal doctor. Galen remained in Rome until his death in 199 AD.

Those of Galen's works which have been preserved in the Greek original fill twenty large volumes of the most recent complete edition, published in 1821ff. Two treatises by the author himself tell us about the number, the titles, and the genesis of his writings. What made him write these two tracts was the circulation of numerous other pieces published under his name: unauthorised lecture notes, excerpts, and plain forgeries. Galen, who was not free from vanity, naturally did not want to see his literary achievement distorted or obscured. His treatises *Of the Sequence of my Own Books* and *Of my Own Books* are of unique value as evidence concerning book production and distribution at the time, and they also provide information about a number of lost works.

As an author Galen did not limit himself to medicine alone. He was well-schooled in Academic-Peripatetic philosophy, and his treatises on logic, psychological theory, and the history of philosophical doctrines are valuable contributions to specialist philosophical literature. Galen also wrote about grammatical and rhetorical-stylistic issues; and in doing so he showed remarkable insight into the artificiality of literary Attic, the mastery of which most of Galen's contemporaries took as the measure of a person's education. Galen's views expose this kind of assessment as inadequate.

For Galen, his lifelong interest in philosophy was highly relevant to his work as a physician. Since the age of Hellenism, there had been a continuous debate as to which activity of the human mind was the most important. The most widespread opinion put those 'arts' which serve practical purposes and are performed to earn a livelihood on the lowest level. Above them are the so-called Liberal Arts, including all mathematical and linguistic disciplines, serving that education which prepares men for attaining moral-political virtue. The ultimate access to this highest goal of intellectual effort was promised to those who pursued philosophy or rhetoric, the two disciplines which vied for pride of place. This hierarchy had been developed with a view to general education, and that is why it did not have a place for specialised science, pursued as an end in itself or for the increase of human knowledge. Neither did it accord a place to medicine, whose worth lies in a unique synthesis of theory and practice. Hence it is easy to see why exact scientists and physicians would persist in claiming the status and the appellation of philosopher, which meant a claim to the highest rank in the educational hierarchy. Around 400 BC Democritus had established a precedent by calling the philosopher the physician of the soul. Galen even devoted an entire treatise to the contention that a true physician must always be a philosopher as well. The argument is based on parallels between the three Classic philosophical disciplines logic, physics, and ethics (see p. 200), and the individual branches of medical science. Galen puts particular emphasis on the comparison between medical therapy and ethics, as both combine a theoretical and a practical part.

In all of Galen's writings, his fundamental philosophical beliefs shine through the records and the interpretations of observations on anatomy, physiology, pathology, or medical therapy. He keeps presenting ever-new examples to demonstrate that there is not a single natural event which does not have a clearly marked purpose, recognisable to human understanding. This idea also comes into a description which Galen gives of the hair covering different parts of the human body. The result is a violent polemic against the Jewish and Christian belief in a sovereign divine creator, with a power unrestricted by any natural laws. According to Galen's philosophical creed, it is blasphemous to assume that the God who created the world is free to turn a lump of clay into a cow or a man, just as he pleases. The God whom Plato taught people to worship creates only that which is rationally possible: but in his perfection, he chooses always the best one among the possible options. This makes man as a rational being able to recognise and appreciate ours as the best of all possible worlds: to see, for instance, that the divine creator of the universe has given people eyelashes which serve a different purpose and are thus structurally different from the hair covering the head.

Platonism was the dominant philosophy during Galen's lifetime when its efforts were mainly directed at giving a correct interpretation of the school founder's writings. It was believed that Plato himself, but also Aristotle, had already expressed all the essential truths (see p. 71); and Galen applied exactly the same approach to medical science. He subscribed to none of the schools that were in vogue at the time, Empiricists, Methodicists, or Pneumaticists (see p. 143). Like Rufus of Ephesus two generations earlier (see p. 144), Galen produced a varied and prodigious literary *oeuvre* in which he tried to summarise and analyse all existing medical knowledge in the light of the Hippocratic tradition.

Hippocrates, who had led the medical school on the island of Kos to its greatest achievements around 400 BC, may well be called the founder of strictly scientific medicine. One reason is that for the first time ever, his school demanded a complete physiological-pathological explanation of the causes of individual symptoms diagnosed, and a corresponding justification of the recommended therapy. At the same time, however, the Hippocratic school insisted on a permanent awareness of the fact that all theory needs constant improvement. This is why the school never stagnated in rigid dogmatism and never came to reject medicine that was based exclusively on experience. The scientific tradition of Kos found its most significant continuation in the medical research carried out in Alexandria during Early Hellenism. In contrast, the schools of Late Hellenism and the Early Empire favoured a medicine that was easier to teach, being reduced to a rigid dogmatic system derived from philosophical sources, or to mere empiricism.

The teaching of the school of Kos was made available in a vast collection of works on individual topics and problems. Some of these writings are still extant; all of them bore the name of Hippocrates. It is indeed possible that Hippocrates himself did produce several of the texts, which at least were written when he was alive. But Hippocratic treatises were still being published during Galen's lifetime such as, for instance, an interesting tract on the ethics of the medical profession, entitled *Of True Decency*, and written in pre-Classic Old Ionic. Polybus, Hippocrates son-in-law, was the author of a treatise on the nature of man which explains the most influential part of Hippocratic medicine, the doctrine of the body fluids or qualities and their mixtures, the so-called temperaments.

Through adopting this doctrine and developing it further with the help of recent theories and observations, Galen helped it to a worldwide influence which lasted well into the Modern age. In his lengthy commentaries on the relevant treatise as well as on other writings of the Hippocratic corpus, he was not merely trying to explain the archaic-Ionic texts. Instead, he integrated them into the medical knowledge of his own epoch by establishing references to his own observations on diagnosis and therapy as well as to other medical sources, and by developing their theoretical-dogmatic approaches.

The influence of Hippocratic ideas can also be seen in Galen's many longer or shorter specialist treatises on aspects of anatomy, physiology, surgery, dietetics, pharmacology, and other medical disciplines. These works not only give us a comprehensive picture of the author's medical knowledge and his manner of scientific argumentation, but they also provide insights into general medical practice of that period, and furthermore into the world of ideas of an educated person whose thinking was largely determined by contemporary philosophy.

More than post-Classical Europe, the Graeco-Roman world regarded medical knowledge as a part of general education. This is why many extant Classical texts on medicine, including some of Galen's works, were evidently written for a lay public. One example by Galen is the *Protreptikos*, a pamphlet promoting the study of medicine. The tradition of this literary genre dates back to Aristotle, whose own *Protreptikos* was unfortunately lost. However, extant fragments show that it was designed to promote the life dedicated to philosophy. A Latin imitation of this text in Cicero's *Hortensius* had also been lost, although Augustine, in his *Confessions*, gives us a very detailed description of the effect which Cicero's writing had on him. Galen's promotional pamphlet has a close affinity with the philosophical tradition of the genre, both because the author was very much at home with philosophy, and because he was keen to present the professions of the physician and the philosopher as identical.

A totally different piece of writing, if also designed for use by laymen, is Galen's dietetic advice for the treatment of an epileptic boy, instructions which he gave without having a chance to see the patient. In Classical medicine, dietetics did not only include nutrition, but all physical aspects of lifestyle. This branch of medicine was then much more important than it is today, not only with regard to its therapeutic potential, but also particularly as giving instructions for proper living to the healthy. This is why the author Galen could assume that his patient's parents would accept the detailed practical guidance, accompanied in each instance by more general physiological-pathological reasons. The author also points out the fact that in view of the particular circumstances of the case, he is unable to give an exact diagnosis.

As I have already said, Galen's aim was to keep Hippocratic medicine alive by means of a modernisation, with a comprehensive inclusion of recent advances in medical knowledge. The philosophy of the period was likewise dominated by the endeavour to show that, correctly read, old equalled right as well as progressive. In Galen's work this is best illustrated by a long treatise in which the author sets out to prove a fundamental agreement between the teachings of Hippocrates and his school and those of Plato. In one longer section of this work Galen refers to an ancient debate which had been carried on among the Stoics of the first century BC. According to Stoic doctrine as it stood then, all seemingly irrational stirrings of the soul – emotions, affections, and impulses – did not emanate from specific parts of the soul which lay outside reason but had to be interpreted as the results of misguided rational judgment. The philosophical consequence of this axiom was that all spontaneous, irrational urges to act had to be classified as errors.

The learned Stoic Posidonius modified this doctrine of his school by adopting Plato's and Aristotle's assumption that the soul has an independent irrational part whose impulses are useful and necessary, in so far as they are controlled by reason. Posidonius was one of the first exponents of a 'modern' school of philosophy which had originated during the age of Hellenism, going back to the 'ancient' philosophers Plato and Aristotle, and freely combining elements of 'Classic' and 'Hellenistic' origin to form new doctrines.

Galen subscribed completely to Posidonius' views concerning the nature and the origin of the human soul's affections; however, he complemented Posidonius' doctrine with elements borrowed from Hippocratic physiology. There he had found information concerning a question which was of special interest to him as a physician: to what extent are affections purely products of the soul, and how far does their genesis involve the body? It was not only in the abovementioned context, but also in an entire separate treatise, that Galen dealt with this question, raised from the point of view of the physician, but leading him even closer to Plato and Aristotle. Unlike the Stoic materialists, both of them had based their view of man and the world on a dichotomy between mind and matter. Continuing Platonic thought, Aristotle in particular had given special attention to the problem of transition, or the conjunction of mind and matter in the living soul. In the tradition of Platonic teaching, with its many borrowings from Aristotle, this had always remained a key issue; and it was here that Galen could enrich the discussion with his knowledge of Hippocratic physiology, getting closer to his goal of proving that there was indeed an agreement between what was taught by the greatest physician and the greatest philosopher among the ancients. Galen's liberal use of Posidonius' treatise on the affections documents the unbroken tradition of scholarly research. In Galen's case, going back to an admired ancient model did not lead to that blind faith in authority which, ironically enough, was invested in himself by a good number of people in many later generations who read his works. Galen never let his reverence for the ancients inhibit his own original thought, and neither did he underestimate achievements of a more recent origin. To posterity, however, he became a medical authority as unassailable as Ptolemy was in geography and astronomy.

11 CHRISTIAN LITERATURE

Apologists

In documents from the early second century AD, such as the historical works of Tacitus or the letters of the Younger Pliny, we see that educated Romans viewed the Christians as no more than members of an obscure sect. It might be distinct from Judaism, and it might have a sizeable lower-class following in some parts of the Empire, but on the whole its grotesque superstitions warranted but little attention. But in the second half of the same century, a professional Platonic philosopher called Celsus saw reason enough to write a long pamphlet attacking the Christians and their doctrine. This document can be reconstructed from the refutation which Origen produced about fifty years later. I have already discussed Galen's views, expressed at around the same time as Celsus', about the belief in a sovereign divine creator, as a notion common to both Jews and Christians (see p. 291).

The development of Christian writing corresponds fairly accurately to the difference in the amount of attention paid to the Christians by the educated classes in the first and second half of the second century AD respectively. But what remained unchanged until the end of the century was that all Christian literature was written in Greek, a fact that tells us much about the membership of Christian communities even in Rome or Gaul.

The literary forms of the first half of the second century AD are those with which we are familiar from the New Testament. There were letters, mostly addressed to Christian congregations, as well as moral instructions, reports of visions, liturgical prayers and hymns, and of course evangelia or gospels, that is accounts of Jesus' life and works. During the second half of the century a lengthy process of selection from the numerous writings of this kind which had been produced in the first and second centuries AD led to the formation of an established canon. This process was not without a fair amount of controversy: in the East, for instance, the canonisation of John's Apocalypse was resisted for many years, whereas another piece of apocalyptic writing only temporarily accepted in the West, the *Shepherd of Hermas*, remained in the Eastern canon for a long time. In the third century AD, however, the Christians finally had an established New Testament, the second sacred book used in worship beside the Septuagint, the Greek version of the Old Testament, which initially had been the only Holy Scripture recognised by Christians and their Jewish predecessors alike.

The linguistic-literary standard of Christian texts from the second half of the second century AD is not very high. We find only rare attempts at elaborating a passage by means of some of the common devices of rhetorically formed prose. In most cases the language is relatively close to the vernacular, if not exactly identical with it. Among the features which indicate this are occasional Latinisms, which had found their way into Greek through oral communication between native speakers of Greek and Latin. The reason for the generally greater frequency of Semitisms is not that the authors of Christian texts were bilingual in Greek and Hebrew: those influences do not come from any spoken Semitic idiom, but from the Septuagint, with which Christian writers and readers were very familiar. The language of the Septuagint shines through not only in literal quotations, but likewise in many idioms and forms of expression. Many Old Testament pericopes were part of Christian liturgy, and for Christian authors, allusions to the Greek text of the Bible – which as a translation of course keeps recalling the language of the original – were the most important means of raising the linguistic level in their writings.

A document from the last years of the first century AD is a letter from Rome to the congregation of Corinth, designed to help resolve disputes within that community. Very early on this letter was ascribed to a certain Clement, who according to traditional lore was a disciple of the apostle Peter, and his successor as Bishop of the Roman church. A text known as the second letter by Clement is in fact a Christian sermon which dates from about forty years later. This is the earliest extant example of a literary genre which was to be developed widely within the Christian church.

Like John's Apocalypse, Clement's first letter already mentions the persecution of Christians by state officials. From a rescript by the Emperor Trajan to a question put by Pliny as governor of north-western Anatolia (see p. 226), we know that Christians were at that time regarded as followers of an illegal cult. Since their secession from the synagogue, they could no longer claim that tolerance which the Roman state was willing to extend to the exclusive monotheism of the Jews, as well as to any other religion which was absorbed in the process of the Roman Empire's growth. However, an exclusive monotheism which prohibited its followers any other form of religious worship was still regarded as a sign of Godlessness, and the general opinion was that such a phenomenon should not be allowed to arise within the Roman Empire. The diversity of gods and forms of worship was regarded as crucial to the religious legitimacy of the Empire's legal order, which bound so many different nations together. This, however, did not preclude the possibility of speculative thought about the oneness of the divine. Such a belief was expressed by many philosophers, who nevertheless saw no reason why they should not participate in the many existing forms of ritual worship of specific deities.

It seems that initially the Christians were regarded as too insignificant to warrant a major effort at the persecution, and thus the elimination of this group, whose existence was not protected by the legal order. However, each governor was free to take measures against Christian individuals or communities – for example, in the case of a denunciation – and he could impose corporal punishment if he saw a threat to public order. The death penalty was the norm for a confession of the Christian faith under interrogation, and likewise for a refusal to perform ritual acts belonging to the cult of another deity, or that of the Emperor's genius. In view of the special status to which the Christians themselves laid claim resentment and slanderous rumours could arise only too easily, and lead to denunciations.

The conditions described above were those under which the extant letters from the period were written. Ignatius, Bishop of the Christian diocese in Antioch in Syria, wrote a number of epistles to Christian communities in Asia Minor, as well as to his colleague Polycarp of Smyrna. The texts of Ignatius' letters were subjected to later editorial changes. Of Polycarp, we have an epistle to the Christian community of Philippi in modern-day Macedonia. Ignatius died as a martyr in a Roman arena during the reign of Trajan, while Polycarp was burned at the stake in 156 AD at the age of eighty-six (see p. 308). Their letters illustrate the organisation of Christian communities and their links with one another, as well as giving us details of the religious ideas of their members. Especially interesting is a letter from around 130 AD, ascribed to the apostle Barnabas, a companion of Paul's. Its explanations of the proper Christian reading of the Old Testament document the process of separation of the church from the synagogue. The unknown author uses the method of allegorical interpretation as it was also known to Greek-speaking Jews, in his attempt to prove that Biblical ritual laws, the observance of which bound Jewish communities together, should be understood as expressions of spiritual truth, and were not at all meant to be followed literally. As by that time most members of Christian communities were converts from a pagan milieu, such a reading of the relevant parts of Christian Holy Scripture was virtually inevitable.

Of course Christian communities also developed their own sets of rules for worship and social life, as well as for the private lives of the individual members. Some passages concerning such issues can be found even in the earliest extant Christian letters. From the first half of the second century AD, we have the *Didache*, the oldest comprehensive and completely extant set of rules for a Christian community, followed by other texts of that kind in the third and fourth centuries AD.

From a literary point of view, the most interesting piece from the period in question is the *Shepherd of Hermas*, an apocalyptic text written in Rome, temporarily canonised, and translated soon after its appearance into Latin as well as several Oriental languages. It is divided into three parts, respectively containing visions, instructions, and parables. The title refers to an angel who approaches the visionary in the form of a shepherd, and communicates some of the messages recorded in the text. Others come from an old woman who reveals her true identity as the incarnation of the church. The main topic is the doctrine about a baptised sinner's second chance to repent and to be forgiven, before the impending day of judgment. This is an obvious attempt to vindicate the orthodox church practice of penance which had prevailed, in spite of more rigid views claiming that after the act of baptism which washes all sins away there could be no more sins which needed to be forgiven. Apart from comments on this subject, the *Shepherd* gives eschatological instruction and moral guidance which tells us a lot about social interaction within the Roman congregation. There are also several visionary descriptions of scenes that invite an allegorical interpretation as images of the Christian community, such as, for instance, the one about the building of a tower.

The *Shepherd* has very little structural unity and consequently there have been many different theories about its time of origin and its exact genesis. Its linguistic-stylistic features show that the author was not a very educated person, but nevertheless the work echoes many literary and philosophical motifs from the pagan environment. There are scenes of a type that definitely stems from the erotic novel; but those scenes have a spiritual twist in them. We also find images or parables borrowed from the paraenesis current in popular philosophy. Close parallels exist with the so-called *Tabula* of Cebes (see p. 88), and the revelatory speech introducing the *Corpus hermeticum* (see p. 283). Thus the *Shepherd* fairly accurately reflects the literary-philosophical milieu of that semi-educated class to which the most eminent members of Christian communities belonged at that time; as the most eminent, of course, we must regard those who left us a literary legacy.

The earliest exponents of Christianity who had a full share in the philosophical-literary life of their environment are presumably to be found among the Gnostics. Of special importance are the names of the men who created major Gnostic doctrinal systems and schools, such as Basilides and Valentinus. Both are said to have been well acquainted with Platonic philosophy, without whose terms and methods we could hardly even begin to explain the concepts behind their systematics. However, our knowledge of Christian-Gnostic literature, which according to our sources used a whole range of different forms, is based almost exclusively on short quotations, on accounts given in anti-Gnostic polemics, and on some Coptic translations of Gnostic treatises. This scanty evidence makes it very difficult to arrive at any literary-stylistic evaluation of Gnostic writing.

The Christian Gnostics based their doctrines on ideas which had been discussed in many places, including the Jewish world, long before the appearance of Jesus. Their aim was to interpret the new Christian message in a way that led beyond Jewish-Biblical tradition, by putting it into a cosmological context, and neglecting the belief of Jesus' first followers that his actions were historical events which fulfilled the prophecies of the Old Testament. According to Gnostic doctrine the empirical world is the creation of a lesser or even an evil god, who left the realm of true being which is the immaterial world of light. Our cosmos, as many Gnostics asserted with explicit reference to the Biblical account of creation, has no intrinsic worth. It is able to exist merely because some particles from the world of light have been trapped in it, and have forgotten where they came from. Such particles are first and foremost all or some human souls, or at least their most valuable components. Being no human, but a messenger from the world of light appearing in human form to deceive the cosmic powers, Christ has once again reminded the immaterial cores of men of their origin. By an act of cognition, which is what the term Gnosis refers to, they can now achieve reunification with the luminous substance which belongs to them. In doing so, they cease to be part of the visible-material cosmos, which is abandoned to its inevitable dissolution.

The similarity of this scheme to the spirit/matter dualism of the Platonic tradition is as evident as the fundamental difference between the Gnostic world view on the one hand, and both the Greek-Platonic and the Biblical one on the other. To the Gnostics, the cosmos is neither the perfect creation of the sole, sovereign God, nor is it the mirror-image which reflects the beauty and the order of an intelligible world. This explains why, in the long debate with the Gnosis about the worth of creation and the historical nature of the process of salvation as documented in the Bible, Christians would again and again refer to philosophical ideas about the sublime quality of nature. This was done in spite of the knowledge that the Gnostics themselves had used philosophy to develop their tenets into systematic doctrines.

The formation of that which was later called orthodox or Catholic Christianity was a long and slow process, as each new doctrine, even if it was later labelled a heresy, began with the claim to put the Christian message across in its purest form. The dogma as recognised by the church took shape only in the confrontation with ever-new doctrines; and Paul's letters show that this development had already set in at the time of the apostles. It was continued in the great dogmatic controversies of the fourth and fifth centuries AD when delegates from all over the known world were called to those councils which were to arbitrate.

The Christian community in Rome already played a key role in the second century AD when its members still spoke Greek. The aforementioned Gnostic Valentinus, a highly gifted pastor, came very close to becoming Bishop of Rome. Another candidate for the same office around the middle of the century was Marcion, who came from a rich family in Asia Minor. However, he was then soon branded as a heretic and left the Roman congregation after a few years to found his own church which survived for a long time in Rome as well as in the Syrian regions east of the Empire's frontier. Marcion regarded the God of the Old Testament as a divine being of secondary rank, and the creator of an imperfect world. Christ was the messenger of the true, intelligible God who came to deliver men from this world, and also to teach them love instead of justice. Consequently Marcion rejected the Old Testament and limited the canon of the New Testament to the writings in the tradition of Paul, that is, to Paul's letters and Luke's evangelium which were the only texts in which he saw a liberation from the Israelite-Jewish tradition.

Like Valentinus and like Basilides, who taught in Alexandria, Marcion was a highly educated man and a stylish author. Each one of these three proclaimed doctrines which were condemned by the church sooner or later, and we can do no more than speculate as to the extent to which they influenced the development of specifically Christian manners of argumentation, or literary forms (see p. 379).

Better known than the original works of the Gnostics is the apologetical literature of the second century AD, of whose authors at least some belonged to the educated upper classes. Their apologies for Christianity, its doctrines and its communities, must be seen in the context of the legal situation of the Christians, as described above (see p. 296). This situation explains why the defensive treatises of the apologists put special emphasis on portraying the Christians as people who led peaceful, morally irreprehensible lives and who were above all loyal to the state. Their description of worship and social interaction in Christian communities was to counteract the many current rumours claiming that ritual murders and other kinds of outrageous horrors were common practice among the Christians. In an appeal to educated readers, the defence of exclusive Christian monotheism, basically unacceptable in Graeco-Roman culture, linked it to philosophical monotheism, which was actually quite a different phenomenon (see p. 296). The most important apologies extant are those by Aristides, Justin, and Athenagoras; there were others which we know only from quotations.

Justin's apology was accidentally handed down to us in two parts; but although they are quoted as separate publications, the work was originally one whole, dedicated to the Emperor Antoninus Pius. Aristides dedicated his apology to Hadrian and Athenagoras named the two Emperors Marcus Aurelius and Commodus as recipients of his dedication. However, the literal truth of the dedicatory remarks is more than doubtful, and it is even more unlikely that copies of the works thus introduced reached the Imperial addressees they cited. In all likelihood the three authors merely saw their gesture as a way of underlining their writings' claim to public attention.

Aristides' apology is the oldest one among the three. We have only a Syrian translation, several papyrus fragments, and a later Byzantine edition; and hence it is difficult to form an adequate judgment of its literary merit. The work contains lengthy polemics against the religions of the Greeks and Jews, as well as against barbarian religions: that is those of exotic nations outside the Graeco-Roman world. This is followed by a relatively short description of the Christian concept of God, and of Christian ethics.

Justin came from the city of Flavia Neapolis, modern-day Nablus in Palestine. He had a comprehensive education in philosophy, and became a convert to Christianity only after some years of wandering as a professional philosopher. Justin continued his migrant life after his conversion, now using his erudition to serve his new faith. Together with six companions, he was tried and executed in Rome in 165 AD. This martyrdom is documented in a very old report (see p. 308).

Justin's apology begins with a refutation of accusations levelled at the Christians; this is followed by a description of the Christian faith and of the life of Christian communities. The most interesting passages in it are those dealing with liturgy which illustrate how the Old Testament was used to justify the belief in Christ. Apart from the apology, Justin also wrote a report about a debate which he claims to have conducted with a learned Jew called Tryphon, who may be identical with the Rabbi Tarphon mentioned in the Talmud. Besides much autobiographical detail, this work contains a controversy about the validity of Mosaic law; a discussion of the question of whether the worship of Christ can be reconciled with Biblical monotheism; and a defence of those people who came to Christianity directly, without the detour via Judaism.

Justin was not aiming for any literary excellence. Nevertheless, every page of his elegantly written piece documents his familiarity with the content and the methods of contemporary philosophy, although the author never denies that his convictions are rooted in the Old Testament faith. Justin's work is the earliest evidence of an author's attempt to find a theological expression – namely, one that uses the means of Platonic and Stoic ontology – for the concept of Jesus' status as the Son of God, and the working of the Holy Ghost.

Justin's endeavour was directed at presenting Christian concepts, clad in current philosophical terminology, to educated people: and in the process the content was inevitably coloured by the form. The Biblical account of the creation of the world, for instance, is interpreted as the shaping of matter without qualities, through the divine spirit. This was certainly incompatible with the idea of a creation out of nothing, as it was first formulated by Paul, and as it was later established as an essential part of the faith. But still, a philosophically educated Christian would not necessarily balk at the contradiction, because Plato and his followers asserted that mere matter as such did not have any being in the true sense of the word.

The Stoics taught that the spirit which gives form, life, and consciousness to the world exists everywhere, in different concentrations of the very finest, all-pervading matter. Justin transfers this notion of the *logos spermatikos* to the spirit of God as mentioned in the Bible, and to its working in history. He claims that the spirit which God used to create the world revealed the nature and the will of its creator to the Jews, through Moses and the prophets. It was the same spirit that taught the Greeks and their philosophers to understand the world, and the norms of morality. The whole truth was not brought to light until the incarnation of the spirit in Christ: but still, Justin says, Moses and many of the Greek philosophers may well be called Christians before Christ.

The endeavour to find a meaningful correlation between the Greek and the Christian tradition was naturally also meant to underline the contention that Christians led inoffensive, lawful lives within the Roman state, and more: that their possession of the ultimate truth made them able to render invaluable services to this state because they alone were truly capable of evaluating legal and institutional justice, and the actions of the rulers. The same idea is also expressed in another apology, the letter to Diognetus, which even compares the role of the Christians within the Empire with that of the soul as the body's inhabitant. Albeit implicitly, Luke's evangelium already claims that the growth of the Roman Empire had been brought about by divine providence as a condition for the spreading of the Christian faith, and that Imperial Rome and Christianity were thus closely related. A lengthy presentation of this idea can be found in a text written in the second century AD by the Bishop Melito of Sardis, who also wrote a lost apology dedicated to the Emperor Marcus Aurelius; and likewise in the apology by Athenagoras, which I shall discuss below. Melito was, moreover, the author of an Easter sermon which has been preserved on papyrus. This is an early specimen of a genre of Christian prose literature which was to develop fully in the subsequent centuries (see p. 517). In Melito's text, the rhythmical patterns do not follow the traditional rules of Greek literary prose, but rather reflect the influence which Semitic, and above all Syro-Aramaic verse forms had on the emerging Christian literature.

The apology by the Athenian Athenagoras does not go beyond a defence of the Christians against accusations of godlessness, and of ritual crimes. A contemporary work dedicated to Athenagoras was Boëthus' treatise on the intricacies of Plato's use of language. This underlines the fact that like Justin, Athenagoras was one of those Christians who had a full share in the intellectual life of their pagan environment, and who bore the title of philosopher. Beside the apology, he also wrote a treatise about the bodily resurrection of the dead, a notion which must have struck educated people as particularly repulsive. The argument for it is presented in a very subtle way, starting with the commonly accepted Platonic doctrine about the immortality of the soul. Athenagoras holds that this immortal soul still needs a body which is able to suffer, so that the soul can fulfil its destiny beyond the threshold of physical death, and be punished or rewarded for good or evil deeds.

A treatise which may likewise be classed as an apology is *To Autolycus* by the Bishop Theophilus of Antioch, although this tract contains more polemics against Classical mythology and philosophy than statements in defence or in explanation of the Christian faith. The transition from defence to attack, however, has always been one of the options open to the apologetical writer. Pure polemic is found in the *Speech Against the Hellenes* by the Syrian Tatianus, one of Justin's pupils. The majority of the apologists tried their best to prove that Graeco-Roman culture and Biblical-Christian tradition were in many ways related to one another; Tatian condemned anything produced by the Hellenes or Greeks, and thus by heathens in general, in their poetry or rhetoric, science or philosophy, fine arts, mythology, or religion. There was hardly any other author as radical as Tatian in the expression of the belief that Classical culture and Biblical-Christian faith were mutually exclusive.

Tatian came from Syria, lived in Rome for some time, and joined the ascetic sect of the Encratites after his return home. In spite of his vehement polemics against Greek intellectual life as a whole, Tatian's contributions to Christian literature do reflect literary interests and abilities. In the late first century and throughout the second century AD the spreading of Christianity had been the immediate cause of the production of two kinds of writings in very different circles: there were letters under the names of the apostles, and evangelia, reports about the works of Jesus (see p. 210). But the sacred text of the Christians was the Old Testament, and the new Christian literature was at first not used in ritual worship. Only very gradually, Christians began to think that among the texts documenting the life of Jesus and the apostles, there was a limited number of particularly valuable ones which could form the corpus of a second part of Holy Scripture. In many Christian groups there was considerable displeasure caused by the fact that this corpus should include four evangelia which differed in content. The Gnostic Marcion, for instance, suggested around the middle of the second century AD that only Luke's evangelium should be regarded as canonical. His reason for this choice was the link between Luke's text and the apostle Paul whom Marcion held in particularly high esteem. Tatian, on the other hand, harmonised the reports of the four evangelia in a synthesised account written in the Syrian language. This so-called *Diatesseron* temporarily found official recognition in the Syrian church. It was also translated into Greek, Latin, Armenian, and later into Old High German.

Heretics and anti-heretics

Some of the authors named as apologists in the previous section, for instance, Theophilus and Justin, also wrote treatises belonging to the context of disputes within the Christian faith. We know of pamphlets against advocates of various Gnostic doctrines, as well as against Marcionites, Encratites, Montanites, and many more. The most important work of this kind is undoubtedly that by Eirenaios, known in Latin as Irenaeus of

Lugdunum, modern-day Lyons. Irenaeus died as Bishop of his native city shortly before the beginning of the third century AD.

The Christian community of Lyons, which suffered severe persecutions in 177 AD, was a Greek-speaking one like its counterpart in Rome. Like the trade along the Rhone Valley, the spreading of the Christian faith in that part of the Empire emanated from the Greek cities in the region now known as Provence. Among the extant Christian texts written before the beginning of the third century AD we find not a single work by a Latin author. In the second century AD all the areas where Christian communities existed in larger numbers were in Greek-speaking regions, above all in Asia Minor and northern Syria. Even the Syriac-speaking lands inside and outside the Roman Empire seem to have had a greater share of Christians among their inhabitants than the Latin world, although immigration from the East had led to the establishment of large Greek-speaking communities in all western cities. Greek was also spoken by all the Jews in the Roman Empire, except for the ones who lived in Palestine who spoke Syro-Aramaic.

The five books of Irenaeus' major work contain detailed descriptions of Gnostic systems, which are refuted in several different stages of Biblical-theological as well as philosophical argumentation. In the context of these refutations, Irenaeus presents many positive results of his own theological reflections, including the earliest known versions of some individual doctrines which were to become of fundamental importance in later Christian dogma. One example is the doctrine of apostolic succession, based on the claim that through the continuous line of their predecessors, all rightful bishops have been indirectly ordained by the apostles themselves. This unbroken continuity is cited as guaranteeing the authority of the bishops on questions concerning doctrine, the constitution of Christian communities, and moral living. Irenaeus' manner of thinking and arguing was to a large extent determined by that notion of order on which the Roman state was founded; and Irenaeus in turn was to a large extent responsible for passing this notion on to the Christian church, which became more and more of an established institution.

It is difficult to say much about the specifically literary qualities of Irenaeus' work, as we have only parts of the original Greek text. The only extant complete version is a very old Latin translation dating back to the fourth century AD. It is obvious why Irenaeus' text should be less elaborate in style than the contemporary apologies; but none the less it shows the author's complete mastery of the current means of expression used to formulate philosophical and scientific arguments. In this respect, his work is particularly good evidence of the Christians' entry into the educational world of Graeco-Roman culture. Of course lengthy accounts and refutations of the doctrines of those with whom one disagreed already existed in a time-honoured genre of philosophical literature; and in the following section of my book, I shall discuss the most important extant example of this kind of scientific-philosophical writing (see p. 323). But while its author Sextus Empiricus follows the tradition of Skepticism in basing his refutations on methodically constructed chains of argument, Irenaeus, who was equally familiar with that approach, still chooses to use Biblical authority as the main arsenal in internal Christian controversy.

To borrow or deduce arguments from authoritative texts was quite a common habit in the environment in which Christianity grew. Above all in the school of Plato, but also elsewhere in the philosophy and the science of the Empire, we find plenty of cases where authors attempted to present their own teachings as the correct interpretation of ancient authorities, and to prove this by a corresponding reading of ancient writings. The bone of contention between Christians and Jews was ultimately the correct reading of the Bible. Its authority as the basis for all discussion was never really denied by either party, except for a growing number of Jews from the second century AD onwards who refused to continue accepting the Greek translation of the Bible as authentic. On the Christian side there were only very few people who rejected Biblical-Jewish traditions altogether, such as Marcion, who in the second century AD founded a separate church that recognised only Paul's letters and Luke's evangelium as Holy Scripture. But nobody who participated in the complex debate about the proper faith could steer clear of controversy about the correct reading of the Biblical text.

In this context, the writing of commentaries was of course a particularly important activity. In the interpretation of what was later called the Old Testament, Christians in the first and second centuries AD could draw on the products of a rich Jewish literary tradition in Aramaic as well as Greek. Not only the works of Philo (see p. 161), for instance, but also parts of the New Testament contain abundant illustrations of its interpretational practice. It took a long time, however, until comparable efforts were made to interpret those texts which came to form the New Testament canon during the second and third centuries AD. As in the development of well-structured doctrinal systems, the Christian Gnostics seem to have been the pioneers in this field. Most members of Gnostic groups were from the educated classes and it is indeed significant that one of the few pieces of Gnostic writing of which we have the complete original text in Greek should be an elegantly styled edificatory letter explaining Valentinian doctrine. The author is Ptolemaeus, a teacher from Valentinus' school, who addressed his epistle to a noble lady named Flora, in the second half of the second century AD.

From the same period we have lengthy fragments of a commentary on John's evangelium by the Gnostic Heracleon. The Gnostics were fond of illustrating doctrine by reference to a rich mythology, and this is in keeping with Heracleon's use of allegorical interpretation, a method from the Stoic exegesis of Homer which had already been adopted by Greek-speaking Jews (see p. 163).

We know that even the earliest Christian communities had their own liturgical chants; their poetic form, however, can only be approximately reconstructed on the basis of evidence from later periods, or by means of analogies drawn from information about synagogue ritual. Some Gnostics are cited as authors of psalms and hymns, as for instance the aforementioned Valentinus, but also Basilides and his school. The close links of those Gnostics with the Platonic tradition suggest that their poetic works were produced according to the rules of Greek versification. This is certainly the case with one anonymous *hymnus* from the Gnostic sect of the Naacenes, whose doctrine put particular emphasis on the story of the serpent that persuaded Adam in paradise to eat the fruit of the Tree of Knowledge. An entire collection of hymns from the second century AD is extant in a Syrian translation, and parts of it in Coptic; but the original Greek text was lost. These so-called *Odes of Solomon* stem from the Encratites, as do the *Acts of Thomas* which I shall discuss below (see p. 307). The Encratite circles combined esoteric teachings about the human soul with strict ascetic practice. Their texts must have been of great poetic beauty in the original Greek: even in the translations, we recognise a rich imagery with a particularly large number of bold metaphors, more often than not coined to express motifs and notions which were alien to Biblical tradition. In this respect the poems document the impact of religious syncretism, which affected the early Christian church as well as Judaism within the Graeco-Roman world, and beyond its eastern borders.

Of course the rich literary production of the Gnostics or of circles close to them included also evangelia: that is reports about the life of the Saviour, and above all lengthy accounts of the travels and the adventures of the apostles. This genre of literature for edification and entertainment contains all the formal characteristics and motifs of the Greek novel (see p. 236), and it was extremely popular among educated readers. In most of these works the specific doctrines of the groups among which they originated are hinted at rather than spelled out, while the entertaining-edifying elements of the narrative are put in the foreground. This explains why later readers failed to recognise the heterodoxical character of these writings, which remained part of the established church tradition, and were spread throughout the Christian world by translations into several Oriental languages, Latin, and later also Church Slavic. Many episodes from such narratives inspired representations in the fine arts.

Not all of the apocryphal *Acts of the Apostles* can be dated precisely, but we may assume that they were all written between the second and the fourth centuries AD. An early specimen are the *Acts of Paul and Thekla*, which describe not only the apostle's career with many ornamental additions, but which also contain a detailed physical depiction of Paul, undoubtedly intended to make the account more vivid. A favourite feature of such narratives is the description of long journeys and exciting adventures in distant countries. The authors send their heroes to India and Africa to meet cannibals and wild animals, and they make them escape dangers and perform difficult tasks aided by God-given miraculous powers. Thus, the apostle Thomas is said to have travelled through the desert with the help of wild donkeys which obeyed his command. Another common feature in the *Acts* are stories concerning the miraculous success of conversions: Thomas, for instance, who is taken to India as a slave, becomes court architect to a Rajah, who gives him a large sum of money intended for the construction of a palace. Thomas, however, gives it all away to the poor, and is thrown into prison when he is found out by the King. But then the King dreams that he enters heaven, and is directed to a place said to be his property. Baffled, he asks how this heavenly palace was created: and the answer reminds him of the charity which Thomas practised with his money. The King awakes, Thomas is set free, and the way is clear for the preaching of the Gospel.

Most reports, however, culminate in descriptions of the heroes' martyrdom: and this is a point in which the *Acts* resemble a different and much more simple genre of edificatory writing (as described below). The *Acts* also contain a fair amount of realistic features, such as geographical detail, exotic names or descriptions of exotic milieus, or references to the customs or doctrines of the groups among which the texts were produced. The *Acts of John*, for example, mention a dance of Jesus' disciples at the Last Supper, and thus hint at a ritual which has survived only in marginal branches of the church tradition. The *Acts of Bartholomew* contain a geographical introduction which illustrates the contemporary image of countries around the Indian Ocean.

The most interesting of the *Acts* are undoubtedly those of Thomas. Their lost original version was presumably written in the Syrian language in Edessa, around 200 AD. The extant Greek version is only slightly more recent, and closer to the original than the extant Syrian text, which seems to be a retranslation from the Greek. The *Acts of Thomas* illustrate the bilingualism of Christian life on the eastern fringes of the *Imperium Romanum*. They contain a *hymnus* of great poetic beauty, in a metre which is clearly of Semitic origin and whose Greek version does not seem at all influenced by Greek versification. This text narrates the story of a king's son who travels to Egypt and then returns to his father's court: a tale meant as an allegory on the soul which loses its divine home, but whose destiny it is to return to it.

The most voluminous work among these Christian novels are the so-called *Pseudo-Clementines*, produced in the third and fourth centuries AD, mostly by authors with a Jewish-Christian background. The stories, of which there are two extant versions, focus on different individuals: the apostle Peter, his disciple Clement of Rome, and his adversary Simon Magus, of whom we also know through the canonical history of the apostles. Simon Magus was regarded by the church as the founder of Gnosticism. The twenty books of *Homilies* contain missionary sermons ostensibly preached by Peter, with accompanying narrative. The ten books of *Recognitions* apply the popular novelistic motif of the separation and reunion of a couple of lovers to Clement, his parents, and his brothers.

Both the Greek and the Latin text which we have of the Clementines are from the fourth century AD: they are the result of much editorial work and include many additions. The narrative framework is all but obliterated by theological reflections, moral paraenesis, and excerpts from the constitutions of Christian communities. This complex product may likewise be based on an original in the Syrian language, written among the Jews of Palestine. It gives us important clues about the faith and the general way of thinking of those second-century Christians who still regarded themselves as belonging to the synagogue.

The apocryphal *Acts of the Apostles* represent a fairly high-brow type of edifying literature. A much simpler type of writing is exemplified by the *Martyrs' Acts*, which were widely read in ecclesiastical circles. The oldest specimens centre on accounts of interrogations by the Roman authorities, recorded in direct speech, which suggests that official transcripts were either used, or at least closely imitated. To the words spoken by the steadfast confessor, the authors would add reports about his former life, his arrest, his imprisonment, and above all his execution and the faith and courage which he showed on that occasion. The earliest *Martyrs' Acts* are those of Polycarp, Justin, Carpus, and Apollonius, all written in the second century AD, and invariably very short and very plain. Those richly embellished acts which are mostly of little value as historical sources were not produced until much later. The eagerness of Christian groups for authentic information about people who proved their faith in their *martyrium* is illustrated by a letter from the congregations of Lyons and Vienne (see p. 304), which describes the persecutions they suffered in 177 AD. This letter was addressed to the Christian communities in Asia Minor, and included in the ecclesiastical history of Eusebius 150 years later. However, it does not simply tell of the martyrs' steadfastness, and of Christian solidarity under persecution, but moreover mentions instances of apostasy and betrayal. Together with the aforementioned edifying literature, such reports about martyrs formed the basis for a rich literary production of legends and lives of saints in later centuries.

5

THE SEVERAN ERA

1 GENERAL REMARKS

The reign of Marcus Aurelius, the last of the Antonines, saw the first forebodings of a crisis which was to put an end to a whole system of political and social order. The safety of the Empire was seriously threatened by Germanic as well as Iranian Sarmatic tribes, who pushed against the Danube border. At the same time, there was warfare on the Eastern frontier, where the Euphrates marked the border with the Parthian state. The Emperor and the army proved their ability to cope with this military challenge, with the eastern war being fought under the command of Verus, the Emperor's brother and temporary co-regent. However, the sheer duration of the war effort put too much of a strain on the Empire's finances and the economy was further weakened by an equally prolonged epidemic which decimated the population. Finally, the Emperor abandoned the principle of succession by adoption in 177 AD when he made his son Commodus his co-regent. Commodus succeeded Marcus Aurelius as sole ruler in 180 AD.

The return to the dynastic principle took its toll on relations between the Emperor and the economically and culturally dominant classes of the population, the educated upper bourgeoisie of Greek and Roman cities, and first and foremost the Senatorial nobility. Harmony between those groups and the Emperor had produced peace and prosperity: the basis for this harmony was the idea that education and wealth were necessary conditions for exercising public influence and taking on any kind of public responsibility. People generally believed that the reigning Emperor must consider these facts in choosing the best man as his successor, instead of acting only as the bearer of a charisma belonging to his family. If he made the right choice, then even the religious exaltation of the Emperor's dignity could ultimately be reconciled with that ancient Roman-Republican tradition as whose guardian the Senate saw itself.

During the twelve years of Commodus' reign this monarch developed into a despot. When the Senate showed him its dislike the Emperor retaliated with executions and confiscations of property. Commodus adopted an extravagant lifestyle and came to regard his divine status more and more as appertaining to his person and not to his office. Like Nero and Domitian before him, Commodus was finally thought of as a bloodthirsty tyrant by the educated people, while he loved to pose as a charismatic benefactor of the underprivileged rural folk, and as a protector of the poor against the tyranny of the rich. Commodus' reign wrought enormous damage to the Empire's finance and administration, as well as to the military. After the murder of the monarch the succession was contested in a bloody war between the most powerful commanders: once the principle of adoption had been given up the Senate was completely sidelined. At long last Septimius Severus, commander of the troops on the Danube, defeated Clodius Albinus and Pescennius Niger, generals of the forces in Gaul and Germany respectively, as well as the supreme commander in the East. As in the Year of the Three Emperors 69 AD; the destiny of the state was thus decided by the army. The victorious Septimius Severus reigned for eighteen years, trying to recreate a stable order in the Empire.

The memory of the 'good' Emperors of the second century AD was still so much alive that Severus claimed to be Marcus Aurelius' adopted son and took the family name of Antoninus. Severus came from an equestrian family in the north African city of Leptis Magna, modern-day Tripoli. He had risen to the ranks of the Senatorial nobility through a meteoric career in the army and the administration. While holding a command in Syria, Severus married his second wife Julia Domna, who came from the powerful dynasty of the priests of Baal at the temple of Emesa in Syria. This clan had developed a very peculiar synthesis between their country's religious traditions, and the status and lifestyle of the Greek upper classes.

In spite of his ostentatious link-up with the Antonines, Severus' politics often went against the interests of the bourgeois upper class. All his measures and innovations were aimed at funnelling private wealth and the profits of economic activity into the ever-empty coffers of the state, so that he could keep the army generously equipped for military campaigns, as well as for protecting his own power. Severus had no qualms about confiscating the fortunes of Senators suspected of an oppositional stance, or about imposing cruel punishments and oppressive taxes on the populations of entire cities. He transformed the personal guarantee of officials from the municipal nobility for their communities' tax payments into a collective liability of their class, and he inflicted a heavy burden on many specific regions by requisitioning excessive amounts of services for the troops.

On the other hand Severus introduced a large number of collective privileges, especially exemptions from taxes and other duties, for such professional groups whose work appeared to be of vital importance for the state and the army. Among them were shipowners, merchants who supplied goods to the military, people in the transport business, and domain as well as tax leaseholders. This was the beginning of that subordination of all economic activity to the interests of the fiscus which was characteristic of the Late Classical and the Byzantine state, and which led to economic decline as well as to the mushroom growth of bureaucracy. On the other hand the granting of privileges to certain professions and other groups among the population indicated a tendency which worked against the centralistic nature of the state, and foreshadowed the division of estates in the feudal order of mediaeval society. Soon after Severus' measures were introduced, some privileged individuals managed to amass large fortunes and great power, within the framework of the tyrannic state but yet beyond its immediate reach.

Severus curbed the political influence of the Senatorial class by giving people of equestrian rank many of those administrative and military posts which were by law and tradition reserved for Senatorial families. He also encouraged the rise of soldiers from the lower ranks to the equestrian officers' commissions, increasing the influence of the troopers in the army at the cost of that of the educated bourgeoisie. In his legislation, Severus did his best to promote the interests of the *humiliores*, the lowly people, whom he tried to protect against exploitation by the *honestiores*, the wealthy upper classes. This gives Severus' laws a humanitarian character which contrasts strangely with his ruthless governmental practice.

While the 'bourgeois' emperors of the previous century had for the most part tried to improve military discipline, Severus kept on increasing the army's pay, and thus gave the mainly rural soldiers the feeling that they belonged to a more and more privileged class. The Emperor ensured the legal recognition of the habitual concubinages of long-serving soldiers as marriages, and he thus encouraged the settlement of soldiers in the garrisons which were then most often situated in their respective recruitment areas. In the border provinces this led to the creation of settlements which may well be called military cities.

Finally, Severus did away with the last privileges which still distinguished Italy from the provinces. He dissolved the Praetorian guard, stationed regular troops in the vicinity of Rome, and made his regime more secure by enlarging the police forces. Severus' administration was commonly regarded as oppressive in all parts of the Empire, except for his own native region in north Africa, and also the Syrian homeland of his wife.

Severus' son Caracalla continued his father's practices in an even coarser fashion. He ordered the murder of his brother Geta, who had been his co-regent for only a few years; and his dislike of the educated bourgeoisie found vent in a horrible massacre in Alexandria. Like his father, Caracalla had a certain amount of success in military campaigns against the Parthians. In 212 AD he introduced a law which granted Roman citizenship to all but a few free inhabitants of the Empire. This *constitutio antoniniana* marks a turning point in legal history; but still, it had very little practical importance at a time when, in one way or another, everybody suffered from an increasingly despotic government.

In 217 AD, during the Parthian War in Syria, Caracalla became the victim of a conspiracy led by a senior officer called Macrinus, whom the troops then proclaimed as Emperor. Macrinus, however, tried to discipline the army and to bring about a return to the politics of the previous century. This led to a new civil war in which Macrinus himself was killed. The victorious party was commanded by Elagabal, an eccentric young man from that Syrian dynasty of priests into which Severus had married. In the decades in question this clan produced quite a number of female characters who were as influential as they were fond of intrigue. Elagabal was pushed to the fore by his mother and his grandmother, who persuaded the Syrian legions to proclaim him as the new monarch. He introduced the worship of Baal of Emesa as the highest official cult in Rome, and when his outrageous policies had deprived him of any support which he might have had, Elagabal was forced by his grandmother to accept his cousin Severus Alexander as his co-regent. Elagabal repeatedly tried to get rid of this rival, but finally, after a reign of three years, he himself and his mother were beaten to death by soldiers.

Severus Alexander was a well-intentioned, well-educated young man, but like Elagabal, he was entirely under the influence of his mother and grandmother. He reigned for thirteen years until 235 AD, making an honest effort to restore the politics of the Antonines and the former status of the Senate. Alexander's failure was due to his ineptitude as a military commander. This was a crucial issue not only because the army alone could ultimately protect the monarch's power over the Empire. A more important factor was the increased pressure on the Roman Empire's eastern border, where a new military challenge had appeared after the demise of the Parthian dynasty, who were succeeded by the far more enterprising Sassanids. Like his predecessor and cousin, Alexander was killed by soldiers, together with his mother Julia Mammaea. His death marks the end of an epoch in so far as it heralded the breakdown of the new order which Septimius Severus had after all created, even if that order was of a much cruder kind than the one which preceded it. Alexander's death was followed by a period of quarrels over the succession, a time during which disorder reached the level of complete anarchy.

2 ROMAN JURISPRUDENCE

Scientific jurisprudence is arguably the most precious legacy which the Romans left to posterity. The development of Roman legal science, which has not a single parallel in the history of all other civilisations in the Old

World, resulted from the specific social and political conditions in ancient Rome.

Before the Romans, the Greeks had already created a highly sophisticated legal culture. One of its most important features was the steadfastness with which people under the most diverse political circumstances upheld the idea that nothing should be allowed to happen within a community which was not justified by its laws. This explains the high prestige enjoyed both by legislators and law-abiding citizens. Another characteristic of Greek legal culture was the early pursuit of reflections about the nature of law and justice. Naturally such speculations were first and foremost based on problems from constitutional and criminal law, as both areas suggested viewing individual cases in the context of a fundamental contemplation of human co-existence much more strongly than, for instance, a disputed inheritance or right of way. Because of the basic philosophical approach to law most of those Greeks who had a comprehensive and detailed legal knowledge were in fact philosophers; and as well-documented individual cases show, philosophers were equally numerous among the legislators.

On the other hand the Greek world never really knew that kind of legal specialist whose knowledge is strictly confined to the framework of the current legal order. This can be explained by the fact that from a very early stage, legal-judicial practice in most Greek states was in the hands of people's courts. Their work was always governed by strict procedural rules, and yet the numerous members of their juries expected to be persuaded by the spokesman of a party, rather than to be convinced by legal technicalities. This is why the training of advocates, the only specialists in legal practice, was entirely dominated by rhetoric from the fifth century BC onwards. Of course a legal orator had to know the relevant laws, but his art was not the specific skill of jurisprudence, which consists of using the legal order as a whole to deduce reasons in favour of one's cause which are not explicitly stated in the law itself.

A Greek advocate had rather to find arguments which would be immediately convincing to anybody, because of their appeal to the jury's common sense, unburdened by specialist knowledge; to their general moral consciousness; or to their emotions. Rhetoric as taught to legal orators would thus concentrate on the technique of argumentation, and psychological-ethical rather than legal knowledge. Neither advocates nor philosophers who were concerned with a potential or the actual legal order would be interested in an exact definition of the borderline between what is good and just on the one hand, and what is dictated or permitted by the law on the other. A philosopher or legislator looked at justice within the given law; an advocate tried to promote his client's cause by presenting the law as being in harmony with the jury's sense of morality.

In ancient Rome, the situation was entirely different. For much longer than the Greeks, the Romans had adhered to a belief in the religious nature of all jurisdiction. This notion seems common in all archaic communities without a developed executive, where it provides a means of ensuring that legal decisions are respected in practice. In Rome the delivery of expert legal opinions in disputed cases thus remained for a long time the task of a council of priests, the *pontifices*, who acted as guardians of a largely unwritten legal tradition. The extreme conservatism of the Romans also explains the long survival of a custom which made the pronouncement of certain formulas, initially certainly believed to have magical-binding power, a condition for the validity of any legal transaction. Such pronouncements were often accompanied by symbolic gestures. This formalism reflected the stubborn adherence to tradition that made the Romans suspicious of all legislative processes, which, as a rule, respond to newly arisen necessities, and hence contain an element of innovation.

The codification of the so-called Twelve Tables, made under Greek influence after the fall of the Roman monarchy in the fifth century BC, remained in force until well into the Imperial age, with only very few laws added to it by the people's assembly on occasions that required urgent action. At the same time, economic and social conditions changed fundamentally, as Rome was transformed from an agricultural community into the centre of a global empire. Consequently there was hardly any law in the Twelve Tables which could still be applied literally, and the language of this legal code had in any case become incomprehensible to all but a few scholars. These were the reasons why Romans for centuries saw themselves forced to come up with ever-new readings of the law, in order to make ancient and still valid legal rules suit newly arisen needs.

The most important condition for coping with this perennial task was provided by the stable, aristocratic character of the Roman state. A significant trait of its political order was the *imperium*, the power of disposition and command given to holders of high offices from the Roman nobility, who wielded it with almost no restrictions, but never for longer than one year. The two lawlords or Praetors, for instance, could make any kind of legal decision, confirming or overruling those of their predecessors. However, they had to remember that their successors in office would have the same power, and that their reputation was at stake, as were their prospects in the permanent competition between the members of their class, who all aimed for the same careers. This explains why centuries of annual change in office still led to the fixing of a growing number of decisions and procedural rules, as tried and tested in Praetorian legal practice, and in the interpretation of the old-fashioned, inflexible *ius civile*, the Roman civil law code. This process created a law of office or *ius honorarium*, confirmed each year in the Praetors' edict at the beginning of their term, with such minor additions as seemed necessary. This law of office could thus be described as self-codifying, and was in turn liable to become the subject of a process of interpretation. In the following, I shall give a few examples of how the *ius honorarium* adapted the old *ius civile* to the changing demands of economic and social life.

Like other agricultural societies, the early Romans regarded the wilful felling of slow-growing fruit or olive trees as a particularly grave crime, with correspondingly heavy sanctions. When people in Latium began to grow vines, the wording of the law which mentioned only trees could not cover damage done to vineyards. However, the Praetor would simply rule that during his term of office, vines were to be regarded as trees; and this decree of course then entered the permanent *ius honorarium*. Another case in point concerns those laws of the *ius civile* which dealt with property, the family, or inheritance. These laws were only valid for Roman citizens and consequently those who had been taken prisoners of war and thus lost their citizenship would be left with no legal means of preventing irreparable damage to their property, or to their personal rights. However, the Praetor's office enabled him to decree that until the return of such a person, his citizenship was dormant, but not invalid; and thus the rights and the property of that man could be protected.

The greatest influence exerted by the Praetors was on the laws governing legal procedure. The *ius civile* prescribed no more than a small number of strictly formalised types of legal processes, the so-called *legis actiones*, which had to be adhered to by those who wanted to make a claim based on precisely defined parts of the legal code. Those *legis actiones* often turned out to be totally inadequate to the more and more complicated reality of economic life, with its overseas trading, and its incipient credit business. For conducting legal disputes in such cases the Praetor could offer the concerned parties independently drafted forms. Those forms, either self-designed or adopted from his predecessors, were usually publicised when a Praetor took up his office. Quarrelling parties could then demand the issue of a corresponding procedural contract, granted by the Praetor with a theoretical preliminary verdict on both parties' claims, an assessment which informed the final decision of that judge whom the Praetor appointed for the hearing of evidence.

The annual change of officeholders led to a steady increase in the number of men with considerable legal experience among the Roman nobility. Anybody who considered taking legal action was well-advised to consult such a person first in order to be enlightened about the prospects and the possible developments of the case. Such a step seemed all the more logical if the family of the person consulted was closely linked with one's own by those relations of clientele or patronage which played such a dominant role in Roman political life, with regard to elections, the appointment of administrative assistants, or matters of social welfare. Legal advice solicited in the aforesaid circumstances was given publicly, in the presence of young noblemen eager for learning, and this is why it came to replace the religiously protected private dispensing of legal expertise by the *pontifices* (see p. 314). Over the generations the process of spreading legal lore more and more widely among the nobility had a considerable impact on general public consciousness. The best proof for this influence is the fact that legal terminology features in Roman poetry and literary prose from their very beginnings as, for instance, in the comedies of Plautus which were after all written for a very mixed audience. This seems to suggest that we would find the same phenomenon in everyday linguistic usage, if we had the necessary evidence. But however widespread legal notions had become, what was expected from the legal advisor or *iuris consultus* of the period was above all a specialist knowledge of the law, and not the art of persuasion.

The flexible interpretation and enlargement of a rigid, old-fashioned legal code was a development that happened under the protection of a socially accepted fullness of power, wielded by successive officeholders. In the process the legal consciousness of the general public was also affected, and opened up to new ideas. The Roman people became aware of principles that had to be observed in legal transactions between Romans and foreigners, and this led to the notion of a *ius gentium*, a law governing relations between citizens of different states. This concept was developed above all with regard to the work of the *praetor peregrinus* who had to deal with such cases.

In legal practice laws that were too rigid or that had become meaningless were routinely watered down or circumvented, and this led to a growing appreciation of legal adequacy, practicability, and rationality. Thus, for example, the old civil law prescribed the *patria potestas*, the absolute power of the male head of the family over all its members. According to the code, a son might be an adult, or even holder of a high public office: but he was still legally a minor as long as his father was alive. This caused major problems in families which, for instance, were engaged in extensive trading. However, there was a way in which a son could be exempted from the *patria potestas*, if his father had sold him into slavery three times, and if the son had been freed and returned into his father's power twice. This legal provision had long become obsolete, but it became a useful means of getting rid of the cumbersome tie of the *patria potestas*, whenever that became a nuisance to all family members involved. If, for example, the owner of a family estate wanted his son to be responsible for managing a plantation on that estate, he could invite a number of friends to attend the public staging of a triple pro forma sale and release in fulfilment of the letter of the law.

During the second century BC Rome absorbed more Greek thought than ever before, and many members of the upper classes in particular became familiar with Greek philosophy and rhetoric. Roman legal lore, with its practical origins, was consequently transformed in the Greek philosophical-rhetorical fashion by way of systematising, defining its terms and concepts, and making it a common theme in literature.

We know that the first Roman legal literature consisted of compilations of forms for legal procedure, and of commentaries on the Twelve Tables, which were written in the early second century BC. These were followed by collections of general legal principles, and systematic treatises on specific areas of the law. Our sources tell us that such works were occasionally in the form of dialogues, which quite clearly shows the literary influence of Greece. The authors were without exception such members of the Senatorial nobility who had held high public offices, and who had distinguished themselves in the judicature. In the relevant sources we come across the names of very many friends of Scipio the Younger, a man who had a special interest in promoting Greek education. One of his friends was the great legal scholar Q. Mucius Scaevola, Consul in 95 BC as well as holder of the office of Pontifex Maximus, who wrote the first comprehensive survey of the *ius civile*. Two generations later Servius Sulpicius Rufus, Consul in 51 BC and legal instructor of Cicero, wrote a number of works including a commentary on the Praetorian Edict, which was then already regarded as a closed code.

The early representatives of Roman scientific jurisprudence were much indebted to Greek philosophy, which had made them aware of the need for exact terminological definitions and inspired their endeavour to arrive at a systematic-complete presentation of legal facts. From Greek rhetoric, which for psychagogical reasons had incorporated a doctrine concerning general rules of moral conduct and categories of moral judgment, Roman legal scholars learned the skill of finding adequate expressions for those maxims that all legal practice should follow, especially in the interpretation of rigid laws: for instance, the principle of *aequitas* or justice, or that of *bona fides* or trust. The Stoic philosophical doctrine about the *ius naturale* or the natural origin of the law helped to formulate a more precise definition of the relationship between the *ius gentium* and the *ius civile*, the law governing the interaction between people of different nations, and the one concerning relations between Roman citizens. All of these developments contributed to the creation of an exact legal hermeneutics.

An excellent illustration of this process is a documented legal case from the year 93 BC where the two quarrelling parties were represented by L. Licinius Crassus, the most famous orator at that time, and the likewise highly prominent legal scholar Q. Mucius Scaevola. The facts of the case were as follows: a testator had named an heir in tail as well as a reversionary heir, and the heir in tail had died before the testator. According to the letter of the will, this meant that the intestate succession had to be followed and that the reversionary heir whom the testator had named would inherit nothing at all. Crassus prevailed with his opinion that a decision had to be made in accordance with *voluntas* or intention of the testator, and not according to the *verba* or wording of the will. This case established the prominence of one of the most important hermeneutical methods in Roman law: the objectification of the intention as expressed in words or actions, prior to the application of the letter of the relevant law. This method had no Greek precedent, for among the Greeks reflections on purpose and intention operated only within the confines of psychological and moral aspects. These were the very issues which Roman legal theory ignored, in its strict limitation to the interpretation and application of existing laws as it was called for in legal practice. The creation of a specific legal definition of intention illustrates particularly well how Roman jurisprudence became a separate science, distinct from ethics, political theory, general anthropology, and other related disciplines.

The Empire saw the heyday of Roman legal science. The Emperor Augustus made his explicit permission a condition for at least the public *respondere* or delivery of legal expertise, traditionally given by a competent Senator. Augustus' policy meant that the *responsa* or expert assessments delivered by such privileged men acquired a status similar to that of Imperial edicts and laws, as acts of legislation. Imperial law, which replaced the Republican law of office, was thus complemented by jurisprudential law. Augustus and his early successors respected the tradition of the legal profession in so far as they permitted only Senators to give expert statements *ex auctoritate principis* or with Imperial authority, although more and more legal scholars from equestrian families came to be employed as private legal tutors, counsellors, solicitors, and experts in Imperial service. But when Tiberius granted the knight Masurius Sabinus the Senatorial privilege, this was a great exception. M. Antistius Labeo, the greatest legal scholar of the preceding generation, had never been thus honoured, unlike his Senatorial rival M. Ateius Capito, Consul in 22 BC.

The flowering of legal science continued throughout the first and second centuries AD. The Emperor Hadrian took a particularly great interest in jurisprudence, actively encouraging legal instruction, and trying to make legal studies a condition for entry into public service. From then on many legal experts from the equestrian class became Senators through their careers in public office.

The second century is commonly regarded as the High Classic epoch of Roman jurisprudence, represented by such men as L. Javolenus Priscus, Salvius Julianus, P. Juventius Celsus, Neratius Priscus, Titius Aristo, and Sex. Pomponius. Apart from the latter two who seem to have worked exclusively as legal instructors all the others held high posts in the administration and in the army. The last of the Empire's great legal scholars – Aemilius Papinianus, Julius Paulus, and Domitius Ulpianus – lived in the early third century AD and also served the state as holders of high offices. Papinian was a friend of the Emperor Septimius Severus; Ulpian was the closest advisor of the Emperor Alexander Severus. Both were killed during the quarrels about the succession following the deaths of their patrons.

It would be easy enough to add even more names to this list of famous legal scholars, all of whom belonged to one of two school traditions, the Sabinian or the Proculian. The large number of eminent individuals is matched by a correspondingly wide range of forms and types of legal literature. Beside collections of *responsa* by legal experts of the past, there were commentaries on different legal codes, especially the Praetorian edict and the old Roman *ius civile*. In the so-called *quaestiones* and *disputationes*, authors discussed individual cases. The so-called *digestae* were excerpts from older legal writings, from edicts or rescripts of the Imperial administration, or from older laws. Those excerpts had a systematic structure, with divisions according to specific legal areas or problems.

The literary genres mentioned so far were texts to be used in legal practice as well as in instruction, whereas the so-called *institutiones*, short but comprehensive surveys of the entire legal system, were exclusively written for teaching purposes. The same goes for systematic descriptions of specific legal areas, for collections of basic legal principles known as *sententiae* and *regulae*, and for compilations of legal terms and fundamental concepts under the headings of *differentiae*, *definitiones*, or *opiniones*. Of particular interest to the modern reader is an *enchiridium* or textbook by the abovementioned Pomponius, a work which has been preserved among the *Digests* of Justinian (1, 2, 2; see below), and which contains a survey of the history of Roman jurisprudence.

Pomponius' work is only one specimen of a rich literature whose accumulation over the years is documented in the fifty books of the *Digests*, collated in the sixth century AD at the order of the Emperor Justinian, by legal scholars from the school of Berytus, modern-day Beirut. The volumes were published in the context of a comprehensive codification of the *corpus iuris* or current law, together with a didactic treatise or *Institutiones*, and with a collection of Imperial laws entitled *Codex Iustiniani*. In the *Digests* we find excerpts from older literature grouped according to topics. In their large number, and often considerable length, these excerpts give us a fairly good idea of many legal scholars' way of working, talking, and arguing. Occasionally, the *Digests* also reflect the great formal diversity of legal literature.

From this great profusion of writing, only one document is extant in a complete, or at least a nearly complete form. This is a textbook by a certain Gaius, rediscovered on a palimpsest, a parchment where the original writing was washed off and replaced by a new layer of different text. We know no biographical details from Gaius' life; he seems to belong to the period around 160 AD but was presumably unknown to the eminent legal scholars at that time, and lived and worked in a provincial setting: not in the capital or in one of those centres of legal learning such as Berytus where Latin was the medium of instruction. The earliest known references to Gaius are found in works from the Late Classical age, where his name is mentioned alongside those of the Classics in the context of endeavours to revive ancient legal culture, a trend which began in the fourth century AD. We may infer that by then, Gaius' book was widely used in teaching; this assumption is also borne out by the discovery of fragments of the text on Egyptian papyri. Even in the Late Classical age, there were still authors who produced epitomes and paraphrases of Gaius' work. A textbook commissioned by the Emperor Justinian follows Gaius' *Institutiones* very closely in more than one passage. Justinian's *Digests* also use material from other writings by Gaius, such as a commentary on the Twelve Tables, and another on the Urban Praetor's edict.

Gaius' extant work is characterised by great systematic precision. His textbook was presumably designed for a beginners' course in legal studies covering all aspects of civil and procedural law; it reflects the high degree of refinement in contemporary legal terminology and dogmatics. To a literary historian, the most fascinating feature of Gaius' writing is the clarity and precision of diction, influenced by none of the successive, and occasionally even overlapping stylistic fashions of literary prose. In its strict objectivity, its exact correspondence of expression and content, and its avoidance of all words and phrases which could evoke distracting connotations, Gaius' work is typical of the features common to all legal literature, in spite of some noticeable differences as to degrees of tortuousness or wordiness in the writings of individual legal scholars.

Gaius, who was virtually unknown in his own lifetime, was a kindred spirit to the great legal personalities of the High and the Late Classical age, because of his conscious subordination to a strict linguistic discipline produced by a long tradition of legal practice and instruction. The strict objectivity and the imperturbable constancy of legal prose is crucial to a proper understanding of Roman linguistic art, as a foil to those ever-new artistic devices of literary prose which were all derived from rhetoric, and meant to have a psychagogical effect in persuading the hearer or reader, or in appealing to his emotions.

Beside the legal texts, there were also other textbooks and expert treatises written without the rhetorical arsenal of literary prose. But no other discipline had such a time-honoured tradition of endeavours to express facts precisely: and no other discipline produced such convincing results. The many legal terms and allusions which appear in all kinds of Latin literature indicate that jurisprudence had a considerable influence on the thought and the speech of educated people (see pp. 315 and 351). This is certainly one of the reasons why school instruction and the educational tradition in general returned again and again to a kind of Latin which has that precision and that monumentality which is generally admired, as a phenomenon viewed in isolation from the very different path which leads from the spoken Latin of the Classical age to the Romance languages. The importance of legal language in the history of Latin literature is best illuminated by comparing Latin legal texts with their Greek translations, of which we have only a few from the Early Empire, but quite a large number from the Late Classical age. The Greek translators never achieved that degree of linguistic perfection which was demanded by the Latin originals; and it took the Greeks a long time to acquire at least a sense of precision in the rendition of those terms which for many years dominated the edicts and decrees of the Imperial administration, because of the influence of legal scholars.

3 LATIN SCHOLARLY LITERATURE

With the exception of jurisprudence and Christian writing there was only a modest amount of literary activity in the Latin West during the Severan era; and in the later part of the third century AD we find hardly any evidence of literary life at all.

One of the areas where the early third century AD saw at least a certain degree of productivity was grammatical-philological scholarship. From around 200 AD we have a commentary on the poems of Horace, a piece of writing which contains some astute linguistic-stylistic perceptions. The author, Pomponius Porphyrio, shows a profound knowledge and a great love of Old Latin poetry, whereas he is not much impressed by post-Classic products in the poetic genre. Of Porphyrio's background we know nothing at all.

A slightly older writer whom Porphyrio quotes is Helenius Acro, like himself the author of a Horace commentary, but also of commentaries on the comedies of Terence. However, Acro's works were lost; an extant commentary on Horace which was handed down to us under Acro's name actually dates from a much later period.

Charisius, a famous grammarian from the fourth century AD, keeps referring to the work of a certain Julius Romanus as an authoritative source. Romanus compiled a collection of grammatical examples and quotations. From what we know of the authors he himself quoted, Romanus seems to have lived not long after 200 AD, and probably came from the province of Africa, roughly identical with modern-day Tunisia. As in the case of Romanus' collection, we have only indirect access to the work of Serenus Sammonicus who seems to have been a very capable grammarian and antiquarian. His writing was copiously used and occasionally quoted by Macrobius (see p. 445). Sammonicus had close ties with the Severan dynasty, and this cost him his life during the conflict between the brothers Geta and Caracalla.

A man who was certainly of African origin was Sammonicus' contemporary Terentianus Maurus, by whom we have a set of three didactic poems on the pronunciation of the letters of the alphabet, on the quantitative values of syllables, and on metres. The change in Latin pronunciation, and in particular the disappearance of quantitative distinctions, created the demand for a theoretical description of the linguistic basis for Classic-Latin versification, required by readers of Classic poetry as well as by those who wrote poetry during the Severan era, and who invariably and faithfully copied Classic metrical patterns. The metrical theory of Terentianus Maurus is explicitly presented as a sequel to the work of Caesius Bassus (see p. 112).

A collection which presumably also dates from the third century AD is that compiled by the African Nonius Marcellus who lists in lexicographical order peculiar linguistic phenomena found, for example, in word meanings, verb and noun flexions, and names for items of clothing, for colours, or for family relationships. Nonius' vast compilation contains a wealth of quotations, above all from Old Latin literature that was later lost; his work thus documents the unflagging interest of grammarians in that particular part of the literary tradition. However, we may assume that Nonius' writing as well as most other comparable ones were largely based on the rich tradition of such collections, rather than on a reading of the primary texts.

Roughly contemporary with Nonius' work is the major compilation by C. Julius Solinus. The author lists pieces of information concerning the history of Rome, as well as curious facts from the world of plants, animals, and human beings. The overall structure of the work, however, is determined by geographical aspects; and Solinus features geographical information about the entire world as it was known at that time. His most important sources were Pliny the Elder's *Natural History* (see p. 180), the geographical survey by Pomponius Mela (see p. 151), and Suetonius' lost collection that bore the title of *Prata* or *Meadows*. Solinus' compilation was widely read in the Middle Ages, and thus he must be ranked as one of the major communicators of Classical knowledge to the educational world of the Latin Western world.

Virtually impossible to date is a small compendium called *Liber memorialis* written by an otherwise unknown L. Ampelius, who may well belong to the third century AD, or possibly even a later period. His work contains cosmological, geographical, mythographical, and historical information, the latter mostly taken from Livy and Cornelius Nepos, but also from authors of the Imperial age. Ampelius' slim volume is not altogether without interest, as it illustrates the structure and the extent of the knowledge possessed by an average educated person.

A grammarian whose life we can date exactly is C. Censorinus, who in 238 AD dedicated his book on aspects of chronology to an otherwise unknown Q. Caerellius. This short work begins with general reflections on human life, before it turns to questions concerning the segmentation and the counting of time: hence the title *De die natali* or *Of the Birthday*. In the scholarly tradition of the Classical age, the discussion of chronological problems had set in very early, because of the many difficulties involved in any attempt to locate dates and years in a supra-regional framework. This was largely due to the common habit of distinguishing years by reference to eponymous officeholders, instead of counting them from a fixed zero point in time. Further complications arose from the fact that each municipal community had its own calendar of festivals with its own date for the beginning of the year. Censorinus' treatise shows a fair amount of expertise, and a good choice of authorities, such as Varro (see p. 24) or Suetonius (see p. 258). At least for some time, Censorinus was presumably quite a famous grammatical scholar: his lost work about word accent in Latin is occasionally quoted by later authors, and several older as well as more recent tracts have been handed down under Censorinus' name. One of these is the earliest extant work on Roman metrics, a treatise which appears to date from the late first century AD.

4 PHILOSOPHY

Throughout the third century AD the Greek East saw much more literary activity than the Latin West, and this is especially true with regard to philosophical writing. In philosophy the traditions of the different schools had survived in spite of all those syncretistic tendencies which had been at work from the first century AD onwards. The schools ran well-established institutions in several different cities of the Empire, but above all in Athens.

It is probably no more than a coincidence that two major compilations which give us invaluable information about the entire history of Greek philosophy should date from the very same period, the years shortly before or after 200 AD. One collection consists of eleven books written by Sextos or Sextus, a physician of the Empiricist school, and hence known in Latin as Sextus Empiricus. Sextus' work challenges all those who believe that sure and verifiable knowledge can be gained in any field. His rejection of all dogmatics marks Sextus as the last author known to us as a representative of the Skeptic school. This school had originated around 300 BC when Pyrrho had taught the impossibility of reliable knowledge, a doctrine meant to help him guide his disciples towards the goal of unshakeable serenity. During the third and second centuries BC Skepticism had merged with the Platonic school tradition, as Plato's followers put the Socratic art of ignorance in the place of positive doctrines, and consequently saw their main task in the refutation of rival school dogmas. In the first century BC, when the Platonic school returned to a dogmatic system of its own (see p. 71), Skepticism once again became independent. This time, however, the focus was less on an ethical goal than on the invention of extremely elaborate and ingenious methods of argumentation, to be used in refuting any claim to the possession of secure systematic knowledge. Sextus himself describes such methods in an extant treatise called *Outlines of Pyrrhonism.*

His major anti-dogmatical work, *Adversus mathematicos*, gives meticulously argued reasons for denying the possibility of attaining verifiable knowledge in the areas of logic, physics, ethics, grammar, rhetoric, geometry, astronomy/astrology, and musical theory. For all these fields, the author refuses in good Skeptic fashion to recognise any other facts than empirical data, and he backs up this stance with logical as well as historical arguments. It is this strategy which made Sextus feature numerous excerpts and pieces of information from literature that was later lost; and not only from philosophical writings, but also from poetry and the prose literature. As Sextus was a man with an exceptionally astute intellect his arguments are always worth considering. He also shows great skill and diligence in the choice and the presentation of quotes, where he rarely commits those errors by which other authors frequently distort the meaning of a quoted text in their excerpts, and diminish the documentary value of their quotations.

Thus, for instance, Sextus' work contains extremely valuable evidence of a longstanding dispute about the points of view and the criteria which should go into the formulation of a system of rules that describe a language, and that serve as a basis for assessing the correctness of an expression. Although attacking the exponents of logic, Sextus' book is still our most important source of knowledge about the Hellenistic, post-Aristotelian logic of different schools, whose original writings were largely lost. Similar credit is due to many other parts of Sextus' tract.

We have no reliable information about the background and the life of Diogenes Laertius, the author of the other major philosophical collection from the period in question. Diogenes Laertius appears to be the last follower of Epicurean philosophy who left us a literary legacy. Among the educated people of the Empire, the Epicureans had a bad reputation for three reasons: their doctrine about gods who do not care about the world and leave everything to chance; their staunch materialism; and their alleged amoral hedonism. All the same, the second century AD saw something like a revival of the Epicurean school which enjoyed the special patronage of Plotina, the wife of the Emperor Trajan. During Trajan's reign, an Epicurean held a chair with a state salary in Athens, beside exponents of the other three major philosophical schools. From the third century AD onwards, however, there is no evidence at all of Epicurean philosophers, even if philosophical texts of varied origin still sometimes feature ideas from the Epicurean tradition along with sayings of their school's founder. In his many attempts at a critical discussion of Epicurean doctrines Plotinus does not make any obvious reference to living exponents of that philosophy, whereas we know that he conversed with contemporary Stoics.

Diogenes Laertius wrote a work whose ten volumes constitute something like a history of Greek philosophy. Each book deals with one specific school tradition: but whereas there is not the slightest doubt about the existence of a coherent Stoic or Platonic school philosophy, some of the other school traditions which Diogenes Laertius describes are entirely fictitious. In each of his books the account consists of biographical sketches of the exponents of a certain school philosophy. These biographies vary greatly in length according to the importance of the person described and to the availability of source material.

Another difference concerns the range covered in the listing of philosophers from different schools. The enumeration of pre-Socratic philosophers is complete, whereas Platonic philosophers feature only up to the second century BC, Stoics until the first century BC, and philosophers from the Empire are not mentioned at all. The biographies of the respective school founders are often followed by what purports to be a comprehensive survey of their teachings, but is in fact invariably the systematic doctrine of the school tradition as it stood in the second or first century BC. In Book 10, which deals with the philosophy of Epicurus, the presentation of his doctrines is complemented by the full texts of three of his didactic letters. This last volume likewise differs from the rest in focusing entirely on the person and the teachings of the school founder.

The longer biographies follow a recognisable pattern even if there are many variations; but there is no indication of any effort on the author's part to make his account of any individual life a literary-artistic product. What we find is normally a chronological report on origin and family background, childhood, adolescence, education, and any other facts concerning the life of the person described before his admission into the circle of professional philosophers, and his decision to become the disciple of a specific teacher. This chronological report is followed by a for the most part unsystematic account of the protagonist's work as a philosopher, his position in his chosen school, his social prestige, and, if applicable, his public influence. This part of the biography, in most cases interspersed with anecdotes and famous sayings of the person described, also talks about friends and acquaintances, everyday habits, and specific features of his teachings. Each biography closes with a report about the last days of the protagonist's life, often with a character portrait attached. Finally, Diogenes Laertius features the text of the protagonist's last will, and a list of his publications.

The many variations of this pattern were the inevitable result of differences in the availability of source material. The value of Diogenes' work as a source of information about Classical philosophy is undisputed; but the question as to which sources the author had at his disposal has occupied modern-day scholars more than any other aspect of his writing for more than the past century.

When Diogenes quotes one of the many authorities he refers to we cannot always tell whether he had direct access to the relevant text, or whether he knew the original only through an intermediate source. A rich tradition of biographical lore about the philosophers existed since the days of Plato. Biographical information was first passed on within the schools and the first published compilation of such material, arranged according to different school traditions, was produced by the Alexandrian scholar Sotion in the early second century BC. Sotion's work was definitely one of the main sources for Diogenes' writing.

Outside the schools, however, there was also a demand for information about the lives of ancient and recent philosophers, from a public that was not really interested in the content of their philosophy. Since the age of Hellenism the general public had known philosophers as people who claimed to teach the art of proper living, and this suggested judging their claims by taking a close look at their own lives. It is exactly this motivation which is documented for another authority drawn on by Diogenes, Antigonus of Carystus, who lived in the third century BC. Antigonus was a versatile writer without any special interest in philosophy; some of his accounts of philosophers' lives contain highly amusing descriptions of those philosophers whom he had got to know personally in Athens.

The authors whom I have mentioned are not the only writers of biographical literature in the narrower sense whose works Diogenes used. His own writing, however, also documents an acquaintance with information which was presumably inaccessible outside the philosophical schools where, for instance, the text of the founder's last will and testament as well as the catalogue of his writings would be guarded and handed down from one generation to another. Moreover, Diogenes was also closely familiar with doxographical writing where the doctrines of individual philosophers were recorded. The rich tradition of doxography dates back to Early Hellenism, and I have already had more than one occasion to point out its importance in the intellectual life of the Empire.

The historical range of Diogenes' account is proof enough of the author's total dependence on source texts, none of which is extant. Still, most recent research has quite rightly complemented the identification and reconstruction of sources with the attempt to assess Diogenes' own intentions and achievements. There are many instances where the author shows a genuine philosophical interest, and his endeavour to illustrate the diversity and the development of philosophy is inspired by much more than the industry of a mere collector. Diogenes indeed deserves to be recognised as an author in his own right. The fact that he focuses almost exclusively on periods from a distant past, in a work that clearly illustrates the importance of philosophy in his own lifetime, must be understood in the light of the entirely backward-orientated education of his epoch.

The survival of institutionalised school philosophy during the Severan era is most impressively documented in the writings of the Peripatetic

Alexander of Aphrodisias in Asia Minor. In 198 AD he was appointed to the Peripatetic chair among those four professorial posts in Athens which were endowed with a state salary. We know this from the dedication to the Emperor and his co-regent which is prefaced to Alexander's treatise on fate and man's freedom of choice. This treatise attacks the Stoic doctrine of *heimarmenē*, the all-embracing coherence which determines each event in advance, and excludes coincidence from the world. From the Stoic point of view, human freedom appears as a state of consciousness arising from a recognition of the world order as beneficent and optimal, an insight which enables people to choose freely and without coercion to do and to suffer whatever fate has ordained for them. Against this view, Alexander pitches a Peripatetic doctrine which had already been formulated by Aristotle, asserting that the natural order, chance, and man's free choice are forces operating as on one and the same plane to determine the course of events, and that nature is in command only in as much as it defines the limits of the possible.

Alexander wrote a number of other treatises, dealing with a variety of subjects such as the soul, or problems in the explanation of natural phenomena. Especially important, however, are his extensive commentaries on didactic writings by the school founder. Of the five extant specimens, the most interesting is that on the *Metaphysics*. Alexander's strictly methodical, ingenious, scholarly, and matter-of-fact approach to interpretation made him one of the most outstanding Classical commentators. Later Peripatetic commentaries on Aristotle rely largely on Alexander's work; but he was held in great esteem also by the Neo-Platonists, who became ever more keen to understand Platonic and Aristotelian philosophy as one. In the biography of his teacher Plotinus (14) Porphyry says that Alexander's commentary on Aristotle's *Metaphysics* was particularly highly recommended by Plotinus. Modern-day scholars dealing with Aristotle likewise keep going back to the helpful explanations which Alexander's commentaries offer to the reader of difficult Aristotelian texts.

5 CHRISTIAN LITERATURE: THE GREEKS

In that generation which preceded the Severan era there were no more than a few Christians who had shown a fairly close acquaintance with contemporary philosophy and science as, for instance, the martyr Justin (see p. 300). In the Severan era, however, we find quite a considerable number of advocates of the new religion who could claim to have reached the general standard of scientific-philosophical education, or even to be on a par with its foremost exponents. Such Christians would use the means of Greek philosophy to explicate their faith in ever-more intricate and refined dogmatic systems. This was partly done with a view to the outside, as an apologetical effort directed at the pagan educational world which surrounded the Christians. Another motivation, however, was the internal debate among the Christians about the true faith and about its appropriate terminological expression.

Clement of Alexandria

Clement of Alexandria is clearly the first author whom I must mention in this context. He came from a pagan family who were presumably resident in Athens, and acquired Roman citizenship as early as the first century AD. T. Flavius Clemens, as was his full name, seems to have received a thorough education, and travelled widely. We do not know when he was converted to Christianity but it was around 200 AD that he arrived in Alexandria where the Christian Pantaenus taught him theology. Scholars still argue about whether or not this happened within an institutional framework established by the Bishop of Alexandria. A local persecution of Christians caused Clement to emigrate to Asia Minor where he died not long after 215 AD; as far as we know without ever having held any ecclesiastical office. Clement's literary *oeuvre* shows him as a man of comprehensive philosophical-literary erudition. No less than 360 different authors are quoted in the extant parts of his works, and even if many of the quotations are likely to be second hand, Clement's writing also often indicates that he had read and appreciated the original.

Clement's earliest work is a *protreptikos*, a speech intended to admonish or to convert educated pagans. In this oration, the author first attacks the cults of the ancient gods as foolish and immoral, a verdict which he backs up by precisely those arguments which Classical philosophy had already used to condemn popular religious notions. Hence it is no more than consistent if Clement presents philosophy as well as Mosaic law as preliminary stages of Christian revelation given to the heathens by the divine *logos*, and ultimately completed through its incarnation in Christ. This notion had already been propounded by Justin; in Clement's *protreptikos* it ushers in an appeal to the audience to accept the full revelation of divine grace.

The second treatise written by Clement, the *Paidagogos* or *Tutor*, is the earliest known comprehensive account of Christian ethics. It is addressed to already converted heathens who now need to be familiarised with the Christian lifestyle. The author deals at length with aspects of everyday living down to the most trivial detail, which is why this work has become a valuable source of information for the cultural historian. Clement's intention is not to teach an ascetic ideal: on the contrary, his counsels for family life, eating, drinking, or clothing stem from the old philosophical principle of naturalness as defined in the Platonic-Peripatetic tradition. This did not condemn the enjoyment of creature comforts and pleasures, but saw moderation as the way to realise an ideal rule of reason over instinct and emotion. A recent ecclesiastical historian has quite aptly described Clement as a 'liberal puritan'.

In the introduction to the *Paidagogos*, the author announces his plan to write a third work called *Didaskalos* or *Teacher*, which was to contain a doctrine of the Christian faith. It seems that this plan was never put into practice; instead we have the eight books of the unfinished and posthumously edited miscellanies entitled *Stromata*, literally *Carpets*. The title labels this work as part of the so-called poikilographical genre, which comprised unsystematic collections of all kinds of factual material, as well as of reflections or short treatises on diverse subjects. Clement's *Stromata* deal mainly with the relationship of the Christian faith to the philosophically moulded culture of its environment, to the Classical literary tradition, to the Old Testament, to contemporary Gnostic doctrine, and also to 'Barbarian philosophy' or the wisdom of exotic peoples. All of these issues are discussed on the basis of a comprehensive knowledge of literary sources. Book 8 of the *Stromata* illustrates Clement's systematic manner of studying, as do extant fragments of two other pieces of writing. Those excerpts from the Gnostic Theodotus and the Old Testament prophets which Clement left us in his literary legacy were most certainly not intended for publication.

Among further writings by Clement which were lost, or of which we have no more than fragments, there are unfortunately also the eight books of the *Hypotyposeis* or *Sketches*. This work, occasionally used by later theologians, contained scientific-theological interpretations of selected Biblical pericopes. The extant treatise *Which Rich Man will be Saved?* is a sermon meant for a larger and more mixed audience, on the story of the rich young man from the Gospel of Mark (10.17ff.). In elegant but plain language, Clement explains that not the possession of wealth, but only its sinful use could exclude a rich man from heaven.

Like most of his educated contemporaries, Clement relied mainly on the fundamental tenets of Platonic philosophy, by then generally thought to differ only in detail from the Aristotelian. When Clement applied the spirit/matter dichotomy to the Biblical teachings about God and his creation, as well as to Christian anthropology, this was in the true Platonic sense: God is spirit, as the Bible confirms, and he created the world by forming the cosmos in its perfect beauty from unordered and hence non-existent matter. Thus the Christian Clement agrees with Plato in seeing spiritualisation, or liberation from the bonds of the flesh, as the way of moral ascent, and as the means of attaining eternal perfection.

Although Clement's fundamental philosophical beliefs are Platonic, he makes liberal use of Stoic terms in psychological and moral casuistics. Such terms, however, are sometimes radically reinterpreted. The Stoics had, for instance, used the word *synkatathesis* or 'assent' to describe the simultaneous recognition and approval which reason gives to an idea emerging in the human mind which implies a need for action, thus creating the urge to act. Clement, however, uses the word to signify the righteous striving of the faithful, as an endeavour independent of all rational cognition.

The endless repetition of an attempt to describe and explain the content of the faith with the means of philosophy led Clement, like most theologians after him, to the notion that faith and knowledge must ultimately coincide, and that the perfect Christian is one who knows: that is a Gnostic. Clement did not hesitate to use this term, even if he had as little time for Gnostic doctrine as the philosophers did. Like the latter, Clement firmly rejected the Gnostic denigration of the empirical cosmos. To the successors of Plato, the universe had an intrinsic worth as a mirror-image of the perfect order and beauty of the world of ideas whose character is thus shown to men. To a Christian the cosmos was simply the perfect work of the divine creator.

Greek philosophy was first and foremost ontology, the study of being. Especially in the dominant school traditions in the Empire, all enquiry was based on the assumption that the structure of the world and of all forms of being is accessible to rational understanding. The universal creator, who had formed the world according to Plato and his followers, had to be a rational being, too. This idea clashed with the Biblical tradition which spoke of a God whose plans and intentions cannot be known by man: a God who made the world intelligible to human beings but who also confronts them personally with inexplicable demands, gifts, and promises, expecting obedience and trust, but not comprehension. If philosophical ontology was needed to explain the message about this God, theologians would inevitably be compelled to present his actions and his promises as rational, and thus as intelligible to man. All early Christian theology is pervaded by this conflict between the central Biblical statements about God and the fundamental postulates of Greek philosophy. In the works of Clement, who went further than most in his Hellenisation of the Christian message, these contradictions emerge with particular clarity.

A contemporary of Clement was Bar Daisan of Edessa, capital of the small kingdom of Orrhoëne, which enjoyed a precarious independence between the Persian and the Roman Empire. Its monarchs had been converted to Christianity as early as the second century AD. People in that region spoke a form of Syriac, and it was with the Edessan translation of the Bible that Christian-Syrian literature began. At the time this particular corner of the world was a crossroads of cultural influences from the Graeco-Roman and the Iranian world. The Neo-Platonist Porphyry has preserved a Greek text in which Bar Daisan recorded the description of a Buddhist monastery which was given to him by an Indian delegation stopping at Edessa on their way to Rome. This is a good illustration of the largely cosmopolitan character of life in that region, where many people spoke more than one language.

Like many of his contemporaries, Bar Daisan – known to the Greeks as Bardesanes – was interested in astrological lore, whose rigid definition of fate could hardly be reconciled with the Jewish-Christian faith that emphasised the sovereignty of the divine creator, as well as the freedom and responsibility of man. We have a Syriac text, as well as quotations in works by Greek authors, of a treatise written in Bardesanes' school; this tract illustrates how Bardesanes explained fundamental astrological concepts to Christians, with the help of Platonic and Peripatetic doctrines. In the mathematically precise motion of the stars, Platonic philosophers of the Empire saw proof of their status as superhuman rational beings, entrusted with an important role in cosmic government. Philosophers in general agreed that all rational-spiritual beings must have the same freedom of choice as human souls.

The Peripatos taught that all events in the world were determined by three factors: the natural order, chance, and man's free choice. Bardesanes adopted this threefold structure but with an important modification. Because Biblical statements about divine providence made it impossible for Jews and Christians alike to accept chance as such as a determining factor, Ba rdesanes interpreted chance as the result of free decisions taken by stars, demons, and other spiritual beings. Like humans, those are also free to use their power of choice against the divine order of creation: and the outcome of this is what man calls coincidence. Contrary to Gnostics and Marcionites, Bardesanes maintained that the order of creation is perfect and that each single creature has all the faculties it needs to live a conflict-free life in harmony with this order. This is why all spiritual beings, humans, angels, stars, and demons alike, will ultimately be taken to account for how they have used their freedom of choice, as each and every violation of the universal order must be atoned for.

Bar Daisan is also known as the author of hymns and songs. Of those, however, hardly anything is left, for his followers soon seceded from the official church and developed further doctrines which resembled those of the Gnostics. What is extant of Bar Daisan's writing constitutes a good example of how Greek philosophy influenced the development of Christian religion, even outside the boundaries of Graeco-Roman culture.

A little younger than both Bardesanes and Clement was the Roman Presbyter Hippolytus, who got himself elected as rival Bishop after a dispute with the Bishop Callistus. During a later persecution of Christians Hippolytus was banished to Sardinia together with the second successor of his opponent. Hippolytus died in exile in 235 AD. At that time Greek was still the ecclesiastical language of Rome, as the capital's Christian congregations recruited their members mainly among the Greek-speaking part of the metropolitan population.

Hippolytus wrote two major treatises against the Gnostic sects. The original text of the longer one has been handed down to us under the name of Origen, and the other we know in partial Latin translations. The *Refutation of all Heresies* identifies and denounces the different systematic doctrines of no less than thirty-three Gnostic sects. In this tract Hippolytus drew upon some older anti-heretical writings, especially the major work by Irenaeus (see p. 303). Nevertheless, the treatise proves that its author examined many of the incriminated writings himself; and his work remains a valuable source of information about the Gnosis, even now that Coptic translations of original Gnostic texts have been discovered. All known later anti-Gnostic writings – as, for instance, those by the Bishop Epiphanius of Salamis in Cyprus – are based on Hippolytus' treatise.

Like other anti-Gnostics, Hippolytus was convinced that the erroneous doctrines of those heretics had their roots in Greek philosophy. This assumption encouraged efforts to try and link specific Gnostic doctrines to well-known philosophical school traditions; and the results of such endeavours were often far-fetched. This phenomenon seems particularly remarkable in view of the fact that at the same time, Christians also kept on borrowing from philosophy in their refutation of Gnostic doctrines (see p. 303). Thus, for example, philosophical ideas about the reasonable order and the beauty of the universe were often cited as evidence against the Gnostic belief that our world has been created by a lesser or evil god, to serve as a prison for the cores of human souls, which come from the luminous world of true being. Gnostic assertions about the cosmic predestination of the fall and reascent of the human souls were frequently refuted by reference to philosophical views of man's reason as the basis for his freedom of choice, and for his responsibility for his own actions.

Of Hippolytus' exegetical writings, we have some in Georgian, Armenian, or Old Slavic translations. Large parts of one work, the commentary on the Book of Daniel, are also extant in the Greek original. This commentary was written in 204 AD under the pressure of the anti-Christian persecutions ordered by Septimius Severus.

If many Christian texts from this period express a positive view of the Roman Empire and its culture, there is not always an apologetical intention behind it. Such statements could also represent a widespread Christian motif of which a rudimentary form was already present in Luke's Gospel: the idea that the unification of the civilised world under the sceptre of Rome had been brought about through divine providence at the same time as the appearance of Jesus, to create the conditions for an instant worldwide spreading of the message of salvation. Another notion frequently encountered in Christian texts is that though the Roman-pagan state was not an instrument that ensured the rule of righteousness as desired by God, it still created an order that was indispensable for human co-existence. The first expression of this latter concept is found in Paul's Letter to the Romans.

In his interpretation of the visions in the Book of Daniel, Hippolytus expresses a radically different opinion. To him, the Roman state was bad all through. It was a vessel within which injustice grows from generation to generation, until it reaches its peak with the coming of the antichrist. That was to be followed by the end of the world, the last judgment, heralding the eternal rule of God. Hippolytus held that the apocalyptic events would also prove that only the church had previously practised the rule of righteousness in the communal life of its members, and could thus be recognised as presenting a positive counter-image to the existing state.

That the communal life of Christians creates the rightful order which God wants to exist among men is a notion which also dominates the ecclesiastical constitution edited by Hippolytus. Parts of the original text are extant, as well as parts of translations. This piece of writing illustrates the conscientious efforts made to formulate precise and reliable rules for solving social and moral problems that faced Christian communities; for instance, questions arising in connection with a member's choice of profession, or about the proper way of dealing with a recidivist sinner. Documents like this ecclesiastical constitution help us understand why the church should have proved to be far more resilient than any other social group in the turmoil of the third century AD.

Hippolytus' special interest in eschatological questions is also evident in his short treatise on the antichrist, a work which we have in the Greek original, and in which the description of apocalyptic events follows that given by Hippolytus' teacher Irenaeus. Hippolytus' reflections on eschatology stop short of chiliastic speculation; and in what seems to be his most important scientific work, a *World Chronicle*, extant in fragments of the original as well as in later editions, Hippolytus even included an explicit warning against this kind of speculative chronology.

I have already said that it was the specific conditions in the Graeco-Roman world of the Classical age, which had led to the establishment of chronology as an independent scientific discipline (see p. 247). As Christians confronted the culture which surrounded them, they saw themselves faced with the task of relating Biblical chronology to the chronological systems of the Greeks and Romans. Hippolytus' *World Chronicle*, which covers the time from the creation of the world to the year 234 AD, is an early example of Christian chronography, but not the earliest: the genre tradition was established with the slightly older work by Sex. Julius Africanus.

That so little of Hippolytus' *oeuvre* is extant, and that we frequently have to rely on nothing more than fragments and translations, is not really due to his being classed as a schismatic because of his election as anti-bishop. The Christian community in Rome even counted him among the martyrs because of his death in exile; and on his Roman tomb they erected a statue in his memory, a piece of sculpture which was rediscovered in 1551. The fate of Hippolytus' works was not sealed until Latin became the official language of the church of Rome shortly after the middle of the third century AD. After that the West saw a steady decline in the numbers of those who had a command of Greek. This development had a particularly strong effect among the educated classes, to which most authors and readers belonged.

An inscription on the abovementioned funeral statue gives us a catalogue of Hippolytus' writings. This list is incomplete but it does tell us that Hippolytus was among those who wrote about one chronological problem which had been hotly debated since the second century AD: the calculation of the dates for Easter in the years 222–3 AD. In Asia Minor Christians had until then always celebrated the Feast of the Resurrection on the Jewish Passover day, the 14th of Nisan. This custom was condemned by the Roman church: according to their calculation, Easter fell on the first Sunday after the first full moon after the first day of spring. The Roman rule came to be more and more widely accepted, and was ultimately observed by Christians everywhere in the fourth century AD.

Sextus Julius Africanus, who came from Jerusalem, was a contemporary of Hippolytus, and likewise a capable scholar. He received his education in Alexandria where he made the acquaintance of the great Origen. Sextus corresponded with the theologically-minded royal family of Edessa (see p. 330); and the Emperor Alexander Severus commissioned him to build up the stocks of that Roman library which the monarch himself had founded.

What Sextus Julius Africanus founded was Christian chronography. Of his *World Chronicle*, which covered the time up to the year 217 AD, we can reconstruct no more than an outline from existing fragments and from evidence of its influence on other writings. It seems to have contained tables synchronising dates from global history, according to both Biblical and Graeco-Roman tradition. The chronology followed a strict chiliastic scheme: the duration of the world's existence was computed at exactly 6,000 years, with the birth of Christ happening in the year 5500, and the Millennium lasting from the years 6000 to 7000.

Dedicated to the Emperor Alexander Severus were the twenty-four books of Sextus' *Kestoi* or *Embroideries*, a motley mixture of excerpts and treatises from areas of knowledge as diverse as agriculture, medicine, and even magic. Of this work, too, we have no more than fragments. The only completely extant writings by Sextus are two letters: one addressed to Origen, the other to an otherwise unknown Aristides. The first letter questions the authenticity of the story of Susannah from the Old Testament apocrypha; the second discusses the discrepancies between the genealogies of Jesus given by Luke and Matthew respectively. Both texts illustrate the emergence of Christian Biblical scholarship which used the methods of Hellenistic philology.

Origen

Another Christian author who belongs to the Severan era is Origen of Alexandria, one of the truly great men in the history of early Christian literature. He was born to Christian parents around 185 AD, and as early as 203 AD he succeeded Clement as the first officially appointed teacher of theology in Alexandria, installed by Bishop Demetrius. It seems that upon his appointment Origen immediately began to design a systematic curriculum. Among the subjects were grammar or philology, for which he won his friend Heraclas as an assistant teacher, and also philosophy: both disciplines were given a place as propaedeutics to Bible studies and theology. At the time when he drafted this theological curriculum Origen himself still continued his philosophical education in the Platonic school of Alexandria.

The year 212 AD saw Origen in Rome, where he made the acquaintance of Hippolytus. In 215 Origen gave some well-attended lectures in Caesarea in Palestine, and soon after that he returned to Alexandria. He travelled again in 230 AD, this time to Greece. When he broke his journey at Caesarea, Origen was jointly ordained as a priest by the local Bishops of Caesarea and Jerusalem. The two dignitaries, however, had violated ecclesiastical law in bestowing this favour, and the Bishop of Alexandria, to whose diocese Origen belonged, responded with his excommunication. It is possible that accusations of heterodoxical teachings may have already played a part in these events. In the following years Origen lived in Caesarea where he kept up a didactic routine described in full detail in an oratorical expression of gratitude to the teacher written by his pupil Gregory Thaumaturgus. When the Empress Julia Mammaea was staying in Antioch, Origen's reputation as a scholar was reason enough for her to invite him there to lecture in her presence. After the Emperor Decius had unleashed a major campaign of persecution against the Christians, Origen was imprisoned, and tortured so cruelly that he never recovered. He died soon after in 253 AD at the age of seventy.

Origen was an amazingly prolific scholar, and certainly the most important writer of Biblical exegesis in the early church. His tracts, scholarly commentaries, edifying sermons, annotations, letters, and dogmatic-apologetical writings were numerous enough to fill an entire library. We know of a well-organised secretarial service which a rich patron donated to Origen to help him with his literary work. For a long time afterwards the library resources which Origen had gathered in Caesarea offered the world's best facilities for theological studies.

In spite of his vast literary output, we have only relatively little of Origen's *oeuvre* in the original Greek. More is extant in Latin translations made by Hilarius, Rufinus, and Hieronymus towards the end of the fourth century AD. Much, however, was lost, because doubts about Origen's orthodoxy already existed very early on, and were confirmed by a definitive ecclesiastical condemnation in the sixth century AD.

Origen was the first scientific theologian who took the question about the authenticity and reliability of the Biblical text really seriously. In its emergence from the Jewish faith of the Classical age, the early church had adopted the so-called Septuagint, the Greek translation of the Old Testament, as its sacred text. As the church detached itself from the synagogue, this Holy Scripture was searched for arguments to be used in the Christian dispute with Judaism. The Jews responded by paying more attention to the Hebrew text, of which new and more exact translations into Greek were produced in the second and third centuries AD. The outcome of the Bar Kochba uprising (see p. 170) was another factor that favoured a Jewish break with Greek culture, and a return of Jewish scriptural scholarship to the Hebrew-Aramaic form of the text. The Septuagint, which had its own long history dating back to the third century BC, was not at all an accurate rendition of that original, from which it frequently deviated in meaning as well as in length.

Origen was well aware of the philological problems arising from these facts, all the more so because he maintained contacts with Jewish rabbis. Thus he began working on a complete scholarly edition of the Old Testament in six parallel columns: the first two featured the Hebrew text in Hebrew and Greek script respectively; columns three and four contained the recent translations by Aquila and Symmachus; column five showed the text of the Septuagint as used in Christian liturgy; and the last one was reserved for another recent translation by Theodotion. Passages from the latter version were transferred to the Septuagint column, wherever there were parts of the Hebrew text not featured in that Greek translation. Those passages were then marked with an asterisk; and the passages from the Septuagint which had no equivalent in the Hebrew text with an obelisk, a horizontal line. The same symbol also indicated translators' errors in the Septuagint, for which marginal corrections were also provided.

This colossal scholarly work by Origen is an impressive testimony of the continuation of scientific philology, as developed during the age of Hellenism. It was not meant to be reproduced and distributed in multiple copies; instead, interested scholars could come to consult the original, as the learned Hieronymus did. What was copied many times was the Septuagint text recorded by Origen, a text which played a major role in the subsequent history of the Bible's Greek version. A few people would also copy all four columns with the different Greek translations; and many references to the so-called Hexapla can be found in different documents from early Christian literature.

The extant parts of Origen's exegetical writings represent only a small remainder of the whole. Our sources refer to 574 sermons, of which we have twenty-one in the original Greek and 186 in Latin translations. This is enough, however, to give us a fairly clear idea of the goal and the methods of Origen's exegesis. What we have least evidence of are the so-called scholia – that is to say commentaries on specific passages which presented special grammatical or semantic problems. Origen's commentaries on longer sections of Biblical text are clearly the products of extremely well-informed scientific scholarship, interweaving the actual reading of the text with detailed discussions of different opinions, digressions on questions of dogma, or references to parallels in pagan as well as Christian literature. This explains why, for example, the commentary on John's Gospel alone filled twenty-eight books, of which eight are extant in the original Greek. Another consequence of this manner of composition is that Origen's commentaries also contain explanations of very specific doctrines of his own and hence statements which one would rather expect to find in dogmatical works.

Alexandrian scholars in particular had upheld the method of allegorical interpretation, a well-established tradition ever since Homer's writings and Greek myths about the gods had been read as allegories illustrating cosmological-physical or moral phenomena. The allegorical method was popular with grammarians and philosophers of the Empire, who used it to adapt ancient and well-known traditional lore to the intellectual taste of educated people. Philo had applied it extensively to the stories of the Old Testament as a tool enabling him to present the meanings of these stories as in keeping with philosophical ideas and to explain away the rather frequent features which were obviously offensive to philosophers. Moreover, the Stoic-Platonic philosophy of the Empire had produced the doctrine about a cosmic sympathy of events happening on all levels of the universal order, and in all parts of the universe. This doctrine provided the ontological justification for the assumption that, for instance, a mythological account of a battle could have a connection with a cosmic event and could hence be interpreted in that sense.

The traditional method as Origen found it had one major weakness beside the abovementioned merits. This flaw was that one and the same story or character could easily be read as representing very different allegorical meanings. Evidence of this exists, for example, in a short manual by the Stoic Cornutus from the first century AD, where the author offers several different and sometimes even contradictory allegorical interpretations for each of the divine personages from Greek mythology. Origen tried to avoid such ambiguity by making the allegorical method more systematic. He taught that the Bible has a threefold meaning, which he defined according to Platonic anthropology. Hence the first exegetical task was to find the physical-literal or grammatical-historical sense of a Biblical text; then the psychological or moral one; and finally the pneumatic or spiritual. To Origen, however, each part of the Bible had a spiritual meaning, but not necessarily a grammatical-historical one: and thus the door was open for a return of the old ambiguity.

Origen's use of the allegorical method had an immense impact on posterity. His procedure may strike us as alien but it appears less strange if one takes into account its long history, the sacred character of the texts Origen dealt with, and finally the fact that there is hardly any poetic or literary text at all which is not intended to signify more than its wording would represent in ordinary discourse. Language styled in a literary manner always contains images, metaphors, formal conventions, and other means of pointing beyond the literal meaning of the words as understood by a naive reader: there is something else, and to define this something is the task of any exegesis. This is particularly obvious in the case of a sacred text, and this is why for several centuries Biblical exegesis kept going back to the allegorical and the typological method.

The allegorical reading of Homer had already come under attack during the age of Hellenism, and the corresponding Bible exegesis, as practised above all in Alexandria, met with equally strong criticism. A case in point is the Antioch school of Biblical exegesis, whose existence is documented from around 300 AD onwards, where scholars insisted on the supremacy of literal-historical interpretation. But because of the fact that the allegorical method of reading was matched by a long tradition of allegorical writing which produced texts explicitly labelled as allegories, the allegorical method dominated the approach to textual interpretation for hundreds of years afterwards.

The homilies or sermons of Origen follow the same interpretative principles as his commentaries, but they carry a much smaller load of scholarly paraphernalia, and belong primarily to the history of piety. These texts are far less influenced by the art of rhetoric than the famous sermons written during the following two centuries; and Origen's homilies are also more to the point with regard to the task of explaining the selected text. They indicate that Origen knew large parts of the Bible by heart and was completely immersed in Biblical images and phrases.

There is hardly any part of the Old or the New Testament on which Origen did not produce a homily or a commentary. He could cite textual parallels effortlessly, linking separate Biblical passages with no other help than his memory, and making connections which may often surprise even the modern-day exegete with his abundance of convenient aids, such as dictionaries or concordances. Origen's familiarity with the Bible can also be seen in two shorter writings which must be grouped alongside the homilies because of their pastoral intention. The beautiful treatise on prayer contains in its second part an interpretation of the Lord's Prayer; the other one, a topical piece written in 235 AD, is an appeal to Christians to be steadfast under persecution. Origen's own father had died during an earlier campaign of anti-Christian persecution in 202 AD.

The two most famous works by Origen were produced fairly late in his life, around the year 230 AD. We have the eight books in the original Greek of his refutation of the *True Word*, in which the Platonic philosopher Celsus had attacked the Christians about sixty years earlier. Celsus' charges had focused on two points. First, he claimed that Christianity was a religion for stupid and uneducated people, allowing themselves to be intimidated and misled by old wives' tales about Jesus and his followers. Second, Celsus held that by rejecting the worship of the Graeco-Roman gods, the Christians had excluded themselves from the community of civilised nations, and had thus become a threat to the state. According to Celsus, the divine cannot be fully recognised by any individual, and only the diversity of existing religions and cults safeguards the proper relationship between men and divine being, including the one supreme God.

Origen's reply has preserved large parts of his adversary's treatise in lengthy quotations. In his apology, Origen puts great emphasis on historical evidence, and – like other apologists before him – on insisting that Christians led exemplary lives in loyalty to the state, which made them the virtual guarantors of social order. Unlike, for example, Tatian (see p. 303) or Hippolytus (see p. 331), Origen did not try to denigrate Graeco-Roman civilisation, which he cherished as much as Celsus did. Another peculiar feature of Origen's refutation is the lack of any obvious stylistic-rhetorical ambition, although this context would have given the author plenty of scope for displaying his argumentative and stylistic skills.

Origen's four books *Of Principles* contain the first comprehensive system of Christian dogma which is on a par with the standard of contemporary philosophy. As this work features the clearest expression of those doctrines which met with disapproval and finally condemnation on the part of ecclesiastical orthodoxy, we have only one complete version of it in Rufinus' translation. The merits of Rufinus' text can be assessed by comparison with various longer quotations from the original in works from the fourth and sixth centuries AD.

There were hardly any other theologians who went as far as Origen in his effort to prove that Biblical revelation is ultimately in accordance with reason (see p. 337). Origen did not only borrow his method from contemporary Platonic philosophy, which he had studied thoroughly: he likewise adopted some of its crucial basic axioms and opinions. Thus he went along with Plato in teaching the pre-existence and the repeated incarnation of all human souls, which implies that although just reward and punishment for human deeds are often lacking in the span of one lifetime, they can yet be expected over a period of several reincarnations.

The Biblical tradition concerning the Fall was read by Origen in the sense of Platonic metaphysics. According to this, all spiritual beings, including human souls, have fallen from their state of communion with the supreme One, and have become entangled in matter to various degrees. Their task is the individual endeavour to enter the path of reunification, a goal to be reached in a series of reincarnations. Divine grace supports such striving by guidance and assistance, and at the end of time, all spiritual beings, men and fallen angels alike, will be reunited with their God in an intelligible cosmos. This doctrine of *apokatastasis*, the preordained restoration of an original state as a process which unfolds as inevitably as the working of a natural law, was particularly offensive to orthodoxy. One important reason why Origen incorporated so many philosophical concepts into Christian doctrine was certainly his desire to prove that man's independent moral endeavour was a necessary condition for salvation: and such proof could only be given if moral standards and divine justice were shown to correspond. Hence the statements about the incomprehensible election or condemnation by the judgment and the grace of God made in Chapter 9 of Paul's Letter to the Romans had to be reinterpreted as a rationally intelligible moral admonition.

Of Origen's own numerous letters we have no more than two, one to his disciple Gregory the miracle-worker (see p. 335), and the other to Sextus Julius Africanus (see p. 333). Origen's literary *oeuvre* as a whole marks a first peak in Christian intellectual life. In spite of early criticism, his contemporaries and his early successors recognised him as a great man. At the beginning of the fourth century AD, the learned Eusebius worked in Origen's library in Caesarea; and it is Eusebius' ecclesiastical history which contains the many biographical data which give us a relatively detailed picture of Origen's life.

6 RHETORICAL LITERATURE

The extant writings of Philostratus, as well as miscellaneous pieces of biographical information which we have about him from other authors, give us some interesting insights into the literary life of the Severan era. Philostratus came from a distinguished family whose home was the island of Lemnos, and which had produced several sophists. Since the reign of Nero this title had been officially given to professional teachers of rhetoric and travelling lecturers who displayed their art in public orations about political, moral, antiquarian, and many other different topics (see p. 173). The sophists enjoyed a particularly high social prestige in the second century AD: this is evident in the fact that quite a few of them entered successful careers in independent municipal administrations, and obtained Roman citizenship. Some sophists even rose to the Senatorial class, or at least paved the way to such a promotion for their sons, as Philostratus did. The name Philostratus was a very popular choice within his lineage, and three different namesakes, with several different writings for each one, are listed in the so-called *Suda*, a Byzantine encyclopaedia of linguistic and general knowledge. Unfortunately the data given there do not quite tally with the extant works under the name Philostratus. Most of these, however, were doubtlessly produced by Flavius Philostratus of Lemnos, who married Aurelia Melitene. The couple had three children, and one of them rose to the ranks of the Senatorial nobility.

Flavius Philostratus received his rhetorical education in Ephesus and Athens, where his father had worked as a sophist before him. Apart from numerous speeches, we know that he also wrote tragedies, presumably for reading rather than for the stage, and a treatise on the theory of drama. None of the latter works has survived; but it is possible that an extant treatise on gymnastics which has been handed down among the works of Philostratus' son is actually the one which is documented for the father. The younger Philostratus became much more famous than his progenitor and this fame may have saved his father's treatise from oblivion, although a confusion between the two men could easily have been avoided by reference to the elder Philostratus' different patronym.

After his rhetorical training, Flavius Philostratus seems to have begun working as a travelling sophist. Our sources indicate that he spent some time in Rome in the entourage of the Empress Julia Domna who took a great interest in literature. Philostratus is also mentioned as being part of the Emperor's train in Gaul. That he later taught in Athens is documented on the rediscovered base of a lost statue erected by that city in honour of Philostratus himself, his wife, and one of his sons. Another inscription in honour of Philostratus was found in Olympia.

The one work by Philostratus which was most widely read by subsequent generations, and also translated into Latin, is a biography of the Pythagorean philosopher and miracle-worker Apollonius of Tyana from the second half of the first century AD. The figure of Apollonius came to interest more and more people as philosophy focused on religious issues and as efforts were made in many different places to form doctrines of salvation appealing to faith, from elements of traditional, rationally based philosophy. According to Philostratus' own testimony, it was the Empress who suggested that he should write a life of Apollonius. In keeping with this assertion is a piece of information recorded by a pagan historian from the Late Classical age about the Emperor Alexander Severus, the last monarch of his dynasty. According to that authority, the Emperor's *Lararium*, the traditional domestic chapel of all Roman houses, contained effigies of Abraham, Orpheus, Jesus, and Apollonius of Tyana.

Philostratus' description of Apollonius' life fills as many as eight books. The lengthy account has all those characteristics which we know from the legendary lives of saints. It is meant to prove that a charismatic person who increases his capabilities through a strictly ascetic life in the sense of Pythagorean philosophy will finally be in a position to perform all sorts of supernatural feats and to bring all those whom he encounters on his chosen path instruction, help, consolation, and eternal salvation. In Philostratus' work the reader is first told of miraculous events in the hero's youth, before the author takes him along on the protagonist's extensive wanderings through the entire Roman Empire and as far as Persia, India, and Ethiopia, where Apollonius converses with exotic sages. Everywhere the hero shows his supernatural power, protected and increased through asceticism. Apollonius fearlessly confronts the tyrannical Emperor Domitian, reconciles quarrelling cities or factions, subdues proud and crude Parthian Satraps, tracks down demons, and proves his sagacity in talks with potentates, with exponents of traditional Greek philosophy, or with wise priests and ascetics in India. He demonstrates his ability to describe events happening far away or even in the future, and he helps people to recover from illness or mental distress: but, above all, he answers all questions which are raised about the proper worship of the gods. One issue on which the author places particular emphasis is that of blood sacrifices which Apollonius rejected because of the Pythagorean doctrine about the transmigration of souls.

Apollonius was a historical character, of whom we even have some letters, and thus the most obvious question to ask is how much truth Philostratus' account contains. What must be considered here is that Philostratus' life of Apollonius follows the tradition of Pythagorean biographies, which did not really attempt to tell the true life story of the historical personality from the sixth century BC, a story which had soon been overgrown by legend anyway. What the lives of Pythagoras tried to do was to portray an exemplary lifestyle according to the rules of Pythagorean philosophy; and by analogy, we may assume that only very few episodes in the life of Apollonius have any kind of factual basis. However, this should not prevent us from reading the work also as a document of cultural history, for its descriptions of different milieus are actually largely realistic. From them, we get some fairly reliable information about life in the Greek cities of the Empire, about public appearances of philosophers and sophists or rhetors, about the relationship between Roman provincial government and independent municipal administrations, about theatre, music, sport, and many other subjects. This can even be said of those parts of the narrative whose settings are in Iran and India. Beside reminiscences of Alexander's campaign – which is ultimately the model for Philostratus' travelogue – these chapters also contain accurate and up-to-date information about north-western India, which was ruled by Iranians at the time when the work was written.

In one part of the biography Philostratus does not take the stance of an authorial narrator in his own right, but claims to be retelling the account of a certain Damis, said to have accompanied Apollonius on his travels. It is still not certain whether this Damis actually existed or whether Philostratus invented him. The second possibility seems the more likely one, in view of the fact that the narrator's claim to have obtained his information from a companion of the hero represents a common motif found in all kinds of hagiography.

The religious interest which is documented in the book on Apollonius also dominates Philostratus' short treatise on heroes. According to ordinary Greek linguistic usage, heroes were dead men worshipped in sepulchral cults as individuals whose exceptional achievements or qualities shown during their lives enabled them to exert more power from their graves than other deceased people could muster. Because of the close connection with the earth in which they were buried, those heroes were thought of as helpers in times of distress, and as bringers of blessings and fertility to the surrounding land. There are many stories about their deeds: thus, for instance, the Attic heroes are said to have miraculously appeared to fight beside the hoplites of Athens, at the Battle of Marathon. In order to bring their benign power closer, some Greeks would dig up the bones of a particular local hero, and reinter them at their home. Naturally enough, people thought of the heroes as less distant from the common man in his common needs than the great gods, whose temple cults were a matter for the political community. In popular piety the heroes thus had a role resembling that played by the saints in large parts of the Christian world. Educated people, on the other hand, would often look on this side of religious practice with great skepticism, especially in the centuries that followed the Classic period.

Philostratus' short treatise is written as a dialogue, in which a vintner in northern Greece defends the faith in heroes against the unbelief of a guest from Phoenicia. The vintner tells a great number of stories about the appearance of heroes, some from of other people's reports and some from his own experience. He even claims, for example, that the hero Protesilaus, whom the epic tradition named as the first Greek killed in the Trojan War, appeared to him and told him some previously unknown details about that event. Thus this writing by Philostratus is a valuable piece of evidence for the growing influence of folk belief on the religious notions of educated people. This influence was strongest in the Late Classical age, whereas the ideas of the post-Hellenistic educated classes were largely influenced by the rationalistic legacy of that period.

The image which Philostratus had of his own profession is illustrated by his two books of sophists' biographies. As we can infer from the dedication to the Proconsul Gordian, this work was produced before the year 238 AD. In older Greek usage, the word sophist had meant as much as 'wise man' or 'expert'. It acquired terminological status in the fifth century BC when the title of sophist was claimed by a group of travelling teachers, who thus alleged that they were competent instructors in moral and political virtue. Their medium of teaching was first and foremost the art of argumentation and oratory and the introduction of pupils to unprejudiced reflections about the facts of human life. Plato and the philosophical tradition then used the term sophist in a pejorative sense, because they saw the educational programme of those men as directly opposed to philosophy, the incessant search for truth. In the Empire the title of sophist became fashionable once more, and people used it again in the original sense to mean orators who would go beyond rhetorical instruction by giving expression to the concerns and ideas of educated people in public speeches and lectures on the most diverse topics, but above all on aspects of politics and morality. I have already talked about the prestige enjoyed by these new sophists who finally came to enjoy the status of a legally privileged class, like professional grammarians, teachers of literature, physicians, or philosophers (see p. 7).

Philostratus wrote the history of the older and the newer sophists and their *métier*, as described above, in a series of short biographical sketches. These sketches are not biographies as such, because they do not attempt to give comprehensive accounts of moral personalities, even if personal-private matters are occasionally mentioned. But Philostratus' aim is above all to portray the development of sophistic eloquence in the Empire and the achievements, the rank, and the influence of its exponents, as well as its relationship to philosophy as the other educational force. What transpires is the author's desire to make his own profession appear in a proper light, and to explain its genesis. Philostratus' treatise, written in a plain style, contains valuable information about individual representatives of this branch of literary education, including many men of whom we know nothing else. Philostratus also tells us about the centres of this art, which spread above all in western Asia Minor; and likewise about the different stylistic trends which existed in this most demanding area of literary prose.

Typical products of rhetorical practice are Philostratus' letters, most of which have an erotic content and therefore belong to a class which constitutes a particularly large share of extant rhetorical exercises and examples. The only genuine letter in the collection is the seventy-third epistle, addressed to the Empress Julia Domna. A further example of rhetorical writing by Philostratus is *Nero*, a fictitious report by the philosopher Musonius about the tyrannical whims of the Emperor during whose reign Musonius was banished. This piece can be grouped alongside a work called *Pictures*, containing a series of artfully written descriptions of paintings. It is not clear, though, whether those paintings were real or invented. In any case, extant textbooks prove that the *ekphrasis* or description was a particularly popular type of rhetorical exercise. Philostratus' published specimens are especially artfully styled, and embedded in a narrative framework, according to which Philostratus describes the pictures which he has seen at a gallery in Naples, to the son of a friend he is staying with.

Beside the *Pictures*, we have a second series of much less elaborate descriptions of paintings, likewise written by a Philostratus. Its prooemium declares that the author of that second work was trying to emulate the model of his grandfather's writing. Yet another work handed down under the name of Philostratus is a letter with a lengthy discussion of the question to what extent official administrative messages should be formulated according to the rules of the rhetorical art. The author of this epistle was presumably the nephew and namesake of the 'great' Philostratus, who had already mentioned the controversial topic in his lives of the sophists.

The aforementioned treatise on gymnastics (see p. 341) stands outside the boundaries of rhetorical literature. It contains descriptions of individual disciplines, instructions for training, and discussions of specific medical issues; but the author also deals with those degenerative trends in contemporary sport which were a consequence of its largely professional character. Besides the countless inscriptions referring to sportsmen and sports competitions, this short work is our most important source of information about sport in the Classical age.

The writings handed down under Philostratus' name reflect many different facets of the culture and the literary life of the Late Empire. It is this that makes them so valuable, and not any special stylistic or compositional merits. The texts are among the very last documents which reflect a balanced education, guided by the endeavour to give equal dues to religion, philosophy, rhetoric, science, art, and politics, without subscribing wholeheartedly to any opinion or conviction. During the crises of the following decades such an attitude was naturally of little use to people who were looking around for sources of spiritual strength.

In a totally different way, the education and the literature of the Severan era are also epitomised by a most peculiar piece called *The Learned at Banquet*. Its author Athenaeus, who came from the ancient Greek city of Naucratis, chose the conventional form of table talk, which had been a much-used literary device since the days of Plato. In Athenaeus' work the host is a Roman knight whose learned friends talk for one whole day about meals, cooking, drinks, dishes, recipes, table manners, and virtually anything else that belongs to this range of subject matter. The dialogue is of monstrous dimensions, filling a total of fifteen books, of which some are only extant in excerpts. The value of this document lies mostly in the thousands of those quotations from largely lost poetry and prose which the speakers produce as evidence for their statements. Without Athenaeus' work we would, for instance, know very little of the so-called Middle and New Comedy that existed in Athens between the fourth and the second centuries BC; and his text has likewise preserved invaluable quotes from the historical work of the great philosopher Posidonius from the first century BC, and from the elaborate chorus lyrics of the fourth century BC. Athenaeus displays his voluminous collections of relevant passages from ancient literature with an unmistakable pride. This is to show that education, philosophy, and science alike were guided by the very same principle. The leading idea was that the ancients were the ones to emulate: their works had to be properly interpreted, as the only possible sources of knowledge and guidance.

7 HISTORIOGRAPHY

In Roman historiography of the Severan era, the most noteworthy figure is the author of a lost work which documented in several different ways a reorientation of historical interest. Next to the different kinds of oratory in the narrower sense, Romans as well as Greeks had long regarded historiography as the noblest, stylistically most demanding, genre of eloquence, a general term for all formal literary prose in the Classical age. In Rome this aesthetical-moral evaluation was matched by the social prestige of the historiographer's art: especially in the ancient Roman tradition, it was regarded as a fitting pursuit for an aristocrat unlike, for instance, grammatical or philosophical scholarship. Tacitus was only one among many who were conscious of this special dignity of historiography, and he expressed this awareness very unequivocally in his choice of stylistic devices. At the same time, however, he deplored the lack of subject matter commensurate to the sublime nature of the historiographical tradition. According to Tacitus, the reason for this was that under the rule of the emperors only what the monarch did or did not do had any historical significance and this meant that the historiographer could no longer ignore everyday trivialities.

Such trivia from the life of the monarch and his entourage are found in abundance in Suetonius' lives of the emperors, which were not meant to be read as historiography, but still painted a broad panorama of conditions in the capital and the Empire under successive monarchs. These biographies belonged to the tradition of stylistically plain scholarly writing on antiquarian issues or aspects of culture. In Suetonius' lifetime such learned activity had long lost its social stigma, and Suetonius himself is a good example for the high-ranking men among those who thus occupied themselves.

Suetonius' complete sequence of Imperial lives began with Augustus and ended with Nerva. In the third century AD, Marius Maximus read the series as a historiographical work, which he continued with further biographies of the monarchs from Nerva to Elagabal. Marius Maximus' writing was in turn used by an anonymous historiographer of the fourth century AD who portrayed Roman history from Hadrian to Diocletian in a series of emperors' lives, and could thus use Maximus' writing as a source for the years from 117 to 222 AD, a period of just over a century. The introduction to one of the emperor's biographies by the anonymous author of the so-called *Historia augusta* (see p. 476), as well as critical remarks by the historian Ammianus Marcellinus from the second half of the fourth century AD, indicate that then, the Imperial lives by Marius Maximus as well as those by his predecessor Suetonius were regarded as historical writings. In comparison with historiography in the manner of Livy or Sallust, they were thought to be stylistically inferior, but at the same time more detailed and reliable.

Up to the second century AD historiography and biography had been regarded as two separate genres fundamentally different with regard to intention and style (see p. 188). What we know of Marius Maximus shows a development that had taken place since the lifetime of Suetonius: it had become fashionable to write history as the story of great men's lives, which at that time meant first and foremost the biography of monarchs. This convention survived throughout the Late Classical age and the Middle Ages, and well into the Modern age, beside a kind of historiography which focuses on periods, countries, nations, or chains of causally linked events. The new tradition cited Suetonius as a model in spite of the fact that Suetonius certainly did not intend to found a new genre. Its popularity was virtually unaffected by critics such as Ammianus, who spoke up for the other, higher kind of historiography. Ammianus characterised the new type of historical account with the deprecatory comment that it reported no more than what the Emperor said at the dinner table.

Marius Maximus came from an equestrian family; his rise to the Senatorial class was the result of a meteoric career documented in several inscriptions as well as in literary sources. He held high command posts in the army, and was Consul twice.

The biographical reorientation of historiography can also be observed on the Greek side. A good example is the historical work by Herodianus, whose eight books deal with events from the death of the Emperor Marcus Aurelius in 180 AD up to the succession of Gordian III in 238 AD. This period largely coincides with the lifetime of the author who was presumably an Imperial freedman. The divisions of his account follow neither years nor clusters of events, but periods defined by emperors' reigns. He gives an explicit reason for this: he saw the difference in historical events as a consequence of the different stages in their lives at which monarchs began their reigns, as well as of their diverse temperaments, talents, and intentions. Although Herodian was far removed from that historiographical tradition which Tacitus sought to follow as a Roman and a Senator, the two authors agreed in the view that the reigning Emperor had a paramount influence on the course of events.

Neither Herodian's class nor his family background suggested reminiscences of the Republican past, or the idea that there was a contradiction between civil liberty and monarchy. That a religiously legimitised emperor should rule a state which united the entire civilised part of mankind was a virtually natural fact to Herodian, whose attitude was very much in keeping with the prevailing view among wealthy educated citizens in the urban communities of the Graeco-Roman world. However, this basic tenet did not preclude criticising monarchs whose government did not match the moral norms upheld by educated people, values which found ever-new expression in semi-philosophical writing about monarchy and the duties of a ruler. A key concept expressed in such literature was that a monarch had to show those very virtues which distinguished the educated citizen, and that he must substantiate this by maintaining a harmonious relationship with the Senate, the most eminent group among the wealthy bourgeoisie. Any ruler who neglected to do so and relied solely on the army could easily be suspected of being a tyrant.

Herodian's historiography is the work of a man of letters without personal experience or expertise in matters of warfare, high politics, or administration. Methodical criticism of source material and philosophical reflection on the nature of state and society were not his forte either. But within the limitations thus indicated the information he gives us on his chosen historical period does have its value, even if it is neither free of errors, nor particularly well ordered. Herodian's work was frequently and liberally used by later authors, in spite of its unambitious style.

Of an entirely different nature is the major historical work by Cassius Dio Cocceianus, who came from a distinguished family resident in Nicaea, in the north-western corner of Asia Minor. He became a Senator under Commodus, went through a career which led to high posts in the army and the administration, and held the Consulate twice, the second time in 229 AD as the Emperor's counterpart. Cassius Dio spent the last years of his life in his native region of Bithynia.

All these and other facts about Cassius Dio's biography can be gathered from his extant historiographical writing, in which he also mentions some earlier literary products. Among those lost works were a book on the interpretation of dreams, a history of the civil war that followed Commodus' death, and a biography of his fellow Bithynian Arrian, who had lived about a century before him (see p. 241). Cassius Dio's main work is his Roman history which contained eighty books, twenty-four of which are extant. These deal with the years from 68 BC to 47 AD; of the others, we have no more than fragments and excerpts incorporated into the accounts of Byzantine historians.

Cassius Dio is a typical exponent of a group which we come across with growing frequency in sources from the second century onwards: Greeks from the urban upper classes whose service for the Empire led them into the highest ranks of the Imperial nobility; men who never denied their Greek linguistic and cultural background, but still identified completely with the political and historical tradition of Rome, as upheld above all by the Senatorial families. The complete integration of the Greek part of the populace into the order of the Roman Empire explains why the Greeks kept calling themselves Rhomaeans or Romans well into the nineteenth century, or were called thus by their Oriental neighbours. In the case of Cassius Dio the romanisation of a Greek is also reflected in his adoption of conventions from Roman historiography, in contrast, for example, to his predecessor Appian (see p. 244).

In keeping with a Roman tradition still recognisable in the works of Tacitus, Cassius Dio's history has an annalistic structure. However, this is not adhered to too rigidly, as the author followed the traditional Greek convention of including theoretical reflections on history in the chronological account. Among the topics of such digressions are fundamental problems of political theory, as well as the different conditions for historians who rely on documents from either a Republican or a monarchic period.

Cassius Dio used high-quality historiographical sources, including a large number of Latin authors such as Livy. It is interesting that for the history of the Early Empire he did not base his account on Tacitus but preferred older, presumably Latin authors. Hence Cassius Dio's report provides a convenient foil to Tacitus, although the comparison sometimes reveals instances where both writers drew on the same authority. Occasionally, however, Cassius Dio's work also clearly reflects the influence of biographical source material, even if we cannot identify any specific author.

Cassius Dio was generally a more ambitious writer than Herodian, also in purely literary terms. In some of his books we find an extensive use of stylistic devices, especially in the many speeches which he included in his account to illustrate the intentions of the participants, after the manner of Thucydides who had provided the model for all high historiography. Particularly interesting is a speech in Book 52, where Maecenas, trusted counsellor of the Emperor Augustus, gives detailed advice for the establishment of a monarchic order. The political theory put forward here does not fit into the Augustan era at all and rather seems to express the author's own political credo.

His rich political-administrative experience enabled Cassius Dio to subject received information to expert scrutiny. This is, of course, particularly obvious in the part of his writing which deals with events of his own lifetime. Unfortunately this very part – which according to the author himself was especially detailed – is only extant in fragments and such excerpts as mentioned above. But even in this form it is our most important source of knowledge about the history of the early third century AD.

Cassius Dio represents a social class which conducted the Empire's political affairs, but which, during the following decades of the third century AD, was progressively ousted by less educated and less scrupulous men, mostly with an army background. It is significant that Cassius Dio was unable to take up his second Consulate in Rome because he had made himself unpopular with the Imperial guard through his firm insistence on military discipline in his different commands. Another telling fact is the murder of the great legal scholar Papinian by the very same troops.

8 CHRISTIAN LITERATURE: THE LATINS

The Severan era saw the beginning of a Christian literature in Latin. This, however, did not come about in Rome whose focal role in Greek Christian as well as pagan writing I have pointed out on more than one occasion. The development which I shall outline in the following took place in Roman north Africa whose overall output of Latin writings in the second century AD had already surpassed the capital's. But even in the north African genesis of Latin Christian literature, Greek influence should not be underestimated, and a good case in point is one text which has long been looked upon as one of the earliest specimens of genuine Christian-Latin writing. This piece, of which we have a Latin and a Greek version, is a report on the trial, imprisonment, and execution of Vibia Perpetua, a young noblewoman from Carthage, with her female slave Felicitas, and three catechumens from the city's Christian community. The account is based on statements made by Perpetua under interrogation and it gives us an authentic impression of the procedure followed in trials of Christians, as well as an idea of how individual Christians conceived of life after death. It was not until fairly recently that a French scholar managed to prove that this work was originally written in Greek. The opposite seems to be true in the case of a slightly older report which is also extant in two different versions, describing the martyrdom of six Christians in the north African city of Scili in the year 180 AD.

Particularly with regard to north Africa, we may well assume that at least parts of the Bible were translated into Latin in the second century AD, and thus the basis for a tradition of Latin-Christian linguistic usage was established. The true founder of the Christian literary tradition in Latin was the African Q. Septimius Florens Tertullianus, a man with an exceptionally volatile temperament, great erudition, and unique linguistic talent. Tertullian was born in a pagan family around 160 AD; his father served as a Centurion in the Roman army. He made sure that his son received a sound rhetorical and legal training, after which the young man worked for several years in Rome, as a solicitor and legal orator. It seems that Tertullian became a convert to the Christian faith during this sojourn in Rome but the exact circumstances of his conversion are unknown. Upon his return to his native city Carthage in 195 AD Tertullian began his prolific career as a writer for the cause of Christianity; he did not, however, hold any ecclesiastical office. Around 207 AD he even turned his back on the established church and joined the Montanites, a sect which had originated in Asia Minor. The Montanites were a strictly ascetic community which rejected the view of ecclesiastical office held by the meanwhile firmly institutionalised church, and which recognised only personal charisma as given to people by the divine spirit. Tertullian died around 220 AD.

No fewer than thirty-one pieces of writing by Tertullian have been preserved, eight of them from the time when he belonged to the Montanite sect, and bitterly attacked the secularised church. We know some titles of other lost works, and in a number of cases we also have an idea of their content. The list of those writings features short exhortational pieces and pamphlets, as well as scholarly treatises in several books. In all of Tertullian's works, however, we find literary paroxysms of his violent temper, to which he gave vent with all the rhetorical devices at his command, and often in the most unlikely contexts. His *oeuvre* thus abounds with cutting satire, pointed puns, paradoxical formulas, and outbursts of scorn and hate. In the introduction to his treatise on patience Tertullian admits that he is setting out to describe a virtue which he himself does not possess, like a sick man extolling the merits of good health.

It is above all the clever and sometimes overly crafty argumentation in which Tertullian's writings reveal his astute intellect, sharpened through good philosophical and rhetorical education as well as through legal training. The reader encounters specifically legal patterns of thought and expression with a frequency that makes it obvious why it has been suggested that the ecclesiastical writer is identical with the lawyer Tertullian who is quoted once in Justinian's *Digests*, even if there is no way to prove this assumption.

One of Tertullian's anti-heretical works, for instance, is entitled *De praescriptione hereticorum*. As a legal term, *praescriptio* meant an accused person's invocation of a clause in the law which ruled out the institution of court proceedings. Tertullian applies this legal figure of argumentation to the relationship between the church and individual or sectarian heresies. He begins with the axiom that the tradition of Christian teaching has been passed on in lawful succession, as described by Irenaeus, from Christ to the church, via the apostles. Therefore, only the ecclesiastical authority is legally entitled to interpret the meaning of Holy Scripture. As the heretics have no such legal basis, the church can thus claim the principle of *praescriptio*, and decline to offer them the chance for pitching their own reading of the Bible against the orthodox one in a kind of public trial. The bottom line is that exponents of church theology do not really need to discuss the content of Gnostic or other heretical doctrines at all: but there is a certain irony in the fact that Tertullian himself spent a lot of his time doing just that.

This example of legal argumentation along with other comparable passages in Tertullian's work signify much more than a merely metaphorical use of legal terminology. What lies behind Tertullian's method is rather a fully developed image of the church as a legal order to which one may quite naturally apply ideas and norms from the legal order of the state.

This notion was extremely hard to reconcile with the spiritual definition of ecclesiastical community, a definition that had never been seriously challenged. Still, Tertullian's idea came to be widely accepted, above all in the Latin West where it exerted a much earlier and also much more fundamental influence than in the Greek East, or in the churches outside the Graeco-Roman world. It decided the destiny of the Roman church by giving it the means to assert its legitimacy as a successor to the Roman state, in its capacity as the guarantor of a legal order.

The underlying definition constituted a characteristic difference between the ecclesiastical traditions of Roman and non-Roman provenance; a difference which, significantly enough, appeared to be unaffected by the varied level of agreement between the church and the political order in different historical circumstances. For centuries to come, the East saw a much more unproblematic co-existence of church and state than the West. Nevertheless, the Roman-Latin image of the church retained its legal flavour, as indicated already in the very first beginnings of a Christian-Latin literature.

For the first two centuries AD, the debate about the formulation of Christian doctrine had been conducted exclusively in Greek, even in Rome or Lyons. Under the influence of Greek philosophy, such discussions had led to a remarkably high degree of terminological abstraction and precision by the end of that period. Tertullian's Latin entry into those debates shows an astonishingly sure-footed approach, with the most astounding feature being his ability to go one better than Greek in finding simpler and more manageable Latin expressions for complex problems such as those of christology. That he had a full command of Greek is evident from his abundant use of Greek literature.

His terminological dexterity, however, does not make Tertullian's work easy to digest. He obviously took great delight in displaying his linguistic virtuosity, in using rhetorical devices, and especially in coining neologisms, and hence he frequently created argumentative and syntactic structures whose meanings are only revealed by a very close reading. There is a strange contrast between such difficult and sometimes very obscure passages, and individual formulas which are so immediately striking and memorable that they have entered all kinds of manuals and collections of quotes. Examples of the latter are his description of the *anima naturaliter Christiana*, the human soul as naturally Christian or disposed to receive the Christian faith; his characterisation of pagan cults and rites as *sacrum facinus* ('sacred crime'); or his maxim *adversus regulam nihil scire omnia scire est* ('to know nothing against the rule of faith is to know all'). Among such famous phrases, however, there are also quite a few which were wrongly ascribed to Tertullian, such as the notorious *credo quia absurdum* or 'I believe because it is absurd (and hence unknowable)', which can certainly not be located in any of Tertullian's extant writings.

Tertullian's gift for linguistic creation is probably best illustrated by the fact that statistics of the Latin language feature nearly a thousand words as first documented in his writings. It is true that we may not regard all of those as Tertullian's own inventions, in view of the large share of Latin literature which was lost, or of our ignorance about the vernacular. But in quite a number of cases Tertullian is almost certainly the creator, especially of words which relate to the Christian faith, and have since entered that vocabulary which is specific to Christianity.

One concrete example may serve to illustrate the nature of this special Christian idiom. Greek as well as Latin had different words for sacredness and holiness, to refer either to the numinous power of hallowed people, objects, or actions; or to denote purity, innocence, and perfection as qualities ascribed to the hallowed, or to those people who establish the proper kind of relation with it. In Greek, this distinction was expressed by the words *hieros* and *hagios*, and in Latin by the words *sacer* and *sanctus*, whereas Biblical Hebrew knew only the one word *qadoš* for all aspects of sacredness and holiness. Greek-speaking Jews and Christians avoided the word *hieros* which in pagan ritual language evoked the numinous power of gods whose divine status the Christians denied, whereas they were quite ready to believe in their existence as demons. Consequently the Christians went against genuinely Greek linguistic usage, in applying the word *hagios* to the entire semantic range covered by the Hebrew adjective. The word *hieros* returned to Christian Greek only when its speakers became used to an organised form of worship in which the holy was taken to be materially present. A similar situation existed in the early Christian use of Latin. If Tertullian called a pagan cultic ritual a *sacrum facinus* or sacred misdeed, this was in keeping with his general avoidance of the word *sacer* in a Christian context, where he would substitute it by *sanctus*. At the same time, the paradoxical formula alluded to the laudatory meaning of the word *sacer* in a pagan environment, as a fact well known to Christians. Later on, after the conversion of large parts of the population and the institutionalisation of Christian worship, the word *sacer* re-entered Christian Latin, just as its equivalent *hieros* became acceptable in Christian Greek. This case shows quite clearly how the new religion affected the meaning of old words, especially of course in religious language.

The catalogue of Tertullian's writings suggests a division into sections according to differences in content. Many of the works cited are anti-heretical tracts, attacking above all Gnostic doctrines or individual advocates of Gnostic teachings. Thus the treatise against Hermogenes denounces the Gnostic claim that the empirical world is the inferior creation of a lesser god, while the treatise about the bodily existence of Christ condemns Gnostic docetism – namely, the belief that the divine saviour had only the semblance of a physical body. Both topics feature also in the tract against the Valentinians. Tertullian's treatise against Praxeas defends the doctrine of the trinity; and his tract on baptism belongs to the context of the debate as to whether baptism was valid if it had been performed by a heretic.

Beside these and other shorter treatises on similar kinds of subject matter, this section of Tertullian's *oeuvre* also contains two longer works. The five books against the teachings of Marcion (see p. 299) were written in 207 AD, and the similarly anti-Gnostic treatise on the soul a few years after that. The attack on Marcion is much more systematically structured than the also largely polemical later piece, but the tract on the soul does document Tertullian's astounding degree of familiarity with the different psychological doctrines of the philosophical schools better than any other one of his works. Tertullian's own doctrine about the soul may well surprise the reader because it incorporates much of Stoic teaching as expressed in the work by the physician Soranus of Ephesus (see p. 143). Of course, however, the Christian Tertullian would not go as far as to accept the strict materialism of the Stoic world view.

The second group among Tertullian's writings comprises his mostly paraenetical works on practical ethics, pieces whose main value is as documents relating to cultural and moral history. In his tract against the theatre the author emphasises the links of drama with pagan ritual and mythology which are his main reason for branding it as dangerous with the label *pompa diaboli* ('the Devils pomp'). Another tract in this group attacks the frills of female fashion. But beside such polemics, we also find the aforementioned treatise on patience, as well as one on repentance and the ecclesiastical practice of penance. Tertullian's treatise on praying features an interpretation of the Lord's Prayer, as does the corresponding slightly later work by Origen. Finally, we have a short treatise which Tertullian addressed to his wife, giving her instructions for the event of his own death: she is either to live as a widow after that, or to choose none other than a Christian partner for a second marriage.

Tertullian's behests to his wife are a particularly good illustration for the difference in the author's convictions before and after joining the Montanites in 207 AD. In two tracts written afterwards, a treatise on monogamy and an appeal for chastity, he explicitly denies the permissibility of second marriages which the church at that time only forbade to bishops. In his treatise on the wreath, Tertullian denounces the traditional decorations which were bestowed, for example, in acknowledgement of military distinction. The author declares that this habit is pagan and goes on to prohibit army service to Christians. His tract on the worship of idols extends this prohibition to all professions which might in any way be related to paganism, as for instance the job of a schoolmaster might force him to teach Classic poetry and its mythological background. In this respect Hippolytus' ecclesiastical constitution is much more liberal (see p. 331).

The progressive radicalisation of Tertullian's views is also evident in his two appeals for steadfastness under persecution, treatises written around

200 AD and 212 AD respectively. In a tract on the veil, a piece which like the second one of the aforementioned works was produced after his conversion to Montanism, Tertullian insists that all virgins should be veiled whenever they appear in public. In his tract on fasting, he denounces the orthodox ecclesiastical practice, which differed from the Montanist custom, in the most violent tone as being virtually dictated by the cravings of the stomach. In the treatise on the cloak he defends his habit of wearing the short *pallium* of the philosopher, as an expression of his ascetic outlook on life.

Tertullian's treatise on chastity deals with basic aspects of the dispute between the established church and the Montanites. The author takes a circular from an unnamed bishop, a letter talking about penance and the forgiveness of sins, as occasion for denying that an ecclesiastical office conveys the power to pardon sins in the name of Christ. Tertullian's Montanist view is that this prerogative is reserved for spiritually gifted charismatics, such as the apostles or prophets. The question whether the effect and the validity of the sacraments depended on the official legitimacy or on the charismatic endowment of the acting person was a perennial bone of contention within the church. The debate could be rekindled by prophetic-ecstatic movements like the Montanites, and likewise by proven ascetes or steadfast confessors who claimed that their unwavering faith shown under persecution qualified them to administer ecclesiastical rites. Another way of reopening the discussion was to raise questions about the worthiness of holders of church offices in general. Tertullian's treatise on this topic already contains almost all the arguments which were put forward in this controversy over the subsequent centuries.

Without any doubt, Tertullian's fame among later generations was largely based on his reputation as an apologist. Among the five extant apologetical works from his hand the one most widely known is the *Apologeticum* of 197 AD. The treatise addressed to the heathens seems to be a preliminary sketch for his major apology, while a short treatise on the *Testimony of the Soul* is a mere supplement to it. The latter work is meant to prove that nature gave the heathens basically the same ideas about God and man as the Christians. Tertullian's epistle to the notorious anti-Christian Scapula, Proconsul of the province of Africa in 212 AD, warns the addressee of divine punishment. In a short treatise against the Jews the author explains the contrast between the avenging nature of the Old Testament God, and the mercy of the Christian God, who will even speak to the heathens.

In this group of writings, however, the *Apologeticum* certainly is the one major achievement. In comparison with other early Christian apologies, Tertullian's work stands out because it is the first Christian document which sheds proper light on the legal aspects of anti-Christian persecutions. Tertullian's legal argumentation provides the framework for all the other apologetical motifs featured: the preposterousness of all moral accusations against the Christians whose lifestyle actually sets an example for the pagans and their philosophers; the loyalty of the Christians to the Emperor and the Empire; the absurdity and immorality of pagan ideas about the gods; and the true facts about Christian doctrine and Christian life.

Tertullian shows great skill in exposing the precarious legal basis for the suppression and persecution of Christians in the Roman state where the policy of the authorities towards the Christians was indeed highly questionable from a legal point of view. The fundamental guidelines were still the definitions of the relationship between the state and its Christian citizens given by the Emperor Trajan in his rescripts to enquiries from Pliny the Younger (see p. 226). According to these texts, it was forbidden and thus punishable to belong to the church, defined as the organisation of an illegal religion. But at the same time Trajan had commanded the executive to refrain from taking independent measures to track down Christians and bring them to trial, saying that legal investigations and, if necessary, legal retributions should only follow specific and non-anonymous accusations. Sentences were to be handed out only if an accused person refused to demonstrate his being part of the great religious community of all the Empire's inhabitants by performing a sacrifice to the gods under the auspices of one of the many recognised cults. It was exactly this demand, however, which the exclusive monotheism of the Christians did not allow them to fulfil. This legal situation, which lasted until the middle of the third century AD, explains why there were many local persecutions of very limited scope and duration, while at the same time, in large parts of the Empire, Christian communities could live and multiply without any interference on the part of the state. After all, the likelihood and the frequency of public accusations depended very much on how hostile or how amicable their non-Christian neighbours were, and the severity of legal action varied greatly according to the sympathies or antipathies of individual state officials.

In his *Apologeticum*, Tertullian exposes this fundamental inconsistency in Imperial legal practice, by asking the obvious questions. How can anyone declare having the *nomen Christianum* or being a Christian a punishable offence, but at the same time prevent the authorities from initiating legal action against the offenders? How can it make sense that in normal criminal proceedings, sanctions such as torture are used to extract a confession of his deed from an accused, while in Christian trials the same means are employed to force the accused to deny his crime? Tertullian's apology places a particular emphasis on such legal arguments which sound all the more convincing because the author could express a genuine loyalty to the Emperor and to the legal order, as well as a genuine pride in the culture which the Roman Empire embraced.

I have already pointed out on more than one occasion that during the period in question the word philosophy meant the lore of proper living, which is why people recognised a philosopher first and foremost because of his lifestyle. In this sense, Christianity could be called a philosophy too: and Tertullian used the application of the term for his apologetical purpose. Why, he asked, are only the Christians persecuted, and not the philosophers, if many of the latter are equally critical of the traditional worship of the gods, and some even deny their existence altogether? In this context, Tertullian naturally ignored the many attempts of Greek philosophy to reconcile its cosmological view of the divine with religious traditions. His intention was to establish a parallel between philosophy and Christianity, and for this purpose he needed to prove that both rejected traditional religious beliefs. The parallel was developed further in a definition of philosophy as a distortion of divinely revealed truth through human arrogance. Tertullian put this down to the influence which the pagan gods exert over men as evil demons, who are ultimately also behind the persecution of Christians.

Tertullian's apology closes with a highly emotional appeal to the provincial governors to whom the treatise is addressed, urging them to acknowledge the futility of the persecutions, as they must realise that the proven steadfastness of the Christians has actually helped them to spread their new faith. In this context, Tertullian uses a phrase which is frequently quoted, but more often than not incorrectly: *semen est sanguis Christianorum* ('the blood of the Christians is seed').

Like Cicero, Petronius, and Tacitus, Tertullian is undoubtedly one of the most eminent authors of Latin prose: at the very least, he is one of its most original exponents and far superior to his contemporaries. But it is only fair to say that many of his instantly striking statements do not appear all that convincing if subjected to a close scrutiny. Tertullian went for effect rather than for accuracy, and this makes him a very typical representative of a post-Classic Classical education which was entirely dominated by rhetoric. His famous dictum, *Quid ergo Athenis et Hierosolymis?* ('What on earth has Athens got to do with Jerusalem, or the Academy with the church?'), is proved wrong most clearly in his own writings. Each page of Tertullian's literary legacy documents the impact which Graeco-Roman culture had made on him; and what makes Tertullian's own influence unique is that he was the first to introduce the tradition of Roman law into the Christian world of ideas.

There are extremely close parallels in content which link Tertullian's *Apologeticum* with another apology, a dialogue by M. Minucius Felix which has been handed down to us under the title *Octavius*. The label refers to the man to whom this fictitious conversation was dedicated and who was already dead at the time of writing. Taking part in the talk are three friends who are on an excursion from Rome to Ostia: the author and Octavius, advocates working in Rome and some provincial setting respectively, and finally Caecilius, a pagan who comes from north Africa. The dialogue is not written in the Platonic style but follows the tradition developed by the Peripatos and used in Cicero's philosophical works, as can be seen in two features: instead of short questions and answers, we find longer statements in which the speakers express their opinions; and the author himself appears as one of the participants in the conversation.

The discussion is triggered off when Caecilius blows a kiss to the statue of a deity which the three men walk past. This common gesture of religious veneration in the Classical age leads to a controversy among the three friends with their different religious views. They agree, however, that Octavius and Caecilius should conduct a disputation, whose outcome is to be judged by Minucius. Caecilius begins by defending pagan religious traditions with the argument that the divine is ultimately unknowable, and hence observing tradition is the only rational form of religious behaviour. He claims that Rome's greatness proves the power of its gods who have rewarded faithful veneration with benevolence. Finally, Caecilius brings up the common contemporary charges against the Christians, asserting that they are ill-educated people, and perform immoral rituals.

Octavius responds to these points one by one, in carefully chosen words. He affirms the old philosophical principle that human nature is designed for the cognition of truth, and that truth must be sought in spite of the fact that ultimately God cannot be known. But such truth as has been brought to light reveals that the ancient gods were actually prehistoric men whose achievements earned them particular honours. This so-called euhemeristic view was already a time-honoured motif in the philosophical criticism of religion. Octavius goes on to say that the greatness of Rome was built on iniquity and violence, and that the slanderous allegations against Christians are nothing but lies, instigated by the demons who see their power over mankind threatened. At this point, Caecilius admits defeat, and all that is left to do for the authorial arbiter is to express his joy about the result of the debate.

For all their similarities in content, the apologies of Tertullian and Minucius Felix could hardly be any more dissimilar than they are with regard to style as well as to the tenor of the message. Minucius Felix wrote an elegant dialogue among friends who use polite language and who refer to a common educational background. Tertullian produced an epistle addressed to Roman officials whom the author expected to order the bloody persecution of his fellow believers: hence his vehement language, his sarcasm, his threats, and his acrid way of making legal points. The smoothness and elegance of Minucius Felix's style mark his work as one of the most perfect emulations of the Ciceronian norm, while Tertullian's diction is characterised by deliberately crude violations of the very same set of rules and by the use of neologisms and rhetorical devices to give the reader surprise after surprise. But what makes the juxtaposition of the two texts so strange is that their apologetical aims are absolutely identical and that the number of obvious parallels rules out coincidence as the explanation. The seemingly endless debate about which work came first now seems to have been finally settled with a verdict in favour of Tertullian.

It is very likely that Minucius Felix was an African like his fellow author. That he set his dialogue in the urban-Roman milieu does not contradict this assumption, in view of the particularly close relations existing between the capital and the province of Africa and documented, for instance, by what we know about the life of Tertullian (see p. 350). Such close ties were not least the result of regular grain imports from that province; but, as the slightly more recent correspondence of Cyprian shows (see p. 384), the far-reaching effects of the strong traditional links between Rome and Africa can also be detected in the development of their respective churches.

In very different ways both Tertullian and Minucius Felix have provided us with evidence of one and the same process: the gradual social and intellectual integration of Christian communities into the cultural environment of the Roman Empire. One important factor in this development was the establishment of a terminology with which Christians would explain and promote, but also modify the faith which had initially made them aliens on their native soil. In the process, Christianity made increasing use of the full range of tools provided by the Graeco-Roman educational tradition. On the Greek side we can trace the beginnings of this development back as far as the first century AD. On the Latin side the earliest evidence from the time around 200 AD shows that the process was already in full swing by then.

6

THE CRISES OF THE THIRD CENTURY AD

1 GENERAL REMARKS

The period between the murder of the Emperor Alexander Severus in 238 AD and the succession of the great reformer Diocletian in 284 AD may well be described as the bleakest time in Graeco-Roman history. Catastrophes on a hitherto unknown scale shattered the very foundations of the Roman Empire: its political and legal order, which seemed to have been made to last for ever. Germanic hordes which had fused in the Alemannic tribe broke through the section of the Empire's border that was marked by the Limes. Their looting raids penetrated deep into Gaul, and it was only after tremendous effort that the Romans managed to secure the northern frontier once again. That they took this threat very seriously indeed is attested by the construction of a new wall around the city of Rome. This fortification, of which large parts still stand to this day, was the first one undertaken since the fourth century BC. Other Germanic tribes, Goths and Heruli, raided the border along the Danube. From the Black Sea coast, they also launched piratical forays into the Mediterranean where they laid siege to Athens and plundered Delphi.

In the East, the Empire had been involved in continuous warfare with the Persians who had become a major power under the rule of the Sassanid dynasty from 226 AD onwards. One reigning Emperor, Valerian, was taken prisoner by the victorious Persians after a battle, and he died in captivity. Of this unprecedented humiliation of Rome, we still have evidence in the trilingual inscription and the rock relief of the High King Sapur in Naqs-i-Rustam, near today's border between Iraq and Iran. Later on the Persians might well have conquered the entire eastern part of the Roman Empire had it not been for the firm stand of Queen Zenobia in the desert city of Palmyra. For a while this monarch reigned over an independent state formed of the Empire's eastern provinces, and it took a toilsome military campaign under the Emperor Aurelian to bring these territories back under Roman rule.

The political and military difficulties were aggravated by economic ones.

Ever-new issues of money were necessary to cover first and foremost the pay for the soldiers. This inflationary policy weakened the Roman currency so much that the world of finance and long-distance trading collapsed and large parts of the population found themselves living within an economy that had been reduced to a primitive state.

In this general distress it was the army which had to secure the survival of the Empire time and again. Being conscious of their importance, troops on the threatened borders were naturally most likely to try and decide the Imperial succession by proclaiming one of their generals as Emperor. But many of the generals were now officers who had risen because of active service at the front, as opposed to members of the educated bourgeois upper classes who had gone through a regular administrative-military career. This meant an institutionalisation of the conflict between the army and the Senate as representing those upper classes, and upholding the longstanding claim that the Senators should have the final say in selecting a candidate for the throne. The acrimonious nature of this conflict stemmed from the animosity existing between both camps because of social distinctions. The latent tension had already led to occasional bloody eruptions during the Severan era, but then the unity of Empire as such had never been seriously at risk (see p. 309). Now, however, the quarrel between army and Senate became the dominant factor in internal politics.

The result was a chaotic situation, which repeatedly reached the state of complete anarchy. It happened more than once that different people were proclaimed Emperor at the same time, and this unleashed an endless series of bloody battles within the Empire's borders. It was exceptional for one of the wearers of purple of this period to die a natural death: most of them were either murdered or killed in battle.

The historiographical tradition provides us with no more than scanty information about this epoch; all of it was processed by writers who were either close to the Roman Senate or at least belonged to the educated urban classes. Hence their tendency to give bad marks to the soldier emperors, many of whom came from the rural population of the Illyrian and the Danubian provinces. They are mostly portrayed as ill-educated, cruel monarchs, hostile to the Senate. This is certainly unjust, for there were quite a few among them who undertook heroic efforts to avert the worst. Decius and Claudius, for instance, fended off the threat from the Goths; Gallienus, the son of the captive Valerian, introduced a comprehensive military reform which banned the Senatorial class from armed service; and Aurelian managed to restore the Empire's unity by defeating Zenobia.

The religious policies of the Emperors of this period, and especially their attitudes towards the Christians, will be discussed in a following section (see p. 379). In this context, I must mention two different political and social phenomena which also have a certain relevance for the assessment of literary life in the third century AD. One is the changing role of Rome, the metropolis which remained the focal point of Imperial ideology throughout the era in question, but which was no longer unrivalled as the centre of administration, and the Emperor's place of residence. It became imperative for Roman monarchs to move closer to the threatened borders, and thus the status of temporary capitals and residences fell to Cologne, Trier, Milan, Nish in modern-day Serbia, Nicaea on the Sea of Marmara, Antioch in Syria, and Alexandria in Egypt. This was yet another factor undermining the influence of the Senate, which remained tied to Rome. The concerns of this political body were thus limited to the preservation of Roman traditions, or at best to municipal administration.

The virtual paralysation of the state apparatus had another far-reaching effect in favouring a development that points ahead to the Latin Middle Ages. The Emperor and the state could not but welcome the fact that major landowners in Asia Minor or north Africa would take over their tasks in administration and jurisdiction and in turn guarantee the payment of taxes in their regions. The rural population could no longer expect anything from the state's representatives and consequently came to depend socially and legally on such landowners, to whom they turned for protection.

This formation of states within the state had a parallel in the increasing importance of professional associations among the urban middle classes. Through a close alliance, groups like bakers or haulage contractors could achieve greater social security. If the state wanted to make demands on such groups – for instance, because of the army's requirements – it could deal with the representatives of corporations instead of separate individuals. In the following centuries various degrees of privileges were granted to, or various obligations were imposed on professional groups *en bloc*, while the professions themselves became hereditary. Such a legally prescribed differentiation between the estates had not been unknown in the society of the Early and the High Empire, in whose social framework a large number of co-operative and municipal institutions constituted levels between the individual citizen and the central power of the state. During the third century AD, however, there was a marked proliferation of such collective intermediaries in the Roman Empire's society. Classic Roman law had laid particular emphasis on a notion derived from Greek philosophical thought, according to which the sovereign state ultimately has the individual citizen as its partner. This idea was gradually replaced by an attitude which saw the individual as first and foremost the representative of a group with certain rights and duties, a group mediating between him and the state.

The radical changes in the economy, society, and politics of the Graeco-Roman world were mirrored by corresponding developments in intellectual life. What came to dominate the world view of educated people was a feeling of uncertainty and of pessimism concerning human reason's capacity to create the physical and spiritual conditions for happy, fulfilled living. Such an optimistic trust in human reason had prevailed in the fifth century BC, when it aided the development of philosophy and science and favoured the creation of rationally organised states. Public and private life in the Roman Empire were likewise influenced by this optimism; and yet throughout the Imperial age we can notice a growing interest in transcendental matters, arising from the hope that meaning could be given to human lives by a power beyond the limits of human experience and human calculation. The fundamental crisis of the third century AD led to a significant weakening of the faith in human reason; instead, people tended to look fearfully or hopefully towards powers or forces which human reason could approach, but not completely fathom, and far less master.

It is not surprising that literary and scientific activity was severely hampered by the turmoil of this epoch. Outside the Christian church there was virtually no literature written in Latin at all. On the Greek side, too, there was a widespread decline in literary productivity, although the educational tradition was hardly disrupted in areas such as grammar, rhetoric, or philosophy. Noticeably affected were sciences like medicine, geography, or astronomy, whose progress depended on observation and the collection of data. But a completely opposite development took place in mathematics and speculative philosophy, and there was an even bigger boom in Christian theology into which a great deal of intellectual effort flowed.

The division of Imperial power between several rulers in the third century AD was at first understood as an exceptional measure in response to a state of emergency, although it later became an institutionalised phenomenon. This development fostered similar divisions in intellectual life where the most significant development was the growth in the importance of the linguistic border. During the second century AD an educated citizen of the Empire's western half would normally be bilingual, and I have mentioned plenty of writers who used both languages in previous chapters. Things were not entirely alike in the East, but many educated Greek-speaking people – for example, Plutarch – were able to read Latin texts. Moreover, the East had centres of Latin education such as the legal school of Berytus or Beirut; and among the literary papyri from Greek Egypt we find ones that carry writings by Virgil, Livy, and Sallust. But evidence from the third century AD onwards documents a steady decline in linguistic competence in Greek among educated people in the West, even within the framework of ecclesiastical life, with its strong links between geographically separate Christian communities. Even the ecclesiastical history of the period indicates what was going to take place in the Middle Ages, with effects that we can still perceive today: a radical separation of the Christian world into a Greek East and a Latin West.

2 GREEK PROSE LITERATURE

A considerable number of extant texts and other pieces of information from the third century AD prove that there were indeed some centres in the East which preserved a continuity of education and knowledge in this time of crisis, and which prevented the complete disruption that took place in the West. This is best illustrated by the life of Cassius Longinus, about whom we know a great deal because of frequent mentions in a biography of Plotinus by the Neo-Platonist Porphyry. Longinus lived between about 210 and 273 AD. He came from a distinguished family, travelled widely, and received a thorough philosophical and scientific education in Athens and Alexandria. From about the middle of the century to 267 AD he was head of the Platonic school in Athens, whose chair was endowed with a state salary. In 267 AD Longinus went to Palmyra at the invitation of Queen Zenobia (see p. 360), whose offer to become her counsellor he accepted in obvious emulation of Plato's Sicilian adventure. Longinus was executed in 273 AD at the command of the Emperor Aurelian, after the defeat of Zenobia, and the reintegration of her domains into the Roman Empire.

We know some of Longinus' philosophical doctrines from Late Classical commentaries on Plato, while we can deduce others from Plotinus' critical remarks. According to those, Longinus was very conservative and very well-read and Plotinus thought him more of a philologist than a philosopher. Longinus wrote about Plato's style, about Homeric exegesis, and about other philological problems which he also lectured on. A didactic treatise on rhetoric from his hand is partly extant. All this shows that scholarly-philological and rhetorical studies continued to have an audience and were even cultivated within the framework of school philosophy in Athens and elsewhere.

It is rhetorical literature in particular of which we have quite a few examples from the third century AD. These writings include two treatises on the theory and the didactics of epideictic eloquence; both of these bear the name of Menander of Laodicaea in Asia Minor, but they were certainly written by different authors. Our sources tell us that Menander also published rhetorical exercises known as *progymnasmata*, as well as a commentary on the rhetorical manual by Hermogenes (see p. 256), and perhaps further commentaries on Classic-Attic oratory.

Around the same time as Menander lived Apsines of Gadara in Syria, a man who taught for a while in Athens, and attained the Consulate in 240 AD. Philostratus knew Apsines personally. We know of a number of his works, but the only extant one is a *technē*, a manual of rhetoric. Another piece that seems to have been written during the crises of the third century AD is a very original treatise on rhetorical theory. This is featured in a manuscript kept in Paris: the anonymous author has been named

Anonymus Seguerianus after the French nobleman to whose collection the manuscript belonged.

A very long didactic treatise on rhetoric, a piece which was handed down to us among the works of Dionysius of Halicarnassus, also seems to date from the third century AD. This tract is composed of very different parts; it is especially informative on aspects of Classical stylistic theory. There are detailed instructions and stylistic examples for various genres of epideictic eloquence, such as speeches for weddings or funerals. We also find descriptions of frequently occurring errors in diction, of forms of composition, of rhetorical figures, and much more. The many examples which illustrate the rules are mostly taken from poetry, particularly that of Homer. This illustrates very well what function the reading of ancient poetry had in the system of higher education in the Empire. The cultivation of linguistic-stylistic judgment through such studies was an important factor in the shaping of general attitudes in public and private life. Its influence is all too easily underestimated by people living in our day and age, where notions of education are largely content-orientated.

Among those Greek novels of which we have not only older papyrus fragments but also the full texts as featured in mediaeval manuscripts, the one written last is at the same time the longest, of the highest literary quality, and the most important because of its influence on European literature from the seventeenth century onwards. It is not quite clear whether the author Heliodorus belonged to the third or the fourth century AD. His plot follows the familiar pattern of the erotic novel, with the separation, adventures, and happy reunion of two lovers. Heliodorus' choice of exotic settings followed a convention for which I have already cited a number of examples (see p. 236). In this case the locations are Egypt and Ethiopia, which explains why the work is known as *Aethiopica.*

What makes Heliodorus' novel special is the artful construction of a rich and varied story, the attempts at a psychological deepening of characterisation, and in particular the religious concern of the author, which has no parallel in the novelistic genre. Heliodorus makes the adventures of his protagonists appear as trials testing the piety of these individuals: above all other positive qualities which they share, piety is the one that most clearly distinguishes the good characters in the book from the bad. Expressions of religious veneration are mostly directed at the sun god, a fact which has been taken as a clue by scholars trying to date the work. The cult of the sun god was officially promoted under the Severan dynasty, and the solar deity was sometimes identified with Baal of Emesa whose worship the Emperor Elagabal had imported into Rome. Aurelian tried to secure general acceptance for the cult throughout the Empire.

Such details, however, are of the little help in the dating of the novel. The worship of the sun was similarly widespread as a cultic expression of pagan piety in the fourth century AD. From the Emperor Julian, who abandoned Christianity, our most important evidence of his individual faith is a long speech about the sun god. Around 400 AD the learned pagan Macrobius explained how the many deities of mythology were to be interpreted as manifestations of that same one sun god (see p. 446). This drift towards a solar monotheism was doubtlessly influenced by the worship of the sun that existed in some Oriental countries, and that converged with the notions of educated people which were dominated by Platonic philosophy. To them, the sun's place in the visible world appeared as equivalent to that held by the supreme universal God in the true existence of the intelligible, spiritual cosmos.

In any case, Theagenes and Chariclea, the hero and heroine of the novel's ten books, prove to be blameless worshippers of the sun god. The moral and religious stance which dominates the entire narrative is so marked that later generations invented a whole biography for the author, as early as in the fifth century AD. He was alleged to have been a Christian who wrote the book as a young man, who later became Bishop of Tricca in Thessaly, and – another fabrication inspired by the exemplary chastity of the hero and heroine – who first introduced celibacy for priests in his diocese.

From the third century AD, we have the oldest extant version of a narrative of which ever-new editions and translations into nearly all oriental and European languages kept appearing well into the Middle Ages. This work tells the story of Alexander the Great and his deeds, transposed into the realm of the fantastic and the legendary in the form of a complete, continuous narrative. The earliest version from the third century AD is in Greek.

The immense achievements of the great Macedonian had created a deep impression on contemporaries and subsequent generations. Contemporary historical accounts already featured all kinds of exaggerations of fact; it was above all the miraculous experiences of Alexander and his soldiers in distant India which inspired the historiographers' imagination. They elaborated not only the wonderful nature of the country, but also the encounters between the King and pupil of Aristotle with the exponents of Indian wisdom, the Brahmins and gymnosophists, the 'naked sages' or yogis. The latter motif was particularly important in the mostly very critical philosophical debate about Alexander's person, for this debate dealt with the question whether divine-charismatic talent or philosophical-moral education made the ideal monarch.

All of these elements were taken up by the novelistic tradition about Alexander, which we encounter in ever-new and only loosely linked productions, none of which we can ascribe with certainty to any known author. One type, the Alexander dialogue which shows the King conversing with Indian sages, seems to have originated in the age of Hellenism, presumably among Cynic philosophers. The earliest evidence of this tradition was once again found on a papyrus scroll. Of similar antiquity –

even if it became documented much later – is in all likelihood the type of writing which features letters to and from Alexander. There are fictitious correspondences between Alexander and his teacher Aristotle about the curiosities of India, as well as letters ostensibly exchanged between him and his mother Olympias, his bride Roxane, the Indian King Poros, or Indian sages.

Another rich tradition consists of anecdotes focusing on Alexander. It contains reports about acts of bravery and other notable deeds, about witty remarks and rejoinders as well as expressions showing the King's magnanimity; but also about events in which his counterpart in conversation emerges as superior, as in the stories connecting Alexander with Diogenes. Finally, this complex popular tradition also features stories which give Alexander's person numinous characteristics, in keeping with official monarchic ideology. In the great oasis of Egypt, for instance, the god Ammon – commonly identified with Zeus – was said to have addressed Alexander as his son. This gave rise to the legend about the monarch's birth, according to which the god had mated with Alexander's mother in the shape of a snake.

All the motifs which I have enumerated can be found in the Greek Alexander novel of the so-called A version, the oldest extant one. They are embedded in a continuous narrative which basically follows the historical sequence of events. Later extant versions of the novel are not merely copies of this older one, but new editions which were all based on more than one source, so that we find even very old details only in relatively late versions. This form of popular literature never knew any kind of authoritative editing.

The A version is ascribed to Callisthenes, a nephew of Aristotle who accompanied Alexander on his expedition. He became involved in a conspiracy and was executed at the King's command. His historical work, extant only in small fragments, seems to have showed the author's special preference for the grandiose, and it is perhaps because of this that he became known as the author of a novel with whose writing he certainly had nothing to do at all.

The novel's diction is occasionally close to spoken language and thus deviates from the linguistic standard of Atticist literature. Another remarkable feature consists of long verse interludes, as in Menippean satire (see p. 99). This proves that such verse interludes belonged to a kind of writing aimed primarily at entertaining its readers; hence also their occurrence in the novel by Petronius (see p. 129). The Alexander novel is only one example of a process by which historical or mythical events became a matter for popular literature, having first been dealt with in poetry and historiography, and then antiquarian or mythographical works, that is, on the whole, writings belonging to high or scientific literature.

In the Late Classical age as in the Middle Ages, there were two very well-known and widely read prose works in Latin which told the entire story of the Trojan War in a popular manner. The books, presumably from the fourth century AD, bear the names of Dictys and Dares. The Dictys book is ostensibly the eye-witness account by one who took part in the war, written in Phoenician after his return to his native Crete. The author is supposed to have taken the work to the grave with him in a tin container; in the thirteenth year of Nero's reign the grave is said to have been opened by an earthquake, whereupon the container was brought to the Emperor who commissioned a Greek translation of the text which was in turn translated into Latin by a certain L. Septimius, a process resulting in the extant version. A papyrus find in the early twentieth century has shown that there was indeed a Greek version of the Dictys, presumably from the first century AD, and reproduced fairly exactly in the Latin translation from the fourth century.

The Dares book, on the other hand, seems to be a free and enlarged rewriting of the Dictys. The Dictys text, however, is a good example of a kind of non-artistic popular literature, bringing the story of the Trojan War which each educated person would know well from other sources to a far less demanding reading public, with the miraculous story of the introduction trying to claim the credibility of an eye-witness report. The interesting thing about both books is a tendency to provide rationalistic explanations for the miraculous elements of the tale; and where the latter is too improbable there are sometimes even changes in the known course of events. This shows that in the eyes of the author the Trojan War was a historical happening. If we consider how many pictorial representations of this story were to be found in any Classical city, we can assess the demand for information concerning this event particularly in those circles with a lesser degree of Latin education. But the existence of such a popular literature also provides a further clue as to the small number of illiterate people, at least among the urban population.

In the Byzantine chronicles of the Middle Ages, mostly written by monks for a little-educated reading public who were to be comprehensively informed about the Classical and the Biblical tradition, we find many indications of the authors' use of such popular retellings of ancient Greek myth and history. In that milieu, both were once again regarded as part of a whole.

There is another popular book of Greek origin which is only extant in its Latin translation from the fourth or fifth century AD; this is the story of Apollonius, King of Tyre. It contains ancient fairy tale motifs alongside others – above all erotic ones – from the Greek novel; there are also historical reminiscences of the Diadochian epoch. A summary of the complex adventure plot would easily fill a few pages. Like Dictys and Dares, the book contains absolutely no trace of the influence of Christian ideas, and this is why the Greek original cannot really be dated any later than the third century AD – if it is at all justified to speak of an original in this case. That Christians also had a need for similar reading matter is exemplified by the apocryphal *Acts of the Apostles* and the major Clement novel (see p. 306).

From the historiography of the period, I should mention one author who was himself involved in the political-military events of the crisis of the third century AD. Dexippos (his full name, which shows that he held Roman citizenship, was C. Herennius Dexippus) came from the most ancient circles of the Athenian nobility. In the independent municipal administration of the city he rose to the very highest office, that of the Archon Eponymos, after whom the year was named. In 267 AD he gathered a militia of two thousand men and repulsed the Heruli. However, the inscription which has been preserved on his tomb does not make any reference to this brave deed and merely refers to Dexippus' literary achievements. In contrast, someone had written an epigram for the grave of Aeschylus which says nothing at all about his tragedies but mentions the fact that he took part in the Battle of Marathon.

Dexippus wrote a universal history in twelve books which covers events from prehistoric times up to the year 270 AD. We have a very short excerpt, as well as a larger number of literal quotations featured by Byzantine authors. Besides, he produced a history of Alexander the Great's successors in four books, presumably based on the work by Arrian (see p. 242), and a work called *Scythica*, dealing with the raids by Germanic tribes between 238 and 274 AD. From the latter book, much was adopted by Late Classical historiography in Greek as well as in Latin, in accounts of the great migrations of the fourth and fifth centuries AD, and especially of the history of the Goths.

Dexippus was an educated man; his historiographical works are based on the writings of Thucydides, but, as far as we can tell from the existing fragments, his own political-military experience put him in the position to make individual judgments about traditional accounts.

We have quite a lot of information about Greek historiographers from the third century AD. There is a certain C. Asinius Quadratus who produced a Roman history covering the time up to the year 225 AD; this work was written in the Ionic dialect of Herodotus. A member of the family of Philostratus who lived during the reign of Aurelian 270–5, produced an account of Zenobia's and her husband Odaenathus' war against the Sassanid Sapur; and an otherwise unknown Eusebius wrote a history that began with the reign of Augustus and ended with that of the Emperor Carinus who was on the throne until 285 AD. These and other historiographers are mentioned by Byzantine authors who often quote fairly long passages from their works.

3 PHILOSOPHY

Plotinus

In the very midst of the turmoil of the third century AD, there came a renewal which marked teaching in the Platonic tradition, a development which was to be a decisive factor in the transfer of philosophical thought from Classical to European culture. The man who instigated this renewal was Plotinus, whom historians of philosophy today regard as the founder of a new kind of philosophical movement – Neo-Platonism. This reputation is not without a certain irony in view of the fact that Plotinus himself certainly had no intention of establishing anything like a distinct new school.

In relation to what we know about comparable personalities of the Classical age, the amount of information which we have about Plotinus' life seems fairly extensive. His best-known and most talented pupil, Porphyry, left us a biography of his teacher. Besides, Plotinus commissioned him to produce an edition of his works, a task which Porphyry performed with great philological diligence. Thus Plotinus may be said to be the only Classical author of whom we have a complete edition of collected works, all of them dated and grouped according to topics.

There are some biographical facts, however, which remain unknown, as Plotinus himself never revealed his origin and family background even to his closest pupils. This was certainly a very eccentric kind of behaviour in the Classical age when the full name of any person would include the patronym and the home town. Plotinus' reason for concealing these facts was his conviction that the corporeal existence of man was unimportant and that the true origin and home of the human race lay in the intelligible realm of true being. Consequently the lifelong endeavours of men had to be directed towards the goal of a return to that realm.

Plotinus studied in Alexandria, a city which was not only the seat of a reputable school of Platonic philosophy but also still a centre for the sciences. At that time one of the teachers there was Diophantus, the most outstanding arithmetician in the history of Greek mathematics; another famous one was the versatile Longinus (see p. 364). As he tells us himself, Plotinus was not satisfied with philosophical and scientific instruction, until he found a teacher to whom he remained a faithful disciple for eleven years. The man whose disciples Plotinus joined at the age of twenty-eight was Ammonius, later also known as Saccas or sack-carrier, although this epithet does not appear in contemporary sources. Like Socrates, Ammonius exerted a strong and lasting influence over many gifted pupils through his teaching and through his exemplary living, without leaving any piece of writing to posterity and without teaching in any kind of institution. Late Classical commentaries on Plato identify only very few individual doctrines in the Platonic tradition as stemming from Ammonius. It is thus difficult to ascertain how much of the specific details in Plotinus' philosophy come from his teacher, and this question has given rise to much controversy until the present day.

After the death of Ammonius, Plotinus joined the campaign of the Emperor Gordian against the Persians. Porphyry tells us that this was done in the hope of coming into contact with Indian philosophy. In 244 AD, after the military failure of the expedition, Plotinus went to Rome where he opened a school of Platonic philosophy and gathered around him a large number of pupils, mostly of Eastern origin. He gained high personal respect even among the Senatorial nobility, a fact which is documented by Plotinus' being allotted the guardianship of many orphans. He had a plan for establishing a large community which was to live by the principles of Platonic philosophy; for this purpose, he envisaged a rebuilding of a Campanian city which lay in ruins. This scheme is said to have had the support of the Emperor Gallienus, but all the same it was never realised. Plotinus died in 270 AD on a friend's country estate outside Minturnae, near the border between Latium and Campania.

Plotinus' literary legacy contains fifty-four didactic treatises of different lengths. Porphyry divided these according to subject matter into six groups of nine works each. This systematic ordering is complemented by chronological information contained in the biography which accompanied Porphyry's edition. The original elements in Plotinus' philosophy were already appreciated by his immediate successors; but none the less Plotinus did not see himself at all as an innovator. He was convinced that everything of philosophical importance had already been said in Plato's works, and was confirmed by its agreement with ancient 'Barbarian wisdom'. To Plotinus, his philosophical task was the correct interpretation of the works of the school founder. In doing so, his approach and his method remained within the framework of the existing school tradition. There were, however, two novel elements which I shall discuss in the following.

All philosophical schools in the Empire had returned to the study of the works of their founders, through whose correct interpretation they sought to develop a coherent and complete school dogma. This naturally led to a special appreciation of the value of philological scholarship. During the age of Hellenism the information which had been gathered through scholarly work in different areas had above all provided an arsenal for argumentation in the debate between rival schools. In the Empire, however, scholarly knowledge became mainly a tool of exegesis. Besides, the acknowledged common aim of all philosophical studies led to frequent borrowing of individual doctrines and methods between different school traditions. Middle Platonism had been particularly willing to adopt concepts from Stoic ethics, Aristotelian logic and metaphysics, and

Pythagorean religious thought. A side-effect of this was the accumulation of a large amount of scholarly knowledge in the Platonic school.

Many passing remarks in his writings prove that Plotinus was well read in the different branches of philosophy and science. But unlike what seems to have been the attitude of his contemporary and schoolmate Longinus, Plotinus categorically regarded all learning only as a means towards an end: namely, the deepening of philosophical understanding. There is not a single passage of his works where he indicates even the slightest interest in scholarly knowledge for its own sake. Nevertheless, Plotinus' learning does tends to surface in the course of his writing, especially in philosophical studies which are based on the interpretation of authoritative texts.

When he was philosophising himself, Plotinus stuck to the good Platonic tradition of concentrating on the doctrine of being, which he ultimately understood theologically as the doctrine of the Supreme Being. All branches of speculative philosophy, including ethics, appeared to Plotinus as derived from a thus-defined ontology. This is why Plotinus' philosophical endeavour achieves such an admirable degree of conciseness and logical consistency; and this explains his lasting influence in the history of European thought, albeit largely through the mediation of his pupil Porphyry.

I shall now outline the ontological plan at which Plotinus arrived through his study of Plato, as well as through the free use of older concepts found in the school tradition. To Plotinus, all being or reality has its roots within the *One*, in whose purely spiritual substance known and knowing, thought and thinking, becoming and decaying, enduring and changing are continually and perpetually reunited. From its inexhaustible richness, the *One* releases the *Nous*, the spirit. This hypostatic entity enables one spiritual being as a perceptive subject to recognise another one as a perceived object. From the *Nous* emerges the hypostasis of the *psychē*, the soul. This enables matter, which by itself does not exist at all, to receive its share of being from the spiritual world as form, life, and consciousness. The result is an unfolding of matter in a series of hierarchical hypostases, creating the cosmos as it is visible to us.

Because it is ultimately the creative power of the highest *One* which moulds the cosmos through the multitude of mediating entities, even his lowest creations reflect some of the beauty and order of intelligible Being. On the other hand the birth of every new hypostasis also means that a part of true Being has descended or fallen, and thus become alienated from its source. This is why a part of every creation has the desire to become reunited with the previous hypostasis, from which it received being and existence, and with which it is thus able to communicate. As this desire pervades the entire cosmos, the emergence or *prōhodos* of all beings from the superior ones in the cosmic hierarchy is paralleled by the reverse movement of return or *epistrophē*, ultimately directed at the unification of all being with its source, the One or *hen*.

Plotinus saw this plan not so much as a description of the world's creation at some point in time, but rather as an image of eternal reality in which life, that is growth and decay, perpetually emerges from constant, unchangeable Being. In the tradition which Plotinus took up, Being is located nowhere else than in the realm of the intelligible, which is why it is seen as exclusively accessible to thought. To this process of cognition, a perennial obstacle exists in the combination of spirit and matter in the empirical world, in both the perceiving subject and the perceived object. The goal of a fulfilled life as formulated by the Platonic school, (i.e. the approximation of a god-like state) is reached by the liberating of human reason from its ties to the empirical-material world, and thus enabling it directly to recognise the true Being. Man is thus shown the path of discursive thought, by which he may approach this Being in a succession of methodical steps. Each stage of man's ascent marks at the same time his intellectual and his moral progress. But when he comes to the last stage the complete union between the subject and the object of cognition, the tool of discursive thought, fails. Like Plato, Plotinus can do no more than describe the ultimate ecstasy, the emergence of man from his individuation, as an experience of mystic vision which is probably enjoyed by no more than a few sages, who are thus allowed a glimpse of their existence after death, liberated from matter. Such a preview, however, can only be attained at the end of a long life which is full of the most rigorous intellectual endeavour.

Unlike many of his disciples and successors, Plotinus never succumbed to the temptation to turn to supernatural revelation or religious ritual as a source of help for that last step towards perfection. He did not bother to waste even a single written word about the so-called Chaldaean oracles (see p. 283), a text written in the second century AD and read and interpreted as divine revelation by Plotinus' disciple Porphyry. The dichotomy between true Being and empirical world was formulated more radically by Plotinus than in the Platonic tradition which he got it from, but it certainly did not lead Plotinus to that kind of contempt for the world which was taught by the Gnostics. His view is that wherever spirit loses itself in matter the intelligent observer will perceive forms which reveal nothing other than the beauty of the spiritual world. To Plotinus, the material world is not false, and especially not evil: this is what he says in a long treatise attacking the Gnostics. Plotinus wrote an entire separate treatise about evil, defining it as a lack of substance of true Being in those hypostases which are particularly far removed from the One, the source of all being. The beauty of the cosmos and the existence of evil show the ambivalence of the inherent urge of the One to emerge from itself: the creation of the world is bought with the progressive decrease of perfection and unity, a loss which only a return from matter may mend.

As I have mentioned before, however complex Plotinus' speculative constructs may be, he never loses himself in scholarly detail; that kind of information receives no more than marginal attention. What may particularly surprise the modern reader, though, are large numbers of extremely subtle psychological observations going far beyond that knowledge about the workings of the human mind which previous Classical psychology had accumulated. Thus, for example, Plotinus was the first author to give a correct analysis and description of the difference between self-knowledge and self-awareness.

Plotinus' works rank among the most difficult texts in the Greek language. But as soon as the reader has managed to follow the argument of a passage, he will perceive linguistic beauty of a highly original kind. In Greek there was a long tradition of prose which presented the results of philosophical and scientific research without any conscious effort at literary-stylistic ornamentation, aiming to present the facts which had been found as accurately as possible. Plotinus' writing follows this tradition, and besides, many passages show characteristics of informal oral language, of the improvised lecture. But the intensity, the exactness, and perhaps we may even say the selflessness of this speculative thinker give Plotinus' language a beauty beyond all intentional stylishness and all stylistic conventions, an aesthetic effect based solely on the beauty and the order of the argument. It was precisely the author's unerring endeavour to attain objectivity which created a style more individual and unmistakable than that of any other work in post-Classic Greek literature.

Porphyry

Plotinus' most famous pupil was a man totally different from his teacher for whom, however, he had the utmost respect throughout his life. He was born in 234 AD in the Phoenician city of Tyre and was originally called Malchos, a name derived from the Semitic *melek* or king. Malchos later changed his name to Porphyry, which means 'the purple one'. He received his first philosophical education in Athens, where at that time Longinus (see p. 364) was head of the Academy. From there Porphyry went to Rome, where he became acquainted with Amelius, the only one among Plotinus' pupils who came from the West. At first Porphyry took a polemical stance against one of Plotinus' doctrines which was put forward by Amelius. This concerned the question whether the ideas, which in Plato's philosophy represented the only true existing models of the creatures and of all the phenomena in the material world, were to be located in the divine *Nous* – later Christians talked of ideas as the thoughts of God – or to be taken as having an independent existence.

In 263 AD Porphyry became one of Plotinus' pupils and he very soon occupied a prominent position in this circle. As we know from his biography of Plotinus, five years later Porphyry suffered from severe depression, and followed the advice of his teacher to seek a cure in Sicily. There he stayed until after Plotinus' death, but in the following year he returned to Rome to become his successor as head of the school. His age was already fairly advanced when he married Marcella, the widow of a friend, who had seven children to look after. He died in Rome in the early years of the fourth century AD.

In various ways, Porphyry's work took up the threads of the school tradition before Plotinus. This is true above all of his scholarly writing from which his teacher's legacy profited first and foremost (see p. 370). We know of no less than sixty-six titles of books which Porphyry wrote, and some of them were fairly substantial volumes – for instance, major commentaries on Plato and Aristotle, but also ones on Homer and the Chaldaean oracles. His scientific interests are documented by specialist treatises whose topics range from rhetoric to musical theory, and from grammar or the interpretation of poetry to historiography. The philosophical subjects he dealt with concerned ethics and psychology, logic, the history of philosophy, and doxography; but also particular aspects of Platonic ontology like the origin of evil or the relationship between *Nous* and ideas, and not least the question of the extent to which Plato and Aristotle were in agreement.

Only eight or nine mostly shorter treatises are extant from Porphyry's *oeuvre*; of the others, we have only fragments quoted in commentaries on Plato and Aristotle from the fourth to the sixth century AD. The reason for this almost total loss was a lengthy treatise in fifteen books, written in Sicily, in which Porphyry attacked the Christians: he was thus condemned as one of the arch-enemies of the victorious new religion. In 448 AD the work was publicly burned at the command of the Emperor Theodosius II. Still, it was Porphyry from whom the Christian theologians of the fourth and fifth centuries AD acquired the terms and the methods of Neo-Platonist ontology, which they used in their debate about the precise wording of the trinitarian dogma. Patient research over the last hundred years has shown that a significantly large number of Christian texts contains entire chains of argumentation from Porphyrian philosophy. It was Porphyry alone who made the bulk of Plotinus' philosophy accessible to posterity, as direct access to Plotinus' works was not regained until the Renaissance.

One of the extant works by Porphyry, entitled *Helpful Advice for Approaching the Noetic World* – mostly quoted as *sententiae* – is designed as an introduction to Plotinus' doctrines. It is a kind of catechism of his teachings, in parts very close to the original texts. The emphasis is on the ethical implications of Plotinian ontology and the booklet was meant to be read as a guide to practical living, with a description of the successive steps on the upward path to perfection. Its central idea, namely that the same virtues were to be tested in different, new forms at every successive stage attained, was a direct borrowing from Plotinus.

The custom of producing such summaries of a particular philosophy had a long tradition, going back to the sententiae or central doctrines of Epicurus. Among references to Porphyry's works, we find mention of the titles 'Kephalaia', 'Epicheiremata', and 'Hypomnemata', all of which could belong to such a catechism. It is an open question, however, whether they refer to the work I have mentioned or whether they were titles for commentaries on Plotinus' texts.

I have already mentioned Porphyry's biography of Plotinus which accompanied the edition of his works, and which contains a wealth of information relating to the history of philosophy. The biography belongs to the context of school teaching; the same goes for the two extant and the one lost commentaries which Porphyry wrote about Aristotle's treatise on categories. The latter is featured as the first piece in the standard version of Aristotle's didactic writings, an edition produced in the first century BC. For the commentator, this meant the necessity of discussing the systematic order of Aristotle's works and his biography, and hence the need to give a general introduction to Aristotelian philosophy and a special one to its first part, logic.

Porphyry adopted and modified a fixed didactic plan of Platonic school philosophy, a scheme which predated Plotinus. This plan began with an introduction to Aristotelian philosophy on the basis of selected writings. This was to be followed by the study of Platonic dialogues, likewise selected and ordered according to didactic considerations. In the process, the Hellenistic tripartite division of philosophy into logic, physics, and ethics took on a new shape. Physics was henceforth only concerned with insight into the cosmos of the spiritual world, and ethics, whose goals were to govern philosophy as a whole, was supplemented by *epoptics*. That term was borrowed from the language of the Mysteries where it meant the witnessing of the secret ritual; it was now used to refer to the guidance towards the ultimate and highest truths which Plato had declared the object of dialectics.

The longer of the two extant introductions, written at the request of a Roman nobleman with an interest in philosophy, is a systematic explanation of the basic terms in one of Aristotle's treatises. As a fundamental aid to the student of logic in the Middle Ages, it was translated into several languages and became itself the subject of commentaries. The other introduction, written in a question-and-answer form known as *erotapokriseis*, was also widely read in the Middle Ages. The lost major commentary on Aristotle's treatise about categories, dedicated to another great Roman, can be reconstructed – at least in its outline – from adaptations written in the fifth and sixth centuries AD.

From the Neo-Platonist tradition, Porphyry got his strong interest in Pythagoreanism and its doctrines concerning practical living. This interest is shown in his extant life of Pythagoras, which follows the tradition of writing which sought to illustrate the principles of the Pythagorean lifestyle by reference to the legendary biography of the school founder (see p. 73). Porphyry's pupil Iamblichus (see p. 236) also wrote such a life of Pythagoras. Pythagorean ideas are likewise found as an important element in the longest one among Porphyry's extant tracts, his four books about abstaining from eating meat. The doctrine of the transmigration of souls – which Plato had borrowed from the Pythagorean tradition and which his school had always preserved – suggested very strongly that the eating of meat should be forbidden if people believed that souls could be reborn in either human or animal form. In this context there was a problem which was controversially debated between Stoics and Platonics: the question whether the animal soul contained an element of reason, that is a piece of the highest substance or potential appertaining to the soul. There was also a basic disagreement as to whether blood sacrifices could please the divine being. Porphyry treats these issues from the point of view of a strict asceticism in keeping with his other ideas about morality. In the process, the author refers to a large number of literary sources, including some that were later lost. Among those is a treatise on piety by Aristotle's pupil Theophrastus, a book which is known to us almost exclusively through the work by Porphyry on abstaining from meat.

During the last years of his life Porphyry wrote an epistle to his wife Marcella, giving her instructions about proper, philosophically guided living. In this letter special emphasis is laid on piety, the proper relationship with the divine in ritual worship and prayer, which is presented as having the four basic elements of trust, truthfulness, love, and hope. Time and again, this passage has been compared to Chapter 13 of Paul's First Letter to the Corinthians.

Porphyry's treatise on the grotto of the nymphs is the only fully extant example of an allegorical interpretation (see p. 162) of a Homeric pericope in the sense of Platonic philosophy. In Book 13 of the *Odyssey* we find the exact description of a cave inhabited by nymphs, that is lesser goddesses which give life to nature. Porphyry reads this episode as a reference to the place where the soul is endowed with a body prior to its entry into earthly life.

The philosophical tradition offered a twofold justification for the convention of interpreting poetry and myth in an allegorical way and thus arriving at a philosophical meaning. For one, Plato had repeatedly used myths to express central doctrines of his philosophy and those myths demanded allegorical readings just like the inventions of poets. There was also the Stoic doctrine of cosmic sympathy according to which all events in the world are interrelated and thus form part of one meaningful causal connection, a view which had been widely accepted in the Platonic school in the form set out by Posidonius. With this background one could quite plausibly argue that, for instance, a battle reported in some ancient tale had a real correlation with some cosmic event, and that there was therefore a concrete basis for interpreting the account as the coded report of a natural phenomenon.

Judging from what we know, Porphyry's literary output as a whole lacked that impressive unity of thought which the reader finds in the work of Plotinus. Porphyry's interests were too diverse, his temperament was too uneven, his intentions were too contradictory. What we have to admire was his astuteness and his intellectual honesty wherever scientific research was concerned. In his tract against the Christians he was the first to give irrefutable proof that the Book of Daniel dates from the second century BC, a fact which Porphyry established through exact observation and correct deduction. All previous Jewish-Christian exegesis had been founded on the assumption that this piece of apocalyptic writing came from the man whose name it bears, a legendary prophet from the sixth century BC, the time of King Nebuchadnezzar. But Porphyry had not only a scientific but also a pious mind, and not merely in the sense of philosophical religion. He also showed an unmistakable love for the supernatural, for that which was given through divine revelation or inspiration, prior to all speculative thought. This was a major point of distinction between him and his teacher.

It was only recent research which revealed that a considerable part of Christian-trinitarian doctrine was formulated with the help of ideas coined by Porphyry to complement the Plotinian plan. Such ideas were contained in several lost writings in which Porphyry commented on the Chaldaean oracles, to him a text possessing divine authority.

Plotinus' ontology describes a kind of vertical unfolding of the cosmos, from the highest *One* down to the phenomena of the sensual world. It never occurred to Porphyry to change this model which he instead complemented by a horizontal one, stating that on each level of being this unfolding also takes place in another direction. A distinctly Plotinian notion is that the pure, omnipresent Being has the intrinsic urge to create life and thus movement. This movement, at first random, is then structured by reflective reason as a contribution to the formation of a cosmos which is both alive and meaningful. Like Plotinus' plan, Porphyry's ontologically explained sequence of three steps was not so much meant cosmogonically – that is as a model for the creation of the world – but rather cosmologically, as a model reflecting the co-existence of being and becoming. Porphyry's theory is derived from much more vague speculations on the trinity expressed in the Chaldaean oracles, and by the Pythagorising Platonic Numenius from the second century AD. Those speculations had described an immovable, eternal and paternal God, then a Goddess as the life-giving principle, and a second *Nous* or Spirit creating the rationally ordered cosmos from both principles, being and becoming. This background illustrates that Porphyry's possibly most influential achievement in the field of systematic philosophy originated from the desire to find a suprarational justification in authoritative texts for his firm individual belief in salvation.

Through the works of the Latin Platonic Marius Victorinus, but presumably also through the study of Porphyry's writings, Augustine became acquainted with the aforementioned doctrine. He used it in his major work on the Christian doctrine of the trinity; however, this application was not made without some fundamental changes (see p. 561).

During the last two or three decades of his life, a time which he spent in Rome, Porphyry had numerous pupils who developed Neo-Platonism in some completely different directions. Porphyry's influence was particularly strong on Latin Neo-Platonism as increasingly distinct from the fourth century AD onwards, and consequently on the world of ideas of the Latin Middle Ages.

4 CHRISTIAN LITERATURE

General remarks

In my discussion of Tertullian's writings (see p. 350), I have described the peculiar legal status of Christians living in the Roman Empire as a fact which explains why certain communities suffered repeated persecution, while elsewhere the church could develop in entire regions without any interference. This situation changed around the middle of the third century AD. On the one hand the internal and external turmoil of the time of crisis increasingly brought home to the holders of power the fact that the church, with its firm organisation and the strong social ties between Christian believers, represented a considerable force. There was no other institution or group which remained similarly unshaken. At the same time, though, especially the religiously-minded people among the holders of high offices in army and administration were susceptible to the idea that the distress in which the Empire found itself could be explained by the fact that large parts of its population had turned away from the traditional worship of the gods. The anti-Christian polemic by the philosopher Celsus shows us that to educated people in particular, diverse forms of worship were in fact expressions of a religion perceived as one whole, and this whole in turn as part of one global civilisation. The religious unity of a state's population was among those notions taken for granted in the political thought of the Classical age when political community was invariably perceived as religious community.

Such were the conditions under which the Emperor Decius decided to take a drastic and previously unprecedented measure in 249 AD: all inhabitants of the Empire were to prove their loyalty to traditional religion by taking part in a ritual sacrifice under public control, with an official certificate issued by the authorities. Those who refused – and this clearly meant the Christians – were to be forced to return to the old religion by sanctions whose extent was presumably to be determined by local authorities. This method was very successful: large numbers of Christians deserted from their faith, but many others suffered imprisonment, torture, and even death. There were likewise quite a few who obtained the necessary certificate of sacrifice through bribery; incidentally, specimens of such documents were found among the Egyptian papyri.

Decius' departure for the war against the Goths brought the anti-Christian campaign to a standstill. The church was left with the difficult question of how the different categories of lapsed Christians who wanted to rejoin the communities were to be dealt with. In 257 AD the Emperor Valerian opened a second major wave of persecution, this time directed mainly at the clergy. They were forced to perform sacrifices on the pain of death; all worship in churches was forbidden; and Christian members of the Senatorial nobility who refused to take part in the sacrifice were threatened with the loss of rank and fortune, and, in case of repeated refusal, with death. Christians in public service as well as women from the upper classes were to be banished or sentenced to forced labour for the same offences.

This attack on the Christian leadership proved to have no effect at all. There were numerous martyrs, but no apostates; and when Valerian was taken prisoner by the Persians in 260 AD it was not only the Christians who saw this as a divine punishment for what he had done. His co-regent and successor Gallienus chose to pursue a categorical policy of tolerance, a strategy which was continued by all successive emperors until the major persecutions begun by Diocletian in 299 AD. The murder of Aurelian prevented him from carrying out his own plans for the persecution of the Christians, in the context of his endeavour to establish a unified form of worship in the Empire after his victory over Zenobia (see p. 360).

In the long run the persecutions of the third century AD were beneficial to the prestige and the social influence of the church. It proved its ability to cope with the material and moral difficulties, which did not result from the persecutions alone, within the framework of its tried and tested organisation. In the end it managed to retain its place as a major spiritual power and as a force of order in the Empire's society. This was unaffected by the internal disputes within the church, including even the persistent quarrel about the formulation of Christian doctrine, which led to the secession of ever-new separate groups. This is the background against which we have to see the literary life of Christian communities in East and West.

The East

In the further course of the third century AD literary-theological life in the East was entirely dominated by the influence of Origen (see p. 334). As head of religious instruction in Alexandria, he had been succeeded by his friend Heraclas, and then by his pupil Dionysius who became Bishop of the city in 247 AD. From the large literary output of Dionysius, we have only very little, mostly in the form of quotes in the major ecclesiastical history by Eusebius (see p. 422). As Bishop of one of the most important sees, Dionysius was involved in many internal church disputes in the whole Empire, and some of his writings, such as his statements on the doctrine of the trinity or on the perpetually re-emerging chiliastic doctrines, may well be taken as expressing something like the official opinion of the church. But the extant fragments of his writings also show his interest in historical and philosophical issues. Dionysius wrote a treatise against Epicurean physics and argued against the assumption, upheld by the church, that the last book of the New Testament had been written by the apostle John. His successors as heads of the Alexandrian catechism school, Theognostus and Pierius, were also writers; but none of their works is extant.

At the time of Dionysius official church documents such as synodal decrees, episcopal edicts and letters, or letters on the occasion of Easter, already had fixed forms. These are known from early examples in the aforementioned ecclesiastical history by Eusebius but also from other compilations, as well as from later collections of texts concerning church law. All of them reflect the intensity of ecclesiastical life, the disputes about dogma and ecclesiastical law, and the strong communicative links between the separate communities. Like the rich Christian literature of letters and sermons, the official church documents are often carefully styled in the manner of the rhetorical tradition. This indicates a natural integration of the church once it had acquired power and influence into the educational world of Classical culture. The same impression is conveyed by new forms of literary communication, arising from the special features of ecclesiastical life.

Another pupil of Origen was Gregory, known as the Miracle-worker. I have already mentioned this man, who lived well into the eighth decade of the century. From him, we have a speech of thanks to Origen, a text which gives us exact information about the content and the method of the Alexandrian school curriculum. The only other extant document from his rich literary production is a letter about the practice of confession, and a formula for professing the Christian faith. Gregory worked as Bishop of Neocaesarea, in northern Asia Minor.

Alexandria was not the only centre of Greek-Christian education. An interesting exponent of a tradition forming in Antioch in Syria was Paul of Samosata, Bishop of Antioch as well as local governor during the short reign of Queen Zenobia over the Empire's eastern provinces. He was deposed after being condemned as a heretic by a synod in 268 AD; this is why none of his writings is extant.

The real founder of the scholarly-theological tradition of Antioch was Lucian, the teacher of Arius. He was likewise regarded as a heretic because of his teachings on the trinity. In the persecution of 312 AD, during which Lucian was killed, he seems to have made his peace with the Antiochian community. Lucian comes first in a long line of Antiochians famous for textual criticism and exegesis. He launched a new edition of the Greek text of the Bible on the basis of Origen's *Hexapla*, in which he also included what had meanwhile become the fixed canon of the New Testament.

About the life and work of Methodius, a self-confessed enemy of Origen's theology, we know very little. He seems to have lived in Asia Minor, but it is not certain where exactly he worked, or whether he held any ecclesiastical office. All the information we have about him is from later and not very reliable sources. However, we may safely assume that he lived during the later years of the third century AD.

Several of Methodius' works, such as tracts about the resurrection and about free will, are extant only in Old Slavic translations. Others, such as a refutation of Porphyry's accusations against the Christians, have been completely lost. We do have, however, the Greek original of a very peculiar work, which was to compete with one of Plato's major writings. This is the description of a banquet where the guests are ten virgins praising, in well-chosen words, chastity, and not, as in Plato's work, Eros. The final part of Methodius' writing is a *hymnus* in twenty-four stanzas in which Christ and the church are celebrated as bridegroom and bride.

Anyone familiar with Plato's *Symposion* will note the radical transformation of the theme, and likewise Methodius' replacement of urbane conversation and speeches of most subtle irony as well as deep seriousness, with a number of bombastic lectures. From this point of view, Methodius' work appears to be no more than the product of a hopelessly degenerated taste. By contemporary standards, however, Methodius' *Symposion* must be seen as a piece of very successful prose writing, which showed its author's formal training and literary knowledge to such an extent that he acquired a high regard among the educated classes. However new the aim of Christian writers might be, the overwhelmingly rich heritage of Classical literature and the strict formalism of rhetorical training were something from which they could not escape. Writers were forced to refer time and again to Classic models in language, style, and content. This was certainly in some ways a factor that inhibited artistic creativity, but on the other hand it ensured the survival of an educational and moral tradition which was jeopardised again and again over the centuries.

The *hymnus* with which Methodius concluded his work is not the only extant example of Christian hymns. Hippolytus (see p. 331) quotes a hymn from the Gnostic sect of the Naacenes and the second work by Clement of Alexandria (see p. 328) also finishes with a *hymnus* on Christ. All of these poems, including that by Methodius, are purely literary products apparently unrelated to the liturgical chants which, as our evidence shows, existed very early in Christian communities and were certainly related to comparable songs from synagogue ritual. The metres followed ancient tradition and could only be realised visually in reading, but no longer acoustically. The reason for this was the change in Greek pronunciation during the second and third centuries AD, a process resulting in the loss of the phonetic distinction between long and short syllables, on whose alternation the old metre was based. A dynamic stress replaced the old musical one which had been marked by a rise in pitch.

To give verse an acoustically perceptible rhythm it now became necessary to abandon an old convention based on the quantifying nature of the language, according to which two short syllables equalled one long one. Instead each line now had to contain a fixed number of syllables. This was complemented by the necessity to make at least certain stresses reoccur at exactly the same place in each line, in order to achieve a correlation between stress and the rhythm of the line that had been unknown in ancient poetic art. Verses of the new kind, in which the old metres were used with mainly equal numbers of syllables, and with the regular distribution of one or more stresses, can be found in texts from the second to the fourth century AD. It is significant that most of those texts are not of a very high literary standard. Examples are the verse interludes of the Alexander novel (see p. 366), the fables of Babrius, and, above all, short poems or songs, mostly in the anapaestic rhythm short-short-long, preserved on Egyptian papyri. There are, for instance, two shanties and a collection of *skolia* – 'Songs to be sung at wine'. From the fourth century onwards poems with a Christian content also feature.

The abovementioned examples of earliest Christian hymns may be unrelated to liturgical chants of the period; they do, however, resemble a large number of 'scholarly' poems of non-Christian origin, likewise preserved on papyri as well as in the form of inscriptions. The authors of those poems had to have acquired a knowledge of the distinction between long and short syllables, likewise of the rules of versification, and the tradition of poetic diction. We do not know how such texts were recited or sung: but any rendering would have required a violation of either the new rules of Greek pronunciation, or of the old ones which corresponded to the metres used.

Methodius' *hymnus* is remarkable because on the one hand it has the qualities of scholarly poetry in diction and style, while at the same time it shows the author's efforts to build his verses on stress as well as on quantities. Thus, this hymnus foreshadows a development in poetic art which only came to a full flowering in the fifth and sixth centuries AD, prevailing first in ecclesiastical poetry which was sung, and then much later in spoken verse too, where the new metrics gained ground against the Classic or scholarly metrics which was still practised (see p. 570). In the new poetic art the only rhythmic elements were the regularisation of the numbers of syllables and of stresses, as we know it from poetry in modern European languages.

The West

Latin Christian writing in the third century AD was still dominated by the province of Africa, represented by the impressive figure of Thascius Caecilius Cyprianus. From his large literary legacy and from his biography written by the Deacon Pontius, we get a fairly vivid picture of his life and work, even if the biography is rather problematic as a historical source because of its legendary aspects.

Born in the early years of the century, Cyprian's origin and character make him appear as a *grand seigneur* with a thorough rhetorical and legal education. He became a convert to Christianity in 246 AD and Bishop of his native city of Carthage only two years later. This illustrates the significant role played by members of the upper classes in the church whose strength was growing. During the persecutions under Decius Cyprian went underground but kept on guiding his parishioners through numerous letters from his place of hiding. After the persecutions had abated, Cyprian's main worry was about the Confessors, who claimed the right to receive the apostates back into the fold at once, while Cyprian, as a responsible official, insisted on a strict practice of penance. The consequence was a schism in the church of Carthage. A synod presided over by Cyprian failed to resolve the disagreement, but the leaders of the dissenting party then emigrated to Rome. During the subsequent years Cyprian showed himself as the most influential figure in the north African church, skilful in managing synods and never afraid to argue with the Bishop of Rome. During a severe epidemic he established a well-organised nursing and relief service which impressed even non-Christians. At the time of the persecutions under Valerian in 258 AD, Cyprian was arrested, interrogated, and executed.

The most impressive document in the literary legacy of Cyprian is the collection of his letters. There are ones written from his hide-out, giving instructions to his congregation, and letters to the Bishop and the clergy of Rome which express his opinion in the debates about the validity of baptism performed by heretics, and about Novatian's schism (see p. 389). Others, addressed to the clergy of Cyprian's diocese, concern various aspects of church discipline and liturgy. Sixty-five letters by Cyprian are complemented by sixteen addressed to himself or the clergy of Carthage;

some of the latter were written by the Roman Bishops Cornelius, Lucius, and Stephanus, and two by the Roman Presbyter Novatian. Novatian was the one who established a fairly long-lived dissenting church after the dispute about the Confessors' right to accept penance.

Most of Cyprian's letters are carefully styled in a manner that reflects the author's rhetorical training. In rhetorical instruction the writing of letters played an important part, and the letter had become a recognised form of artistic prose as early as the fourth century BC. Consequently letters were frequently written with a view to publication, but mainly as pieces of fictional literature for entertainment and edification, a type of writing to which large parts of the extant collections of non-Christian letters belong.

Most of the Christian epistolography of this period can be regarded as literature, also in the sense that the letters in question were written with particular attention to style and were thus fit to be published and read long after their production by people other than the addressees. The type of the purely fictional letter, however, occurs only occasionally in Christian writing. With but a few exceptions, Christian letters are communications arising from well-defined situations and discussing a great variety of current issues concerning church law and dogmatics. This is why so many Christian letters were preserved, especially if they were written by well-respected holders of ecclesiastical office or by theologians: their epistles were regarded as authoritative documents to be drawn on in discussions of dogma and ecclesiastical law. The first survey of ecclesiastical history, written by the learned Eusebius in the early fourth century AD, is largely based on letters, frequently reproduced in the original wording.

Cyprian's style is entirely different from that of Tertullian, in spite of Cyprian's high regard for the man who had established the theological fame of the African church, and despite his frequent references to Tertullian in his choice of phrases as well as his selection of topics. Cyprian wrote a Latin that is almost Classic, regular, and free of all extravagances. The impression thus created is that the dignity and the burden of the episcopal office itself find expression in the forms of the Roman tradition.

In one respect, however, Tertullian and Cyprian appear to be very close to one another, in spite of all their differences of temperament: both are very much influenced by Roman legal thought. But while in the case of Tertullian this shows above all in his dispute with the heretics and the representatives of the state, Cyprian displays the same characteristic whenever he expresses his concept of the church, its order, and its offices. Entirely in keeping with Roman legal and political thought, Cyprian saw the church as a legal order, deriving its legitimacy from the appointment of the apostle Peter according to Matthew (16.18) and hence endowed with the power of government and jurisdiction. In this view the unity of the church is guaranteed through the episcopal office, whose numerous holders are in turn bound together by the apostolic tradition in which they were ordained. Participation in Christ's work of salvation is, according to Cyprian, only possible for those who belong to the established church. This is the very reason why he saw ecclesiastical offices as so important; and consequently he rejected in a categorical fashion all claims to authority or function within Christian communities which were founded on charismatic gifts or recognised moral achievements. What we know of Cyprian indicates that this hardline stance was exceptional in a man who was otherwise urbane and tended towards compromise.

In his short working life – just over a decade long – Cyprian wrote a large number of treatises. Their style is very similar to that of the letters; their most remarkable quality is not so much theological or philosophical acumen as practical insight into pastoral, moral, and administrative problems.

Written as a monologue is the short treatise addressed to Donatus, a work comparable to Augustine's *Confessions*, in which Cyprian tries to describe his state of mind after the reception of baptism.

There is a problem of categorisation with some of Cyprian's writings in that they could be either treatises or sermons. The pieces that seem to be most obviously of the former type are: the work about the lifestyle of the anointed virgins; the refutation – addressed to Demetrian – of the accusation that the Christians were responsible for the Empire's distress; the admonition – addressed to a certain Fortunatus – to be steadfast in persecution; and most likely also the piece about the Lord's Prayer. To be counted among the sermons are the writings on patience, on envy, on the giving of alms, and on mortality; the latter was written during the epidemic of 254 AD.

The three books of Cyprian's *Testimonia* are dedicated to a certain Quirinus; they contain a collection of quotations from the Bible with selected passages concerning the doctrine of trinity and ethics in general. This material was meant to provide arguments in the Christian debate with Judaism. Cyprian's most important work is his treatise on the unity of the church. With an appendix about the proper penance to be imposed on apostates, it was sent to the Roman Confessors in 251 or 252 AD, to impress upon them the importance of ecclesiastical office, and to combat Novatian's schism.

Cyprian's fame was so great that numerous contemporary ecclesiastical writings which are partly extant were handed down under his name. Ironically enough, they even include a piece which explicitly attacks his own point of view in the debate about baptism performed by heretics – Cyprian had denied the validity of such an act. Others are a tract against Novatian, a treatise which for the first time demands that priests should be celibate, and a piece which deals with the calculation of the date for Easter and is meant to correct the statements made by Hippolytus. The most interesting writing in this group is a sermon which condemns the playing of dice; this is written in an idiom which comes close to the vernacular, and is thus the earliest example of Christian popular literature in Latin.

The first examples of Christian poetry in Latin, written by a man called Commodianus, also appear to come from an African milieu. Even to those who lived soon after the author's death, the poems themselves were the only source of information about him; in recent years there has been a heated debate on when exactly he lived. The texts, however, appear to be written with a very specific background of church organisation and dogma, a background which definitely suggests the third century AD.

The first poetic work by Commodian is a didactic one with the title *Instructions*; it contains eighty shorter pieces in two books. Book 1 is an apology for Christianity against attacks by Jews and pagans: Book 2 contains instructions for a Christian lifestyle, addressed to members of Christian communities. The second poetic work, a long poem consisting of more than a thousand lines, is a *carmen apologeticum*; thus its content is similar to that of Book 1 of the *Instructions*, which demonstrates the truth of the Christian faith to pagans and Jews.

Commodian's poems are in many ways remarkable. For instance, he attacks not only the Jews but also Judaising Christians. It is not clear whether by this he means real Jewish Christians – who by the third century AD were very rare and more likely to be found in Syrian-Palestinian regions – or whether he condemns Christian doctrines in which he saw a return to the Jewish religion. Commodian's moral ideas are marked by a leaning towards asceticism; they do not yet, however, go so far as to suggest organised monastic life. His statements about the trinity show a largely unrefined terminology.

Commodian was particularly interested in eschatological speculations. In his *Instructions*, he supports the theory claiming that the world was going to perish six thousand years after its creation. A long passage in the other poetic work describes in all detail those events which would herald the imminent end of the world. It was most probably Commodian's chiliastic attitude which prevented the inclusion of his poems into the list of reading matter recommended by church orthodoxy.

The most striking features of the poems, however, are their diction and metre. The language is far removed from the tradition of Latin poetic diction, being full of vulgarisms and Biblicisms. Those – and not any reminiscences of High Latin poetry – are the means with which the author achieves pathos and immediacy. The verses are doubtlessly meant to be hexameters and in this the author follows the genre tradition of Classical didactic poetry. However, he shows a sovereign neglect of the rules of quantitative versification, apparently using stress to achieve poetic rhythm when necessary; however, his intentions are not always quite clear.

As in Greek, the distinction in pronunciation between long and short syllables disappeared in Latin also, and the importance of stress grew accordingly. It is significant that on the Latin side there were earlier and more radical attempts to make the new pronunciation the basis for a new versification. On the Greek side the normative force of the Classic tradition was stronger, and made authors cling tenaciously to conventions which no longer had anything to do with spoken language, and could only be recognised in reading.

On the other hand we find a co-existence, over many centuries, of Classic-quantifying and modern-accentuating metrics in the Latin West as well as in the East; and here as well as there texts whose rhythm was based on the new system alone were refused recognition as poetry. Grammar as well as musical theory stuck to the categories handed down from the ancients. But people in the West showed an earlier and greater willingness than those in the East to try the new versification for texts of a higher literary standard. In the Latin church, though, the early hymns, certainly designed for practical-liturgical use and hence for singing, still followed Classic metrics. Their authors, Ambrosius and Hilarius (see p. 577), were highly educated men, quite unlike Commodian.

Commodian certainly did not intend his poems to lack artistic-stylistic elaboration: in the *Instructions*, this is indicated by the fact that every single poem is an acrostic (i.e. the first letters of each line form a saying which sums up the poem's content). This technique was common outside Christian literature, but there, too, predominantly in religious poetry. It was first and foremost a device to ensure the completeness of texts passed on orally, although later it became a purely artistic device. The abovementioned *hymnus* by Methodius is a so-called *abecedarius* in which the successive lines begin with all the successive letters of the alphabet in turn. An early example of this type of acrostic is found in Psalm 119.

A change which had important consequences occurred in the Christian community in Rome. Presumably just before the middle of the century Greek came to be replaced by Latin as the language of liturgy and church administration. This suggests that the majority of Christians in the capital came from a Latin milieu, unlike during the early years of the Roman church. At first, the linguistic change did not have any immediate effect on the links between the church of Rome and those of Alexandria and Asia Minor. Still, a development had begun which was to lead to an increasing division between the Latin and the Greek provinces of Christianity. For the sixth decade of the century, Cyprian's letters already show that Latin only was then used in the offices of the Roman Bishop, even if we may certainly assume that educated people in the West were still bilingual at that time. Bilingualism, however, became rarer and rarer during the remaining part of the third and the two following centuries. Augustine, the leading theologian of the late fourth century AD, only had a modest knowledge of Greek.

As early as the middle of the third century AD the Roman Christian community could boast a member who was able to give adequate Latin expression to subtle theological speculation. This was Novatian, who in 250 AD seems to have been a particularly well-respected member of the Roman clergy, in whose name he wrote two letters to Cyprian during the time when the see was vacant. In the following year Novatian quarrelled with Bishop Cornelius about his practice in receiving people who had abandoned their faith during the persecutions back into the Christian community. Novatian rejected Cornelius' leniency towards the apostates, and formed a dissenting church, as whose bishop he had himself anointed by other Italic bishops. In the East as well as in the West, his church survived well into the fifth century AD. The information that Novatian died as a martyr stems from a long time after his death; none the less, it was corroborated by the discovery of his grave with a funeral inscription in a Roman catacomb.

Apart from the aforementioned two letters to Cyprian, we have four treatises written by Novatian. They were all handed down under the name of either Cyprian or Tertullian, but Novatian's authorship can be established without any doubt. One tract about the Jewish laws concerning food is meant to prove that Christians are not bound by the dietary rules laid down in the Old Testament. However, the author warns Christians not to eat the meat of animals which were slaughtered during pagan rituals and whose meat was later sold in butchers' shops. The treatise about actors, similar to a comparable piece of writing by Tertullian, orders Christians not to go to the theatre or the circus. The treatise about chastity gives us a comprehensive picture of prevalent Christian attitudes to sexual morality.

The longest work by Novatian is a treatise on the trinity. It is distinguished by a clear structure, precise terminology, and extensive reference to Greek precedents as well as to the writings of Tertullian on the subject. Ascribed to Tertullian, this tract was never criticised by church orthodoxy; and quite rightly so considering that the real author Novatian had caused a schism because of a dispute about matters of church discipline alone and not because of any controversy about dogma.

It is especially in his treatise about the trinity that Novatian comes across as a man with a high degree of philosophical, literary, and rhetorical education. He knew and used Classic Latin literature, and seems to have gleaned most of his knowledge of Stoic philosophy from Seneca. Novatian was extremely adept at structuring ideas clearly and expressing them effectively. His Latin follows Classic norms without any pedantry; there is no stilted shunning of biblical expressions or words from theological jargon, and likewise no frantic endeavour to keep coining new and surprising phrases. In this Novatian is as different from the idiosyncratic Tertullian as Cyprian was; however, he is far superior to the latter in terms of literary talent and philosophical knowledge.

Another new phenomenon that appeared in the third century AD was Biblical exegesis in Latin. The writings of Tertullian already document the existence of a Latin translation of the Bible in Africa and the works of Novatian tell us of one in Italy. The earliest commentaries on individual books of the Old and New Testaments which we know of are, however, those by the Bishop Victorinus of Poetovio, modern-day Ptuj on the Drava in Slovenia. According to the account given by Hieronymus in his collection of biographies of Christian authors, Victorinus died as a martyr in the persecutions under Diocletian in 304 AD.

Hieronymus tells us of a large number of individual commentaries by Victorinus; of these, the only extant one is that on the Apocalypse of John. We also have a short treatise about the creation of the world. Hieronymus edited this commentary and, as the extant original version shows, suppressed the author's chiliastic doctrines. Those found much more interest in the West than in the Eastern church, which also displayed, for several centuries, a great reserve towards the Apocalypse.

Hieronymus criticises the author of the commentary saying that his Greek was better than his Latin. But from a modern-day point of view, Victorinus' Latin usage appears clear and correct. Yet Victorinus may well have been of Greek origin since until the fourth century AD we find men from the East, such as Hilarius of Poitiers, among the important authors of Latin-Christian literature. As regards his exegetical interests and methods, Victorinus seems to be influenced by Origen, and hence his work is the first evidence of the long-lasting influence which Origenism was to have in Latin Christianity.

7

THE ERA OF DIOCLETIAN AND CONSTANTINE

1 GENERAL REMARKS

The diligence and competence of the soldier emperors of the third century AD, mostly men from Illyria and Pannonia, had saved the Empire from a military collapse. By the end of the century, however, its political and economic order was in ruins. All incipient reforms such as those attempted by the Emperors Gallienus and Aurelian were foiled by the violent deaths of the respective monarchs. Only Diocletian managed to see through a comprehensive work of reform, but in doing so, he radically altered the character of the Roman state, institutionalising the consequences of those unplanned changes which had come about in politics and society during the third century AD.

Like many of the preceding emperors, C. Aurelius Valerius Diocles, as he was called before his accession to the throne, came from the Illyrian-Dalmatian region and had begun his career as a private soldier. By 284 AD he had managed to rise as far as the command of the Imperial bodyguard, the *protectores domestici*. In that year the reigning monarch Numerian was murdered at Nicomedia in Asia Minor, and the soldiers proclaimed Diocletian as the new Emperor. Diocletian fought successfully against a rival for the throne and achieved victory in arduous campaigns against Germanic and Sarmatian tribes, as well as against the Persian Empire. He also triumphed against an usurper in Britain and rebelling peasants in Gaul. After all this, he set out to implement a major reform programme, whose results I will now outline.

The precarious situation on the borders had made it necessary to decentralise the military command as well as the administration. Diocletian introduced a new system of government, with a quadripartite structure. Two superior *augusti* and two *caesares*, adopted as sons and successors by the former, resided in four different places, and governed four different parts of the Empire. The residences were at first York, Trier, Milan, and Nicomedia. This quadripartite system soon proved to be impracticable, but from this time onwards the basic idea of a division of power became the rule rather than an exception. Only very strong monarchs like Constantine or Theodosius I managed to hold on to undivided supreme power.

A further measure taken was the reorganisation of the provinces. Diocletian did away with the distinction between Senatorial provinces, where the governor was appointed by the Senate, and Imperial ones, where the choice was made by the Emperor himself. The only remaining hierarchy among the provinces was established by the comparative ranks of governors, all, however, appointed by the Emperor. Italy and Egypt were brought under regular provincial administration; the number of provinces was increased to nearly a hundred by dividing larger ones, and the new provinces were in turn grouped into twelve dioceses. The army was enlarged, and once again accommodated in garrisons; but contrary to Old Roman tradition, civilian and military administration were separated.

Military expenditure and lavish public building put an immense strain on financial resources. Building concentrated on Rome which, in spite of its and the Senate's lack of political importance, remained the symbolic centre of the Empire and was thus exempt from taxation. In order to raise enough money for public spending demands for payments in kind and indirect taxes were complemented by a new system of levies, a scheme which prescribed a new tax to be paid *per capita* for each person working on a piece of land. Thus the state had an interest in allowing no land to lie fallow. This tended to restrict the freedom of the peasants through legislation which tied them to their estates.

In view of the massive public expenditure which the state incurred it is not surprising that Diocletian's plans for rehabilitating the weakened Roman currency failed. In 301 AD he released an edict which was to curb the galloping inflation. Maximum prices were fixed for all goods and services, from dried meat to private lessons given by teachers of grammar. We may assume that this measure had very little success, but all the same, the extant text of the edict is one of our most important sources about Late Classical economic history.

Diocletian tried to heighten the dignity of the Emperor and Empire first of all by strengthening the hierarchic features in the army, the administration, and Roman society as a whole. Most important, however, was his introduction of what was very much an oriental style of courtly life, with countless courtiers, eunuchs, and other such adjuncts, ruled by a protocol which bore a fundamental resemblance to that observed in the neighbouring Persian Empire of the Sassanids. There was a new visible expression of the sacred and superhuman status of the Emperor's person, and this exceeded whatever previous Roman Imperial thought had borrowed from Hellenistic monarchic ideology. Mediaeval manifestational forms of monarchy go back to those innovations introduced by Diocletian, lasting throughout the Late Classical age, and documented by products of courtly art, such as those in S. Vitale in Ravenna, until the present day.

To us, the new image of Emperor, court, and state seems to have lost all Graeco-Roman features; but nevertheless, Diocletian saw himself as the restorer and preserver of the traditions of the Roman state. In the administration, he preferred men with a legal education to those qualified by general knowledge acquired through mainly rhetorical training. In this context, the change of name is significant: when he became Emperor, he Latinised the Greek Diocles into Diocletianus. A member of Diocletian's crown council or *consilium* was one of the last major legal scholars who presumably also held the high office of *praefectus praetorio*. This man, Hermogenianus, put together a collection of Diocletian's legislation from which much material entered into Justinian's *Corpus iuris*; he also wrote a manual in six books which is likewise frequently quoted in Justinian's *Digests*.

The conservatism of the Emperor is best visible in his religious policies. When he established the tetrarchy, he referred to the *augusti* as *Iovii*, representatives of the ancient Romans' supreme god Jupiter; and the *caesares* he called *Herculii*, placing them under the special protection of Hercules, Jupiter's son, a human whose prowess and perseverance had earned him a place among the gods. The bestowing of those titles reflects the fact that Diocletian's religious ideas were deeply rooted in tradition, and consequently, in an edict released in 297 AD, he made the worship of Jupiter the official cult obligatory for all citizens of the Empire. In the same year, there followed an edict against the Manichaeans, followers of a religion which had developed on the basis of Gnosticism in Persia, and which began to find more and more believers in the Roman Empire also. Understandably enough, those were regarded as sympathisers of the Empire's eastern enemy.

Around the same time, there had been several instances of Christian soldiers in the Roman army refusing to obey orders. The very fact that there were such individuals in the armed forces proves how freely Christianity had been allowed to spread since the days of the Emperor Gallienus. After repeated insubordinations, the Emperor took action to remove the Christians from the army, by forcing those who refused to perform the sacrifice to resign from military service. In 303 AD at last, and not without prior consultation of the Delphic oracle, Diocletian pronounced the edict which initiated the most severe persecutions ever. All Christians from the upper classes lost their rank, fortune, and public office; all Christians serving at court were made slaves. All churches were to be destroyed, all Christian writings burned, all church possessions confiscated, and all Christians without exception were to be regarded as having no legal capacity. These measures caused a good deal of unrest, which prompted another edict ordering the imprisonment of all ecclesiastical officeholders. They were to be forced to perform the sacrifice and torture and execution awaited them if they refused. Yet a further edict extended the enforcement of the sacrifice to all Christians, naming hard labour or death as penalties for refusal.

It is hard to assess how rigidly these laws, pronounced in the names of all four regents, were applied. Constantius Chlorus, the *caesar* who ruled in Britain, seems to have paid little heed to them, while the other *caesar* Galerius is portrayed as the real instigator in Christian sources. In any case, their superiors, the *augusti* Maximian and Diocletian, were extremely meticulous in putting the edicts into practice.

A serious illness forced Diocletian to abdicate in 305 AD. Prior to that, he had persuaded Maximian to do the same, had promoted the two *caesares* to the status of *augusti*, and had appointed two new *caesares*, Severus and Maximinus Daia. Diocletian himself lived on in peace for eight more years, in that palace on the coast of Dalmatia whose walls harbour the old town of Split to the present day.

Immediately after the abdication, long-lasting quarrels and some bloody wars broke out between the four successors whom I have named and additional rivals. The man who finally emerged as victor and sole ruler in 324 AD was Constantine, the son of Constantius Chlorus and his wife Helena, landlady of a bar, and the man whom posterity called the Great. Throughout the preceding period there had been persecutions of Christians on the basis of Diocletian's edicts in some parts of the Empire but not in Constantine's steadily growing sphere of influence. He favoured the Christians from the beginning, agreed on an edict of toleration with Galerius in Milan in 311 AD, and finally, after his victory in 312 AD over one of his many rivals called Maxentius at the Milvian bridge outside the gates of Rome, he publicly joined the ranks of the Christians.

This sudden change which turned the persecuted and humiliated Christians into worshippers of a God on whose benevolence the future of the Roman Empire was now to depend made a deep and lasting impression on contemporaries and posterity. From our point of view, it is difficult to pinpoint Constantine's motives in detail. However, the facts are that he tried in a most generous way to compensate for injustices that had been done to Christians; that he gave to the high clergy the privileges of public dignitaries; that he started a comprehensive programme of building new churches; and, most importantly, that he himself took the initiative to restore the unity of Christianity, which had been jeopardised by the Arian debate about christological dogma, and by the secession of the Donatist church in Africa.

Constantine presided over the famous council of Nicaea in 325 AD and in the apostolic church of the new capital he had chosen his tomb amid the relics of the first messengers of the faith. That he was only baptised on his deathbed was in keeping with a widespread convention: even to the persecutors, someone who studied the catechism prior to baptism was already a Christian. The belief in a complete forgiveness for all sins in the act of baptism suggested that especially the great men of the Empire who could wield legal power should put off baptism until the hour of their death approached: thus the pardon given could no longer be affected by any subsequent action which might be inevitable in the interest of government. Constantine's open intervention in matters of faith and the church set an example for many centuries of Late Classical and mediaeval history. In the future, the monarch's position within the framework of ecclesiastical life was seen as one of the most important features of his reign.

None the less, as much as Constantine emphasised the fact that he saw Christianity as the then and future religion of the Roman Empire, he never attempted to suppress pagan belief. What he did was merely cautiously and gradually to distance himself from the old titles and cultic acts which bound the monarchy to the old religion. It was only his successors who began to deny the pagan cults privileges and financial means, and who in the end made them illegal.

Constantine's governmental practice largely followed the paths mapped out by Diocletian. Constantine was a military genius and he continued the reform of the army by adding mobile rapid deployment forces to the firmly garrisoned border troops. By introducing a gold standard he managed to stabilise the Roman currency. This was a measure from which foreign trade benefited greatly, as is proved by the fact that Roman coins found in India and Ceylon date from before as well as after this period, but not from the time of crisis in the third century AD. But the mushrooming bureaucracy and the unbearable pressure of taxes and other charges levied by the monarchy to finance the military, the court, and public building, remained like a cancerous tumour. In spite of all political stability, it paralysed the productive forces so effectively that the prosperity of the High Empire was never regained. Another factor which influenced the economy was the aforementioned progressive exemption of major landowners from the state's economic and financial system (see p. 310) and the growing legal restriction of large parts of the population to their inherited profession and place of residence.

Constantine was much less inclined to respect Roman political traditions than Diocletian, the most obvious reason for this being his Christian faith. This attitude is reflected in his legislation which has a much lesser degree of juristic precision; and also in his tendency to prefer the rhetor over the lawyer in public service. That is to say he favoured the type of men who paid more regard to common ethical notions than to the strict terminology of legal scholarship. What Constantine retained was the elevation of the Emperor's person to a sacred state in his titles as well as in court protocol, even though his Christian beliefs no longer allowed a deification of the monarch. But the growing readiness of the public to accept hierarchies in all parts of social life likewise demanded such an elaborate representation of the monarch at the top of the social pyramid.

Apart from his Christianisation of the state, the most consequential historic deed of Constantine was certainly the foundation of the Empire's new capital, on the site of ancient Byzantium. The restored monarchy seemed to be asking for a new residence, whose location was to reflect the shift of political weight to the East, which was less threatened by barbaric raids. Diocletian had already governed mainly from Nicomedia, right across the water from Byzantium. Another factor was that the traditions of the capital Rome were difficult to reconcile with a Christian monarchy. Constantine made the new capital a second Rome, with all the institutions and privileges which the old one possessed: a Senate, circus games, and free food for the urban proletariat. The establishment of a new metropolis took no more than four years, from 326 to 330 AD. At its official inauguration the ritual also included those time-honoured ceremonies used in the founding of all Roman cities, in spite of the Christian character of the new capital. In Constantinople the eastern half of the Roman Empire acquired a cultural, economic, and political centre which ensured its survival there for a thousand years longer than in the West.

The period between Diocletian's accession to the throne in 284 AD and the death of Constantine in 337 AD was in many ways a transitional one. During those years foundations were laid for a culture which was Christian but at the same time inseparably linked to the Roman Empire. This culture flowered in the following two centuries and has determined our cultural vision to the present day.

2 LATIN PROSE AND POETRY

A literary reflection of the general stabilisation which marks the years after 300 AD can be seen in the collection of the *Panegyrics*. These texts, widely read and imitated in the Late Middle Ages, are eulogies on different emperors. The oldest pieces, numbers 5 to 12 in the collection, are anonymous, with one exception only. All were written in Gaul between 289 and 311 AD, and each one is addressed to an emperor who reigned during those years, such as Constantius Chlorus, Constantine, or Maximian. The collection is completed by four pieces which do not belong to the timespan outlined above. There is a *panegyricus* on the Emperor Trajan which was delivered in 100 AD by Pliny the Younger, a speech on the Emperor Theodosius given by Pacatus in 389 AD, a speech of thanks to the Emperor Julian delivered in 362 AD by the newly appointed Consul Mamertinus, and a eulogy on Constantine from 321 AD by a certain Nazarius.

In spite of great individual stylistic differences, all the speeches have a high linguistic standard which indicates that the authors were thoroughly and comprehensively educated. Thus these texts prove the survival of rhetorical education beyond the caesura of the third century AD. Apart from their documentary value as recording certain historical events of the period, they belong to our most important sources of knowledge about monarchic ideology in the fourth century AD. This ideology seems to be highly homogeneous during the whole period covered by the collection, and it shows no trace of the influence of Christian ideas at all.

This confirms an observation which has been made on the basis of other, non-literary evidence, suggesting that the elevated, sacred position of the Emperor was founded on the cosmic role which he had to play; a role expressed, for instance, in the Imperial orb, as a symbol of the globe. The Emperor was taken as a visible representative of the universal God; he was the man whose task it was to implement the eternal, perfect order of the universe in the form of justice among men. Because of its cosmic legitimacy, this task implies the claim to global rule, a claim which Christian kings of the West have never rejected in principle, in spite of their large number which means that the claim can never be put into practice, and can only be contemplated in the form of theoretical political hypotheses such as the assumption of family relationships existing between all crowned heads. In any case, with regard to the cosmic justification of their office, there was no difference between the pagan and the Christian emperors of the Roman Empire, a state whose size and whose power could very well be described as global, and in which global rule was popularly defined as the political unification of all civilised nations.

The most interesting one among the older speeches of the *Panegyrics* is not one about an emperor, although it does contain a eulogy on the monarch. It is addressed to the governor of Lugdunum or Lyons, asking him to persuade the Emperor to consent to the reopening of a local school, to which the author Eumenius has donated one annual salary – a state stipend – which he earned as professor of rhetoric in Augustodunum or Autun. The speech, delivered in 297 AD, tells us, moreover, that the author's grandfather came from Athens and had taught rhetoric first in Rome and then in Autun. Prior to his appointment as professor, the author himself had been employed in the Emperor's offices, where he earned a salary of 300,000 sestertiae a year, and hence about half of his emoluments as a professor. Eumenius' statements give us an insight into the recovery of education which had suffered particularly badly in Gaul because of the raids of looting Alemannic tribes and because of internal unrest. Now, after the stabilisation of the border which had been pushed back to the Rhine, there was a new educational boom.

The leading region in Latin literature, though, was still Africa. However, it is perhaps only a result of chance that we have among our evidence of this fact the seven books against the heathens written by the rhetor Arnobius, a man from the small African town of Sicca Veneria, presumably just before 300 AD. Arnobius seems to have produced the work shortly after his conversion: it is not really so badly argued or formulated, but it does betray the author's total ignorance of Christian doctrine. On the other hand Arnobius has recorded much valuable information from grammatical-antiquarian literature, to which he refers extensively in his attempt to prove that pagan cults and myths are absurd and immoral. Arnobius explicitly rejects any attempt to give myth a moral or cosmological meaning through allegorical reading. He seems to have been unaware of the fact that this method of interpretation was at that time already well established in Christian-Biblical exegesis.

Much more influential than Arnobius was his pupil L. Caelius Firmianus Lactantius, likewise an African, who came to be quite rightly called the Christian Cicero. In 303 AD Diocletian made him professor of Latin rhetoric at his residence of Nicomedia. In 307 AD Lactantius was dismissed from his post because of his Christian faith, and in 317 AD Constantine employed him as tutor to his son Crispus who grew up in Trier.

Lactantius is the most brilliant exponent of the intellectual life of the period, even though all of his numerous writings on grammar, rhetoric, and philosophy have been lost, and the only extant ones are Christian in content. One is a book on the creation of man, outlining an anthropology which is Christian in character, but fundamentally influenced by Platonism; this work describes the eternal life of the soul after its separation from the body as the final destiny of human nature. There is also a book on the wrath of God, a concept which was naturally odious to philosophical thinkers: the Bible spoke of an angry or a jealous God, whereas philosophical faith saw the perfection of God largely in the fact of his nature as a purely rational being, incapable of any irrational-emotional impulse. Using established traditional doctrine, Lactantius removes this bone of contention by explaining the wording of the Bible as a concession to the readers' limited power of understanding.

Another work by Lactantius is apologetic in character, describing in glowing colours how all those Roman emperors who persecuted the Christians died a miserable death. The book is of considerable interest because it is the only extant example of a whole genre of writing describing the circumstances surrounding the deaths of famous men. From the letters of the Younger Pliny, we learn about other works of this type which were, according to him, hybrids of historiography and oratory, and were dedicated – with a panegyrical or paraenetical intention – to the victims of the 'evil' emperors' persecutions among the Senatorial nobility.

Lactantius' main work is the *Divine Instruction*, a description of the Christian faith in seven books written not entirely without apologetical intent. We have a complete version as well as an excerpt made by the author himself, with his own corrections. The book addresses the educated pagan reader, and it consequently tries to demonstrate that Christian instruction is primarily concerned with acquiring the proper knowledge of God. The first two books are a refutation of pagan religion, describing its gods either as dead people given divine honours in the euhemeristic tradition, or as demons. Book 3 attacks philosophy whose teachings contradict one another and do not lead to salvation. Book 5 is about justice which has disappeared among men and will come back again only when people recognise one another as children of God. In Book 6 we have a description of the knowledge of God communicated by Christ, eliminating sin – defined as ignorance – from the world, and leading to the true love of God and humans. Book 7 finally contains an eschatology.

There is one point on which Lactantius obviously shares the opinion of the Gnostics, and that is the view of the process of salvation, crowned by baptism, as the acquisition of knowledge. The content of the revelation is wisdom. This and other 'Gnostic' elements in his work do not necessarily prove the direct influence of Gnostic doctrines. They may also stem from the author himself, in his effort to present Christianity as philosophy to philosophically educated people. From Arnobius' writings we know that, especially in north Africa, a popularised kind of Platonism was at that time widespread among educated people as a doctrine of salvation. It is on the very same level that Lactantius' apologetical and missionary argument operates.

Lactantius was a master of Latin prose. He followed a Classicist stylistic tradition after the model of Cicero, a manner of writing which became more and more popular among pagans and Christians in the fourth century AD. On the other hand his writings show no philosophical or theological expertise, and astute reflection and argumentation were not his forte either. Unlike Tertullian and Novatian, whose works illustrate the entry of the philosophically based Eastern theology into Latin, Lactantius and his Western contemporaries achieved no more than a mainly formal adaptation – guided by rhetoric – of Christian literature to the Classical world of education.

A very peculiar phenomenon in the literature of the early fourth century AD is constituted by the works of Julius Firmicus Maternus, a member of the Senatorial class who lived in Sicily. During the last years of Constantine's reign Maternus wrote a comprehensive astrological treatise in eight books, dedicated to his friend, the then governor of Campania. This work gives us valuable information about astrological notions and methods current in this period; it shows that the author had an extensive knowledge of specialist literature on the subject. Moreover, Book 1 contains a lengthy defence and moral justification of astrology, a piece similar to that which Vettius Valens had produced two centuries earlier. Astrology, deeply rooted as it was in the belief of the divine nature of the cosmos, clashed with the Jewish-Christian concept of a sovereign divine creator who communicated with man directly, and not only through his creations. Consequently astrology was strongly condemned by the church.

Firmicus must have become a convert to Christianity very soon after he wrote his astrological textbook: only ten years after its publication he wrote the most violent polemic against paganism in all known early Christian literature. In it he asks the reigning monarchs Constans and Constantine II to eradicate the pagan cults once and for all. The unrestrained polemics of this tract about the errors of pagan religion are repulsive in tone, and of little literary merit. But no other anti-pagan writer has left us as much information as Firmicus about the cults of the Late Classical age, including the Mysteries of Mithras, and others. This is why his book is an invaluable source for the religious historian.

During the Diocletian-Constantinian period we also have a re-emergence of poetry. A later historiographer tells us about didactic poems on fishing, hunting, and navigation, dedicated to the reigning Emperor Carinus by the poet Nemesianus from Carthage. The beginning of the poem on hunting is extant, including the dedication; it shows that the author mastered the poetic technique of the didactic poem in the tradition of Virgil. There are also four bucolic poems, eclogues in the Virgilian tradition, which were written by Nemesian, although they were handed down under the name of Calpurnius Siculus, a poet from the time of Nero's reign. This is another proof of the survival power of a genre tradition which, taken up after a long interruption, could still help reasonably talented poets to achieve fairly respectable results.

The figurative poems of Publilius Porfyrius Optatianus had the value of literary curiosities, but the impact of major poetic achievements. The texts are dedicated to Constantine on the occasion of the anniversary of his succession in 325 AD; their effect was permission granted to the poet to return from banishment. The relevant edict by the Emperor is featured alongside the poems in an edition launched by the author himself some years later. The history of the figurative poem begins in the age of Hellenism from which we have a few specimens, and it continues right into the Baroque period. Its basic technique is the use of different line lengths, resulting in the typographical representation of the shape of a tree, an altar, or other objects. Other techniques are to make the first or last letters of lines form words; to write entire poems which can be read back to front without violating the metre; to form lines in which each word is one syllable longer than the preceding one; and more such poetic sleights-of-hand.

Under the name of Lactantius we have a longer poem written in elegiac distichs telling the tale of the bird Phoenix, incinerating itself and being reborn from the ashes. This story was extremely popular in the Empire; it was read as an allegorical description of eternity and, because of the Egyptian elements it contains and which Herodotus had already pointed out, as referring to the perennially renewed and hence eternal rule of Rome. The Christians soon came to interpret the story as alluding to the resurrection of Christ.

Words to that effect can be found, for instance, in the *Physiologus*, the standard work in the Latin, Greek, and Oriental Middle Ages about the symbolical and typological significance of animals, plants, and stones. Among the extant versions of this popular book in many different languages, the Greek one is the oldest. It comes from the fourth century AD but we can reconstruct earlier forms of the text which originated in Alexandria in the High Empire and thus completely unaffected by Christianity. From this book, for example, people knew the story of the pelican, which was said to open its carotid artery with its beak in order to feed its young; the account came to be read as a reference to Jesus' sacrifice of his life. This illustrates that Christians adopted a fairly common means of interpreting real or invented natural paradoxes.

Such a background explains why it has been impossible to this day to establish the authorship of the poem about the Phoenix. The text merely tells the story without any interpretation. It is smooth in metre and diction, and there is nothing in form or content which would jar with the assumption that Lactantius is the author; but at the same time we cannot say for sure whether the poem was written by a Christian author at all.

A text which is unmistakably of Christian origin is a poem in about 150 lines, closely following the Virgilian model, which describes a miracle that occurred in Gaul around 320 AD. This poem ends with congratulations to the Emperor Constantine, as does the work of a poetess named Probina who retells the Biblical story of creation and of the early history of mankind in 694 lines from Virgil. During the fourth century AD it became more and more fashionable to compose such *centos* of Virgilian material; there is also an entire Medean tragedy in this form, a play written by a certain Hosidius Geta.

More important than these works are the four books by the Spanish priest Juvencus, also written during the reign of Constantine. In more than three thousand hexameters, they contain a retelling of the story of the gospels, harmonising the four different accounts, but largely following that of Matthew's evangelium. Here, too, diction and metre follow as closely as possible the Virgilian pattern, which anybody with any kind of education would know from reading the *Aeneid* at school. Juvencus' example shows that the West preceded the East in the development of Biblical poetry; this suggests that the Latins had fewer scruples about modifying their non-Christian poetic tradition to suit Christian purposes. Biblical poetry in the Homeric style was written only after Julian's edict in 362 AD forbade the instruction in Classic-Greek poetry to Christian schoolteachers, in order to exclude Christians from higher education (see p. 429).

We have two more short poems in hexameters under the names of Tertullian and Cyprian. They are about episodes from the Bible and may come from the later years of Constantine's reign.

Under the conditions set by the development of the language, the revival of Christian and pagan poetry presupposed a thorough grammatical education on the parts of poets and readers alike. It is true that we have no texts from the Diocletian-Constantinian period which give us proof of literary productivity in this field, though there is a large number of such texts from the late fourth and fifth centuries AD (see p. 439). Those must be seen as the product of a very conscious cultivation of the literary heritage; it is possible that they replaced their predecessors because of their number as well as their quality.

3 GREEK PHILOSOPHY

A fair amount of information about the numerous philosophers who worked in different corners of the Empire around 300 AD is contained in the *Lives of the Sophists* written by Eunapius of Sardes around the end of the century. The author had begun his own studies in philosophy and rhetoric in Athens in 336 AD.

The dominant figure of this era was the Syrian Iamblichus. He was taught by the Peripatetic philosopher Anatolius, a prominent mathematician besides. After being instructed by Anatolius, Iamblichus belonged to Porphyry's circle of pupils, and lived in Athens for some time. Throughout the last years of his life, between 330 and 340 AD, Iamblichus taught in the Syrian city of Apamea.

Iamblichus' philosophy was a development of stimuli which he received from Porphyry, although the pupil was later only too keen to stress his independence from his teacher. Going beyond the Plotinian-Porphyrian plan, he tried above all to arrive at an even closer description of the hypostases of the intelligible Being. A similar endeavour to arrive at an ever-more detailed metaphysics, based on the belief that this alone could help to interpret the sensual world as well as the nature and the destiny of the human soul, can also be observed in the works of Theodorus of Asine. That man nevertheless tended to follow Porphyry much more closely in such reflections than Iamblichus did, and consequently there was a lot of tension between the two contemporaries.

Porphyry, in obvious contrast to his teacher Plotinus, had already chosen to see the study of the occult, the immediate contact with the numinous in cult and magic, as the crowning of philosophical endeavour to attain knowledge beyond the limits of sensual perception and discursive thought. Iamblichus went a good deal farther on the same road. He believed that he could find the means for making contact with the divine, above all in the cultic and magical practices of exotic peoples, in spells and invocations. The theoretical basis for such efforts can be found in the works of Porphyry: according to him, the world is full of good and bad demons surrounding men and influencing their actions in various ways. As a theurgist, a man who is capable of supernatural actions, the philosopher can establish a direct communication with those demons.

Among Iamblichus' many pupils there were quite a few who distinguished themselves chiefly through exhibiting magical-theurgical powers. It was the influence of those men which later moved the Emperor Julian to reject his Christian education and to embrace a paganism defined in a Neo-Platonist sense. We may well assume that large parts of the public in the fourth and fifth centuries AD were of the opinion that a proper philosopher had to prove his credentials by working miracles: this was the ultimate evidence of his attainment of the philosophical idea of perfection, as an approximation of a divine state.

The frightful obscurantism which at that time dominated a considerable part of philosophical education was often coupled (and frequently in one and the same person) with astonishing ingenuity, as shown in the construction of metaphysical-ontological systems, and above all in the interpretation of Platonic and Aristotelian texts. In the works of Iamblichus we find the earliest instance of a fully developed method of interpreting Plato which achieves a degree of independence from the sequence of the text, and no longer only tries to unravel the meaning consecutively, passage by passage. As in Origen's Bible exegesis (see p. 336), the new method suggested that for every passage three levels of meaning must be found: the empirical-physical, the moral, and the metaphysical-ontological sense. This was a way of applying to the interpretation of texts a principle formulated by Plotinus and Porphyry, describing the intellectual and moral ascent of man towards the goal of spiritualisation and approximation to the divine: on each new level one was asked to practise the same virtues in new and different ways.

The leaning towards the supernatural and miraculous was something which Christian theologians and Platonic philosophers had in common, as well as their meticulous interpretation of a set canon of writings. The Christian saint, who around this time first appears as a well-defined type, corresponds to the Late Platonic philosopher, a worker of miracles, and a morally perfect man. This concept, however, could also be traced back to Pythagoreanism, which had become more and more popular since the second century AD, especially among the Platonics.

The nucleus of the literary production of Iamblichus together with that of his pupils and contemporaries was constituted by commentaries on Plato and Aristotle. We have only one completely extant work of this kind from the fourth century, but all the more texts from the fifth and sixth centuries AD. The latter ones contain frequent quotations from older exegetical literature; in good scientific manner, the authors mostly provide a very serious discussion of earlier interpretative efforts. But of course they also quote from other, non-exegetical writings among older philosophical literature. From such sources we get a fairly good impression of the exegetical methods of Iamblichus, Theodorus, and other scholars.

The only completely extant commentary on Aristotle is the one on the *Categories*, written by Iamblichus' pupil Dexippus. This man is certainly not identical with the historian Dexippus (see p. 369), but beyond that, we know neither where he came from nor where he taught. Dexippus' reading of Aristotle's treatise on categories follows the line of argument shared by Porphyry and Iamblichus; in this particular instance, the two agreed in their rejection of Plotinus' evaluation.

From the large number of Iamblichus' writings which he produced beside the commentaries, quite a few are extant, among them an anti-Porphyrian tract called *About the Mysteries*. Under this title, which was added later, Iamblichus' work deals with the significance of cultic-magical formulas. He sees especially those from the religious tradition of Egypt, whose meaning is not to be decoded by reference to normal linguistic usage, as means of a supernatural communication with the divine.

Of Iamblichus' major collection of works on the Pythagorean tradition, we have about half of the material that originally filled ten books. There is a description of the Pythagorean-philosophical lifestyle, written as a biography of Pythagoras, and a *protreptikos*, a tract promoting this way of life. In this work the author quotes lengthy passages from Aristotle's lost writing with the same name. There are also three tracts by Iamblichus which constitute an introduction to Pythagorean-Platonic mathematics and numerical speculation, disciplines which are presented as constituting the foundation of metaphysics.

It is only from textual fragments that we know about Iamblichus' philosophical doctrines, which were apparently as important to him as his own were to Theodorus of Asine. For Iamblichus, the theory of the transmigration of souls played a central part. The relevant fragments are found in the abovementioned commentaries from later centuries, especially those by the Neo-Platonist Proclus on Plato's *State* and *Timaeus*. More material exists in the major collection of excerpts compiled by Bishop John Stobaeus in the former Yugoslavian part of modern-day Macedonia. This collection also contains numerous excerpts from Porphyry's writings.

Iamblichus enjoyed an extraordinarily high esteem until the end of the century; his pupils continued his teaching in many places throughout the Empire. The most influential man among them was Aedesius from Asia Minor, who founded a school in Pergamum and died in 355 AD. Exponents of the school, such as Chrysantius, Priscus, or Maximus, were still to be found one generation later. Maximus in turn founded a school in Ephesus, where he taught the future Emperor Julian. Alypius, another pupil of Iamblichus, was from Alexandria, where he went back to teach for the rest of his life. Some people from this circle even found favour at court, in spite of their insistence on the old religion. Sopatrus was called to the court as a counsellor to Constantine but later fell out of favour for reasons unknown to us and was finally executed. There was also a second generation pupil of Iamblichus called Eustathius, a man who had some rhetorical talent as well as philosophical knowledge, and was sent to the Persian court as an envoy of the Emperor Constantius II. Eunapius tells us that Eustathius was married to the daughter of a rich landowner in Cappadocia in eastern Asia Minor, and that his wife also had a reputation as a professional philosopher.

With the exception of the aforementioned Alexandrian Anatolius, we know hardly anything about philosophers outside the Platonic school tradition at that time. A most peculiar piece of information in our sources claims that the Peripatetic Anatolius wrote, among other things, a book about the calculation of the date for Easter which would, of course, lead to the assumption that he was a member of the Christian church. However, around the year 300 AD it would have been very unlikely indeed to find a professional philosopher who was a Christian, and thus we have to reckon with the possibility that this is a case of mistaken identity between two authors of the same name.

Another Platonic philosopher was Alexander from Lycopolis in Egypt, the author of a short tract against the Manichaeans which appeared about 300 AD. Around the middle of the third century AD Mani, a man who came from the Iranian nobility, had created a new religion from Christian-Gnostic teachings and the traditions of a Mesopotamian sect of Baptists. For the spreading of the new creed he had won the support of the Sassanid King Šapur; but under Šapur's second successor Zoroastrian priests contrived to turn the monarch against him. Mani was interrogated, imprisoned, and died in jail in 273 AD. Mani's untiring missionary work in the provinces was accompanied by a rich literary production in Syriac, the only exception being a treatise that was handed to King Šapur and hence written in Persian. The different dialects of the Syriac language were spoken all over the Mesopotamian-Syrian region, that is the western regions of the Persian and the eastern provinces of the Roman Empire.

Unlike the Gnostic sects, most of whose followers did not leave the church out of their free will, Mani's converts chose to become members of a new religion, related to Christianity but with its own organisational forms, its own offices and ordinational degrees, and above all, its own canon of Holy Scripture. Mani's doctrine, clothed in a complicated mythology, was based on a radical dualist view of the world. In it, light and darkness, spirit and matter, soul and body, good and evil, are independent cosmic powers hostile to one another. Their eternal conflict is not moderated by any divine omnipotence. Man is forced to take sides in this quarrel, in order to fulfil the destiny of his true nature, liberation from matter and return to the spiritual world.

Being at once belligerent and ascetical, Mani's teachings soon came to extend their influence beyond the borders of the Persian Empire. As early as 297 AD Diocletian released an edict against the Manichaean religion whose provenance from the country of the archenemy made its followers as suspect as Christians were in the Persian Empire from the reign of Constantine onwards. Manichaean texts have been discovered in the sands of Egypt, partly in Coptic translations, but also partly in Greek. A few years ago the first part of a life of Mani from the Cologne collection of papyri was published, a text in Greek found written in tiny letters on a parchment codex from the fourth or fifth century AD. During the second half of the fourth century AD no lesser man than the church father Augustine was a member of a Manichaean community for over ten years.

Alexander's polemic against Manichaeism is based on the world view of the Greek-philosophical tradition; and yet his criticism largely coincides with Christian attacks on the Manichaeans in later years. To Gnostics as well as Manichaeans, the empirical world has life only because it contains particles from the spiritual world of light, but it is still predominantly the playground of evil, which equals matter. Platonists did not doubt that spiritual being was of infinitely higher value than material but to them, reality down to the minutest creations in the empirical world was a continuum, with beauty and order reflecting everywhere the power of the divine being, purely spiritual, which created them. To Jews and Christians as well, the world was the work of a sovereign creator, who had once and for all found it good. In the Late Classical age, philosophers and Christians shared the longing for a union with the divine, as well as the idea that this spiritual goal can only be reached through asceticism, the suppression of impulses emanating from the human body. All the same, both could not but reject the radical dualism of the Manichaeans. Neither the religious veneration of the cosmos, which embraces the sensual and the spiritual, nor the Biblical belief in creation could tolerate the denigration of our world as the empire of evil, the counter-reality to the spiritual world.

It is significant how Alexander, in his refutation of Manichaeism, was led towards a concept which was originally alien to philosophy and which was not generally accepted until philosophical methods were used to formulate the Christian faith. The first philosophically educated theologians had interpreted the Biblical account of the creation of the world as meaning that God had formed it from matter which had neither shape nor qualities, and was thus non-existent in that sense. It did not seem to occur to them that this doctrine implied that there was matter existing beside the eternal God prior to the creation of the world, as, for instance, postulated in Aristotelian cosmology. It was not until later that the Biblical story was read as referring to a creation from nothing, with the creator's will being the world's only reason to exist. It is the latter notion, alien to the philosophical tradition, that appears in the works of Alexander. In order to emphasise the unity of the entire sensual and spiritual world, and to nip in the bud any idea of its division between good and evil, he radicalised the concept denying the pre-existence of mere matter, devoid of form and qualities prior to being formed by the spirit. Alexander explicitly states that there is no independent existence of any kind of matter at all, and that everything is created by the divine spirit. In this form, the doctrine of the *creatio ex nihilo* was indeed a logical continuation of Platonic-Plotinian thought.

4 CHRISTIAN TEXTS IN GREEK I: THEOLOGICAL LITERATURE

Without any doubt, the most important part of the Greek literature of the period in question is of Christian origin. During the epoch in which the church suffered the greatest pressure and saw its greatest triumph, there was also the beginning of an internal dispute about dogma which had far-reaching historical consequences. This dispute seemed to have been resolved in the Council of Nicaea, chaired by Constantine in 325 AD, but it flared up again soon afterwards, and was not finally settled until the Council of Constantinople in 381 AD. The settlement itself, however, gave rise to new controversies about the proper formulation of the faith, controversies which were similarly vehement and led to further divisions.

Even if we take into consideration our own religious experience, we in the late twentieth century will find it hard to understand that such great emotional, intellectual, and political energies were invested in the debate, not about the faith itself but about its terminological description. We can comprehend that it was important to preserve the religious – even though we might rather tend to say ideological – unity of the members of a political community. But according to our way of thinking such fundamental beliefs do not allow a strict terminological fixation, and this is all the more so when the relationship between the individual and the divine is concerned. Even the religious unity of a Classical state was, after all, expressed in cultic acts performed by the people and not in the terminology of a credo.

The crucial historical importance of the dispute about dogma must be explained by reference to a certain historical constellation. Greek philosophy, the dominant educational force in post-Classic Antiquity, had taught those who took an active share in education to see the given, immutable natural order which made life and growth possible as a rational order. This implied that the rational, discursive, communicative, objectifying thought of men was able, however imperfectly or incompletely, to recognise the eternal, unchangeable, final order of being or of the world. In the systematics of the philosophical schools, theology was part of physics, the study of nature. Alien to all Greek philosophy was any kind of notion implying that there could be a relationship between God and man independent of the common, objectively existing order of being and hence impossible to describe in the same categories. Everything that defied ontological categorisation was quite simply ignored.

Such an ontological perspective also influenced the first Christians who operated within this educational context, trying to express the Biblical faith in creation and salvation in a discussable form. Hence they attempted to come up with an objective terminological rendering of the message of salvation contained in Biblical scripture, even where the texts speak very explicitly of the incalculable actions of God, inexplicable on the basis of the order of creation; or where the Bible mentions God's direct revelations to man, and his mysterious plans. In the process of their work Christian theologians could exploit the fact that contemporary philosophy focused mainly on the intelligible Being which was beyond sensual verification and that thence philosophers used terminological language to discuss the invisible and transcendental. Thus there seemed to be a good chance of constructing an ontological framework for the content of the Christian faith. It was only Augustine who introduced the idea that what the Bible talked about could be seen and described from a point of view which took no more into account than the relationship between God and the human soul and which excluded the objective order of being.

Origen's major plan for a comprehensive description of the Christian faith (see p. 335) remained within those limits of philosophical ontology which I have just outlined. Throughout the following decades this plan inspired several attempts at completion, correction, and above all specification. One of these attempts was undertaken by the learned Arius, taught by Lucianus in Antioch, and later serving as a presbyter in the church of Alexandria. Arius defined the Biblical statements describing Jesus as the Son of God by reference to the Neo-Platonist doctrine of the hypostases of the supreme level of Being, as emanating in hierarchical succession (see p. 372). This was applauded especially by philosophically educated theologians, but there was also some criticism, most notably from the clergy of his own church. The most important counter-argument was based on the contention that, according to the ecclesiastical interpretation of the crucifixion, God had sacrificed himself in his son for the salvation of man, contrary to which view Arius' doctrine separated the Saviour from the supreme divine Being, and made him a part of creation. This, it was said, infringed the fundamental belief in salvation. In 320 AD Bishop Alexander of Alexandria expelled his presbyter from the church, whereupon Arius went to join Bishop Eusebius of Nicomedia, who was the Emperor's friend, and later on baptised the monarch on his deathbed.

Among other issues, the question Arius had raised was discussed at the Council of Nicaea in 325 AD with the result that Arius was condemned and banished by the Emperor. But this was not the end of the dispute in which the Alexandrian faction prevailed against the majority of Greek theologians, first and foremost with the support of the Latins. The Emperor himself changed sides shortly before his death, and Arius was rehabilitated. This led to the deposition and banishment of Athanasius of Alexandria in 335 AD. Athanasius had succeeded Alexander as Bishop in 328 AD, and had been one of the most fervent advocates of the doctrine postulating the identical nature of Father and Son. Being mainly interested in the unity of the church, emperors until the Council of Constantinople in 381 AD which finally confirmed the decision taken at Nicaea, tended to support anti-Nicaean doctrines, later rejected as Arian; the only exception was the short period of pagan reaction under Julian. This is why the converted Germanic tribes received Christianity in an Arian form which many of them preserved for several centuries.

In this context, I cannot go into the details of the dogmatical and ecclesiastical history of the period when both major parties were soon divided into numerous factions and intermediate groups. However, much of the rich literary production of Christian theologians throughout the fourth century AD emerged from the dogmatic dispute in which the monarchy took a vivid interest for obvious political reasons. But, as our sources prove, the discussion was followed equally keenly by large parts of the population.

Arius' own literary output, which was not very extensive, is only known to us from a number of quotations. His major work entitled *Thalia* contained prose and poetry. According to the few extant fragments of the latter, it seems that he had adapted old metres to suit current pronunciation. Much more of Arius' theology was spread through the works of friends and followers who all had connections with the exegetical school of Antioch. Most of their works were handed down under the names of orthodox theologians. A case in point is the Job commentary of the Arian Julian, written around 300 AD and ascribed to the orthodox Julian of Halicarnassus. Then there were the sermons of Asterius the Sophist, thus called to distinguish him from the later Asterius of Amasea. Fragments of these texts on the subject of the Psalms have been handed down under different names, mostly in so-called *catenae* (see p. 515). Asterius belongs to the third and fourth decades of the century; he was a pupil of Lucianus, the founder of the Antiochian tradition of Biblical exegesis, some of whose interpretations are recorded in Julian's writings as information based on oral tradition.

Much better known is the literary work of Athanasius, a man who was at the centre of ecclesiastical developments for nearly fifty years until his death in 373 AD, even though he was deposed and banished several times. His lifetime mostly coincides with the era of the Christianised Roman Empire, but his thought and his reputation were entirely rooted in the preceding transitional period to which this chapter is dedicated.

Two extant early writings of Athanasius – the speech against the pagans and another about the word becoming flesh – are wholly in the tradition of early *apologetica* directed against pagans and Jews. More important are his three speeches against the Arians, written between 330 and 350 AD. With a carefully thought out terminology based on Platonic philosophy, but also with an impressive array of metaphors, these tracts argue the doctrine of the identical nature of Son and Father, seeking to invalidate the Arian objection that this would mean denying the unity and the uniqueness of God. Athanasius explains that the light cannot be separated from the flame, nor the water from the source, neither spatially, temporally, or substantially; likewise, he claims, Father and Son belong together, prior to time and creation.

Of Athanasius' exegetical writings, we have only few fragments, whereas his works concerning ecclesiastical politics are for the most part extant. There are letters to the parishes in his diocese, to synods and to other bishops; there are also writings defending his views and his work, including reports about his activities with enclosed documents. These have different addressees, one among whom is the Emperor himself. We also find pieces in which Athanasius expresses his opinions about synodal resolutions. All of these writings are mainly of interest to the ecclesiastical historian, but in them especially, Athanasius shines as a master of rhetorically styled argumentation who may well be compared with Classic legal and political orators. From a literary point of view, however, Athanasius' most notable work is his life of the hermit Antonius, with which he established the tradition of Greek lives of the saints. This book will be discussed in the following section.

5 CHRISTIAN TEXTS IN GREEK II: MONASTIC LITERATURE

Ascetical movements of many different kinds had existed in Christian circles from the very beginning, even without a generally recognised institutionalisation of ascetic life. There was no difference between Christians and Jewish, Gnostic, or Baptist sects, or indeed many philosophical groups, in their common view that asceticism was a way towards moral or religious perfection, and in their corresponding respect for people who chose an ascetic lifestyle. But during a period when every Christian community had to be prepared for persecutions setting in at any time, the possible reputation of an ascete could hardly match that of a steadfast confessor, and far less that of a martyr who shed his blood for the faith. The possibility for such ultimate proof of one's faith disappeared with the official recognition and the privileged status of Christianity: and thus the hour of the ascete as the model Christian had arrived.

The first distinct form of asceticism which attracted widespread attention was represented by the Anchorets. Especially in Egypt, where cultivated land and desert bordered directly on one another, pious hermits sought solitude in a life without any material comforts and without any contact with other people, in caves, huts, or ancient tombs. The desert was known as the home of the demons who – according to the notions of these simple sons of peasants who often spoke no Greek, but also according to educated philosophers – surrounded and influenced people everywhere. Prepared through fasting, waking, and praying, the hermits would challenge those demons to combat during long nights, again and again trying to master them in the name of the Saviour, in order to break their power over men. The fight against the demons by the Anchoret, who had left house and land and family behind, replaced the trial of faith under persecution, the latter likewise thought to have been brought about by demons.

Through their way of life which was contrary to any ideas of the 'normal', and through their spiritual gifts proved in a life of constant contact with the numinous, the Anchorets came to enjoy great respect among the clergy as well as among the common people. Spiritual advice and help were often asked from such desert saints whom one trusted because of their charisma not because of any particular knowledge or office and about whom people told miraculous stories of healings, the taming of wild animals, prophecies, and such like. The gifts that visitors brought would frequently ensure the hermits' survival, if they did not earn a bit of money themselves by weaving mats or making baskets.

A very good insight into the world of early desert ascetes is provided by a collection that contains the religious sayings of such dwellers in the wilderness. The so-called *Apophthegmata of the Fathers* were compiled in the fourth century AD, partly from older oral tradition; most of the sayings are embedded in anecdotal accounts of the events which gave rise to the remarks. The book is written in Greek, although most of the Anchorets quoted in it were Copts who knew no Greek at all. Latin translations of such collections of sayings were made as early as the fourth century AD and there were also new revised editions in Latin, such as that by John Cassianus from modern-day Dobrudja. He lived as a monk in Palestine and Egypt and became one of the fathers of Latin monastic life through the foundation of monasteries in Massilia or Marseilles, as we now know it.

One of the most famous Anchorets was Antonius, the son of a Coptic farmer, who turned his back on the world at the age of twenty and retired ever deeper into the desert, as increasing numbers of visitors became attracted by what they had heard about his saintliness and his miraculous powers. Antonius died in 356 AD at the age of 105. Athanasius' life of this man (doubts about the authorship of the work must be taken seriously, but do not seem to invalidate the traditional assumption) is more than a mere compilation of the great wealth of miracle-stories which circulated about Antonius. In his carefully arranged account the author shows how the hermit, relying solely upon himself, carries on his never-ceasing battle with the demons until he reaches the highest level of human perfection.

Having arrived at this goal, he is in a position to demonstrate the superior power and the understanding belonging to the pneumatic, the spiritual man whose insights have penetrated far beyond all efforts of scholarship; a fact which he can prove in his social dealings with all kinds of men, from simple peasants to bishops and governors. A most impressive part of Athanasius' work is the description of Antonius' emergence from a tomb, as a reborn new man at the age of fifty-five, after having spent ten years underground fasting, praying, and battling with the demons without so much as even talking to anybody.

With the typical lives of the philosophers, Antonius' biography shares the idea of successive stages in the ascent to perfection; there are quite a few episodes in Athanasius' work that remind us especially of the common Pythagorean biography. This is certainly not coincidental, even if so far it has not been possible to establish a convincing link in detail between the form of the life of Antonius and the Pythagorean tradition. Like the perfect philosopher, the perfect ascete was seen as an exemplary human being; this idea we come across again and again in the collection of the *Apophthegmata*. Thus the hermit, like the philosopher, could serve as a model to each empirical man, regardless of great differences in moral or religious achievement. It is this concept which justifies the writing of such biographies as a means of moral or religious admonition. The life of Antonius was translated into Latin in the same century as it was written, and it served as the archetype of a long tradition of hagiography.

Even in the earliest layer of tradition about the desert saints we find mention of the fact that some ascetes – for example, old men with their disciples – lived in the wilderness in groups rather than alone. From such colonies, the first monasteries arose. Among them, the most important ones were those founded by the Copt Pachomius around 320 AD, because they were the first to be organised according to a set of rules laid down in writing. Of those rules, originally written in Coptic, we have editions and translations, fragmentary or complete, in virtually all languages of the Christian West and East. These were the earliest in a long series of codifications of the rules of monastic life, among whose authors we find such eminent figures of ecclesiastical history as Basil, Augustine, Cassiodorus, and Benedict of Nursia.

From Pachomius' laws, but also from his life – however uncertain we are about the relevant dates – and from literature describing monastic life which developed in the course of the fourth century AD, we see how the ideal of Koinobite monastic life differed from that of the hermits. The battle with the desert demons was substituted by the fight to overcome one's own faults and weaknesses, the demons in one's own heart. Another important demand was to maintain humility and the willingness to help monastic brothers and sisters, as well as people outside the order who often would appeal to the monasteries as centres of Christian life, for material and spiritual help. We know of many instances from Egypt, and later from the capital, where monasteries, including urban ones, catered on a large scale for ill people and travellers, with entire aid programmes being carried out when a catastrophe occurred. A case in point is the invasion of war-like nomads in upper Egypt in the fifth century AD when, as our sources tell us, the Abbot Shenute of Atripe co-ordinated a major relief operation.

In monastic life the most extreme forms of asceticism were excluded. One had to make allowances for the sick and the weak, secure the basis of the community's existence through craftwork or agriculture, and, not least importantly, come together in worship and the celebration of religious festivals. In their early days monasteries were not yet centres of learning, but all the same strongholds of orthodoxy. The piety of the monks, mostly uneducated people, was without any theological subtleness. It found its expression in ritual worship, prayer, and asceticism, and, whenever there were disputes about the faith, in an unhesitating and unconditional support for the doctrinal authority of the local bishop. This shows a humble subordination to the holders of ecclesiastical office, an attitude which was also expressed in all Egyptian monks' refusal to be ordained as priests, because they did not want to be in any way superior to their fellow humans. Late Classical thinking was, after all, wholly dominated by the concept of hierarchy, and thus people could also see ecclesiastical office only in the categories of higher and lower rank. Alexandrian Patriarchs sometimes prevailed in disputes about ecclesiastical politics and dogma by calling large numbers of monks from the Egyptian monasteries into the streets of their capital and see. Those monks would stage demonstrations, which frequently turned into full-scale riots. Such outbreaks of violence can perhaps also be seen as a compensation for the limitation of ascetic practice through social obligations.

But Koinobites and hermits agreed at least on the ideal of ascetic life, which was to foreshadow the perfection of the transcendental existence, liberated from matter. This is why the monk's cowl was known as the angel's garment and why Pachomius' rules call the joining of the community of ascetes a second baptism, just as earlier the martyrdom of an unbaptised Christian had been seen as an act of baptism which opened heaven's gate to the blood witness. That the true monk was also the true human being was a notion essential to the Anchoretic as well as the Koinobite ideal, and presumably also the reason for choosing the name monk, meaning 'the unique one'.

Asceticism developed slightly differently in the Syrian region. Here, particularly in the parts beyond the Roman Empire's borders, there were large groups within the church which demanded an ascetic life of all baptised Christians, and allowed worldly pursuits only to the catechumen, the Christian preparing for baptism. This explains why the hermits or

Anchorets who appeared in Syria around the same time as in Egypt tended even further towards extremes which they preserved until the sixth century AD. From the early fifth century onwards, there were, for example, the Stylites, who would sit still for years on the capital of a high column, suffering the burning heat and the bitter cold of the desert climate. This proved their supernatural gifts to the general public and it ensured them immense respect as well as an often considerable influence on state officials. The most famous Stylite was the saint Simeon; even when he was still alive a monumental church was erected around his column, which became the goal of pilgrimages for centuries. The ruins of Kalat Siman are still the most impressive monument of Syrian architecture. Another form of asceticism found mainly in Syria was supposed to demonstrate the homelessness on earth of the citizen of heaven, which caused many ascetes to lead a travelling life. Then there was also the type of holy ascete who feigned madness for several years in order to emulate Christ in being entirely despised by the world. The latter motif occasionally appears also in texts from Egyptian monastic literature.

Most of the monastic communities founded in the Syrian region from the fourth century onwards were more or less based on Egyptian models, and there were strong links between the monasteries of Syria and those of Egypt. But there were also some ascetic communities which were typical of the Syrian church alone. A case in point is the movement of the Messalians, which included the Akoimetes, 'the sleepless ones'. They were a group of migrant ascetes whose self-appointed task entailed an uninterrupted, endlessly repeated, singing of the song of praise of the heavenly beings from Isaiah's Vision, a song which had entered the liturgy of the early church as the 'Thrice Holy'. Walking and singing, the Akoimetes roamed for years through the East of the Empire until they were given a monastery in Constantinople to bide in.

In and around the monastic life that was spreading and quickly becoming institutionalised, there was a literary production with a corresponding growth rate. I have already mentioned the *Apophthegmata*, the collection of sayings of famous desert monks; and likewise the codification of the rules of monastic life. Texts of both types also existed in Latin, partly as translations, partly as revised editions or imitations. The same applies to the biographies of famous ascetes for which the life of Antonius provided the model. We find them throughout the following centuries, on the Greek as well as on the Latin side and, quite naturally, in many varieties with very different literary and historical merit. These texts, written for the edification of a fairly broad reading public, include many which were not written in standard literary language, but contain elements of contemporary oral usage.

An example of such rather popular biographies is the life of Hypatius, a well-respected and influential abbot of the monastery of Chalcedon in north-western Anatolia. Without investing too much energy in style and literary composition, his biographer Callinicus has produced an account which includes extremely interesting details of ecclesiastical and social life in the early fifth century AD. Such biographies of monks are also invaluable sources for ethnologists, as they give deep insights into the world of ideas and the types of behaviour found especially among the common people. This is also true of the series of lives of the ascetes written by Cyrillus of Scythopolis on the River Jordan in the first half of the sixth century AD. A man who lived in the second half of that century was John Moschus, who was for many years a vagrant ascete in Egypt and Syria, and fled to Rome because of the Persian invasion in the early years of the seventh century. Cyrillus produced a widely read collection of individual miracle-stories from the monastic tradition, a compilation to which he gave the pretty title of *Spiritual Meadow*. The tradition of hagiography written in monastic circles for a little-educated public continued in the eastern Roman Empire well into the eighth century AD. To the linguist, such writings provide valuable clues as to current vernacular of which we have only very little information and very few examples.

The co-existence of these edifying writings in popular language with a theological literature which was completely adapted to the rhetorical, scientific, and philosophical linguistic tradition of its pagan environment, reflects an issue much discussed in the church. The question was whether Christianity could really and truly be reconciled with the old education, and whether a Christian should not really try to emulate the language of the uneducated fishermen who became Jesus' first disciples, rather than that of rhetors and philosophers. Tertullian, Hieronymus, Basil, and many other writers had discussed this problem. That the debate was finally settled in favour of the educational tradition is shown especially clearly in the handed-down hagiographical writings. In the tenth century the learned Symeon, known as Metaphrastes or 'the translator', rewrote all the hagiographical literature accessible to him in literary language, an effort which caused the loss of many of the older versions. But we still have a large enough number of those older texts from between the fourth and sixth centuries AD to give us a fairly exact picture of the linguistic differences.

In any case, there was a linguistic development within the Christian community which led to a kind of literary standard usage that was independent of the Classic tradition. This language was formed on the basis of those phrases in the Greek translation of the Bible which reflected a Hebrew or Aramaic wording, and hence differed from spoken Greek. This Biblical Greek and the cultic language of Greek Judaism were the medium in which Christian liturgy had evolved since the first century AD. Liturgy was only influenced by the philosophical-rhetorical linguistic tradition when it admitted formulas that had been coined in dogmatic controversies.

The earliest among the Latin lives of ascetes are the three works by

Hieronymus. He wrote about the lives and miracles of the three legendary Anchorets Paul, Malchus, and Hilarion, who are said to have lived in different regions of the Christian Orient. The hermit Paul seems to be Hieronymus' invention: the author describes him as the teacher of the monastic father Antonius, and this is an all too blatant giveaway of Hieronymus' attempt to outdo the famous life of Antonius written by the great Athanasius.

Unlike Hieronymus' hagiographical writings, the life of Melania the Younger is of great value as a source of historical information. That lady from the high Senatorial nobility of Rome spent many years travelling to famous strongholds of monastic asceticism. She made contact with leading personalities in the church at that time and she died in a monastery near Jerusalem which she had founded herself. Her biography, written soon after her death in the first half of the fifth century AD, exists in a Greek and in a Latin version. It is not sure which of these languages was originally used by the author, the monk Gerontius. A work written around the same time is the life of Honoratus, the man who had founded the famous monastery of Lerinum near Marseilles, and who later became Bishop of Arles. The author Hilarius lived as a monk at Lerinum, and went on to succeed Honoratus as Bishop.

Beside individual biographies, which were written not only about monks but also about bishops or other religious people with a special reputation (see p. 523), other books of mainly biographical content described the lives of entire monastic communities. The interest shown in this kind of writing resulted mainly from the fact that hermits' colonies and monasteries had soon become the destination of pilgrimages. The best work of the kind is the monastic history by Palladius dedicated to the Imperial court official Lausus, and hence called *Historia Lausiaca*. Palladius had himself lived for many years as a monk in Palestine and Egypt, before becoming Bishop of a see in Asia Minor.

The *Historia Lausiaca* was written in the early fifth century AD, but it is based on much older, partly oral traditions. It gives us a very vivid impression of the lives of the Egyptian Anchorets and Koinobites, reporting not only miracles and spiritual sayings, but also events of a much more mundane nature. The work was soon translated into Latin as well as different Oriental languages, because of its popular appeal as a smoothly written edifying book. A work with a similar impact was the *History of the Egyptian Monks*, written around the same time by an author whose identity has not been fully established. This book was often edited in one single volume together with the *Historia Lausiaca*. Rufinus, the friend and later adversary of Hieronymus, translated it into Latin.

The so-called *God-pleasing History* by Theodoretus, who was Bishop of Cyrrhus in Syria during the first half of the fifth century AD, contains biographical sketches of thirty Syrian ascetes. The accounts were put together from written and oral tradition, but also from the author's own experiences. The work is written in a highly elevated and flowery style: it is different from most monastic literature in its use of mainly rhetorical devices for the glorification of the heroes and the edification of the readers. This book is of considerable value as a historical source, for in spite of its many miracle-stories, it contains important clues as to the situation within the eastern regions of the Roman Empire. There, the urban population was bilingual, whereas most of the rural people spoke only Syriac, and it was the cultural gap in particular which exposed them to the tyranny of the landowners from the urban aristocracy, and to that of the state's officials. The spiritual authority of the ascetes frequently offered protection to a lower class to which some of them had once belonged themselves.

The attraction which the strongholds of asceticism possessed, above all those on the sacred soil of Palestine, will be understood by anyone who reads the early pilgrims' reports. The oldest one was written by an anonymous author from Burdigala or Bordeaux in 333 AD, but this account includes no more than a list of stations *en route* between his native city and Jerusalem, via Milan and Rome. Much more interesting is the report by a noble lady called Egeria or Aetheria, who went on a pilgrimage to Palestine in the late fourth century AD. She describes churches, martyrs' tombs, and hermitages, together with the religious services which she attended, thus giving us a vivid picture of the religious life of the period. This short book, unfortunately not completely preserved, was discovered only in the late nineteenth century; it is of particular interest to the linguist. The author did not in the least try to achieve a literary style in her report and hence the text is a unique piece of evidence of spoken Latin in the Late Classical period, when it had already moved very close to the later Romance languages.

The quick spreading of monastic life during the fourth century AD must be ascribed to a number of very different factors. One was the success in finding enthusiasts for ascetic life among members of the upper classes, both males and, very importantly, females. This not only raised public esteem for the monasteries but also opened them to education and led to a whole series of generous donations for the foundation and the furnishing of such establishments. For the late fourth century AD this is proved by the correspondence of Hieronymus who himself founded several monasteries in Bethlehem and made them places of study with the financial help of noble ladies from the Senatorial class of Rome. His rival Rufinus managed to enlist similar support, and quite a few of the lady patrons became nuns themselves, or pledged one of their children to ascetic life. By the fourth century AD many new bishops were recruited from the monasteries – a fact that, in view of the political importance of this office, also indicates the ever-rising social and intellectual status of monastic communities. Moreover, it became common for high dignitaries to move into monasteries after retirement, or after dismissal. Finally, we hear of several bishops who lived in a kind of monastic community with the clergy of their respective cities, as, for example, Augustine did in Hippo.

All this should explain why theological literature from the fourth century onwards dealt with aspects of monastic life in the most varied contexts, and why hardly any of the more important authors of the fourth and fifth centuries AD was entirely uninfluenced by monastic ideas. There was, moreover, a fair amount of criticism of monastic life. The state passed laws in order to prevent slaves from shaking off their masters by becoming monks, peasants from abandoning their land in times of economic distress, or members of the municipal nobility from choosing the same way out in order to avoid liability for their city's duty to the state. The orator Libanius complained bitterly about the savage behaviour of fanatical mobs demolishing heathen temples; another accusation against the monks which he raised was that they only pretended to be ascetes and were in reality extremely fond of good food and drink.

There were also critical voices raised among the Christians. Around the year 400 AD Hieronymus wrote two polemical tracts against Vigilantius and Jovinianus. The former had not simply questioned the value of the relic cult and other forms of popular piety, but also stated that the active life of a Christian was more important than spiritual contemplation. The other one had declared marriage and the raising of children to be more valuable than sexual asceticism and virginity. It is significant that the answers by Hieronymus are extant, whereas the original texts by the other two were not preserved.

In the rich theological literature of the period, there are not only such results of what one is tempted to call an inevitable concern with asceticism and monasticism. There are also writings which emerged from monastic life itself, and made it the object of their reflections. First, I must name the large corpus of the *Homilies*, spiritual orations handed down under the name of the Anchoret Macarius who lived around the middle of the fourth century AD in the Scetian desert in Egypt. That man himself presumably never wrote a single word in his life, but his orthodoxy was never in doubt. The *Homilies*, albeit re-edited, seem to come from ascetic circles in Syria or Mesopotamia, and, as was revealed about fifty years ago, their author appears to be a certain Symeon, the man who was believed to have founded Messalianism, a movement later condemned as heretical. None the less, it is by no means certain that the *Homilies* were all written by the same author.

Those circles among which they originated placed great emphasis on prayer and meditation. The psychological and religious experiences thus gained led them to expect salvation from an inner absorption of the faith, and not from ritual and instruction. Their religious attitudes became very individualistic and entirely spiritual. Written by and for men who had devoted their whole lives to introspection, the texts are often difficult to interpret. But some passages, such as that about the liberating power of prayer or about the aim of creating room in one's own soul for the coming of divine grace which nobody can bring about by himself, are among the most beautiful products in the rich mystical tradition of the church.

Much more concrete are the instructions for ascetic life compiled with much effort by Euagrius from northern Asia Minor. Around the mid-fourth century AD he had embarked on a promising career as a preacher, but then withdrew into the Nitrian desert to join a community of monks. According to Palladius he earned his keep by copying books; this is yet another indication of education taking hold in the monasteries.

Euagrius wrote numerous works for practical use by monks and nuns. There were collections of *sententiae* and Biblical quotations as instructions for proper living and as a means of overcoming depression or evil thoughts. We find instructions concerning individual aspects of dogma, arranged in groups of a hundred each; then there are also pastoral letters and comprehensive surveys of monastic life. Euagrius explicitly distinguished between chapters addressed to uneducated ascetes, and those meant for educated monks.

Euagrius' reputation is illustrated by the fact that these works were at once translated into Latin, Syriac, and Armenian. Today, though, it is almost exclusively the translations which are extant. The original Greek text was lost because Euagrius' theology was based on Origen whose teachings were finally condemned in Byzantium in the sixth century AD and whose writings were destroyed wherever they were found, while in the Orient and in the West there was not so much clarity about heterodoxical elements. But in spite of the later fate of his books, Euagrius had a considerable influence on Eastern monastic life, and in Egyptian monasteries, the influence of Origen's theology persisted for a long time.

A role similar to that which Euagrius played in the internal development of Eastern monasticism can be ascribed to John Cassianus, one generation younger than Euagrius, in the Latin West. Cassian came from modern-day Dobrudja, was ordained as a priest in Rome, lived for many years with the monks of Palestine and Egypt, and finally founded several monasteries in Massilia, modern-day Marseilles.

The twelve books of his manual, written in excellent Latin modelled on Classic archetypes, first give a very detailed description of the institutions, customs, rules, and living conditions in the monastic communities of Egypt and Palestine, which Cassian knew from his own experience. He tells us virtually everything that is of any interest whatsoever: conditions for admission, the order of prayer and service, clothing, food, disciplinary rules, and much more. All of this is supposed to provide guidelines for new monasteries in the Latin West. The main part of the book, however, is about the inner life of the monk, with the text divided into eight chapters according to the eight principal vices which he has to combat throughout his life.

A doctrine which put together a catalogue of major vices or sins had already been developed in the second century AD. A point of contention was the question whether there were transgressions of the divine commands which were too grave to be forgiven, at least if committed after baptism; hence, this was an issue concerning the practice of penance. Most writers mentioned in this category the sins of apostasy, manslaughter, and adultery. In the third and fourth centuries AD a different view came to prevail. It called for an explanation of sin that included psychological elements, based on the philosophical theory of the emotions, above all the Stoic theory of the four basic affections pleasure, pain, fear, and desire. These terms were sometimes reinterpreted in a demonological sense. The main goal was to provide a counterpart to the generally accepted canon of the four moral cardinal virtues of philosophy, and the three 'spiritual' virtues named in Chapter 13 of Paul's First Letter to the Corinthians: faith, love, and hope.

In monasticism, the experience of meditation and self-scrutiny led to a refinement of those schemes by authors who sought to incorporate the accumulated wealth of psychological and psychagogical insights. The catalogue of the eight major vices was widespread because of Euagrius' writings; he had been able to adopt it ready-made, as we know from its appearance in the monastic theologian Nilus of Ancyra's works about virtue and vice. Cassian put the scheme of the eight vices into Latin; he did not refer to Euagrius as a source, but named the otherwise unknown Egyptian abbot Serapion instead.

In institutionalised monastic asceticism, the fight with the demons intruding from outside was replaced by the fight with the evil stirrings of one's own heart, also frequently interpreted in a demonological sense. This kind of striving for perfection was the basis for the careful classification of vices or sins to be fought in a lifelong inner battle, because they could be practised even in thought, without any practical action: for instance, gluttony, effeminacy, greed, anger, sadness, arrogance, weariness of ascetic life, pride, and the craving for fame. Elsewhere Cassian even comes up with a list of eighteen different vices.

The paedagogical and pastoral zeal which was to be felt in monastic communities had its effect also on Christians outside the monasteries. Here the doctrine of vices became very important, in a version with a shorter canon of seven. This is first found in the *Battle for the Soul*, an allegorical poem by Prudentius (see p. 583), and then in the writings of Gregory the Great. With the number seven, it constitutes the exact match to the catalogue of virtues, with its four cardinal and three spiritual ones.

Cassian, whose edition of the desert monks' sayings I have mentioned before (see p. 411), was not only an elegant stylist, but also an educated theologian. Beyond his role in the development of monastic life in theory and practice, he had a lasting influence on Christian doctrine in the West through his stance in the Pelagian debate (see p. 545). For monasticism, Cassian's work meant an important contribution to its full integration into the educational world of the Late Classical age.

Euagrius' writings – in which Origen's influence is obvious – and their continuing reception in the West document a symbiosis of monastic life and theological reflection which had been alien to monasticism in the beginning. Between the fourth and the sixth centuries there were also other writings which illustrate this aspect of monastic life.

In an Egyptian monastery lived the learned Isidorus of Pelusiun, about thirty years younger than Euagrius. We have nearly three thousand of his letters which deal with questions of dogma and exegesis. Most importantly, though, these short texts give theologically reasoned instructions for the proper life of a monk. Isidorus was a man with a very good philosophical and theological education who took an active share in the debate about Arianism and the incipient Monophysitism. Moreover, this writer was a brilliant stylist who in all likelihood had also had a thorough rhetorical education.

From a monastery in Ancyra, modern-day Ankara, we have letters and short treatises for the instruction of monks. These can be compared in many ways to similar texts by Isidorus, and were written around the same time by the authors Nilus and Marcus. The latter was called the Hermit because he withdrew into the Syrian desert for the last years of his life. Slightly more recent are the treatises of Diadochus, Bishop of Photice in Epirus in Greece. These works describe the ascete's path to spiritual perfection, and have some features in common with the homilies of Symeon-Makarius (see p. 418). Comparable writings existed in the West, in the tradition established by Cassian. In the mid-fifth century AD Bishop Eucherius of Lyons wrote, beside several works on Biblical exegesis and the first literary account of the legend about the Theban legion's martyrs, two treatises on the spiritual life of the ascete.

The combination of scholarly theological work and monastic living which this literature documents, became the decisive factor in the further development of Western-Latin monasticism. As early as the fifth century AD, the aforementioned monastery of Lerinum had become a centre of theological studies. In the sixth century AD the monastic rules of Cassiodorus and Benedict explicitly named the cultivation of the educational tradition as one task of monastic communities. Ultimately, the monasteries came to play a vital part in the history of European intellectual life.

As shown by the texts I have discussed, Eastern monasticism also knew the cultivation of theology and other areas of scholarship, but there it never came to dominate monastic life in the same way. The main reason for the difference is certainly that for centuries a real educational tradition could, in the West, survive nowhere else than behind the walls of monasteries. In spite of the cultural caesura which the intrusion of Islam into the eastern provinces, and the dispute about icons brought also to the eastern Roman Empire, there remained several possibilities of access to the wealth of the educational tradition, without, as well as within, ecclesiastical life.

In this section about the literary heritage of the monastic movement I have referred to times long after the epoch of Constantine. This calls for some justification. But monasticism established itself and spread surprisingly quickly in all the countries of the Roman Empire, parallel to the Christianisation of state and society, that is the process of integration of Christianity into a culture to which it had been more or less hostile before. The rise of monasticism can thus be understood as an effort to cling to the old position of the true Christian in an environment hostile to him and even to his God. This constellation was to be preserved even under changed circumstances in order to keep showing the people what a true, uncompromising Christian life was. Part of the outside world was now also the church with its believers and the official clergy who enjoyed a high social status.

The urge towards asceticism which arose during the era of Constantine survived for centuries in Eastern as well as Western monastic life, even if there was necessarily a periodical secularisation and a constant interaction with the universal church. But the idea that the monastic lifestyle could preserve a genuine, almost pre-Constantinian Christianity, was never lost. In the East, this showed in the fact that monks were always more concerned than any other exponents of the church with the lower social classes, the oppressed people who did not represent the recognised culture, the political and social order with which the official church had meanwhile associated itself. This function of the monk was shown again and again in the history of the Eastern churches, down to the example of the *starets* in the solitude of the Russian forest. Even in the West, where all monasteries developed into something more like educational institutions, they were also the milieu in which nearly all movements towards church reform began.

6 CHRISTIAN TEXTS IN GREEK III: EUSEBIUS OF CAESAREA

The learned Eusebius was the most influential figure among the Christians during the Constantinian era. He was born between 260 and 270 AD and began his scholarly studies as a slave of Pamphilus, presbyter of the church in the Palestinian city of Caesarea and owner of the large library of Origen. Pamphilus was executed during the persecutions under Diocletian, and Eusebius fled to Egypt, where he was put into prison. After the edict of toleration, he became Bishop of Caesarea, and took part in the Council of Nicaea as an advisor to Constantine. His stance in the dogmatic dispute changed as that of the monarch did, and he has been called the 'prototype of the spineless State Bishop'. Nevertheless, he was rewarded with the honour of being called upon to deliver the oration on the thirtieth anniversary of Constantine's reign. Eusebius' own theology is based on that of Origen whom he held in high regard. This explains why Eusebius' views can be connected with those of Arius.

Even before the outbreak of Diocletian's persecutions, Eusebius published a universal chronicle, giving a survey of the history of the Oriental nations as well as of the Greeks and Romans by parallel tables synchronising important events in individual years. The apologetical intention was to prove the greater antiquity of Biblical tradition whose beginnings with the divine call on Abraham Eusebius dated in the year corresponding to 2015 BC of our reckoning, a system which was not introduced until long after his lifetime. The fact that Eusebius left out the chronology between the creation and Abraham, which by then had long been deduced from the text of the Bible, shows his correct assessment of the mythical character of the relevant parts of the Old Testament. Eusebius' chronicle is only extant in fragments of the original which was published in 303 AD; but there is a complete Armenian translation and of the second half, we have a Latin re-edition by Hieronymus, continued up to the year 378 AD. The latter especially was much read in the West over a long period of time. The chronicle preserved valuable information from lost historiographical works; in Hieronymus' additions, for instance, we find facts from Roman literary history which were taken from the scholarly works of Suetonius (see p. 260).

With his ecclesiastical history, Eusebius established a new literary genre. The work is extant in many versions, partly translations, in mediaeval manuscripts; these prove that there were several editions of it published by the author himself. As his account took in contemporary events, and as the happenings between 304 and 324 AD created ever-new constellations in ecclesiastical and general politics, the work had to be rewritten time and again. The first edition in seven books appeared before the persecutions under Diocletian, and the last one after Constantine's victory over his temporary co-regent and his last rival Licinius in 324 AD. Licinius had broken an agreement on religious tolerance by ordering the persecution of Christians living within his sphere of influence. The last two editions of the ecclesiastical history included an eighth book, dedicated to the martyrs of the last persecutions in Palestine, Eusebius' native region.

Eusebius presented ecclesiastical history within the framework of a universal historical plan. The dominant idea is that divine providence has ordered the coincidence between the birth of the Roman Empire and the birth of God's Son as a man, because the global, peaceful order established by Augustus was the condition for the unhindered spreading of the message of salvation. This notion could already be found in Luke and it had kept reappearing in many Christian writings since then. In the eyes of Eusebius' contemporaries, the Christianisation of the Empire under Constantine was an impressive confirmation of this assumption.

According to literary rules in the Late Classical age, historiography was a part of high literature which is why the historiographer had to do more than just plainly describe the results of his research. His subject matter demanded a high standard of presentation, even if the author's true aim was to give a complete, faithful account of events and their causal connections. This demand had several consequences, one being that documents cited as historical evidence could never be quoted literally, but only in a style which was in keeping with that of the narrative.

Eusebius' text does meet the demands of the historiographical tradition. He displays a considerable rhetorical-stylistic artistry, producing ornate and elegant prose in introductions, summaries, assessments of great men, and also narrative passages. But the documents on which he bases his account – for example, synodal resolutions, Imperial edicts or rescripts, or Christian literature of a narrative, apologetical, or theological kind – are quoted extensively in the original wording. This method traditionally belonged to grammatical-antiquarian literature which made do without any artistic elaboration of language. By combining two principles Eusebius created a new and lasting genre tradition; and I do not really need to emphasise the fact that his quotations have preserved large parts of writings that were otherwise lost without trace.

In the preface to his work Eusebius presents a full list of those themes which he intends to highlight in the account. His book lives up to the declared goal, particularly as regards two motifs. First, he not only deals with the external events affecting Christianity's fate, but also stresses the growth of Christian doctrine, including the many individual groups which broke away from the official church as heretics. Second, his work is marked by a vivid interest in biography, which makes Eusebius a fellow spirit of contemporary non-Christian historiographers. He paints vivid portraits of martyrs, bishops, and theologians, and the whole of Book 6 is really a biography of his hero Origen. It is a truly historiographical biography in the sense that Origen is described again and again in the context of external events and the internal development of church doctrine, and thus his life becomes the mirror of a whole epoch in ecclesiastical history.

Eusebius' history of the church was soon translated into Latin by Rufinus who also updated the account. Another early translation was into Syriac. There followed numerous imitations and continuations in Greek, Latin, and several Oriental languages. The standard of those varied greatly but all followed the same principles as Eusebius, thus establishing that extremely rich tradition of ecclesiastical historiography which survived well into the Middle Ages.

The usual inclusion of the writings about the Emperor Constantine among Eusebius' historiographical works is not entirely justified. There is the so-called *Vita Constantini*, a panegyric on the Emperor in four books, written in pretentious language and full of the most exaggerated praises. Peculiar is the fact that, quite contrary to the formal laws of courtly panegyrics, this work also includes documents in literal quotation. The second work of this kind, featured as one whole in manuscripts, consists of two parts. One is an oration praising the Emperor on the occasion of the thirtieth anniversary of his reign in 335 AD; the second is an introduction to the Christian faith addressed to educated pagan readers and dedicated to Constantine. Finally, we have a Good Friday sermon delivered by the Emperor, a piece which seems to be a translation from Latin. This indicates that the author in this case may not have been Eusebius, but rather one of Constantine's theological advisors from the West.

Eusebius' Constantinian writings are invaluable as sources telling us about the change in attitude of many Christians towards the nature of the state and the monarchy under the new conditions. As I have stated several times before, the monarchy based its legitimacy on the notion that the Emperor was to practise justice among men as an implementation of the eternal, unchangeable world order. The Christians could not recognise this cosmic justification of the monarch's power because to them the world was a fallen creation doomed to perish, and the only acceptable standards of justice could be derived from God's commands. The church expected perfection in this world only at the end of history through the direct intervention of God at an unpredictable point in time.

Eusebius has the daring to ascribe an eschatological quality to the events of the early fourth century AD. To him, Constantine is the new Moses; the victory over his rival Maxentius at the Milvian Bridge is the salvation of God's people at the end of history, as forecast in the Old Testament account of the Israelites' march across the Red Sea, and of the destruction of the pursuing Egyptians. Such passages in the Constantinian writings reflect a political theology in which an eschatological justification of the monarchy complements the enduring cosmological one (see p. 395). This concept of the Christian monarchy was expressed most often in later periods when the Empire was under serious threat, as during the Gothic invasions of the late fourth century AD. Augustine rejected this view most categorically.

Two further extant works by Eusebius are scholarly writings in fifteen books each, the *Praeparatio evangelica* and the *Demonstratio evangelica*. In the first the author draws on a vast amount of evidence in order to prove that the 'philosophy of the Jews' (i.e. the teachings of the Old Testament) are far superior to the Greek and especially to the

Greek-philosophical tradition in Antiquity in age and value; and that Plato had tacitly made use of the Old Testament. This work is particularly valuable because of extensive quotes from lost philosophical writings. The *Demonstratio evangelica* contains a comprehensive account of so-called scriptural proof, a method dating back to the time of the apostles, by which all the texts of the Old Testament, including historical accounts, psalms, or legal codes, could be interpreted as prophecies fulfilled in the deeds and teachings of Jesus (see p. 207).

Of the numerous other dogmatic, exegetical, and apologetical writings of Eusebius, we have only a few fragments. Among the lost works there is unfortunately also a much-praised commentary on the Psalms, a book of which there was also a Latin translation, and a reply in twenty-five books to Porphyry's attack on the Christians. Extant is Eusebius' answer to an anti-Christian tract published by Hierocles, governor of Egypt during the great persecutions, under the title *Lover of Truth*. An interesting fact is that Hierocles seems to have presented Apollonius of Tyana as the true saviour to the Christian addressees of his treatise. Two shorter writings concerning the dogmatic dispute are levelled against Marcellus of Ancyra, and advocate the resolution of Nicaea, of which Eusebius had been a supporter at the time. However, from the fourth decade of the century onwards, Constantine as well as his successors favoured that party to which Eusebius then belonged, propounding a doctrine of the *logos* incarnate developed on the basis of Origen's teachings.

7 GREEK POETRY

Papyrus finds prove that throughout the Imperial age until the conquest of Egypt poems in hexameters, iambics, anapaests, or elegiac metres were produced on the most varied occasions. Existing fragments stem from mythological, didactic and historical epics, hymns to the gods, congratulatory and matrimonial poems, homages, and much more. On top of this, we have a large number of funeral epigrams in the form of inscriptions. The study of poetic texts was the most important part of grammatical instruction. The rhetorical training which followed the grammatical did not merely only include reference to stylistic models of a poetic kind but featured as exercises the transformation of poetic texts into prose and the writing of verses. Some products of such exercises have also been preserved on papyrus.

Among educated people the ability to produce poems must have been as widespread then as it was in nineteenth-century Germany. From the third century AD, for example, we have a hexametrical song of praise on a gymnasiarch; from the fourth century there are poetic eulogies on two professors teaching at the legal school of Berytus or Beirut. These texts are likewise written in hexameters, and have iambic introductions. Then there is an iambic poem in praise of a man who served his native city of Tyre as an emissary at the Emperor's court. From the epoch around 300 AD we also have fragments of an epic about the creation of the world, of an epic retelling of the story of Telephus, and of an epic about a topical subject, the Persian War waged by the Emperor Galerius. Apart from these, we know of hymns to several deities.

The continuity in utilitarian and occasional poetry does not seem at all surprising; but there was also a particular boom in epic poetry during the second half of the third century AD, a trend which continued until the end of the fifth century AD. The first person to be mentioned in this context is Quintus of Smyrna, for a long time believed to have lived around 500 AD by scholars who assumed that the entire epic renaissance had taken place during the lifetime of the Egyptian Nonnus (see p. 598) around the middle of the fifth century AD. That Quintus' last Classical editor still dated his work correctly in the third century AD has been splendidly confirmed by a recent papyrus find.

Being a Greek, Quintus himself wrote his name as Kointos. He was the author of an epic in fourteen books, intended to close the narrative gap between the *Iliad* and the *Odyssey.* It tells of events in the Trojan War between the death of Hector and the fall of the city, and of the return of some of the Greek heroes, but of course with the exception of Ulysses.

The mythological-historical subject matter dealt with by Quintus had first been put into epic form in the so-called *Kyklos*, a series of epics produced by different authors in the seventh and sixth centuries BC. Those seem to have been the first written versions of an oral tradition, produced with obvious reference to the *Iliad* and the *Odyssey* in their narration of episodes of the kind described above. The entire *Kyklos* was lost apart from a few quotations and a summary adopted by a Byzantine scholar from a grammarian of the second century AD. But prior to that it had given plenty of inspiration to dramatic poetry and the fine arts. However, the epics it contained were no match for the *Iliad* and the *Odyssey,* either in quality or quantity.

Quintus presumably still knew the *Kyklos*; but by his lifetime the stories it contained had long been made much more easily accessible in mythographical manuals (see p. 235), and it is such a source which he seems to have followed. As models for the elaboration of individual scenes or characters, he used a large number of passages from Classic and Hellenistic poetry. He also drew on the tragedies of Sophocles and Euripides, the epic about the Argonauts by Apollonius of Rhodes from the third century BC, and other Hellenistic authors. Scholars differ as to whether he also used Latin sources, above all Virgil and Ovid, but that seems at least very likely. We may assume that it is this reference to a time-honoured poetic tradition which he sees as his justification for occasional changes to the plots of his sources, a method which was alien to major epic art, but common in minor Hellenistic epic, and above all in writing for the stage.

The title *Post-Homerics* shows Quintus' claim to be a successor of that great epic poet; he justifies it in as far as he establishes a wide narrative framework and uses Homeric techniques of composition in individual passages, for instance when he employs elaborate similes to illustrate a situation. In detail, however, his language and diction are modelled predominantly on later Greek epic. He does not achieve the monumental character or the immediacy of Homeric poetry, nor that psychological deepening of epic narrative which is one of the outstanding features of those achievements of Hellenistic poets which influenced Roman epic art.

There is some evidence which indicates that Quintus' *Post-Homerics* were used as a model in the writing of a short epic about the fall of Troy, a work handed down under the name of Triphiodorus. Besides the version in a mediaeval manuscript, there is also a small fragment on a papyrus which dates from around 300 AD and hence the poet's lifetime. The *Suda*, a Byzantine encyclopaedia that contains many short biographies, tells us that Triphiodorus came from Egypt and worked as a grammarian. He wrote a book on Homer's similes together with epics about the Battle of Marathon and the Amazon Hippodamia, and also a new version of the *Odyssey* which was marked by the absence of certain letters of the alphabet. Thus he appears as a scholar who was a philologist as well as a poet, a man of a type frequently found in Hellenism, and then again later in Italian Humanism.

The Conquest of Troy is not a very attractive poem. Like Quintus' work, it is based on a retelling of the tale in a mythographical manual. What is of interest, however, is the liberal use of Virgil (i.e. of a Latin model).

A most peculiar text has only recently been discovered on papyrus. Its hexameters, not too flowing, but correct and full of Homerisms, describe a vision of heaven experienced by the Christian Dorotheus, the son of Quintus. The 350 lines of this poem are extremely difficult to comprehend because of many gaps caused by holes in the papyrus. But one thing which is clear is that the vision is that of an audience with the King of Heaven. The spirits who serve there bear titles and perform functions known from the protocol at the Roman Emperor's court. The narrator is asked to perform some task – it is not quite clear just what it entails – of such a heavenly courtier. He is not altogether up to the job, and is punished severely for his failure, but finally Christ pardons him. The reconciliation is effected through a heavenly act of baptism, and the narrator is finally sent away with good counsel for his life on earth.

In Books 7 and 8 of his ecclesiastical history, Eusebius mentions two men called Dorotheus who both lived around 300 AD, either of whom could be the author of this work. One belonged to the clergy of the church in Antioch and was known for his Greek education; the other was an official at the court of Diocletian, executed during the Emperor's major persecution of Christians.

From nearer the middle of the fourth century AD is the work of a certain Naumachius, a didactic poem about the proper behaviour of a wife, of which several lines are featured in the aforementioned *Florilegium* by John Stobaeus. Moral-didactic poetry of this kind was also written by Christians. A papyrus from about the same period contains a poem with twenty-five stanzas of three anapaestic lines each; the lines of each stanza in turn begin with the same letter of the alphabet. The text gives instructions for Christian living. As in Methodius' *hymnus* (see p. 382) and some popular shanties likewise preserved on papyrus (see p. 383), the metre shows a slight uncertainty in the treatment of quantitative distinctions, and a partial consideration of stress.

When in 362 AD the Emperor Julian barred all Christians from teaching grammar, claiming that only the followers of the old religion were entitled and able to explain Homer and other ancient poets, the Bishop Apollinaris or Apollinarius of Laodicaea in Syria wrote long poetical works for use in Christian schools. He recast stories from the Old Testament in Homeric hexameters, but also in the form of tragedies and comedies after the manner of Euripides and Menander, and as Pindaric odes. He also composed songs and hymns for church services. Unfortunately, we only know about them from ecclesiastical historiography of the fifth century AD, when this poetry was still read.

A paraphrase of the Psalms in very elegant Homeric hexameters has been handed down under the name of Apollinarius, but its authorship is uncertain, all the more so because this kind of Biblical poetry which had begun one generation earlier on the Latin side (see p. 401), was produced well into the fifth century AD. Apollinarius was a learned theologian who never shied away from debate. In a large number of treatises, he expressed his opinion on the main issues discussed in the late fourth century AD. In questions concerning the doctrine of the trinity he sided with the view sanctioned by the Council of Nicaea and later recognised as orthodox. However, his christology (i.e. his attempt to define the relationship between the human and the divine nature of Christ) was finally condemned as heterodox; and hence all his writings, including the poetical works, were lost.

Even though Apollinarius' poetical production may well have been inspired by the controversy between Christians and pagans, the speed at which it was written as well as its later continuation prove how small the practical distinctions between Christian and pagan literature had become by the mid-fourth century AD when both drew on the same educational tradition. What is true of poetry also applies to grammatical and antiquarian scholarship. Likewise, both parties used the same methods of philosophical analysis and argumentation, in spite of the fact that their basic ideologies differed especially with regard to philosophical issues.

8 RHETORIC, GRAMMAR, AND SCIENCE

I have already mentioned Eunapius' collection of lives of the philosophers, which also contains much information about the famous teachers of rhetoric in the fourth century AD, especially the professors in Athens who were paid by the state. Around 300 AD one of them was Julianus of Cappadocia who taught a large number of students including he who was to be the most prominent sophist of the next generation. This was a man called Prohaeresius, a Christian from an Armenian family, who was temporarily forced to stop lecturing during the short reign of the Emperor Julian. Before coming to study in Athens Prohaeresius had been taught by the rhetor Ulpian in Antioch. Another of Julian of Cappadocia's students was the Arab Diophantus, the main rival of Prohaeresius. Such rivalries were often quite violent and the animosity between the teachers led to fights among their disciples. One incident involved a fight between the students of Prohaeresius and those of the Spartan Apsines; during this fight there was even some bloodshed and the matter was taken to court where the professor Julian – then already quite an old man – pleaded for his student Prohaeresius who had been named as responsible for the events.

Many of the rhetors or sophists of the period also wrote textbooks, and theoretical treatises on the art of oratory; but we have no extant texts from those rhetorical writings of the period which we know to have existed. One man who seems to have produced no such works at all is Prohaeresius, whose influence as a teacher is, however, described in the writings of Himerius and Libanius, much more famous figures than Prohaeresius, being the most prominent orators of the second half of the century.

Apparently for didactical reasons, rhetorical training was sometimes combined with medical education. We know of the iatrosophist or physician-cum-rhetor Zeno from the island of Cyprus, an older contemporary of Julian, which indicates that most of his lifetime fell into the third century AD. Zeno had several students who also worked in both capacities. One of them was Magnus of Nisibis, a Syrian city east of the border marked by the Euphrates. Magnus later taught in Alexandria; his colleague Oribasius of Pergamum went on to become the Emperor Julian's court physician. At the monarch's request, he compiled a huge collection of excerpts from older medical writing. Twenty-five of its seventy books are extant; they are one of our most important sources of information about medicine in the Hellenistic period and in the Imperial age. Oribasius also edited a concise version of this collection in nine books, likewise extant, as well as a comprehensive work in four books for domestic use by laymen. The existence of Latin, Syrian, and Arabic translations of Oribasius' writings prove their wide and lasting influence. They are the result of medical research carried out exclusively at the desk, and a good illustration of what the profession of iatrosophist was about.

During this period grammatical studies which aimed at the conservation and interpretation of the Classic literary heritage went on largely undisturbed. This was the basis for the rapid development of Christian Biblical exegesis. I have already mentioned that some poets also distinguished themselves as grammarians; commentaries and encyclopaedias from the Byzantine Middle Ages also feature a number of names which seem to belong to the early fourth century AD, but those do not include any especially prominent or innovative exponents of this discipline.

On the Latin side the revival of grammatical studies in the period of incipient reforms is documented by the textbook written by Marius Plotius Sacerdos towards the end of the third century AD. This work was produced in several stages, as the prefaces to the individual books tell us. The author began with a conventional survey of phonetics and word formation to which he then added first a book on inflection, and then one on metrics.

In contrast to grammatical studies, mathematical research in the fourth as well as in the third century AD did produce some outstanding results. This includes also the application of mathematical methods in astronomy, geography, and mechanics. In all of these areas, there were still productive thinkers in the sixth century AD. During the reign of Diocletian, the famous mathematician Pappus taught in Alexandria. Much of his large literary output is extant, including a commentary on Euclid's *Elements* in an Arabic translation. He also produced a partly extant commentary on Ptolemy's major work, the *Almagest*. Pappus' greatest achievements are documented in a collection of eight individual treatises, a work of which a small part was lost, whereas the last two treatises seem to have remained unfinished. The author discusses a great variety of problems and solutions from older mathematical literature, to which he adds his own further reflections. In the Armenian language, there is a book about the geography of the inhabited parts of the earth, written by Moses of Chorene, one of the founders of the Armenian church and Armenian national literature, in the fifth century AD. Moses tells us that his geography was based on the corresponding lost work by Pappus.

In the late fourth century AD one of the mathematicians who worked in Alexandria was Serenus. His writings are partly extant; they were about the theory of conical sections, following the classic authority in this field, the mathematician Apollonius of Perga from the third century BC. A man who appears to belong to the same period as Serenus is Theon who also lived in Alexandria where his daughter Hypatia later taught Platonic philosophy. In 415 AD she was lynched in the streets of the city by a Christian mob incited to riot by the Patriarch.

Theon wrote several commentaries on the astronomical works of Ptolemy, and produced a critical edition of the *Elements* and other Euclidian writings from the third century BC. This is typical of the period in question when it was above all pagans who made efforts to preserve Classic texts in their pure form, and not only literary Classics in the narrower sense. The extant mediaeval manuscript versions of Euclid's work are based on Theon's edition.

More information about Theon – for instance, concerning his interest in astrology – is found in the rich Byzantine scholia commentaries on the didactic poem about astronomy by Aratus, a work from the third century BC. These commentaries, featuring scholarly observations amassed over several centuries, are a mine of information from older, lost writings on astronomy and mathematics. The same can be said for the extant commentaries which Eutocius of Ascalon wrote in the first half of the sixth century AD on works by Apollonius and Archimedes, the mathematical Classics of the third century BC. Eutocius was a student of the mathematician and architect Isidorus of Miletus, the man commissioned jointly with Anthemius of Tralles to build the church of Saint Sophia in Constantinople. Isidorus also wrote commentaries on works by Archimedes, and on the book about the construction of vaults by Heron of Alexandria (see p. 145). The dome of the Hagia Sophia which Isidorus erected collapsed after only a few years, but after repair work carried out by his eponymous nephew it held, and still does to this day.

Isidorus' colleague Anthemius was also a writer who produced among other things a partly extant work on the making of a burning glass. The continuity of such scholarly work even in the Late Classical age is indicated by the fact that two of Anthemius' brothers distinguished themselves as physicians, and another as a grammarian.

Finally, I must mention the writings of the land surveyors, the *gromatici* or *agrimensores*, texts preserved in a Late Classical corpus. From the very first the Romans had paid great attention to the observance of religious rules when choosing the site for a temple or a settlement. Those rules were presumably of Etruscan origin, for the apparatus used in taking the necessary measurements was called *groma*, a word derived from the Greek *gnomon* via the Etruscan language. The reason was that the Greek world had provided the mathematical foundations for the construction and the use of this fairly complicated piece of equipment. The practice of surveying continued throughout the Imperial age, also in the service of administration and jurisdiction. Each legion, for instance, had its team of surveyors and to this day the ground plan of a legion's camp can be detected in many cities on the soil of the Empire. The practice of surveying found frequent literary expression, for the necessary techniques had to be taught and passed on. This is why the Late Classical corpus features only part of the older writings in their original form. Most of them were shortened and adapted to the linguistic and material conditions of later times. As a source of information for the cultural and linguistic historian, the collection is of enormous value.

As before (see p. 422), I have looked forward to the final years of Classical culture; so once again, I must return to that stage in the chronological order of events which my account has reached.

8

THE CHRISTIAN EMPIRE

1 GENERAL REMARKS

Late Classical culture with its characteristic features completed its development on the foundation created by Diocletian and Constantine. During the Middle Ages it found a continuation in two different ways, in the Latin West and Greek East respectively.

After the turmoil of the third century AD and the complicated quadripartite government of Diocletian, Constantine had once again established a true dynastic rule. His claim that his father Constantius Chlorus descended from Claudius, the conqueror of the Goths, was presumably a piece of purely fictitious genealogy; however, it put Constantine in a position to proclaim the advent of a new Flavian dynasty. This dynasty found an early end with the death of Julian in 363, AD but that event did as little damage to the lasting impact of the dynastic idea as had the bloody dramas enacted within the reigning family under Constantine and his successors.

The distribution of power between several regents remained a common practice: Constantine's immediate successors, for instance, were his three sons Constantine II, Constans, and Constantius II. Collective rule could seem advisable for security reasons: for example, when wars had to be fought on different borders simultaneously, or when none of those men qualified for the succession had a sufficient power base to ensure that he would be an undisputed sole ruler. Thus Constantius II did not become the only holder of power until 340 AD, after conquering a usurper who had killed his brother Constans, the latter in turn having killed Constantine II in a civil war. When government was divided between the two sons of Theodosius II in 395 AD, this was only one of many such measures and not – as it was later read – a deliberate separation of the Latin West from the Greek East.

The Christianisation which Constantine had begun became the dominant trait of the Roman state's development. If only for the sake of preserving the unity of the Empire's population, each one of Constantine's successors was forced to become involved in theological-dogmatical debate, whose successive quarrels caused a corresponding series of ecclesiastical schisms. At the same time, the social and political influence of ecclesiastical office-holders grew. Constantine had already given the bishops some privileges normally reserved for high-ranking state officials, as for instance the use of the *cursus publicus*, the state's courier and transport service. This was soon followed by the granting of jurisdictional powers and frequently, in times when the state machinery was defunct, administrative and political acts were performed exclusively by the bishops and their clergy.

Such a state of affairs came about with particular frequency in the west of the Empire, where the great migrations brought much more chaos than in the eastern provinces. Consequently, people in the West were particularly likely to see the church not least as a legal order; and it is in the West that we find great ecclesiastical leaders like Ambrosius of Milan, who forced the reigning orthodox and victorious Emperor Theodosius I to do penance in public, or Pope Leo I, who did not hesitate to use all the diplomatic and administrative power of his office when Italy was under a military threat. It was the social status and the administrative experience of the Popes, and not any theological superiority, which ensured their final say in dogmatical controversies.

Soon after the death of Constantine, Constantius II introduced the first measures to suppress the practice of pagan religion. How strictly the rules were applied depended first on regional variables and it was not until the reign of Theodosius II that official policies had major effects, such as the destruction of great and famous shrines and temples. Still, around 360 AD Julian already noted with great displeasure that the practice of the old religion was declining, even without official interference.

On two occasions paganism replied with an open counter-reaction. The first is linked with the name of the Emperor Julian, a nephew of Constantius II; it ended instantly with Julian's death on the battlefield, after no more than two years during which he was sole regent. The other reaction had an even smaller impact; it originated from unconverted families among the Senatorial nobility of Rome, who wanted to use the short reign of the Imperial usurper Flavius Eugenius, a professor of rhetoric proclaimed in Rome by a Germanic general, to reinstate the old cults. The defeat of Eugenius in the civil war against Theodosius I in 394 AD put an early end to this endeavour.

It is significant that neither of the two leaders of the church at the respective times, Athanasius and Ambrosius, took the pagan reaction too seriously. Bloody persecutions of Christians only occurred in the context of street riots, and not on the basis of official decrees. The same goes for the suppression of heretics or pagans by the Christian state, in spite of the fact that plenty of bishops were banished by Emperors. This happened also during the dogmatical controversies which threatened the unity of the church, when the measure of banishment would be followed by the appointment of an exponent of current orthodoxy to the vacant see. The belligerent Athanasius incurred this fate no less than five times. What caused general horror, however, was the execution of Priscillianus in 384 AD. This man, who had established a separate church with an ascetic orientation in Spain, was put to death together with some of his companions at the order of the usurper Emperor Magnus Maximus who resided in Trier, on the pretext of serious legal offences.

The most consequential historical event of the period in question was the battle of Adrianopolis in 378 AD. The Goths had been forced out of their settlements in southern Russia by the invading Huns from central Asia. On their search for new land they crossed the border along the Danube, completely annihilating the Roman troops who opposed them. During the fighting Valens, one of the two reigning Emperors at the time, was killed. The Barbarian raids which now continued for decades were different from those in previous centuries, when the raiders had only been out for loot, whereas now Goths and Gepidi, Vandals and Burgundi, Franks and Suevi intended to settle in the cultivated and developed lands of the Empire. After the first catastrophe, the standard reaction of the Roman state was to make allies of the intruders by allocating them land near the frontier and at the same time entrusting them with the defence of the border against new attackers following after.

The Germanic and Sarmatic tribes formed only a small minority among the traditional residents of the provinces, but they were much more accustomed to warfare. Their superior military strength, combined with the pressure of new migrating groups, thus made them head for the richer regions of the Empire. During the fifth century AD, this caused the creation of tribal states in Italy, Gaul, Spain, and north Africa, as territories which were *de facto* independent and only nominally under the authority of the Emperor. The tribal communities would live there according to their own laws, as a military nobility and as the holders of political power, beside those indigenous residents of the provinces who by then had become very much Romanised. The Germanic tribes were also an alien element as regards religion, for they had all been converted during the middle years and the second half of the fourth century AD when they accepted the creed which was then the official one favoured by the Emperor. The Germans held on to their faith even when the Council of Constantinople in 381 AD condemned all forms of Arianism, and confirmed the formula agreed at Nicaea. The only exception were the Franks, a mixed tribe which at roughly the same time crossed the lower Rhine and settled in northern and central Gaul. They at once adopted the Nicaean creed, and could thus be much more easily Romanised, once they had arrived on Gallic soil. The instant Christianisation of all intruders, however, also shows their general readiness to accept the superior culture of the conquered country which they admired.

This latter attitude was particularly well exemplified by the many Germanic individuals who rose to the very highest offices in the Imperial army and administration, and who without any exception proved to be loyal servants of the Empire. One example is the Vandal Stilicho who managed to ensure the safety of Italy for many years during which he acted as supreme military commander and representative of the Western Emperor Honorius, a man hardly fit to govern. When Stilicho was murdered at the behest of the Eastern Emperor Arcadius, the Visigoths were able to invade and loot the city of Rome; this, of course, was an event which made a deep and lasting impression on contemporaries.

The facts which I have stated in this outline indicate clearly enough that since the reign of Diocletian the centre of the Empire had lain in the East. Only in the Latin West, target of the deflected flow of migrating tribes, we find such phenomena as the formation of Germanic states on Roman soil, and the official abandoning of entire provinces, like that of Britain to the Anglo-Saxons, and of the region between the Danube and the Alps to the Bavarians. This development was at last also legally concluded with the abdication of the last emperor residing in the West in 476 AD. The recovery of Italy and north Africa, connected with the destruction of the Ostrogothic and Vandal states, was an enterprise rooted in the foreign and military policy of the firmly established eastern Roman Empire, which had a particular interest in establishing political ties between Constantinople and the Pope of Rome as the spiritual centre of the church.

Around the same time as the last Emperor in the West was dethroned by a Germanic adventurer, the East managed to free itself of the individual influence of German personalities and families. They were replaced by even more uncivilised and unspent soldiers from eastern Anatolia and Armenia; those, however, were men whose homes had been part of the civilised world for centuries, and who were thus not regarded as Barbarians. In the East, the Roman Empire preserved its unity which it had successfully defended against the Persians for centuries. The regions of the West, on the other hand, developed progressively different physiognomies, and lost their strong cultural and linguistic ties with the East. This can be explained as a consequence of the regional symbiosis between the Roman population and different Germanic tribes: a problematic development, especially at the beginning, but one which in the long run produced relationships that were indeed peaceful and conducive to cultural endeavour.

The new co-operation was first put to the test at the Battle of the Catalaunian Plains in central France, where in 451 AD the last attack of the Huns was repelled by Visigoths from southern Gaul and Franks from northern Gaul, supporting the efforts of Aëtius, the last local representative of an orderly Roman provincial administration. The reign of the Gothic King Theodoric around 500 AD favoured the late flowering of Latin intellectual life in Italy. It outlasted even the fall of the Ostrogothic state, and only became extinct when the Langobardians invaded in 568 AD. In the state of the Visigoths in Spain and southern France, there was a considerable amount of literary activity in Latin until the Islamic conquest in 712 AD, and a similar survival can be observed during the much shorter period of Vandal rule in modern-day Tunisia between the early fifth and the mid-sixth centuries AD.

Political history from the second half of the fourth century AD onwards was marked by the dissolution of the Empire in its western half, by heavy fighting with the Persian host on the eastern border, and not least by perennial state demands exceeding the economic capacity of the population, in order to cover expenses for the military, for the mushrooming bureaucracy, and for the luxurious life at court. Nevertheless, this epoch saw many cultural achievements, including ones of a literary kind. In spite of the flooding of some of its territories by Barbarian invasions, the Roman state, renewed by the reforms of Diocletian and Constantine, offered once again the fixed framework which the third century AD had lacked. Moreover, Asia Minor, Syria, and Egypt remained entirely unaffected by the torrents of the migrations, which in the East were only felt in Greece and the northern Balkans. Hence intellectual life was at its richest in non-European regions, and that break of cultural continuity which enables the historian to talk of the end of the Classical age was not experienced in the eastern Empire until about 600 AD, in the wake of the temporary Persian and the permanent Arab conquest of Syria, Palestine, and Egypt.

The reign of Justinian in the mid-sixth century AD was characterised by a particularly large number of different and very conscious borrowings from Classic traditions. A good example is his major legislative work through which Roman legal tradition was preserved for posterity in a Latin form. Classicist trends in this sense can be observed repeatedly in the Late Classical age as, for example, under the Emperor Theodosius II in the fourth and fifth decades of the fifth century AD when legal studies were likewise particularly promoted and a re-established university in Constantinople was endowed with chairs for Greek and Latin grammar and rhetoric. This conscious return to tradition was an important element in the conservation of the Empire's unity. In the West, on the other hand, the process of regional differentiation led away from the global cultural uniformity of the Roman Empire, even if there were individual efforts to preserve parts of the Classic heritage. In this context, the dethronement of Romulus Augustulus by a Germanic *condottiere* in 476 AD appears as an event of great significance, however small its practical, political impact may have been at the time.

2 GRAMMARIANS AND ANTIQUARIANS

I have already talked about the unbroken tradition of specialist scientific writing, particularly in the mathematical sciences and in medicine (see p. 431). An even stronger continuity can be observed in grammar, the basis of the entire educational tradition with its literary orientation.

The continued presence of grammatical writing in the East is documented above all by a long series of commentaries on works of canonical status, produced throughout the Late Classical period and well into the Byzantine Middle Ages. In such commentaries the original texts were usually quoted extensively, which is why, although the commentaries frequently came to replace the originals, most of the original text was preserved. The most famous examples are commentaries on the systematic grammar by Dionysius Thrax from the second century BC, on the monographs by Apollonius Dyscolus about individual aspects of grammar from the second century AD, and on the works of Apollonius' son Herodianus, especially those about phonetics and accentuation.

A prominent figure from the late fourth century AD is Theodosius, who worked in Alexandria and wrote a much-used book on Greek inflexion, a study based on the work by Dionysius Thrax. Theodosius' book in turn became the subject of a commentary by Choeroboscus in the sixth century AD. The latter author was one of the professors of Greek grammar at the university of Constantinople, an institution re-established by the Emperor Theodosius II in 432 AD. Choeroboscus also wrote about rhetorical figures, and about orthography; and besides, he was the author of a grammatical commentary on the Psalms.

There was a growing demand for systematic textbooks on grammar, as spoken language moved farther away from canonised literary usage, based on the rules of Attic prose as written in the fourth century BC. Consequently there was no fundamental difference between the respective roles played by the professors of Greek and Latin grammar whom Theodosius II appointed: all of them were concerned with the cultivation of an idiom which a Rhomaean, a Greek-speaking Roman citizen, had to acquire and use like a foreign language.

A good example of how in this period solid traditional knowledge could sometimes be combined with strange speculation, is the work by Horapollon. In the fifth century AD, this Egyptian from Nilopolis used the Coptic language to write a treatise about the interpretation of ancient Egyptian hieroglyphs; the extant version is a Greek translation by an otherwise unknown Philippus. The curious fact is that some of the characters are read correctly, although neither the author nor the translator had any idea at all about the system of hieroglyphic writing. The reasons given for the author's *Readings* are merely speculative and sometimes pretty fantastical at that. This contradiction proves the existence of a traditional lore about some of the characters of hieroglyphic writing, which was still to be seen on many Egyptian monuments at that time, although knowledge of the system as a whole had disappeared, and the hieroglyphs were perceived merely as mysterious symbols. Traces of such a lore can be found also in the report by the historian Ammianus (see p. 347) about an Egyptian obelisk erected in Rome.

In poetic exegesis, another branch of grammatical studies, an innovation of the period in question was the form of the scholia commentary. Commentaries had originally been published as separate books, whereas in Byzantium it gradually became common practice to present the original text side by side with a running commentary, compiled from records of older interpretation. Such run-on scholia commentaries certainly had more predecessors than only the originally Hellenistic custom of explaining difficult words in a text by marginal or interlinear glosses. The most important inspiration may have come from the so-called *catenae* commentaries of Christian authors (see p. 409), who collated interpretations of individual Biblical passages from different exegetical works. Nevertheless, some writers in the Christian Empire still produced independently published commentaries, as we know from references in the scholia. Zosimus of Ascalon, for example, a scholar from the fifth or sixth century AD, is quoted as the author of exegetical works on Classic prose, as well as of biographical studies on Classic writers.

Besides scholia on literary texts, and commentaries that began as supplements to older theoretic-grammatical works and developed into scholarly publications in their own right, the most important way of passing on the results of grammatical scholarship was through lexicons. There were very different types of such reference works, produced from the Early Imperial age until the very last epochs of Byzantine history. The largest and most important of those lexicons designed as aids for readers of ancient poetry was published by Hesychius of Alexandria in the fifth century AD. He based his writing on the subsequently lost work by Diogenianus from the second century AD but used also older dictionaries and commentaries. Hesychius' work has preserved hundreds of words from ancient Greek literature which would otherwise have been lost with the texts in which they were contained. Nevertheless, the semantic explanations which Hesychius gives are of very varied validity, and information on the sources is extremely scanty. In too many cases the vocabulary is simply passed on or copied without any deeper understanding.

Another type of lexicography during the period in question is represented by the so-called *etymologica*, although the earliest completely extant examples date from the Byzantine age. Those, however, contain a lot of material from the large *oeuvre* of the Alexandrian Oros, called the Black, who lived in Constantinople in the fifth century AD. He produced etymological studies based on Herodian, as well as writings on orthography, accentuation, nomenclature, and semasiology. Orthography was something which teachers had to devote particular attention to, because spelling followed the pronunciation of Classic Greek.

Partly extant is the etymological dictionary by the Egyptian Orion, who like Oros worked in Alexandria and Constantinople in the fifth century AD. Classical studies in etymology were different from the ones in our day and age, because of the lack of insights provided by the comparison of related Indo-Germanic languages. We find some fairly obvious derivations based on the identity of word components and semantic elements, but there are also frequent speculations about the relationship between the form of a word and that of the material object it signifies, as well as speculative reflections about the genesis of language as such. It was this factor which prevented the development of a sound method for etymological research, as it had been achieved, for instance, in the study of inflexion or accentuation.

We know that Orion also wrote an Atticist dictionary, in which common expressions from the Greek vernacular were listed beside the corresponding words and phrases from literary Attic. This type of reference work already had a long history, too (see p. 254).

An encyclopaedic work from the tenth century AD bears the strange title *Suda*, meaning fence or stockade, and indicating its very mixed content. Among other things, it features an alphabetically ordered sequence of biographies of famous intellectuals. This is a particular variant of the genre of works 'about famous men', including short biographies and bibliographies of great men in history, art, philosophy, and literature, compiled to record and communicate knowledge pertaining to the educational canon. The author of the biographical encyclopaedia in the *Suda*, Hesychius of Miletus, lived around the turn of the fifth and sixth centuries AD. He also wrote a history of the world which above all contained curious facts; an extant excerpt is the account of the history of the city of Byzantium until the foundation of its successor Constantinople. This excerpt is not really historiography, but rather a compilation of antiquarian material.

From the beginning of the sixth century AD, we have a voluminous geographical encyclopaedia written by Stephen of Byzantium who used a large number of sources in his compilation. Besides the major geographical accounts by Strabo and Ptolemy, Stephen's work is by far our most important source of knowledge on Classical geography and toponymy. It has even preserved entire passages from the very earliest geographical writings of the sixth century BC.

Grammatical-antiquarian knowledge can be found in the extant writings of John Laurentius Lydus, who was born around 490 AD. During the reign of the Emperor Justinian Lydus made a career as a scientist as well as an administrator. He wrote a work about the months, in which he deals with aspects of chronology, but above all with festivals and customs linked with individual dates; his information is taken from literary sources. Another treatise is about all kinds of omens and their interpretation, and yet another is concerned with officials and their titles in the Roman republic and the Empire. These two were likewise the product of library research alone.

It may well be seen as characteristic of this kind of antiquarian literature in Greek that even its Christian authors in no way emphasised Christian elements. This shows that a Classicist trait in education survived even in Christian Late Classical society. This fact was explicitly recognised by the church as early as the fourth century AD, as we can see, for instance, in Basil's letter about the treatment of pagan-Greek Classic authors. Even the abovementioned biographical encyclopaedia of Hesychius did not include any Christian writers. When Hieronymus wrote his Latin treatise about famous men of the Christian era, his preface emphasised the intention that his work should be ranked beside the corresponding writings in the pagan tradition.

In this last period of Classical culture, the tradition of Latin grammatical studies is represented by several short as well as some longer works, which remained influential far into the Middle Ages.

Several shorter specialist grammatical treatises on aspects of orthography and metrics were handed down under the name of C. Marius Victorinus. Hieronymus reports the erection in 353 AD of a statue in Rome's Forum of Trajan which was then the site of two libraries, in recognition of Victorinus' merits as a teacher of rhetoric and grammar. We also learn from the same source that Victorinus was converted to Christianity as a very old man, and that in 362 AD he was one of the Christian teachers of grammar whom the Emperor Julian's edict barred from exercising their profession. More important, however, was Marius Victorinus' role as a translator and communicator of philosophical texts, especially of the Neo-Platonist school, and as a theological author taking part in the debate on Arianism (see p. 408).

A contemporary of Marius Victorinus was Hieronymus' teacher, Aelius Donatus. His textbook in two parts, for beginners and advanced students respectively, was used for centuries as the basis for instruction in Latin grammar; the first commentaries on the work appeared already in the Late Classical age. The short beginners' section is divided according to the eight parts of speech or different word classes, and the longer second section has a division into three books, after the manner of the *ars grammatica*. Both formats were already well-established conventions at the time Donatus was writing; we know nothing, however, of his immediate predecessors or models.

Donatus also wrote commentaries on six comedies by Terence. Five of those commentaries are extant, as well as the introduction to one on Virgil, with a biography of the poet. A long extant commentary on Virgil's

Aeneid likewise bears the name of Donatus, but it was actually written one generation later by Tib. Claudius Donatus.

A number of textbooks which give us an insight into the teaching of Greek have been handed down under the name of an otherwise unknown Dositheus, a grammarian who presumably lived in the second half of the fourth century AD. A Latin-Greek textbook structured after the familiar pattern of the *ars grammatica* is most probably genuine, even if its long use in instruction has led to much distortion through omissions and additions. An extant Greek–Latin glossary, on the other hand, is more likely a much later fabrication.

A contemporary of Dositheus was the learned Flavius Sosipater Charisius, mentioned by Hieronymus under the presumably misspelt name Charistus. In Hieronymus' edition of Eusebius' chronicle, this Charistus is described as a famous grammarian from Africa, under the heading of 358 AD. Charisius' *ars grammatica* in five books is extant with only a few gaps. It offers what may well be described as the most comprehensive source material for the reconstruction of grammar in the earlier Empire, as represented by names like Remmius Palaemon, Julius Romanus, or Flavius Caper. Charisius not only deals with grammar in the narrower sense: his first book treats basic concepts like word, syllable, or sound, and Books 2 and 3, the parts of speech and inflexion; but the following two volumes also feature some rhetorical chapters, as well as accounts of the theory of stylistic qualities and of metrics.

Shortly after Charisius came the grammarian Diomedes, whose *ars grammatica* in three books also took in poetics and metrics. Like the anonymous author of an *ars grammatica* found in the monastery of Bobbio, Diomedes used Charisius' work on top of other sources which were not drawn on by that unknown writer. The last among the authors of extant Latin grammars is Priscianus, who was a professor in Constantinople around 500 AD and came from the city of Caesarea in modern-day Morocco. Priscianus' *ars grammatica* is the most voluminous and the most valuable of its kind. It contains eighteen books, and is limited to grammatical subjects in the narrower sense of the term: word classes, inflexion, word formation, and syntax. The information given exceeds by far the requirements of schoolteaching. Numerous examples from literary texts document the phenomena discussed, and source material is frequently quoted at length. Some of the statements on linguistic theory are literal translations from Greek grammarians, and quite often Priscianus also refers to Greek texts in comparison. Priscianus' grammar became very popular, which is why it is extant in more than a thousand mediaeval manuscript versions.

Besides his comprehensive *ars grammatica*, Priscianus produced a short version of Books 6 to 13 of his major work for use in schools, as well as other writings. A metrical and grammatical commentary on the first verses of each of the twelve books in the *Aeneid* was styled as an *erotapocrisis*, in the form of questions and answers. Then there was a book about numerical signs, a treatise arguing the poetic character of Terence's comedies which were read as prose at the time, a translation of the rhetorical exercises of Hermogenes, and a poetic translation of Dionysius' didactic poem on geography from the second century AD.

The interpretation of poetry remained the most valued activity of all grammarians. Like their Greek counterparts, Latin scholia commentaries – for example, those on Lucan or Juvenal – have preserved fragments of Imperial exegesis. The most important evidence of this tradition is the major commentary by Servius – an extremely famous man in his time – on the three main works of Virgil, the *Eclogues*, the *Georgics*, and the *Aeneid*.

Like other comparable works, Servius' commentary on Virgil has not been handed down in its original form, but with considerable additions, as first noted by the Dutch philologist Daniel in the seventeenth century. Directly or through an intermediate text, those additions seem to stem from the abovementioned lost commentary by Donatus. Donatus' two *artes grammaticae* are the subject of two separate extant commentaries by Servius.

Like the *Saturnalia* of Macrobius (see p. 445), Servius' Virgilian exegesis documents a concern which was clearly widespread at that time among the educated classes. Those were loyal to the old, pre-Christian tradition, and thus keen to collect, order, and hand down traditional knowledge as comprehensively as possible. In the West where social and political structures were put to more severe tests it was naturally the tradition-conscious Senatorial nobility who were most prominent in such efforts. Servius' commentary tries to explain all aspects of Virgil's poetry, and to prove that the author was not only a master of the poetic craft, but also exemplary with regard to each and every kind of philosophical and general erudition. This gave Virgil the place which Homer had in the East, as father of all philosophy and science, and hence Servius repeatedly tried to refute any criticism of Virgil, as had been expressed occasionally in the tradition of grammatical scholarship.

Besides extensive linguistic-grammatical explanations which sometimes develop into digressions leading far away from Virgil's text, we thus find allegorical interpretations aimed at finding the philosophical or religious meaning of individual verses, as well as analyses of the rhetorical shaping of the text, and many individual illustrations of a mythological or antiquarian kind. It is especially the latter ones which make Servius' work a valuable source for the religious or cultural historian. None the less, the wealth of individual interpretations designed to convey factual information somewhat obscures those goals which a modern reader would have in mind: the summary and explanation of the argument, as well as the structural analysis.

Servius could already look back on a long tradition of Virgilian exegesis, which in turn had been fashioned on the model of Homeric exegesis begun three centuries earlier. Hence there are surprisingly close parallels between Homeric scholia and Servius' commentaries on the *Aeneid*, corresponding to the imitation of Homer in the Virgilian text which Servius interprets. The abovementioned additions to the commentary concern mainly aspects of rhetorical form, and aspects of mythology in the poem; from this, however, we can hardly infer the nature of the source. Some shorter works by Servius, all on metrics, are also extant. Others have been ascribed to him such as, for example, a Latin–Greek glossary of uncertain origin.

Virgilian exegesis as a means of structuring and handing down encyclopaedic knowledge can also be found in the *Saturnalia* by Ambrosius Theodosius Macrobius. This book was one of the main vehicles for the transfer of Classical learning to Latin-mediaeval culture.

Macrobius belonged to the circle of those Roman Senators who took an interest in literature. It is possible that he was the same Macrobius whose name is mentioned in a legal text as the *praefectus praetorio Italiae*, the chief administrator of Italy in 430 AD, to whom Avianus dedicated his poetic fables. The *Saturnalia* follow a long tradition, established by Plato, of using dialogue as a literary form in order to communicate philosophical or scientific information.

The narrative frame in the work describes the fictitious situation as follows: on the three holidays of the Saturnalia – the great popular festival which the old Roman calendar dated in the month of December – the leading Roman intellectuals of the period around 400 AD come together for scientific discussion. There is the famous orator and city prefect Q. Aurelius Symmachus Eusebius, to whose son Macrobius' work is dedicated; then his friend P. Vettius Agorius Praetextatus, also a holder of high offices and famous for his thorough knowledge of ancient Roman religion and pontifical law; their fellow Senator Nicomachus Flavianus, whose learned father had been the major instigator of an attempt to revive the old religion during the short reign of Eugenius and had committed suicide after Theodosius' victory; and finally, the poet Avianus, the aforementioned Servius, as well as some minor characters.

The conversation revolves around the poems of Virgil, whose rhetorical skill and whose erudition is to be proved by the mention of ever-new examples quoted from his work and explained. The discussion draws on a wealth of material from astronomy, rhetoric, pontifical law, mantics, cult, mythology, philosophy, chronology, and calendrics. It is spread out over seven books, of which the fourth and the sixth are only partly extant.

The work is based on a large number of literary sources and, corresponding to the multitude of topics mentioned, it is extremely varied in its content, perfectly in keeping with the conversational tone in which the whole thing is presented. But, in spite of the unsystematic variety, there is indeed a continuing thread, not only provided by Virgilian exegesis. Beyond that, the author pursues a theological intention, revealed in his interpretation of the many details from mythology and cultic tradition mentioned in the conversation, as references to the one universal God, in the sense of Neo-Platonist theology. Notwithstanding the respect expressed for the traditions of the old religion, the work still shows a rejection of polytheism and teaches the worship of one sole deity, to all practical intents and purposes identical with the sun god. The sun which we see every day, however, is seen as no more than a form of expression or a symbol of the purely spiritual universal God whose position in the spiritual world is matched by that of the sun in the visible one.

Such a henotheistic reinterpretation of the many cults and deities with the sun as the recipient of practical worship can also be observed in the attempt by the Emperor Julian to restore the old religion. By means of allegorical interpretation, likewise the pet tool of Macrobius, the old religion with its kaleidoscopic multitude of cults was to be endowed with a unified theology, and thus enabled to meet the challenge of Christian monotheism. The terminological arsenal was provided – like that for Christian theology – by Neo-Platonist philosophy; but beyond that, Neo-Platonism also provided the basic cosmological tenets, whose nature as irreconcilable with the Biblical belief in creation was not always perceived by contemporaries. The philosophically-educated pagans agreed with Christians in their rejection of the old myths and cults in their naive understanding that the reality with which men sought to connect on the path shown by religion was a purely spiritual one.

Some people have suggested that Macrobius' *Saturnalia* were, somewhat like the two major theological speeches by the Emperor Justinian, manifestos of a resurgent paganism. This view is almost certainly erroneous. Among educated people there were quite a few who saw no major difference between Neo-Platonist and Christian theology and who consequently even as Christians promoted the respectful cultivation of old religious traditions as part of a culture which was threatened in its entirety. Through allegorical-philosophical interpretation, the relevant mythological parts of Classic literature would lose their religiously offensive nature to any observer but a trained Christian theologian involved in the dogmatic debate. Some facts even suggest that Macrobius himself was a Christian. In any case, Christians as well as pagans belonged to those aristocratic circles in the city of Rome who, in the fifth and sixth centuries, made major efforts to preserve the literary tradition.

Another work by Macrobius is his long commentary on *Scipio's Dream*. This text concludes Cicero's monumental dialogue *Of the State*, which competes with Plato's treatise of the same name. In Cicero's work the main speaker in the dialogue, Scipio the Younger, is promised future glory by his grandfather, the conqueror of Hannibal. In a grand vision the old man shows him the greatness and the beauty of the cosmos, and enlightens him about the shortness and the insignificance of human life on earth as well as about the immortality of the soul. Scipio is admonished to work only for the good of the fatherland and thus to earn his soul a quick return to its home above the heavens.

Macrobius' commentary tries to interpret the image which Cicero spun together from older philosophical doctrines, in the sense of Neo-Platonist cosmology and psychology. In the process he mentions facts from many disciplines which were part of traditional philosophical teaching: for instance, astronomy, geography, or musical theory. Naturally, Macrobius knew Plato's treatise on the state; he was particularly keen on removing any possible contradiction between Plato and Cicero and, wherever possible, to find a verse from Virgil to confirm his interpretation. Especially in the form given to it by Porphyry, Neo-Platonist philosophy had become widely known in the Latin West, and was occasionally even developed further in the medium of Latin. In the following, I will mention some other traces of this Latin Neo-Platonism. Macrobius' commentary on Cicero was one of the fundamental influences on the world view of the Latin Middle Ages. Another work by him, dealing with the comparative grammar of Greek and Latin, is only partly extant.

A generation or so after Macrobius came Martianus Capella, about whose life and whose origin we know hardly anything at all. His most peculiar work gave the Middle Ages the canon of the Seven Liberal Arts of higher education. The encyclopaedic account in nine books is presented as an allegory: the god Mercury is wed to Philology, the personification of science. In honour of the couple, there are speeches in which the seven disciplines – grammar, dialectics, rhetoric, geometry, arithmetic, astronomy, and musical theory – present themselves and their basic teachings, often in a form that is so much abridged as to become incomprehensible. In some cases we can pinpoint the authors used as a source for the relevant parts of Capella's work. Like Macrobius, he interprets the deities in the sense of Neo-Platonist theology. His narrative contains occasional verses after the fashion of Menippean satire which, incidentally, also appears among the allegorical personifications.

The third communicator of grammatical learning to the Middle Ages besides Macrobius and Martianus Capella was Isidorus, a seventh-century Bishop of Hispala or Seville in Spain, which at that time was under the rule of the Visigoths. His most famous and most used work are the *Etymologies*, an encyclopaedic collection in twenty books. The first three contain an account of the seven *artes liberales*; the rest a kind of encyclopaedic dictionary featuring interesting facts from the most diverse branches of knowledge under individual word headings. Isidorus made extensive use of the works of Suetonius which were accessible to him in a much more complete form than they are to modern scholars. This is how he preserved valuable material from older grammatical studies.

Isidorus is the most important case in point for the modest late flowering of Classical culture under the Visigoths whose kingdom was conquered by the Arabs in 711 AD. His main achievement was the handing down of a wealth of knowledge to the Middle Ages. Much less successful in this respect was the grammarian Fulgentius, who worked in north Africa during the era of Vandal rule in the second half of the fifth century AD and who should not be confused with his younger namesake, the Bishop of Ruspe (see p. 552). Fulgentius' writings show clearly the manner in which at that time the knowledge of ancient mythology and its allegorical interpretation, the understanding of ancient linguistic usage, and a general knowledge of history were passed on. We may assume that such learning was common among his educated contemporaries, for the late flowering of poetry in the manner of the ancients demanded a public which was aware of those facts (see p. 595).

Three books by Fulgentius contain summaries of myths used by Virgil and instructions for their interpretation as providing insights into moral philosophy; they also feature explanations of archaic words and phrases in Virgil's diction. In a fourth book the author gives a most peculiar survey of world history, divided according to the twenty-three letters of the alphabet. Each of the twenty-three short descriptions of different epochs is written without the use of one respective letter. Such linguistic plays on letters and words were also common in contemporary poetry (see p. 400); their primary purpose was presumably to demonstrate the writer's skills, but, as in this case, they occasionally also served to facilitate the memorising of a text.

Mediaeval manuscripts featuring Fulgentius' works give his full name in different forms. This is not surprising considering that during the Late Classical age members of the upper classes bore particularly many names. But all these sources call this grammarian a *vir clarissimus*, that is a man of Senatorial rank. This shows once again that the didactic use of ancient literature had by that time long become a pursuit which was deemed fitting for upper-class people. To a large extent, the long late flowering of poetry in the ancient diction and metre (see p. 593) was also a result of the efforts of upper-class landholders, especially in the territories of the West where the power of Imperial government had steadily diminished. Both kinds of efforts, the grammarian-antiquarian and the literary-poetic, were complementary.

3 RHETORIC: THEORY AND LITERARY PRACTICE

In this sphere of intellectual life, which may well be called the most important one for the Classical educational tradition, the epoch of the

Christian Empire is represented by particularly many and particularly excellent achievements. Teaching had never been seriously disrupted in the major scholarly centres such as Athens, Ephesus, or Alexandria. We know this from the biographies written by Eunapius (see p. 402) which also contain information about famous professors of rhetoric. In the late fourth century AD Antioch came to surpass all other cities as a centre of rhetorical education. This ancient Seleucid city on the Orontes was not only one of the oldest Christian strongholds in the Orient and the early seat of an independent tradition of exegesis and theological instruction. It was also regarded as the most elegant city of the Empire, whose inhabitants indulged in tasteful luxury like nobody else.

Antioch owed its fame as the most acclaimed centre for rhetorical teaching to the work of Libanius. This man's vast literary legacy comprises sixty orations, most of them presumably written as pamphlets or public lectures; fifty-one declamations, that is exemplary speeches based on fictitious situations and designed for instruction; and well over 1,500 letters. From all of these together we get a fairly detailed image of the author, especially because the lectures include no less than five autobiographical pieces.

Libanius came from a distinguished pagan family in Antioch, where he was born in 314 AD. He was educated in Ascalon and Athens where a professorship was offered to him as early as 340 AD. He then taught in Nicomedia, and, at the Emperor's special request, in the capital Constantinople. In 357 AD, however, he returned to his native city, where his work until his death in 393 AD made him extremely famous. Libanius was a close friend of the Emperor Julian, but was also held in high regard by the Christian monarch Theodosius I. This enabled him to act as spokesman for Antioch in several memoranda addressed to the Emperor, seeking to avert draconian punishments after street riots, or protesting against the destruction of precious temples by fanatical hordes of monks. Among Libanius' most gifted pupils were the Christians Basil and John Chrysostom. The addressees of his letters include all but a few of the prominent politicians and intellectuals of the period.

Like Aelius Aristides, Libanius had studied Classic literature to such an extent that his mastery of the Atticist literary language very soon led to the recognition of his writings as stylistic models equivalent to Classic texts themselves. He had a special love for the speeches of Demosthenes, which he read again and again. Such literary studies were pursued as a means of formal linguistic training, and the extensive mythological and antiquarian knowledge which they brought came as a natural by-product. But the curiosity for facts, for instance, the desire to know what was the name of the Amazon queen conquered by Theseus, or which court in Athens had tried cases of murder by poison in the fourth century BC, had nothing to do with scientific history. Its aim was to reassure the person who possessed such knowledge of being part of a living unbroken tradition, reaching back to the time of idolised Classic Greece.

Hence, Libanius and his pupils would have been much less inclined than the modern reader to regard certain pursuits as ivory-towered or anachronistic. In the context of his rhetorical teaching, for instance, Libanius wrote an apology for Socrates, referring to the bill of indictment by the sophist Polycrates, which was published soon after the trial of 399 BC and which itself was a piece of largely literary-fictitious character. We must also consider that the dedicated cultivation of the Classic tradition was meant to protect a civilisation which was perceived as threatened not only by the attacks of the Barbarians, but also by Christianity. This was a logical assumption in view of the fact that there were still strong anti-educational forces within the church, especially among the monks, who rejected Classic tradition as objectionable.

Libanius was not really interested in either philosophy or specialist sciences, and the Roman-Latin educational world remained alien to him. This is why he complained bitterly when, in the general context of a legal Classicism, the Imperial administration under Theodosius I recruited more and more legal scholars for public service and showed less preference for candidates who had acquired a formal and literary education in rhetorical schools. The medium of legal instruction at the time was Latin, in the West as well as in the East, at the famous legal school of Berytus or Beirut.

Beside the letters, which were all written with a view to publication and which deal with personal as well as public and literary matters, Libanius' topical writings are of particular interest. This part of his literary legacy contains petitions in which the sophist or professor of rhetoric acted in time-honoured fashion as advocate and spokesman for his native city. There are also eulogies on the reigning Emperor in which the official monarchic ideology is expressed from a pagan point of view; speeches expressing grief for the victims of natural catastrophes; public appeals; an obituary on the Emperor Julian after his death in battle, praising a man with whom Libanius agreed in his desire for the preservation of the old religion; lectures for the moral instruction of his fellow citizens, and much more.

Since the time of Isocrates rhetorical instruction had never abandoned the claim that formal training also served the purpose of moral instruction according to generally recognised principles. While philosophical schooling sought to achieve this by providing insights into the natural order, the rhetorical schools pursued the same goal by constantly restating, in a convincing linguistic form, those principles which were deemed good and just by all men. Hence the cultivation of a sententious manner of expression had a double function: first, to find the most economical and thus the most effective expression of an idea, and besides, to make the pupil remember the rules of proper living. It was only the ethical implications of an otherwise purely formal schooling which enabled rhetoric to rival philosophy as an educational force for so long, and with such great success. Because of this fact, Libanius would preach morality to his fellow citizens, as Dion of Prusa had done three hundred years before him; for example, in his fifty-third speech, which censures excessive indulgences during the numerous festivals in the Antiochian calendar. Very similar statements can be found in the sermons which Libanius' pupil John Chrysostom delivered in his episcopal church in Constantinople.

Born around the same time as Libanius was his friend Himerius, whom Libanius met in a rhetorical contest in Nicomedia in 350 AD. Himerius came from Prusias, modern-day Brussa, in northwestern Asia Minor. He taught for a long time in Athens, until the unpleasantness of quarrels with his rival Prohaeresius (see p. 430) caused him to leave in 362 AD, when he joined the court of Julian in Antioch. After Prohaeresius' death in 368 AD Himerius returned to Athens where he seems to have lived until the penultimate or the last decade of the century.

Readers in the Classical age had access to about eighty speeches by Himerius; thirty-two of those are extant in mediaeval manuscripts, if mostly in a much shortened form. Himerius' reputation among contemporaries and subsequent generations did not match that of Libanius, but nevertheless he had among his pupils some major ecclesiastical personalities, such as Basil and Gregory of Nazianzus. Most of Himerius' speeches belong to the context of teaching. We find the common declamations about fictitious subjects, but also addresses to his Athenian students, and the latter pieces give us a fairly detailed impression of the atmosphere in Athens, as a relatively small city which kept its importance because of its ancient fame and the constant influx of young students. There are also some pieces by Himerius which are not didactic, such as an obituary on his son and speeches on the occasion of weddings; but unlike Libanius' work, political pamphlets or lectures are absent in this category. Himerius occasionally hints at professional difficulties which he incurred as a firm follower of the old religion.

Himerius' style was soon ridiculed by his contemporary Libanius. Himerius belonged to a stylistic tradition opposed to Atticism, in as much as it included all means of poetic expression in oratory, and did not recognise the strict limitation of certain words and phrases to specific literary genres. Thus Himerius' speeches are full of quotations and reminiscences from ancient lyric and epic poetry, and his diction is more flowery and bombastic than that of any other rhetor. He also goes farther than anyone else in the rhythmic regularisation of literary prose; this fact likewise shows his ambition to equal the poets. Among the prose writers which Himerius chose as models, Plato ranked first; but this preference did not go together with any serious interest in philosophy. Another noteworthy fact is that to Himerius as to other contemporary rhetors, the orators of the second century AD, such as Aristides and Dion, ranked as Classics who deserved to be imitated just as well as the Attic prose authors of the fourth century BC.

However, not all those who cultivated rhetoric were indifferent or even hostile to philosophy. From the period in question we have quite a few impressive examples of the type of philosopher appearing already at the time of Favorinus and Dion: the type of man who would express his philosophical convictions and teachings with the means of the orator's art.

The first one to be mentioned here is Themistius. He came from a noble landowning family in eastern Asia Minor but spent most of his life in the capital Constantinople, where he was head of a school in the final years before his death around 390 AD. In spite of being a pagan, he was well-respected by all the reigning emperors during his lifetime. He became a member of the Senate and Prefect of Constantinople, and Theodosius I even employed him as tutor of the crown prince Arcadius. All of Themistius' speeches, extant partly in Syrian translation and partly in the Greek original, are Imperial eulogies, written on occasions such as jubilees, or acts of clemency. They give us valuable insights into the monarchic ideology of the period. Themistius' teaching, however, seems to have mainly centred on philosophy, although his method was not didactic discourse among a small circle of pupils as was common in the philosophical schools of Athens or Alexandria, but rather rhetorically styled lectures offered to a wider audience. This preference is mentioned in the extant text of one of his speeches.

Looking at those of Themistius' writings which were handed down to us, we may well see a reflection of the aforementioned manner of teaching. Although we have none of his exegetical works, which were still read by the Patriarch Photius in the ninth century AD, some of Themistius' paraphrases of Aristotle's didactic writings are extant. The *Pragmatica* of the Aristotelian corpus are lecture scripts or notes not intended for publication and thus without literary embellishment. By rewriting them in standard literary language, they were to be made accessible and comprehensible to a wider public with its well-established reading habits.

What is particularly remarkable is the one-sided preference which Themistius professed for Aristotle. In most of the philosophical schools of the period, the teachings of Plato were dominant, in the renewed form created by Plotinus and his successors. Nevertheless, Aristotle was also widely read in those schools (see p. 375). He was held in high regard as a representative of ancient or Classic philosophy, and the conviction that Plato and Aristotle had essentially taught the same justified the use of Aristotelian terms to explain Platonic thought. Porphyry, pupil and successor of Plotinus, had written those commentaries on Aristotle's works which were to be the standard ones for centuries, as an introduction to the study of philosophy in general. Yet the world view which all philosophical teaching of the period shared, and which it defended not least against Christianity, was based on Plato. Some scholars have suggested that Themistius' Aristotelianism can be put down to his desire to mediate between philosophy and Christianity in the capital of the Christian Empire, where an open declaration for Plato could at that time only be taken as an anti-Christian stance. This was without any doubt the case in the centres of philosophical teaching in Athens and Alexandria.

The second name among the philosophical rhetors is that of the Emperor Julian, Flavius Claudius Julianus, born in 331 AD as the great-nephew of Constantine. Miraculously, Julian and his stepbrother Gallus survived the bloodbath perpetrated among their family by mutinous soldiers. The reigning Emperor Constantius II regarded Julian with much suspicion, and his brother Gallus was even executed for a trivial offence in 354 AD at the Emperor's order. Julian grew up under close surveillance, but far from the court, at ever-new locations chosen by Constantius. When he was in Nicomedia and in an Imperial domain in eastern Asia Minor Julian's tutors were the two Bishops Eusebius and George, who were close to the court; but he also came into contact with Libanius. At that time Julian developed a profound contempt for those high-ranking churchmen who were involved in courtly intrigues. In Ephesus, where he was moved next, he got to know the philosopher Maximus, and under his influence Julian secretly became a convert to the Neo-Platonism of Iamblichus' school, that is of the mystical-theurgical kind. In the wake of Gallus' alleged conspiracy, Constantius ordered Julian to come to Milan, where he was saved by the Empress's intercession on his behalf.

After a short stay in Athens, Julian was called to Milan once more in 355 AD: this time, however, in order to be appointed as *Caesar* or co-regent, and to be married to the Emperor's youngest sister, as well as to be entrusted with the supreme command of the troops stationed in Gaul. Known to all as a bookworm, the prince nevertheless turned out to be a competent general. He drove the Franks out of Cologne, routed the Alemannic tribes in a major battle near Strasbourg, secured the border on the Rhine, and established regular shipping between Gaul and Britain. In 360 AD, when Constantius ordered Julian to send him part of his army for the intended campaign against the Persians, Julian's soldiers rebelled and proclaimed him as *Augustus*. Julian's own declarations of loyalty were not trusted by the Emperor, and he had no other choice but to lead his troops towards the East for the decisive battle. But this never took place because of Constantius' sudden death, and as early as 361 AD Julian could settle in Constantinople as sole ruler.

After a comprehensive purge in court and administration according to the strict standards of the ascetic Emperor, Julian released a series of edicts in which he now openly professed his paganism, and attempted to restore the former status of the old religion. A general edict of toleration not only reopened the temples and revived their cults, but also marked the end of all state intervention in ecclesiastical disputes; all banished bishops thus returned to their dioceses where they had to face the new holders of the sees. The next step was an edict ruling that only those who professed the old faith could teach grammar, as Classic literature could only be adequately understood and explained on this religious basis. However, a total repaganisation of army and administration was no longer feasible, even if Julian quite naturally gave preference to pagans wherever he could, and reintroduced the old military ensigns which Constantine had abolished in the army. Julian was unable to carry out his plan for a rebuilding of the Temple in Jerusalem, where Jews had not been allowed to live since the reign of Hadrian, but nevertheless he systematically favoured the Jews.

The revival of pagan religious practice was encouraged not simply through generous financial support. Julian attempted to form a supra-regional organisation of the different priesthoods, which were originally completely independent of one another. He wanted to pave the way for a unified theological interpretation of the different cults according to Neo-Platonist philosophy, to educate the priests as models for moral living, and to make the temples centres of organised social welfare. After the manner of Christianity, the pagan religion was to become teachable, and serve as the basis for a specific morality.

Although some of the edicts, such as the orders to restore the temples and their financial assets, could create major problems for the Christian population, it was not the Emperor's intention to instigate brutal persecutions against the church. Where there were cases of violence against the Christians, as in Alexandria or the Syrian city of Bostra, they were acts of revenge perpetrated by pagan mobs.

Beside the measures taken to implement his religious policies, Julian also worked feverishly to reform financial and military institutions. All this was interrupted by the Persian campaign for whose preparation the Emperor went to Antioch in 362 AD. In that city, which was at the same time Christian and given to indulgence in the pleasures of life, the pagan-philosophical ascete on the throne was anything but popular and Julian became extremely disappointed by the lack of appreciation for his programme of reform. In the spring of 363 AD the Roman army entered Mesopotamia. But there was no major battle, for after tiring marches the Emperor was wounded in a vanguard skirmish and died within a few hours. The army proclaimed a Christian officer as the new Emperor.

In spite of the brevity of Julian's reign as *Caesar* and *Augustus*, he left behind a rich literary production. A large corpus of the Emperor's letters reflects his continued philosophical and literary interests. It contains communications addressed to Libanius, Iamblichus, and his philosophical mentor Maximus; but the largest part of his epistles was written in the context of his religious policies. Those letters are addressed to urban communities and priests, explaining the Emperor's intentions, refuting possible objections, and showing the burning zeal of the reformer.

As *Caesar*, Julian wrote several speeches in honour of Constantius II and the Empress Eusebia; and there is also a beautiful obituary on his friend Sallustius. But the most interesting speeches are the theological ones which illustrate the fundamentals of his religious beliefs. The major oration about the sun god Helios contains – in a sometimes not quite logical and hence obscure argument – Neo-Platonist theology as developed by Iamblichus, with which the author Julian justifies the restoration of the old religion. To him, all those deities worshipped in the many cults are different manifestations of the one universal God whom men can see in the shape of the life-giving sun. In our imperfect sensual world, however, the sun is only the representation of a higher, spiritual God, who reigns over all spiritual beings, and whom humans can know because they are endowed with reason. Above this God, in turn, rules the Supreme Being, the One, which embraces all opposites and to which man has access not through thought, but only through mystical vision at the end of the path of rational cognition. Thus the cults of the old religion, combined in the worship of the sun, have a point of reference beyond themselves in the comprehensive oneness of spiritual reality.

Another speech deals with the Mother of Gods, a deity whose worship had a rich tradition in Asia Minor; this contains an allegorical explanation of the strange mythology of the Attis Mysteries. The allegorical interpretation of myth was widely practised among the Neo-Platonists (see p. 377), and hence it also features largely in Julian's writings. A defence of this method is given in a speech directed against the Cynic Heraclius. Being firmly opposed to all dogmatism, the Cynics regarded such attempts to find meaning in ancient traditions by applying philosophical doctrines as illegitimate. They saw no need for any theoretical justification of their lifestyle, whose accordance with nature was, as they thought, self-evident. During the reign of Julian the lifestyle of the Cynic philosopher, with its renunciation of the comforts of civilisation, its asceticism, and its contempt for all convention, still attracted many people, even among Christians. The Emperor himself sought to emulate it as far as his office permitted, but he himself did not share the aversion of the true Cynic towards any kind of scientific studies, philosophical speculation, and rhetorical education. Thus, his Cynic speeches are attempts to prove that Cynic lifestyle, philosophical theory, and literary culture belonged together.

His ascetic way of living, which was reflected in his unkempt attire, had prompted the more worldly Antiochians to ridicule the Emperor. Julian's retort was a pamphlet called *Misopogon*, whose irony and self-mockery was most probably not understood by the spoiled urbanites.

A major polemical work by Julian was directed against the *Galileans*, the Christians. It can be reconstructed from the refutation by Cyrillus of

Alexandria, published nearly a hundred years later. Completely extant is a satire in the style of Lucian (see p. 237), written as a contribution to the jesting at the *Kronia* or Saturnalia festival. In it, the gods give a banquet to which all of Julian's Imperial predecessors are invited, some of them having been elevated to the status of divine beings. Many are unanimously banished from the assembly of the gods, above all Constantine, but also, for example, Tiberius and Nero. Others find some advocates among the gods, but only a few are welcomed unanimously, as in particular Marcus Aurelius, the philosopher on the throne. Although it contains some grotesque details, Julian's short piece does not really achieve the light-hearted tone of Menippean satire; however, it expresses quite unambiguously the Emperor's judgment on the history of Imperial Rome.

Julian was certainly neither a creative philosopher nor a major author. He was an intellectual with an all-round education and a strong temperament, to whom chance, through Imperial power, gave the opportunity of exerting political influence on the basis of convictions which were no longer rooted in the thought and the feeling of the masses. But then again, nobody can tell what success his endeavours would have had if he had reigned longer.

Among the rhetorically trained and at the same time philosophically orientated authors of the Late Classical age, the most interesting figure is without any doubt Synesius from the Greek city of Cyrene in north Africa. He came from a prominent family of landowners, spent several years in Alexandria where he received a very thorough education in Neo-Platonist philosophy, and then lived a squire's life on his domains, only occasionally fulfilling public functions, such as, for example, leading a delegation to the Emperor's court. In 410 AD, when he was about forty years old, Synesius was elected Bishop by the Christian community in his native city, although he was unbaptised and married, and had explicitly stated his disagreement with parts of Christian doctrine because of his philosophical convictions. He was chosen in spite of all that, because only he was thought capable of organising the defence against the raids of dangerous nomadic tribes, as head of the ecclesiastical and Imperial administration. In the few remaining years until his death, Synesius fulfilled all military and administrative expectations.

The collection of his 156 letters tells us a lot about Synesius' diverse activities, his connections, and his ideas. He was an astute observer and equally good at description, and thus his letters are among the most vivid pieces of writing extant in Late Classical prose, regardless of whether they discuss aspects of military organisation, appointments to public offices, social welfare, or his experiences during a sea-voyage in the most diverse company of passengers. The only comparable collection of letters in Latin is that of Hieronymus (see p. 565).

From the years in which Synesius led a relatively leisurely life, we have a number of treatises or speeches, as well as a collection of nine hymns in Classic, anapaestic and Ionic-anacreontic metres, written in an artificial poetic language composed of Ionic, Aeolic, and Doric elements. The hymns are addressed either to the Christian God, to the trinity, or to Jesus, but their invocation, praise, and prayer reflect ideas and doctrines much closer to Neo-Platonist theology than to contemporary Christian dogma.

At the time in question the expression of theological doctrine in the form of the *hymnus* after the Classic pattern already had a long tradition. We find it in the Orphic hymns (see p. 270), in fragments of Gnostic poetry (see p. 388), in the works of the Christian writers Clement of Alexandria, Methodius (see p. 382), and Gregory of Nazianzus (see p. 605), and in those of the Neo-Platonist Proclus from the later part of the fifth century AD. Synesius puts particular emphasis on literary models in ancient Greek lyrics; in his ninth *hymnus*, for instance, he presents himself explicitly as one who continues the Ionic poetry of Anacreon, the Lesbian verse of Alcaeus and Sappho, and the great Doric chorus lyrics in the style of Pindar. Synesius' mastery of long-extinct dialects and metres shows his literary erudition, but the encoding of philosophical content in ancient poetic language also makes the interpretation of the hymns extremely difficult.

The choice of such poetic forms goes back to a very old motif of Greek piety, sublimated in philosophy. The hymns talk again and again of the splendour, the sublime nature, and the beauty of the divine and the created order, as well as of the aesthetic pleasure enjoyed by the person who approaches it by rational cognition. Using an entirely different language, but likewise in keeping with time-honoured Greek tradition as revitalised by Plato, Plotinus had already repeatedly praised the beauty of the order of the spiritual world, and also of its creations in the world of our sensations. Synesius' artful poetry tries to match this notion of the divine. Although the details of the doctrines expressed in this attempt are mostly philosophical in origin, the general mood and the piety conveyed are in fact comparable to those in later Christian art, where ever-new productions of liturgy, music, and fine arts were likewise created in response to the beauty of the divine.

The analysis of the poems in the light of the history of philosophy has shown that Synesius' philosophical understanding was far superior to that of the Emperor Julian. Further evidence of this is found in Synesius' philosophical prose works – the three tracts about providence, for instance. Here, the Neo-Platonist doctrine of freedom and predestination is combined with detailed allegorical interpretations of the Egyptian myth of Isis and Osiris, which had by then long become a part of Greek tradition.

In one of his speeches entitled *Dion* Synesius explicitly calls himself a successor of Dion of Prusa (see p. 228), who finally found the meaning and the goal of his life on the path shown by philosophy without ever denying the merits of his rhetorical education and of his early work in oratory. Synesius emphatically rejected rhetoric as a source of meaning in life, but likewise he distanced himself from the anti-educational ideology of Christian monks, and thus touched on a problem hotly debated within the church. The link between the Classical educational tradition and institutionalised ecclesiastical asceticism was a result of the efforts of the major figures in the monastic tradition, such as Basil, Hieronymus, or Cassian. But many of the monastic communities of the fourth and fifth centuries AD were far from such a synthesis. Those monks who, as Libanius reports, directed their destructive rage against the temples and who lynched the Neo-Platonist philosopher Hypatia, the teacher of Synesius, in the streets of Alexandria, were motivated by a deep-seated hatred of all education (see p. 450). This hate was not only religiously motivated: it was also the hostility of a rural population which had been underprivileged for centuries, towards a culture entirely limited to the urban milieu; a culture which since the reign of Constantine could continue to enjoy the protection of the state only if it integrated itself into ecclesiastical life.

Synesius follows Dion of Prusa also in his speech about monarchy, a guide for princes which can be compared to similar speeches by Themistius and Julian. Some shorter speeches are ostensibly written as addresses on the occasion of barbarian invasions into the territories of Cyrene and Ptolemais; those, however, are most probably literary exercises. Synesius did not neglect those rhetorical exercises in which one had to prove one's skills by treating a subject as obscure or even absurd as possible. A case in point is his praise of baldness, a piece designed to rival one by the admired Dion which praises hair.

Another representative of Late Classical education with its synthesis of the philosophical and the rhetorical was Eunapius of Sardes, who lived between 345 and 420 AD. He was taught philosophy in Athens by Chrysanthius, a follower of the Neo-Platonist Iamblichus (see p. 404), but he became known mainly as a man of letters or rhetor. Modelled on Philostratus (see p. 340) is a treatise with short lives of the philosophers and rhetors of his period, beginning with biographies of Plotinus and Porphyry, the two major philosophers of the previous century. Eunapius' sympathies lay with the old religion, likewise favoured by most of the authors he portrayed; these sympathies also pervade a historical work which was meant to continue the historiography of Dexippus of Athens (see p. 369). Eunapius began this work in 396 AD at the suggestion of his friend Oribasius, who had been court physician to the Emperor Julian, and written an extant medical encyclopaedia with many excerpts from older writings. The patriarch Photius, whose *Bibliotheca* preserved an excerpt from Eunapius' historiography, calls Eunapius' work a eulogy on the apostate Emperor Julian, and, as a churchman would, makes some angry comments. Indeed those parts of Eunapius' writings which we still have today give us a good insight into the thinking of pagan-oppositional circles on the literary scene.

From the West we also have evidence of considerable activity in the field of rhetoric. I have already mentioned the collection of panegyrical speeches, the latest of which dates from 389 AD. Beside illustrating monarchic ideology, these texts prove that after the decline of education in the preceding time of crisis, representative prose authors had regained the mastery of traditional linguistic and stylistic forms. Eumenius' speech comments on this, with reference to the history of educational institutions.

The reascent of the educated classes had some particular features in the city of Rome, where it concerned first and foremost the Senatorial aristocrats who had remained pagan. Rome had long ceased to be the Emperor's residence; this role had been taken over by Trier and Milan, Nicomedia and Antioch, but above all by the newly founded city of Constantinople on the Bosporus. It was the very distance of the reigning Christian Emperor, however, which facilitated the cultivation of the former world capital's tradition, as closely linked with thc old religion. The resident Senatorial nobility, who owned large amounts of land, enjoyed high social prestige, although their public functions were limited to some traditional offices in Rome and the western provinces, the ancient priesthoods, and legal scholarship. Only a few representatives of this class were found in key positions of the Imperial military and civilian administration.

The most prominent figure from this group in the fourth century AD was Q. Aurelius Symmachus Eusebius, who may well be called the most famous Latin orator of the period. The name tells us that his family, which produced also other high dignitaries and legal scholars, came from the Greek East; this, however, did not affect their loyalty to the old Roman tradition.

Symmachus was born around 345 AD and quickly rose to the rank of Prefect of Rome and that of Consul. Although he twice took the side of a usurper – the second time, as other members of his class, hoping for a restoration of paganism – he enjoyed the favour of the reigning Emperors until his death in 402 AD. In 384 AD he asked the Emperor to cancel legal measures taken against paganism: in particular, to restore to the temples their financial assets which had been confiscated for the state or the church, and also to bring the altar of the goddess Victoria back into the Roman Senate's assembly room. This petition is extant as impressive evidence of the author's loyalty to the great tradition of the city of Rome. Ambrosius, the great Bishop of Milan and counsellor to the Emperor, immediately wrote two letters arguing against the demands (see p. 534), and even in the year after Symmachus' death, the Christian poet Prudentius (see p. 585) still wrote a long polemical poem which tried to invalidate the argument of the petition.

There are altogether eight extant speeches by Symmachus, including eulogies on the Emperors Gratian and Valentinian I, plus no less than nine hundred letters which his son published after the father's death. Symmachus writes a correct and cultivated Latin which testifies to his training in the Classics. He masters all the devices of the art of oratory as taught by rhetorical schools, as well as the simple and elegant style which is demanded by the letter form. His epistles are of great interest because they tell us much about political and social conditions of the period and of its intellectual life, and because they introduce many important figures of that era to the reader. The speeches, on the other hand, are rather rhetorical showpieces, meant to demonstrate the writer's skill more than to convey any kind of message.

Symmachus was one of the members of the late Roman Senatorial aristocracy who did a lot for the preservation of Classic Roman literature such as the works of Virgil and Livy, and for their interpretation through scholarly commentaries, as well as for the cultivation of Roman jurisprudence. Of course all this was connected to endeavours to preserve the old religion which was seen as an essential condition for the proper access to the literary tradition. Still, the cultivation of the Classic Roman literary heritage remained a concern even in those Senatorial families who embraced Christianity during the fifth and sixth centuries AD. There is also much evidence to indicate that in the East as well as in the West, members of the educated classes could maintain friendly connections even if they were of different faiths because of a common interest in philosophy and literature.

Another particularly remarkable representative of this group was Symmachus' brother-in-law Virius Nicomachus Flavianus, to whom several of Symmachus' letters are addressed. Flavian held offices comparable to those of his relative, who was about ten years his junior; and like him he supported the usurper Eugenius. After Eugenius' defeat at the Battle on the Frigidus in 394 AD, Flavian committed suicide, presumably because he felt very strongly committed to the cause of the old religion. He was a versatile author, and translated into Latin Philostratus' life of Apollonius of Tyana, a man who was of great interest to the educated pagans of the period as a counter-figure to Jesus. Like a historical work by Flavian, this translation was lost. Flavian's son, who became a high dignitary like his father, also shared his literary interests, and similarly his concern for the purity of the texts and the scholarly interpretation of Classic literature.

Symmachus, Nicomachus Flavianus, their common friend Agorius Praetextatus, an expert in ancient religious law, and Servius, the learned commentator on Virgil, are all found in Macrobius' *Saturnalia*, together with other participants in the discussion. I have already dealt with this work (see p. 444); I am mentioning it again in this context because in its description of the three days of the Saturnalia festival virtually all the elements of general education are present: the grammatical-antiquarian, the philosophical, and the rhetorical. This is why the work, like the natural history of Pliny the Elder and the peculiar compilation by Martianus Capella, was a source of much Classical knowledge to the Middle Ages, albeit in an incomplete form.

As the Greeks since Hellenism had regarded Homer, so did the Romans, proud of their tradition, see in their national poet Virgil the original expression of all wisdom, science, and philosophy. I have already pointed out (see p. 455) how allegorical interpretation was used to demonstrate this for philosophy, and antiquarian erudition to show it for religion as well as for science. It was, however, of special importance to present Virgil also as a model of rhetorical virtuosity.

The ability to appreciate the stylistic devices of artistic prose and their active mastery distinguished an educated person; hence they also had to be found in Virgil. The search was not in vain, for rhetoric had indeed exerted a great influence on Virgil's poetry. In his case it made a lot of sense to use, as was the common habit, the reading of poetic texts for a rhetorical training aimed at the mastery of literary prose. Like Servius' commentary, Macrobius also highlights again and again Virgil's stylistic qualities, and emphasises that to him the many fields of knowledge which are touched upon in conversation in the *Saturnalia* are not only part of philosophical, but also of rhetorical education. The way for an incorporation of poetic texts into rhetorical instruction had been opened up by the transformation of rhetoric since the time of Isocrates, from a method of writing legal speeches to a theory of adequate linguistic expression, as a means of general education.

Scipio's Dream is not as interesting as the *Saturnalia* with regard to the rhetorical aspect of this educational literature: and in the work of Martianus Capella, a different feature of educational ideas in the post-Classic Classical age is dominant.

Between the rivalling forces of philosophy and rhetoric, scientific research which merely aimed at more knowledge was in a difficult position. Unlike the case in modern educational theory, not all persistent, never-ending search for facts was regarded as having an educational value during at least the post-Classic Classical age, which in this respect followed the opinion of Isocrates and not that of Plato. Scientific research could, in the eyes of the people of the period, be of practical use, for instance, in medicine; and it also held its own in philosophy, where the schools disputed the proper way to a fulfilled life. But in other areas science was seen as justified only in a propaedeutical function. Provided it dealt with the right subjects, it could prepare students for philosophical instruction by sharpening the intellect and communicating indispensable factual knowledge.

From the basis of this view of science as a means of education between the elementary level and the higher philosophical or rhetorical level, the canon of the so-called Seven Liberal Arts was developed. First in evidence in the period of Hellenism, these were seen as suited to the education of freeborn children who were not obliged to do any manual labour. The seven arts were grammar, dialectics or logic, rhetoric, geometry, arithmetic, astronomy, and musical theory. The selection of disciplines corresponded to the requirements of subsequent higher education, whether of the philosophical or of the rhetorical kind. Martianus Capella's compilation from specialised literature in the individual sciences is founded on this definition of the function of scientific education.

To close this section I will finally give a survey of the theory and didactics of the higher art of oratory in this epoch. On the Greek side, beside the aforementioned declamations of Libanius (see p. 449), we have the so-called *Progymnasmata* by his pupil Aphthonius. This work has fourteen chapters, each giving a precise definition of a central term of rhetorical theory, and then an example for detailed explanation. The book was extremely popular in Byzantine schools, and hence became the subject of numerous commentaries. From Aphthonius, there are also a series of fables, partly original and partly adapted; these also belong to the context of rhetorical education. Such training began with exercises in the art of simple narration or *chriē*, and of description or *ekphrasis*. Only after that came the introduction to the art of invention, and the structuring of an argument. Aphthonius' declamations were lost, although they were still read by the Patriarch Photius in the ninth century AD.

The life of the famous teacher of rhetoric Nicolaus of Myra belongs entirely to the fifth century AD. He was a compatriot of the Neo-Platonist Proclus, and had philosophical interests himself. As professor at the university of Constantinople, an institution founded by Theodosius II where also the most prominent grammarians of the fifth and sixth centuries AD were teaching, Nicolaus wrote a detailed textbook (*Progymnasmata*). This textbook was incorporated into a later anonymous commentary on the work by Aphthonius, although parts of it have also been preserved independently. Other rhetorical writings mentioned in Nicolaus' extant biography are lost.

I have already mentioned C. Marius Victorinus (see p. 442) as the author of grammatical treatises; his philosophical and theological works will be dealt with in subsequent sections. Victorinus' great success as a teacher in Rome, as reported by Hieronymus and Augustine, was in the field of rhetoric. He was even honoured by the erection of a statue in the Forum of Trajan in Rome, where, as I have said before, there were two major libraries for Greek and Latin literature. Having converted to Christianity at an advanced age, Marius Victorinus had to give up teaching in 362 AD because of the Emperor Julian's edict which barred Christians from giving professional instruction in Classic literature.

There are a number of shorter treatises on rhetoric from the fourth and fifth centuries AD, all of them new attempts to deal with traditional aspects of rhetorical technique, such as the doctrine of the stylistic levels, or of the parts of speech. Some of these treatises are anonymous, while others have been handed down under names which are unknown to us. Occasionally, teachers of rhetoric as well as grammarians (see p. 141) would use verse as a didactic medium. Most of such treatises were not from Rome, but from the educational centres of Gaul (see p. 397), Spain, and north Africa.

Finally, rhetorical schools saw a late flowering in the East which provided a smooth transition to the distinctive Byzantine civilisation. The most remarkable phenomenon in this field was the tradition which was established in the Palestinian city of Gaza. Those of its exponents whom we know from the fifth to the seventh century AD were all Christians, and in some cases also known for their Biblical exegesis. The fame of the school of Gaza was founded by Procopius, who lived between 460 and 530 AD. He was educated in Alexandria, and then taught rhetoric as a professor in public employment in his native city, to which he remained faithful throughout his life in spite of prestigious job offers elsewhere. People read and admired Procopius' speeches on the occasions of festivals or deaths, his descriptions of paintings, his declamations, and other texts belonging to epideictic rhetoric; of those a panegyric on the Emperor Anastasius is extant. Procopius had a thorough knowledge of Classic-Attic as well as of Atticist prose literature from the second century AD, whose elegance he tried to emulate. Besides, he also wrote commentaries on several books of the Old and the New Testaments.

The prose texts from the school of Gaza are particularly distinguished by their rhythmical organisation. In Hellenistic and Imperial literary prose, a method had been developed for the rhythmic shaping of texts by regulating the succession of long and short syllables of the final words in sentences and clauses, after a few exactly defined patterns. This method was also adopted in literary prose of the elevated style in Latin. From the fourth century AD the rhythmic patterning of clause endings in literary prose followed a different convention which had arisen because of the loss of the quantitative distinction between syllables in living, spoken language, and the replacement of the musical stress by a dynamic one (see p. 252).

The rule for the new rhythmic pattern is called Meyer's Law, after the man who discovered it at the end of the nineteenth century. This law prescribes that at the end of a clause the last two stressed syllables should always be separated by an even number of unstressed ones. This was meant to avert a rhythm with alternating stressed and unstressed syllables at the end of syntactic units, a rhythm which was nearly automatically produced by secondary stresses in reading aloud. The reason was that such a pattern was considered to be a characteristic of spoken verse. The aim to avoid the common rhythms of spoken poetry had already determined the form of the clauses which were regulated according to the succession of long and short syllables; the final cadence of the hexameter, for example, was at the time especially frowned upon if occurring in prose.

In the school tradition of Gaza, Meyer's Law was made even stricter, permitting only clause endings where two unstressed syllables came in between the last two stresses, the second of which had to be followed by two more unstressed syllables. This detail illustrates the principles according to which prose texts of a high standard were styled in this period. At this literary level, authors used the vocabulary, the grammatical forms, and even the syntax of a long-dead language; but for the sound of the text in its oral presentation they developed rules which suited the conditions of the contemporary spoken idiom.

Procopius of Gaza had many pupils. The most famous one among them was his compatriot Choricius, who succeeded his teacher in office, and also delivered his extant funeral oration. Other extant texts by Choricius are several encomia or eulogies which, like the abovementioned funeral speech, occasionally contain valuable information on contemporary history. There are also other speeches on funerals and weddings, but also declamations about subjects from Classical mythology, and on fictitious legal cases from the Classic period. These declamations, which belong in the context of rhetorical teaching, are prefaced by short theoretical discussions which reflect the survival of the traditional notions which motivated rhetorical education. Choricius did not write any theological works, but he did produce writings on popular philosophy, as discussions of moral issues in an intentionally artless style.

As a stylist, Choricius' contemporary Aeneas of Gaza also belongs to the school tradition of this city, but in his work as a teacher in Gaza and other cities in the Syrian region, he dealt also with philosophical and theological subjects. This is particularly so in his writings. Aeneas had been taught by the Neo-Platonist Hierocles in Alexandria and, as his dialogue *Theophrastus* shows, he tried at the same time to defend basic Christian doctrines such as that of creation against the philosophical view of the world, and to show fundamental philosophical concepts such as that of the pre-existence of the soul – condemned by Christian orthodoxy – as Christian in nature.

The uninterrupted influence of the rhetorical school tradition as cultivated in Gaza in particular, can still be seen in the literary legacy of the Patriarch Sophronius of Jerusalem, who died in 638 AD after the Caliph Umar had conquered the holy city. Sophronius' eulogy on two Egyptian saints, his sermons, and also some neatly finished religious poems in the anacreontic metre indicate that their author was firmly rooted in an educational tradition which had derived all of its formal elements from Classic Greece. Sophronius himself had presumably worked for some time as a teacher of rhetoric, before joining a monastery near Jerusalem, from where he was called to assume the office of Patriarch.

4 HISTORIOGRAPHY

From the Late Classical age we have important works of historiography in Greek as well as in Latin. There seem to be several different reasons for this late flowering of the genre, which in the Greek East continued throughout the entire Byzantine era well into the fifteenth century, while the Latin West produced nothing comparable for a long time after the fifth century AD. Christianity had introduced educated people to a concept of time and history which was fundamentally different from the Classical notion. In the former Graeco-Roman world all historical processes had been conceived of on the basis of an analogy with natural ones. This is the ground for Thucydides' opinion that historical events repeat themselves in similar forms because human nature remains the same, as well as the basis for the comparison between a nation or humanity as a whole and a living organism which goes through youth, manhood, and old age. Likewise it explains the widespread conviction that the succession of historical events is determined by cycles corresponding to those in the sphere of the stars.

In contrast to all this, Jewish-Christian eschatology presumed a goal and an end to all history. What was to follow was not a return of the golden age or of a prehistoric world free of conflict, a notion which was especially common in Classical monarchic and political ideology. Instead something entirely novel and unprecedented would be created. This view was rooted in the belief of the Israelites that they were the chosen people, and it had become particularly important in Jewish apocalyptic thought since the second century AD, in the context of Judaism's separation from Greek civilisation. The idea had a decisive influence on the growth of Christianity, in whose original message the notion of the imminent end of the world had been a prominent factor, only gradually giving way to a long-term perspective, and resulting Christian efforts to find a place within their environment. Eusebius' ecclesiastical history as well as his life of Constantine indicate how the glorious victory of the church could be immediately integrated into this perspective and consequently interpreted as an eschatological event, meaningful in a linear and teleological course of history as introducing the promised final stage.

Another reason for the vivid interest in history was the impact of the Barbarian raids in the fourth and fifth centuries AD. After the severe crises of the third century, likewise accompanied by Barbarian invasions, the decisive action taken by Diocletian and Constantine had brought renewed stability to the Empire, and once more confirmed the belief of its inhabitants that civilised humanity was and would remain separated from the

Barbarian world by stable borders under military protection. This feeling of security vanished with the Germanic raids of the late fourth and fifth centuries AD. Not only were the army and the administration now interspersed with Germanic individuals and contingents, but Germanic and Sarmatian tribes established permanent settlements in the western half of the Empire, being at first admitted because of their military prowess which was to protect the borders against new intruders. This soon led to the formation of independently governed territories where the local residents came under direct Barbarian rule, even if the chiefs or kings of the new inhabitants were prepared to recognise the Emperor as the supreme authority.

Such were the conditions for the gradual creation of new nations around the western Mediterranean, with the idea of a unity of all civilised humanity surviving only within the church, which had its centre in Rome, the ancient global capital. Politically, the Roman Empire in the West had to be re-established later, in changed circumstances. From the Greek East, however, the Barbarian tribes were expelled at a very early stage, and likewise, Germanic officers and officials disappeared from Imperial service from the fifth century AD onwards. Thus the Imperial tradition, which had found a new centre in Constantinople, the second Rome, remained a political reality in the East for another thousand years. Until very recent times, the bearers of Greek language and culture called themselves Rhomaeans, a name which also entered the language of their Turkish conquerors from the eleventh century AD.

The conquest and the sacking of Rome by the Visigoths under Alaric in 410 AD were recognised already by contemporaries as a key event for any understanding of the course of history in the fourth and fifth centuries AD. People had kept thinking of Rome as the global capital, in spite of the relocation of the administrative centres, and its fall made pagans and Christians alike reconsider the question of the meaning of history. Was the turning away from the ancient gods who had protected the global Empire responsible for the catastrophe? Or did that event only confirm their powerlessness? Or was it in fact a just punishment for centuries of worshipping idols in a religion which had some particularly fervent followers in Rome even in the Christian Empire? Or was it even the beginning of the Apocalypse itself?

Ammianus

The most important historian of the whole epoch was without any doubt Ammianus Marcellinus, born in Antioch in Syria around 330 AD. He saw Gaul and Mesopotamia during his service as an army officer, and he took part in the Persian campaign of 363 AD in which the Emperor Julian died. Afterwards he seems to have led the life of a well-heeled private man, first in Antioch, and then in Rome where he was connected with members of the Senatorial aristocracy who cultivated a literary interest. His work documents several journeys which he undertook at this stage in his life, for example to Egypt. He died just before the turn of the century.

His historical work in thirty-one books is written in Latin, which was not his native language. It is a continuation of Tacitus' *Annals*, beginning with the death of Nerva in 98 AD, and ending with the death of the Emperor Valens in the Battle of Adrianopolis against the Goths in 378 AD. The extant Books 14 to 31 deal with the events from 353 to 378 AD, in other words, with contemporary history, for which Ammianus claims to have needed no literary sources.

Ammianus was one of a large number of members of the urban upper classes in the Greek East who could identify entirely with the Imperial Roman tradition, and even with the cultivation of ancient Roman traditions by Senatorial families in the old capital. I have already mentioned this phenomenon several times in my account (see, for example, p. 348). That Ammianus takes up his history where Tacitus left off indicates much more than merely a chronological continuation of the *Annals*. Like Tacitus, Ammianus was a fervent advocate of old Roman tradition, a man convinced of the greatness and the dignity of Rome, which called for historiography written in the sublime style. One passage in Ammianus' work expresses his contempt for a popular contemporary form of historiography (see p. 347) in which everything was related to the person of the respective reigning Emperor and where consequently Imperial history and Imperial biography were equated. Ammianus regarded this kind of historiography which tried to record 'what the Emperor said at the dining table', as pure gossip.

This is why his work reflects his effort to concentrate on major events and to match the greatness of the subject by using all the devices of rhetoric. It is this very endeavour which makes his style frequently difficult to follow. In spite of his colloquial command of Latin which he acquired during his military career and later through contact with literary men in Rome, Greek expressions often provided the basis particularly for his choicest phrases, a literary technique which was possible because the rules of rhetoric were largely the same for both languages. But even where he did not imitate Greek expressions, Ammianus' endeavour to create a linguistic impact on the reader occasionally led him to be more daring than any author with Latin as his mother tongue would have been.

Ammianus followed Tacitus in his continuation of the great and quasi-official Senatorial historiography of Rome, also by at least superficially structuring his material after an annalistic pattern. However, he found himself compelled time and again to insert lengthy passages which broke up the chronology by offering previews or retrospectives.

Historiography as Imperial biography – the genre which Ammianus rejected – referred to the authority of the learned Suetonius. It made lesser claims to stylistic excellence but greater ones to exactness and detail, especially where apparently trivial facts were concerned. Ammianus on the other hand followed the older convention of stylistically elaborate historiography, and used scholarly sources, as for instance geographical or ethnographical literature, only in digressions.

A catastrophe occurring during Ammianus' lifetime was the Battle of Adrianopolis, which resulted in the death of the Emperor Valens and the opening of the way for permanent Gothic settlements on Imperial soil. Without ignoring the importance of this defeat, Ammianus maintained his trust in the greatness and the power of the Roman Empire: he did not live to see what happened in 410 AD (see p. 466).

Ammianus was a pagan, but his work is free of any venomous, or even merely polemical attacks, on Christianity. His relatively critical stance towards the Emperor Constantius II, in whose reign ecclesiastical matters played a particularly important part, was not so much religiously motivated as based on the view that Constantius was the antagonist to Ammianus' hero, the Emperor Julian. The report of Julian's death in 363 AD in Book 25 was presumably first intended to finish the whole work. Book 26 opens with a new preface, and thus begins a continuation which may not have been written and published until after the appearance of Books 1 to 25. We know of many other such enlarged new editions, as for example the one of Eusebius' ecclesiastical history (see p. 423).

Ammianus' work is an invaluable historical source. With an understanding trained by long military experience, the author excelled in his description of military operations; he had a good idea of the mechanisms and forces in the Roman Empire's administration; he understood the power games at the Emperor's court; he communicated with leading personalities in political and social life; and was able to collect and use historical evidence systematically. All this is obvious in his work, and in all of these aspects Ammianus was even superior to his model Tacitus. In the understanding and description of characters, as manifest in historic action, he almost equalled the older author. But in the art of phrasing, that is in the wide field of rhetorically shaped expression, Tacitus was superior by far. In the writing of Ammianus we find no sentences which are so immediately memorable as the phrases that Tacitus produced, with their extreme conciseness, or their rich content implied rather than stated with very few words. In this respect Tacitus has no serious rival. Nevertheless, there is hardly any other epoch in Roman history of which we have such an illuminating and reliable account as in Ammianus' report about the events of his own lifetime.

In ancient Rome, political life had been greatly influenced by attempts to look into the future through the practices of the official cult. This is why the records of state priesthoods meticulously listed all sorts of omens and public reactions to them as precedents, and why such facts were thus firmly incorporated into the traditional lore of earliest Roman historiography. This tradition survived for centuries, and after the advent of philosophy, it merged with reflections on the problem of freedom versus determination in ever-new considerations of historical philosophy. What determined the course of events, the free decisions of the agents, coincidence, or the predetermination of fate? While Tacitus in a famous chapter of the *Annals* leaves this question open, Ammianus expresses his conviction that there is an inevitable fate, but that this fate, as Virgil had already said, decreed the lasting greatness of Rome.

Among the Greek historiographers of the same period we know only from fragments several who wrote their works after the manner of Herodianus (see p. 347), as descriptions of the deeds or the lives of certain emperors. Praxagoras of Athens and Bemarchius wrote histories of Constantine, Eustochius one of Constantine's son Constans, and Magnus of Charrae an account of the deeds and the life of the Emperor Julian. The few extant fragments do not indicate whether these authors were Christians or pagans. Definitely pagan was Olympiodorus of Athens, who in 412 AD accompanied an Imperial delegation to the Huns. In the ninth century AD the Patriarch Photius wrote a summary of Olympiodorus' work. In it, he found the earliest discussion of a question arising in the dispute about the altar of Victoria (see p. 459) and gaining added relevance through the events of 410 AD: namely, whether the Christian Empire's neglect of the old gods and their cults had been responsible for Rome's distress.

Augustine and Orosius

The question I have cited at the end of my previous section inspired one of the most important works in European philosophy of history, Augustine's *City of God*, which I shall discuss in the present context because it was of great influence on later historiography. Augustine, whose other works I shall deal with in a following section (see p. 502), wrote his monumental treatise, which must also be seen as the last great apology for Christianity, not simply to refute the opinion that the fall of Rome had been caused by the people's betrayal of the ancient gods. He also argued against Christians such as the Archbishop Ambrosius of Milan and the great scholar Hieronymus who read the turmoil of the period eschatologically, identified the Goths with the nations of Gog and Magog in John's *Apocalypse*, and saw the Christian Empire as uniting the people of God who were to be saved after the world perished. Against this view, Augustine set the doctrine of the two *civitates*, the two communities among men, none of which can be equated with any of the numerous states and empires in history.

To Augustine, the church in its historically shaped form is not the City of God either. He claims that within all communities established by men, the bad people belong to the kingdom of the earth or the devil, and the good ones to the Kingdom of God. History is the perennial struggle between the two. Both intermingle in all events on earth, and only at the Day of Judgment, when every human deed is laid open and rewarded or punished, will the two be separated for ever. Only then will full justice be established among the members of the divine kingdom; but even before that, in the historical states, each created order which becomes the basis for communal living testifies to the presence of citizens of the Kingdom of God. They are the ones who follow God's command in having only God and their fellow humans at heart, while the citizens of the other state aim for nothing but self-assertion, power, and the domination of others. As all states produced by history included individuals of both categories, they contained not only strife, violence, and injustice, but always likewise 'a kind of justice', without which any state would be no more than an organised gang of robbers. However, this worldly justice should not be confused with the perfect one in the ultimate Empire of God.

The twenty-two books of Augustine's vast work were written and published successively between 417 and 426 AD. His scholarly input was immense. The first ten books, meant to prove that even when the ancient cults were unchallenged the Roman state was not exempt from catastrophes and crimes and hence the old gods did not at all guarantee human happiness, contain a wealth of material relating to cultural history. This evidence is taken from the rich antiquarian literature, especially from the writings of Varro, a contemporary of Cicero. Augustine's attack on the old religion culminates in the reference to the Christian hope for eternal salvation in the other world, something to which the ancient gods have nothing at all to contribute.

The plan of his philosophy of history in the narrower sense is contained in Books 11 to 22, which contain the doctrine of the two empires or communities which I have sketched above. Augustine continued the efforts of older Christian authors to establish a correlation between the Jewish-Christian view of history as a process directed by God towards a definite goal, the eternal salvation of his chosen ones, and the historical knowledge accumulated in the Graeco-Roman tradition. In such attempts the providential significance of the Roman Empire was of special importance: it was part of God's plan of salvation, because its international peaceful order made the spreading of the Gospel possible. Such notions are already indicated in the Gospel of Luke; this made it seem natural to read the successive events of the Empire's Christianisation and the catastrophes of the great migrations as the beginning of the Apocalypse, the time in which the people of God were to be led into the last fierce battles with God's enemies.

Following ideas expressed in Paul's letters, Augustine's plan emphasises the basically provisional character of all historical events and situations, and thus also the inseparable intermingling of good and evil in all happenings among men. According to him, the end of history, with its universal judgment resulting in the only valid and final separation of good from evil, will be brought about by direct divine intervention, which is why it is not to be foreseen by any man, not even on the basis of contemporary historical events. Hence Augustine's historical interpretation of Biblical statements about the end of the world and the universal judgment refuted any claim that human actions could lead to a state of lasting happiness and perfect justice, not even on a Christian basis. This claim was made again and again in Augustine's lifetime and subsequent centuries and it was an essential part of all forms of monarchic ideology of the Classical age and the Middle Ages.

Even while he was writing the *City of God*, Augustine encouraged the presbyter Paulus Orosius who had fled to north Africa after the invasion of the Vandals in the Pyrenean peninsula, to supplement his own historical-theological plan by a corresponding account of global history. The resulting work, the *Historia adversus paganos* or *History Against the Pagans*, shows its apologetical nature even in its title. The seven books contain a survey of the time from the creation of the world, dated in the Jewish-Christian tradition on the basis of Old Testament chronology, to the year 417 AD. Orosius could use Christian chronography, a fully developed genre at the time, and especially Eusebius' chronicle, which was later translated into Latin by Hieronymus (see p. 423), for his portrayal of the history of salvation, divided according to the events of the creation, the Fall, the calling of Abraham, the giving of laws at Mount Sinai, and the incarnation and the expected return of the Son of God. Eusebius' chronicle had already established connections between important dates of Graeco-Roman history and the Biblical system. In his account, which was to present not only chronological tables but also a brief narrative of historical events, Orosius also used a number of older and contemporary historical surveys by pagan authors. Of those works, I have already mentioned that by Justin (see p. 300), and I will deal with that by Eutropius in a following section (see p. 475). Orosius' evident use of Livy was presumably based on one of the many excerpts from this Classic author, but we can no longer identify that intermediate source. Orosius' report about the last years of the time he covered is not based on literary material but the author's own knowledge. This part, more detailed than the rest, may hence be described as a primary historiographical source.

Written in fairly simple language, the book was widely read in the Middle Ages, and like no other it influenced common ideas about the course of world history in the Latin West. In the work the apologetical tendency of Augustine's *City of God* is amplified by the author's effort to prove that humanity before the advent of Christ not only suffered from an equal amount of catastrophes, but from an even greater number, and even more severe calamities.

Orosius also communicated to the Western world the idea of a fourfold division of history up to the beginning of the final period, based on the eras of the four great Empires of Assyria, Persia, Macedonia, and Rome. This notion came from the apocalyptic Book of Daniel from the second century BC; at the time it had been meant to give a historical-theological interpretation of the dichotomy which had arisen between the Israelite-Jewish tradition and the dominant global civilisation of Hellenism. This periodisation was greatly influential until well into the Modern age, but it was never unchallenged. Augustine himself had suggested a division into six periods in an earlier treatise directed against the Manichaean Faustus.

Like other contemporaries, Orosius was one of the large number of Greek and Latin authors expressing their pride in the greatness of Rome and of its Empire even in this late epoch, when the Roman state was shaken by crises and catastrophes. Among them were not only pagans such as Ammianus (see p. 466) or Symmachus (see p. 459) who stood for old Roman tradition, or Greek intellectuals like the historian Zosimus (see p. 440), to whom Greek civilisation and Roman state formed an inseparable unit. The idea of Rome, in which the political and cultural self-confidence of the global Empire's citizens had had its focal point for centuries, also influenced Christian thought. Before the Christianisation of the Empire, the concept of the Roman state as the tool of divine providence, but also – for example, in the works of Origen (see p. 334) – as the foundation of a recognised civilisation, had been in conflict with its evaluation as the creation and the instrument of powers hostile to God, and worshipped in pagan religion. Now the Christianisation of the Empire could not only be seen as signalling the ultimate battle against the forces opposed to God, as stated by Eusebius and other authors (see p. 425); but also, and even more so in a period of external threat, as a renewal of the Empire in order to protect that civilisation which it represented.

These ideas are found in a whole number of Christian writings, as for example the works of the poet Prudentius (see p. 582). They were condensed in that Christian concept of Rome which achieved a historical importance which can hardly be overestimated, for the Western Popes and Emperors, but also for Constantinople and Moscow, the second and third Rome. However, this process was not without conflicts and contradictions: was it really justified for a Christian to be the guardian of Cicero's legacy, as Hieronymus asked himself? And, as Salvianus of Marseille put it to his contemporaries, could the message of the Gospel not find much better roots among the unspoiled Germanic Barbarians than in the civilisation of the global Empire, being time-honoured but marked by various degenerations? In spite of such doubts, though, perennially nourished by the ascetical and anti-civilisatory elements in the Christian tradition, what dominated in the long run was a consciousness in which the Christian message of salvation was combined with the Classical educational tradition. The intruding Barbarians gradually integrated themselves into this Christian-Classical civilisation and accepted the political and military task of its preservation, and this determined the future course of European history in which the idea of Rome in its very complex Christianised form became an essential factor.

Ecclesiastical history

Orosius' work is no ecclesiastical history in the manner of Eusebius but a world or universal history in the tradition of Classical profane historiography. The kind of ecclesiastical historiography pioneered by Eusebius was adapted in Latin by the learned Rufinus of Aquilia, a friend and later opponent of Hieronymus. In 403 AD he translated the nine books of Eusebius' work, if not without deletions and additions; he also added two further books in which he continued the account up to the year 395 AD. The text of those was without any doubt formulated by Rufinus himself, and the most interesting parts for the modern reader describe the big temple of Sarapis in Alexandria and its destruction at the order of the Emperor Theodosius I. But Rufinus could draw on Greek authors who had continued the work of Eusebius. The most important one among them is Gelasius, the second successor of Eusebius as Bishop of Caesarea, whose work was unfortunately lost, so that it is now impossible to say whether it really formed the basis of Rufinus' account in Books 10 and 11. The year when Gelasius died is the same with which Rufinus closes his account.

Also lost was the ecclesiastical history published around 435 AD by Philippus of Side in Asia Minor, while of a slightly earlier one by Philostorgius long fragments survive in the *Bibliotheca* by the Patriarch Photius (see p. 480), and in hagiographical texts. Philostorgius supported the views of Eunomius, the most radical partisan of the christology based on Arius' doctrine. This is why Philostorgius' work was not more widely read and copied in orthodox circles. The extant fragments give very interesting insights into relations between the Christian Roman Empire and countries such as Abyssinia, southern Arabia, and India, relations which were at the same time political-diplomatic, missionary, and, not least importantly, commercial. To Rome, Christian communities in that region also meant bases for the economic and political-military confrontation with the Iranian Sassanid Empire. Most of what we know about the Christianisation of the Goths also comes from Philostorgius' fragments.

One of the distinctions between pagan and ecclesiastical historiography was the use of documents, letters, and other source material which ecclesiastical historians quoted literally without adaptation to the style of their account (see p. 424). The different manner of coping with this stylistic element, which was at odds with Classic demands, among Eusebius' successors is shown in the extant works of Socrates and Sozomenus. The former wrote his account of the years 305 to 439 around 440 AD in Constantinople. The latter, likewise working as a lawyer or legal scholar in Constantinople, wrote his work about ten years later. He deals with the years 324 to 425 AD and occasionally uses Socrates' book as a source.

Without excessive stylistic ambitions Socrates aimed for the greatest possible exactness, which is why he quotes original documents at length and gives fairly little room to the legendary detail which formed a large part of the ecclesiastical tradition. Sozomenus' goals were entirely different, even if he could not escape the by now completely fixed demands of the genre and hence featured original documents in his text, including some not quoted by his predecessor. But Sozomenus' effort was directed at an artful, elegant account shaped according to the rules of rhetoric, serving to edify the readers. This is why he gives ample room to legends.

In view of the unity of Roman state and Christian church established by Constantine and unchallenged since Theodosius I, it is not surprising that both Socrates and Sozomenus paid much more heed to the events of profane history than Eusebius. The same is true of the work of Philostorgius, as well as the extant brief ecclesiastical history written later by Gelasius of Kyzikos. More cases in point are the works by Hesychius of Jerusalem and John Diacrinomenus, extant only in fragments; those by Zacharias Rhetor and John of Ephesus, extant in Syrian translations; and that by Euagrius Scholasticus, of which we have the original. This enumeration, which can do no more than indicate the richness of the genre, already reaches well into the sixth century AD. But among the many authors who all followed the model of Eusebius, three were given a virtually canonical status at an early stage: beside the aforementioned Socrates and Sozomenus, the third one was Theodoretus of Cyrus in Syria who also wrote other kinds of literature. His ecclesiastical history, produced around 450 AD, has a strong resemblance to those of the two others, but lacks the literary quality of Sozomenus' work as well as the strength of Socrates as critical historiography. Theodoretus dealt with the years 325 to 428 AD.

Around the middle of the sixth century AD the *anagnost* or *lector* Theodorus of Constantinople put together four books of excerpts from the ecclesiastical histories of the three 'Classics', to which he added his own account of the years until 527 AD. Theodorus' work served as a model for Cassiodorus, Senator of the city of Rome, high official in the service of the Gothic King Theodoric and his successor, and during his long life possibly the most productive and versatile literary man of his period. His *Historia tripartita* or *Tripartite History* in twelve books refers to the same three 'Classic' ecclesiastical historiographers. Cassiodorus also wrote other historiographical works, including a world chronicle and a history of the Goths.

Profane history

Orosius was an exception in profane historiography of the fourth and fifth centuries AD, in which on the Greek as well as on the Latin side the authors were predominantly followers of the old religion. In Latin we have above all three or four works obviously written in an endeavour to maintain the accessibility of traditional historical knowledge in a concise and easily understandable form, because in those troubled times there was apparently the fear that such knowledge would be lost. One of these works is Eutropius' *Breviarium*, a brief, elegant, and well-structured survey of Roman history from its beginnings to the year 364 AD, without any polemical or apologetical tendency. According to Eutropius himself, he had taken part in Julian's Persian campaign of 363 AD and gone through a successful career in army and administration. He wrote his account at the request of the Emperor Valens who died in 378 AD in the Battle of Adrianopolis against the Goths. Eutropius' source for the Republican period was Livy, or rather an excerpt from his work; and for the Imperial age he used Suetonius' lives of the emperors as well as a lost Imperial history whose traces have also been found in other historiography of the fourth and fifth centuries AD. At that time the idea that the ancient history of Rome was one of the Roman people and its more recent history one of the Roman emperors, was firmly rooted in the historical consciousness of educated men and determined the choice of historiographical form. Ammianus' aforementioned dissent (see p. 467) was rather an exception.

Eutropius' work was widely read and frequently copied in the Middle Ages. Christian authors around 400 AD, such as Orosius and Hieronymus, already used it; and an otherwise unknown Paenius translated it into Greek soon after its publication. During the reign of Charlemagne, the Langobardic author Paul the Deacon wrote a supplement, and this example was followed by other writers in the Latin West.

Much more modest, but likewise produced during the reign of Valens and similarly emphasising the gradual growth of the Roman state, is the *Breviarium* of Roman history by Festus of whom all we know is that he held an office in the Imperial administration. It also deals with the time between the origins of Rome and 364 AD, the year when the Emperor Jovian died. It is based on the same sources as Eutropius' book, in addition to which, as has been established, the author also used the work by Florus (see p. 227).

Four minor treatises have been handed down under the name of Sextus Aurelius Victor, even if only one was genuinely written by that author. He came from the province of Africa and became governor of the province of Pannonia or Hungary under Julian, and Prefect of the city of Rome under Theodosius I in 389 AD.

The first treatise is entitled *Origo gentis Romanae* or *The Origins of the*

Roman Nation; a title perhaps taken as referring to the whole collection by the editor of the four texts. The first of them contains an account of the Italic legends surrounding the foundation of the city of Rome, with plenty of references to older authorities, partly authors from the Republican period. Without any doubt this work originated among the circles of Roman men of letters who reacted against the victorious Christian faith by trying to revive religious and mythological traditions by means of antiquarian scholarship. I have already mentioned such efforts, which were supported by the Senatorial nobility of Rome who had remained pagan (see p. 460).

The second treatise in the collection contains eighty-six very short biographies of personalities from Roman history, including also women and non-Romans. This part is hardly of any literary value; it seems to be only a summary of general educational material, arranged in biographical form.

Much more interesting is the treatise written by Aurelius Victor himself entitled *Caesares*, a history of the Roman Empire from Augustus to Julian. The chapter divisions follow the lives or reigns of individual emperors, on whose personalities and achievements the account focuses. Hence this work belongs to the tradition of biographical historiography, which I have already frequently referred to. Aurelius Victor was the first to try to define longer epochs in Imperial history, distinguishing between the Julian-Claudian and Flavian dynasties, the Antonines, the soldier emperors of the third century AD, and the Dominate beginning with Diocletian. He strove to explain the always problematical and frequently changing relationships between Emperor, army, and Senate, without pronouncing any rash verdicts. The detailed character portraits of the individual monarchs were to enable the reader to form a political and moral judgment, and the author's view of the rise, flowering, and decay of the Imperial state transferred the perspective of Late Republican historiography to the Empire. On the whole, the treatise of Aurelius Victor indicates a heightened awareness of the instability of political order, in consequence of the only partial Christianisation of society, and the military and economic burdens of the state.

In spite of its artificial diction which is often hard to comprehend, the *Caesares* were frequently used in the fourth and fifth centuries AD, and that they were also widely read in the Middle Ages is indicated by the numerous mediaeval manuscript versions. An early testimony to this popularity is the fourth part of the collection which was presumably put together under the name of Aurelius Victor as early as the end of the fourth century AD. This fourth part is a series of concise emperors' biographies from Augustus to Theodosius I, with the first eleven chapters largely based on Aurelius Victor's *Caesares*.

One of the strangest prose works from the Late Classical age is the so-called *Historia augusta*. This is a complete series of Imperial lives from

Hadrian, whose reign began in 117 AD, to Numerian, the immediate predecessor of Diocletian, who reigned until 284 AD. According to the prefaces, the biographies were by the six authors Aelius Spartianus, Julius Capitolinus, Aelius Lampridius, Vulcacius Gallicanus, Trebellius Pollio, and Flavius Vopiscus. Different addresses distributed among the texts dedicate the work to the Emperors Diocletian and Constantine, which indicates that it was finished around 330 AD. None of the authors' names can with any certainty be identified with those of other personalities from the early fourth century AD mentioned in our sources.

The biographies vary greatly in length but all follow Suetonius' manner of presentation (see p. 260). The reader learns much about lineage, character, attitudes, and habits of the emperors, as well as about their friends and relatives, frequently in the form of anecdotes which emphasise the more peculiar aspects. The political and military events of the monarchs' reigns are mentioned only briefly, and mostly without any chronological order. Reports are primarily focused on the city of Rome; events in the provinces or on the borders are rarely mentioned; and the crucial criterion in judging an emperor is his favourable or hostile attitude towards the Senate. Christianity is frequently referred to, without any pronounced sympathy or antipathy, even if occasionally there is praise for an emperor's tolerance. More attention is given to cultic practices and other events from religious life.

In this work there are frequent expressions of pride in the splendour and the power of Rome; and especially in the mention of catastrophic events during the crises of the third century AD, the authors emphasise the ultimate victory of Roman arms, or prophecies of future greatness. Apart from occasional retrospectives to the great and good emperors of the older period – Augustus and Trajan – it is above all Alexander Severus who is idealised, with particular emphasis on his divine calling, his piety, his tolerance and moral purity, and finally on his close relationship with the Roman Senate, with which he willingly shared the power of government. These qualities are outlined against a foil provided in his cousin and predecessor Elagabal, who imported all kinds of oriental corruptions into Rome. While little is said about the Empire's population outside the Senatorial class, there are many negative comments about the Barbarians, but also about the military.

There is hardly any other period in Classical history of which we know so little as the time of crisis in the third century AD. Hence the *Historia augusta* would be an invaluable historical source if we could really rely on the abundance of detailed, sometimes wholly anecdotal, facts it offers beside plenty of Senatorial minutes and emperors' letters, along with quotations from and other references to authors of lost works. But it was not long until scholars discovered many incorrect statements in the account, whose style and content is that of entertainment literature rather than historiography. There are, for instance, fictitious names, quotations from works by fictitious authors, forged documents, or anachronisms in the references to people, institutions, or events. The simultaneous dedications to Diocletian and Constantine were also suspect.

Since the last decade of the nineteenth century, many hypotheses have been offered to explain these facts, but in spite of intensive efforts particularly in recent years, there has so far been no agreement on the authorship, the date, or the purpose of this peculiar work. A frequently uttered opinion, which is, however, far from being generally accepted, states that the authors' names were only to mystify the readers, and that the book was written by one single person. But in trying to date this assumed author or a supposed editor different people have claimed virtually every single decade between the early fourth and the mid-fifth century AD. Attempts to identify and date the author – both naturally closely related – were partly based on real or assumed parallels in older and later works, but partly also on the interpretation of the political and religious tendency of the book, for which scholars sought a fitting historical situation.

The only certain reference to the *Historia augusta* was found in the history of the Goths written by Cassiodorus around 520 AD (see p. 474), and extant in the edition by Jordanes. Thus we have at least a *terminus ante quem*. Evident parallels with the works of Eutropius and Aurelius Victor are of a kind which suggests that one text was used as a model for another, or that all used an identical source. Parallels with the works of Ammianus, Hieronymus, and Eunapius (see p. 480) are so vague that they do not allow any conclusions at all. Of the many sources named in the *Historia augusta*, only the complete Greek work by Herodianus (see p. 347) and fragments of that by Dexippus (see p. 369) are extant. Of Marius Maximus' lives of the Emperors which continued Suetonius' Imperial biographies and which were presumably a major source for the first half of the *Historia augusta* we know exclusively through the latter. Considering all this, it is difficult to date the *Historia augusta* on the grounds of parallels or discrepancies in comparison with its known or presumed sources, for errors may well have been copied from those earlier texts.

As regards the tendency and the intention of the work, it can first of all not be disputed that in many individual statements, it expresses the values and the aspirations of the Senatorial aristocracy of the city of Rome and thus presumably originated in their circles. But we cannot tell whether the authors belonged to or were affiliated to the Senatorial class in which there were always men with a literary interest, and productive writers. All we can say with any certainty is that the treatise is based on the ideal image of a state in which the Emperor governs in close co-ordination with the Senate and where the Senate and not the army with its officers is thus the second most important force beside the monarch. At any time after the period of the Antonines, this state of affairs existed only in Utopian visions, and because of this the relevant passages in the *Historia augusta* give us no clues as to the date when it was written.

Many scholars have favoured the view that the work is a piece of pagan, Senatorial apologetics directed at the Christianised monarchy. This has been seen in the context of the pagan reaction under Julian and of its failure, and also of the revival of pagan religious life in Rome under the usurper Eugenius. Eugenius, a Christian rhetor, was declared Emperor by the Roman Senate in 392 AD, at the instigation of the influential general Arbogast, an officer with Frankish ancestry. Eugenius' army, however, was routed by the troops of the Emperor Theodosius I in a bloody battle in northern Italy in 394 AD, when the usurper himself was killed.

During the short reign of Eugenius, educated Senators, and first and foremost the learned Nicomachus Flavianus (see p. 445), were working hard to revive the worship of the ancient gods. Constantius II had made it illegal, but the law had not been rigidly enforced; however, the loss of their income threatened the extinction of the ancient cults, even before they were violently suppressed under Theodosius I. The short-lived efforts of the circle around Nicomachus are also documented by a polemical Christian poem (see p. 587). Against this background, the *Historia augusta* has been seen as an apology directed at the victorious Theodosius, a work whose references to the behaviour of the former 'good' emperors towards the Christians were now to urge the monarch to be similarly tolerant towards the pagans. But other scholars have thought that the context for the appeal for tolerance towards the pagan tradition, as cultivated especially in Rome's Senatorial circles, was to be found somewhere near the beginning or during the middle years of the fifth century AD during the reign of Theodosius II.

Such interpretations and tentative datings, however, have not remained unchallenged; it must be admitted that the motif of religious tolerance and the apology for pagan traditions is not dominant enough in the text to warrant a conclusive interpretation for the whole work.

The one certain fact remaining for the literary historian is that in one of the prefaces, that of the life of the Emperor Probus, the *Historia augusta* is explicitly declared to be a piece of historiography in the tradition of Suetonius and Maximus Probus. This is strange in so far as to Suetonius himself, his Imperial biographies were certainly not historiography, but scholarly-antiquarian, or perhaps also characterological writings (see p. 261). But Ammianus also tells us that Imperial biography, in which much attention was given to the Emperors' private lives, was at that time seen as a form in competition with major historiography, which focused on political-military events. The author of the preface to the life of Probus says that biographical historiography was less ambitious in stylistic matters but aimed at greater accuracy.

The *Historia augusta* is indeed 'accurate' in as much as it furnishes the most astonishing detail – but at the expense of many proven errors, and the invention of names, documents, and authorities. It cannot always be told whether these fictions were created by the authors of the *Historia* itself, or come from the anecdotal tradition on which it is based, and which also infiltrated the works of some serious historians. Furthermore, studies – for instance, of the names mentioned in the *Historia augusta* – have shown that beside fictitious or dubious details, it also contains much relevant and correct information about a period of the Roman Empire's history which is obscure, and badly documented. Those recent scholars who see the *Historia augusta* as nothing but a piece of writing for entertainment share Ammianus' verdict on all biographical historiography. But it is worth asking why, at a time when even the entertainment value of prose literature was largely measured in terms of the formal qualities of the presentation, a negligently written and artlessly composed and formulated book would have been intended to serve that very purpose. In spite of the rich anecdotal material they contain, Suetonius' *Caesares* were still the result of scholarly research, and certainly not written for entertainment. All told, we shall have to accept that, for the time being, the interpretation and the dating of the *Historia augusta* has to close with a verdict of '*ignoramus*'.

On the Greek side the tradition of ambitious profane historiography continued uninterrupted until the fall of Constantinople. Beside the aforementioned authors from the fifth century AD, the most important writers are above all Eunapius and Zosimus.

I have already referred to Eunapius as a Platonic philosopher, and as a biographer of the philosophers and rhetors of the third and fourth centuries AD (see p. 458). His major historical work in fourteen books, dealing with the years between 270 and 404 AD, continued the histories of Dexippus (see p. 369). The Patriarch Photius was still able to read it in a complete form, and tells us that it was full of anti-Christian polemics, with the author idealising the Emperor Julian as a heroic figure.

Almost completely extant is the historical work by Zosimus who may have still been alive in the early years of the sixth century AD. The six books deal with the time from the very beginnings of Rome until the eve of its conquest by the Goths under Alaric in 410 AD. The work was presumably unfinished at the author's death, and the extant text has one major gap; what is lacking is apparently the account of the years around 300 AD.

Zosimus' writing is carefully composed and full of references to motifs and perspectives, as well as to the vocabulary of the rich Greek historiographical tradition which, since the work of Polybius in the second century AD, had also included Rome's early history and its rise to global power. Zosimus obviously follows Polybius in introducing his account with general reflections on Rome's global role and aspects of its political constitution. In this context he also gives a very brief survey of Greek history, followed by a brief account, slightly more detailed only in a few parts, of Roman Imperial history from Augustus to the end of the third century AD. Then, after the aforementioned gap, comes the detailed account of Roman history in the fourth century AD which takes up Books 2 to 6.

This arrangement of the material corresponds to time-honoured tradition, as do the digressions on details of religious law, geography, or antiquarian matters. Zosimus' language is plain and without much rhetorical ornament. He does not invent speeches in which the major historical personalities explain the motives and the goals of their action, a method largely established by Thucydides, which offered all later historiographers the chance to prove their literary-historical skills, in keeping with the view of historiography as part of eloquence. But in spite of all its simplicity, Zosimus' diction is full of allusions to Classic historiography. His work is, moreover, an early example of a convention widespread in highly styled literary historiography of the Byzantine period, that is the habit of replacing the names of nations or the titles of officials current at the author's lifetime by equivalents from the time of Classic literature. From the Roman tradition Zosimus borrowed the annalistic structure of the main narrative, a structure which nevertheless remains superficial, and dictates neither the composition, nor the division into books.

Zosimus paid particular attention to the rhythmic patterning of the text and followed the aforementioned Meyer's Law (see p. 463) throughout. (This convention, by the way, survived in literary prose until the end of the Middle Ages.) What is remarkable about it is that a rhythmic rule following the actual sound of the spoken language was, in all higher literature, combined with a vocabulary and a syntax which came from a long extinct form of the language. In poetry, where the old verse forms remained in use, the situation was different. But something similar existed in Latin, where the varieties of the so-called *cursus* had replaced the old quantifying syntactic clauses of artistic prose. The new rhythms following the stresses were likewise used in texts whose vocabulary was more or less vulgar, as well as in ones with traditional or Classic diction.

Zosimus held a high office in the Imperial financial administration in Constantinople, although he was a pagan. His account of events from the recent past shows a pronounced anti-Christian tendency. He is very scathing about Constantine who incorporated Christianity into the Roman state, and about Theodosius I, the first to suppress rigidly the old religion. On the other hand he describes not only Julian but also the last pagan emperors, such as Aurelian and Probus, with particular sympathy. As mentioned before, the report concerning the reign of Diocletian is unfortunately missing. Zosimus saw Christianity and the renouncing of the old gods as the cause for the decline of Roman power: that is he upheld the very view of history which Augustine and Orosius had argued so vehemently against, about a century earlier.

The events reported in detail by Zosimus belong to a period which preceded his own by one or one-and-a-half centuries, and he seems to have had no time left for an account of the recent past, not to mention contemporary history. Hence the historical value of his account depends largely of that of his sources, and here, we have to rely mostly on inferences. Zosimus quotes the historians Olympiodorus and Magnus of Carrhae (see p. 469), but only once in each case, which is not enough to indicate a broader use of their works. It is logical to assume that he did use Eunapius' historical work, given that both authors had a similar anti-Christian stance. It is likewise logical to suspect that this tendency was responsible for occasional errors and distortions detected by recent historical research, but we can no longer tell if such inaccuracies stem from him or from the authorities he drew on. The antiquarian digressions indicate that he was well read, presumably also in Latin, but here as well we cannot name authors with any certainty.

Slightly older than Zosimus was the rhetor Priscus from a minor city in Thrace, a man who was part of the train of a high court official leading delegations to Rome and to various other places, including the court of King Attila of the Huns, in the fifth century AD. These episodes were narrated in detail in the eight books of his historical work, presumably dealing with the time from the fourth to the eighth decade of the century. His highly interesting and vivid account of these experiences was preserved in one of the major collections of excerpts made at the order of the learned Emperor Constantinus Porphyrogennetus in the tenth century AD. This collection contains, among other writings, reports on the missions of delegations as given in older historiography. Priscus' work served as a source for the Latin history of Cassiodorus (see p. 412), which survived in the edition by Jordanes.

The account of Priscus was continued in the eight books by the Syrian Malchus, who also lived in Constantinople as a rhetor. The Patriarch Photius, who read and made excerpts from the work in the ninth century, tells us that it only dealt with the years 473 to 480 AD, while the data in the *Suda* encyclopaedia have it begin with Constantine I. We may assume that Malchus' account was structured similarly to the histories of Zosimus, narrating recent events in detail, and older history only in brief surveys.

The extant excerpts indicate that Malchus' historiographical work was of very high quality with regard to both historical accuracy and language and style. It contained, for instance, speeches by the chief historical personages, and the author also followed Classic traditions in other respects. Whether he was pagan or Christian, we cannot tell.

In the period of a comprehensive restoration policy under the Emperor Justinian there was a rich flowering of historiography. Its main exponent was Procopius from Caesarea in Palestine. That he came from a high-ranking family is suggested by his sympathies for aristocratic people and values. After a legal education, he was at least until 540 AD part of the staff of the great Belisarius, taking part in his campaigns on the Empire's eastern border, in Africa, and in Italy. For the subsequent ten or twelve years Procopius lived in Constantinople where he produced his historical writings. A work in eight books dealt with the Empire's war against the Persians, Vandals, and Ostrogoths, up to the year 553 AD. The *Anecdota*, his secret history not intended for publication, was according to the preface a companion piece to the war history, as a record of internal events in the Empire narrated with regard to the biographies of the Emperor and Empress. But in fact it was a scathing pamphlet against Justinian and Theodora. Finally, there were six books describing Justinian's architectural activities, divided according to countries; and this work turned out to be a eulogy of the Emperor.

Procopius' war history stands in the tradition of Classic historiography, especially that of Thucydides, and its objectivity and expertise does anything but disgrace this tradition. The only factor qualifying the author's objective view is the honest admiration which he had for Belisarius, a man fallen out of favour as early as 542 AD. However, a much less positive picture of Belisarius is drawn in the secret history, which is of that type of biographical historiography of which Ammianus disapproved (see p. 467), a manner of writing which had become extremely popular since the second century AD. Procopius' work illustrates very well that this genre of writing always came dangerously close to mere gossip. His own account of Imperial architecture is not only of interest to the archaeologist, but also furnishes much of our knowledge of Early Byzantine monarchic ideology.

Procopius' view of history has some remarkable features. The idea that events are influenced by people who are wise enough to reckon with the superior and unpredictable power of chance was a notion from Classic historiography which, in Procopius' view of the world, did not apparently clash with the Christian belief in a divine providence. The secret history expresses the author's firm belief in demons: in it Justinian is the representative of demonic powers, described in the language of eschatology.

Procopius' work was continued by the lawyer or *scholasticus* Agathias of Myrina in Asia Minor. Agathias had a better literary education than his predecessor but was much less important as a historian. He is also known for his poetic epigrams (see p. 123). Agathias continued the account of the war history up to the year 558 AD, and even more than Procopius had done, he sought to imitate the language of Thucydides. However, his work falls short of that of his immediate predecessor as regards factual exactness, depth of analysis of situations and motives, and clarity of description of historical processes. Both authors nevertheless document the wide geographical horizon of educated people of the period, by dealing in detail with events in the Middle East. According to his own statement, Agathias even had Persian sources translated.

Procopius and Agathias are the first in a series of famous Byzantine historians who have given us a complete record of events up to the end of the Middle Ages. Agathias' work was continued by the Protector (i.e. a member of the Imperial bodyguard) Menander whose writing is extant in fragments. He in turn was succeeded by Theophylactus Simocattes whose work covers the years up to 602 AD. In the Latin West there was nothing to match this continuous writing of historiography on a high literary level; it documents the vital force of the Classical tradition in the East, unbroken in spite of all changes, crises, and catastrophes.

Chronography

I have already said that chronography and chronology, separate from literary historiography but still relevant to it, had for many centuries been pursued scientifically in order to co-ordinate the many chronological systems and had gained added importance in Christianity because of the efforts to establish a correlation between Biblical data concerning the history of salvation and the major dates of the Graeco-Roman tradition. Milestones of this development are the chronicles by Sextus Julius Africanus and Hippolytus from the early third century AD, and the chronographical work by Eusebius from the early fourth century AD which was soon translated into Latin, as well as into the languages of the Christian orient.

From the fourth century AD onwards, there was a growing number of chronicles in which human history is described briefly but comprehensively; these appeared in the West as well as the East. They offered a chance for the spiritual edification of especially the less educated reader, for example, by putting emphasis on particular events and pointing out the providential course of history; or even by communicating certain historical-theological doctrines such as, for instance, chiliastic ideas, by corresponding divisions of epochs. I have already mentioned the edition of Eusebius' chronicle by the learned Hieronymus. The latter was guided by the aim of incorporating names and dates from the Latin tradition, above all from intellectual life, into the Christian plan, and he found the material for this in the antiquarian-grammatical writings of Suetonius (see p. 258).

A Latin edition of Hippolytus' chronicle, continued up to the year 334 AD, is featured in an anonymous collection from the year 354 AD, a work which likewise contains a calendar of the pagan as well as of the Christian festivals of the city of Rome. From the year 397 AD, we have a short world chronicle by an African bishop who was a follower of chiliastic doctrine. Frequently translators and editors of such chronicles would add appendices describing events from their own lifetime, with more detail than featured in the main narrative, and hence of particular value for modern historians. Here chronography and historiography are seen to overlap.

A case in point is the very carefully written and styled world chronicle by Sulpicius Severus from the early fifth century AD. He was a friend and biographer of Martin of Tours, arguably the most important figure in the ecclesiastical history of Gaul in the fourth century AD. Similar additions are also found in editions of the chronicle of Hieronymus – itself an edition of Eusebius' work – published towards the end of the fifth century AD by Tiro Prosper from Aquitania in southern France, and by the Spanish Bishop Hydatius. A similar case is the sixth-century chronicle by Marcellinus Comes which is written in Latin, in spite of the fact that it was produced in Constantinople, and deals exclusively with events in the Greek East.

Unfortunately not extant are two other world chronicles written in Alexandria around 400 AD by Panodorus and Anianus. They were used as models for a large number of later chronicles, also in oriental languages, and the imitations came to replace the originals. Panodorus and Anianus were monks and with very few exceptions, the series of Byzantine chronicles which reaches far into the Middle Ages was produced in monasteries. In these works, mostly written with very little literary ambition and in an idiom close to the vernacular, the dominant element is edification, combined with the communication of a Christian view of world history. But they also show the influence of the solid scientific work of Classic and early Christian chronography, and they contain some important pieces of information. Like the pastoral care directed at large groups of the urban population, these chronicles addressed a wider public. This is also true of the earliest completely extant example of the series from the sixth century AD, even if this particular work was not written by a monk. The voluminous world history in eighteen books by John Malalas from Syria is the oldest known work of Byzantine literature written in the vernacular.

5 PHILOSOPHY

In my previous sections on the Christian Empire, I have repeatedly emphasised the influence of Neo-Platonist philosophy on those writings which reflect the literary education of the period. Cases in point are the speeches by the Emperor Julian (see p. 455) as well as Servius' commentary on Virgil (see p. 444), or Macrobius' *Saturnalia*. The world view and the terminological categories of this philosophy determined to a large extent the manner in which Christians as well as pagans gave linguistic expression to religious phenomena, and in which they wrote and interpreted literary texts.

The East

During the period I am dealing with in this section of my account, school philosophy had several centres of teaching and research, the most prominent being Athens and Alexandria in the East, and Rome and Milan in the West. In this last phase of Classical philosophy the distinctions between the four major schools of the Hellenistic age were no longer of any significance. The heads of the Athens schools all regarded themselves as successors to Plato, but none the less for a long time the fixed course of instruction in Platonic philosophy began with the study of Aristotle's works. Within the tradition of Platonic doctrine there was some debate as to whether there were any real differences between Plato and Aristotle, but the last philosopher who appears to us as a Peripatetic was the aforementioned Anatolius (see p. 402). Frequent reference was still made to details of Epicurean and Stoic doctrine, but the last philosophers who called themselves Epicureans or Stoics belonged to the second and third century AD respectively.

Central terms and concepts of Stoic ethics had long been integrated into Platonic-Peripatetic philosophy, which had also incorporated many elements from the Pythagorean tradition. Iamblichus in particular (see p. 402) had attached great importance to a comprehensive absorption of Pythagoreanism. What became more and more evident was the effort to see the philosophy of all schools and trends, including the traditional wisdom of exotic peoples as well as the Orphic writings of religious revelation and the Chaldaean oracles, as communicating one and the same truth. Again, it was Iamblichus who finally secured the acceptance of theurgy (see p. 402), the approaching of the divine or the Supreme Being by means of cultic practices or ritualistic-magical formulas, as an alternative path to that of philosophical thought.

A curious fact is the survival of Cynic traditions in this late period. Cynic circles equated philosophy with ascetic living, shunning the comforts of civilisation, and hence being in accordance with nature; Cynic doctrine aimed to prove that not only the desire for rank and riches but also that for theoretical knowledge was a product of human vanity. From the biography of the Neo-Platonist Isidorus (see p. 493), we learn of a certain Sallustius who enticed a pupil away from the great Proclus, head of the Platonic Academy for almost fifty years.

A certain number of Christians would also identify with the Cynic tradition through their choice of clothing and their lifestyle, but naturally they replaced the model of Hercules by that of Christ. The church had no objection to this as it had a high regard for ascetic practice. During his brief service as Bishop of Constantinople Gregory of Nazianzus befriended the Christian Cynic Maximus. He was, however, ill rewarded for this friendship by Maximus, whose pose as a Cynic served to disguise his penchant for fairly easy and extravagant living.

Intellectual life of the period was dominated by the notion that, ultimately, only ancient traditions have the power to justify vital decisions and value judgments. This idea was most clearly expressed by the professional philosophers. The corresponding orientation of all philosophy according to the content of the school founders' canonised writings had already begun in the first century BC. Besides, it seemed natural to ascribe a similar authority also to obscure texts presenting themselves as exotic or ancient wisdom, and to extract the desired meaning through purposeful interpretation.

This is why commentaries on the works of the two great philosophers account for most of the philosophical literature handed down to us from the time between the middle of the fourth century and the end of the Platonic Academy in Athens at the beginning of the sixth. It is not at all surprising that there is an exceptionally large number of such commentaries from this last and final period in the history of Classical philosophy. Wherever scholarly efforts in the same field were pursued over several generations during the Classical age, the resulting publications usually included all that their authors found useful in older books, complemented by the results of new research. In this manner a younger textbook or commentary often came to replace its predecessor, for unlike in literary works of art, formal excellence does not necessarily guarantee the continued interest of later generations in scholarly writings of the past. The only exceptions from this process of replacement are works which have acquired some kind of an authoritative status and are thus perhaps themselves commented on. An example is the *Eisagoge* by Porphyry (see p. 374), a survey of Aristotle's works on logic, written as an introduction to the systematic study of philosophy.

Around the middle of the fourth century AD the tradition of Platonic teaching in the East was largely dominated by the pupils of Iamblichus (see p. 402) who taught in several different places. Yet it seems that, apart from the philosophical motifs in the works of the Emperor Julian, only the school traditions of Athens and Alexandria are documented in literature. Between those two, there were many personal links. The only writing which cannot be ascribed to any definite school is the short work by Sallustius on the world and the gods, a brief survey of Neo-Platonist ontology and theology. The author was presumably close to the Emperor Julian.

We learn about the school tradition of Athens from two biographies which Marinus and Damascius dedicated to their respective teachers Proclus and Isidorus. These books, of which only the first is completely extant, give us valuable insights into the history of the Academy, its intellectual and social context, and the development of its teaching. But above all, they illustrate contemporary notions concerning the nature and the task of the philosopher. The life of Proclus resembles Athanasius' biography of Antonius (see p. 410) in presenting the great teacher's progress towards moral perfection via exactly those stages which Neo-Platonist ethics had postulated since Plotinus. At that time moral perfection was seen as liberation of the spirit from all restrictions of corporeal existence in the empirical world. This liberation was to manifest itself in a life of intense prayer, in experiences of mystic vision which transcend discursive thought, and in the ability, created by the close link with the world of purely spiritual beings, to perform actions which seem impossible according to the laws of the material world. This perfection is the basis for the authority of the true philosopher as teacher, helper, and counsellor. In this late period of Classical culture the philosopher occupies that position which is given to the saint in the Christian community. Thus the aforementioned interest in theurgy (see p. 486) was matched by notions of the moral-religious perfection of man.

The first of the late Athenian Neo-Platonists was Plutarch of Athens who lived to a very old age and was head of the Academy until 431 AD. From quotations in later commentaries, we know some passages from his own commentaries on different works by Aristotle and Plato. Plutarch was succeeded by Syrianus, whose commentary on Aristotle's *Metaphysics* is partly extant. While Syrianus followed the convention of the latter-day Academy in beginning philosophical instruction with the study of Aristotle, he did place particular emphasis on the divergence between the Platonic doctrine of ideas and Aristotelian metaphysics, in total contrast to the dominant trend in late Platonism, which saw the philosophy of the two Classics as a non-contradictory whole.

According to the list of his writings found in the so-called *Suda* encyclopaedia from the tenth century AD, Syrianus must have been an exceptionally prolific scholar. His pupils as well as subsequent generations held him in very high regard. He wrote commentaries – frequently not styled as literary works, but rather in the form of lecture notes – on several philosophical treatises as well as on Homer, on Orphic and Pythagorean writings, and even on the doctrine of ideas developed by the rhetor Hermogenes (see p. 256). Syrianus' interpretation of philosophical texts followed the principles established by Iamblichus (see p. 402), and it would be extremely interesting to know more of his methods of reading poetical works allegorically in the context of his philosophy.

The most famous men among the many pupils of Syrianus chose to follow different paths. The Jew Domninus turned his back on philosophical teaching and took up mathematical studies. Hermias, of whom we have an extant commentary on Plato's *Phaedrus* which consists of notes presumably taken from Syrianus' lectures, returned to his native city Alexandria where his son Ammonius became the celebrated teacher of a whole series of productive philosophers. Proclus, who was head of the Athenian Academy until 485 AD, became the most important figure in Late Platonic systematics, and the most influential communicator of Platonic philosophy to the Middle Ages.

Proclus came from a family resident in Lycia in south-western Anatolia. He was born in Constantinople; before moving to Athens shortly after 430 AD, at the age of about twenty, he was a student of grammar, rhetoric, and law in Alexandria. There he was also first introduced to Plato's philosophy.

The Platonic philosophers of Alexandria were a little less devoted than others to those theological and ontological speculations which Iamblichus had developed to a new extreme. They attached greater importance to the study of mathematics as well as of other sciences, and the scientific orientation of their philosophy caused a particular interest in the writings of Aristotle. At the time a teacher of mathematics in Alexandria was the female philosopher Hypatia, daughter of the famous astronomer Theon. Her violent death I have already mentioned (see p. 431). One of her pupils was Synesius of Cyrene (see p. 456), who, even as a Christian and a Bishop, remained faithful to the Neo-Platonist doctrine to which she had introduced him. This is particularly evident in his Christian hymns (see p. 606), in which Christian and Neo-Platonist elements are inseparably united.

Between the Platonics of Alexandria and Athens, there was a constant exchange. Hierocles, for instance, head of the school in Alexandria from 420 AD, was a pupil of Plutarch. From him, we have a commentary on the so-called *Golden Poem*. This piece of hexametrical didactic verse from about the second century AD contains, in a popularised form, the essentials of the Pythagorean tradition, which was held in particularly high regard by the Athenian Platonics, as well as the gist of the so-called Chaldaean oracles, likewise from the second century AD (see p. 283). From the *Bibliotheca* of the Patriarch Photius, we also know longer excerpts from Hierocles' tract on destiny and free will. The doctrines expressed in these two writings have only few features which could be called Neo-Platonist in the narrower sense and appear rather as a mixture of familiar older Platonic, Aristotelian, and Stoic motifs. What is peculiar is that, in spite of its definitely philosophical origin, Hierocles' doctrine of providence is akin to Christian ideas. Divine providence to him no longer establishes a rigid, irrevocable nexus of predetermination, as it had appeared to the Stoics. Like Christian theologians who emphasised this particularly when arguing against the Stoa or astrology, Hierocles saw providence as the all-embracing, but free providential acting, of the divine matched by the freedom of human decision.

The tradition of philosophical teaching in Alexandria received new impulses through Hermias, who had for some time been a fellow student of Proclus under the teacher Syrianus (see p. 488). After moving to Athens, Proclus was first taught by Plutarch, and then, after Plutarch's death, by Syrianus, who chose him as his successor to the headship of the school. Proclus took up this office as early as 437 AD and retained it until his death in 485 AD. We know the titles of more than fifty works by Proclus, including some fairly voluminous writings; this literary production was closely connected with his teaching. Proclus' biographer Marinus tells us that his working day was strictly regulated, and that he always tried to put down in writing the results of the discussions following his lectures.

Proclus interpreted the writings of Plato and Aristotle as well as those of the 'ancient theologians', (viz. Orphic poetry and the Chaldaean oracles). Extant works include a major commentary on Plato's *Timaeus* which shows the influence of Syrianus, as well as commentaries on the dialogues *Parmenides*, *Cratylus*, and the *Great Alcibiades*. There is also a longer writing on Plato's *State*, which is less of a running exegesis than a series of treatises on selected problems. Some of these commentaries, like the writings on systematics which I shall discuss hereafter, are extant in Latin texts, for Proclus' philosophy entered High Scholastics through Latin translations. The extant systematic writings are the *Platonic Theology*, the *Elements of Platonic Theology*, and three specialist treatises exclusively extant in Latin, discussing providence, free will, and the nature of evil.

In Proclus' world of ideas, we find a synthesis of strict scientific method with the unceasing attempt to achieve a direct vision of the supreme, divine being at the end of the path of discursive thought. This explains why he attached equally great importance to mathematical or astronomical studies and to the interpretation of ancient religious poetry, or rather such poetry which he regarded as ancient. His desire to achieve an exact systematisation of Platonic doctrine based on the reading of the founder's works is as obvious in his writing as his very profound piety, based on philosophy but practised in meditation, prayer, and ritual. Impressive evidence of this is found in his divine hymns, which express a philosophical religiousness close to that found in the poems of Synesius (see p. 456).

Proclus brought a systematic conclusion to the philosophy of Plotinus, in particular to his doctrine of being, by interpreting the works of Plato after the method developed by Iamblichus. Iamblichus had already attempted to solve the task inherent in Plotinus' plan (see p. 402), that is to give a plausible explanation for the emergence of the variety of the visible and intelligible cosmos from the primal one. Iamblichus postulated that the spiritual being differentiated itself into ever-new hypostases or entities prior to all shaping of matter and suggested that the difference between the knower and the known, the creator and the created, could be understood on the basis of the manifold structure of the spiritual world.

Plotinus had completely excluded the supernatural, in other words, that which is inaccessible to discursive thought, from his explanation of the world and of being. He once declared that philosophy must not have anything to do with 'sorcery'. Porphyry, on the other hand, had been inclined to give some room to that component of philosophical speculation, presumably first and foremost because of his scholarly interest in the wealth of relevant traditions. Consequently he introduced, among other material, comments on the Chaldaean oracles into philosophical teaching. Iamblichus, who for a while was a pupil of Porphyry in spite of being almost the same age, and who later became a stern critic of his teacher, scorned the enlargement of philosophical doctrine with the help of extensive scholarly research. Like Porphyry, he used many pre-Plotinian elements of the Platonic tradition, but always with a view towards giving a fixed method to the interpretation of 'holy' writings of philosophical or ancient-exotic origin. This was meant to contribute to the creation of a unified system incorporating not only discursive thought but also theurgy. Iamblichus was not too interested in any scholarship and science outside the context of philosophy.

Proclus went further on this path of methodical systematisation, showing a particular preference for the assumption of three kinds of being or action on each respective level of the order of being. This resembles Christian theology's doctrine of the trinity, but it is very unlikely that Proclus' philosophy was influenced by that. The triad scheme had existed long before in traditional Platonic teaching: for instance, in the Chaldaean oracles and their interpretation from which the Christians adopted it for the formulation of their dogma. Proclus, for example, distinguishes between three manners of being as being, living, and thinking; and between three classes of spiritual beings, intelligible ones which can be mentally comprehended, intellectual ones which mentally comprehend, and one mixed form which he interpolates as a middle layer in this ascending hierarchy. He speaks of three forms of appearance of the divine, forms which mediate between the all-embracing universal God and the beings of the material world, as angels, demons, and heroes; and he also mentions three stages on the path towards human perfection, namely love in the sense of the Platonic Eros, truth in the sense of recognising the order of being, and faith in the sense of a union with the supreme One, transcending discursive thought. Again and again, these definitions document the idea of successive steps in the ascent towards the highest One, which are in turn the stages through which the One communicates itself to the world in which we live.

The old threefold division of philosophy into dialectics or logic, physics, and ethics, had acquired a new meaning in Late Platonism. Now, regardless of the adoption of Aristotelian logic as a general introduction to philosophy, dialectics was defined according to Plato's use of the term, as a method for approaching the transcendental being. Accordingly, physics became the science of man's liberation from matter. But although the basis had changed, the systematic order which Proclus strove for was no less rigid than in school philosophy during the age of Hellenism.

Proclus was the first Greek philosopher who postulated a force in the soul above the power of discursive thought and rational cognition, a force which enables man to perform the union with the supreme One in ecstatic vision. The only comparable concepts existed in Jewish and Christian theology, in which the ability to follow God's commands – not to be explained rationally – through one's own free choice, was occasionally defined as man's peculiar capacity, beside his rational one. This is the root of our notion of conscience.

We may well assume that Proclus would have rejected any modern classification of that power of the soul which he saw beside the faculties commonly recognised in philosophical psychology, as being something irrational or extra-rational. In spite of all his preference for mysterious self-revelations of the divine in the old traditions of Greek and Barbarian sages or theologians which called for interpretation, Proclus remained a true Platonic in seeing the final step of cognition, the immediate and illuminating vision of the divine as the ultimate end of lifelong effort, as reasonable and hence communicable. Rational cognition and mystic-ecstatic illumination were an inseparable unit to him, first and foremost because both were directed at the same goal. Consequently he saw no real distinction between religion and philosophy, for as an effort to know the highest One, the latter was both theology, the doctrine of God, and morality, that is guidance for living. In this the religiously orientated philosophy of Late Platonism differed fundamentally from Christianity, which made as much use as possible of terms, methods, and basic concepts of contemporary philosophy in the elaboration of its theology, but which maintained a clear-cut distinction between the content of the faith, based on direct divine revelation and made palpable in ritual worship, and its terminological explanation in theology.

Proclus was an extremely erudite man who knew the works of his predecessors very well. This is why above all his extant exegetical works offer us a wealth of information about traditional philosophical teaching, especially in Middle and Neo-Platonism. Time and again, Proclus refers approvingly or disapprovingly to older philosophers' attempts at interpreting certain passages in Plato's dialogues: that is to authors whose works have mostly been lost. In contrast to that, Proclus' systematic works contain much fewer references of this kind, as there the author's main goal was to present a logical argument or system. Still, the commentaries also contain longer passages that are systematic in content, sometimes about subjects which are less well represented in the mainly ontological-theological systematic works, such as ethics, aesthetics, anthropology, mathematics, musical theory, or astronomy.

I have already referred to Proclus' influence on High Scholastics; he was also held in high esteem by the Platonists of the Byzantine Middle Ages and the Renaissance, when scholars gained access to his works in the original language. Proclus' reputation sank in the nineteenth century, the time when people cherished all that in their opinion could be observed and understood in its genesis, development, and mutation. The scholars of that age, who were interested in contemplating what was alive and what could be described empirically, were disgusted by Proclus' strict limitation to the spiritual world which can only be approached through speculation and introspection, as well as by his striving for a strict systematisation of all knowledge. This was considered ivory-towered, over-subtle, and scholastic in the negative sense of the term. It was not until recently that a different and ultimately more just view of Proclus prevailed once again, recognising his unerring struggle for intellectual honesty and precision, based on the firm conviction of the immutable primacy of spiritual being. The humanising effect of a philosophy with this kind of an orientation is certainly of a particular significance in times in which the external circumstances of social life seem to have disintegrated into disorder, distress, and hopelessness.

Two pupils of Proclus succeeded him in the scholarchate, one shortly after the other: the Samaritan Marinus and Isidorus of Alexandria. I have already mentioned more than once Marinus' biography of Proclus because it contains valuable information concerning the history of philosophy. Marinus portrays the life of the master as the path to *eudaimonia* or perfection, via those stages outlined in the ethical theory of Neo-Platonism. In his doctrine Marinus placed particular emphasis on the mathematical component of Platonic philosophy, for to him as to many other Platonic philosophers, only mathematics could show the way from the empirical world in which man is trapped, to the invisible world of the spirit.

Isidorus is best known through the biography written by his successor Damascius (see p. 487). Before he became a pupil of Proclus, he studied and taught Platonic philosophy in Alexandria; afterwards, however, he seems to have followed Proclus' teachings extremely faithfully.

Damascius from Damascus in Syria had also begun his philosophical studies in Alexandria, under Ammonius (see p. 488) and Isidorus, whom he succeeded in Athens. In 529 AD, when the Emperor Justinian closed the Athenian Academy as a stronghold of pagan science, Damascius and six other colleagues from Athens and Alexandria were invited by the great Persian King Chusrō Anōsharvān to establish a new centre of philosophical teaching at his court. The seven learned men accepted, but went back to the Roman Empire after a few years. The Byzantine historian Agathias (see p. 483) tells us that one of Chusrō's express conditions in a peace treaty with Justinian was a guarantee of free philosophical inquiry for the seven on their return.

Apart from excerpts of the aforementioned life of Isidorus, the Patriarch

Photius has recorded parts of a collection of reports about occult events, as compiled by Damascius. Three other works by Damascius are completely extant, two of them being commentaries or marginal notes from classes on the Platonic dialogues *Parmenides* and *Philebus*; the latter has been erroneously ascribed to Olympiodorus of Alexandria. The third is a treatise on the doctrine of principles. We know of further works through quotations, but none of them are extant.

A contemporary and pupil of Damascius was Simplicius who was first taught in Alexandria and later emigrated to Persia with Damascius. There are particularly many extant commentaries by Simplicius on Aristotelian writings, but unfortunately the most important one on the *Metaphysics* has been lost. Simplicius' commentaries are different from the other exegetical works of the Neo-Platonists in showing fewer traces of originating from instruction, and rather appear as the results of scholarly research. Beside some partly very astute individual readings of Aristotelian texts, they feature plenty of references to older philosophy. The commentary on the *Physics*, for instance, provides us with a large number of literal quotations from pre-Socratic writings.

A totally different piece is Simplicius' commentary on the so-called *Enchairidion* by the Stoic Epictetus (see p. 200), a short catechism of basic moral doctrines of the Stoa, based on notes taken in Epictetus' lectures. Simplicius believed himself capable of proving that in this field of practical moral teaching as well as in that of ontological speculation, the fundamental teachings of the philosophers of the past had never contradicted one another; above all, those of Plato and Aristotle, but also those of the Stoics and pre-Socratics. He maintained that through correct interpretation, the reader could again and again repeat the unchanging recognition of the truth achieved in all philosophy. It is this basic tenet which led to the preservation of many passages from lost texts for posterity. But, strangely enough, we know of no commentary by Simplicius on Plato.

As literary evidence of the Persian episode, we have the Latin translation of a short treatise on logic by Simplicius' colleague Priscianus, a work dedicated to King Chusrō. From the same author there are also parts of the interpretation of a treatise by Aristotle's pupil Theophrastus.

The Alexandrian tradition of Neo-Platonism was revived above all through the teaching of Ammonius, a contemporary of Proclus. To distinguish him from the other men of the same name who were the teachers of Plutarch (see p. 188) and Plotinus (see p. 370), this Ammonius is always cited with his patronym Hermiou (see p. 488). Of his hand, there are several extant commentaries on Aristotle's writings about logic, but he became more famous through his pupils John Philoponus, Asclepius, and Olympiodorus.

By Olympiodorus, we have commentaries on the Platonic dialogues *Gorgias*, *Phaedo*, and the so-called *Great* or *First Alcibiades*, as well as a life of Plato compiled from earlier biographies. It belonged to the Alcibiades commentary since in the curriculum of the Academy the interpretation of that dialogue opened the proper study of Plato and was combined with a general introduction to Plato's philosophy. As I have said before, the reading of Plato followed the study of Aristotle. We also have didactic tracts about the latter by Olympiodorus: namely, an introduction to Aristotelian logic and commentaries on the treatises on categories and on meteorology respectively. Further commentaries on Aristotle which illustrate the method of Olympiodorus were written by his pupils David and Elias. Beyond Aristotle's writings on logic with which the study of philosophy began, Olympiodorus' exegesis includes the introduction to those works written by Porphyry. Thus in this late period we find commentaries on commentaries (see p. 376).

By far the most famous representative of the Alexandrian tradition was the Christian John Philoponus, for a while a fellow student and colleague of Simplicius. His extant commentaries on Aristotle's writings about logic are among the best we know of in Classical exegetical literature. They have come to be properly appreciated only in the last three decades when new developments in the field of logic led to a reappraisal of logical theories of the Classical age.

John Philoponus' scientific interests, in keeping with the tradition of Alexandria, are also reflected by the fact that he wrote several treatises on mathematical, astronomical, and grammatical subjects. Besides, there is an extant tract from his hand which refutes the dogma about the eternal nature of the cosmos which the Platonic tradition had upheld for centuries. The question of whether the world is temporal or eternal was central to the debate between the Classical world view and the Jewish-Christian belief in creation. In his *Timaeus*, Plato had taught that the empirical-material world owes its existence to a creator, and thus has a beginning in or with time; but to him, the world was formed after the model of the eternal, intelligible world of ideas, of whose nature it thus had a share. Jews and Christians such as Philo of Alexandria or Justin had already interpreted the account of creation in the Book of Genesis in this sense, thus bridging the gap between Greek and Biblical concepts. But such a compromise was not sustainable, as the Biblical belief in a sovereign God did not permit the recognition of a world order without a beginning, nor an immutable one. In philosophical terminology the only notion that corresponded to the Biblical faith was the doctrine about a creation from nothing which implied the temporal nature of the intelligible as well as the empirical world.

In Late Platonism, this idea appears twice, in the work of the aforementioned Hierocles (see p. 489), and then in that of Philoponus. There have been repeated suggestions of Christian influence in these cases. But none at all is in evidence for Hierocles; and as to the treatise of the Christian

Philoponus, his argument also contains no single element from the Christian tradition in a strictly philosophical account which features, among others, Stoic motifs. In the materialistic world view of the Stoics universes were born and perished in regular cycles, and the only eternal thing was a fiery-pneumatic substance which time and again created form, movement or life, and finally consciousness.

Philoponus also distinguished himself as a theological author. He produced one of the many commentaries on the Biblical account of creation in which Christians, understandably enough, challenged the cosmological doctrines of philosophy again and again. There is also a short but learned treatise about the calculation of the date for Easter. Philoponus' major theological work, however, was an effort at mediation in the debate about the Monophysite doctrine (see p. 421). He elaborated his plan for a comprehensive doctrine of trinity with the help of Aristotelian terms; the result was condemned as heretical by the orthodoxy, and thus survived only in a Syrian translation, apart from a few quotations in the original language. Philoponus' reputation is reflected by the fact that two commentaries on Aristotle written during or shortly after his lifetime were handed down under his name.

Although some of its representatives joined their Athenian colleagues in their exodus, the tradition of philosophical teaching in Alexandria did not come to the same abrupt end as the Platonic Academy in Athens. One reason for this was, of course, the far greater prestige of the school founded by Plato himself which could be quite rightly called a stronghold of pagan philosophy. But another factor must be seen in the closer ties of the Alexandrian philosophers with the specialist sciences, while the Athenians had concentrated entirely on philosophical speculation and the interpretation of Classic school texts.

Alexandria remained a centre of specialist scientific research, with continued remarkable achievements in mathematics, astronomy, medicine, and grammar, and thus with a considerable influence on intellectual life far into the sixth century AD. The best example is probably the architect Anthemius from Tralles in Asia Minor who, with Isidorus of Miletus, built the Hagia Sophia in Constantinople, consecrated in 532 AD. Both architects also produced writings on mechanics, mathematics, and optics. Isidorus' pupil Eutocius was a prominent mathematician, and Anthemius' three brothers were well respected as physicians or grammarians respectively.

Nevertheless, science in this period was likewise dominated by an interest in the works of the past. Isidorus, for instance, produced a commentary on Heron's treatise from the second century AD about the construction of vaults, while Eutocius wrote commentaries on the works of Archimedes, and those of Apollonius of Perga from the third century BC. The geographical and astronomical plans of Ptolemy (see p. 285) became the subject of commentaries as early as the fourth century AD. The author of those was Pappus, also a distinguished mathematician working in Alexandria. Pappus also compiled a collection of important texts from the mathematical literature of Hellenism, with original additions and explanations. This work is one of our most important sources of knowledge about older mathematics.

This background explains why the borders between philosophy and the specialist sciences were less marked in Alexandria than in Athens where science had never been cultivated in a comparable way. This is why the Platonic Domninus seems to have turned his back on his Athenian colleagues when he began to devote himself entirely to his mathematical interests (see p. 488). In contrast to this, Olympiodorus and Damascius quote the Alexandrian Platonic Asclepiodotus in their discussions of philosophical issues and hence as a colleague, even though he seems to have been mainly interested in mathematical and medical problems, and, as Damascius explicitly criticises, he disliked the mysticism of Orphic and Chaldaean texts.

As late as in the seventh century AD a scholar from Alexandria was called to Constantinople by the Emperor Heraclius. This was Stephanus who, like his predecessors during the five centuries before him, wrote commentaries on Aristotle and mathematical treatises. Some of his writings are even extant but this tradition died completely after Stephanus and was not revived until the ninth century in Constantinople.

Neo-Platonist philosophy became firmly rooted also in the west of the Empire, above all through the reception of Porphyry's writings. I have already mentioned its influence in the context of the scholarly cultivation of Classic Roman literature and its exegesis. It is debatable to what extent we can class the learned Cornelius Labeo among the philosophers; neither can we be certain of the life dates of this man, whose works were used by Macrobius (see p. 444), and who was the target of polemics by Arnobius and Augustine. However, his writings on the old Roman religion seem to have interpreted it in the sense of Neo-Platonist theology.

The same is definitely true of the works of Vettius Agorius Praetextatus who was close to the Emperor Julian and was the most eminent figure among the pagan Senatorial aristocracy in Rome during the second half of the 4th century AD. I have already mentioned him as a confidant of Symmachus (see p. 445). Vettius' effort at a scientific cataloguing of ancient Roman religion was meant to contribute to its revival. That he used philosophical theology may be inferred from the fact that he made a Latin translation of Themistius' (see p. 452) paraphrases of Aristotle's *Analytics*. This indicates a serious philosophical interest which is undoubtedly evident in the works of Macrobius from the early fifth century AD where it likewise appears in the context of antiquarian studies.

Such a permeation of scholarly research by the ideas and terms of contemporary philosophy could also be observed in the East, quite independent of their use as tools of Christian theology. Towards the end of the fourth century AD, for instance, the Christian Bishop Nemesius of Emesa in Syria wrote a textbook or manual of anthropology, whose title refers to a famous treatise in the Hippocratic corpus, and whose text likewise draws on a large amount of medical writings. But the author also cites many philosophical authorities, whose words are interpreted in the sense of Neo-Platonist doctrine, just like the Christian sources used by the author.

The doctrine about the nature of man was traditionally part of philosophy's subjects, and thus the extensive use of philosophical literature in Nemesius' treatise need not surprise us. Much more striking are the borrowings from Neo-Platonist philosophy which abound in the grammatical-antiquarian writings by John Laurentius Lydus from the sixth century AD (see p. 441). The author's good command of Latin, however, is not so exceptional for one writing in Constantinople during the reign of Justinian.

The earliest major extant work of true specialist philosophical literature in Latin Neo-Platonism is the translation of the main source for Platonic cosmology, Plato's *Timaeus* dialogue, accompanied by a detailed commentary. The author Calcidius seems to have lived around 400 AD. The work is dedicated to a man named Osius; there are several reasons which preclude an identification with the Bishop Ossius of Cordoba, the Emperor Constantine's advisor on ecclesiastical politics.

In his interpretation of *Timaeus*, Calcidius closely follows Porphyry, but also refers to older Platonic writings, above all from the second century AD, which he presumably got to know through that older author. Some parallels also indicate an acquaintance with Iamblichus' writings, but Calcidius' exegesis of Plato shows no trace of Iamblichus' methods, which were never influential in the West.

Calcidius' work documents the high level of philosophical erudition and interpretative art in the Latin West, reflected not only in his literary references and the quality of his exegesis but also in the elegant adaptation of philosophical terminology in Latin. For its specific doctrines, Late Platonism had developed expressions which could not always be rendered in Latin with its philosophical vocabulary, created by Cicero in his effort to present philosophical arguments in his native language.

The creation of a Latin terminology for Neo-Platonist philosophy was the work of C. Marius Victorinus, teacher of rhetoric and grammar. From him we have a number of grammatical and rhetorical writings (see p. 442) as well as several commentaries on letters of the New Testament, and a pamphlet against the Arians. The latter works, writings of high quality produced in Victorinus' old age, will be dealt with in a subsequent section (see p. 561). We cannot be too sure about the dating of Victorinus' numerous philosophical writings mentioned by Augustine and Hieronymus. Augustine became acquainted with the *Platonic Books* of Victorinus during his sojourn in Milan from 383 to 387 AD, when the author was already dead. Hieronymus tells us of a translation of Porphyry's introductory treatise, of a translation-cum-commentary of the treatise on categories, and of a straight translation of Aristotle's *De interpretatione*. He also mentions commentaries on Cicero's philosophical writings and two original treatises on aspects of logic. It is most likely that the *Libri platonici* mentioned by Augustine were translations of works by Porphyry, above all of his most important treatise on the doctrine of the soul, entitled *De regressu animae*. From this wealth of writings the only extant ones are the commentary on Cicero's early work *De inventione* and an excellent original tract by Victorinus which bears the title *De definitionibus*.

Marius Victorinus may well be called the most important communicator of the Porphyrian kind of Neo-Platonism to the Latin West. He himself used this philosophy in his theological writings, and Augustine's philosophical education, which was to become crucial to his theology, was strongly rooted in the study of Victorinus' translations and original works. Marius Victorinus' books were also used by the last philosophical writers in the Latin West, who once more conducted serious philosophical studies during the reign of the Goth Theodoric. They were Cassiodorus and even more importantly Boëthius, the two great communicators of Classical educational knowledge to the Latin Middle Ages.

The example of Favonius Eulogius shows that Christians participated in philosophical studies even in this late period. He was a pupil of Augustine and, like his slightly older contemporary Macrobius, he wrote a commentary on the *Somnium Scipionis*, the final part of Cicero's treatise on the state. Like Macrobius (see p. 446) or Servius in his Virgilian exegesis, Favonius Eulogius also interpreted this text in the sense of Neo-Platonist theology and cosmology.

A man who belongs to the mid-fifth century AD is the rhetor and philosopher Claudianus Mamertus who worked in Gaul and was a friend of Sidonius Apollinaris (see p. 594). By Mamertus we have a treatise on the soul which advocates Neo-Platonist psychology, trying to prove through a number of quotations that it is actually Plato's own doctrine. Closer scrutiny of the text has shown that the quotes from Plato are taken from Porphyry's treatise *De regressu animae*. This was available in Victorinus' Latin translations but Mamertus seems to have read the Greek original, a fact which was pretty exceptional in the Gaul of this period and justifies the author's right to complain about the decline of education, as he does in an extant letter. He himself still had direct access to Greek literature.

The philosophical tradition in the West died with Cassiodorus and Boëthius. Flavius Magnus Aurelius Cassiodorus, who came from a noble Senatorial family of Syrian origin, held high offices of state under Theodoric, although he survived the Gothic rule by several decades, living to the age of nearly a hundred. When the collapse of the Gothic state and the Langobardic invasion brought anarchy, Cassiodorus retired to the monastery of Vivarium which he had founded close to his family estate near the straits of Messina. Its library which he established, and its monastic school to which he himself gave the rules, made it the major educational centre in the following dark centuries.

Cassiodorus was an enormously prolific author. In a grammatical treatise which he produced at the age of ninety-three, he himself gave us a complete catalogue of his writings. They include grammatical, rhetorical, theological, and historical works which I have already mentioned (see p. 474), as well as a collection of his letters and documents as examples for official use, and also philosophical treatises such as a tract on the soul.

Like Cassiodorus and other members of the Roman nobility, Anicius Manlius Severinus Boëthius held high offices under King Theodoric. However, he was later suspected of being involved in a conspiracy, and was executed in 524 AD. Boëthius was a Christian, and we have several theological treatises from his hand. But in detention he wrote a consolatory tract in which he called not upon his faith but upon philosophy to enable him to brave his fate. The short book, which found a large number of readers, is styled as a dialogue between the author and philosophy facing him in the shape of a noble woman. In between discussions of individual problems there are poems in different metres. In its artful composition and its plain style this work is a vivid example of the vital power of a philosophical tradition which had for centuries been able to show people the meaning and the purpose of their actions, by instructing them to lead their lives according to the laws which reason can recognise in the order of nature. The personification of philosophy in Boëthius' work reminds the protagonist of this same principle at the very beginning of the dialogue. In the talk an issue of particular importance is naturally the question about the relationship between fateful predestination through the world order, and free human decision which establishes responsibility. In the discussion of this problem, the author shows an especially close familiarity with the traditional teachings of the different philosophical schools, a wisdom with which he seeks to justify his own attitude to life.

Boëthius' writings had a great influence on the educational world of the Middle Ages. His plan to translate Aristotle's collected works into Latin remained unrealised, with the exception of some of the treatises on logic to which he also produced commentaries. He likewise wrote one on the *Eisagoge*, Porphyry's introductory treatise, on the basis of the translation by Marius Victorinus. But later on Boëthius produced his own translation from the Greek as well as a new commentary, which is another of the rare examples showing a good command of Greek in the Latin West at that time. Because of the commercial, administrative, and military relationships with Byzantium, there were certainly many individuals in the West who mastered Greek vernacular at any point in time during the Late

Classical age, whereas the knowledge of high and literary Greek suffered a rapid decline which had already begun in the third century AD.

Boëthius also wrote commentaries on works of Cicero, and besides, he produced textbooks for the teaching of the seven disciplines known as the *artes liberales*; of those books, only the ones on arithmetic and musical theory are extant. Boëthius' work marks the end of a long and venerable tradition, and the grateful and frequent users of his writings in the Latin Middle Ages knew and appreciated this.

6 TECHNICAL WRITINGS

I have already discussed the continuation of research in the exact sciences (see p. 431). In other specialist areas there is much clearer evidence of how those ties to authorities of the past which are so typical for the intellectual life of the Empire made it difficult to carry on independent and productive scientific work. Authors who aimed for original achievement often saw no other path than that of obscure speculation, or concentrated all efforts on the appeal of their literary presentation. This was a state of affairs particularly marked in the Late Classical age.

Publius Vegetius Renatus, a high official in the Emperor's financial administration, wrote a long treatise on military matters, a work which was used as a textbook in teaching until well into the Modern age, and has thus been handed down in numerous manuscript versions. It was dedicated to an Emperor, presumably Theodosius I, which would mean that it was written around the end of the fourth century AD. The four books deal with the training of recruits, the structuring of a legion, aspects of strategy and tactics, and warfare involving fortifications as well as naval units. In writing his work, Vegetius used a large amount of specialist literature which he listed conscientiously. Those works, however, referred to armies in the Hellenistic age, or the Roman forces of the Late Republic or the Early Empire. Thus the reader is told about the war elephants of the Diadochian hosts, the sickle chariots used in the Battle of Gaugamela, or the infantry training of the Classic Roman legions. Besides all this, we find only occasional references to the author's own lifetime, in which the cavalry had become the most important branch of the Roman military, with whole contingents of Gothic or Sarmatic warriors fighting on the side of the Romans, using their own armament.

Vegetius was an elegant and erudite author, but of military matters he knew as little or as much as anyone can learn from old books. A similar verdict can be made about his second book on veterinary medicine, a work likewise compiled from all kinds of specialist writings. The author once tells us that he occasionally tried a hand at breeding horses, but this did obviously not make him an authority on veterinary issues. However, for the readership which he envisaged the appeal of the literary form was obviously more important than the practical use of such works.

A totally different impression is created by a roughly contemporary memorandum which an anonymous author wrote in Greek. This man makes suggestions aimed at strengthening the defence forces of the Empire and, interestingly enough, the proposals include not only military but also economic points. This short treatise, however, lacks any kind of literary polish.

From the tenth century AD we have a collection of texts belonging to the science of agriculture. The so-called *Geoponica* were compiled at the request of the learned Emperor Constantinus Porphyrogennetus. Their bulk is borrowed from two authors of the fourth and fifth century AD respectively: Anatolius of Berytus and Didymus of Alexandria. Greece had possessed a rich literature on agriculture since the fourth century BC and the Romans had taken up this tradition with much enthusiasm from the time of Cato the Elder (see p. 151). Anatolius' compilation accurately preserved valuable information on efficient farming as collected by earlier writers, while the work of the younger Didymus was full of instructions derived from bizarre speculation or crass superstition.

In the Imperial age there was a great demand for compilations of knowledge in all kinds of different areas and this demand grew even stronger in the Late Classical period. The great legal texts of the fifth and sixth centuries AD, the *Codex Theodosianus* and the *Corpus iuris* of the Emperor Justinian, were written because of this demand; the same is true of the *Office Book* by John Lydus (see p. 498), and of the *Notitia dignitatum*, a table of state officials of the early fifth century AD; and likewise of the so-called *Synecdemus* by an otherwise unknown Hierocles, a catalogue of the sixty-four provinces and 935 cities of the Roman Empire during the reign of Justinian.

The literary reflection of changes in the geographical view of the earth will be discussed in a subsequent section (see p. 562).

7 CHRISTIAN-THEOLOGICAL LITERATURE

General remarks

Between the middle of the fourth and of the fifth century respectively, the central tenets of the Christian faith were at last officially formulated. The Council of Constantinople in 381 AD confirmed and fine-tuned the formula agreed in 325 AD at Nicaea, thus putting an end to the so-called Arian debate, a dispute during whose last phase the dogmatical challenge had been met with some very different doctrines, all developed from approaches used in the writings of Arius. The Council of Ephesus in 431 AD separated the orthodox dogma about the saviour as a person from the view held by the followers of Nestorius; the Council of Chalcedon finally formulated the orthodox creed in a reaction against the teachings of the so-called Monophysites.

However, those groups whose doctrines had been out-voted in the respective councils continued to exist as churches with their own hierarchies and organisations. Thus, for example, all Germanic tribes in Gaul except for the Franks had adopted Christianity in a form which was condemned as Arian in 381 AD, even though it had been favoured by the reigning Emperor at the time when those heathens were converted. This is why an Arian church survived within the Empire as long as it contained territories ruled over by Arian Germanic tribes, such as the Ostrogoths in Italy, the Visigoths in Spain, and the Vandals in north Africa. A Nestorian church with Syriac as the language of liturgy developed east of the Roman Empire in the Sassanid state, from where it launched extensive missionary campaigns reaching as far as China. Monophysitism finally became the accepted doctrine among many of the Syrian and Egyptian Christians within the Roman Empire. The resulting schism could not be healed by the Emperors in Constantinople, in spite of efforts that lasted for more than a hundred years; the division paved the way for the Islamic conquests of those countries in the seventh century.

The epoch quoted here as the one in which the dogma was ultimately fixed was at the same time the Classic period in early Christian literature. Within the framework of a literary history, I cannot attempt to describe the development of Christian dogma in detail. But as in the case of philosophy, an assessment of the literary forms created through it and with it would hardly be possible without reference to the spirit and the content of philosophical thought; and likewise the specific phenomena in Christian literature cannot be explained without mention of basic facts concerning dogmatical and ecclesiastical history. This necessity has already been exemplified in my remarks on ecclesiastical historiography, a genre which expresses a new attitude to history which differed from the Classical tradition, and which thus produced new literary forms (see p. 469).

In my sections on the literature of the third and early fourth century AD, I have repeatedly emphasised the fact that during this time more and more of the leading representatives of Christian communities came from the traditional upper classes or attained an equivalent social prestige. Parallel to this development was the advance of productive Christian theologians and authors to places among the foremost exponents of intellectual life. Around the middle of the fourth century AD this process had been completed, even if pagan literary works are in evidence until the sixth century AD, and Christians still had only a minor share in professional philosophy, the ideological backbone of paganism until that period. But none the less, Christian theologians fully adopted the methods and the terminology of contemporary philosophy, as a means of explaining the content of the

Christian faith in a manner corresponding to conventions of thought and expression in the surrounding educational world. The speech in which Gregory the Miracle-worker thanked his teacher Origen (see p. 335) is sufficient proof of the fact that theology as taught by the latter began with systematic instruction in school philosophy. It is evident why the novelty of the challenge thus put to philosophical thought frequently led to developments that appear as something like extensions of philosophical approaches.

The development of ecclesiastical dogma outlined above is a particularly good example for such an application of philosophy. The reason for this is that during the whole of the period I have outlined the level of ontological inquiry was the only possible location for any attempt at a terminological definition of the vague and ambiguous statements Biblical texts made about God the Creator and the Father, about the man Jesus of Nazareth as the Son of God, and about the work of a Holy Ghost. After all, Late Classical philosophy as summed up in Platonism was first and foremost ontology – the knowledge of being and of its eternal order which culminated in the divine. In the Arian debate the question arose whether the Son and Saviour was or was not of the same nature as the Father, and consequently, whether the salvation proclaimed by the church had been the work of the divine being itself, or of a creature blessed by that divine being in an earthly life. This question aimed at ascertaining objective facts, seen as independent from individual faith; yet quite obviously, the terminological clarification of those facts was thought a necessary condition for any adequate discourse about the hope for salvation which was based on them.

The controversies caused by Nestorian and Monophysite doctrines document the same philosophical perspective. The appearance of the divine *logos* in the man Jesus of Nazareth was the most important content of the Christian message. Thus the doctrine claiming the equal nature of Father and Son led to the question in which relationship divine and human nature stood within the historical person Jesus. Three answers were suggested: that the divine nature had entered an existing man; that both natures were from the beginning inseparably combined in a single and unique being; or that from the start the two natures existed separately within the one person. All three answers try to describe the nature of the Saviour not with regard to his relationship with the faithful and the saved, but instead objectively, in ontological categories. The mystery on which the Christian faith centred was to be described in its relationship with that order of being which is the object of discursive and communicable thought, and hence of philosophy.

It is true that there was also a motif from popular piety in the Monophysite concept of two strictly separate natures in the person of Jesus. The cult of Mary as the woman who gave birth to a divine being was especially popular in Egypt, presumably because of reminiscences of the role Isis had in the ancient local religion. The Nestorian doctrine, which spoke of a divine nature given to the already existing human Jesus, denied Mary this status. But the theological position of Monophysitism was derived from an ontological problem, as were all other trinitarian and christological doctrines of Greek theology. The point of view changes only with Augustine (see p. 557), that is to say with a representative of Latin tradition.

The dogmatical controversies of the fourth and fifth centuries AD show us in what sense the first centuries of Christian theology can be described as a continuation of the philosophical tradition. A similar statement can be made with regard to ethics, and thus it is not surprising that quite a few authors during this period described Christianity in all naivety as a new philosophy. At that time philosophy was first and foremost a way of living according to certain principles. But the philosophy of the Hellenistic-Roman era had taught rules for living which were quite rigidly deduced from a rational understanding of the order of being, and consequently demanded a life in accordance with nature. Jews and Christians, on the other hand, got their instructions for proper living directly through the revelation of divine commandments. To them, a rational comprehension of the world order did not necessarily lead to the fulfilment of the divine will, and they rather heeded the words of the prophet Micah: 'To you, O man, it is told what is good, and what the Lord demands of you'. All early Christian theology, however, was busy trying to apply those terms and categories designed to express the rational ethics of naturalness, to the statements of the Bible which reveal the divine commands. This means that the norms of ethics changed, but the terms in which they were expressed remained the same, as did the view of the world in which they were to be practised. For this process, I will give only one example in the following.

Philosophical ethics had worked for centuries with a psychological dualism, claiming that where the same reason which is capable of recognising the rationally structured cosmos also dominates human actions, those actions will be just, that is in accordance with nature. It is only the irrational urges, passions or emotions, which may prevent men from doing right. Where the philosophical schools differed was the question of whether the goal of moral endeavour was the elimination of irrational urges or their control through reason; in other words whether moral perfection was metriopathy or apathy, moderated passion or eliminated passion. In the Empire philosophers tended towards a combination of both concepts in an ascending scale. For all philosophy with a Platonic orientation, moral ascent meant spiritualisation, liberation from the ties to irrational-unordered matter, in which the roots of all emotions and passions had to be sought.

To a Christian, perfection could be nothing else than freedom from sin, through living and acting in accordance with God's revealed command;

and as early as in the third century AD this was identified with the notion of apathy. The Bible taught that man had been made in the image of his creator. The Platonic definition of human perfection was 'approximation to God' and hence spiritualisation. This suggested referring the Biblical statement about man's resemblance to God exclusively to the soul or its rational part, a connection that was made as early as in the second century AD. After all, the Bible also said that God was spirit, even if the Biblical account of creation certainly meant something other than the immaterial existence imagined by the philosophers. But for educated people in the Empire, it now seemed natural to read the relevant statement as pointing to the intelligible nature of the Supreme Being who is thus devoid of all irrational emotions. The resulting demand of man as the image of God is apathy, a state equated with freedom from sin. Old Testament passages speaking of Jehovah's wrath or jealousy made this logic seem a trifle problematic, but those statements could be read either allegorically, or as expressions adapted to the limited understanding of uneducated readers. The ideal of apathy was the theoretical justification for the ascetic way of living, which Late Classical philosophers valued just as highly as Christian monks. Both sides regarded it as a means of liberation from the constraints of corporeal existence.

Naturally the integration of the new religion into the world of ideas of Graeco-Roman culture concerned many areas of life and thought, from public worship to private life, or legal practice. In the interaction of philosophy and theology, however, this process found its clearest terminological expression. This development had already begun in the first century AD, and it was completed in the century which followed the Christianisation of the Roman state. During all those years, however, there was nothing which intensified and accelerated the process so much as the permanent struggle for a terminological definition of the doctrine of the trinity, and of christology.

As I have said before, the period of these dogmatical controversies is at the same time the Classic era of early Christian-patristic literature, the years when its repertoire of motifs and forms found that shape in which it came to dominate mediaeval intellectual life. Still, the rich flowering of this literature followed paths which had in many ways been laid out in the literature of the Empire. What can be said concerning the role of philosophy in explaining the content of the new creed, may also be transferred by way of analogy to the formal traditions of Graeco-Latin literature. Tertullian maintained that Athens and Jerusalem had nothing in common, and Hieronymus asked himself anxiously if he was not perhaps a Ciceronian rather than a Christian; but notwithstanding that, as well as all assertions that the ornament of pagan rhetoric was not needed for the truth first received and then passed on by the fishermen of the Lake of Genezareth: Christians were less and less able to keep apart from the educational tradition of their environment, the more they became the dominant part of society, and thus the inheritors of its cultural legacy.

Julian's edict which barred Christians from teaching Classic poetry in schools shows very well how strongly even then Christians had come to identify with the surrounding educational tradition. At the same time the prohibition reflects a clear awareness of the importance of the literary tradition for the continuity of the cultural and political consciousness of the Empire's population. Not long afterwards, Basil of Caesarea in eastern Asia Minor, a man equally important as theologian, author, and church administrator, wrote a letter which was to become a famous document. In it he explained that Classic Greek literature should be given ample room in educating the young because it provided an intellectual and ethical preparation for instruction in the Christian faith. Basil himself kept up a correspondence with Libanius, the most eminent contemporary teacher of rhetoric, and Libanius in turn was tutor to John Chrysostom, the greatest preacher of the early church. Moreover, Hieronymus was a pupil of Donatus, the most famous grammarian and interpreter of Classic Roman literature at the time.

As in the High Empire, so did the fourth and fifth centuries AD see a busy exchange between the educated classes in East and West respectively. Western scholars would visit famous educational centres and learned men in the East even much more frequently than such journeys were made in the opposite direction; but nevertheless the knowledge of Greek in the West declined palpably and the Latin as well as the Greek world developed intellectual lives of their own, in which impulses from the other linguistic area could only be received through the medium of translation.

On both sides all Christian literature was written in the high form of the language used, an idiom influenced by Classic models, and very different from the vernacular. The only exceptions existed in edifying literature which aimed at a particularly wide readership. Most of these works were lives of saints, written in monastic circles (see p. 410). Thus Christian literary language shared the Classicism of its pagan equivalent, but it none the less contained certain elements alien to the Classic tradition and not borrowed from vernacular speech. I have already said that Christian texts occasionally tended to avoid and to substitute certain words connected with ideas from pagan worship (see p. 353). But those words lost their objectionable character as time went by and readers were no longer acquainted with any but the Christian cult. Furthermore, Christian literary language naturally included a fair amount of neologisms formed in the context of debates about the proper formulation of the dogma, and hence not part of the given literary tradition. But by far the most important element characteristic of high Christian language consists of reflections of Biblical linguistic usage, known to all Christians mainly because of the inclusion of lengthy Biblical passages in the liturgy. This phenomenon is also found both in the Greek East and the Latin West.

Bible translations

Christianity had first spread in the Greek half of the Roman Empire. Its Holy Scripture was the Greek translation of the Bible, the so-called Septuagint, adopted from the Judaism within which Christianity had originated (see p. 203). From the second century AD Judaism had turned more and more towards the original Hebraic-Aramaic forms of its sacred texts, a process which was largely a distancing from the Christian faith and from Greek civilisation, even among Jews whose native language was Greek. This made Jews as well as Christians reflect on the question as to which was the proper text of the Old Testament; and Origen's *Hexapla* was the first instrument designed to compare and interpret the original wording alongside the different translations. The Septuagint text in the *Hexapla* became the basis of several fourth-century revisions of the Greek Bible in Alexandria, Antioch (see p. 380), and Constantinople. The resulting versions became officially, that is, liturgically valid, and can still be read in the extant original manuscripts.

In the West, there were several translations of the Bible from Greek into Latin, from the end of the second century AD onwards; the oldest Latin version is thought to have originated in Africa. Evidence of such translations is found in the form of quotations in works of Latin authors from the third and early fourth centuries AD. Those versions found their way into liturgical use when Latin came to replace Greek as the common language of worship and ecclesiastical administration. In the city of Rome this happened around the middle of the third century AD. In the Orient too – as, for instance in Armenia or the Syrian city of Edessa – the development of an indigenous Christian literature began with a translation of the Bible.

Towards the close of the fourth century AD the reigning Pope Damasus took exception to the multiplicity of Latin versions of the Bible in liturgical use. He commissioned the learned Hieronymus to revise the texts; Hieronymus began his work in Rome, starting with those books which were most important in the liturgy, that is the books of the New Testament, and the Psalms. He continued this effort after his move to a monastery near Bethlehem in 386 AD, now using the *Hexapla*; afterwards he set out to produce a new translation of the entire Old Testament. Hieronymus mastered Hebrew and Aramaic, and like Origen before him, he also made contact with Jewish scriptural scholars.

Hieronymus' translation met at first with violent criticism. In his correspondence with Augustine, we find a clear expression of the suspicion with which people regarded the original text handed down among the

Jews, and of the conviction that the Greek text of the Bible was divinely inspired. Still, over the centuries Hieronymus' translation, known from the thirteenth century onwards as the Vulgate or 'the common one', became the universally accepted version: a late triumph of philological diligence over prejudices condoned by the church.

The Vulgate is a very good translation, both in detail and as a whole, and this judgment does not need to be qualified by referring to the limited resources which were at the translator's disposal. The text documents Hieronymus' highly developed linguistic and stylistic sensitivity, which enabled him to find adequate Latin wordings for the foreign manner of expression in the two Semitic languages, without drifting off into obscure and unnatural constructions.

In the East as well as in the West, the idiom of the respective Bible translations became part of high or literary language, shunned only by pagan authors such as Zosimus (see p. 480), or in Christian writings whose authors made a conscious effort to stay entirely within the Classic tradition, such as Boëthius' consolatory treatise (see p. 499), or Procopius' historical work. In Christian literature in the narrower sense, however, we encounter a large number of Biblicisms, frequently based on specifically Semitic patterns of thought and expression. But the Biblical element in the Greek and the Latin languages was only an addition to a fully developed tradition of high linguistic usage, and the results can thus not be compared with modern literary German, which as we know it is entirely unimaginable without Luther's translation of the Bible, or with literary Syrian, in whose genesis a Bible translation played a similarly important part.

Commentaries

During the late first and throughout the second century AD Christianity only very gradually detached itself from the Judaism within which it had evolved. Between the Babylonian exile of the Jews and the final destruction of Jerusalem, Judaism in turn had undergone a development in which the importance of ritual worship for religious life declined more and more, and those sacred texts believed to reveal the will of God became evermore important. In the beginning the divine commands expressed there could still be read as instructions for proper preparation prior to the cultic encounter with the divine. But with the end of worship in the Temple, Judaism finally became a book religion, in which all depended on the proper interpretation of the collected canon of Holy Scripture. Understandably enough, this development of the Jewish faith had been anticipated by those Jews who lived outside Palestine. Hence the interpretation of what Holy Scripture said became the most important task for the leading men in religious life.

In spite of their novel content, the earliest known pieces of Christian preaching, first among the Jews and then also among pagans, belong entirely to this interpretative tradition. The life, death, and resurrection of Jesus were explained as fulfilling statements in the Bible, which even to the emerging Christian communities was still only what later came to be called the Old Testament. A second canon had formed only gradually from the second century AD onwards, through a selection from the rich literary evidence of Christian preaching. The so-called New Testament then itself became the subject of exegesis: for Christians adhered to the Jewish tradition in believing that the revelation of the divine will through the written word was of prime importance for the salvation of man. This belief endured even though it was soon complemented by newly developed cultic forms, in which the divine was thought to be in immediate presence, and the process of salvation to become accessible to sensual perception. Hence the proper interpretation of scripture remained an ever-renewed task.

A natural consequence of the integration of the Christian church into the Classical educational tradition was the arising of a rich literature of commentaries, in which the forms and methods of poetic and philosophical exegesis were applied to Biblical texts. I have already mentioned a similar phenomenon in Greek Jewish writing (see p. 154), which is a predecessor of Christian literature also in this respect. Jews and Christians agreed with the exponents of Imperial or Late Classical philosophy in the notion that a handed-down canon of works, properly interpreted, enabled them to penetrate to the ultimate truth, or at least to approach it to a degree which sufficed for proper living, and for the lasting salvation of the soul. The philosophers also believed that the whole truth had already been expressed in writing, albeit in the works of Plato, and that it needed no more than correct interpretation to bring it to light.

In the works of Origen (see p. 334), we already find all the forms of Christian exegesis fully developed; and some recent studies have illustrated particularly well, that this was a continuation of traditional Greek as well as Rabbinical practice. From the early fourth century AD onwards, such fully fledged Biblical exegesis existed also in Latin, with the works of Victorinus of Pettau and later Hilarius of Poitiers (see p. 336). In the late fourth and fifth centuries, there ensued an abundant flowering of this exegetical activity, which has extremely close parallels in works by contemporary commentators in the philosophical schools.

In all this, Origen's role as the pioneer of Christian Biblical exegesis was well established. This is shown by the fact that Hieronymus as well as his friend and later opponent Rufinus of Aquileia translated several of Origen's commentaries into Latin; and Basil and Gregory of Nazianzus jointly produced a collection of exegetical passages from Origen's works, to which they gave the title *Philocalia*. Protected by the names they were published under, these translations or excerpts have preserved large parts of Origen's works, while the originals were lost after Origen was finally condemned as a heretic in the sixth century AD. A contribution to the development of a Latin terminology for ecclesiastical and theological matters was another effect of this translation work. Translations were also made of the great Alexandrian's systematic studies, in this case by Rufinus, as well as of writings by Gregory of Nazianzus and Basil the Great, Sextus' collection of sententiae (see p. 82), and the aforementioned tracts by Euagrius (see p. 419).

As in the works of Origen, three types of exegetical literature existed in the Classic era of the church fathers. There were stylistically unpolished notes from lectures or rough drafts for oral interpretation; elaborate scholarly commentaries meant to be read by a theologically educated audience; and edifying-exegetical works, containing tracts styled as homilies, beside sermons actually given to Christian congregations, and later published from audience notes or in a revised form of the original draft.

The first group contains numerous commentaries on Old Testament writings produced by the blind Didymus who was for a while the teacher of Hieronymus in Alexandria. In his method as well as in his theological doctrine, Didymus was a close follower of Origen whom he greatly admired. This is why Didymus' commentaries were nearly completely forgotten, and did not become widely known again until a papyrus find a few years ago. Many of his texts quite obviously show their origin in teaching, because they record student interjections and the resulting digressions on the part of the teacher, and because their syntax is often rather accidental.

The other group of texts contains, among other writings, several commentaries on the first chapters of the Book of Genesis. There are extant texts by Basil and his brother Gregory of Nyssa, and as a sequel to those, Ambrosius of Milan wrote no less than six books of commentary on the Biblical account of the six days of creation. Such works are particularly interesting, because they gave their authors scope for a detailed discussion of cosmological and cosmogonical doctrines of philosophy, as providing the terminological and ideological framework for the interpretation of the Biblical text. To name but one example, it was almost taken for granted that in accordance with Platonically orientated philosophy, the Biblical statement about the creation of man after the image of God was related only to the spiritual substance of man, in other words the soul or its rational part; this was a view that had already been argued by Irenaeus. Ambrosius wrote, beside many other exegetical works, a major commentary on Luke's Gospel. This commentary comprises sermons as well as learned theological treatises. Ambrosius' commentary on the *hexaemeron*, or the six-day work of the world's creation, is moreover full of nature descriptions of a kind for which there are but few parallels in Classical literature.

Hieronymus, who was not only the translator of Origen's commentaries but also the author of numerous original ones, mainly on books of the Old Testament, wrote among other works of this kind an exegetical treatise which uses selected examples from the Book of Genesis to demonstrate the necessity of using the Hebraic original text in interpretation.

Particularly interesting exegetical works are the Latin commentaries on Paul by an anonymous author and handed down under the name of Ambrosius. Paul, one of the two 'apostolic princes' of the earliest church, had always been held in high regard, and thus numerous commentaries had been written on his letters between the third and the fifth century. But with the exception of the radical Paulinism of Marcion (see p. 299), those commentaries failed to detect much of what is special about Paul's theology. One case in point is the doctrine of freely given divine grace as a gift to which the moral and religious endeavour of man may respond, but which it can in no way earn or evoke.

In contrast to this, communal piety and theology in the first centuries of Christianity had had a synergistic orientation. This term describes the notion that both elements, the helping grace of God and the individual effort of man, are crucial to attaining salvation. This idea corresponded to the emphasis which early Christian doctrine, not least under the influence of philosophy, put on moral practice. Its importance was seen not only in the shaping of the earthly life but also in making a human contribution to the achievement of one's own eternal salvation. Origen's interpretation of Paul's Letter to the Romans shows this in an exemplary fashion. The first signs of an understanding of the specific characteristics in Paul's theology, apart from previous views held only by extremists such as Marcion, can be found in the commentary of the pseudo-Ambrosius or Ambrosiaster. From such beginnings, Augustine developed a well-founded theological position in the debate with Pelagius (see p. 545).

Under the name of Augustine, we have a book with the discussion of several dozens of exegetical problems from the Old and the New Testaments. This book was written by the aforementioned author commonly known as Ambrosiaster or False Ambrosius, a man who worked in Rome between 360 and 380 AD. His work belongs to a type of exegetical literature for which there are also numerous other examples, including some from philosophical writing. It is related to the so-called testimonial collections, compilations of Biblical passages which were to provide arguments in the debate with Jews, heretics, or pagans (see p. 386).

As regards the methods of scholarly exegesis, there were two opposing trends in the early church. In Alexandria, following the poetical exegesis of the Stoics and the Platonics whose principles had already been adopted by Greek-speaking Jewish scriptural scholars (see p. 161), the dominant method presupposed a multiple meaning of the Biblical text. The reading of the grammatical and historical content was thus to be followed by the finding of the moral meaning, which was in turn crowned by the spiritual-supernatural understanding gained with the help of allegorical interpretation. Origen had brought this approach to perfection (see p. 334). In contrast to this, the tradition established in the Syrian metropolis of Antioch around 300 AD advocated a strict limitation of exegesis to the immediate literal meaning of the text.

Eminent theologians were also to be found among those who followed the school of Antioch. The two most prominent ones were Diodorus, who died around 390 AD as Bishop of the Cilician city of Tarsus, and Theodorus, thirty years younger than Diodorus, Bishop of Mopsuestia in Cilicia, and like John Chrysostom a pupil of the great rhetor Libanius. After the Council of Ephesus in 431 AD these two men came to be regarded as forerunners of Nestorian doctrine which was condemned as heretical. This is why their vast exegetical work, dealing with all the books of the Bible, is extant only in a few Greek fragments, and in partly very bad translations by Syrian followers of Nestorius. But even those remnants document the exceptionally high quality and precision of a textual interpretation in which the traditions of Hellenistic philology lived on down to the smallest detail. In Theodorus of Mopsuestia's reading of the Psalms, for instance, there is an insight into a stylistic feature of Hebrew poetry in which all essential statements are repeated in variation, a technique resulting in a parallelism of parts. Other interpreters had tried again and again to read a deeper meaning into these double statements, which are familiar to every reader of the Old Testament.

Among the theologians recognised as orthodox, it was above all John Chrysostom and Theodoretus of Cyrus (see p. 416) who followed the Antiochian principles, while the learned Gregory of Nyssa, for instance, preferred the Alexandrian tradition. The latter dominated throughout the Latin West, a fact linked with the close ties between Alexandria and Rome. There were, however, exceptions: Hieronymus, for example, was also influenced by the Antiochians, whose accurate perception of grammatical, lexical, and stylistic detail suited his intentions.

What has to be said here also is that we should not imagine the divergence between the two methods as being too clear cut. The advocates of multiple meanings conceded that not every Biblical passage allowed such a reading, while on the other side the possibility of a typological interpretation was not excluded. This meant, for instance, that statements from the Old were read with reference to the New Testament, and this in turn meant that such an exegesis could not but go beyond the purely literal sense of the word. Such, however, is the task of any interpretation which seeks to explain metaphorical expression in the widest sense of the term, quite independently of the religious or otherwise authoritative status of the text concerned. Julian of Aeclanum, Augustine's main opponent in the Pelagian debate (see p. 544), finally developed a doctrine claiming that Biblical texts must be read on two, and not three, levels of meaning.

The problem posed by the existence of several translations of the Bible and different exegetical methods led to early reflections on methodology. I have already referred to the correspondence between Hieronymus and Augustine (see p. 508), a man who spoke no Hebrew at all and had only an imperfect command of Greek. Around 380 AD the Donatist author Tyconius wrote a compendium of the art of Biblical exegesis, and Augustine's treatise *De doctrina Christiana* on the same subject was produced only a little later. Special exegetical problems dealt with in monographs were also treated with explicit reference to the method of interpretation such as, for instance, the differences in the accounts of the four evangelists about which Augustine wrote a short tract.

Naturally the repeated interpretation of the same Biblical texts kept posing similar or identical problems. I have already mentioned the discussion of philosophical cosmology in the context of exegesis concerned with the Biblical account of creation. Particular difficulties arose in commentaries on the Song of Solomon, a collection of Old Hebraic love songs incorporated into the Jewish canon at quite an early stage, if not without resistance from scriptural scholars. Pharisaic-Rabbinical exegesis had interpreted these pieces of erotic poetry as references to the covenant between Jehovah and his people, a relationship which the prophets' speeches had already compared to that of a loving married couple, and consequently those who betrayed Jehovah could be accused of adultery.

Christian exegesis of the Song of Solomon began with Origen and the ingenuity with which interpreters came up with ever-new readings of individual passages of these love poems had a deep influence on the forms of expression of piety, an influence which lasted for centuries. Origen's commentary is extant in the Latin translation by Rufinus; the authors who followed him were Gregory of Elvira in Spain, Nilus of Ancyra in Asia Minor, Gregory of Nyssa, and many others in a succession continued well into the Middle Ages. The Song of Solomon was held in high honour particularly in the West. Following Jewish exegesis, its statements were most frequently interpreted as references to the relationship between God or Christ and the church but later on also as a description of the union between the soul of an individual man and its heavenly Lord. This reading is expressed, for instance, in Gregory of Nyssa's fifteen homilies on the Song of Solomon.

The exegesis of the Book of Job forced interpreters to come up with ever-new reflections on, among other things, the problem of undeserved suffering, and hence of justice in the divine direction of human fate. Commentaries by the blind Didymus (see p. 511) and the Arian Julian show attempts to explain this narrative with the help of philosophical doctrines about fate and liberty, doctrines which were very different and could hence only be used selectively. The Stoic notion of an all-predetermining and beneficial, but impersonal destiny was in keeping with

Biblical statements about God's all-comprehensive providence whose direction is ultimately to the good of all men; but it did not go with admonitions saying that man should obey the personal orders of God, and thus expect reward and well-being to result from his own responsible actions. The role which Peripatetic doctrine gave to coincidence was also unacceptable for Christians, but not so the notion which that philosophy had about man's freedom of choice. What the Platonics had taught about levels of providence effected by gods and demons in the different layers of the world, was well suited to Christian angelology and demonology; but no Christian could warm to the idea that God as supreme world ruler governed only indirectly through subordinate beings, and never interfered with the details of human fate in person. Finally, it was extremely difficult to give a philosophical explanation of the Christian doctrine concerning the Fall of mankind and original sin.

The treatment of such problems in commentaries on the Book of Job shows attempts to find solutions through a method that is extremely eclectic, using ever-new combinations of terms from different philosophical school traditions. Thus it is not surprising that the major commentary on Job in thirty-five books which Pope Gregory the Great wrote around 590 AD became an important means of communicating Classical and early Christian ideas to the Middle Ages. For centuries this work was among the most frequently read theological books. Ambrosius and Augustine also had a go at interpreting the Book of Job, the former in a series of explanations of selected passages, the latter in a major sermon. Like most others who attempted an exegesis of Job, these two put the greatest emphasis on presenting Job as first and foremost an example of patient resignation to the will of God.

Rich and varied was also the tradition of interpreting the Psalms. Some of the large number of authors who followed Origen as exegetes of this book were Hilarius, Augustine, Hesychius of Jerusalem, and Theodorus of Mopsuestia (see p. 513). Christian communities were very familiar with the Psalms because of their frequent use in worship. Moreover, all of them were regarded as the works of David, Jesus' ancestor, whose reign in the history of the Israelites foreshadowed the future reign of Christ as King at the end of all history. Thus even the earliest Christian readings of the Psalms, as shown already in the accounts of the evangelists, saw them as prophecies of the earthly life of Christ, his suffering, and his return as universal ruler and judge. This is why the christological debates of the fourth and fifth centuries likewise referred to the Psalms again and again.

Finally, special problems were also posed in the exegesis of the apocalyptic books of the Old and New Testaments, the Book of Daniel, and John's Apocalypse. Their language, abounding with imagery, could not be read in any other way than allegorically, and it seemed natural to use those texts in chiliastic speculations about the date when the world would end. Examples are the commentary on Daniel by Hippolytus (see p. 331), and the one on the Apocalypse by Victorinus of Ptuj or Pettau (see p. 390).

In his own commentaries on these two books Hieronymus explicitly rejected such speculations, as shortly before him the aforementioned Tyconius (see p. 514) had done in a commentary on John's Apocalypse. This chapter of early Christian Biblical exegesis was written mainly in the West. In the East the very inclusion of John's Apocalypse in the canon of the New Testament was doubtful until the fifth century AD. Ecumenius' commentary on this book, presumably written in Syria, dates from the sixth century AD and so does that by Andrew of Caesarea. Under the influence of the Islamic threat, the seventh century saw a rising interest in apocalyptic writing also in Byzantium, an interest that had been kept constantly alive in the Latin West because of the Germanic raids of the fourth and fifth centuries.

These examples of ever-new commentaries on the same books of the Bible explain a phenomenon which is in evidence from around 500 AD. Biblical commentaries had for some time included occasional references expressing agreement or disagreement with the opinions of predecessors, but now people also wrote so-called *catena* commentaries on individual books of the Bible. Those recorded either in literal quotations or in summaries what had been said in explanation of each passage of the text over the past two hundred years. For centuries such *catena* were copied, abbreviated, or extended, so that there is hardly a single case where we can be certain of their original form. They obviously contain valuable information from lost original commentaries, but research on the many *catena* manuscripts from the Middle Ages is still in its beginnings. Until today we do not even know who first compiled such a commentary from older exegetical works. Some early *catenae* on the first eight books of the Old Testament as well as on the Book of Kings and the Book of Isaiah, commentaries which are partly extant in the Greek original and partly in Latin translations, go back to the rhetor Procopius (see p. 463), who taught at the famous school of oratory in Gaza in Palestine at the beginning of the sixth century AD.

From the same period, however, there are also some extant original commentaries. They partly follow the Antiochian tradition in trying to elaborate the literal sense, and partly the Alexandrian one in trying to define the spiritual meaning. Such texts come from the whole breadth of the eastern Roman Empire, from the then still predominantly Greek-speaking island of Sicily to Syria or Egypt.

Sermons

Among exegetical writings, the third group I will be discussing comprises sermons, in as far as they deal with the interpretation of the Bible. This qualification is necessary because by no means all homiletic literature does so (see p. 518). Of exegetical sermons, the most famous are the major sermon cycles by John Chrysostom, the greatest preacher in the Greek church, and by Augustine. Of the former, we have, for instance, seventy-five homilies on the Book of Genesis and fifty-eight on the Psalms, as well as ninety and eighty-eight respectively on the Gospels of Matthew and John. Extant sermons by Augustine include 142 on John's Gospel and ten on John's first letter. In view of such figures it does not seem surprising that especially in homiletics, we find many pieces which were wrongly ascribed to one of these famous names.

We cannot always tell whether extant texts in this category are drafts or audience notes from sermons that were actually given, or if the respective author wrote a version of his speech especially for publication. There are many references to the situational context in such pieces, and not only because of the initial address to the congregation. For example, preachers sometimes complain about the popular practice among audiences of giving loud applause; and because, unlike in modern services, the preacher usually sat while the congregation stood, there are some mentions of listener fatigue.

In the sermons, understandably enough, the precise and scholarly interpretation of the Biblical text recedes behind the intended spiritual and moral application, or in other words, the preacher's pastoral appeal. Still, there is quite frequent mention of the theological debates of the period, as discussions which according to an explicit comment by John Chrysostom did in fact interest large groups among the urban population. Thus giving a sermon did in no way oblige a speaker to conceal his exegetical-theological schooling. John Chrysostom, for example, follows the principles of Antiochian exegesis also in his Biblical homilies, while those by Augustine make extensive use of the possibilities of allegorical interpretation.

How well congregations were informed about dogmatical debates is shown by the numerous extant Easter letters. In those, the head of a church province – the Patriarch of Alexandria for example – would comment not only on aspects of liturgy, church discipline, and general morality, but indeed also on dogmatical-theological issues, in order to show his flock of believers the right path. That popular interest in dogma was taken for granted by the preachers is reflected particularly well in a sermon by the Patriarch Proclus of Constantinople. It was given in 429 AD when its author was still Bishop of the city of Cyzicus on the Sea of Marmara, and it refutes the christological doctrines of the Nestorians who denied any basis for worshipping Mary as the mother of God. Proclus' argumentation is theological even if the issue belongs to the realm of popular piety.

All homiletic literature, in the East as well as in the West, was dominated by the rules of the rhetorical art. Augustine and John Chrysostom, to name but two cases in point, had undergone a thorough rhetorical training; and the aforementioned applause of congregations for their preachers was not least a reward for clever psychagogy, a technique which the audiences apparently understood very well. John was given the epithet 'Goldmouth' because of his splendid eloquence, and even the modern reader cannot but marvel at Augustine's art of phrasing and his complete mastery of the means of rhetoric, a quality which is by no means limited to his homilies. The demands of the church sermon once again opened up a wide field for the practical application of the Classical art of oratory, a range of possibilities which had neither in the East nor in the West survived the death of Republican states and their political life. In the cities, largely autonomous until well into the Late Classical age, political life was a matter of the urban upper classes. Rhetorical skills were indeed in demand – for instance in court, in the municipal council, or in delegations to the Emperor; but on those occasions, speakers would invariably address a limited audience of peers with a common educational background. The Christian preachers, on the other hand, were truly popular orators, like the politicians in ancient Athens or Rome.

I have already said that not all sermons in the early Christian church interpreted Biblical text. Some extant homilies by John Chrysostom, for example, are polemics against the Jews or against the imitation of Jewish customs within the Christian community. We likewise find attacks on theatrical or circus shows in the cities, criticism of popular superstitions, or refutations of astrology. This group of texts is of particular interest to the cultural historian. Other sermons deal with penance and church discipline, but also with contemporary dogmatical controversies; yet others are celebratory sermons given on the occasion of a high festival in the ecclesiastical year, or in honour of a saint.

A similar variety of subjects is found in the sermons by Zeno of Verona, by Gaudentius of Brescia, and by Pacianus, Bishop of Barcelona. All of these authors belong to the late fourth century AD, and their extant homilies show how widespread the art of preaching was throughout the West and the East at that time.

Particularly impressive is a cycle of sermons given by John Chrysostom as Bishop of Antioch on a most unique occasion. During one of the frequent street riots in the city, statues of the Emperor had been knocked down and damaged, and because of this the citizens expected severe punishment. In this awkward situation, John proved to be a model pastor, trying at the same time to cheer the spirits of his congregation and urging them to repent. Another especially remarkable homily dates from the year 403

AD when malicious intrigues had cost John his throne as Patriarch of the capital and he was banished by an Imperial order. His farewell sermon expresses a rock-solid belief in the ultimate invincibility of a church which stands united in the true faith. Another slightly earlier sermon takes the fall of the all-powerful minister Eutropius as an occasion for reflections on the ephemeral nature of earthly glory. A similarly topical piece was a sermon by Ambrosius, ostensibly an attack against the Arian Bishop Auxentius but in reality against the Emperor Valerian II, who in 386 AD had ordered the handing over of the episcopal church of Milan to the Arian party.

There are extant homilies or sermons by a very large number of authors, preserved because people were reading and rereading them as edifying literature, but sometimes also simply kept in reverent memory of the authors or of the saints who were honoured in the text. One example concerns the artfully styled sermons by Basil of Seleucia, in the region of Isauria in Asia Minor (see p. 524). The texts were written in the early fifth century AD and most of them deal with individual characters from Biblical history. Basil's influence extended to the ecclesiastical poetry of the next century (see p. 576), and in the context of my account he will be mentioned once again as a hagiographer.

Extant homiletic literature also occasionally contains works by heretical authors; for example, the sermons on the Psalms by the Arian Asterius from the middle of the fourth century AD. His namesake from Amasea in Asia Minor, about fifty years younger, wrote several homilies on the festivals of different saints and martyrs, sermons in which he attacked the continued practice of pagan customs at festivals: but with as little practical success as enjoyed by Augustine and other preachers who criticised the same phenomenon. Ambrosius of Milan was another famous pulpit orator, and so was Gregory of Nazianzus (see below), even if most of the sermons extant under the latter name were actually written by Augustine.

According to his biographer Possidius, the fifth century read a total of 279 sermons by Augustine, mostly as taken down by stenographers. Today we know of about 650 sermons ascribed to Augustine in mediaeval manuscripts. Recent research has classed about four hundred of them as genuine, but in individual cases there may still be doubts for quite some time to come. Like those of other preachers, Augustine's sermons also deal with very diverse subjects. Some of them are styled in a way that was quite modern at the time, and did not feature in the repertoire of Classical rhetoric, namely as rhymed prose. The choice of this medium seems to have been made with regard to the linguistic taste of the audience.

Quite different in character are the famous five theological sermons by Gregory of Nazianzus. They were delivered in 380 AD, shortly before the Council of Constantinople, as polemical attacks on the Arian doctrines held by Eunomians and Macedonians, and finally excluded from orthodoxy at that council. Gregory was especially highly praised as a pulpit orator and his sermons surpass those of the younger John Chrysostom in stylistic virtuosity, even though they lack the gripping immediacy of John's appeals to the audience. Among Gregory's forty or so homilies there are sermons on saints, funeral speeches on dead relatives and friends, and individual polemics and apologies; however, we find no interpretations of Biblical texts. Gregory's contemporary and namesake Gregory of Nyssa, the brother of Basil (see p. 510), wrote exegetical sermons on the Song of Solomon (see p. 514), the Lord's Prayer, the blessings in the Sermon on the Mount, and the titles of the Psalms; but also homilies on moral or dogmatical topics – for example, the custom of delaying baptism until the hour of one's death, or the divine nature of the Holy Spirit.

Again quite different are the ninety-six short sermons given around the middle of the fifth century, and mostly during Lent, by Pope Leo the Great. These homilies are concise and perfectly well-phrased texts which give us insights into the life and the customs of the Christian community in Rome, as well as containing information about the dogmatical debates in which the stance of the Bishop of Rome carried much weight with people in the East as well as in the West.

A special category within homiletic literature are the so-called *catecheses*, lectures given to candidates for baptism, who were still mainly adults in the fourth century AD. The most voluminous specimen of the genre is the collection of twenty-four sermons given by the Bishop Cyrillus during Lent in the church of the Holy Sepulchre in Jerusalem, around the middle of the fourth century. They contain a complete, systematic instruction in Christian doctrine, ecclesiastical rites and customs, as well as the principles of Christian living, as knowledge which laymen were to receive before baptism. A comparable cycle of catechetical sermons was written by the most eminent exponent of the exegetical school of Antioch, Theodorus of Mopsuestia; those, however, survive only in a Syrian translation.

Texts related to such instruction can also be found among the works of Ambrosius, Gregory of Nyssa, Rufinus, John Chrysostom, and Augustine. They are not always written directly for the education of catechumens or ignorant Christians, but sometimes also give directions as to how those are to be taught. An example is Augustine's treatise *De catechizandis rudibus*; the name *rudis* for novices in the faith was taken from military jargon, where it originally meant *recruit*. A late instance is the treatise entitled *De correctione rusticorum*, written by Martin of Bracara, modern-day Braga in Portugal, for his Bishop. It dates from the middle of the sixth century, and is meant to serve the education of a rural population that had been Christianised only in a superficial way, with many pagan ideas and customs remaining alive among them.

Such catechetical tracts must be distinguished from treatises about the office of the priest, as written by John Chrysostom and Ambrosius. The latter works are clearly meant for a reading public, giving an introduction to the nature and the tasks of Christian priesthood. Ambrosius styled his work after the model of Cicero's treatise *De officiis* or *Of Duties*, a fact which means that he aimed at an educated readership. The same can be said for another piece by the aforementioned Martin of Bracara, a survey of Christian ethics divided according to the four Classical cardinal virtues which closely follows a lost work by the philosopher Seneca. Martin's treatise is dedicated to the King of the Visigoths who reigned over the Pyrenean peninsula at that time.

Edifying-didactic treatises

Any discussion of the treatises cited at the end of the previous section will highlight a problem concerning the evaluation of large parts of Christian literature, as a predicament similar to the difficulty in understanding texts from the so-called Second Sophistic Movement (see p. 173). In the fourth and fifth centuries AD the difference between formulating a written and a spoken text was still much smaller than it is today. For a start, the common practice of reading aloud kept the written word within close reach of the spoken one, and Augustine still commented on silent reading as something fairly exceptional. This is why criteria of form and content do not always make it possible to distinguish between a sermon actually given and then published on the one hand, and a theological treatise on the other. This, of course, is only the case if the treatise in question was aimed at a reading public of interested laymen, and not meant as part of a scholarly debate.

Thus the literary conventions largely adhered to by Christian authors, above all since the integration of the church into the social order of the Roman Empire, appear as corresponding to those of the past: stylistic forms developed for oratory had to be transferred to texts written for reading, if one wanted to meet any higher aesthetical standards. Correspondingly, texts presented orally in public could always be published in writing for private readers. The large number of religious or moral treatises written in Latin as well as Greek for the instruction and edification of a Christian readership can thus be dealt with in the same context as homiletic literature in the narrower sense, that is writing meant for the pulpit.

Gregory of Nyssa's aforementioned homilies (see p. 520) about the blessings of the Sermon on the Mount or about the Lord's Prayer can be read equally well as sermons or treatises. John Chrysostom's treatises, however, are clearly distinguished from his sermons, in spite of a style which is close to that of oratory. This concerns his tracts on the education of children, on virginity, and against remarrying, as well as his consolatory treatises, directed at a wider audience in spite of being addressed to individuals in various kinds of distress.

Such moral-paraenetical writing, which continued the tradition of a philosophy popularised on different levels of literary education, is particularly well represented in the work of Ambrosius. He wrote several tracts on virginal life, on penance, and, as I have mentioned before (see p. 521), on the nature and the duties of priesthood. Significantly enough, his funeral orations on his brother Satyrus and two emperors also belong to this group, because the fact of their publication marks them as being consolatory treatises at the same time as occasional speeches. Augustine's vast literary output also contains tracts of moral-paraenetical content, dealing with lies, patience, marriage, virginity, and much more.

The question of the worth of 'virginal' existence, that is a life of celibacy and asceticism, was of particular interest in this period in which monasticism became more and more important. It is not easy to decide to what extent the writings related to this issue must be regarded as part of monastic literature in the narrower sense, which I have dealt with comprehensively in a previous section (see p. 412). Many of the men known to us through Christian literature as authors or influential clerics spent part of their lives in monastic communities or were at least strongly influenced in their religious notions by the spirit of institutionalised asceticism. Two cases in point are Hieronymus and his contemporary Rufinus. In their younger years both lived for a while in a monastery near Aquilia in upper Italy, and both spent the last period of their lives in monastic colonies near Jerusalem and Bethlehem respectively. Prior to that they spent many years on travels for the purpose of various studies and ecclesiastical work, in the course of which they saw Rome, Constantinople, Antioch, and Alexandria. The monastic colonies where they finally settled had been established with finances donated by noble women from the city of Rome who had been convinced of the worth of the ascetic ideal. Hieronymus' treatises in defence of monastic life (see p. 418), as well as his biography and that of his rival Rufinus, show how scholarly theological work, practical cultic piety, and ascetic striving for perfection were combined.

The biographies and the works of two of the great men in ecclesiastical life, Basil of Caesarea and Augustine, contain some different evidence of the share which monasticism took in the development of specifically Christian forms of thought and imagination in the fourth and fifth centuries AD. Both men were eminent theological thinkers and, in their later years, brilliant organisers of ecclesiastical life and inspired pastors. The motives guiding their work in this field were strongly influenced by the ideal of communal ascetic living, even if these two churchmen never lost sight of the facts and necessities of life in the profane world. Both Basil and Augustine wrote rules for monastic communities, texts which were very influential in the development of monasticism in the following centuries. But their belief in the ideals of ascetic communal living is also particularly well reflected in the rich correspondence of both men about ecclesiastical matters such as the establishment of dioceses, the mediation in disputes, church discipline, or the administration of ecclesiastical wealth.

Since the Christianisation of the monarchy, the church had become in many ways beholden to the bearers of political power and was thus permanently in danger of adapting to social and political demands to such an extent as to betray its task of proclaiming that kind of justice which could never be realised by any political power or order. Even monastic communities could not always avoid this danger, as they also became firmly established parts of Late Classical society; but still the ideal of 'angelic' life which they incorporated remained a fixed framework of orientation for the whole church. The ideal of ascetic-monastic living was diametrically opposed to those conditions of social and political life which Christians perceived as natural; and it was this very negation which enabled groups or individuals who followed the monastic ideal to provide a fundamental and credible opposition to actually existing evils in the world. It is certainly no coincidence that efforts directed at ecclesiastical reform, which in turn influenced social life as a whole, again and again originated in monasteries. The monastic communities also kept providing advice and sanctuary to those outcasts of society who were exposed to the tyranny of the holders of power. This was another way of preserving their role as a permanent corrective of political and social conditions which the official church had more or less accepted. In this manner, the tradition of the Anchorets lived on (see p. 410).

I have already mentioned that monks wrote most of the different types of edifying literature in the Late Classical age and the Byzantine period, as texts whose style did obviously not reflect high linguistic usage, but rather everyday vernacular. Examples are the aforementioned chronicles (see p. 484), numerous lives of saints (see p. 412), and edifying books such as John Moschus' *Spiritual Garden*, a collection of miracle-stories from the sixth century. Comparable texts are the short poems about famous monks written in Syriac by his contemporary and namesake John of Ephesus, the Monophysite who was for some time Patriarch of the capital Constantinople, enjoying the patronage of the Empress Theodora.

Biographies and autobiographies

Another distinct group of edifying works comprises all the biographies written by Christians. The most important prototype of this genre was Athanasius' life of the desert father Antonius (see p. 410), but in detail, such texts show also the influence of other models, such as reports about the deaths of famous martyrs or funeral orations praising the lives which the deceased had led (see p. 520). I have already dealt with the rich biographical production by monastic authors, mostly addressing readers with fairly little education (see p. 410). Those biographies written outside monastic circles are all very different in character, even if they serve the same purpose: to edify and to admonish the reader with an account of an exemplary life.

At the instigation of Augustine, Paulinus, who had gone to Africa after serving the Bishop Ambrosius as a secretary, wrote a biography of his employer twenty-five years after Ambrosius' death. The work presents the life and work of the Bishop in an encomiastic tone and for the edification of the readers, but it nevertheless contains much interesting information. Augustine's life was described in a similar manner, not long after his death, by his pupil Possidius. As is customary in Classical lives of philosophers, the account is complemented by a catalogue of Augustine's writings.

Even closer to the Classical tradition are the works of Palladius which I have already mentioned as belonging to monastic literature (see p. 416). Palladius was a friend of John Chrysostom, a man who died an early death in 407 AD, worn out by the years of his two periods of banishment to the eastern shore of the Black Sea. A year later Palladius, then resident in Syene in Egypt, wrote a life of John as a dialogue modelled on Plato's *Phaedo*, which describes the death of Socrates. This indicates the level of education of Palladius' intended readers. Apart from biographical elements in some of the Platonic dialogues, there were also some Classical precedents for entire biographies in dialogical form. In the third century AD, for instance, the grammarian Satyrus wrote such a life of the poet Euripides.

The figure of Socrates, the martyr for truth, was of great interest to early Christian theologians. This is why Plato's *Phaedo*, combining the description of Socrates' death with a record of his last conversations about the immortality of the soul, found many imitators among them. After the manner of Plato, Gregory of Nyssa wrote a dialogue shortly after the death of his sister Macrina, a piece in which the deceased talks about death and resurrection just before the hour of her demise. This dialogue is no biography, but like Plato's *Phaedo* it uses a biographical motif.

The three biographies cited at the beginning of this chapter are in many respects similar to the numerous extant funeral orations and obituaries from the Late Classical age. Those include the aforementioned funeral orations by Ambrosius on his brother and the two Emperors Valentinian II and Theodosius I (see p. 522), but also several longer letters by Hieronymus which describe and praise the lives of recently deceased people (see p. 566).

Of an entirely different kind are the legendary biographies in which reports of miraculous events are nearly as prominent as in the popular legends about saints. Around the middle of the fifth century AD Bishop Basil of Seleucia wrote a life in two books of the Saint Thekla, legendary female companion of the apostle Paul, and much revered throughout Asia Minor. The tradition concerning Thekla had already found literary shape in the apocryphal *Acts of the Apostles* (see p. 306). Basil was a famous preacher who had all the means of rhetoric at his command and who left us a large number of homilies. He gives a detailed description of the life of Thekla, and of the miracles worked by the saint whose grave at the seat of his episcopal see was a place of worship. The author uses all the devices of the art of rhetoric in his choice of words and rhetorical figures, and this shows once again the close similarity between spoken and written language as far as the latter follows the rules of the rhetorical art.

Different again, but likewise a continuation of Classical tradition, is a last type of biography in which the events of a lifetime represent no more than landmarks in a spiritual ascent to a state of perfection. Here the only aim of the account is the description of the path to perfection as travelled by the 'inner man'. For a long time, the prototype of this special biographical form had been the ever-new retelling of the life of Pythagoras. Pythagoras' biography had become dominated by legendary material at a very early stage and it created a renewed interest especially from the third century AD onwards (see p. 376). The biographical method outlined had already been applied to the Biblical tradition by Philo of Alexandria who used individual personages from the Old Testament to exemplify certain virtues. Of particular importance in this context is his work on Moses (see p. 164) whose life Philo saw as an ascent to the knowledge of God or, more precisely, to the final and complete understanding of the fact that God cannot be known.

Gregory of Nyssa, of all ecclesiastical authors possibly the one most influenced by philosophical, and especially Platonic thought, took up this very subject. On the basis of the Biblical tradition he likewise wrote an 'inner biography' of Moses whose life he saw as an incessant search for the knowledge of God. This was a notion with a Platonic origin. Plato had taught that the highest form of the Eros, love, to which the world owes all creation, is the unappeasable desire of the human soul for a knowing union with the true Being. To Plato, this desire could only be fulfilled when the soul leaves the body, and is free to unfold its power of cognition. Consequently the Neo-Platonists considered the ecstatic union with the highest One as the goal of all philosophical endeavour. By defining the fulfilment of human existence as the insight into the fact that God cannot be known, Philo tried to adapt the Platonic concept to the Biblical image of God, according to which the unbridgeable distance between creator and creature precluded any perfect and knowing union of God with the human soul.

In his own life of Moses Gregory went one step further. He did not see the finding of a fixed point in a secure knowledge as the transcendental fulfilment of human life and endeavour, but rather defined perfection and bliss as the unimpeded, but never completed, search for God. It was a Socratic-Platonic idea that the right path of cognition was more important than the goal, but this radicalisation had to appear as alien to Classical thought. Plato had formulated his concept in the firm conviction that, ultimately, human reason and the order of being were capable of congruity; and he had thus limited the priority of human endeavour to the empirical, imperfect existence of man. The Biblical concept of God, however, precluded any notion of a state of spiritual union between the creature and his creator. Hence the formula 'approximation to God', which Platonic philosophy had used for centuries to describe the goal of human endeavour, could only be interpreted as meaning a perpetual movement and not any kind of final state. In this way, a basic philosophical-ontological tenet was radically reinterpreted.

Especially that type of Christian biography which I have just mentioned documents an obsession with the inner life, a desire to observe the processes within the soul on the road to salvation. The same interest guides the psychological and psychagogical reflections found in abundance in monastic literature. It was shared by philosophy which over the centuries had shifted its emphasis from the explanation of phenomena perceived sensually to the knowledge of the spiritual world order. However, there was a major difference between pagan-philosophical and Christian introspection, even if both produced enduring psychological insights. In the tradition of Greek thought the philosophers were first and foremost concerned with the relationship between man's inner life and the objectively given order of being, or of the world. Christians saw themselves as faced with a God whose revelations, orders, or actions concerned them individually, independent of any comprehensible world order. This explains why autobiography, the literary description of one's own life, thought, and actions, necessarily gained a new function.

The Graeco-Roman Classical age had produced a large number of autobiographies belonging to various literary types. In the fourth century AD already the orator and author Isocrates had used the form of a fictional application for an exchange of fortunes, as detailed in Attic procedural law. This was in a long work styled as an oration, intended to give a public account of his life, his professional and political career, and his political objectives. We know that kings and statesmen of the Hellenistic age, such as Pyrrhus of Epirus or Aratus of Sicyon, would publish their memoirs; and so did great Romans of the Late Republic, such as Rutilius Rufus or Sulla. Some of them used Greek: for instance, Cicero and several Roman emperors including Augustus. But among the authors of autobiographies we also find authors of lower rank, for example Nicolaus of Damascus who lived at the court of Herod, and the Jew Flavius Josephus.

The works by the authors mentioned, as well as comparable writings, must all be understood as accounts primarily intended as self-justification, for which purpose inner motives may, of course, be mentioned to explain the writers' deeds. In moral-philosophical literature, autobiographical elements were of a different kind, with actions playing only a minor role, at best included for the purpose of exemplification. The emphasis here is on the description of the changing inner state, as indicating how far the author has got on the path of moral ascent. Plutarch wrote a whole treatise on this subject, and the so-called *Meditations* of the Emperor Marcus Aurelius, or more properly, the *Treatise Addressed to the Author Himself* (see p. 279), as well as many of Seneca's letters (see p. 93), show how philosophical education with the goal of moral perfection was accompanied by permanent self-scrutiny, the keeping of an ever-renewed account of one's own spiritual state.

What all the forms of autobiographical writing originating in the Graeco-Roman Classical age have in common is that the spiritual state is expressed and evaluated in the same categories which also serve the general, communicable rational cognition of the world or of nature. Hence the authors locate their own spiritual condition – albeit on very different levels of reflection – on a plane of existence which it shares with the other objects of rational cognition.

The Christians had an entirely different view. To them, the inner man ultimately comes face to face with God outside the referential framework given by nature, and becomes directly exposed to the expressions of the divine will. The empirical world offers him the chance to assess his own state only in the ever-changing and unpredictable constellations of human society. The experiences resulting from this situation can neither be generalised, nor communicated in categories relating to a general perception of the world. The only way to tell others about them is via a kind of detour, with the help of images, analogies, or similar devices. This notion shows that the new concept of God and world also brought a hitherto unknown and more meaningful concept of the uniqueness of each individual human life.

It is one of the great works of world literature, and moreover one of the few within the historical scope of this study, which first gave literary form to this new image of man, and of his relationship to God and the world. Augustine's *Confessions* painted the new picture with a clarity that may very well be described as unique and unrivalled.

The thirteen books of this major work were written between 397 and 401 AD. The first nine books are a very detailed account of the author's earthly career and his inner progress, including the humiliating confession of his own errors as well as the extensive description of hard spiritual struggles and decisions. This is why there is no other individual from all the centuries of Graeco-Roman history of whose character, temperament, and way of thinking we can form such a detailed assessment as in the case of Augustine.

Augustine was born in 354 AD to a Christian mother in the minor city of Thagaste in north Africa. It was in this province that he received his rhetorical education and at the early age of twenty he began teaching rhetoric in his native city, a career which he continued in the provincial capital Carthage between 375 and 383 AD. At the time, Augustine was not at all attracted by the religion of his mother and in 373 AD became a follower of the Manichaean creed instead. His acquaintance with philosophy remained superficial, as he only got to know it through the works of Cicero which featured in rhetorical instruction, and he never achieved a full command of Greek.

In 383 AD Augustine went to Rome where the pagan City Prefect Symmachus secured his appointment as a publicly salaried professor of rhetoric in Milan. Augustine began teaching there in 384 AD, entering the sphere of influence of the great churchman Ambrosius, and becoming an avid listener to his sermons. He gained admission to a circle of philosophically educated friends who were closely acquainted with Ambrosius; those men taught him a deep understanding of Neo-Platonist philosophy, and of its application in the terminological definition of the Christian faith.

It was this influence which caused Augustine's final renunciation of the Manichaean faith and his opting for a lifestyle guided by Christianity and philosophy. He left the woman he had lived with for ten years, and who had borne him a son. In 386 AD, after long studies, inner struggles, and many consultations, he decided to ask for baptism. He gave up his professorship, retired for six months to a friend's country estate at Cassiacum near Milan, and was christened by Ambrosius in 387 AD, together with his son. This brought about a reconciliation after many quarrels with his extremely pious mother who had followed him to Milan. Soon after his baptism, Augustine set out to return to Africa with his mother and his son. The mother died on the journey during a sojourn in Rome. After that, from 388 to 391 AD, Augustine lived in a kind of monastic community with some friends in his native city, concentrating entirely on the literary projects which he had taken up in Milan. His son died during this period. When Augustine was visiting nearby Hippo in 391 AD the local Bishop Valerian ordained him as a priest – much to Augustine's surprise and actually against his will – and designated him as his successor. Augustine became Bishop of Hippo in 395 AD and worked in this office with untiring energy until his death in 430 AD, at a time when Hippo was besieged by the Vandals.

The *Confessions* were written during a stage in his life when Augustine was already firmly established in ecclesiastical office, and could evaluate the struggles and confusion of his first thirty years in retrospect. Consequently the last four books of the *Confessions* contain something like a portrayal of the religious and world view which the author has achieved, although it is not cast in the shape of a systematic or didactic treatise. Augustine's musings about God and creation, sin and forgiveness, body and soul, or time and eternity are a peculiar mixture between declarations of faith and philosophical reflections, which are to highlight again and again the limits of human understanding. The individual statements are only loosely linked in a text which Augustine wants to be understood as a praise of God, and as an expression of gratitude for the guidance granted to him through inexplicable divine grace.

As an entirely unique psychogram, the *Confessions* have naturally kept attracting the interest of readers throughout the Modern age, and there is indeed hardly any other work in world literature which exposes the inner life of a man to such an extent. However, a good deal of caution is needed in any attempts at psychological interpretation. Augustine's frank account of his sexual experiences, for instance, has been evaluated in many different ways, according to the Victorian or Freudian bias of readers. But statements about the psyche of a man from a past age can only be understood adequately if seen against the background of contemporary conventions. Of those, however, we often plainly know too little. It is far easier to evaluate statements which can be related to well-known, explicit philosophical concepts of which Augustine was definitely aware; or, to ecclesiastical doctrine as based on Biblical passages. However, many of the psychological insights expressed by Augustine could presumably be understood immediately by anyone at any given time in history.

The reports and reflections of the book are shaped in very diverse linguistic ways. Narrations of individual events alternate with general contemplations, descriptions with prayers and ejaculations, rhetorical questions with self-accusations, and original observations with elements of philosophical and ecclesiastical doctrine. Augustine mastered the means of expression in Latin, as refined through the rhetorical tradition, with an ease unequalled by any but Cicero. Like Cicero, Augustine was no purist, and hence he did not let his language be governed by the strict norms of Classic prose, but also used words, word forms, or phrases from the contemporary spoken idiom. This, however, did not detract from his stylistic consciousness, something which the modern reader is easily led to underestimate by the exceptional, emotional vividness of his diction. Augustine's long professional experience of rhetoric gave him an infallible sense for the effect of the expressions he could choose from in any given case. In this respect the *Confessions* resemble his sermons, and it is especially important to remember in the reading of this unique text, entirely non-traditional in content and seemingly spontaneously formulated, that its stylistic form is wholly created by the exponent of a long rhetorical tradition.

The artful and deliberate shaping of the work is particularly obvious in the way in which quotations from the Bible and from Classic authors are used. The text is studded with hundreds of quotations, mainly Biblical, but also from the Latin Classics. A study of the largest group among the Biblical borrowings, quotations from the Psalms, has shown that they are important elements which simultaneously structure and interpret the content. They establish a correlation between every single piece of detailed information which the author gives about his inner life at the different stages of his spiritual-emotional development, and declarations of the faith as known and recognised by all Christians. The composition of the text, which ostensibly deals with no more than very specific problems of an individual life, can thus be understood on the basis of a religious experience shared by the readers. This method also justifies the communication of the most intimate details of an individual's psyche, in reference to revealed common knowledge.

Augustine's *Confessions* do not only tell us about the author's way to Christianity and to the spiritual and administrative responsibility of the episcopal office. They also map out the path which led him to philosophy, with which he had at first become only fairly superficially acquainted during his study of rhetoric. Among his Milanese friends, however, he managed to achieve a familiarity with Neo-Platonist doctrines which, in spite of his insufficient knowledge of Greek, gave him the basis for independent philosophical enquiry. This is shown not only in the treatises he wrote on purely philosophical themes, but also in many parts of the *Confessions*. One example is the chapter in Book 11 in which Augustine puts forward his own very original theory of time in words which may well be regarded as a worthy continuation of the discussion in Aristotle's *Physics*.

The productive continuation of philosophical thought in the Latin Late Classical age was made possible through the translations of Marius Victorinus (see p. 498), through the work of Platonically-orientated philosophers above all in north Africa and Milan (see p. 528), and not least through a lasting compulsion felt by theologically interested Christians in the West. If they wanted to be up to date with Christian intellectual life, they had to duplicate in their own language those disputes over dogma with philosophical means which had without exception begun in the East. Hence there was a constant transfer of theology into Latin from the Greek in which it had been formulated; and some aspects of this situation warrant a comparison with the time of Cicero. But unlike in the previous Roman Empire, the developments of the Late Classical age led inevitably towards the creation of an intellectual life in which the Latin Middle Ages were largely separated and independent from the Greek East. Greek language and Greek thought had to be rediscovered and re-received in the West during the age of Humanism.

As an old man Augustine continued his autobiographical writing in the *Retractationes*. This book, begun in 427 AD, remained unfinished; it contains many explicit references to the *Confessions*, references which are in some cases corrections of earlier statements. The particular value of the later work is the list of his own writings which Augustine included. Two hundred-and-fifty years before, the physician and philosopher Galen had also written a book about his own literary output (see p. 290). Galen's motivation, however, had been to define the body of writings authorised by him as opposed to forgeries or lecture notes published without permission, whereas Augustine's intention was in the main purely autobiographical. The inclusion of a catalogue of works was also in keeping with ancient tradition, for such a list had been an essential part of philosophers' biographies for a long time, as in the work of Diogenes Laertius (see p. 324), or the different lives of Aristotle. Porphyry, on the other hand, had added a biography of his teacher to his edition of Plotinus' collected works following a convention of Hellenistic grammarians who prefaced editions of Classic poetry and prose with lives of the authors.

For the years up to 427 AD Augustine cites no less than ninety-three titles belonging a total of 232 volumes, that is 232 standard papyrus scrolls. This list includes neither the many letters, though written in a literary style and highly publishable, nor the countless sermons extant in the form of notes. The figures reflect the tireless activity of Augustine since his Milanese days, but they also indicate the ease with which he formulated and wrote down his thoughts. Even at an advanced age, and under the burden of those pastoral, ecclesiastical-political, and theological chores documented in his correspondence, his literary creativity did not wane. His perhaps most important work, the fifteen books about the trinity (see p. 559), were written in the first two decades of the fifth century AD, and contain a theological plan with which Augustine entered upon entirely new ground, a field hitherto untouched by the Greek approach which had so far dominated all theology.

The autonomy from a Greek-dominated tradition which Augustine shows here is also reflected in other chapters of his theological work, as well as his autobiographical writing. This phenomenon may well be linked to the fact that his educational background was limited to Latin. Augustine proves his great familiarity with Classic Latin poetry; his style betrays his training in the imitation of the great prose authors of Latin literature; he made extensive use of grammatical and antiquarian literature in Latin; and he was well acquainted with Cicero's philosophical writings. However, he himself admits that he never found access to Homer, whose work was the basis of all Greek education.

Any search for models or precedents for Augustine's peculiar kind of autobiographical writing on the Greek side is thus bound to be in vain. The only work that can be seen as roughly comparable is Cyprianus' short tract addressed to Donatus, to whom he tries to describe the spiritual state of a new convert. However, the long tradition of European literature of confession and conversion definitely began with Augustine. The earliest work of this group comes from the epoch discussed here. Ennodius wrote his *Thanks for his Own Life* as Bishop of Pavia; he held this office from 514 AD and he was also a major figure in ecclesiastical politics of the period. His large literary legacy also includes poetry (see p. 597), and his autobiography closely imitates Augustine's *Confessions*.

There are some important biographies extant from especially the late phase of Patristic literature in the Latin West. The life of Martin of Tours, for example, the most eminent man in the ecclesiastical history of fourth-century Gaul and still a most popular saint, was written by his pupil Sulpicius Severus whose work became about as important for the hagiographical tradition in the West as the great Athanasius' life of the hermit Antonius was in the East. Before his conversion to the ascetic life, Sulpicius had been a professional rhetor, and I have already mentioned him as the author of a world chronicle (see p. 485). He had a good eye for historically significant detail and thus his biography became a valuable historical source, in spite of the large room given in it to miracle-stories.

Martin's eventful biography included a short career in the Roman army, after which he met Hilarius of Poitiers (see p. 547); he finally became Bishop of Tours after several periods of time spent in ascetic seclusion. His life was very vividly described by the trained rhetor Sulpicius shortly before the death of the saint in 397 AD. By then Martin had done much for the Christianisation of Gaul, including its rural population which there as everywhere else in the Empire held on obstinately to their old religious customs for a long time. In his missionary efforts, Martin had not shied away from any kind of confrontation, whether it was with the advocates of paganism, the zealous enthusiasts who followed Priscillianus, or the holders of secular power. When Priscillianus was executed at the order of the Emperor Maximus, Martin did not hesitate to express his indignation quite explicitly.

Sulpicius later complemented his biography by an account in the dialogical style, describing the miracles worked by the saint. During the following centuries, the life of Martin was repeatedly re-edited, imitated, and even put into verse form (see p. 598). Among the authors who dealt with this saint, who was revered above all among the Franks, we find Gregory of Tours, their first historiographer (see p. 597).

Through a fortuitous accident in the tradition, we have the life of Wulfila written by his pupil, the Arian Bishop Auxentius. The work is styled as a letter which was incorporated by Maximinus, one of the Arian opponents of Ambrosius and later also of Augustine, into a pamphlet directed against Ambrosius, and which is extant presumably because of this very fact only. Wulfila was the son of a Gothic father and of a mother from a family that was abducted by the Goths from Asia Minor. He had become a convert to Christianity when he took part in the mission of a Gothic delegation sent to the Emperor Constantine's court. During the reign of Constantius II Wulfila had converted parts of the Gothic tribes, who then still lived north of the Danube. Until his death in 383 Wulfila was Bishop of the Goths, including those tribes who had settled in the Empire after the Battle of Adrianopolis in 378 AD. All of them preserved Christianity in that form which had been supported by the Emperor Constantius II, but which was finally condemned as Arian by the council in 381 AD. Wulfila's translation of the Bible is our most important source of knowledge about the extinct language of the Goths.

Soon after 496 AD the aforementioned Ennodius (see p. 531) wrote the life of Epiphanius, his predecessor as Bishop of Pavia. After that he produced a biography of the monk Antonius from the famous monastery of Lerinum near Marseilles, a centre of theological scholarship. Roughly contemporary with these two lives is the work which can well be called the most valuable historical source among the biographies of the period, Eugippius' life of the saint Severinus, who died in 482 AD.

In the second half of the fifth century there was a complete collapse of the system of Roman administration in Noricum, the region between the Danube and the Alps. Large parts of the Romanised population saw themselves forced to leave the country because of the pressure of Germanic immigration. In this situation Severinus carried out some impressive work, not only as a comforter and pastor of people in distress, but also as instigator and organiser of comprehensive aid. His skilful negotiating and the authority which he had even among the Germanic tribes and their chiefs would often prevent violence and helped to diminish the suffering caused by the migration of populations. His pupil and biographer was an eye-witness to most of the events he describes; his work aims at edification, but does not put too great an emphasis on miracle-stories, so that the insight it gives us into everyday life at the time of the great migrations is hardly equalled by any other source.

The work of Victor of Vita stands in the tradition of the *martyria* – Christian reports about the suffering and the death of witnesses to the faith – and at the same time in the tradition of a Classical literary genre dealing with the notable deaths of great men. The author was Bishop of a minor city in north Africa; his writing is an account of the persecution of Catholic Christians, especially the clergy, under the first two Vandalic kings who reigned there from 428 to 484 AD, and who, unlike the provincial population over which they ruled, followed the Arian creed. This book was presumably written in 488 AD.

Finally, I must mention two treatises which were produced entirely without literary ambition but which are nevertheless important parts of literary history. They belong to the Christian side of the genre of works 'about famous men', a genre not to be confused with literary biography, the description of a life as a moral or spiritual example for the instruction of the reader. The aforementioned genre aims at the collection and ordering of biographical data concerning philosophers, poets, architects, prose authors, generals, or statesmen: in short, men who are of interest to the scholar as well as in the context of general education. Books of this kind were not styled according to rhetorical rules and belong more to the tradition of scientific writing than that of artistic prose.

Hieronymus' short treatise *About Famous Men* explicitly follows Suetonius' work with the same title (see p. 259). The church father was a frequent user of Suetonius' scholarly tracts – for example, in his edition of Eusebius' chronicle (see p. 484). His treatise contains, in chronological order, concise facts concerning the life and work of those Christian authors in Greek and Latin whom he knew. In the preface Hieronymus puts those authors side by side with writers from the pagan past, and thus illustrates the Christian claim that they were legitimate heirs of the Graeco-Roman educational tradition. Hieronymus also sees his own scholarly collection as a straightforward continuation of the work of Greek and Latin grammarians who published similar writings before him. Nevertheless, he laments the fact that unlike those predecessors, he could not profit from any earlier efforts, except for those parts of Eusebius' ecclesiastical history which deal with literature (see p. 423). Hieronymus' short tract is an important source because of the chronological data it contains and because it features information about authors whose works are no longer extant.

Hieronymus found successors in Greek as well as Latin. An extant extract from a work wrongly ascribed to the Patriarch Sophronius of Jerusalem (see p. 464) was made by Photius in the ninth century AD. Completely extant is the continuation of Hieronymus' work produced by Gennadius, a priest in Marseilles, between 480 and 500 AD In mediaeval manuscripts this is attached to Hieronymus' survey as Hieronymus' second book. Gennadius followed the structure set up by Hieronymus, adding information on ninety-five more authors in addition to the 135 featured originally. In the last chapters of their respective works both Hieronymus and Gennadius give an account of their own literary output: in the case of Gennadius, this consists of treatises directed against Pelagians, Nestorians, and Monophysites.

Apologetical writings

After the Christianisation of the Empire there was hardly any further call for Christian apologies directed at educated pagans. One exception was the short reign of the Emperor Julian, who had accompanied his endeavours to restore the old religion with a vehement literary attack on the Christian faith. This polemic can be partly reconstructed from a long counter-treatise written by Cyrillus of Alexandria half a century after the death of the great apostate. Of the thirty books by Cyrillus, the ten extant ones tell us the gist of the first three books in Julian's work.

Apologetical in content, in as much as they try to prove the superiority of the Christian religion over the pagan faith, are two long letters which Ambrosius addressed to the Emperor Valentinian II. Ambrosius argued against a motion brought forward by Symmachus who wanted the statue of the goddess Victoria re-erected in the assembly room of the Roman Senate in order to ensure that the ancient gods under whose auspices Roman greatness had grown could receive the traditional worship which was their due. The dispute over Victoria's altar lasted from 384 to 392 AD (see p. 534), but it had much longer repercussions. Prudentius did not write his poem against Symmachus until 403 AD (see p. 583). The lasting impact of this debate can certainly be at least partly explained by the high literary standard of Symmachus' and Ambrosius' statements. Both men knew how to argue without undue pettiness or malice, and both proved to be excellent stylists.

The real bone of contention in the debate was, however, the question of whether the Empire's distress had been caused by its turning away from the ancient gods; or, on the contrary, whether the worst could be averted only by turning to the God of the Christians. This issue became even more topical when Rome was taken and sacked by the Goths under Alaric in 410 AD. In this situation, Augustine wrote his major work on political and historical theory, a publication which contains the most comprehensive apology for Christianity extant from the period of the Old Church, and which is at the same time much more than just an apologetical writing.

Augustine's major book on the *City of God* has already been discussed in the context of Late Classical historiography (see p. 469). Apart from its apologetical and historical-theoretical themes, it also contained many other motifs from philosophy and theology. Augustine maintained that in social life good and bad alike arise perennially from the ever-new choices of men. Those choices determine which of the two kingdoms individuals belong to, that of God or that of the devil; at the end of history, those who have thus become God's people will be saved and elevated to an existence of perfect bliss. This notion was very closely linked with the question concerning the nature and the working of divine grace. Why did the creator not destine all men for his own community from the very beginning? This was a problem troubling Augustine at the time of writing the *Civitas dei*, not only in the context of historical theory, but also in a completely different one which I will explain later (see p. 544). In his theory of history, however, Augustine also shows a more profound understanding of Paul's letters than that achieved by any of his predecessors. This is particularly evident in the case of Paul's Epistle to the Romans.

I have already said that Orosius used Augustine's theoretical-historical plan in his own historiography, and thus made his own contribution to the discussion of the events of 410 AD (see p. 466). Those events were echoed by other, similar happenings in the following decades. In 452 AD Rome was threatened by the Huns who had invaded upper Italy, and three years later there was a second occupation and sacking at the hands of the Vandals under Geiseric, who had established a kingdom in north Africa.

Thus there were indeed plenty of occasions for continuing reflections such as those of Augustine. One case in point is the writing of Salvianus of Massilia or Marseilles, a man who was a monk in the famous monastery of Lerinum (see p. 472) from 425 to 439 AD and then worked as a priest in his native city until the penultimate decade of the century.

Around that time Gaul suffered from continuous raids by Franks, Huns, Goths, and Vandals, who all caused great distress to the Romanised population, mostly orthodox Christians. The intruders were either heathens or heterodox Arians. The question of divine protection thus appeared quite independent of the justification of the Roman Empire's ancient cults, for fortune also seemed to favour Barbarian heretics. Salvianus began his reflections by trying to refute the notion that the divine power was indifferent to human welfare; a thought which had been cropping up again and again since the fourth century, and which appeared as a logical conclusion to many people at the time. Salvianus did not explicitly interpret contemporary troubles as heralding the imminent end of the world, but in his treatise on divine world rule he maintained that God's final judgment is meted out even before the end of history. To him, the sufferings of Christian countries were a punishment for immorality and injustice among their populations. Consequently in another treatise Salvianus formulated entirely practical, but none the less radical, demands for distributing the private wealth of the clergy to the relief of the poor. Salvianus admonished his readers by referring to the Barbarian tribes as being much more puritanical, more pious, and above all more generous than the Christians of the Roman Empire, in spite of the erroneous religious beliefs held by the intruders.

The eight books of Salvianus' work have frequently been exploited as a source of information on cultural and moral history, and certainly many of his descriptions, especially those of specific events, are of great informational value. But we must not overlook the fact that preachers of morality will always draw a one-sided image of reality, a picture in which the addressees must appear in a thoroughly negative light if the message is to be brought home. The literary motif of a community's moral decline can be encountered throughout the centuries by any reader who studies accounts from periods of crisis in highly developed civilisations, and the same goes for the motif of the noble savage who compares favourably with the corrupted representatives of civilised nations. Tacitus had already used words to that effect in his *Germania* and in doing so, even he could refer to a time-honoured literary tradition (see p. 217). Nevertheless, Salvianus himself became the founder of another long-lived tradition in literature with his idea of world history as universal judgment. Salvianus' style proves that he was a well-educated man, and his work together with that of other authors of the fifth century documents a late flowering of literary life especially in Gaul. The emergence of literary figures whose influence was limited to one region also foreshadows the development of western European nations during the Middle Ages.

Much of Christian literature from the time of the founder fathers of the fourth and fifth centuries AD is of a polemical nature. This is not surprising in view of several facts: the intensity of the debate carried on in this epoch about the philosophically convincing formulation of the dogma, the formation of many factions during this dispute, and lastly, its repercussions on society and state, after the monarchy had espoused the cause of the church.

In this period the importance of polemics against non-Christian opponents receded behind that of internal debates among the Christian factions. This is why, unlike before, texts discussing Judaism are found only occasionally in the literature of this epoch. One of the few examples is a fictional disputation between the Jew Simon and the Christian Theophilus, written by the otherwise unknown Gallic presbyter Euagrius.

What endured for a long time, however, was the Christian view of philosophy as an opponent outside the church, even long after Christian theology had appropriated philosophical terms and methods. But what Christians perceived quite accurately was that philosophy was the only vital element left of pagan intellectual life. The Emperor Julian's attempt to restore the religious practice of paganism relied largely on interpretations of religious and cultic traditions as developed by Platonic philosophy, and firmly integrated into the philosophical view of the world. Gregory of Nazianzus' vehement speeches, styled with the utmost possible amount of rhetorical devices and, as the author himself proclaims, designed to 'pillory' the apostate even after his death, make no explicit reference to the philosophical motifs in the restoration campaign; and Julian's philosophical teachers are mentioned with only a few disparaging comments. But Gregory was himself extremely well versed in philosophy, and well aware of the fact that there was a potentially lethal threat to the church in Julian's endeavour to establish a pagan monopoly on philosophy and literature or rhetoric and to cut the Christians off from the educational tradition founded on these disciplines. Christians had every reason to be interested in a use of philosophy in the sense of orthodox Christian dogma, in spite of the often repeated judgment of earlier anti-heretics that all Christian heresies were the offspring of philosophy.

A work that has unfortunately been lost is a long apology written by the extremely erudite Apollinaris of Laodicaea, originally a friend and partisan of Athanasius. His attack was directed against Julian, and above all against the anti-Christian treatise by the Neo-Platonist Porphyry. Apollinaris' numerous writings of dogmatical and exegetical content were nearly all lost because the christological doctrines of the author, who lived until the final years of the fourth century AD, were condemned by the Council of Constantinople in 381 AD. Partly extant is only one refutation of

Porphyry, albeit a very superficial one, written by Bishop Makarius of Magnesia in western Asia Minor around the turn of the century.

Around the middle of the fifth century, the aforementioned Theodoretus, Bishop of the Syrian city of Cyrus, wrote a long treatise against philosophy entitled *Therapy of the Greek Diseases*. According to linguistic usage at the time, the word Greek or Hellene could mean as much as 'pagan' because Greek-speaking citizens of the Roman Empire would call themselves Rhomaeans in recognition of their role as bearers of Imperial civilisation. In his major work Theodoretus chose to juxtapose the philosophical and the Christian answers to the most vital questions concerning God, the world, and man. He shows himself well-read in Greek philosophy, even if most of his quotations are not, of course, taken from the original texts but from compilations, so-called *florilegia*. Around Theodoretus' lifetime the Bishop John of Stoboi near the border between former Yugoslavia and Bulgaria, wrote a *florilegium* with lengthy excerpts from poetry, philosophy, and historiography, excerpts which he grouped according to different topics such as friendship, justice, the substance of the stars, the origin of warmth, or the worship of the gods. That Theodoretus knew very well how to construct a philosophical argument is shown in his lectures on the problem of the relationship between divine providence and human freedom. In this field, the church continued the anti-astrological polemics of the philosophical schools of Skeptics and Peripatetics, from whom they borrowed many individual arguments.

A new opponent of the church arose around the end of the third century AD in Manichaeism which quickly spread all over the Roman Empire from the beginning of the fourth century AD (see p. 405). An extant early Christian tract directed against the Manichaeans dates from the middle of the fourth century. Its author Serapion, Bishop of Thmuis in Upper Egypt, was close to Athanasius and is also known as the editor of one of the earliest collections of liturgical prayers. The blind Didymus, who became famous for his exegetical writings (see p. 502), also produced treatises against the Manichaeans, and so did Bishop Titus of Bostra, capital of the province of Arabia. Titus' work dates from around 370 AD; it is extant partly in the Greek original and partly in a Syriac translation. Its first part shows parallels with anti-Manichaean polemics from Platonic circles, as known through the short tract by Alexander of Lycopolis (see p. 405). Both argued above all against the rigid determinism of the Manichaeans and against their denigration of the visible world. Beyond that, however, Titus also provided a detailed refutation of Manichaean Biblical exegesis. Mani and his followers themselves regarded their doctrine as a complementation and perfection of Christianity, and consequently they also drew on the interpretation of specific Biblical passages.

In anti-Manichaean literature, we also find the form of the disputation in which the exponent of the other side is overcome. The so-called *Acts of Archelaus* are nearly completely extant in a Latin translation. The author, an otherwise unknown Hegemonius, lets an equally unknown Bishop Archelaus win a battle of words with one of Mani's pupils and then even with Mani himself. The motif of the Christian-Manichaean disputation is still found in Early Byzantine hagiography: for example, in the biography of Porphyry, Bishop of the city of Gaza around the turn of the fourth and the fifth centuries, a man who made a name for himself through his zeal in the destruction of heathen temples.

Most of the extant anti-Manichaean tracts were written by Augustine who had himself for ten years followed that religion which he then fought against so fiercely. There are no less than thirteen separate treatises, including the thirty-three books of the work against the Manichaean Bishop Faustus. Again and again, Augustine emphasised his rejection of the cosmic dualism which assumed that there was a specific evil substance; he defended the notion of man's freedom of choice against the doctrine of the fixed destiny of individual souls; and he criticised the radical devaluation of the visible world and the consequences which this had for individual lives. Nobody who has studied the history of religious debates can be surprised by the fact that all anti-Manichean polemics go with personal suspicions and slanders against individuals or against entire groups.

Internal Christian polemics I

In the fourth century AD Christian anti-heretical writing already had a long tradition, with a systematic-cataloguing form that went back to Irenaeus. The material which had been compiled in this genre was time and again re-presented and expanded by a long row of successive new authors, whose works consequently preserved the memory of long-extinct sects and doctrines. The genre stands also in the tradition of philosophical doxography which aimed at a complete and comprehensive survey of individual philosophical systems or of different philosophical doctrines on specific issues.

In the chronology of Christian anti-heretical literature, Irenaeus, who lived in the second century AD, was followed by Hippolytus in the third; then came the Bishop Epiphanius of Salamis in Cyprus. His major work, written in the eighth decade of the fourth century AD, has the handsome title of *Panarion* or *Drugs Cabinet* and contains the detailed refutation – mostly borrowed from older authors – of no less than eighty different heresies. This literary genre also spread on the Latin side: ten years after Epiphanius, Bishop Filastrius of Brescia wrote a more concise book based on Epiphanius' work, in which he deals with as many as 156 sects. From this treatise Augustine just before his death compiled a catalogue of eighty-eight sects.

There are also topical discussions of individual doctrines or sects, works which were produced because of specific controversies. Such discussions are, of course, much more detailed and fruitful than the surveys cited above; and fourth- or fifth-century authors of such works could likewise look back to an old tradition of writings, such as, for instance, Tertullian's treatise against Marcion (see p. 354).

Most Christian polemics, including the most important ones as regards content as well as style, belong to the context of the gradual development of trinitarian and christological dogma, whose milestones were the famous Councils of Nicaea in 325 AD, Constantinople in 381 AD, Ephesus in 431 AD, and Chalcedon in 451 AD (see p. 502). The process was accompanied by the secession of Arian, Nestorian, and Monophysite churches. But as in the two centuries before Constantine's revolution, there were also other occasions for the formation of special factions or separate churches whose existence gave rise to internal Christian polemics, not necessarily dealing with the correct phrasing of central religious tenets.

I have already explained that because of their intense practice of prayer and meditation ascetic communities sometimes developed ideas about man's encounter with the divine which were not approved of by the dogmatic authority of the church (see p. 418). A suspicion that arose with particular frequency against such groups was that their ascetic demands were combined with a strictly dualistic doctrine like that of the Manichaeans, which postulated the opposition between spirit and matter as a primal fact. Such an extreme anti-corporeal dualism, which had already been proclaimed by the Gnostics, was contrary to the Biblical faith in creation as well as to Platonic philosophy.

Towards the end of the fourth century the Bishop Amphilochius of Iconiun in Asia Minor attacked some such communities, which perhaps may be identified as Messalian (see p. 418). At that time the pious Priscillianus had established an ascetic community with an intensive practice of prayer in Spain. It became the subject of misgivings as outlined above, and suspicions were further nourished by the preference of this group for apocryphal literature, that is writings not included in the church canon. Moreover, Priscillianus had a known interest in the occult, and was hence suspected of sorcery.

Ultimately, however, the church also knew that ascetic communities had repeatedly inspired ecclesiastical reforms. Consequently a synod held at Saragossa in 380 AD condemned the formation of conventicles within the church, but shortly afterwards the clergy of Avila elected Priscillianus as their Bishop. In spite of many attempts at mediation, the ensuing conflict led to highly unpleasant suspicions and accusations, and finally to a denunciation at the Imperial court in Trier where the usurper Maximus resided at that time. Priscillianus was called to Trier in 385 AD and sentenced to death for practising magic and fornicating with some of his followers. He was the first heretic ever to be executed in the entire history of the church, and the event provoked outrage on the part of contemporaries who were familiar with its ecclesiastical background (see p. 436). A separate Priscillianic church survived in Spain for more than two centuries afterwards.

Of the writings of Priscillianus and his followers, some are extant anonymously or under other names. Most of these tracts were written with an apologetical intention; in any case they do not tell us about any teachings of the group which deviated from church dogma. Nevertheless, the accusation of Manichaean heresy is repeated in the extant counter-tracts, including a memorandum which Orosius dedicated to Augustine on his move to Africa and an anti-heretical treatise under the name of Hieronymus which Augustine used in the compilation of his catalogue of heresies in 428 AD. The same goes for numerous polemical references to the Priscillianists in works by Hieronymus, Augustine, and others. As in internal polemics between the philosophical schools where, for instance, the Epicureans were again and again quite unjustly described as advocates of an unrestrained libertinism, internal Christian polemics also feature such stereotype accusations, never tested by reference to the primary sources.

One internal dispute which smouldered for a long time within the church concerned the teachings of Origen; it went on from the early years of the fourth century until the final condemnation of the great exegete in the middle years of the sixth century AD. What had been recognised early on was that Origen's Platonising notions about the human soul and cosmic processes could hardly be reconciled with essential parts of church doctrine. However, the piety, the spirituality, and above all the great erudition expressed in Origen's writings ensured the continuation of the Alexandrian's strong influence, especially in monastic circles. In the West his friends Hieronymus and Rufinus helped spread Origen's thoughts and knowledge in the Latin world through translations which they wrote as young men living in monastic communities. But while Hieronymus later joined the critics of Origen and toed the line of ecclesiastical orthodoxy, Rufinus remained an Origenist throughout his life. This caused a vehement literary battle between the two former friends, a quarrel that came complete with personal invectives, and mutual questioning of one another's scientific credentials and basic honesty.

Hieronymus had criticised Rufinus' translation of Origen's dogmatical work *De principiis*, a translation which indeed glossed over some features potentially offensive to contemporary orthodoxy. Rufinus was very keen to preclude any doubt of his own orthodoxy, and to justify his plea for Origen on that very ground. This is shown in a treatise in his own defence which he had already addressed to the Roman Bishop Anastasius, when Hieronymus attacked him with a literal translation of potentially sensitive passages from Origen. Rufinus reacted with a very vehement apology; to this extant text Hieronymus in turn published an answer in three books in 401 AD, going so far as to scrutinise Rufinus' entire literary output, with a lot of personal invective mixed up with the analysis, and condemning it as wholly Origenistic.

The great impact of the dispute about Origen within the church is also documented by a pamphlet which Hieronymus wrote against the Bishop John of Jerusalem some years previously. Origen had many followers among the clergy and the monks of Palestine. That region had seen a survival of the tradition of Caesarea, the place where Origen's library was and where he found his most influential partisan in Eusebius (see p. 422). But theological circles in Egypt also cherished Origen's memory. Like Rufinus, Didymus the Blind, whose Biblical exegesis was entirely along the lines laid down by Origen (see p. 502), also wrote a defence of his admired model against all attacks which doubted his orthodoxy.

An entirely different conflict arose in Africa when rigorists claimed that those who had become apostates under persecution could not be reinstated as Christians by just any ordained clergyman; they demanded a special moral qualification on the part of the officiating priest. Hence the quarrel was not about the true faith but about different ideas concerning the nature of the church and the conditions for the validity of official ecclesiastical acts. Although the Emperor Constantine intervened personally in order to procure an early end to the dispute, it did not take long until a separate church with its own hierarchy and administration was established in Africa. There is not only literary, but also archaeological evidence of the co-existence of two separate churches over two centuries, in the remains of ecclesiastical architecture in many places in north Africa. Hence we may say that there was a deep and lasting schism and not a heresy, for what we have of the literary output of the so-called Donatists – for example, the aforementioned work by Tyconius (see p. 514) – was not produced on the basis of any deviations in dogma. The Donatist church, in which the earliest Christians' charismatic view of ecclesiastical office lived on, had its main following among the underprivileged rural Berbers, while the urban population, most notably the upper classes, supported the Imperial church. This explains why the social unrest which troubled the African province in the fourth century AD fused with the Donatist movement, and why the opposition between the two churches became more and more vehement, in spite of frequent talks and synods held for the purpose of mediation.

The earliest anti-Donatist work was written in 365 AD by Optatus, Bishop of the minor city of Mileve in modern-day Algeria; it was addressed to the Donatist Bishop Parmenianus. In 385 AD it appeared in a second edition, enlarged from six to seven books, including also a collection of relevant documents such as episcopal letters and synodal resolutions. Optatus wanted a reconciliation, realising that the state's action against the Donatists merely amplified their resistance, and caused acts of violence such as the destruction of altars and other sacred objects used in their opponents' ritual. However, Optatus argued against the Donatist view in defending the institutional authority of the official church, as justified and united through tradition. According to him the ritual acts of this church were valid and effective, regardless of the personal worthiness of individual holders of office.

The fight against the Donatists took up a good deal of Augustine's time and energy after he became Bishop of Hippo in 395 AD. This is documented in five treatises, some of them fairly long, as well as in many of his letters. He also wrote a poem against the Donatists (see p. 571); and the doctrines concerning the church and its sacraments which Augustine developed in this context were regarded as so significant that the work of another author about the same subject was also handed down under Augustine's name.

The Donatists had the custom of rebaptising all those who had joined them from the official church, for they regarded baptism given by an unworthy priest as having no validity at all. Arguing against this practice, Augustine formulated what became the official doctrine concerning ecclesiastical sacraments in the following centuries. The Donatist idea of the church as a religious and cultic community was that it is perpetually recreated through proof of the moral and religious worthiness of its members and that any external order is ultimately irrelevant to it. Against this, Augustine set the concept of a church existing as a legal order within the secular world, a group which has to subject its members to a certain power structure for the sake of its spiritual task, and of its unity. Augustine's definition of the church shows the far-reaching influence of Roman legal and political thought which had permeated Latin theology – unlike its Greek counterpart – already at a very early stage. This became the most decisive factor in the ensuing history of the Western-Latin church.

Apart from the development of the trinitarian dogma, which I have mentioned before (see p. 504) and which will be dealt with again in the following section of my account, the greatest controversy was caused by the appearance of a monk from Ireland called Pelagius. He was a learned man with a good command of Greek, and a dedicated pastor who made a name for himself in ecclesiastical circles in Rome, in Africa, and finally in Palestine, through a series of tracts and commentaries which put a new interpretation on Biblical doctrine concerning the working of divine grace. According to Pelagius the natural gifts with which man is endowed enable him to attain eternal salvation by himself through constant moral endeavour. The divine grace to which man owes his existence pardons any past sins but without necessarily affecting later efforts. The moral appeal inherent in this doctrine gained Pelagius a large following everywhere he went, as well as in Sicily and Rhodes. It was not until his arrival in Jerusalem in 411 AD that he became involved in an open conflict with Hieronymus. Prior to that the Roman clergy had not taken any offence at

Pelagius' refutation of longstanding dogmas concerning the Fall, original sin, and the necessity of infant baptism.

Pelagius was given a chance to defend himself at a synod held in Rome in 414 AD; however, a council of African bishops in 416 AD condemned his doctrines, and their judgment was endorsed by Pope Innocent I, albeit not by his successor. The final decision about Pelagius' fate was made by the Emperor Honorius, who banished him in 417 or 418 AD. Soon afterwards Pelagius died in exile, but this did not inhibit the activities of his partisans to any significant degree, and the definite condemnation of Pelagianism did not come about until the Council of Ephesus in 431 AD.

Between 412 and 430 AD Augustine wrote several long letters and fifteen treatises concerning this matter. The two last and longest ones were addressed to Julian of Aeclanum, the leader of the Pelagian party after Pelagius' death. In spite of their basically polemical intention, the importance of these writings, wide ranging in subject matter, lies in the development of a comprehensive doctrine of divine grace and human action, a doctrine based on a reassessment of Paul's letters, especially that to the Romans.

Augustine took the Biblical account of the Fall very seriously and consequently denied empirical man the ability of attaining salvation through his own effort. According to him, eternal salvation and the restoration of the lost natural perfection of man as originally intended by the creator can only be granted to fallen man through the inexplicable, freely given, and irresistible grace of God.

In the long tradition of philosophical ethics, wrongdoing had again and again been explained by the adverse effect of external circumstances or of emotions and passions, irrational forces in the human soul, obstructing the application of rational cognition which leads man to doing right (see p. 505). In his interpretation of the Biblical view of man Augustine detached himself from this explanatory pattern which was drawn on by all theology on the Greek side, with the result that freedom from sin was often defined as freedom from passion. This went hand in glove with the ideal of ascetic life, and the appeal to human endeavour derived from it. According to Augustine, though, the irreparable damage caused by the Fall was not due to reason, but to will. According to the command of the creator, the human will should take the form of love of God, and love of one's neighbour. In empirical man, however, it focuses instead on the bearer of the will himself in the form of self-assertion, pride, desire, and ruthlessness to others.

This basic position which Augustine derived from the Bible explains some apparently paradoxical statements of his: for example, that humility accompanied by all possible faults is better than pride accompanied by all possible virtues, or that people can do anything they like as long as they love. In Augustine's view, man is led to perfection not by the progress of rational cognition and the resulting permanent endeavour as philosophy had taught, but only by the regeneration of his will through divine grace. Proper moral action and progressive cognition are consequently effects of the act of grace. It was this radical doctrine which made Augustine an advocate of infant baptism as a visual token of the giving of divine grace. In his lifetime, infant baptism had already become widespread but still met with some criticism.

Augustine's anti-Pelagian writings contain the first instance of a definition of human will which is still an essential part of the discourse on ethics. The current use of the term 'free will' presupposes the theological reflections of Augustine. His notion that the human will had become unfree through sin did in no way lead him to regard deliberate action as impossible. Like philosophers before and after him, he regarded deliberate action as action based on a rational and free choice of goals and means. In Augustine's view the unfree state of empirical man has deeper roots. In spite of the rational choice of individual goals, it guides human action again and again towards the self-assertion of the agent, instead of the welfare of his fellow humans; and no moral endeavour can liberate man from this bondage.

Without any doubt, it is this idea which underlies the view of man expressed in essential Biblical writings. Augustine was the first to give it terminological shape; and it was in this very context that the modern concept of will was developed. The latter sees human will no longer only as a function or a result of cognition, but as an independent factor of spiritual life, different from the intellect as well as from instinctive-emotional urges. In Augustine's doctrines, the new notion of will also found expression in other contexts (see p. 560).

The Pelagian debate had repercussions which went beyond the condemnation of Pelagian doctrine at the Council of Ephesus. Now people in many different places turned against Augustine's radical doctrine of grace which seemed to destroy the theological foundations of ecclesiastical ethics. Especially monastic circles sought to preserve the importance given to moral endeavour in man's salvation, in taking up an opinion defended by Pelagius who claimed that empirical man's endeavour was by nature free and good and thus preceded the giving of divine grace. People in monastic communities were inclined to emphasise the trust in the universal will of God, aimed at the salvation of all mankind, against the doctrine of divine predestination which Augustine did not explicitly advocate, but which his statements about the freely and inexplicably distributed grace of God invariably suggest: that from the very beginning, some men are chosen for salvation and others for damnation.

It was above all the aforementioned monastic theologian Cassianus (see p. 419) who propounded such doctrines, soon classified as semi-Pelagianism, according to which the attainment of eternal salvation depends on the joint effects of divine grace and human endeavour. This was also the essential point in a short general survey of Christian doctrine called *Commonitorium*, written by the monk Vincent from the monastery of Lerinum in southern France. The author did not mention Augustine explicitly, but he put considerable emphasis on the relevant chapter and exerted a far-reaching influence. Shortly before his death, Augustine himself had sent to the monks of the north African monastery of Hadrumetum two treatises which were meant to dispel doubts about his doctrines. He also found help from some friends – above all in Gaul – who supported him in literary contributions to the debate, and who carried on the discussion after his death. The most eminent man among them was Prosper Tiro from Aquitaine, the region between the Garonne and the Pyrenees, to whom Augustine had dedicated two of his anti-Pelagian tracts and who had himself written several shorter treatises, letters, and also hexametrical poems in support of Augustine against Vincent of Lerinum. Soon after Augustine's death, however, Tiro's position moved close to semi-Pelagianism, and his last treatise advocates that very doctrine about God's universal will for salvation which had been so crucial to Cassianus.

In the East Marius Mercator from Africa promoted Augustine's ideas. He lived as a monk in a monastery near Constantinople and wrote short treatises in Greek as well as in Latin. All of them are polemical in content, attacking the Pelagians as well as the Nestorians (see p. 502); these two groups had indeed grown very close to one another.

By far the largest part of the literature written during the Pelagian debate was, however, produced in the West; the East had never shown too great an interest in the problems discussed in this dispute. In the East the focus was on christological debates where the questions were put and answered from an ontological perspective, whereas the battleground for the Pelagian debate was – in philosophical terms – anthropology. This debate continued well into the sixth century AD. Hieronymus refers to a lost tract written against him by Anianus of Celeda who apparently supported the original doctrine of Pelagius, while all the other opponents of Augustine's doctrine of grace were in the semi-Pelagian camp. In Africa Arnobius the Younger attacked Augustine's teachings on grace in the second half of the fifth century AD; in the first half of the following century, Augustine's position was defended by the eloquent Fulgentius, Bishop of Ruspe.

In Gaul a synod held in Orange in 529 AD brought the debate to a close. Its decision, confirmed by the Pope of Rome, followed in the main the doctrine of grace as developed by Augustine but rejected the strict doctrine of predestination which claimed that a part of mankind is destined for damnation. The day for this moderate Augustinism had been won by the eminent ecclesiastical personality and versatile author Caesarius, Bishop of Arles, who came from the monastery of Lerinum. In the second half of the fifth century AD the debate was dominated by an enemy of Augustine who also emerged from Lerinum, although he was originally from Britain:

Faustus of Reii whose letters are the products of an elegant and educated stylist. At the same time the presbyter Gennadius of Marseilles made a stand for Augustine and against Pelagians as well as semi-Pelagians.

Most of the internal Christian debates which I have discussed so far as giving rise to polemical-dogmatical literature concerned fairly narrowly defined issues. Only Augustine's comprehensive and penetrating treatment of those issues produced literary works which formulated basic questions and insights with a wider impact. However, the Augustinism of early mediaeval theology was not always based on the original writings by the Bishop of Hippo. As in the grammar or philosophy of the Empire, there were collections of excerpts also in theology. Thus the author of a life of Saint Severin (see p. 533) is also known as the man who compiled a treatise consisting of crucial passages from Augustine's collected works.

Comparatively greater in volume, more complex, and richer in content than the category of writings dealt with in this chapter is the extant literature documenting the major debates on the formulation of christology and of trinitarian doctrine. These discussions dominated the fourth and fifth centuries; their beginnings have already been portrayed in a previous part of my account (see p. 504).

Internal Christian polemics II

Today, after the abandonment of all attempts to make our world as a whole comprehensible by means of an ontological plan, we find it difficult to follow such ontological debates as I have described. In the period in question, however, those discussions absorbed a measure of intellectual energy which can hardly be overestimated. But to contemporaries it seemed evident that debates of this kind focused on the most important and the ultimate facts: they sought to describe the process of salvation as something of concern to everybody and ultimately inexplicable as such within the framework of a generally accepted image of the structure and the order of being. This framework for discussion had been established by Greek philosophy and hence it is hardly surprising that the Greek East set the tone in all debates about christology and the trinitarian dogma.

In the first stage of the Arian debate, dominated by the towering figure of Athanasius, the major pamphlets were written by that man himself and by Hilarius of Poitiers, both of whom I have mentioned before. Hilarius' three polemical works demonstrate an astonishing skill in the transfer of Greek terminology to Latin. In this respect, these writings can be likened to the translations of Neo-Platonist texts by Marius Victorinus, of whom we also have three anti-Arian tracts, produced soon after his conversion. In the case of Hilarius, however, it must be noted that the finding of adequate Latin expression for the language and the manner of argumentation of Greek theology, with which he had familiarised himself during his stay in the East, was not his only achievement. Hilarius was a well-trained rhetor and explicitly stated his high stylistic demands for theological literature in particular. This is reflected in his major anti-Arian work about the trinity but also in his memorandum for the synods of Rimini and Seleucia in 359 AD. It shows to a much lesser extent in his account of the history of the trinitarian controversy, in which he addresses the leaders of the opposition. In this book, extant only in an incomplete form, the focus is on documents reproduced in the original wording. Documentary material had already been given a prominent role in the pamphlets of Athanasius, and had been a part of the method of ecclesiastical historiography since the time of Eusebius (see p. 424).

Hilarius attempted to mediate between the factions whose number kept increasing throughout the controversy that led to ever-new schisms. The group favoured by the Emperor Constantius II called themselves Homoeans. The name, which is no more than a general reference to the notion of a similarity between Father and Son, reflected the fact that they saw themselves neither as followers of Arius, nor as in agreement with the Nicaean formula which in their view created misunderstandings because of its excessive precision. The decision of the council in 381 AD, however, subsumed the Homoean position under the heading of Arianism, which was the theology received by converted Germanic tribes at that time.

Although Hilarius was a follower of Athanasius and a supporter of the Nicaean formula, he saw himself forced to take a stand against the more radical exponents of his own party, who rallied around Lucifer of Calaris, or Cagliari as we know it today. This faction soon formed an independent sect which still features in a work written one generation later by Hieronymus, another steadfast supporter of the Nicaean formula. This pamphlet is styled as a dialogue between an advocate of orthodoxy and a Luciferian. In comparison with Lucifer's coarse attacks, the stylistic skill in Hilarius' polemics appears in a particularly impressive light.

The defeat of Arianism explains the fact that only a few remnants of Arian literature have been handed down to us. They include a pamphlet against Ambrosius of Milan written in 383 AD by the Arian Bishop Maximinus who later also spoke out against Augustine. Among the documents featured in this work is the aforementioned letter by the older Bishop Auxentius, describing the life and work of his teacher Wulfila (see p. 532).

A new stage in the Arian debate was introduced by the appearance of the Antiochians Aëtius and his pupil Eunomius, later to become Bishop of Cyzicus on the Sea of Marmara. They claimed that the nature of the Son or *logos* was that of a creature formed within time: a radicalisation of Arius' doctrine that represented the son as being subordinate to the father, by introducing the notion of a fundamental difference in nature between the first two persons of the trinity. Arius himself had never gone that far, and neither had Constantius II's favourites, the Homoeans, who stopped at a very general statement about the similarity between Father and Son, and tried to avoid further specification. A more moderate position was also that of the so-called Homoiousians, the advocates of a doctrine about the similar nature of Father and Son. Their first leader was Basil of Ancyra, succeeded after his death in 364 AD by Macedonius, the Bishop or Patriarch of Constantinople. Under Bishop Eustathius, Antioch had at first been a stronghold of those who supported the Nicaean formula; now Eunomius and his followers made it the centre of a renewed Arianism. With the exception of a few quotations, Eunomius' writings have been lost: but the works produced as part of the debate about his doctrine are among the most important pieces of theology and the most valuable pieces of literature in extant Patristic writings.

The first anti-Eunomian tract was written by the great Basil in 364 AD. In mediaeval manuscripts, it is featured as having five books. However, comparisons with other dogmatical-polemical writings by Didymus the Blind have shown that Didymus is the author of the last two books and Basil only of the first three. Both authors do indeed express the same opinions about the identical nature of Father and Son, but there is a difference in their manner of argumentation.

A similar comparison between Didymus and Basil is suggested by their treatises about the Holy Spirit. The ontological definition of the third person of the trinity, and of its relationship with the Father and the Son, was inseparably linked with the nature ascribed to the second person. Consequently the Arian controversy led to the development of a theological movement whose exponents were called Pneumatomachians, or 'fighters against the Spirit', by their adversaries. They denied the existence of the Holy Spirit as an independent divine hypostasis identical in nature to the creator, and Basil as well as Didymus wrote a pamphlet against them. Didymus' work is extant in a Latin translation by Hieronymus, which in turn served as a model, beside Basil's tract, for Ambrosius' treatise on the Holy Spirit which he dedicated to the Emperor Gratian. All of these writings or translations were produced during the short period between 375 and 393 AD; they document the lively communication between Western and Eastern theologians, but also the existing linguistic difficulties. Didymus' comprehensive work on the trinitarian dogma, extant in the original, originated during the same timespan; it attacks Eunomians, Macedonians, and Pneumatomachians.

In all polemical debates of this kind, one crucial element was reference to Biblical passages, interpreted in a manner that lent authority to one's own position. No theologian could get away with expounding a doctrine without such Biblical justification. Origen had given Biblical proof even for his doctrine of *apokatastasis*, a concept which appears to lead far away from the Christian tradition (see p. 340). The novel and special feature in the theological writing of the Cappadocians – Basil, his brother Gregory of Nyssa, Amphilochius of Iconiun, Gregory of Nazianzus, and John Chrysostom all came from the same region in Asia Minor – seems to be the unprecedented rigour in the way they give Biblical proof for the dogma in coherent, methodically controlled argumentation.

This achievement resulted from a thorough application of philosophical methods to the subject matter: its result was the exact fixation of theologically important terms. It was, for example, not until this period that the endeavour to provide an unambiguous description of a God defined as being at the same time One and Three, led to a clear terminological distinction between being or *usia* and nature, and between hypostasis and person. That is why the dogmatical controversies of this and the following century had a great impact on the development of philosophical and scientific linguistic usage, in Greek as well as in Latin, by posing new tasks to the existing highly developed philosophy of the Late Classical age. The continuing interest in dogmatical issues also ensured the survival of skills in the use of philosophical terms.

Theology was concerned with the content of the faith, as concerning man in another way than the knowledge gathered through everyday experience. Most people wanting to communicate such knowledge to their fellow humans would try to order it with the help of reason. For centuries Greek philosophy had concentrated on the effort to attain a comprehensive view of the world and of being through this very application of reason. For the structure of the world which is accessible only to thought and not to sensual experience, they postulated the same rational order which gives man the faculty of communicable cognition. The application of this ontologically orientated philosophy to Christian religion, however, produced a scientific theology which was in danger of losing its link with religion as practised in worship and everyday life. Its problems were generated internally, being the results of a never-ending discussion as in all scientific endeavour. This is the reason for that rejection of all theology which is a recurrent motif in the history of piety, as well as for repeated efforts from the Christian Classical age onwards to find a new theology without ontological targets (see p. 330).

The writings of Basil's brother, Gregory of Nyssa, reflect the philosophical orientation and the rigorisation of theological discussion even more strongly than those of Basil and Didymus. Today, Gregory's major work is commonly referred to as the *Twelve Books Against Eunomius*, although it consists of four independent treatises written successively. Two attack Eunomius directly; one criticises a treatise, and the other his formulation of the faith proposed at the Council of Constantinople. The two others defend Basil's pamphlets against replies published by Eunomius, which makes them something like a legal duplica, the retort of a defendant to the plaintiff's accusations. There are seven more short treatises by Gregory of polemical-dogmatical content, attacking groups such as Macedonians or

Pneumatomachians and, above all, the doctrine of Apollinaris of Laodicaea (see p. 537). Apollinaris had suggested an escape from the confrontation between theories of identical and different natures: he put the Son not quite on the same level as the Father, but still went further than the radical Arians in making him stand out among the other creatures, by denying that the historical Jesus had a full human nature. This doctrine was also rejected at the Council of Constantinople in 381 AD.

Unlike his older brother Basil, the great pastor and organiser, Gregory was a scholarly man, reluctant in becoming a bishop and inept in being one. But there is no other theologian of the early church who equals his philosophical education, his intellectual energy, and his precision in argumentation and in the definition of terms. These qualities can be found above all in Gregory's dogmatical and polemical writings, including also his *Great Catechesis*, a summary of Christian doctrine which emphatically distinguishes it from Jewish, pagan, and heretical beliefs (see p. 518). His edificational and exegetical works show more of his strong and very individual piety, as expressed in the lavish application of the allegorical method as well as in stylistic verve. However, Gregory's skill at sharp, penetrating argumentation is also coupled with a clear insight into the existence of limits to any human endeavour at communicable cognition, limits that are reached wherever the encounter with the divine becomes the subject of reflection. This is said with particular clarity in Gregory's life of Moses (see p. 525), but also elsewhere in his writings.

Gregory of Nazianzus, a friend of the two brothers, was the third Cappadocian who played a major part in preparing and implementing the credo as decided at the Council of Nicaea in 381 AD. I have already mentioned him as an excellent pulpit speaker with a rhetorical education (see p. 519), and I will deal with his poetry in a later section (see p. 572). His biography is one that befits an intellectual with varied education and interests, a man easily irritated, given to introspection, and unable to settle down to any work environment. Among the many stations of his life were a hermitage where he took temporary refuge, as well as the episcopal chair of the Eastern capital. Gregory himself reports this in autobiographical treatises and in poetry, texts which try to justify his inconstant behaviour. As Bishop of Constantinople, or rather of the small community there which adhered to the Nicaean formula, he resigned after only a few years, feeling unable to cope with the day-to-day business of ecclesiastical politics. He expressed the reasons for his decision in a farewell sermon published by himself; and one of his poems expresses a heartfelt complaint about his life as Bishop of the remote minor city of Sasima where Basil had urged him to go. Gregory had been ordained as a priest against his will by his father, who was at that time Bishop of the minor Anatolian city of Nazianzus.

All this explains why Gregory's collected works should include no systematical contributions to theological discussion formulated in patient labour, even if his astuteness, his comprehensive education, and his elegance in linguistic expression would have well enabled him to perform such a task. But his restless nature rather favoured the popularisation and topicalisation of theological issues for a wider public, and in this field he proved his excellence with the speeches against Julian, but most notably with the so-called five theological sermons given just before the council of 381 AD. Here Gregory showed that he was up to date with theological debate, particularly in his comprehensive and easily comprehensible presentation of the state of the controversy, and of his own position. In the Greek church, which numbers him among its saints, these extremely effective homilies earned him the honorific epithet of 'Theologian' which was also given to John the Evangelist.

The decision of Constantinople by no means signified that Arianism was dead. This is why we still have anti-Arian tracts from the following decades; for example, from the influential Bishop Cyrillus of Alexandria (see p. 455). He was about fifty years younger than the three great Cappadocians, who lived until the last two decades of the fourth century AD.

Arianism had the greatest longevity in the West, as the Germanic tribes – Goths, Gepidi, Burgundians, Suevi, and Vandals – had received Christianity in a form that was condemned as Arian in 381 AD. Being the ruling class in the territories they inhabited, they maintained not only their creed but also their own ecclesiastical organisation against the local Catholic population of the provinces. Under two Vandalic kings, there were even persecutions of Catholics in fifth-century Africa, as reported in detail by the Bishop Victor of Vita (see p. 533); but there were also talks between the religious factions like those which had already taken place at the time of Augustine.

All this is documented by a large number of anti-Arian tracts from Africa; among them, the letters of the Bishop Fulgentius of Ruspe deserve particular mention. There was a more peaceful co-existence of the two major denominations in Italy under the Ostrogoths, at least during the reign of Theodoric the Great. However, the sympathies of the Romanic population for their fellow believers in eastern Rome contributed significantly to the collapse of Gothic rule in the mid-sixth century AD. In 586 AD the Visigoths in Spain saw themselves forced to convert to Catholicism in order to alleviate tensions with the local population. The Burgundi had already joined the established church about one century earlier under the influence of Alcimus Avitus, Bishop of Vienne. The Franks, who did not become Christians until 496 AD, adopted the new faith at once in its orthodox form, and the Anglo-Saxons who had migrated to Britain were converted through missionaries sent by Rome around the turn of the sixth and seventh centuries AD. Thus the survival of Arianism appears to be closely linked to the survival of Germanic kingdoms.

In the late fourth and the fifth century AD the controversy over Arianism was still on the agenda in the entire western half of the Empire. From this period, we have a whole series of Latin pamphlets on this issue, even if their arguments do not go beyond the groundwork done by the Cappadocians. A case in point is one of the two tracts written by Ambrosius on this subject, entitled *De fide* or *Of the Faith*, and addressed to his Imperial pupil Gratian. In 419 AD Augustine wrote a full treatise in reply to an Arian tract, and a special pamphlet was produced in the context of a carefully minuted disputation with the Arian Gothic Bishop Maximinus.

In the controversies leading to the decision of 381 AD philosophical thought had once again taken hold of the content of the faith. People believed in the mystery of God becoming man, and the inexplicable nature of this mystery was never called into question. Still, the contention was that the inexplicable could be described in ontological terms, with a degree of clarity which allowed one to make a distinction between believers and non-believers on the basis of their agreement or disagreement with the formula arrived at. This view at the same time opened the door for the search for further dogmatical fixations. The definition of the identical nature of Father and Son led to the next problem: the question of how to give an unambiguous description of the presence of divine substance in the man Jesus.

The history of the further controversies is easy to sum up as far as dogma is concerned, while the related quarrels concerning ecclesiastical politics appear as extremely complex. Nestorius, born in Antioch to Persian parents, was Patriarch of Constantinople from 428 to 431 AD, but proved to be unable to cope with the political demands of his office. He had formed his theological views as a member of the circle surrounding the great exegete Theodorus of Mopsuestia (see p. 513), who was particularly keen to prevent a polytheistic interpretation of the trinity. It was in keeping with the corresponding christology to explain the union of God and man by postulating an existing man Jesus who was later endowed with divine nature. This interpretation, advocated less by Nestorius himself than by his followers, seemed to threaten the monotheistic character of the Christian religion far less than the idea of an incarnation of a pre-existing divine hypostasis through the birth of a man.

However, the Nestorian concept met with criticism from the Alexandrian theologians whose speculations were inspired by the special popularity which the veneration of Mary as the mother of God enjoyed in Egypt, while the Nestorian point of view denied her this dignity. Another attempt to defend the cult of Mary against Nestorian theology was the sermon given in 429 by Proclus, who later became Patriarch of Constantinople. Cyrillus, the spokesman of the anti-Nestorians (see p. 455), found support in Rome where people had little regard for Nestorius because of his sympathies for Pelagius, and where a synod condemned him as early as

430 AD. In 431 AD a council held at Ephesus at Nestorius' own request branded him as a heretic and took his office away from him. Two years later, under the influence of the Empress Pulcheria, the same Emperor who had not long before supported his appointment sent the famous preacher into exile in Egypt where he died many years later.

His followers, above all in Edessa – the main centre for theological studies in the Syriac language – did not accept the synodal decision as the final word. The school was removed to Nisibis, on the soil of the Sassanid Kingdom, and that was the beginning of the final separation of Christianity east of the Roman Empire's border from the Christian West, because of a dogmatic dispute stemming from Greek thought. In the following centuries the Nestorian church, whose language of worship remained Syriac, excelled all others in its missionary work which penetrated as far as China.

The most important documentation of the Nestorian controversy is to be found in the many mainly polemical writings of Cyrillus produced in this context. Cyrillus presided over the Council of Ephesus and had the support of the Roman Bishop. From Nestorius' rich production, we have only fragments preserved as quotations. In addition to those, there is a short treatise by his follower Eutherius of Tyana, a man likewise condemned at Ephesus.

Among Cyrillus' extant writings, there are several memoranda addressed to the Emperor Theodosius II and to other members of his dynasty, as well as a short condemnation of twelve individual doctrines ascribed to Nestorius, with a detailed justification added. Furthermore, we have a treatise in several books written against a no longer extant collection of Nestorius' sermons; an account of Cyrillus' own activities at the council of Ephesus; two writings meant to justify the veneration of Mary as the mother of God; and fragments of a pamphlet against the christology of the Antiochians Diodorus of Tarsus and Theodorus of Mopsuestia whom Cyrillus regarded as forerunners of Nestorius. Then there are so-called Easter letters, epistles from the Patriarch to the churches in his province which deal with matters of liturgy and church discipline, as well as with dogmatical issues.

Cyrillus was a man of strong temperament and great eloquence, a fact which is clearly expressed in these writings. As Bishop of Alexandria, he could incite fanatical fervour among his congregation and the ensuing pogroms against Jews and Novatian (see p. 388) even brought him into conflict with the Imperial administration. During Cyrillus' term of office, the philosopher Hypatia was murdered in Alexandria by a Christian mob (see p. 489). Cyrillus' behaviour at the council likewise seems to have been unrestrained enough to call for a later self-justification.

In spite of all this, Cyrillus' polemical writings as listed above contain extraordinarily exact and well thought out theological formulas. This points to the meanwhile firmly established tradition of theological craftsmanship and theological propaganda in which the philosophical and the rhetorical component of Classical intellectual life remained alive. What can be described as Cyrillus' most famous treatise, *That Christ be One*, argues that the person of Christ must be seen as a unity from his incarnation and that his divine nature was not given to him at any later stage. This treatise made Cyrillus a key figure for a new movement breaking away from the established church, even if the orthodoxy likewise always counted him among their ranks.

In his fight against Nestorius, Cyrillus had enlisted the support of the well-respected monk Eutyches who taught in Constantinople, a man who cared in particular about the notion of an unmistakable, inseparable unity in the Saviour's person. In two treatises, on the other hand (see p. 416), Theodoretus of Cyrus had taken a stand against Cyrillus and for Nestorius, in the tradition of Antiochian theology. He also disagreed initially with the decision of Ephesus, seeing the danger that laying emphasis on the unity of Christ's person could lead to the notion of a hybrid being replacing the idea of the Saviour's pure and unadulterated divine nature.

Dioscorus, who in 444 AD succeeded Cyrillus as Patriarch of Alexandria and who was yet another man with a strong temperament and a great awareness of power, took up the ideas of Eutyches and radicalised Cyrillus' doctrines in a theology which was soon called Monophysitism. Its core was the idea that in the person of Christ, divine and human nature came together to form an inseparable and unique mixture. Dioscorus' influence on the Emperor Theodosius II allowed him to call a second council at Ephesus in 449 AD, the so-called 'robbers' synod', whose discussions were entirely dominated by Dioscorus, and which without much ado proclaimed Monophysitism as orthodox theology.

Theodoretus, who was deposed by this synod, appealed to Pope Leo the Great in Rome, and the intervention of the Pope brought a new council which met in 451 AD in Chalcedon, the city facing Constantinople on the coast of Asia Minor. In long, patient consultations, a formula was worked out which used subtle distinctions between the terms person, hypostasis, and nature, to steer clear of the Nestorian as well as the Monophysite position. The definition which this formula propounded was that in the person of the Saviour, both divine and human nature should be thought of as existing from the incarnation, side by side, but yet unmingled. The authors of this formula thought it the only way adequately to describe the secret of the divine work of salvation and its implementation in the world of men.

Once more, this decision of the council led to a schism in the church. Monophysitism retained its support in Egypt and found new followers in those parts of Syria which belonged to the Empire, as well as for some time in the capital itself. Even Theodora, the Empress at Justinian's side, was still attracted by the Monophysite position.

For the sake of the unity of Empire and church, there were repeated attempts to bridge the rift; through an Imperial edict, the *Henotikon* of 476 AD from the Emperor Zeno, or through mediatory doctrines. Monoergetism and Monotheletism, for instance, suggested that there were indeed two different natures, but only one manner of action or one will respectively. But all these endeavours were in vain, and what remained in the eastern parts of the Empire, in Syria and above all in Egypt, was the existence of two churches with separate hierarchies, and at odds over dogma. The main backing for the Monophysites came from the people who spoke Syriac or Coptic, and this is why their churches gradually developed in a markedly different way from the Imperial church also in ethnical and cultural aspects, into oriental national churches which still exist today. A considerable number of those Christians greeted the Arab conquest of the seventh century AD as a liberation. However, the controversy reinforced the ties between the Greek and the Latin church. But the church of Ethiopia, initially very close to the church of the Empire, was taken over by the Monophysites. There the Ethiopian translation of Cyrillus' treatise on the unity of Christ's person belongs to the most important pieces of ecclesiastical literature to this day.

Polemical literature against Monophysitism is in evidence until well into the seventh century AD. From its early stage, three treatises by Theodoretus deserve particular mention. One entitled *The Beggar* is styled as a dialogue between a beggar and an orthodox Christian; it belongs to the tradition of popular philosophical writing in dialogue form. The title was meant as a reference to Eutyches who, according to Theodoretus, compiled his doctrine by begging from all kinds of earlier heresies. A large part of the extant literature from the Monophysite and Nestorian controversies is written in the Syriac language. With the development of theological activity from the early fourth century AD, literary Syriac incorporated many words from the Greek, and became a more and more suitable instrument for the rendering of philosophical argument. This prepared the way for the role that Syriac was to play as a transitional medium for the reception of Aristotle, via Greek and Arabic, in the mediaeval Latin of western Europe.

The most eminent Monophysite author in Greek was Severus of Antioch, deposed as Patriarch of Constantinople by the Emperor Justin in 518 AD. Severus then went to Alexandria where the Monophysites dominated in spite of the politics of the Imperial court. His major work against the doctrine of Chalcedon was entitled *The Lover of Truth*; it exists only in a Syriac translation, as do his sermons and letters. Severus also acquired a reputation as a writer of ecclesiastical hymns. The place of his banishment was the same as that chosen for the Bishop Julian of Halicarnassus, the home of the so-called Aphtardocetes, a radical branch of Monophysitism; and Severus and Julian got involved in a full-blown literary feud. Another polemical work by Severus, also extant in Syriac translation only, responds to the treatise in defence of the doctrine of Chalcedon published by the grammarian John of Caesarea in the second decade of the sixth century AD. Severus' piece was meant to show that the decision of the council was in keeping with the doctrines of Cyrillus of Alexandria whom the Monophysites claimed as their particular authority, as well as with the statement from Pope Leo I.

A Monophysite of a very special kind was the Alexandrian John Philioponus, by far the most eminent among the late commentators on Aristotle (see p. 494). His dogmatical work is only extant in a Syriac translation; the author had the audacity to define the three persons of the trinity as having three different natures respectively and being one merely in a terminological sense.

As I have mentioned, the debate about Monophysitism and attempts to reconcile it with the formula of Chalcedon went on for a long time. Nevertheless, the three books of a pamphlet by Leontius of Byzantium, a work written in 543 AD, may be taken as the most comprehensive rejection of Monophysitism as well as of Nestorianism which could be given by any supporter of the Chalcedonian formula. Leontius was a very erudite man who had an astonishingly wide knowledge of dogmatical literature and who certainly knew how to use it in his argument. He also saw the unique importance of Origen for all later theology and was open-minded enough to speak out in the so-called Three Chapters Debate against Origen's definitive condemnation, at the very personal initiative of the Emperor Justinian. In the Latin West, farther away from the court in Constantinople, many voices were still raised in defence of Origen.

Evidence of new patterns of thought

There are a number of short dogmatical writings apparently linked to Monophysitism – although the precise connection is not quite clear – which became of great importance in the Middle Ages. In the literature of the Old Church, they appear as isolated in many respects for, in spite of an obvious borrowing of motifs and concepts from Neo-Platonist philosophy, they show a new way of dealing with this philosophical tradition in a manner which could almost be called naive. In these texts philosophy is no longer primarily a tool for the terminological definitions which make the content of the faith accessible to discursive thought. What we find is a novel unity which blends philosophy with the Christian message to a far greater degree than that achieved by any Christian authors with a marked philosophical background, such as Origen or Gregory of Nyssa. The price for such an amalgamation, however, is the loss of terminological clarity.

The works in question are four relatively short treatises and eleven very short letters purporting to be from the hand of the Areopagite Dionysius who, according to the tradition of apostolic history, was converted by the apostle Paul. Consequently the different addressees are individuals known from that historical period, including the apostle John. Severus of Antioch is the earliest author who speaks about these most peculiar writings, which occasionally feature specific terms from Monophysite theology. Shortly after Severus, at a religious disputation in Constantinople, some Monophysites claimed apostolic authority for these works but their orthodox counterparts were at first reluctant to accept this. However, from the middle of the sixth century onwards these texts were generally regarded as genuine, not only among the Monophysites. In the mid-eighth century AD, the Irishman John Scotus at the court of Charles the Bald produced a Latin translation. A rich manuscript tradition shows that in the East as well as in the West these works were extremely popular throughout the Middle Ages. To the West they communicated essential elements of theological speculation with a Neo-Platonist orientation.

The first treatise deals with the Biblical names for God, illustrating God's characteristics through a partly allegorical interpretation. The second one is about that mystical vision beyond all cognitive efforts in which the soul achieves a union with God. Number three contains a complex angelology derived from Neo-Platonist demonology; and the last treatise describes and interprets the structure of the church, its sacraments, offices, and ranks. The letters deal with subjects such as, for instance, the administration of the sacraments, or issues related to penance.

There can be no doubt of the fact that the ecclesiastical and dogmatical facts on which these texts are based belong to the fifth century; but it is not known for whom and on what occasions the author wrote. In the contemporary debates on dogma and ecclesiastical politics the issues dealt with had no particular importance: neither a hierarchical structure of the church conceived of as a parallel to that of the spiritual world, nor the practice of penance; and least of all speculations on mystical vision, which led away from religion as communal practice as well as from the theological explication of the Christian message. The only parallels are to be found in the mystical piety of Messalian monks in the Syrian-Mesopotamian region; those, however, were not at all interested in any theological-speculative justification of an established ecclesiastical order.

The conundrum posed by these works, written in an extremely complex language, remains without a satisfactory solution to this day. Their far-reaching influence was without any doubt owing to the belief in their apostolic origin; it decreased only as more and more doubts concerning this genesis were raised from the fifteenth century onwards. Their special interest to the literary historian lies in the fact that the author not only uses ideas, terms, and patterns of thought from Neo-Platonist philosophy as tools or aids for understanding and interpretation, but that he makes them the content of his apostolically legitimised doctrine. This marks the end point of the process of amalgamation of Classical and Biblical tradition, a development to which I have referred many times already.

Apart from the special case of these pseudo-Dionysian writings, my present survey of Greek and Latin theological literature in the narrower sense illustrates that the gradual formation of central dogmas and individual church doctrines happened essentially through the medium of a polemical literature mirroring oral discussions at synods or religious disputations. This impression is confirmed by many of the letters (which will be discussed in the following section), and by many extant acts and documents from ecclesiastical life. There are also non-polemical accounts of Christian doctrine: but most of them are summaries, textbooks for teaching, or sermons directed at a lay audience (see p. 520); only a few are creative contributions to the development and differentiation of doctrine, or of theological terminology.

With regard to the persistent pressure of ongoing polemics as a driving force, the development of scientific theology from the third to the fifth century AD is clearly similar to that of philosophy between the end of the fourth and the late first century BC. The unceasing exchange of polemics between the competing schools existing side by side in Athens led to a development and differentiation of doctrine at an extraordinary pace, a situation radically different from that during the Imperial age. Ultimately, both Christian theologians and Greek philosophers were motivated by the urge to define proper living, an issue which had an added dimension for the Christians – and, incidentally, also for the Platonics – because of the view towards an afterlife. The seriousness of the issue of righteous life explains the earnestness and the zeal, but also the bitterness in the dispute about proper doctrine leading to individual salvation. That Christians sought to find this salvation through a more and more precise application of ontological categories to the contents of the Biblical faith may well strike a modern-day observer as over-subtle. However, it was a necessary consequence of the fact that the only ready-made tools for theology were the methods of philosophy as shaped by Platonism. These methods determined the direction of thought and made it possible to transform theological speculation into a methodically controlled science, which in turn passed on Classical forms of scientific thought and discourse via the Middle Ages to the Modern age.

This generalised description of dogmatical literature in the Old Church does not at all fit the case of Augustine's major dogmatical writing, the fifteen books on the trinity which he produced during the first two decades of the fifth century AD. It is true that this work also contains polemical references to dissenting views on details of doctrine; but on the whole, its origin was not tied to topical controversy. In the first half of the treatise Augustine describes the Nicaean doctrine of the trinity which was recognised as orthodox at the time and its Biblical foundations. Victory over the different kinds of Arianism had already been secured, even if the opposition was still represented by separate groups or churches. However, the more important second part of Augustine's work explains the belief in the divine trinity in a way which is entirely different from the models and questions used in the Greek discussion. Augustine was aware of the novelty of his approach and wrote to a friend that he expected his argument to be understood by no more than a few.

In the *Monologues*, an early work, Augustine once states that only God and the soul are topics worthy of philosophical investigation. Later on, he himself violated this principle again and again by reflecting also and particularly, in good philosophical tradition, on being and world, state and society; and by intervening in the ontologically orientated debates on the doctrine of the Saviour's nature. In the treatise on the trinity, however, he entered new paths, entirely in keeping with his early maxim. He was daring enough to attempt an interpretation of the trinity as postulated in the Christian faith according to an analogy drawn from the life of the human soul and hence without reference to any comprehensive, objective order of being because insight into the nature of the human soul came from introspection and not from the study of the external world. In one respect, however, Augustine like many theologians before him remained close to Platonically orientated thinking: to him, the likeness of the creator mentioned in the Bible is only the inner man, that core of man's soul which thinks and gives consciousness.

Where Augustine differed from Plato and philosophers in the Platonic tradition was in his description of spiritual processes inside man. According to Augustine, for instance, the act of seeing is initiated by the human will, which establishes the link between the power of vision and the object of visual cognition. As for thought, the internal cognitive process, the object supplied by memory replaces that in the external world. Will, memory, and cognition thus constitute the whole of inner, mental life. They are inseparably linked and cannot function without one another.

This model was new at the time, for philosophical psychology had known will only as potential cognition or as the consequence of completed cognition leading to action; not, however, as a mental factor in its own right. The elements of the new psychology can be found already in Augustine's *Confessions* as the results of intensive self-scrutiny. In contrast to traditional Classical psychology, his description of life within the soul is unrelated to any idea of an order of being to which psychic phenomena belong. On the contrary, the region of the mind is seen as autonomous.

It was this very model which Augustine used for the interpretation of God's all-embracing spiritual being. To him, the three divine persons of ecclesiastical dogma correspond to the three functions of mental-intellectual life.

In the lifetime of Augustine the notion of a tripartite structure, giving meaning and life, at the top of the pyramid of being was already an old motif of Platonising ontology. It appeared in the Chaldaean oracles (see p. 283), was adopted by Porphyry (see p. 402), and first applied to the Christian belief in a divine trinity by Marius Victorinus (see p. 498). The basic difference between those models and that of Augustine is that the latter does not refer to the eternal, immutable being of God as the top, the centre, or the epitome of an objectifiable order of being, but rather to the divine work as echoed in the human soul. The Neo-Platonist model expressed a mode of thinking which uses the contemplation of an immutable state as an analogy for the comprehension of the supreme, which is beyond sensual experience. The Augustinian model rather corresponds to the idea of successive perception of a process.

In his attempt to give a dogmatical explication of the belief in the trinity, Augustine proceeded with great care and caution. This shows, for instance, in his avoidance of a terminological fixation of the three inner functions of the soul which are to provide clues about the mystery of the trinity: in doing so Augustine takes into account the metaphorical character of his expressions. The names for the three elements change according to whether the creative or the saving power of the divine is focused on. What is never lacking, however, is a reminder to the effect that the perfect will as the expression of God's benevolence must be equated with love.

Of course Augustine knew and used the ontologically orientated plans of older trinitarian doctrines. In this he showed a clear preference for the method of so-called negative theology, as developed in the school of Plato presumably as early as the first century BC. It was based on the assumption that human reason is incapable of understanding divine nature correctly and comprehensively; hence the endeavour to express an image of God must be limited to statements about all that can be said not about God himself, but about the created phenomena of the material or the spiritual world. This is the only way to illustrate the different nature of the divine, which can not be comprehended as such.

As I have said above, Augustine's doctrine of grace had a lasting and permanent influence; in contrast to that, his plan of a trinitarian doctrine looks like a stray boulder in the field of early speculations on the trinity. Studies on the *Confessions* have often led to the question of whether the individual self-scrutiny and self-assessment which they document do not really transcend the categories in which people of Graeco-Roman culture thought and felt. The issue of the demise of the intellectual world of the Classical age and of the opening up of new paths for human sentiment and thinking is raised with the same urgency by Augustine's major work on trinitarian doctrine. The reason is that for a person living at the time of Augustine, the reflection about God was more likely than any other intellectual activity to approach the foundations of individual human existence.

Studying Augustine's major works as well as those of the Areopagite is likely to lead readers to a clearer perception of how and to what extent knowledge and patterns of thought from Graeco-Roman culture were transferred to an intellectual life of a different kind; but similarly it helps to understand which new approaches and motifs were now beginning to govern intellectual and practical living. Nobody, however, should be so presumptuous as to base any calculation of loss and gain merely on outstanding intellectual, especially literary creations. The plexus of those motifs which proved to be fertile in the course of history, and sometimes in the most surprising ways, is far too dense and confusing for such a venture.

Nevertheless, there are indeed literary documents from the transitional period between the Classical age and the Middle Ages which do suggest the drafting of such a balance. I have repeatedly mentioned certain collections produced between the first and sixth centuries AD: for example, Pliny the Elder's natural history, Macrobius' *Saturnalia*, or Stephen of Byzantium's geographical lexicon which passed on knowledge and questions from many branches of Classical science to the Greek and Latin Middle Ages. The process is particularly obvious in the case of geography where every new generation is invariably faced with the task of constructing its own image of the earth on the basis of inherited information, or of newly gathered data.

There are several extant works from the Late Classical age which present – in very different manners, but mostly with only superficial ordering – such material, consisting of geographical information handed down through many stages. Stephen of Byzantium's lexicon from the sixth century AD (see p. 441) lists, in alphabetical order, hundreds of toponyms, with explanatory remarks from geographical literature dating back to the sixth century BC. The editor was more interested in the linguistic form of geographical names than in the wealth of knowledge contained in the many works to which he had access. In contrast to this, the anonymous *Expositio totius mundi* or *Description of the Entire World* follows a logical geographical order in its sequence of descriptions of countries taken from older literature. This work, which is extant in a Latin translation, belongs to the fourth century AD. Around 400 AD Marcianus of Heraclea on the Pontus wrote several excerpts from the scientific-geographical literature of Hellenism and of the Early Empire. His sources were the works by Artemidorus from the second century BC and by Menippus of Pergamum from the first century AD; and thus writings which include mathematical geography and cartography, albeit no up-to-date topographical information. All of these texts document a progressively narrowing flow of individual data, all of them handed down, and many of them not understood. However, they also show the survival of opinions and approaches developed through scientific research. Still, there was no new information added to the picture thus achieved.

An entirely different image is presented by the strange work of the seafarer Cosmas, who went to India in the sixth century AD. The author was a merchant who had made sea-voyages to east Africa, Arabia, and Ceylon. From those travels he brought back some extremely interesting information, including high-quality copies of Greek inscriptions from the Abyssynian port of Adulis, as well as reports about trade and Christian churches around the Indian Ocean. Such first-hand facts are also found in other Christian writings: as, for example, in the account of a voyage from the Red Sea to India around 400 AD, handed down under the name of Palladius (see p. 416), in the preface to a retelling of some of the traditional legends about Alexander.

Cosmas retired to a monastery in his old age. His description of the earth, written from the point of view of a Christian who knew his Bible and was conscious of his own knowledge of the globe, propounds a new world view against that of Greek science, as last described comprehensively by Ptolemy in the second century AD. At the time Cosmas was writing educated people still believed in the plan generally accepted since the fourth century BC, with the globe at the centre of the hierarchical spheres (likewise thought of as round), of the planets, and of the fixed stars. Presumably inspired by Antiochian Biblical exegesis further cultivated by the Nestorians in the East Cosmas tried to justify the Old Testament view of the earth and the world. According to him, the world is shaped like Noah's ark and Moses' tabernacle, with the earth as a rectangular base, and above it the firmament in several stories, supported by outer walls. From some unknown source Cosmas knew of an entirely schematic map of the world drafted before the beginning of Hellenistic science and mentioned by the historian Ephorus in the fourth century BC. This map is cited by Cosmas as further evidence for his theory.

Cosmas' book illustrates a change in intellectual life. Like their pagan contemporaries, Christians in the Late Classical age tried to support their views and standards in life and in scholarship by referring to the authority of the ancients. However, the texts called upon by intellectuals of the Empire or the Late Classical age who sought to understand the external or empirical world had often been written on the basis of a methodical, strictly scientific evaluation of recorded phenomena. This is why the ready acceptance of knowledge expressed in such texts also led to the handing down of scientific approaches to an epoch in which there was much less interest in new, individual observations and analyses than there had been during the age of Hellenism, the zenith of Classical science. In any case, in those areas where observation and experience recede behind pure speculation (i.e. logic and mathematics, but also textual exegesis) the tradition of methodically controlled, scientific argumentation was never lost, but developed further in the tackling of ever-new tasks.

Now, Christian authors were also, and even particularly strongly, inclined to look for authoritative instruction in texts in whose production scientific thought in the sense described above had had no share at all. They expected such instruction also in matters concerning the world of external realities. This was the point where a tradition of scientific approaches had to come to an end even – as in the case of Cosmas – where there was a strong interest in the observation of new facts. This was often more clearly expressed in Christian than in pagan texts simply because Christians were more prone to distancing themselves from the authority of Classic Greek or Latin literature, which they thought of as in any case inferior to the authority of the Bible. But the greater openness to new observation did not lead them to a scientific contemplation of the external world. With them, the intellectual energies necessary for the sustaining and development of scientific-methodical activity were directed, with a progressive exclusiveness, at subjects which concern speculative thought alone; and the phenomena of the material world were more and more sidelined. In this, Christian intellectuals were indeed similar to their pagan contemporaries. But the relapse into pre-scientific patterns of thought and opinion in intellectual life was quicker and more thorough among the Christians. This explains why innovative achievements of speculative intelligence are frequently found in Late Classical Christian authors, while methodical-scientific evaluations of facts observed in the external world are extremely rare.

Epistolography

There is an immense mass of extant letters from the early Christian period. The letter had been a recognised literary form since the fourth century BC, and its composition was an established part of rhetorical-didactic theory. On both sides of the linguistic divide, educated people knew what vocabulary, what syntactic forms, and what stylistic figures were thought of as suitable for the various types of letters. Then as now, of course, there was also an entirely artless communication by letters, in which only certain conventions concerning address or closing formulas were observed. Among the Egyptian papyri there are hundreds of such artless private letters, including ones of Christian origin. But the inclusion of the letter in the number of acknowledged literary forms and hence in rhetorical education meant that especially people of rank or literary reputation wrote even very private letters according to the rules of good style, and thus paved the way for later publication. In such circles, letters were in any case written with a view to a readership larger than the group of addressees.

The publication of letters in the Classical age was anyhow a different issue from what it is today. The practice of reading aloud was enough to detract from that intimate character of the letter which we now take for granted. Also the network of social relations and dependencies particularly among the more important people was more dense and their private sphere therefore differently delineated. This is why many more letters than today were addressed to a bigger group, or even the public at large. Followers and admirers of famous men have also at all times posthumously published letters which the latter had not meant for any wider audience. The extant letters from Cicero to Atticus document this as well as those from Brahms to Clara Schumann. Those letters from the period of the Old Church which are featured in mediaeval manuscripts are without exception from ecclesiastical officials or teachers. This gave also letters of a more private nature, and not directly concerned with ecclesiastical matters, a share in the authority with which posterity endowed the authors, and thus it secured their preservation. Paul's letter to Philemon is the earliest case in point.

In a previous section, I have already talked at length about the collection of Cyprianus' letters from the mid-third century AD (see p. 384). As these originated in very different situations in the author's life, and are correspondingly varied in content, so do the countless extant letters from the fourth to the sixth century AD show a great variety of subject range.

Many individual letters in the collections of Basil's and Augustine's correspondence, for instance, provide insights into the everyday reality of the administration of a diocese or church province; while the extant letters by Gregory of Nazianzus, 245 in all, frequently speak of entirely personal matters, as do the thirty extant ones by Gregory of Nyssa. Naturally those texts which deal with personal everyday experiences are particularly rich sources of information for the cultural historian.

Part of the voluminous collection of Hieronymus' letters is an extended correspondence between him and Augustine, discussing in detail aspects of Biblical translation, with particular view to the question whether the Hebrew or the Greek text has the higher authority, and with many textual and interpretative samples. This exchange of letters records an interesting debate between the philologist Hieronymus, and, on the other hand, Augustine as the representative of the official church tradition and very suspicious of innovations entering church practice because of scholarly research. Although he duly observes the rules of formal politeness when addressing the holder of high ecclesiastical office, Hieronymus' feeling of superiority, which is indeed justified in this case, is expressed with great eloquence, and not without irony. This part of the corpus of Hieronymus' letters also contains a particularly large amount of clues about scientific relations between the territories around the entire Mediterranean about the distribution of books and other matters of a similar kind.

Hieronymus' letters are especially varied in content. There are long biographical obituaries on noble friends or patrons, but we find also detailed advice on the upbringing of children with a view to a later life as part of the clergy. This advice is addressed to noble women, some of whom lived in mixed Christian-pagan families. Other letters deal with theological issues or aspects of monastic life; and quite a few are full of acid polemics.

Ambrosius' letters are important documents concerning major issues of ecclesiastical and legal politics; they reflect the high esteem in which he was held by several emperors. All of John Chrysostom's extant letters date from his years of exile, documenting how the great preacher kept up his strong pastoral ties with his followers in Constantinople through frequent correspondence.

The fifty extant letters by Paulinus of Nola are marked by a particular elegance in style. Their author, whom I shall discuss later as an important exponent of Christian poetry (see p. 581), was a highly educated man from the Senatorial class, whose family estate was situated near modern-day Bordeaux. For a while Paulinus held a high office in the administration of Italy. He maintained connections with many literary personalities, and several of his letters are addressed to such men, even if the epistles are mostly concerned with religious subjects. Paulinus was baptised in 390 AD at about forty years of age; afterwards, he led an ascetic life first in Spain, and then in Nola in Campania. From 409 until his death in 431 AD, he was Bishop of that town. Like Basil's major epistle about the proper approach to ancient literature, some of Paulinus' letters deal with the question of how traditional education, gained through the study of pagan literature, could be reconciled with a Christian lifestyle. This problem had already troubled Hieronymus; with Paulinus it gains special weight in view of his biography, and of his exceptional literary talent which he proved in verse and in prose.

Many letters written in the context of the dogmatic debates not only contain information on relevant disputations, synods, or treatises, providing the historian with otherwise undocumented facts about the course of events. Many of them also have the volume and the form of detailed statements of expert opinion concerning, for instance, a forthcoming synod. Among the letters of Augustine, there are epistles which might just as well have been published as treatises on the controversies with the Donatists and the followers of Pelagius. The few letters of the Patriarch Proclus are official condemnations of the Nestorians; and the extant fragments from Nestorius' correspondence indicate that his letters were of a similar character, albeit arguing the opposite point of view.

This type of letter is most frequent wherever the sender is the holder of a high ecclesiastical office, speaking authoritatively on controversial issues concerning doctrine, rites, or ecclesiastical discipline. The addressee of such epistles may be an entire church province, or its clergy as entrusted with the passing on of the message. Among the extant cases in point are numerous Easter letters by the Alexandrian Patriarchs, including Athanasius (see p. 409) and Cyrillus (see p. 455).

Such letters were also addressed to individual clergymen, to advocates of specific theological teachings and, of course, also to synods which debated the respective controversies. Examples are above all the many extant letters of Roman bishops from the time between the third and the sixth century AD. It was often the opinion of the Pope that swayed the verdict of a synod or a major council: not so much because of his contribution to theological discussion, but rather because of the authority which the episcopal see of the old Imperial capital possessed. This was also the case in theological disputes predominantly originating and largely conducted in the East. Thus Rome's support for the Nicaean formula was crucial to its victory in 381 AD and, without the intervention of Leo I, the resolution approved at Chalcedon in 451 AD would presumably have been a different one.

The long line of letter-writing Popes includes, for instance, Sylvester whose anti-Arian epistles Athanasius quotes in full; Damasus from the second half of the fourth century AD; Innocent I who made a stand in the Pelagian debate in the early fifth century AD; Leo I or the Great whose instructional letter of 449 AD paved the way for the Chalcedonic resolution; Gelasius I who condemned Monophysites and Pelagians in the second half of the fifth century AD; and Gregory the Great of whom we have about 850 extant letters. Nearly all of their predecessors or successors are likewise represented in the extant corpus of letters.

This rich tradition is explained by the fact that the Christian church had very early on established fixed forms of organisation, a disciplinary order for its members, and correspondingly fixed ideas about duties and competences of ecclesiastical offices. This is documented by a series of sets of rules for Christian worship and the life of Christian communities which goes back to the early second century AD. Within the framework of this emerging legal-ecclesiastical order, the decision of a high church official was the equivalent to that of the supreme court in a modern state, whereas the resolutions of synods and councils corresponded to the legislative acts of a modern Parliament.

It is true that most episcopal and synodal decisions concerned the rites and the lifestyles of laymen and clergy: for example, in dealing with the validity of baptism performed by heretics, the correct date for Easter, the permissibility of remarrying, or the practice of penance. But the nexus between the tradition of office and that of doctrine, both of which people sought to derive from the apostles, soon opened up opportunities for answering even questions of faith or of theology in the narrower sense, on the basis of official authority as given to individuals or collectives.

Thus the letters of eminent holders of office, even if they had a theological content, were documents of ecclesiastical law, as were synodal resolutions or minutes. All that was recorded from the early synods – for example, those in the Spanish city of Illiberis (modern-day Elvira) in 306 AD or in Arles in 314 AD – were the resolutions, called *canones*. The earliest known collection of such synodal resolutions dates from 378 AD. The oldest Latin collection, containing translated texts as well as Latin originals, is from around 430 AD.

Later on there were also written records of the debates at the major councils – the first one being that of Ephesus in 431 AD – as well as lists of participants, speeches given at the meetings, and more. According to these documents, dogmatical controversies were even at a very early stage in church history decided on the basis of a formal legal framework; and this not only applies to differences of opinion on aspects of worship and lifestyle. As a result even during disputes before a synod the parties involved would draw on the authority of older documents seen as supporting their view. Athanasius used this method in his apologetical-polemical writings (see p. 409); Optatus of Mileve gave an appendix of documents to his anti-Donatist pamphlet; and Augustine also used a similar technique. Of course it was tempting to forge such documents, if necessary, and it is due to this temptation that we have, for example, the Coptic translation of a collection of fake documents alleged to relate to the Council of Nicaea, as well as many forged individual documents contained in different collections of undoubtedly genuine texts. As Imperial legislation was also concerned with ecclesiastical affairs – for instance in the major codifications of Theodosius II and Justinian – Imperial letters and edicts also entered into collections focusing on ecclesiastical law. A case in point is the so-called *Collectio Avellana*, discovered in a monastery in Umbria, which consists of letters from emperors and popes between 367 and 523 AD.

The letters, decrees, edicts, minutes, and other documents contained in these and in comparable collections should of course primarily be read as sources reflecting the rapid emergence of ecclesiastical law. This is most marked in the West where for centuries there was no strong political authority comparable to the Byzantine monarchy, and where hence the church enjoyed great freedom in the development of its own legal order. It is debatable, however, whether the relevant texts can also be regarded as literary works. If we limit our definition of literature to texts in whose writing a prominent interest in the intended aesthetical effect played a part, then the aforementioned documents certainly cannot be regarded as literary. The same applies to a considerable part of the theological treatises discussed earlier on.

Nevertheless, in deciding this issue two more facts should also be considered. One is that in the Classical age, including the Christian period, the rhetorical (i.e. formal-linguistic component of general education) was so dominant that even texts written for clearly non-literary purposes show its influence on every page. The technique of using rhythmical clause endings, for example, is also found in types of writing whose modern equivalents are normally characterised by the lack of any great regard for aesthetical effect; and a similar observation may be made with regard to the choice of vocabulary. In no less than twelve books, Cassiodorus (see p. 499) published documents officially edited by him as examples of a style suitable for the state administration. Some three hundred years earlier Philostratus had already devoted an entire treatise to the rhetorical formulation of such official writings. Those hagiographical texts which are for the edification of a readership with little education and are hence written in an idiom approaching the vernacular, are less carefully styled than many of the documents on ecclesiastical law, and yet no one would want to claim that they are not literary. At that time the dignity and the effect of any text on an educated public did after all largely depend on its being shaped according to the norms of rhetoric. Virtually the only exceptions in Latin are texts written by members of the legal profession; and in Greek, texts produced for readers with a specialist knowledge of, for instance, mathematics or astronomy. But wherever knowledge is communicated with predominantly didactic intent, and of course in dedications or prefaces, we find the elements of rhetorical organisation even there. Hence the definition of what belongs to the literature of the Empire and the Late Classical age, especially with regard to the heritage of Christian writing, is first and foremost dependent on criteria relating to social background, aesthetical effect, and form, or on combinations of such criteria.

This leads to a second fact suggesting that the definition of literature in this case should be a fairly wide one. The separation and separate study of so-called *belles-lettres* from texts produced in the context of law, politics, science, journalism, economics, and social intercourse is relatively unproblematic if the civilisation in question is either the observer's own, or at least one with which there is an immediate historical link. In such cases, those clues for the understanding of literary works of art which come from non-literary life will to a large extent come to the observer without any special effort because of the background knowledge which he is likely to have gathered at first hand. The situation is entirely different if any culture from a remote past is the subject dealt with. In this case only a complete and comprehensive scholarly use of all existing evidence – something which in any case is possible only in ideal circumstances – will establish the framework for an optimal understanding of individual literary texts. It is this fact which demands that a literary history of the Roman Empire should not have too narrow a selection of material, and look for helpful information in all the extra-literary sources available.

8 GREEK AND LATIN POETRY

Liturgical poetry

The political and social stabilisation brought about by the reforms of Diocletian and Constantine created the conditions for a late flowering of poetry which lasted until well into the sixth century AD, in the East as well as in the West (see p. 426). A large share of its production is extant since the poets of this period came to be regarded as Classics in the following centuries. This opinion was justified in as much as on both the Greek and the Latin side, versifiers stuck to the stylistic and metrical forms and conventions of Classic poetry in their respective language. Consequently the poetry of this late period was largely scholarly. It was taken for granted that poets as well as their audience were familiar with the Classic tradition, especially with Virgil and Homer. The rhythm of the newly written verses did not follow the phonetics and the accentuation of current spoken language: the metres could only be recognised by those readers who knew ancient literature well enough to recognise their linguistic basis.

We can hardly say for sure how this poetry was read aloud but there are good reasons for assuming that a dynamic stress was used to emphasise the long syllables which were the chief parts of the old measures, and that this accentuation went against the correct pronunciation of the word if necessary. In any case, the laws governing the pronunciation of Latin cause a frequent coincidence of the *ictus* or verse stress – originally realised as length, and now dynamic – with a syllable carrying the main stress in a word. Papyri preserving late Greek verses in old metres show the occasional mistake of replacing the long syllable as demanded by the metre with a stressed short syllable. This in turn warrants the assumption that when the verses were read, the long syllables prescribed by the metre were pronounced as stressed syllables. The Greek language made it easier than Latin to follow the ancient metres even after the distinction between long and short syllables had disappeared from the living idiom. The reason was that in most cases the Greek alphabet indicated the old distinction regardless of the change in pronunciation. Late metrics adapted to this by treating syllables written with the vowel signs alpha, iota, and upsilon as dichrona, that is syllables which could be realised as either long or short depending on their place in a metre, notwithstanding their former pronunciation and their resulting functional value in ancient poetry. In all other cases, the quantitative value of the syllable was indicated orthographically.

The survival of the old metres throughout the Late Classical age and the Middle Ages, in spite of radical changes in grammar and pronunciation, reflects the unique normative force of Classic poetry: people were reluctant to abandon its conventions because it remained the most important medium of all literary education. This phenomenon may well be compared to the abundance of ancient relics in the orthography of modern European languages, a fact which interferes considerably with the representation of current phonetics. Cultural traditions are thus also responsible for the plight of schoolchildren in England, Germany, or France, who have to learn spellings that differ a lot from the sounds they know. In the case of Late Classical poetry, however, an additional difficulty was caused by the crucial importance of rhythm in poetic texts; and because of the retention of old verse forms based on a different linguistic usage that rhythm had to be created anew.

Naturally the same period also had a continuing tradition of popular poetry operating within the framework of the living language. But only a tiny fraction of this subliterary poetry is extant, such as, for instance, some short songs of boatmen which were found on papyrus. Further insights into popular poetry and its rhythms are provided by irregularities in the use of ancient metres. In such cases it is not always possible to distinguish between simple mistakes and attempts at metrical complementation or modification through elements which follow the spoken language. Early examples can be found in the works of the Latin author Commodian (see p. 386) and the Greek Methodius (see p. 382).

Certainly intentional was a practice which became widespread from the fourth century AD onwards, although there are also some earlier occurrences. This was the convention to put only stressed syllables at certain fixed places in ancient metres – for instance, at the end of a line or before a caesura – even if this did not make sense within the overall structure of the line. In all Late Classical and Byzantine poetry this custom was followed in the case of the iambic trimeter, the metre of spoken verse in ancient Attic drama. The same convention is also found in verses produced later, at a time when an iambic trimeter would merely consist of twelve syllables chosen at random without any regard to quantity.

Augustine is the first famous author of whom we have an experiment in writing spoken verse regardless of the Classical tradition, that is composed only according to the number of syllables and some of the current word stresses. Of his long so-called 'psalm' against the Donatists the author says in his *Retractations* that it was meant for an uneducated audience. The poem consists of a so-called *hypopsalma*, a prooemium, and a number of stanzas equal to that of the letters of the alphabet, whose sequence determines the initial letters of each stanza. All stanzas are composed of long lines; they are separated by a refrain, which is the introductory *hypopsalma*. The lines consist of sixteen to eighteen syllables, regardless of quantities or the occurrence of hiatus, that is the clash of two vowels at the end and the beginning of two successive words. The lines have a caesura in the middle. At the end of a line the stress always falls on the penultimate syllable, whereas the distribution before the caesura is not regular. All lines end on '-e' or '-ae', whose pronunciation was identical at the time.

This so-called tirade rhyme also occurs in Semitic poetry or poetry that follows the Semitic tradition. What we must consider is that end rhyme as a device of literary art is occasionally found in Classical literary prose but never in Graeco-Roman poetry. Augustine tells us that Parmenianus, the second Donatist Bishop of Carthage, also used this form to spread his heretical doctrines among the public, in Latin as well as in the Punic language of north Africa. In keeping with its intended use, his own psalm, an abecedarius, has simple vocabulary and diction. One can well imagine just how the speaker would deliver the verses with their violent polemics against the Donatists and how the listeners would reply after each stanza with the refrain 'All you who delight in peace, see that you judge well!'.

Another example of early spoken verse whose rhythm follows word stresses is a poetic epistle sent by the Bishop Auspicius of Toul to the Frank Arbogast, a high dignitary in Trier, soon after the middle of the fifth century AD. The text consists of forty-one stanzas composed of four long lines each; each line has sixteen syllables, with a caesura in the middle. The stresses in those words carrying the main meaning are distributed so as to produce an alternating rhythm with each unstressed syllable followed by a stressed one: hence we can speak of accentuating iambs. Syllabic quantities, no longer heard in normal Latin pronunciation at that time, are entirely disregarded. What is remarkable is that the same stanzaic pattern can also be found in several early examples of liturgical – and hence presumably sung – poetry from the Greek East (see p. 574). In the West the number of poems or poetic fragments whose rhythm is constituted by the distribution of stresses increases from the sixth century onwards, in liturgical texts as well as occasionally in verse inscriptions.

On the Greek side two texts comparable to Augustine's anti-Donatist psalm are poems handed down among the works of Gregory of Nazianzus. The rest of Gregory's poetic legacy follows the traditional forms of scholarly poetry. The two pieces in question are a paraenetical poem about virginity as an ascetic ideal and a vespertine hymn addressed to Christ. They consist of long lines of fourteen to sixteen syllables with a caesura after the seventh or eighth syllable, and, with very few exceptions, a stress on the penultimate syllable of each line. There are no stanzaic divisions. The poems appear to be isolated among Gregory's works but they do have some similarities to sung ecclesiastical poetry of the fifth and sixth centuries AD. Some recent studies have denied Gregory's authorship and ascribed the poems to a much later period: however, the issue is as yet undecided.

A different situation exists in poetry which is sung, for a melody can give a text a rhythm which the listener recognises without any problem, even if it does not correspond exactly to the linguistic form. Hence it is more than probable that texts whose rhythmical-poetical styling followed different sets of rules were sung to the same kind of music. Even today, a poem by Goethe, an ode by Horace, or a Biblical psalm may be set to music which follows one and the same set of musical-rhythmical conventions, without giving the listener the impression that the rhythm of any of these texts is being mauled.

Song lyrics are usually meant for practical application and less for reading. This is why information about singing in the early church is so interesting, as ecclesiastical poetry is the only Late Classical poetry for such a practical use of which we know. Moreover, it has a tradition which lasted well into the Modern age on the Greek as well as on the Latin side.

I have already said that the earliest known liturgical texts in Greek from the history of the church – that is, prayers, hymns, and such like – reflect quite clearly the Jewish origins of the Christian cult. Their form is reminiscent of Hebrew poetry which couples phrases of approximately equal length, and with an identical number of important and hence stressed words. Such elements are often linked up in long sequences (see p. 513). The rhythmical principle which they embody is entirely alien to Graeco-Latin poetry; the only possible comparison is with certain forms of literary prose which, however, were unlikely to have any influence on the first beginnings of the Christian cult. But the rhythmical form of the texts in question makes them different also from the extant examples of early Christian hymnic poetry in the traditional forms of Greek metrics – specimens found, for instance, in the fragments of some Gnostic writings (see p. 382) or in the works of Clement of Alexandria (see p. 328).

It seems justified to see the latter texts more as examples of a poetry meant for readers, while the liturgical pieces mentioned were certainly intended for practical use. We do not know, however, whether they were properly sung throughout, or only half-sung and half-spoken to a musical accompaniment. Yet all sources agree that ecclesiastical singing came from the East. Augustine tells us that those innovations in ecclesiastical music which Ambrosius introduced in Milan in the fourth century AD followed oriental customs; and Pliny the Younger speaks of ecclesiastical songs which Christians in Asia Minor had as early as the second century AD. It is difficult to decide whether 'oriental' or 'eastern' as used by Augustine meant as much as 'Greek' or whether we should think of Orientals in the modern sense of the word.

Famous poets are known especially from the early period of the Syrian church. The apocryphal *Acts of Thomas*, originally written in Syriac (see p. 307), contain a *hymnus* that shows impressive poetic imagination. Yet the Greek translation tells us nothing about the metrical form of the original and neither does a later Syriac version. In the early third century AD, Bar Daisan of Edessa and his son Harmonius (see p. 330), whose doctrines were later condemned as heretical, are said to have written some impressive songs. Extant are only some sparse fragments; but it looks as though we may form an assessment of their poetic forms on the basis of a large number of extant poems written more than a century later by Ephrem, the most famous hymnographer of the Syrian church and a zealous partisan of the Nicaean formula.

The three main forms used by Ephrem, called *memra*, *madraša*, and *sogitha*, are fairly similar to one another: they are long sequences of identical stanzas, each stanza consisting of several lines with a fixed number of syllables, and of important or stressed words. The major differences between the three forms concern first the number of lines in a stanza, and then the relationship between lines within a stanza as regards equal or unequal numbers of syllables. The poems contain hymnic and prayer motifs, but they are mainly of a didactic and occasionally of a polemical nature, so that they might be called versified sermons. Of some of Ephrem's poems there are also Greek translations; but those are difficult to date. They preserve the stanzaic pattern and contain lines with rigidly fixed numbers of syllables, thus imitating the originals not only in content but also in form.

In the Greek church poetic texts with a form which resembles the aforesaid Syriac poems appear roughly one century later; this dating of the anonymous texts handed down in all kinds of different liturgical manuscripts is, however, exclusively based on stylistic and metrical clues. The poems are written for certain occasions of the Christian day or year. Their content is hymnic, paraenetic, or didactic; and we also find some prayers. The form is either a sequence of identical long lines structured by a caesura in the middle, or a sequence of stanzas varying between the simple combination of lines into couplets, and complex patterns consisting of individual lines and groups of lines of different lengths. But unlike in the Greek translations of Ephrem's poetry, the rhythm of the verses is regulated not only as to the number of syllables, but also in the distribution of stresses. This indicates a trend leading from the regularisation of stresses at the end of lines and before caesuras towards the fixing of all main stresses in the line, or in other words, the stresses in those words which carry the main semantic content. Some of these texts can be compared in their form to Auspicius' epistle (see p. 572).

This poetic technique was perfected by the melodian Romanus, a converted Jew from Berytus or Beirut, who was one of the clergy of Constantinople's Hagia Sophia during the reign of the Emperor Justinian. His poems were very famous and this explains why the manuscripts in which they were handed down also feature occasional pieces which were written by other authors and then put under the name of the great poet.

The form of these poems is known as *kontakion*. They are long, and divided into many stanzas called *oikoi* or houses; the initial letters of the stanzas always form a word or a word group (*akrostichon*), which is frequently the name of the poet plus the title of the poem. Each text has an initial shorter stanza which is not repeated: this so-called *kukullion* states the subject of the poem. The stanzas consist of strictly parallel lines of varied length which are in turn combined into groups, so that there are three structural planes in stanza, group of lines, and individual line. This artful composition is reminiscent of the chorus songs of archaic lyrics and Attic tragedy. The corresponding lines have not only equal numbers of syllables, but also a consistent distribution of stresses in important words, that is all but the so-called structural words such as conjunctions, prepositions, or such like. The basic rules of composition are fairly obvious, even if some details of the formal principles applied in these verses still need to be clarified in order to ensure a proper understanding of certain deviations and irregularities.

The rhythm of this poetry is governed by word accents and numbers of syllables; it has no connection whatsoever with Classic metrics which were based on quantities. That the texts were sung during communal worship is documented by the information on melody and key recorded for each poem in the relevant manuscripts from the ninth and tenth centuries AD. As in the case of the Old Testament psalms, the *kontakia* were sung to either newly written or already existing melodies. The initial *kukullion* had its own melody and stanzaic form. The *kontakia* disappeared from liturgical use as other, more recent, forms of ecclesiastical songs were favoured in the Greek church in Byzantium from the ninth century onwards. However, this seems to be the very reason why we have a particularly exact knowledge of *kontakia* texts, which remained unaffected by later changes in liturgical practice.

The content of this poetry also indicates its liturgical application. Prayer invocations and hymnic parts alternate with long narrative or didactic passages, and there is even some mention of dogmatic detail. The subjects range from episodes and characters of the Old and New Testaments, above all the person of Christ, to the great festivals and festive seasons of the ecclesiastical year, and the stories of the lives and the sufferings of the saints, including those from the recent past such as John Chrysostom. The general classification as a versified sermon containing elements of prayer, hymn, and doctrine applies to the *kontakion* as well as to the aforementioned types of Syrian church poetry with which there is also a formal similarity. But with regard to the artful composition of stanzas and lines, and thus presumably also of the respective melodies, neither the works of late Graeco-Byzantine ecclesiastical poetry nor the aforesaid Syrian poems are a match to the great *kontakia* by Romanus and his anonymous contemporaries. The sermon-like character of this poetry is confirmed by close parallels between some of Romanus' *kontakia* and homiletical literature, not only in similarities of structure and the choice of topics, but even in the borrowing of entire passages, modified only because of the demand of rhythm. To date, some sources used in this way have been identified among the sermons of Basil of Seleucia from the fourth century AD.

Particularly famous in the Byzantine church was the so-called *Hymnos akathistos*, the *Hymn For Which You Stand Up*, a most impressive *kontakion* on the mother of God. In the tradition it was connected with the relief of Constantinople from the Arab siege, and ascribed to the Patriarch Sergius. Recent scholars have been more inclined to count it among the works of Romanus, even if its alphabetical *akrostichon* – the first letters of the successive stanzas form the alphabet, similar to those in Psalm 118 (119) – has no parallel in Romanus' known poems. There the acrostic always gives the name of the poet, with variations in form, and sometimes the subject of the poem. Romanus also used different poetic forms, and among others, a so-called *stichēron*, a *hymnus* consisting of a sequence of corresponding lines without stanzaic divisions, is extant under his name.

Romanus showed great linguistic artistry. For his *kontakia* he developed an elevated style featuring elements of Greek poetic language, but without their special dialectal forms, as well as incorporating elements from elevated prose, Biblical diction, and the language of liturgy. There are even occasional words from theological debate, and hence from a technical vocabulary. From this extremely heterogeneous material, Romanus created a poetic language which strikes the reader as surprisingly homogeneous, and with the help of this instrument the author managed to produce brilliant phrasings and gripping narratives. Romanus' style gives the lie to all prejudices concerning a stagnation of literary Greek because of the rigid division between written language and vernacular. Particularly impressive in this respect is, for instance, a portrayal of the coming Day of Judgment; and more tender notes are struck in a Christmas *kontakion*.

Romanus was possibly the last really great poet in the Greek language. His work marks at the same time the beginning and the zenith of the tradition of Byzantine ecclesiastical poetry, which was nevertheless represented again and again by men of fairly respectable talent in the subsequent centuries. The technique of versification in this tradition remained that of Romanus, even if stanzaic forms and forms of poems would sometimes change. Beside the enduring cultivation of ancient versification, the construction of lines on the basis of stress became common above all in religious poetry. From song lyrics it was transferred also to spoken verse, where ancient metres were imitated in an accentuating manner, just as in German poetry of the seventeenth and eighteenth centuries. A case in point are the beautiful poems of the so-called New Theologian Symeon from the ninth century AD. Major epics of the Middle and Late Byzantine period, however, used the form of so-called political verse, which was rooted in popular poetry. Of this there are occasional older examples known to us, but its non-literary origins are lost in the obscurity of an undocumented past.

Romanus' fame was great enough for his biography to be included in that treasure of scholarly knowledge handed down by grammarians in the form of commentaries and encyclopaedias for use in schools. The *Suda* encyclopaedia tells the reader about the man and his work, but it counts his poetry as prose because it does not follow the ancient metres. This shows how exclusively the formal educational tradition was dominated by Classic notions.

The accentuating poetry of the Greek Late Classical age, whose development I have outlined above, emerged within the framework of liturgical practice without any closer contact with Classical poetic techniques. That this poetry influenced also the Latin West between the fourth and the sixth centuries may be inferred not simply from Augustine's words about ecclesiastical music in the episcopal church of Ambrosius. By coincidence, an ecclesiastical song with only one stanza has been preserved, a text which certainly predates Romanus and may stem from the fifth century AD. This song has exactly the same form as the aforementioned poetic epistle of Auspicius from sixth-century Gaul (see p. 572). However, the documented beginnings of sung ecclesiastical poetry in the West are entirely different from those in the East.

To this day the Roman church regards Ambrosius as the archegete of its hymnic poetry, and many old hymns which are still sung as part of the liturgy are believed to be his works. Some of them have been proved genuine, or at least very likely so; and some others extant in fragments may even be ascribed to Hilarius of Poitiers, an author who was about twenty years older. This dates the authorship back to the mid-fourth century AD; and it may be assumed that Hilarius also got the inspiration for his hymnic poetry in the East where he lived during an extended period of banishment. Hilarius and Ambrosius both say themselves that their hymns were sung by the congregation and that this fact constituted a liturgical innovation.

In view of this it seems remarkable that the poems or poetic fragments which have been identified beyond any doubt as theirs, show the correct application of quantifying and hence 'scholarly' versification, and not the stress rhythm which corresponded to contemporary Latin pronunciation and which we must assume to have existed in popular poetry. In the extant three long fragments of Hilarius' hymns, we find stanzas composed of lines like those in the lyrics of Horace, as well as groups of two or three iambic senars or trochaeic septenars. These lines with six and seven feet respectively were the most common types used in Roman dramatic dialogue.

The hymns of which Ambrosius' authorship is established beyond any doubt include the famous *Aeterne rerum conditor* and *Intende qui regis Israel*, which is most frequently cited as *Veni redemptor gentium* or *Come, Saviour of the Pagans*, after the beginning of the second stanza. All the texts consist of stanzas of four lines each, with each line in turn containing four iambic feet. This form can also be found in older poetry and was particularly popular in the second century AD. The details of its metrical principle correspond to those of Classic Latin poetry – for instance, the conflation of vowels clashing directly at the end of one word and the beginning of the next one, or of those separated only by a weak final consonant, as well as the occasional substitution of two short syllables for a long one. Other stressed or only loosely rhythmical hymns traditionally believed to stem from Ambrosius – for instance, the so-called Ambrosianic song of praise *Te deum* – were definitely written at least two centuries later; they were ascribed to Ambrosius because of his fame as the father of ecclesiastical song.

Both men, Hilarius as well as Ambrosius, mastered not only the technique of versification, but also the linguistic-stylistic means of expression of Classical poetry, even if their vocabulary is naturally a very different one. But the poetic quality of these hymns, which is certainly to a large extent responsible for their long survival in liturgical practice, rests on an unbroken tradition of the art of versification and of poetic diction, which was now put to use under new circumstances, and hence gained new religious and social significance. Ambrosius' hymns mark the beginning of a long history of Christian-Latin poetry for use in ritual worship, and hence always for singing. In the course of this history Classical metres from Classic-Latin poetry remained in use, applied with varied degrees of skill. Besides those, however, there were soon also stressed imitations of such quantifying metres, as well as an emerging stressed poetry whose forms were invented and developed in total independence from the Classical tradition.

Thus, in spite of the unequivocal evidence in sources which speak of the introduction of liturgical chants into the cult of the Christian West as modelled upon the East, we must note a fundamental difference between East and West in the origin and character of Christian-liturgical poetry as a genre with a genuine practical application. Although the patchy nature of the evidence and our total ignorance concerning real folk poetry urge a good deal of caution, it is possible to give a tentative description of this distinction as follows. The origins of Greek hymnography, which reached its zenith with the works of Romanus in the sixth century AD, were rooted in liturgical practice whose language was from the very beginning influenced by Semitic elements. This is evident if we think of the Greek of Biblical translations or the model of ritual worship in the synagogue. Here the emergence of elaborate poetic forms was largely independent of models from Classic poetry. More likely models were verse forms adapted to the spoken language, as found in popular poetry; of those, though, we know virtually nothing. Classic models, however, dominated the first Christian attempts at literary poetry as is evident in the works of Clement of Alexandria, for instance; the role of Classic poetry here was parallel to that of rhetoric in Christian literary prose.

On the Latin side, on the other hand, the first Christian hymnographers composed lyrics intended to be sung by congregations according to the rules of Classic-Roman poetry, a fact which ensured their success for centuries regardless of that wealth of forms of ecclesiastical poetry independent from these models which developed later. Thus we must assume that the difference between scholarly poetry which followed the rules of Classic versification and those kinds of poetry which did not do so was perceived as much greater in the Greek East than it was in the Latin West. This may be connected with differences in pronunciation, especially as regards stress. In the history of Late Classical poetry this difference has a certain significance, for it is quite obvious that between 350 AD and 600 AD poetic production was much richer in the West than in the East, and while we know no single case from this period where a poet with Latin as his native language even so much as tried a hand at Greek versification, two of the most talented Greek-speaking poets – Claudian in the early fifth and Corippus in the early sixth century AD – wrote their very best poems in Latin.

Scholarly poetry

Decimus Magnus Ausonius, a man from a distinguished family resident in Burdigala or Bordeaux, lived from about 310 to 394 AD. We have a complete corpus of his poetical works, in an edition for which he himself provided an autobiographical introductory poem. Ausonius worked for a long time as a professor of rhetoric in his native city. In 365 AD Valentinian I called him to his court in Trier as a tutor for the princes, and during the reign of his pupil Gratian Ausonius was appointed to high administrative offices and finally attained the rank of Consul. After Gratian was murdered in 383 AD, Ausonius spent another ten years of private life as a squire on his country estate near Bordeaux.

Ausonius' poetical work consists exclusively of occasional poems. There are mnemonic verses on the Roman calendar or on the successive Roman emperors, poetic eulogies on deceased relatives or on professors at the Bordeaux schools, translations of Greek epigrams, poetic epistles to his father and wife, an epithalamium composed of lines from Virgil, funeral epigrams on the heroes of the Trojan War, and much more. Slightly longer than these are two short epics: one describes the natural beauty seen during a voyage by boat on the Moselle, while the other is about a beautiful Alemannic slave girl called Bissula. There are also some extant prose works by Ausonius, including a speech expressing gratitude to the Emperor Gratian, and a collection of letters of which the most important ones are those addressed to his friend and pupil Paulinus, later Bishop of Nola (see p. 566).

There is nothing in his work which could be called great poetry; but all the same, Ausonius was an extremely erudite man who seems to have known by heart much of the Classic poets, especially the works of Virgil, Ovid, and Horace, and hence he found it easy enough to produce verse according to their conventions. He expressed himself with equal virtuosity in epic hexameters, elegiac distichs, or lyrical verse forms. He also frequently showed his excellence in making elegant pointed statements and witty, pretty, or sentimental aphorisms: but wisely enough, he never attempted to take on a major subject in a large-scale composition.

From his letters we know that Ausonius was a Christian, and indeed he would have hardly become tutor to the princes if this had not been the case. But there is not a single line in his poetry which betrays his allegiance to the church. His work belongs entirely to the cultivation of an educational tradition untouched by Christianity, a tradition which at that time upper-class Christians and upper-class pagans approached in very much the same manner.

The epigrams of Naucellius belong to the same context. Naucellius was a friend of Symmachus (see p. 459), and the recipient of some of Symmachus' extant letters. This suggests that he belonged to the Senatorial class but without holding any public office; he did not profess the Christian faith and shared the literary-antiquarian interests of the circle of friends around Symmachus in Rome. The poems which Naucellius sent to Symmachus were rediscovered in a manuscript made in the monastery of Bobbio in northern Italy. This manuscript comprises a fairly large collection of pieces of varied origin. Those fifteen poems of the so-called *Carmina bobiensia* for whom Naucellius' authorship is safely established, are epigrams and short elegies – it is difficult to draw the line between the two – describing his country estate, his own baths and those of a friend, and some paintings in his possession. One of the poems is styled as a prayer to the god Saturn, asking this god of the golden age for relief from the hardships of being old; Naucellius lived for nearly a hundred years. The extant fragment of an autobiographical poem is interesting because in it the poet, born in Syracuse, tells us that his native language was Greek and that he learned Latin only with great pains.

The choice of subjects and the diction of his poems are in the tradition of scholarly poetry which uses a deceptively dilettantish pose, a manner of writing which the Neoteric poets of the Late Republic had introduced in Rome after the fashion of Hellenistic poetry. Its cultivation had long been widespread among aristocrats and their clientele; it presupposed writers and readers who were closely familiar with the different poetic models, and hence able to pick up the offered subtleties. Naucellius' use of words and his poetic technique show him as part of this highly developed, but very artificial, poetic culture whose repertoire also included the Latin rewriting of Greek epigrams. The parallels with Ausonius which have been noted in Naucellius' work result from the common social background of the two men and the identical social function of their poetry.

Another poet from Symmachus' circle of friends who is represented in the Bobbio collection is Anicius Probinus. He came from the Senatorial nobility of the city of Rome, was born about fifty years after Naucellius, and attained the rank of Consul when he was still a young man. His four poems, two of them Latin versions of Greek epigrams, are composed with a slightly looser poetic technique than those of Naucellius. Around 400 AD Probinus' family were already third-generation Christians, and his great-grandmother Probina composed a poetic eulogy on Christ from lines by Virgil (see p. 401).

The middle years of the fourth century AD saw the births of the two most important Christian poets of the Latin West, Paulinus of Nola, whom I have referred to several times before, and Aurelius Prudentius Clemens. I have already outlined the biography of Paulinus (see p. 566), whose life led him – against the express advice of his teacher Ausonius – from the existence of an educated, highly respected administrative official to the ascetic rigour of a hermitage, and finally to an episcopal see. Likewise, I have mentioned his correspondence which linked him with many famous contemporaries. He was highly esteemed not least because of his charity, which led him to donate the fortunes he and his deceased wife Therasia had inherited to the church in Nola, for the construction of hostels, aqueducts, and other installations.

As befits the humility of a good ascete, Paulinus himself published no more than his fourteen poems honouring the martyr Felix, the patron saint of his episcopal city. His remaining twenty-one pieces of poetry, which in all fill a respectable volume, have been handed down among the work of other authors in mediaeval manuscripts. Likewise, Paulinus' poetry does not contain any pieces of autobiographical information, something which his contemporaries would frequently include in their own poems.

With the exception of those about Felix, Paulinus' poems are of paraenetical content. In a language with great emotional appeal, they urge the reader to practise an active Christianity which should be entirely based on simple faith, and make all theological questions superfluous. Personal facts are only found in poems 10 and 11, addressed to his teacher Ausonius, in which the issue of the relationship between Christian faith and traditional education is discussed. It is most remarkable that although Paulinus clearly expresses his lack of interest in theology, and hence also in philosophically orientated reflection about the faith, he was still a most impressive exponent of the old rhetorical-literary education, and in this, in spite of his decision to renounce the world, a true pupil of Ausonius.

Written in hexameters and elegiac distichs, Paulinus' poems like those of Ausonius grew from an intimate knowledge of the Roman poetic tradition. In versification and linguistic usage, they are indeed a credit to this tradition; and the use of mostly allusive borrowings from ancient poetry and from the Bible betrays the trained rhetor, who nevertheless, unlike his greater contemporary Prudentius, does not develop his rhetorically inspired phrases to baroque proportions. High pathos was simply not Paulinus' style.

Among the material used in rhetorical instruction, whose aim was the mastering of artistic expression in prose, was also a great deal of poetic literature, above all Virgilian epic. This was certainly justified, as the style of major poetry had formed under the strong influence of rhetoric, at least since the time of Virgil. Paulinus' writing also reflects this unity of a stylistic sensibility shaped by rhetoric as well as poetry, something which many different works document for Roman literature. It is perhaps because of this high linguistic refinement, coupled with a modest and moderate poetic temperament, that none of Paulinus' extant poems became part of liturgical practice. Those hymns which he himself claims to have composed are lost.

Prudentius was born in 348 AD, five years before Paulinus. He came from a distinguished Spanish family and worked as a high administrative official, first in Spain and then at the court of Theodosius I. Like Paulinus, he later withdrew from political life, and he died in his native Spain presumably during the first decade of the fifth century AD, after a pilgrimage to the martyrs' graves in Rome.

To the Latin Middle Ages, Prudentius was the Classic author of Christian poetry. His vast collected work, about ten thousand lines published by himself, has been handed down in a large number of manuscripts. His great popularity is indicated by the fact that more than three hundred manuscripts are still extant, dating from the sixth century AD onwards.

Recent research has suggested that with his edition of his collected works in 405 AD Prudentius aimed at creating something like a canon of Christian poetry, featuring equivalents and hence also substitutes for the traditional genres of Classical poetry. This conclusion is based on the structure of the collection in which books of entirely different content are numbered together, and also on the resulting sequence of verse types and forms of poems.

Part 1 with the title *Cathemerinon* contains a total of twelve hymns for different times of the day, for Lent, and for Christmas and Epiphany, plus one hymn on Christ for use at any time during the year, and one requiem. These poems are in the lyrical metres familiar from Horace's works. Part 2 with the title *Apotheosis* is a didactic poem in hexameters on the doctrine of trinity. Its prooemium is styled as an epode, the main form of poetic invective adopted by Horace from the Greek; it contains polemics against several heresies. Part 3 also contains a didactic poem, entitled *Harmati-*

genia, which deals with the doctrine of the origin of sin. Its prooemium attacks the Marcionites; it is written in iambs, likewise a popular metre for polemical poetry ever since the times of Archilochus and Hipponax.

The most famous among Prudentius' works is found in Part 4: the poem called *Psychomachia* is the oldest example of Christian-allegorical poetry. In it the seven major vices (see p. 420), represented as seven armed female warriors, encounter the seven Christian and cardinal virtues, and the former are, of course, vanquished in the process.

Part 5 contains the two books against Symmachus, written in hexameters. With those verses, Prudentius took up the old controversy, already twenty years past and nearly as long decided, between Symmachus and Ambrosius, who had argued about re-erecting the altar of the goddess Victoria in the assembly hall of the Roman Senate. The author uses this case for a comprehensive attack on the old religion. The following Part 6, entitled *Peristephanon*, consists of fourteen hymns in lyrical metres in honour of the martyrs. The texts are full of gory descriptions of the martyrs' sufferings, in an account which had a strong influence on mediaeval art. The collection is framed by a prooemium in lyrical stanzas and an epilogue in epodic form in which the poet tells the reader about his life and about his hope that there will be a reward in heaven for his poetic effort.

Prudentius later added a second volume to the first edition. Under the title *Dittochaeon* or *Double Feeding*, it combines forty-eight epigrammatic quartets to give a corresponding number of descriptions of real or fictitious paintings, depicting scenes from the Old and New Testaments. At that time, the description of paintings had long been a traditional subject of epigrammatic poetry. Indeed, the genre of the epigram is missing in the original collection, while the different forms of epic and lyric are featured, and the long dialogues of the *Psychomachia* may well be regarded as the equivalent of dramatic poetry, a classification which would also accommodate the baroque scenery of the battles described. When Prudentius wrote his works poetry in dramatic forms had for centuries been frequently used with a view to reading alone, without any thought of a possible performance.

Prudentius showed an outstanding virtuosity in his mastery of the linguistic, stylistic, and metrical forms of older poetry. His extensive reading of older literature is reflected in many allusions, imitations, and references which could only be understood and appreciated by an equally educated reader. The artistic skill documented in the use of such a method is especially well highlighted because of the content of Prudentius' poems, which is completely different from the poetic subjects of the ancients.

Prudentius' strong poetic temperament vents itself in overflowing pathos in his descriptions, invectives, and eulogies. I have already mentioned the graphic goriness in his accounts of the *martyria*, a feature which is bound to strike the modern reader as unbearable and embarrassing, and occasionally – of course entirely against the author's intentions – even as comical. Full of pathos are also the battle scenes and the combatants' speeches in the *Psychomachia*, which uses the entire arsenal of heroic epic as a vehicle of allegory.

Recent research has shown that Prudentius' aim was to use his sovereign mastery of a linguistic and stylistic tradition for the development of a new, specifically Christian, figurative and poetic language which made use of the older elements and developed the inherited style further. This artistic effort took so much for granted that its result is only accessible to a modern-day reader who has at least some knowledge of the elements it incorporated; and even during the poet's lifetime only a well-educated person would have been able to appreciate his poetic achievement. Nevertheless, Prudentius soon got through to a wider public which did not fulfil these requirements. Some of the hymns of the first part, the *Book of Hours*, found their way into liturgical practice; the fine arts got inspiration from the *Peristephanon* with its reports of the *martyria*; and the *Psychomachia* provided the model for a long line of allegorical poems. This impact is certainly a consequence of the high pathos in Prudentius' diction but of course also of his poetic visualisation of theological positions. Prudentius shows himself well versed in orthodox church doctrine, attacks heretical opinions, and offers plenty of material for reflections on the motifs of communal-cultic as well as individual piety.

The poems of Prudentius document the synthesis of Classical heritage and Christianity, and not only in a formal sense, because of their seemingly natural adoption of traditional Roman poetic language and technique. Prudentius was also the first herald of a Christian idea of Rome. To the educated people of the Imperial age, the city of Rome as being at the head of the Empire which united civilised humanity, was at the core of their political and cultural consciousness. This is perhaps nowhere more clearly expressed than in Aristides' speech on Rome (see p. 232). Rome maintained this place in ideology also after its political and administrative importance receded behind that of the new residences from the third century AD onwards. As reflected, for instance, in Ammianus' account of Constantius II's visit to Rome, the old capital remained the centre of the civilised world, and this gave rise to speculations about its everlasting existence. But this very fact was also a potential cause of conflict between the old cultural world and the new religion; and the Christianisation of the state did not put an end to this state of affairs. It was in particular exponents of the old education who felt, and quite rightly so, that their notions of the permanence of Rome and its world culture as embracing Greek and Roman elements were inseparably connected with religious traditions. This could be perceived in the numerous cults and rites that had always been an important part of acts of state, as well as in the great poems of Homer and Virgil, which like no other works epitomised Graeco-Roman culture, and which, after all, spoke first and foremost about the deeds of the gods.

In several parts of his work Prudentius tries to show the difference between ancient Rome and the new, Christian one. In the hymn on the martyr Laurence he says that in vanquishing the pagan gods, portrayed as demons, the Christian martyrs had helped Rome itself to attain triumphant liberation. Thus, he claims, those outward victories which cast the nations of the globe down at the feet of Rome are finally succeeded by the inner victory, through which Rome itself is freed from the rule of the demons, and now becomes the haven of true civilisation. This corresponds to a statement in the anti-Symmachian poems which rework the dispute about the altar of Victoria, a passage where the right to permanent supremacy is claimed for the new, Christian Rome.

One of the important expressions of the cultural self-definition of the Graeco-Roman world was the demarcation line drawn between its population and the Barbarians. The word Barbarian, originally a neutral term for a non-Greek, thus at first acquired a double meaning in Greek as well as Latin. As referring to the aliens from outside the civilised world, it could carry the connotations 'raw, rude, cruel'; but in view of the interest of educated people in ancient or exotic traditions which confirmed the insights of philosophy, it could still be used in a neutral sense, or even with positive connotations. Those venerable bearers of Egyptian, Indian, or Jewish wisdom, who according to tradition had been the teachers of Solon and Pythagoras, Plato and Democritus, represented a 'Barbarian philosophy'; and authors critical of contemporary culture were particularly inclined to find better human beings among the Barbarians. An early and much-used argument against the Christians was based on the denial of any claim that their new doctrine was 'Barbarian philosophy', because it had been conceived in the womb of the civilised and united world. In the pre-Constantinian church, there were voices who pointed out the Barbarian origin of their tradition, as not to be reconciled with Graeco-Roman culture; but others saw the Christians as the very bearers and protectors of this culture. Tertullian represents the one side and Origen the other (see pp. 350 and 334). Regardless of this difference, though, the common tenet was that the Christian message was directed at all humans alike, a view that was first expressed in Paul's Letter to the Galatians.

However, as Christianity became the state religion at a time when Germanic and other tribes threatened or even flooded the Empire, the question concerning the nature of a Barbarian was put in an entirely new way. The decision was made easier by the fact that the intruding Germanic tribes could be classed either as pagans, or, at least since the council of 381 AD, as Arian heretics. This explains the rapid change in linguistic usage towards an identification of 'Barbarian' with 'non-Christian'. A similar situation had occasionally existed in Jewish-Latin usage, where the *goyim*, the non-Israelites, were called Barbarians.

The word Barbarian became more and more of a polemical term. In letters and edicts the Emperor Julian had again and again made a point of calling the Christians and their doctrine Barbarian; and in turn the Christians retaliated by the identification of Barbarian and non-Christian. The firm establishment of an exclusively pejorative use of the word during the fourth century AD is indicated by the fact that later on Germanic tribes were explicitly excluded from the category 'Barbarian': wherever Germans converted to orthodoxy, for instance, or in Theodoric's Gothic Kingdom with its relatively peaceful symbiosis between the provincial Catholic population and the Arian Germans. On the other hand the word Barbarian was also frequently used to describe unwanted intruders in the context of a violent denunciation of the growing influence of Germans in Imperial army and administration, a reaction which is in evidence from around 400 AD.

These conditions explain why it was almost a matter of course for Prudentius to proclaim a Roman Empire whose citizens' Christianity makes them the representatives of civilisation against the Barbarian world. To him, it is only Christianity, the faith whose blood witnesses liberated the Romans from the yoke of the demons, which enables Rome truly to exercise its cultural mission as described already by Virgil. Prudentius does not try to hide his dislike of the Barbarians, seeing them as infidels as well as enemies of civilisation. Consequently, he makes no mention at all of the 'Barbarian' origins of the new religion.

Prudentius did not live to see the catastrophe of 410 AD. Yet that nexus between the idea of Rome and Christianity which he established could be used as the basis for Christian argumentation, even after the events of that year which posed the question about the significance of the old religion with increased urgency. The essential elements of a Christian image of Rome had already been expressed in the poems on the dispute about the altar of Victoria, a quarrel which Prudentius correctly recognised as being of fundamental importance.

From the lifetime of Prudentius, we have two hexametrical poems which may prove that there was indeed an audience for polemical-didactic epics on topical subjects. The one, handed down among the works of Tertullian, consists of a sharp condemnation of the followers of Marcion (see p. 299), communities which still existed in some parts of the Empire in the fourth century AD. This piece ended up among Tertullian's writings because he was the most famous anti-Marcionite among the Christian authors. Much more interesting is another poem, handed down without an author's name. It is evidently directed against those members of the Senatorial aristocracy in the city of Rome who, during the short reign of the usurper Eugenius, tried once again to revive the old cults and rites. This was the last attempt of the kind, and a locally limited one at that, thirty years after the death of the Emperor Julian. The efforts of the men who carried this movement, including Symmachus, Nicomachus Flavianus, and Vettius Agorius Praetextatus, were based on an extensive antiquarian knowledge (see p. 479).

The cultivation of ancient traditions and the interpretation of Classic literature were indeed very closely linked with the study of ancient cults, customs, and manners; the desire for their revival was a result of loyalty to ancient Roman tradition, at least to the same extent as it sprang from any religious impulse as such. Under these circumstances, the resumption of cultic practice was bound to look very artificial, and it is this very fact that the author of the poem *Against the Pagans* derides with merciless severity. Notwithstanding all the exaggeration in its polemical descriptions, the text gives us valuable historical clues about the religious life of Rome during that period.

Biblical poetry, the treatment of Biblical subjects with the help of the technique of Classic epic, had begun with Apollinaris in the East and with Juvencus in the West (see pp. 429 and 401). In the late fourth century AD it is represented by the otherwise unknown Cyprianus who came from Gaul. His epic, extant only in an incomplete form, is a retelling of the historical books of the Old Testament.

Like Prudentius, the second great poet of the fourth century AD, Claudius Claudianus, died shortly before the fateful year 410. The presumably posthumous edition of his voluminous collected works was commissioned by his patron Stilicho; it consisted of two collections of the major and the minor poems respectively. In later manuscripts both volumes were put together and thus the collected works including some unfinished parts were preserved as a whole.

Claudian was born in a Greek-speaking family in Alexandria. Among his short poems there are some Greek epigrams, presumably early productions. It is not known where and when Claudian managed to acquire a familiarity with Classic-Roman epic that certainly allows us to rank his writings beside the epic poetry of the Augustan and the Flavian era. Shortly after he moved to Rome Claudian began the long series of his major poems which were all written between 395 and 405 AD. In Rome, he made a name for himself with a poetical panegyric on the Consuls of 395 AD. He gained a recommendation to the court at Milan; and in the Vandal Stilicho, who showed sagacity and enterprise in directing the fate of the western Empire on behalf of the young Emperor Honorius, Claudian found a faithful patron, who also procured him an office at court. The reigning Emperors Honorius and Arcadius even had a statue erected in honour of Claudian in the Forum of Trajan; the inscription on the effigy is extant.

While belonging to the closest entourage of Stilicho at the Milanese court Claudian wrote most of his poetical works. There were three poems on the three respective occasions when the Emperor Honorius took on the Consulate, and some poems on the occasion of that monarch's marriage to Stilicho's daughter. The latter include a solemn *epithalamium* as well as so-called *fescenninae* in the ancient Roman tradition – mocking verses which can be compared to jokes cracked at an eve-of-the-wedding party. There are other wedding poems; panegyrical epics on Stilicho's successful wars against the usurper Gildo and the Goths under Alaric; poems on the Consulate of Stilicho and the Milanese philosopher Manlius Theodorus; and finally invectives against Rufinus and the eunuch Eutropius, who were influential advisors to the Emperor Arcadius in Constantinople, counselling policies that ran counter to those of Stilicho. These poems on contemporary history are complemented by ones of mythological content: three books of an unfinished epic about the rape of Proserpina, and the beginning of a *Gigantomachia*, an account of the battle of the gods against the earth-born Giants. It is very likely that some verses from a Greek epic about the same subject, handed down under the name of Claudian, do indeed come from a lost early work of that poet.

Finally, the collection also includes a number of shorter poems. There are epistles in elegiac distichs; idylls in the same metre, after the manner of Alexandrian poetry, on exotic subjects such as the bird Phoenix, the Nile, or the electric ray fish; and lastly epigrams in Latin and Greek. Some of the latter are not genuine, and these almost certainly include the few which have a Christian content. None of Claudian's remaining poetry contains even the slightest reference to anything Christian, even if it was written at a Christian court. Instead there is a vivid poetic visualisation of the world of the ancient gods, not only in the epics on mythological subjects but also in the political-courtly poems. In the manner of the ancient epic tradition, the events reported in the latter acquire a larger, lasting significance through the 'divine apparatus', justifying and interpreting the events described on the human plane by reference to events among the gods which are known only to the poet. Claudian was almost certainly a pagan, but this was obviously not detrimental to his reputation at the court in Milan.

Like Prudentius, Claudian had a perfect command of the language, diction, and versification of Augustan and Imperial epic, whereas to date there has been no proof of any influence of contemporary Greek epic on his style. He seems to have made a conscious choice to embrace the Roman poetic tradition entirely. By far the largest part of his poetry is written in perfectly structured hexameters; some poems, including the prooemia which occasionally precede the epics as well as the *idyllia*, are in elegiac distichs. The *fescenninae* on the marriage of Stilichos daughter have different, but all common lyrical metres.

Part of Claudian's style is an overwhelming mass of references, allusions, names, and other kind of pointers at the mythological tradition which had provided the subject matter for epic poetry for centuries, enriching its manner of expression by offering many possible comparisons, parallelisms, and indirect designations. The corpus of myths was nearly exclusively of Greek origin, but by the time of Claudian a line of poems spanning several centuries had long made it the common property of both educated Romans and Greeks. At the Milanese court, too, there was an audience for a poetry which used that mode of expression developed in dealing with myth, even when writing about topical subjects from contemporary history. Myth of Greek origin was complemented by the history of Republican Rome, elevated to mythical status; thus, Camillus, Scipio, and Cato became the equivalents of Achilles, Hercules, and Ulysses. This tradition, long canonised at the time, is the source of Claudian's standards for assessing the significance of the events and characters which he portrays and praises. By keeping the tradition constantly present, the language which tells of those events gives them dignity and lasting fame.

There was a long, but yet surveyable, line of Roman epic poets who all elaborated their individual style in a conscious contrasting, modifying, or imitating relationship to Virgil. This made it fairly difficult for later authors, with the exception of Christians who had to give form to an entirely new and different subject matter, to find a style of their own. Here Claudian shines above all in his descriptions of scenes or images with a strong emotional effect. The sequential narration of events, on the other hand, recedes in his work. In spite of entirely dissimilar moods expressed, this is so in the political poems as well as in the mythological ones. Claudian also formulated speeches for his epic characters with great skill and psychological understanding, in obvious succession to post-Virgilian epic writing. The extreme graphic detail and the overflowing pathos which dominated Prudentius' diction and manner of presentation were alien to Claudian. In this respect he rather followed the standard set by Augustan poetry.

Claudian was also a zealous partisan for the fame and the greatness of Rome. In the torrents of contemporary history he saw Stilicho, whose achievements he seems to have admired honestly and whose murder he did not live to see, in the role of the great men from Rome's heroic age; measured by the same yardstick, Stilicho's internal opponents Eutropius and Rufinus seemed to fall lamentably short. Claudian had no doubt of the fact that Rome was destined to govern the world; but in his works there is not the slightest trace of any renewal or enrichment of the idea of Rome with Christian motifs. To him, Stilicho's defence of Rome against the Goths is entirely in keeping with ancient Roman tradition. It is true, though, that the poet does not explicitly put Stilicho's achievements down to the help of the ancient gods, whose poetic evocation merely gives palpable expression to the dignity of a tradition, and has no longer any religious significance. But anyhow, how could Claudian have talked about aid from the old gods at a Christian court? Nevertheless, he did leave the Christian God completely out of the picture.

Around the lifetime of Claudian, Avianus wrote his retold fables in elegiac distichs. About the poet's identity and his life dates there has been much discussion. He cites the Greek editions of fables by Babrius (see p. 271) as his model, and the recipient of the book's dedication is Macrobius, the author of the *Saturnalia* (see p. 444). This indicates that Avianus belonged to the wider circle of those educated members of the aristocracy in the city of Rome who were interested in literary and antiquarian studies. Among those men Symmachus himself, for instance, expressed regret about his insufficient command of Greek, while his friend Vettius Agorius Praetextatus carried out philological work on Greek texts, and translated Themistius' paraphrases of Aristotle into Latin. Thus Avianus' own reference to Macrobius' knowledge of Greek must be seen, just like the fables themselves, in the context of endeavours in the aforementioned circles to regain access to Greek literature.

As the existence of numerous manuscripts shows, Avianus' forty-two fables were very popular in the Middle Ages, although neither the use of language nor the poetic technique shows any particular authorial skill. More interesting are the poems of Rufius Festus Avienus who was later often confused with Avianus. Avienus came from a noble family, was a pagan, and held high offices in Rome, as we know from an inscription written by himself. He translated a whole series of Greek didactic poems into Latin, including the hexametrical description of the earth by Dionysius from the second century AD as well as the *Phaenomena*, Aratus' didactic poem on astronomy from the third century BC, whose translation had already been attempted by Cicero and Germanicus, the son of Drusus.

Another didactic-geographical poem in iambs, a work which is extant in an incomplete form, describes the coastlines between northern France and the Crimean peninsula. We cannot tell what source Avienus had for this; the uncertainty is increased because of his habit of incorporating additional material in his translations, and thus lengthening the original poems considerably, as he also did in the case of Aratus' *Phaenomena*. For the *Ora maritima*, which is the title of the aforementioned poetic fragment, he tells us that he also drew on the work of Sallust. What we know for certain, however, is no more than that the *Ora maritima* contains information stemming from a very old periplus, a description of the coasts of western Europe from the period of discovery in the seventh and sixth centuries BC. From which texts Avienus got this information is not clear. Other didactic poems in iambs by Avienus have been lost; there are some which Servius mentions in his commentary on Virgil, including one that is an excerpt from Livy's historiographical writing. Although the literary value of these poems, or rather verse translations, is fairly modest they are impressive documentations of the efforts among educated aristocrats of the period to preserve educational knowledge, and to restore its accessibility.

A text of high poetic quality is the verse narrative by Rutilius Claudius

Namatianus. The poet came from a Senatorial family resident in Gaul and, as we know from the Emperor Theodosius II's collection of laws, he was Prefect of the city of Rome in 414 AD. From Rome he returned three years later to visit his estates in Gaul which had suffered severely from the Gothic invasions. This journey is described in a poem which continues a tradition of poetic travelogue that reaches back to the work of Lucilius in the second century BC and which is represented by Horace and Ovid in Augustan poetry. Rutilius' work consists of two books: beginning and end were lost at some stage of the manuscript transmission, so that we no longer know the title.

The story is written in elegiac distichs, a form which had become common in shorter verse narratives since the age of Early Hellenism, beside the epic hexameter. Rutilius was meticulous in his attention to the rules of Classical versification: for example, with regard to caesura, elision or suppression of vowels, length of words at the end of verses, and such like features. What is noticeable, however, is the peculiar prominence of heavy rhythms. This is produced by a deviation from the norms of Classic poetry in that Rutilius, especially at the beginning of a verse, much more frequently substitutes a dactylus, one long syllable followed by two short ones, with a spondee, a foot of two long syllables.

Rutilius' use of language is dominated by large-scale borrowing from Virgil, and references to Virgil and Ovid which occur above all in digressions of mythological and historical content. Such passages arise in the context of descriptions of places passed on the journey and from detailed accounts of the author's feelings on such occasions. Again and again this leads into comparisons between the past and the present, and also to mentions of contemporary history. The poem is very varied in content not simply because of the inclusion of many different subjects; it also echoes, in line after line, the most diverse words, motifs, and artistic devices of an abundantly rich poetic tradition. There is, however, a kind of unity in the text, as established by an all-pervading melancholy-pathetical mood to whose evocation all its elements contribute. Unlike Horace in his fifth satire of Book 1, which describes a journey from Rome to Brundisium in the company of his patron Maecenas, Rutilius makes a point of not dwelling on the more amusing episodes of his sea-voyage, which must also have occurred at least during the several excursions for the purpose of visiting friends which the author mentions.

Rutilius was a pagan and had a heartfelt dislike for the new religion. Two cutting polemics in Book 1 of his work attack monasticism with expressions of contempt for its lifestyle which he sees as perverse and amoral. Like Claudian, Rutilius was also a fervent partisan of the idea of Rome. His travelogue begins with a long invocation of eternal Rome whose rule has made the whole earth one vast city as the epitome of civilised life within a legal order. To Rutilius, it is clear that after all the dangers it withstood in its glorious history Rome will be able to cope with the Gothic threat too.

What distinguishes Rutilius from Claudian is the simple fact that his verses were written after, and not before, 410 AD. The poem cannot be construed as a direct reply to Augustine or Orosius; but none the less it belongs to the discussion following the catastrophe of 410, a debate whose terms and motifs – for example, the historical succession of global empires – appear in Rutilius' work as well. Claudian had praised Stilicho as the man who would continue the line of heroes of ancient Rome and become the saviour of the Empire. Rutilius witnessed the overthrow and the murder of Stilicho in 408 AD and the ruin of the city of Rome in 410 AD which was largely triggered off by that earlier event. To Rutilius, the policy of the treacherous Vandal was responsible for the disaster: a totally unjust verdict which was, however, in keeping with many other opinions in a widespread anti-German reaction.

Claudian and Prudentius, Augustine, Orosius, and Rutilius: all of these are writers who bear witness to the importance of the idea of Rome in the efforts of educated people to cope intellectually with the turmoil and the catastrophes of the period. But they all give very different answers to the burning question of the day concerning the survival of civilisation and of the Empire's legal order.

The poetry of Sedulius, about whom we have no additional biographical information, leads the reader further on in time, into the middle of the fifth century AD. The poet presumably lived in Italy; a note in one manuscript tells us that the five books of his *Carmen paschale* were published posthumously. The work is a continuation of Biblical epic: Book 1 deals with those events in the history of salvation narrated in the Old Testament, whereas the other four are a loose paraphrase of Matthew's Gospel. Sedulius aimed at poetic and linguistic art in the Virgilian tradition. Later on, he wrote a new version of the *Carmen paschale* in highly artificial rhetorical prose. From an abecedarius, a poem whose stanzas follow the alphabet in their initial letters, two extracts have remained in liturgical use as hymns until today. The poem describes the life of Christ; it is written in iambic dimeters, the quantitative metre of the Ambrosianic hymns, and is thus a part of 'scholarly' poetry. However, a novel element which does not belong to the techniques of this genre is the consistent use of end rhyme, as otherwise found mainly in accentuating poems. Another poem by Sedulius, composed in elegiac distichs, describes parallels between the Old and the New Testaments.

A near-contemporary of Sedulius was the rhetor Marius Claudius Victor, who lived in Massilia or Marseilles and wrote a Biblical epic in three books based on the narrative of the Book of Genesis. This work appertains entirely to the scholarly tradition in poetry, as does the hexametrical autobiography of Paulinus of Pella in Macedonia, a grandson of Ausonius and an older contemporary of Sedulius, as well as the hexametrical life of Martin of Tours written by Paulinus of Petricordia, modern-day Périgueux. The model for the latter work, which was written not long after the middle of the fifth century AD, was the biography of the saint by Sulpicius Severus (see p. 532).

The survival of 'scholarly' poetry in old metrical forms no longer corresponding to the spoken language is documented not only in literary works. Throughout the Imperial age, until its very last epochs, we encounter verse inscriptions, often on tombstones, but also on buildings or as evidence of religious consecration in a pagan or a Christian context. Naturally the poetic merit of such inscriptions is very varied, just like the degree to which their authors mastered the metrical technique and the diction of great poetry. Yet it must be noted that specimens of remarkable quality can be found even from the very latest period of the Classical age, as occasionally featured in collections of poetic literature. This is the case in the Greek East as well as the Latin West.

The distinction between pagan and Christian poets became more and more blurred in the course of the fifth century AD; or to be more precise, Christian poets in the Latin language became less reluctant to deal with pagan subjects such as, for instance, topics from mythology. In the beginning they had shied away from anything of the kind, in spite of their adoption of a rich repertoire of forms from ancient poetry. In the middle years of the century in question lived Flavius Merobaudes, a man who came from Spain, although he had a Frankish name. For a poem celebrating a victory of Aëtius Merobaudes was rewarded by the erection of a statue in his honour in the Forum of Trajan in Rome. The inscription tells us that he held a fairly high administrative position. Aëtius was the last general who managed to bring large parts of Gaul under an orderly administration. In 451 AD, in an alliance with Goths, Burgundi, and Franks, he beat off the final major onslaught of the Huns in the heartland of France.

Merobaudes' relationship to Aëtius corresponds with that of Claudian to Stilicho. The fragments of his panegyrical poetry in honour of his patron show clearly that he imitated Claudian's poems. But Merobaudes also used prose to glorify Aëtius' achievements: mediaeval manuscripts feature some complete texts and some fragments of Merobaudes' shorter poems, such as epigrams, birthday congratulations, and *ekphraseis* or descriptions. Among these pieces there are some of Christian content: two baptismal poems and one versified treatise on the two natures of Christ. These poems resemble some of the non-genuine pieces included in the collection of Claudian's short poems. The difference between Merobaudes and Claudian in their attitude towards religion is a significant indicator for a historical change, all the more so because in the content, function, and style of his poetry Merobaudes is quite obviously indebted to the work of Claudian, a fact which also proves the high esteem enjoyed by the latter.

Another case in point is Sidonius Apollinaris who lived about one generation after Merobaudes. He came from a noble family in the city of Lugdunum or Lyons and became the son-in-law of the short-lived Emperor Avitus. His occasional poems include epigrams, descriptions of paintings, *epithalamia* or bridal poems, and eulogies on several Emperors. All of them are secular in content, full of mythological paraphernalia, and, also in obvious succession to Claudian, committed to the language and style of Classic poetry. They show some elegance in the mastery of its poetic technique and thus also document the relatively high standard of education in Sidonius' part of Gaul, where there was obviously an audience which appreciated such writing. In 469 AD Sidonius was elected Bishop of Averna, modern-day Clermont-Ferrand; there is a large corpus of his letters from the subsequent years. Their epistolary style follows models like the letters of Pliny the Younger or the pagan Symmachus (see p. 459), but they naturally deal with various Christian topics. That the Bishop Sidonius did not stop being a poet is proved by verses, mostly of Christian content, which occasionally appear in these letters. Of Rusticius Helpidius, who presumably belonged to Sidonius' circle of friends, we have exclusively Christian poems, hexametrical or elegiac-epigrammatical, on a comparably high technical level.

Under the rule of the Vandals in north Africa between 431 and 534 AD Latin culture showed an astonishing vitality. I have already mentioned the regional discussion about Augustine's doctrine of grace, a debate which survived its author who died in the year of the Vandals' invasion. I have also talked of the renewed discussion about Arianism, which was the creed of the new masters (see p. 532). In this controversy the central character was Fulgentius, Bishop of Ruspe around 500 AD. Much of his prolific theological writing is extant, and we even have evidence of the fact that he had a good command of Greek.

Among the poets of the region, the outstanding figure is Blossius Aemilius Dracontius, a man from the Senatorial class who had a legal training. As a Catholic and a supporter of the Emperor in Constantinople he incurred the wrath of the King Gunthamund and was imprisoned for several years along with his whole family. Gunthamund's successor was Thrasamund, also a strict Arian but interested in serious theological debate, as proved by Fulgentius' tract in response to his set of ten questions. During Thrasamund's reign Dracontius was set free in 496 AD. While in detention, he had written two major pieces of poetry. The first, entitled *Satisfactio*, is at once a penitential poem addressed to God, and a plea for pardon addressed to the King. It is written in elegiac distichs and its metre and linguistic usage are clearly influenced by the poetry Ovid produced during his banishment. The other piece by Dracontius, *De laudibus dei*, is a hexametrical epic in three books. Book 1 contains an account of the creation and the Fall, followed by the description of Christ's salvation of fallen mankind in Book 2 where the author uses the occasion for biting anti-Arian polemics. Book 3 is a collection of examples of steadfast courage under persecution, as reported in Biblical-Christian as well as in Graeco-Roman tradition, recalled to bring consolation and encouragement to the prisoner.

Of a totally different kind are the poems which Dracontius wrote as a free man and which he presumably gathered himself into a collection entitled *Romulea* or *Roman Matters*. Here we find rhetorical exercises beside *epithalamia* and dedicatory poems addressed to his teacher beside short hexametrical retellings of mythical episodes. Counted among the works of Dracontius is finally also a so-called tragedy, a dialogical, but hexametrical, rendering of the tale of Orestes. We know of more such epic-dramatic versions of mythological subjects, as texts which were suitable for reading with shared-out parts. For instance, presumably in the fourth or fifth century AD, an otherwise unknown Hosidius Geta wrote a Medea tragedy largely composed of lines from Virgil; and a hexametrical version of the Alcestis tale became known only recently through the appearance of a papyrus from the fourth century AD in Barcelona. This text also consists mostly of direct speech by the characters involved, with the dialogue linked by no more than a few transitional lines.

Dracontius was an expressive poet, well able to communicate individual sentiments in the medium of Classical poetic tradition dominated by myth, as well as with the help of the Christian world of ideas clothed in the same linguistic-stylistic forms. It is very probable that he did not find it at all difficult to unite the two systems of poetic communication. Under pressure from the rule of the heterodox Vandals, it was logical to see a unity between the Classical educational tradition – a source of pride to a native citizen of the Roman Empire – and Christian orthodoxy. Both were equally to be upheld against the Barbarian rulers.

Under the name of Dracontius, a few mnemonic verses on the names of the months are featured in the *Codex Salmasianus*, a Spanish manuscript from the seventh or eighth century AD named after the French Humanist Saumaise. It is the most voluminous among the manuscript collections of Latin poems, of which some survive and some are known only from early printed versions, with works from all kinds of authors and periods. There are plenty of forgeries in this compilation, but also such original texts as the short epic about the love affair between Mars and Venus. Its author, an otherwise unknown Reposianus, obviously knew the Ovidian as well as the Homeric version of the episode. Integrated into the *Codex Salmasianus* is a collection of Latin poetry from Vandalic north Africa which was presumably put together in the sixth century AD. This collection features a hundred hexametrical riddles by a certain Symphorius; a series of partly elegiac and partly hexametrical poems – one with a complex play on letters – by a Flavius Felix who describes the baths built by King

Thrasamund; and elegies from the pen of an otherwise unknown Pentadius about the deeds of the goddess Fortuna, with numerous examples from myth, and about the coming of spring. Under the name Florentinus, there is a eulogy on King Thrasamund which at the same time contains a eulogy of his residence Carthage and of its history; ascribed to the same author are also other poems of mythological, erotic, satirical, or moral content. Poems from the Late Classical period are also known from other manuscript collections: as, for instance, the mnemonic poetry by a rhetor called Citherius, whose verses contain enumerations and exemplifications of different rhetorical terms in groups of three hexameters each.

The most interesting figure among the Late Classical poets from north Africa is Luxorius or Luxurius, who seems to have written his works around the beginning of the sixth century AD. Under his name, the *Codex Salmasianus* has preserved ninety epigrams and one epithalamium which contains a liberal amount of literal quotation from Virgil's verses. Like those of Martial, Luxurius' epigrams are written in varied metres, including lyrical ones applied in a non-stanzaic form. Martial was the later poet's model also with regard to language, style, and formulation of witty points. Some of Luxurius' epigrams mock unnamed schoolmasters, chariot-drivers from the circus, physicians, or advocates; others deal with erotic themes in very uninhibited and sometimes crude diction; yet others describe gardens, buildings, tamed wild animals, and more such curiosities. In short, we find the whole wide range of subjects of older literary epigrammatics in Greek or Latin. One longer epigram in twenty-two elegiac distichs is dedicated to a Vandalic nobleman. It describes a park with a pavilion, for which that person commissioned a painting which shows him in the act of killing a boar. This poem illustrates the situation of the poet as part of a clientele.

The sovereign mastery of the technique of versification, and the close familiarity with older epigrammatics also documented by these poems, prove the undisturbed existence of an educational system under Vandalic rule. How people at the time would learn about the many names and events from Classical mythology is shown by the works of the grammarian Fulgentius from the fifth century AD (see p. 448). He also lived in Africa but is not to be identified as the Bishop Fulgentius, with whom he was later often confused.

The last Latin poet from Africa worked and lived in Constantinople. In 534 the great general Belisarius had put an end to Vandalic rule on behalf of the Emperor Justinian. The former province of Africa was thus regained for the Roman Empire, but for a long time afterwards the Byzantines were still struggling with the Berbers of the hinterland. This war was led and finished by the general John, about whom Flavius Cresconius Corippus wrote an epic in eight books called *Johannis*. He followed this with another epic in four books glorifying the deeds of the Emperor Justin II, Justinian's nephew and successor. These are the last examples of historical epic in

Latin which show a full command of the epic tradition; they are matched by Greek specimens of the genre from the same period (see p. 601). Justinian's successes in foreign and military policy, which once more won north Africa, Italy, and parts of Gaul and Spain for the Empire, are the background of this production. In Africa literary life came to an end with the end of Vandalic rule; in Italy a similar caesura is marked by the invasion of the Langobardi in 568 AD. In Gaul and Spain, on the other hand, the respective rule of the Visigoths and the Franks saw a very gradual transition to a culture which is called mediaeval from our point in time.

As the author of letters and theological treatises, I have already mentioned Ennodius of Gaul, Bishop of Pavia in upper Italy from 514 AD. Originally this man was a rhetor and this is reflected in his hexametrical poems and his epigrams of mostly very secular content. His hymnic poetry remains within the tradition established by Ambrosius. Ennodius composed his stanzas of iambic dimeters and lyrical or alcaeic verses, under strict 'scholarly' observation of syllabic quantities.

A pupil of Ennodius was Arator, later a member of the clergy of the church in Rome, by whom we have a long Biblical epic. It contains both a paraphrase and an exegesis of the history of the apostles, in more than two thousand correct hexameters. There is no certainty concerning the author of a short epic about the resurrection and the Day of Judgment, a work which appears to date from the early sixth century AD. In the manuscript tradition, it ended up among the works of Cyprian (see p. 386), a fact which seems to indicate an African origin.

The very last author writing poetry in the living Classical tradition was Venantius Fortunatus. He came from Venetia and visited the grave of Saint Martin in Tours on a pilgrimage at the age of about thirty-five. This was in 567 AD, one year before the invasion of the Langobardi put an end to literary life in Italy. Venantius stayed in Gaul after a conversion to ascetic life, was ordained as a priest in Poitiers, and soon after became Bishop of that city. Venantius communicated with all the important contemporaries in the vicinity, above all with the Bishop of neighbouring Tours, Gregory, historiographer of the Franks, and author of many hagiographical works. He also maintained contacts with members of the Merovingian dynasty, particularly with the royal widow Radegund. This is documented by numerous occasional poems, epistles, and congratulatory poems, which were combined with his hymns in a collection comprising eleven books. Some of the hymns found their way into the liturgy still used today – for instance, the famous *Vexilla regis prodeunt*. A number of hymns on the passion of Christ were written on the occasion of Queen Radegund's receipt of an alleged piece of the true Cross sent to her by the Emperor Justin II. Among the occasional poems, a short epic describing a boat trip on the Moselle deserves particular mention because it quite neatly documents the cultural continuity in Gaul, in being a parallel to the poem Ausonius wrote more than two centuries earlier on an identical subject.

Apart from this collection of Venantius' works, we also have a major epic in four books, which is a poetic version of the life of the saint Martin of Tours as written by Sulpicius Severus about two hundred years before. There are also several hymns on the Virgin Mary, and a hexametrical lament on the downfall of the Thuringian royal dynasty from which Radegund came.

Venantius was a man with a lively temperament and with a great love of company, the central figure of a large circle of friends, and a poet to whom versification came easy. Thus he wrote poems on all kinds of events and encounters in his variegated life, and left us a work which is an extremely valuable source of information on cultural history. Venantius used the most diverse poetic forms and metres and knew his Classics inside out; but nevertheless he was no strict guardian of the great tradition of Roman poetry. His vocabulary is interspersed with many expressions which were alien to that tradition, and in most of his poems the reference to people and events from his own biography is too close and too spontaneous to allow a stylisation according to the laws of Classic poetry. Venantius' poems are often entirely unconventional, particularly in expressions of the author's susceptibility to the beauty of nature and landscape for which there are hardly any parallels in older literature. However, it must be said that linguistic and stylistic ties with ancient literature do dominate in Venantius' poems, much more so than in the prose works of his older contemporary Gregory of Tours. The latter would be a much more unlikely candidate for the title of 'last exponent of Classical-Roman literature' than the poet Venantius Fortunatus.

The outstanding figure among the Late Classical poets of the East was Nonnus from Panopolis in Egypt. His exact life dates are not known but it is most likely that he belongs to the middle of the fifth century AD. Nonnus' major work is entitled *Dionysiaca*. The forty-eight books of this gigantic epic deal with the wealth of tales surrounding the god Dionysus; the main event of the narrative is the expedition of the god and his train to the wonderland of India. Only after his return from India does Dionysus travel through the Greek world, and finally, the son of Zeus is welcomed among the gods of Olympus. Here Nonnus follows a version particularly often interpreted by philosophers which claims that not only Hercules but also Dionysus was included among the gods only at the end of a long career full of deeds for the good of mankind, which is exactly why he can also provide an example for human endeavour.

Nonnus did not leave out any single episode of the vast circle of legends, and neither does his work lack any motif or typical scene of the epic tradition in the succession of Homer. There are descriptions of battles, enumerations of warriors in the train of the god, descriptions of weapons, speeches and quarrels between the gods, competitions, descriptions of places, messengers' reports, and all the other elements of epic narrative in the Homeric fashion. We also find all the more formal characteristics of the epic style without any exception: the repeated invocation of the Muse whenever the action is approaching a climax, similes as visualisations of the emotional content of a situation, and the use of set epithets for gods, men, and objects.

However, there is much in Nonnus' language, style, and composition which transcends the limits of the Homeric tradition. Ancient epic demanded the description of divine interaction, parallel to the account about the events on earth which are governed by it. Nonnus extends this plane beyond the conventional group of divine characters and gives it a cosmic dimension so that sun and ocean, fire and earth themselves are in turmoil. From Hellenistic epic Nonnus borrowed the representation of a psychological motivation of events which is much more detailed and vivid than in Homer's poetry, as well as the description of psychological processes for their own sake.

Ancient epic had already known occasional digressions, which described landscapes or told tales from other contexts as parallels to the main action portrayed. Hellenistic epic had elaborated this detail, padding out the narrative with digressions of scholarly-antiquarian content. Nonnus makes excessive use of this option with the result that occasionally his digressions obscure the main narrative and disguise the overall structure of the epic. In doing so the author shows a keen interest in subjects related to magic and astrology; the latter appear in the context of digressions which retell legends concerning the stars. On the whole this makes Nonnus' epic a goldmine of obscure individual tales and versions, although it is sometimes difficult to assess where a remote or lost source was used and where the poet's own invention took over. Dionysus had already been the subject of numerous Hellenistic epics; and of several corresponding texts from the fourth century AD there are extant fragments on papyrus, namely from Dionysius' and Sotericus' epics with the identical title *Bassarica*, and from several hymns to the god. Thus Nonnus had plenty of material from a rich tradition at his command.

Another possibility that had been opened up during the age of Hellenism was the use of high pathos in the language of epic art. Nonnus magnifies also this trait up to the limits of the possible or of good taste; still, this seems well justified by the chosen content of his epic. There is hardly any other piece of Classical poetry whose language finds such convincing expression for intoxication and ecstasy, states of mind which had always been closely associated with the nature and the deeds of Dionysus.

Nonnus was the last great exponent of the art of versification in Greek poetry. Though the rhythm of the hexameter, governed by the succession of quantities, was no longer recognisable to the ear of an audience used to contemporary vernacular, Nonnus still developed euphonic rules whose rigidity exceeds even the formal demands upheld by the pedantic poets of Early Hellenism. This concerns the distribution of dactyls and spondees, the frequency of certain verse caesuras, and the length of words before caesuras and at the ends of verses. Nonnus' habit of also regularising the last stress of each single line seems to be a concession to the pronunciation of Greek vernacular, for this rule has nothing to do with the quantitative rhythm of the line. Nonnus' technique of versification had a considerable impact, as shown by several other Greek epic texts of the Late Classical age.

Under Nonnus' name, and unmistakably in his style, there is also a hexametrical paraphrase of John's Gospel. In this case there was a great reluctance to acknowledge the authorship of a man who had produced the *Dionysiaca*, a work which reflects a keen interest in astrology and mysteries, as two forms of expression of Late Classical religious thought which were particularly odious to the Christians. It was suggested that the poet must have converted to the new faith between the writing of the two works: but the construction of this hypothesis appears to be a wasted effort, if one considers, for instance, the example of Christian north Africa, where writers were similarly uninhibited in choosing pagan as well as Christian subjects for their poetry. What is remarkable in Nonnus' Biblical epic, however, is the frequency with which Mary is referred to as the mother of God. This suggests that the work was written at the time of the Nestorianic controversies, around or after the decision of Ephesus in 431 AD.

A successor to Nonnus with regard to the art of versification is Colluthus of Lycopolis in Egypt. From his rich production listed in the *Suda* encyclopaedia, only a short epic about the abduction of Helena is extant. Colluthus was alive during the reign of the Emperor Anastasius between 491 and 518 AD. Other fragments of epic poetry from the Late Classical age dealing with mythological subjects have become known through recent papyrus finds.

The subject of a short epic by Musaeus does not come from myth, but from the erotic poetry of Hellenism. The work tells of Leander's love for the beautiful Hero; of how he swam the Hellespont each night to see her because the parents were against the match, and of how he drowned as the lamp which was to show him the way went out. The story is mentioned in Virgil's work and Ovid made it the basis for two of his letters of heroines. A papyrus fragment from the third century BC documents a version in an elegy from the Early Hellenistic period, and the motif keeps resurfacing at different times throughout the history of European literature and fine art. Musaeus was perhaps the same man who is mentioned as a correspondent of Aeneas of Gaza (see p. 464). He knew and used Nonnus' epic, and in turn Colluthus seems to have used Musaeus' work, a fact which gives us some clues as to their life dates.

Papyrus finds have uncovered substantial remains of encomiastic and historical epics from between the fourth and the sixth centuries AD. I have already referred to the fragments of an epic account of the Persian Wars waged by the Emperors Diocletian and Galerius (see p. 427). Several fragments from the fifth century AD describe and praise the achievements of some military commanders on the upper Nile who managed to beat off the attacks of the Blemyes, a warlike nomadic nation. Another fragment is from a didactic poem describing the creation of the world.

Only rarely do such fragments yield any information about their authors, but in one case, the poet seems to have been identified. An astrological treatise from the Byzantine age gives us the horoscope and the biography of a certain Pamprepius of Panopolis in Egypt who lived from 440 to 484 AD. The successive stations of his life were Athens, where he worked as a teacher of grammar, Pergamum, Constantinople, Antioch, and finally Egypt again. He was a staunch pagan, involved in several political affairs, and for a while the holder of a high office in the central Imperial administration; however, he was later murdered in the context of a political intrigue. A slightly more recent papyrus has preserved a poetic eulogy on one of his high-ranking patrons called Theagenes, as well as a pretty epic description of the times of the day and the activities associated with them. This has naturally led to the conclusion that these verses, written in the manner of Nonnus, stem from Pamprepius.

In the early sixth century AD Christodorus of Coptus in Egypt wrote his historical epics; among others, we know of one entitled *Isaurica*. Isauria was a backward region in Asia Minor, infamous for its robbers. From one of its chief families came the Emperor Zeno, originally called Tarasicodissa, who reigned until 491 AD. With the help of Zeno's clan, his predecessor on the throne, Leo, had got rid of the last influential dignitaries of Alanic and Gothic origin and had thus paved the way to the throne for the Isaurian. Anastasius, Zeno's successor chosen at the instigation of his widow, was once again a man from the municipal upper classes. In a protracted war he suppressed a subsequent uprising of the inhabitants of the Isaurian mountains and forcibly settled many of them in northern Greece.

These are the events from contemporary history which Christodorus narrates in one of his epics. The only extant one among his writings, apart from some quotations in works by later authors, is a so-called ekphrastic epic. It describes a series of statues representing characters from Greek mythology; its preservation is due to its inclusion among the epigrams of the *Anthologia Palatina*, in spite of its incongruent form and its great length, on the strength of the fact that the description of works of art was also a favourite subject for epigrammatic poetry. In the *Anthologia Palatina*,

Christodorus' epic fills an entire volume, Book 2 of the collection. Christodorus' verses follow the rules set by Nonnus; but apart from that, they do not show any particularly great poetic talent.

From the reign of Justinian we have two more ekphrastic epics. In a long hexametrical poem with an iambic prologue, the Silentarius or Imperial chamberlain Paul gives a most vivid, precise, and lively description of the architectural wonders of the Hagia Sophia church in Constantinople. The epic was recited at the second consecrational ceremony in 563 AD; an earthquake had destroyed the building twenty years after its first consecration and its re-erection took six years. The work shows its author as an elegant poet who knew how to make full use of traditional epic's potential for linguistic expression. In his verses the deep impression which the grandiose spatial design of the Hagia Sophia still leaves with every modern-day visitor is described adequately and in a way that can be understood by even the modern reader. To the archaeologist, the most interesting feature of this epic is above all the very detailed description of the interior decoration, which has since changed quite a lot over the centuries. Paul's metrical technique is also Nonnianic.

The rhetor John, another contemporary of Justinian, was trained at the aforementioned school of Gaza (see p. 463). His ekphrastic poem in two books, hexametrical verses with an iambic introduction to each book, was also preserved in the *Anthologia Palatina*, where it was interpolated between Books 14 and 15. John, by whom we have also other poems (see p. 603), describes the painting in the cupola of baths in Gaza or Antioch, where the cosmos is portrayed in the form of allegorical figures. John was also a Nonnian, but did not equal the expressiveness and the vividness of his contemporary Paul.

The reign of Justinian saw a late flowering above all of epigrammatic poetry. The aforementioned epic poets Christodorus, Paul, and John, but also the historian Agathias, are represented in the *Anthologia Palatina*, with epigrams of the most varied content. What is striking here is that epigrams were apparently not always written according to the strict metrical rules which dominated a large share of the epic production after Nonnus. However, the regularisation of certain word stresses is also found in the works of several epigrammatic poets of the epoch.

Agathias was probably the most productive among them. From epigrams written by himself and by contemporaries, he put together a collection which was almost completely adopted by Cephalas in his own anthology, compiled around 900 AD. From there it entered the famous *Anthologia Palatina*, thus called after the manuscript kept at Heidelberg, in the tenth century AD. This contains even the epigram with which Agathias introduced his collection. The edition of ever-new collections of epigrams which included its respective predecessors was a custom which had begun in the first century BC, and continued throughout the Byzantine Middle Ages.

Among the many epigrammatic poets from the reign of Justinian, Agathias excels through particular elegance in his phrasings, whether in fictitious consecrational epigrams addressed to Classical gods, or in mourning, descriptive, and mocking epigrams. The imitation of the ancients had been proclaimed several times as an express programme of epigrammatic poetry, and this led to a close emulation of the language and style of certain specific Hellenistic authors from the first heyday of literary epigrammatics. Agathias' contemporary Macedonius, for example, tried to imitate the style of Leonidas of Tarentum from the third century BC.

Epigrammatic poetry had the great advantage of being open to all kinds of subjects, including very topical ones, without any obstacle created by a traditional formal language. This flexibility of the art had already been achieved by the poets of the age of Hellenism. Thus epigrams again and again contain references to what was going on in the capital; for instance, in the circus, in literary circles, or in education. A melancholy and very artful epigram by Agathias, for example, laments the death of a lady distinguished by her beauty who had been an eminent poetess and legal scholar at the same time. The epigram was also a suitable form for courtly poetry: the aforementioned John even dared to use traditional and fairly direct expressions from erotic epigrammatics combined with courtly gallantry, in a poem honouring the beauty of the Empress Theodora. That Christian motifs could very easily be clothed in the epigrammatic form is proved in Book 1 of the *Anthologia Palatina*, which consists exclusively of Christian poems.

Among the educated classes of this period, there was still an astonishingly large number of people who were more or less able to produce epigrams, iambs, or hexameters, in the prescribed linguistic and metrical forms. This is proved by the many extant verse inscriptions, which from the fourth century onwards contain more and more evidence of their authors' Christian faith. This state of affairs is the same for the East as for the West (see p. 578). Another type of vulgarisation of scholarly poetic art is indicated by a group of texts known as the Magical Papyri, whose youngest specimens date from the fifth century AD. Its recipes and instructions for magical actions are intermingled with invocations of gods and demons from a world of ideas which is a motley mixture of Greek, oriental, Jewish, and Christian elements. The invocations, styled as poems, frequently have the form of long hymns, and they are mostly difficult to date. They are written in the verse forms and after the linguistic conventions of literary hymnic poetry; but they also frequently contain errors which give scholars clues as to the working of linguistic change in detail.

A verse form especially popular in the Late Classical age was the anacreontic, whose two types were both spoken verses derived from old song lyrics. It was used in poems which resembled epigrams in subject and length and the *Anthologia Palatina* features about sixty texts in this metre.

One kind was described as hemiambs or half-iambs, because of a shortening of the two rising syllables at the beginning of a verse which made them look iambic: they were perceived as such because the audience was no longer conscious of their lyrical origin. Epigrammatic poetry in the metrical form named after the poet Anacreon from the sixth century BC had already begun in the second century AD. This metre was used by many poets between the fourth and the sixth centuries AD, including, for instance, John of Gaza and Synesius.

The collection of anacreontics appended to the *Anthologia Palatina* contains poems from entirely different periods, and of equally varied literary quality. Some are formed correctly; in others, metrical deviations and the occasional following of word stress suggest either the poet's lack of education, or a very late date of authorship. A similar statement may be made with regard to linguistic features. As befits the man who gave the genre its name, we find toasts and love poems, but also poems of semi-philosophical content, or on subjects which were chosen to surprise the reader, as in Hellenistic epigrams. One poem which became famous through Goethe's translation is dedicated to the cicada, the songstress among the insects.

In the course of the Late Classical age, the anacreontic-hemiambic metre gradually lost its affinity with humorous-witty or sympotic, and with erotic poetry. In the early years of the seventh century AD, the Patriarch Sophronius of Jerusalem, a late and very erudite exponent of Gaza's rhetorical school, wrote twenty-three anacreontic poems on the festivals of the ecclesiastical year, and religious poetry in this metre continued well into the Byzantine era, parallel to the development of epigrammatics.

The discussion of epigram and epic have very quickly brought the present account to the age of Justinian's restoration because the most voluminous and most interesting literary evidence dates from that period. Yet that Christian scholarly poetry in Greek which began in the third century AD already found a Classic author in the fourth century in Gregory of Nazianzus. His large literary legacy enjoyed such a high reputation that quite a few texts which he did not write also ended up among his works, as, for instance, the two aforementioned accentuating poems (see p. 572).

Gregory talked willingly and at length about himself, and this is the reason why we have not only some autobiographical poems, but also a longer piece, likewise written in iambs, which is intended to tell the reader about the meaning and the purpose of his poetic activities. He states, for instance, that he wants to subject his strong temperament to the discipline of versified expression, to pass on Christian doctrine to the young in an appealing form, and to create a Christian counterpart to the rich treasure of pagan poetry. The latter goal had already been envisaged by Gregory's contemporary Apollinaris of Laodicaea, who, under the pressure of Julian's ban on Christian teachers of literature, wrote poetic paraphrases of Biblical texts which were to replace those of Homer in secondary education (see

p. 401). His eponymous father is even said to have written tragedies, dramatic pieces meant for reading, about Biblical subjects. We know also of epic Biblical poetry from the following century by Nonnus (see p. 600), a fact which constitutes a complete parallel to the spreading of the genre in the Latin West.

Gregory, however, chose a different path. His poems are not paraphrases of the Bible, but communicate Christian ideas frequently within expressions of individual thought and sentiment, in various forms and through various subjects. There are hexametrical hymns and prayers; didactic epistles in that same metre as well as in elegiac distichs, which in turn are occasionally used for a *hymnus*, in the manner of the avowed model Callimachus; and there are iambic narratives from the poet's own life, intended to vindicate the author, and at the same time give the reader theological instruction. We find longer and shorter poems of moral and dogmatical-theological content in iambic, dactylic, or elegiac metres and with a didactic intention; sententious-epigrammatic poetry in distichs and hemiambs; and finally also poems, mostly addressed to friends and comparable to many of his letters, which communicate his moods and feelings in a way that is very rare in non-Christian Greek poetry.

These poems as well as the poetical autobiographies are in a way a counterpart to Augustine's *Confessions* and its successors, such as the autobiography of Ennodius. They document a growing interest in psychological processes under the influence of the Christian religion on ideas and ways of thinking. It is true that comparable trends are found also in Late Classical philosophy, but there, the goal of cognition is the comprehension of an objective order of being which, being of a purely spiritual nature, can only be understood by means of insight into psychological processes. The Christian interest, on the other hand, focuses on the question how the individual, unique human soul can meet its God. This approach gives general significance especially to the most individual experiences.

Gregory was exceptionally well read in ancient Greek poetry and everywhere in his poems we find explicit references or implicit allusions to those texts. The natural ease with which he uses the linguistic and metrical forms of the individual poetic genres cannot be imagined without such erudition. Still, his poetical work does not fit entirely into the picture which we can form of so-called scholarly Greek poetry in the Late Classical age. The epic tradition which produced Nonnus and later imitated him was combined with a growing rigidity of metrical rules, which could only be appreciated by scholarly readers, and no longer by those whose sensibilities were shaped by the living language. The same thing may be said for linguistic form and content. In Gregory's work, on the other hand, especially in view of his faithful adherence to traditional (i.e. Classic poetic technique and poetic language), there is a surprising degree of nonchalance in the way he would sometimes also choose the very metrical or poetic forms which tradition reserved for other subjects than the ones dealt with. He also used occasional word forms, words, or phrases which could not but strike an educated person as non-poetic; and he was also unperturbed by sloppiness in metrical composition. As some remarks by Gregory prove, these slight deviations from tradition were conscious, as well as presumably intentional. In any case, his technique helped him to deal with a great variety of themes, and, in spite of its ties to very old conventions at odds with contemporary linguistic reality, to make his poetry the vehicle of a living expression of current thoughts and feelings.

Gregory's special position is best illuminated in comparison with Synesius, one generation his junior; I have already dealt with Synesius' poetry in a previous section (see p. 456). In spite of their Christian content, Synesius' hymns, composed in particularly obscure and elaborate linguistic and metrical forms, belong to philosophical poetry after the manner of the hymns written by the Neo-Platonist Proclus (see p. 490). Both authors attempt to express the insight – gained through discursive thought – into the divine order of the world, which is still at the same time the object of religious veneration, in a manner suited to religious sentiment. To achieve this, Proclus in his hexametrical hymns draws on the world of the ancient gods, whose characters, philosophically understood, give him the opportunity to visualise his philosophical convictions, and at the same time to go back to religious tradition. In Synesius' hymns it is the trinity, especially its second person, which figures as both the addressee of the pious invocation, and the epitome of philosophical knowledge of God.

The poems of both men can be interpreted as evidence of their authors' true piety; but even in such a reading, the subjective element of this piety is not of any particular importance. This type of piety is encountered also in the so-called Orphic Hymns (see p. 270), albeit on a totally different intellectual plane. In Gregory's work the poems with a didactic content feature prominently, and his hymnic poetry does also express the objectifying piety which is characteristic for philosophical-religious poetry of the Late Classical age. However, in other parts of Gregory's poetical work, and not only in the long autobiographical pieces, the reader perceives some very personal and unique notes. These indicate a different notion of the meaning and the purpose of poetic expression in a religious context, a notion which is much more akin to the mediaeval-modern world of ideas as shaped by Christianity, than to Classical sentiment. It is these new notes which are in keeping with Gregory's nonchalance – totally unlike the attitude of a Proclus or a Synesius – in using the familiar repertoire of forms from old poetry. It would be an oversimplification to say that this can be explained entirely by Gregory's temperament, and the insatiable urge to communicate which he doubtlessly had. But in spite of his particular deep-rootedness in the old educational tradition, it is certainly legitimate to see Gregory as the herald of a different age, with other demands on, and other possibilities for poetry.

649474

POSTSCRIPT

During the centuries of the Late Classical age, Graeco-Roman culture finally gained that shape in which it had its lasting impact on posterity. The development which characterises this period was an amalgamation of Graeco-Roman cultural heritage with the teachings and life forms of Christianity whose growth into a world religion took place within the framework and under the permanent influence of this culture. In the present account I have again and again referred to this process only as far as it concerned literature, poetry, philosophy, and science. But of course this metamorphosis affected religious, social, and political life as a whole. It created the conditions for the astonishing continuity with which Classical culture kept informing the entire Middle and Modern ages. Its perennial presence within Christianity itself, and within the world moulded by the Christian faith, ensured that people could at any time also turn to its pre-Christian products. This fact and its historical consequences are more clearly recognisable in legal history than in the vast and complex field of literature. However, the processes which can be observed are very similar in both cases.

The Imperial state of the Late Classical age had many traits which we today are bound to find repulsive. We are, for instance, inclined to criticise the omnipotence of the state, the compulsive character of its social structure, the unfettered exploitation of all economic resources for the purposes of political power, or the religious and ideological conformism of this epoch. In one respect, however, the Late Classical state has undoubtedly left a very valuable legacy to posterity through its best exponents: the knowledge that political order must be recognised and continually re-established as the rule of justice, and that the state must not be perceived as merely the outer form of human rule over fellow humans.

Important achievements in jurisprudence and legislation mark the historic stations of the Late Classical Roman state; and in each case, the respective efforts were motivated by the will to preserve or to revive the legal order under altered conditions. The reform campaign of Diocletian which, in spite of all innovation should be seen as the restoration of an old order, found its parallel in the work of Hermogenes, one of the last legal scholars known to us by name. Theodosius II, who wanted to strengthen the Greek and Latin educational tradition with the foundation of a new university, had a corpus of all Imperial laws compiled and published by legal experts. The digests in the gigantic *Corpus iuris civilis*, inspired by Justinian, were designed to make as much as possible from the wealth of legal skill and knowledge gathered over the centuries accessible for use in legal practice and legal instruction. The editors of the *Corpus* came from the legal school of Berytus or Beirut, where Roman law was still taught in the medium of Latin during the sixth century AD. All these attempts show the repeated acknowledgement of a need to go back, in a 'Classicist' manner, to the roots of a legal culture which was highly developed, but still permanently endangered by oscillations of the level of general education, by changes in political and social conditions, by all kinds of emergencies, and by despotic behaviour on the part of those who held political power.

The influence of this ever-renewed legal tradition lived on in both East and West but with some very characteristic differences. This constitutes a parallel to those distinctions between East and West which are obvious to anyone who tries to assess the impact of the literary and the educational tradition during those centuries leading up to the Modern age. In the eastern Roman Imperial state with its central government, legislation and jurisprudence continued in the old tracks, notwithstanding major changes in legal matter brought about by new social conditions, new political tasks, and new moral-religious notions. Greek had already become the only legal language throughout the eastern Empire at the end of the Justinian era, but there were still Imperial laws of supra-regional validity and comprehensive codifications, as well as works of reference which were meant to help the reader of those collections.

The regionally valid codifications which appeared in the West adapted the elements of the old legal order to the changed conditions in the new states of the Visigoths or Langobards, political structures which were gradually gaining in stability. What survived was thus merely a fragmented form of the old legal system as blended with legal concepts from a different origin. It was only in the vicinity of the papal see that a new movement towards a universal legal order began, and this happened in the context of efforts to create a mainly spiritual and less political order. It was only the study of Justinian's work at the school of Bologna in the eleventh century AD, and the resulting – though much delayed – reception of Roman law in the countries of continental Europe, which created the conditions for a renewed acceptance of the ideal notion of a legal order embracing all civilised humanity. This was once again proof of the power of that cultural and legal consciousness which had kept the Roman Imperial state alive.

The literary part of the Late Classical cultural heritage had a lasting influence in correspondingly different ways in East and West respectively. Crises and catastrophes shook the foundations of the eastern Roman state in the seventh and eighth centuries AD and caused deep-reaching transformations in state and society as well as in people's mentality. The Persian assault, the loss of all the Empire's oriental territories, the long defence against the Arabs who twice laid siege to Constantinople, the restructuring of Imperial administration and army, and not least the repercussions of the quarrel with the Iconoclasts made the memory of the old educational assets recede into the background. The change in the educational world can be seen even in minute detail, such as in forms of handwriting. However, the marked centralism which Byzantium had inherited from the High Empire and which dominated its intellectual life even more than had been the case in the Flavian or Antonine state also paved the way for the sweeping success of every new renaissance emanating from the capital.

Such a rediscovery and revival of Classical tradition did indeed come about in the course of the ninth century AD when the state asserted its power in a determined foreign and military policy and gained social and economic strength within. Classical literature was systematically rediscovered and collected, as by the Patriarch Photius, for instance, whose name has occurred again and again in this book; and the cultivation and the study of the literary heritage continued undisrupted until the very end of the Byzantine state. It is true that this state also saw times of direst distress and danger in the last two centuries of its existence. But the very fact that at the end its territory was limited to its capital seems to have facilitated the transfer of the Greek literary legacy to the Italy of the Humanist movement in the years before and after the fall of Constantinople in 1453. At that time there was no multitude of educational centres but only one single strand of tradition which had to be picked up and continued. The renewed differentiation of this educational tradition in the following centuries belongs already to the cultural history of the individual European nations.

In the ninth century AD the Latin West also saw a renaissance, a rediscovery and revival of Classical heritage. This ran parallel to the restoration of the western Empire whose crown Charlemagne received on Christmas Eve in the year 800 AD when the Frankish Kingdom had united the largest part of western Europe and Charles seemed to the Pope a more effective supporter of his claim to religious supremacy than the Emperor in faraway Constantinople. However, the men who revived the study of Latin authors not only at the court of Charlemagne and his successors, but also in the monasteries of the large Imperial territory, came from totally different regional backgrounds; and there was a corresponding difference between the cultural relics which could serve as starting points for a renaissance in various regions.

In northern Spain and southern France there lived the descendants of those who had been the last bearers of a Classically orientated education in the Visigoth Kingdom, extinguished in 711 AD. In Britain, settled by Anglo-Saxons, Classical elements had long been part of an active literary life which unfolded in the wake of Christianisation, as begun from Rome around 600 AD. With Bede 'the Venerable' this culture produced an important scholar and a systematic collector of knowledge which could be gained from Classical sources, as early as the eighth century AD. Christian missionaries from Britain had then brought the seeds of this education to central Europe during the course of that same century. In remote Ireland, there had been an unbroken tradition of Classical education occasionally even combined with Greek learning. After the consolidation of Langobardic rule in Italy that country – especially its northern parts – had also seen the beginnings of a renewed study of Classical literature; and finally in Gaul, the heartland of the Frankish Kingdom, the fire of Classical literature had never been allowed to go out anyway.

From all these countries scholars and writers came to the court of Charlemagne and his successors: Paulus Diaconus from Pavia, John Scotus from Ireland, Alcuin from Britain, Einhard from the Maingau in Germany, and many more. The resulting richness of intellectual life was just as obviously a product of this background as was its rapid regional differentiation at the break-up of the Carolingian Empire. In spite of the unifying factors of Latin as the language of education and of Christianity as the common religion, this differentiation remained a characteristic of the Latin West, in marked contrast to the Greek East. It was certainly an obstacle to any efforts aimed at the preservation of cultural continuity, but it also gave the Western intellectual world an exceptional degree of openness to outside influences.

This can be seen, for instance, in the reception of Aristotelian philosophy during the twelfth century AD. The Latin translations of relevant texts came partly from the Greek-speaking area, which at that time still included Sicily and southern Italy; and partly also from the cultural sphere of the Arabs. A considerable amount of Greek literature had been translated into Arabic from the eighth century onwards, either directly or via intermediate Syriac versions. The ready acceptance of this literature in the West contrasts sharply with the reluctance of the mediaeval Greek East to embrace cultural influences from outside. Even after the crusades had brought very close contacts with the West, and Latin political entities had sprang up on the soil of the Byzantine Empire, there were hardly any translations from Latin. A Greek Ovid was a great exception, while only folk literature knew frequent mutual borrowings and inspirations. But the haughty exclusiveness and the linguistic purism of the East also helped to preserve the remnants of ancient literature in an astonishingly pure textual form, and to keep this literature accessible through philological work. Without the groundwork of the Byzantines, the study of this literature in the

West, begun seriously in fifteenth-century Italy and exerting a hardly overestimable effect on all European intellectual life, would presumably have had a very slow start – if any start at all.

Regardless of the differences between Latin West and Greek East, the reception and the influence of Graeco-Latin literature, a long historical process whose cataloguing will still occupy whole generations of scholars to come, took place on the basis of that specific form which this literary tradition had gained in the Roman Empire. Among the Empire's exceedingly rich literary production, there may be only few outstanding masterpieces, but in the consciousness of the people of the era, literary activity was presumably the most important part of all culture. Here lies the reason for the diligence with which in the Empire the legacy of a more creative past was not only cultivated within the framework of literary activity, but was moreover creatively applied to contemporary reality. This establishes the ultimate historical importance of Imperial literature.

BIBLIOGRAPHY

In the following bibliography, I have not included any textual editions or translations of the primary sources. Details of those are easily found in the reference works listed below.

Pauly's *Realencyclopädie der classischen Altertumswissenschaft*, new edition by H. Wissowa, W. Kroll, K. Mittelhaus and K. Ziegler, Stuttgart, 1893–1950.

Der kleine Pauly, K. Ziegler and W. Sontheimer (eds), Stuttgart 1964–75.

See also the annual bibliography of all Classical studies:

L'année philologique, Paris 1924ff.

The following titles are only a brief selection, but still the books mentioned will give the reader a general introduction to specific fields of scholarship, or at least provide access to further reading.

Selected original passages from the works of Imperial authors, with German translations and biographical appendices, are available in the following series:

Die griechische Literatur in Text und Darstellung vol. 5, Kaiserzeit ed. by H. Görgemanns, Stuttgart 1988 and

Die römische Literatur in Text und Darstellung vol. 5, Kaiserzeit II ed. by H. A. Gärtner, Stuttgart, 1988.

The most detailed accounts of Greek and Latin literary history in the Empire and the Late Classical age are found in the following manuals in the *Handbuch der Altertumswissenschaft* series:

W. von Christ, *Geschichte der griechischen Literatur*, ed. by O. Stählin and W. Schmidt, part 2 (Die nachklassische Periode), 2 vols, Munich 1920/4.

M. Schanz, *Geschichte der römischen Literatur*, ed. by C. Hosius and G. Krüger, parts 3 and 4, Munich 1914/1922; new edition by R. Herzog and P. L. Schmidt, (forthcoming) *Restauration und Erneuerung – die Lateinische Literatur von 284 bis 374*, Munich.

Less detailed, but more up to date:

A. Lesky, *Geschichte der griechischen Literatur*, Berne 3rd edn, 1971.

Shorter accounts in:

P. E. Easterling *et al.*, *Cambridge History of Classical Literature: Greek Literature*, Cambridge 1985.

E. J. Kenney *et al.*, *Cambridge History of Latin Literature: Latin Literature*, Cambridge 1982.
E. Norden, *Die römische Literatur*, Leipzig 6th edn, 1961.
M. Fuhrmann, *Römische Literatur*, Wiesbaden 1974.

A comprehensive account of Christian literature is given in:

B. Altaner and A. Stuiber, *Patrologie*, Freiburg 9th edn, 1981.
H. v. Campenhausen, *Griechische Kirchenväter*, Stuttgart 4th edn, 1967.
H. v. Campenhausen, *Lateinische Kirchenväter*, Stuttgart 6th edn, 1986.

Information about political, philosophical, and religious history of the Empire is found in:

H. Bengtson, *Grundriß der römischen Geschichte* (Handbuch der Altertumswissenschaft III, 5), Munich 1967.
P. Garnsey and R. Saller, *The Roman Empire – Economy, Society, and Culture*, London 1987.
G. Alföldy, *Die Krise des Römischen Reiches. Ausgewählte Beiträge*, Wiesbaden 1989.
A. Demandt, *Die Spätantike*, Munich 1989.
M. P. Nilsson, *Geschichte der griechischen Religion* (Handbuch der Altertumswissenschaft V, 2) vol. 2, Munich, 3rd edn, 1974.
H. Temporini and W. Haase (eds), *Aufstieg und Niedergang der römischen Welt*, Part II (Principate) vols 16/17 (Römische Religion, Orientalische Kulte), Berlin 1978/84.
H. Lietzmann, *Geschichte der alten Kirche*, 4 vols, Berlin 1932–41.

Encyclopaedic information in:

Th. Klauser, E. Dassmann, *Reallexikon für Antike und Christentum, Sachwörterbuch zur Auseinandersetzung des Christentums mit der Alten Welt*, Stuttgart 1950ff (currently available up to 'H')
A. H. Armstrong, *The Cambridge History of Later Greek and Early Medieval Philosophy*, Cambridge 2nd edn, 1970.

1 INTRODUCTION

1 R. Syme, *The Roman Revolution*, Oxford 1939
2 F. Millar, *The Emperor in the Roman World*, London 1977
2 G. W. Bowersock, *Augustus and the Greek World*, Oxford 1965
8 E. Binder (ed.), *Saeculum Augustum*, 2 vols, Darmstadt 1987/8
17 G. Kennedy, *The Art of Rhetoric in the Roman World*, Princeton 1972
17 M. Fuhrmann, *Einführung in die antike Rhetorik*, Zurich 1984
23 A. Dihle, *Hermes* 85/1957, 170–205 (literary theory)
24 M. v. Albrecht in Pauly-Wissowa, *Realencyclopädie* Suppl. 13 1973, 1237–1347 (Cicero's style)
24 F. Büchner in Pauly-Wissowa, *Realencyclopädie* 2nd series, vol. 13, 1939, 1104–91 (Cicero's philosophy)
25 G. Maurach (ed.), *Römische Philosophie*, Darmstadt 1976
26 J. Bayet *et al.*, *L'influence grecque sur la poésie latine de Catulle à Ovide (Entretiens sur l'antiquité classique 2)*, Vandoeuvres-Geneva 1953
29 E. A. Schmidt, *Catull*, Heidelberg 1987
29 E. J. Kenney, *Lucretius* (Greece and Rome: New Surveys 11), Oxford 1977
30 E. Zinn, *Antike und Abendland* 5 1956, 7–26 (Roman epic)

30 B. Otis, *Virgil – A Study in Civilized Poetry*, Oxford 1963
31 H. Oppermann (ed.), *Wege Zu Vergil*, Darmstadt 1976
34 E. Fraenkel, *Horace*, Oxford 1949
34 C. O. Brink, *Horace on Poetry*, 2 vols, Oxford 1971/82
36 C. Neumeister, *Tibull*, Heidelberg 1987
36 P. Boyancé (see note on p. 26), 169–209 (Propertius)
37 L. P. Wilkinson, *Ovid Recalled*, Cambridge 1955
37 M. von Albrecht and E. Zinn (eds), *Ovid*, Darmstadt 1968
41 E. Burck (ed.), *Wege zu Livius*, Darmstadt 1967
42 K. Latte, *Sallust*, Leipzig 1935
43 V. Pöschl (ed.), *Sallust*, Darmstadt 2nd edn, 1981
43 W. D. Lebek, *Verba Prisca*, Göttingen 1970
43 C. O. Brink *et al.*, *Varron* (Entretiens Fondation Hardt 9), Geneva 1962
43 A. Dihle in Pauly-Wissowa, *Realencyclopädie* 2nd series, vol. 8, 1958, 1636–46 (Verrius Flaccus)
44 Th. Gelzer *et al.*, *Le classicisme à Rome (Entretiens sur l'antiquité classique 25)*, Vandoeuvres-Geneva 1978
48 R. Syme (see note on p. 1)
50 R. Pfeiffer, *History of Classical Scholarship from the Beginning to the End of the Hellenistic Age*, Oxford 1968
53 A. Dihle, *Antike und Abendland* 23 1977, 162–173 (Atticism)
57 E. Norden, *Die antike Kunstprosa*, 2 vols, Leipzig 2nd edn, 1915; reprinted 1958
58 A. D. Leeman, *Orationis Ratio*, 2 vols, Amsterdam 1963
59 A. H. Armstrong, *The Cambridge History of Later Greek and Early Medieval Philosophy*, Cambridge 2nd edn, 1971

2 THE JULIO-CLAUDIAN ERA

64 See note on p. 17 (rhetoric)
64 H. I. Marrou, *Histoire de l'éducation dans l'antiquité*, Paris 3rd edn, 1955; German edn Freiburg 1957
65 I. Hadot, *Arts libéraux et philosophie dans la pensée antique*, Paris 1984
65 M. Winterbottom, *Roman Declamation*, Bristol 1980
66 H. Kornhardt, *Exemplum*, Göttingen 1936
68 D. A. Russell, *Greek Declamation*, Cambridge 1983
69 M. Fuhrmann, *Einführung in die antike Dichtungstheorie*, Darmstadt 1973
70 D. A. Russell, *Criticism in Antiquity*, London 1981
70 K. Heldmann, *Antike Theorien über Entwicklung und Verfall der Redekunst*, Munich 1982
71 J. Hahn, *Der Philosoph und die Gesellschaft*, Wiesbaden 1989
72 P. Moraux, *Der Aristotelismus bei den Griechen*, 2 vols, Berlin 1973/86
72 H. Dörrie and M. Baltes, *Der Platonismus in der Antike*, 2 vols, Stuttgart 1987–90
72 J. Wiesner (ed.), *Aristoteles – Werk und Wirkung*, vol. 2, Berlin 1987
73 W. Burkert and H. Thesleff in *Pseudepigrapha I (Entretiens sur l'antiquité classique 18)* Vandoeuvres-Geneva 1972, 25–102 (Pythagorean literature)
73 W. Speyer, *Die literarische Fälschung in der heidnischen und christlichen Antike*, Munich 1971
74 A. A. Long, *Hellenistic Philosophy*, New York 1974
74 A. A. Long and D. N. Sedley, *The Hellenistic Philosophers: Translations and Texts*, 2 vols, Cambridge 1987

77 J. Glucker, *Antiochus and the Late Academy*, Göttingen 1978
78 D. R. Dudley, *A History of Cynicism*, London 1937
80 W. Spoerri in *Der kleine Pauly* 2 1967, 823–9 (sententia)
80 P. L. Schmidt in *Der kleine Pauly* 2 1967, 324–30 (epistolography)
80 H. Musurillo, *The Acts of the Pagan Martyrs*, Oxford 1954
82 J. F. Kindstrand, *Bion of Borysthenes*, Uppsala 1976
86 G. W. Most in *Aufstieg und Niedergang der römischen Welt II* 36 (1989) 2014–66 (allegoresis)
88 I. Lana, *L. Annaeus Seneca*, Turin 1955
88 M. Pohlenz, *Kleine Schriften* 1, Hildesheim 1965, 384–447 (Seneca)
89 I. Hadot, *Seneca und die griechisch-römische Tradition der Seelenleitung*, Berlin 1969
89 G. Maurach (see note on p. 25) (philosophy in Rome)
91 P. Hadot in *Reallexikon für Antike und Christentum* 8 1972, 555–632 (catalogues of princely virtues)
95 A. Bourgery, *Senèque prosateur*, Paris 1922
96 M. T. Griffin, *Seneca: A Philosopher in Politics*, Oxford 1976
99 O. Weinreich, *Römische Satiren*, Zurich 2nd edn, 1962, Introduction
100 W. H. Friedrich, *Untersuchungen zu Senecas dramatischer Technik*, Leipzig 1933
100 O. Zwierlein, *Die Rezitationsdramen Senecas*, Berlin 1966
100 E. Lefèvre (ed.), *Senecas Tragödien*, Darmstadt 1972
102 A. Dihle, *Antike und Abendland 29* 1983, 162–71 (Roman theatre)
102 M. Bieber, *The History of the Greek and Roman Theatre*, New York 1961
102 P. Ghiron-Bistagne, *Recherches sur les acteurs dans la Grèce antique*, Paris 1976
106 W. Schmid in *Reallexikon für Antike und Christentum* 2 1954, 786–800 (Bucolica)
108 J. van Wageningen in Pauly-Wissowa, *Realencyclopädie* 14 1928, 1115–33 (Manilius)
110 Manilius, *Astronomica*, ed. and trans. G. P. Goold, Cambridge, Mass. 1987 (Introduction)
112 B. Axelson, *Unpoetische Wörter*, Lund 1945
113 Th. Haecker, *Vergil – Vater des Abendlandes*, Leipzig 2nd edn, 1933
113 E. R. Curtius, *Europäische Literatur und lateinisches Mittelalter*, Bern 5th edn, 1965
113 B. M. Marti, P. Grimal *et al.*, *Lucain (Entretiens sur l'antiquité classique 15)*, Vandoeuvres-Geneva 1969
114 W. D. Lebek, *Lucans Pharsalia*, Göttingen 1976
119 U. Knoche, *Die römische Satire*, Göttingen 4th edn, 1982
121 A. E. Raubitschek, L. Robert *et al.*, *L'épigramme grecque (Entretiens sur l'antiquité classique 14)*, Vandoeuvres-Geneva 1967
125 W. Burnikel, *Untersuchungen zur Struktur des Witzepigramms bei Lukillios und Martial*, Wiesbaden 1980
127 J. P. Sullivan, *The Satires of Petronius*, London 1968
128 V. Buchheit, *Studien zum Corpus Priapeorum*, Munich 1962
128 K. Heldmann (see note on p. 70)
131 H. Wiemken, *Der griechische Mimus*, Göttingen 1951
132 N. Holzberg, *Der antike Roman*, Zurich 1986
136 A. Dihle in Pauly-Wissowa, *Realencyclopädie*, 2nd series, vol. 8, 637–59 (Velleius Paterculus)
136 A. Dihle, *Die Entstehung der historischen Biographie*, Heidelberg 1986

139 Ed. Schwartz, *Griechische Geschichtsschreiber*, Leipzig 1959, 35–100 (Diodorus)
141 K. Barwick, *Remmius Palaemon und die römische ars grammatica*, Leipzig 1922
142 H. Fuchs in *Reallexikon für Antike und Christentum* 5 1962, 365–98 (general education)
144 H. Flashar (ed.), *Antike Medizin*, Darmstadt 1971, 308–60 (Celsus)
145 L. Rydbeck, *Fachprosa, vermeintliche Volkssprache und Neues Testament*, Uppsala 1967
145 T. L. Heath, *A Manual of Greek Mathematics*, Oxford 1931
145 O. Neugebauer, *The Exact Sciences in Antiquity*, New York 1962
146 G. E. R. Lloyd, *Science after Aristotle*, London 1973
146 R. J. Forbes, *Studies in Ancient Technology*, 9 vols, Leyden 1955–64
148 G. Aujac, *Strabon et la science de son temps*, Paris 1966
148 G. Aujac, *La géographie dans le monde antique*, Paris 1975
148 F. Prontera and G. Maddoli (eds), *Strabone – Contributi allo studio della personalità e dell' opera*, 3 vols, Perugia 1984/9
152 A. Satini, *Storia delle scienze agrarie*, Bologna 1979
153 See note on p. 146 (Forbes) vol. 1 (water supply)
153 Aeneas Tacticus, *Asclepiodotus and Onasander, with an English translation by Members of the Illinois Greek Club*, London 1923, Introduction
154 S. Sandmel, *Judaism and Christian Beginnings*, New York 1978
154 J. G. Gager, *Moses in Greco-Roman Paganism*, New York 1972
155 M. Hengel, *Judentum und Hellenismus*, Tübingen 2nd edn, 1973
155 O. Eissfeldt, *Einleitung in das Alte Testament*, Tübingen 2nd edn, 1956, 710–87
157 O. Kurfess, *Sibyllinische Weissagungen*, Munich, 1951
165 H. Temporini and K. Haase (eds), *Aufstieg und Niedergang der römischen Welt*, Part II (Principate), vol. 21 (Hellenistic Judaism in Roman Times: Philo and Josephus), Berlin 1983/4

3 THE FLAVIAN ERA

173 G. Kennedy (see note on p. 17) (rhetoric)
173 H. J. Marrou (see note on p. 64) (education); E. W. Bowersock, *Greek Sophists in the Roman Empire*, Oxford 1969
174 E. Lefèvre, *Das Pooemium der Argonautica des Valerius Flaccus*, Wiesbaden 1971
174 W. Schetter, *Das römische Epos*, Wiesbaden 1978
175 E. Wistrand, *Die Chronologie der Punica des Silius Italicus*, Göteborg 1956
176 W. Kissel, *Das Geschichtsbild des Silius Italicus*, Frankfurt 1979
177 W. Schetter, *Untersuchungen zur epischen Kunst des Statius*, Wiesbaden 1960
177 H. Cancik, *Untersuchungen zur lyrischen Kunst des P. Papinius Statius*, Hildesheim 1965
178 A. Hardie, *Statius and the Silvae*, Liverpool 1983
178 N. Holzberg, *Martial*, Heidelberg 1988
180 W. Kroll in Pauly-Wissowa, *Realencyclopädie*, 2nd series, vol. 21, 271–439 (Pliny the Elder)
180 Alfonso and N. Alfieri (eds), *Plinio il Vecchio* (Atti del congresso di Como 1979), Como 1979
183 *Periplus Maris Erythraei*, ed., trans. and comm. by L. Casson, Princeton 1981
183 L. Casson, *Ships and Seamanship in the Ancient World*, Princeton 1971
183 L. Casson, *Travel in the Ancient World*, London 1974

184 E. Norden (see note on p. 57), 314ff. (prose style)
185 A. D. Leeman, *Orationis ratio*, Amsterdam 1963, vol. 1, 287–363 (prose style)
185 M. Winterbottom (see note on p. 65) (declamation)
186 Th. Gelzer *et al.* (see note on p. 44) (Classicism)
187 K. Heldmann (see note on p. 76) (rhetoric)
188 D. A. Russell, *Plutarch*, London 1973
193 R. Aulotte, *Amyot et Plutarque*, Geneva 1965
195 I. Hadot (see note on p. 89) (transmigration of souls)
200 M. Pohlenz, *Die Stoa*, Göttingen 6th edn, 1984, vol. 1, 277–366 (philosophy in the Empire)
203 P. Vielhauer, *Geschichte der urchristlichen Literatur*, Berlin 1975
207 P. Stuhlmacher *et al.*, *The Gospel and the Gospels*
207 H. Cancik, *Die Gattung Evangelium* (*Humanistische Bildung* 4 1981, 63–107)
208 E. Hennecke and W. Schneemelcher, *Neutestamentliche Apokryphen in deutscher Ubersetzung*, 2 vols, Tübingen 1959/1964, Introductions
210 L. Rydbeck (see note on p. 145)

4 THE SECOND CENTURY

215 R. Syme, *Tacitus*, 2 vols, Oxford 1958
215 V. Pöschl (ed.), *Tacitus*, Darmstadt 2nd edn, 1986
216 E. Norden, *Die Germanische Urgeschichte in Tacitus' Germania*, Leipzig 1920; reprinted 1959, 4th edn
223 E. Norden (see note on p. 57), 321–43 (prose style)
225 A. Heuss, *Antike und Abendland* 4, 1954, 65–104 (monarchic ideology)
226 A. N. Sherwin-White, *The Letters of Pliny*, Oxford 1966
227 P. Jal (ed.), *Florus, Oeuvres*, 2 vols, Paris 1967, 1–129, Introduction
227 Ilona Opelt, in: *Reallexikon für Antike und Christentum* 5, 1962, 944–972 (Epitome)
228 E. W. Bowersock (see note on p. 173)
228 C. P. Jones, *The Roman World of Dio Chrysostom*, Cambridge, Mass. 1978
229 H. v. Arnim, *Leben und Werke des Dio von Prusa*, Berlin 1898
232 J. H. Oliver, *The Ruling Power*, Philadelphia 1953 (Aelius Aristides)
232 J. H. Oliver, *The Civilising Power*, Philadelphia 1968 (Aelius Aristides)
232 C. A. Behr, *Aelius Aristides and the Sacred Tales*, Amsterdam 1968
234 K. Thraede, *Grundzüge griechisch-römischer Brieftopik*, Munich 1970
235 R. Güngerich, *Die Küstenbeschreibung in der griechischen Literatur*, Münster 1950
236 T. Hägg, *The Novel in Antiquity*, Oxford 1983
237 R. Merkelbach, *Die Quellen des griechischen Alexanderromans*, Munich 2nd edn, 1977
238 R. Adrados *et al.*, *La fable (Entretiens sur l'antiquité classique 30*), Vandoeuvres-Geneva 1984
240 C. P. Jones, *Culture and Society in Lucian*, Cambridge, Mass. 1986
240 J. Hall, *Lucian's Satire*, New York 1981
241 P. A. Stadter, *Arrian of Nicomedia*, Chapel Hill, N. C. 1980
244 E. Schwartz (see note on p. 139), 361–93 (Appian)
246 Pompeius Trogus, *Weltgeschichte von den Anfängen bis Augustus im Auszug des Justin*, intro., trans. and comm. by O. Seel, Zurich 1972
247 D. Korzeniewski, *Die Zeit des Q. Curtius Rufus*, Cologne 1959
245 E. Schwartz (see note on p. 139) 253–318 (chronography)

248 C. Habicht, *Pausanius – Guide to Ancient Greece*, Berkeley 1985
251 H. Erbse, *Beiträge zur Uberlieferung der Ilias-Scholien*, Munich 1960
254 H. Erbse, *Untersuchungen zu den attizistischen Lexika*, Berlin 1950
256 D. Hagedorn, *Zur Ideenlehre des Hermogenes*, Göttingen 1964
259 A. Wallace-Hadrill *Suetonius*, London 1983
260 A. Dihle, *Die Entstehung der historischen Biographie*, Heidelberg 1986
262 W. D. Lebek (see note on p. 43) (archaism)
264 E. Champlin, *Fronto and Antonine Rome*, Cambridge, Mass. 1980
265 L. Holford-Stevens, *Aulus Gellius*, London 1988
266 J. Fontaine in *Reallexikon für Antike und Christentum*, Suppl. 1 1985, 137–51 (Apuleius)
270 E. Pöhlmann, *Griechische Musikfragmente*, Nuremberg 1960
270 E. A. Lippman, *Musical Thought in Ancient Greece*, New York 1964
270 W. D. Anderson, *Ethos and Education in Ancient Music*, Cambridge, Mass. 1966
270 P. A. Rosenmeyer, *The Poetics of Imitation*, Cambridge 1991 (anacreontics)
271 U. Knoche, *Die römische Satire*, Göttingen 1982
272 R. Schilling (ed.), *La veillée de Vénus*, Paris 1944, Introduction
274 J. Dillon, *The Middle Platonists*, London 1977
276 P. Moraux (see note on p. 72) vol. 2
278 C. Andresen, *Logos und Nomos*, Berlin 1955 (Celsus)
279 M. Pohlenz (see note on p. 200)
280 R. B. Rutherford, *The Meditations of Marcus Aurelius*, Oxford 1989
280 P. Hadot, *La citadelle intérieure*, Paris 1992 (M. Aurelius)
282 E. des Places (ed.), *Numénius*, Paris 1973, 1–41
283 A. J. Festugière, *La révélation d'Hermès Trismégiste*, 4 vols, Paris 1944–54
283 E. des Places (ed.), *Les oracles chaldaïques*, Paris 1971, 1–65
287 E. Polaschek in Pauly-Wissowa, *Realencyclopädie*, Suppl. 10 1965, 680–833 (Ptolemy)
288 F. Boll and C. Bezold, *Sternglaube und Sterndeutung*, Darmstadt 5th edn, 1966
289 O. Neugebauer (see note on p. 146) (sciences)
290 E. Flashar (see note on p. 144), 361–416 (Galen)
295 A. Wlosok, *Rom und die Christen*, Stuttgart 1970
298 C. Colpe in: *Reallexikon für Antike und Christentum* 11 1981, 537–659 (Gnosis, Gnosticism)
302 G. H. Waszink, *Opuscula Selecta*, Leyden 1979, 317–28 (Justin)
303 M. Elze, *Tatian und seine Theologie*, Göttingen 1960
304 A. Benoit, *St. Irénée – introduction à l'étude de sa théologie*, Paris 1960
307 E. Plümacher, in Pauly-Wissowa, *Realencyclopädie*, Suppl. 15, 1978, 11–70
308 H. Musurillo (ed.), *The Acts of the Christian Martyrs*, Oxford 1972, Introduction

5 THE SEVERAN ERA

312 W. Kunkel, *An Introduction to Roman Legal and Constitutional History*, Oxford 1966
312 F. Schulz, *History of Roman Legal Science*, Oxford, 2nd edn, 1953
316 M. Fuhrmann, *Das systematische Lehrbuch*, Göttingen 1960
321 K. Barwick (see note on p. 141) (grammarians)
324 M. Pohlenz (see note on p. 200) (late Stoics)
324 W. Schmid in *Reallexikon für Antike und Christentum* 5, 1962, 618–819

325 F. Leo, *Die griechisch-römische Biographie nach ihrer literarischen Form*, Leipzig 1901
327 R. W. Sharples (ed.), *Alexander of Aphrodisias on Fate*, London 1983
328 M. Pohlenz (see note on p. 88), vol. 1, 481–558 (Clement of Alexandria)
328 H. Chadwick, *Early Christian Thought and the Classical Tradition*, London 2nd edn, 1971 (Clement of Alexandria)
330 H. J. Drijvers, *Bar Daisan of Edessa*, Assen 1966
332 H. Lietzmann, *Geschichte der alten Kirche*, 4 vols Berlin 1932–41, vol. 2, 244–63
334 H. Gelzer, *Sextus Iulius Africanus und die byzantinische Chronographie*, Leipzig 1880/8 (2nd edn, 1978)
335 H. Crouzel in *Reallexikon für Antike und Christentum* 12, 1983, 779–93 (Gregory Thaumaturgus)
337 H. Crouzel, *Origène et la philosophie*, Paris 1962
337 P. Nautin, *Origène*, Paris 1977
337 U. Berner (ed.), *Origenes*, Darmstadt 1981
337 N. R. M. de Lange, *Origen and the Jews*, Cambridge 1976
337 B. Neuschäfer, *Origenes als Philologe*, Basel 1987
338 J. Whitman, *Allegory. The Dynamics of an Ancient and Medieval Technique*, Oxford 1987
338 R. P. C. Hanson, *Allegory and Event*, London 1959 (Origen)
340 Bowersock (see note on p. 173) (sophists)
341 E. Schwartz, *Fünf Vorträge über den griechischen Roman*, Berlin 2nd edn, 1943
341 G. Anderson, *Philostratus. Biography and belles lettres in the 3rd century AD*, Leyden 1986
343 H. Koskenniemi, *Studien zur Idee und Phraseologie des griechischen Briefes bis 400 n. Chr.*, Helsinki 1956
346 Dihle (see note on p. 260) (biography and historiography)
347 W. Widmer, *Kaisertum, Rom und Welt bei Herodian*, Zurich 1967
348 E. Schwartz, *Griechische Geschichtsschreiber*, Leipzig 1957, 394–450 (Cassius Dio)
348 F. Millar, *A Study of Cassius Dio*, Oxford 1964
350 T. D. Barnes, *Tertullian. A Historical and Literary Study*, Oxford 1971
350 J. C. Fredouille, *Tertullien et la conversion de la culture antique*, Paris 1972
350 H. v. Campenhausen, 'Tertullian' in *Gestalten der Kirchengeschichte*, ed. M. Greschat, vol. 1, Stuttgart 1984, 97–120
357 B. Axelson, *Das Prioritätsproblem Tertullian – Minucius Felix*, Lund 1941
357 C. Becker, *Minucius Felix*, Munich 1967
357 P. L. Schmidt in A. Cameron *et al.* (note on p. 397), 101–90 (dialogue in Christian literature)

6 THE CRISES OF THE THIRD CENTURY AD

361 E. R. Dodds, *Pagan and Christian in an Age of Anxiety*, Cambridge 1965
364 D. A. Russell and N. G. Wilson (ed.), *Menander Rhetor*, Oxford 1981, Introduction
365 Holzberg (see note on p. 132) (novel)
366 Merkelbach (see note on p. 237) (Alexander novel)
366 H. van Thiel (ed.), *Leben und Taten Alexanders von Makedonien*, Darmstadt 1974, Introduction
369 R. Helm, *Der antike Roman*, Göttingen 2nd edn, 1956

370 H. R. Schwyzer in Pauly-Wissowa, *Realencyclopädie*, 21, 1, 1951, 471–592; Suppl. 15 310–28 (Plotinus)
370 J. M. Rist, *Plotinus*, Cambridge 1967
372 G. O'Daly, *Plotinus' Philosophy of the Self*, Shannon 1973
372 E. R. Dodds *et al.*, *Les sources de Plotin (Entretiens sur l'antiquité classique 5)*, Vandoeuvres-Geneva 1960
373 C. Zintzen (ed.), *Die Philosophie des Neuplatonismus*, Darmstadt 1977
374 H. Dörrie *et al.*, *Porphyre (Entretiens sur l'antiquité classique 12)*, Vandoeuvres-Geneva 1965
377 J. Pépin in H. Dörrie *et al.*, 229–72 (allegorical interpretation in philosophy)
379 P. Hadot, *Porphyre et Victorinus*, Paris 1968
382 J. Farges, *Les ideés morales et religieuses de Méthode d'Olympe*, Paris 1929
382 V. Buchheit, *Studien zu Methodios von Olympos*, Berlin 1958
384 J. Kroll, *Die christliche Hymnodik bis zu Klemens von Alexandreia*, Darmstadt 2nd edn 1968
384 M. M. Sage, *Cyprian*, Cambridge, Mass. 1975
384 *The Letters of St Cyprian*, trans. and annot. by G. W. Clarke, vol. 1, New York 1984, Introduction
385 U. Wickert, 'Cyprian' in *Gestalten der Kirchengeschichte*, ed. M. Greschat, vol. 1, Stuttgart 1984, 158–75
387 H. A. M. Hoppenbrouwers, *Commodien*, Nijmegen 1964
389 P. Lampe, *Die stadttrömischen Christen in den beiden ersten Jahrhunderten*, Tübingen 1987
389 Novatianus, *De trinitate*, ed. H. Weyer, Darmstadt 1962, Introduction

7 THE ERA OF DIOCLETIAN AND CONSTANTINE

397 A. Cameron *et al.*, *Christianisme et formes littéraires de l'antiquité tardive en occident (Entretiens sur l'antiquité classique 23)*, Vandoeuvres-Geneva 1977
397 H. Hagendahl, *Von Tertullian zu Cassiodor. Die profane literarische Tradition in dem lateinischen christlichen Schrifttum*, Göteborg 1983
398 A. Wlosok, 'Laktanz' in *Gestalten der Kirchengeschichte* vol. 1, ed. M. Greschat, Stuttgart 1984, 176–88
400 Boll and Bezold (see note on p. 288) (astrology)
400 H. O. Schröder in *Reallexikon für Antike und Christentum*, Stuttgart 1969, 524–636 (belief in fate)
400 Iulius Firmicus Maternus, *De errore profanarum religionum*, ed. K. Ziegler, Munich 1953, Introduction
400 W. Schetter and C. Gnilka (eds), *Studien zur Literatur der Spätantike*, Bonn 1975
400 M. Walla, *Der Vogel Phoenix in der antiken Literatur und der Dichtung des Laktanz*, Vienna 1969
401 A. Wlosok, 'Die Anfänge christlicher Poesie lateinischer Sprache' in *Information aus der Vergangenheit*, ed. P. Neukam, Munich 1982, 129–67
401 O. Seel, *Der Physiologus*, Zurich 2nd edn, 1987
402 J. Fontaine, *Naissance de la poésie dans l'occident chrétien, IIIe-VIe siècle*, Paris 1981
402 B. D. Larsen *et al.*, *De Jamblique à Proclus (Entretiens sur l'antiquité classique 21)*, Vandoeuvres-Geneva 1975
405 G. Widengren, *Mani und der Manichäismus*, Stuttgart 1961
405 M. Dibelius in *Reallexikon für Antike und Christentum* 1 1950, 270–1 (Alexander of Lycopolis)

409 H. von Campenhausen, *Griechische Kirchenväter*, Stuttgart 6th edn, 1986, 72–85 (Athanasius)

410 B. Lohse, *Askese und Mönchtum in der Antike und in der Alten Kirche*, Munich/Vienna 1969

410 P. Brown, *The Cult of the Saints*, Chicago 1981

411 R. Reitzenstein, *Des Athanasius Werk über das Leben des Antonius*, Heidelberg 1914

411 P. Cox, *Biography in Late Antiquity*, Berkeley 1983

411 K. Holl, *Die schriftstellerische Form des griechischen Heiligenlebens – Gesammelte*, Aufsätze, Tübingen 2nd edn, 1928, 249–69

412 M. Fuhrmann in A. Cameron *et al.* (see note on p. 397)

414 M. van Uytfanghe in *Reallexikon für Antike und Christentum* 14 1988, 150–80

416 J. Wilkinson, *Egeria's Travels to the Holy Land*, London 1971

417 B. Kötting, *Peregrinatio Religiosa*, Münster 2nd edn, 1980

418 H. Fuchs in *Reallexikon für Antike und Christentum*, 2 1954, 346–62 (education)

418 K. Thraede, *Untersuchungen zu Sprache und Stil des Prudentius*, Göttingen 1965, 21–72

418 P. Brown, *The Body and Society*, New York 1988, 213–338

418 H. Dörries, *Symeon von Mesopotamien*, Berlin 1941

418 G. Quispel, *Makarios, das Thomas-Evangelium und das Lied von der Perle*, London 1967

418 A. and C. Guillaumont in *Reallexikon für Antike und Christentum* 6 1966, 1088–1107 (Euagrios)

419 O. Chadwick, *John Cassian, A Study in Primitive Monasticism*, Cambridge 1950

422 A. A. Morshammer, *The Chronicle of Eusebius and Greek Chronographic Tradition*, London 1977

423 T. D. Barnes, *Constantine and Eusebius*, Cambridge, Mass. 1981

423 R. M. Grant, *Eusebius as Church Historian*, Oxford 1980

427 F. Vian, *Recherches sur les Posthomerica de Quintus de Smyrne*, Paris 1959

427 K. Thraede in *Reallexikon für Antike und Christentum* 5 1962, 983–1042 (late epic)

429 H. Lietzmann, *Apollinarios und seine Schule*, Berlin 1904

430 O. Temkin (see note on p. 144), 417–68 (Late Classical medicine)

431 Heath (see note on p. 145), 434–65; 518 *et passim* (mathematicians)

432 G. L. Huxley, *Anthemios of Tralleis*, Oxford 1959

8 THE CHRISTIAN EMPIRE

439 H. R. Robins, 'Dionysius Thrax and the Grammatical Tradition' in *Transactions of the American Philological Society* 9 1957, 67–107; K. Barwick, *Probleme der stoischen Sprachlehre und Rhetorik*, Berlin 1957
A. D. Saglione, *Ars Grammatica*, The Hague, 1970

439 G. Boas (trans), *The Hieroglyphics of Horapollon*, New York 1950, Introduction

440 *Lexica Graeca Minora*, ed. K. Latte, Hildesheim 1965, 1–11; 231–82

441 E. Honigmann in Pauly-Wissowa, *Realencyclopädie*, 2nd series, vol. 3, 1929, 2369–99 (Stephen of Byzantium)

442 R. T. Schmidt, *Die Grammatik der Stoiker*, Brunswick 1979

442 L. Holtz, *Donat et la tradition de l'enseignement grammatical*, Paris 1981

443 K. Barwick, *Remmius Palaemon und die römische ars grammatica*, Leipzig 1922
443 M. Glück, *Priscians Partitiones und ihre Stellung in der spätantiken Schule*, Hildesheim 1967
444 K. Büchner in Pauly-Wissowa, *Realencyclopädie*, 2nd series, vol. 8, 1958, 1468–76 (Classical Virgilian exegesis)
444 M. Mühmelt, *Griechische Grammatik in der Vergilerklärung*, Munich 1965
444 R. A. Kaster, *Guardians of Language: The Grammarian and Society in Late Antiquity*, Berkeley 1988
445 E. Türk, *Macrobius und die Quellen seiner Saturnalien*, Freiburg 1962
446 J. Flamant, *Macrobe et le Néo-Platonisme à la fin du 4e siècle*, Leyden 1977
447 F. Le Moine, *Martianus Capella. A Literary Re-evaluation*, Munich 1972
447 J. Fontaine, *Isidore de Sevilla et la culture classique dans l'Espagne wisigothique*, 2 vols, Paris 1959
447 P. Courcelle, *Les lettres grecques en Occident de Macrobe à Cassiodore*, Paris 2nd edn, 1948
449 G. Kennedy, *Greek Rhetoric under Christian Emperors*, Princeton 1983
449 G. Fatouros and T. Krischer (eds), *Libanios*, Darmstadt 1983
449 A. J. Festugière, *Antioche païenne et chrétienne*, Paris 1959
449 J. H. W. G. Liebschuetz, *Antioch*, Oxford 1972
452 W. Stegmann in Pauly-Wissowa, *Realencyclopädie*, 2nd series vol. 5, 1934, 1642–80 (Themistius)
453 J. Bidez, *La vie de l'empereur Julien*, Paris 1930; German edn, *Julian der Abtrünnige*, Hamburg 1956
453 J. Geffcken, *Der Ausgang des griechisch-römischen Heidentums*, Heidelberg 1929; A. Momigliano (ed.), *The Conflict between Paganism and Christianity*, London 1963
455 Dudley (see note on p. 78) (Cynics)
456 C. Lacombrade, *Synésius de Cyrène*, Paris 1951
456 H. v. Campenhausen (see note on p. 409), 125–36 (Synesius)
458 H. Hunger, *Die hochsprachliche profane Literatur der Byzantiner*, vol. 1, Munich 1978, 279ff. (Eunapius and other historiographers)
459 R. Klein, *Symmachus*, Darmstadt 2nd edn, 1986
459 R. Klein, *Der Streit um den Altar der Victoria*, Darmstadt 1972
463 H. Hunger (see note on p. 458), 92–123 (Procopius and Aeneas of Gaza)
465 Y. A. Dauge, *Le Barbare. Recherches sur la conception romaine de la barbarie et de la civilisation*, Brussels 1981
466 F. Paschoud, *Roma aeterna*, Rome 1967 (idea of Rome)
466 I. Opelt and W. Speyer, *Jahrbuch für Antike und Christentum* 10 1967, 251–90 (Barbarian)
466 K. Rosen, *Ammianus Marcellinus*, Darmstadt 1982
469 P. Brown, *Augustine of Hippo*, London 1967
469 H. Chadwick, *Augustine*, Oxford 1986
471 F. Paschoud (see note on p. 466), 276–92 (Orosius)
473 F. X. Murphy, *Rufinus of Aquileia*, Washington 1945
474 *Philostorgius, Kirchengeschichte*, ed. J. Bidez and F. Winkelmann, Berlin 2nd edn, 1972, Introduction
474 Theodoros Anagnostes, *Kirchengeschichte*, ed. G. C. Hansen, Berlin 1971, Introduction
475 A. Momigliano, *Studies in Historiography*, London 1969, 181–210
475 W. den Boer, *Some Minor Roman Historians*, Leyden 1972
476 J. Schlumberger, *Die Epitome de Caesaribus*, Munich 1974

476 J. Straub, *Heidnische Geschichtsapologetik in der christlichen Spätantike*, Bonn 1967 (*Historia augusta*)
478 R. Syme, *Ammianus and the Historia Augusta*, Oxford 1968
478 A. Lippold in *Reallexikon für Antike und Christentum* 15, 1989 (*Historia augusta*)
480 F. Paschoud in Pauly-Wissowa, *Realencyclopädie*, 2nd series vol. 10, 1972, 795–84 (Zosimus)
482 M. E. Colonna, *Gli storici bizantini dal IV al XV secolo*, Naples 1956
483 B. Rubin in Pauly-Wissowa, *Realencyclopädie*, 23, 1954, 273–599 (Procopius of Caesaraea)
483 Averil Cameron, *Procopius and the Sixth Century*, London 1985
484 Gelzer (see note on p. 334) (chronography)
485 Colonna (see note on p. 482) (John Malalas)
486 Dudley (see note on p. 78) (Cynics)
490 W. Beierwaltes, *Proklos Grundzüge seiner Metaphysik*, Frankfurt 1965
490 Saloustios, *Des dieux et du monde*, ed. G. Rochefort, Paris 1960, Introduction
491 C. Zintzen (see note on p. 373), 391–426 (philosophical theurgy)
492 K. Praechter, *Schulen und Richtungen im Neuplatonismus (1911) Kleine Schriften*, Hildesheim 1973, 165–216
493 Proclus, *Théologie platonicienne*, ed. H. D. Saffrey and L. G. Westerink, Paris 1968, Introduction
498 P. Hadot, *Marius Victorinus. Recherches sur sa vie et ses oeuvres*, Paris 1971
499 F. Bömer, *Der lateinische Neuplatonismus und Claudius Mamertus in Sprache und Philosophie*, Bonn 1936
499 P. Courcelle (see note on p. 447), 318–88 (philosophy in the western Empire)
499 R. Helm in *Reallexikon für Antike und Christentum* 2 1954, 915–26 (Cassiodorus)
499 R. Schlieben, *Christliche Theologie und Philologie in der Spätantike*, Berlin 1974
499 A. Momigliano (see note on p. 475) 181–210 (Cassiodorus)
500 H. Chadwick, *Boethius*, Oxford 1981
501 A. R. Neumann in Pauly-Wissowa, *Realencyclopädie*, Suppl. 10 1965, 992–1020 (Vegetius)
501 E. A. Thompson, *A Roman Reformer and Inventor*, Oxford 1962 (anonymus *de rebus bellicis*)
507 G. Q. A. Meershoek, *Le latin biblique d'après S. Jérôme*, Nijmegen 1966
508 B. Fischer, *Beiträge zur Geschichte der lateinischen Bibeltexte*, Freiburg 1986
508 H. Hagendahl and J. A. Waszink in *Reallexikon für Antike und Christentum* 15 1989 (Hieronymus)
508 N. R. M. de Lange, *Origen and the Jews*, Cambridge 1976
510 W. A. Bienert, *'Allegoria' und 'Anagoge' bei Didymos dem Blinden v. Alexandria*, Berlin/New York 1972
512 E. Dassmann, *Der Stachel im Fleisch. Paulus in der frühchristlichen Literatur*, Münster 1979
512 A. Stuiber in *Reallexikon für Antike und Christentum* Suppl. 1 1985, 301–10 (Ambrosiaster)
512 K. Staab, *Paulus-Kommentare aus der griechischen Kirche*, Münster 1933
513 C. Schäublin, *Untersuchungen zu Methode und Herkunft der antiochenischen Exegese*, Cologne 1974
514 E. Dinkler in Pauly-Wissowa, *Realencyclopädie*, 2nd series, vol. 6, 1936, 849–56 (Ticonius)
514 W. H. C. Frend, *The Donatist Church*, Oxford 2nd edn, 1971 (Ticonius)

515 J. Doignon, *Hilaire de Poitiers*, Paris 1971
516 H. Lietzman, *Catenen*, Freiburg, Leipzig and Tübingen 1897
518 E. Norden (see note on p. 57), 538–58 (homiletic style)
518 H. v. Campenhausen (see note on p. 409), 137–53 (John Chrysostom)
518 G. Gentz in *Reallexikon für Antike und Christentum* 1 1950, 520–2 (Apollinaris of Laodicea)
519 H. v. Campenhausen, *Lateinische Kirchenväter*, Stuttgart 6th edn, 1986, 77–108 (Ambrosius)
519 K. Holl, *Ges. Aufsätze zur Kirchengeschichte*, Tübingen 2nd edn, 1928, 249–69 (lives of the saints)
523 G. Luck in *Jahrbuch für Antike und Christentum*, Suppl. 1 1964, 230–41 (lives of the saints)
523 M. Fuhrmann in A. Cameron *et al.* (see note on p. 397) (lives of the saints)
525 E. Mühlenberg, *Die Unendlichkeit Gottes bei Gregor von Nyssa*, Göttingen 1964
527 H. J. Marrou, *S. Augustin et la fin de la culture antique*, Paris 2nd edn, 1949; reprinted Paderborn 1981
527 P. Courcelle, *Recherches sur les Confessions de S. Augustin*, Paris 1950
527 St Augustine, *Confessions*, trans. with an Introduction by H. Chadwick, Oxford 1991
528 P. Brown (see note on p. 469) (Augustine)
528 H. Chadwick (see note on p. 469) (Augustine)
529 G. N. Knauer, *Psalmenzitate in Augustins Konfessionen*, Göttingen 1955
529 E. A. Schmidt, *Zeit und Geschichte bei Augustin*, Heidelberg 1985
532 B. R. Voss, *Der Dialog in der frühchristlichen Literatur*, Munich 1970, 308–15
533 F. Kaphahn, *Zwischen Antike und Mittelalter*, Munich 1949 (Eugippius)
533 C. Courtois, *Victor de Vita et son oeuvre*, Paris 1954
534 Hagendahl and Waszink (see note on p. 508) (Hieronymus)
535 J. Wytzes, *Der letzte Kampf des Heidentums in Rom*, Leyden 1976 (altar of Victoria)
535 A. Schindler in *Theologische Realenzyklopädie* 4 1979, 646–98 (Augustine)
535 P. Courcelle, *Histoire littéraire des grandes invasions germaniques*, Paris 2nd edn, 1964
536 J. Badewien, *Geschichtstheologie und Sozialkritik im Werk Salvians*, Göttingen 1980
537 G. Gentz (see note on p. 518) (Apollinaris)
538 B. R. Voss (see note on p. 532) (dialogues)
538 H. Dörrie in Pauly-Wissowa, *Realencyclopädie*, Suppl. 8 1956, 1260–7 (Serapion)
539 W. Schneemelcher in *Reallexikon für Antike und Christentum* 5 1962, 909–27 (Epiphanius)
540 H. Chadwick, *Priscillian of Avila*, Oxford 1976
541 Ilona Opelt, *Hieronymus' Streitschriften*, Heidelberg 1973
541 H. Marti, *Übersetzer der Augustin-Zeit*, Munich 1974
544 H. Chadwick (see notes on p. 469), 38–43; 107–19 (Augustine)
544 G. O'Daly, *Augustine's Philosophy of Mind*, London 1987
547 J. Doignon in *Reallexikon für Antike und Christentum* 15 1989 (Hilarius)
549 H. v. Campenhausen (see note on p. 409), 86–100 (Basil)
550 H. Dörrie in *Reallexikon für Antike und Christentum* 12 1983, 863–95 (Gregory of Nyssa)
551 B. Wyss in *Reallexikon für Antike und Christentum* 12 1983, 793–863 (Gregory of Nazianus)

553 G. Jouassard in *Reallexikon für Antike und Christentum* 3 1957, 499–516 (Cyril of Alexandria)
558 R. Roques in *Reallexikon für Antike und Christentum* 3 1954, 1075–1121 (Dionysius Areopagita)
559 M. Schmaus, *Die psychologische Trinitätslehre des hl. Augustinus*, Münster 1927
560 G. O'Daly (see note on p. 544) (Augustine)
562 H. Hunger (see note on p. 458), 508–42
564 K. Thraede (see note on p. 234) (epistolography)
564 E. Dassmann in *Theologische Realenzyklopädie* 2 1978, 362–86 (Ambrosius)
565 J. N. D. Kelly, *Jerome*, London 1975
566 W. Erdt, *Christentum und heidnisch-antike Bildung bei Paulin von Nola*, Meisenheim 1976
567 R. Manselli in *Reallexikon für Antike und Christentum* 12 1983, 930–51 (Gregory the Great)
569 S. Krautschick, *Cassiodor und die Politik seiner Zeit*, Bonn 1983
570 W. Meyer, *Abhandlungen zur mittellateinischen Rhythmik*, Berlin 1905, vol. 2, 1–201, 342–65
572 B. Wyss in *Reallexikon für Antike und Christentum* 12 1983, 793–682 (Gregory of Nazianus)
573 J. Kroll (see note on p. 334) (hymnodics)
575 E. Wellesz, *A Handbook of Byzantine Music and Hymnography*, Oxford 2nd edn, 1961
575 C. Hannick, 'Byzantinische Musik' in H. Hunger, *Die hochsprachliche profane Literatur der Byzantiner*, vol. 2, Munich 1978, 181–218
575 J. Grosdidier de Matons, *Romanos le mélode et les origines de la poésie religieuse à Byzance*, Paris 1977
576 *Sancti Romani Melodi Cantica*, ed. P. Maas and C. A. Trypanis, Oxford 1970, Introduction
576 J. Quasten, *Musik und Gesang in der Kult der hiednischen Antike und der christlichen Frühzeit*, Münster 2nd edn, 1973
577 J. Szöverffy, *Die Annalen der lateinischen Hymnendichtung*, vol. 1, Berlin 1964
579 *Opere di Decimo Magno Ausonio*, ed. A. Pastorino, Turin 1971, Introduction
580 W. Speyer, *Naucellius und sein Kreis*, München 1959
581 K. Kohlwes, *Christliche Dichtung und stilistische Form bei Paulinus von Nola*, Bonn 1979
581 R. Herzog in A. Cameron *et al.* (see note to p. 397) (Paulinus of Nola)
582 K. Thraede, *Studien zu Sprache und Stil des Prudentius*, Göttingen 1965
583 R. Herzog, *Die allegorische Dichtkunst des Prudentius* (München) 1966 Munich
583 W. Ludwig in A. Cameron *et al.* (see note to p. 397) (Prudentius)
585 W. Speyer/Ilona Opelt in *Jahrbuch für Antike und Christentum* 10, 1967, 251–90 (Barbarian)
586 Th. Mommsen, *Kleine Schriften* vol. 7, Berlin 1909, 485–98 (*Carmen adversus paganos*)
587 A. Cameron, *Claudian Poetry and Propaganda at the Court of Honorius*, Oxford 1970
587 J. L. Charlet, *Théologie, politique et rhétorique* in *La poesia tardoantica*, Messina 1984, 259–87 (Claudian)
588 S. Döpp, *Zeitgeschichte in Dichtungen Claudians*, Wiesbaden 1980
590 J. Küppers, *Die Fabeln Avians*, Bonn 1977
590 F. R. Adrados *et al.*, *La fable (Entretiens sur l'antiquité classique 30)* Vandoeuvres-Geneva 1984

590 J. O. Thomson, *History of Greek Geography*, Cambridge 1948, 53; 329–30; 375 (Avienus)

590 M. Fuhrmann in *Der kleine Pauly 1*, 1964, 788–9 (Avienus)

591 E. Doblhofer (ed.), *Rutilius Namatianus, De reditu suo*, 2 vols, Heidelberg 1972/77 Introduction

592 K. Thraede (see note on p. 427) (Late Classical epic)

593 G. O'Daly, *The Poetry of Boethius*, London 1991

594 A. Loyen (ed.), *Sidoine Apollinaire, Poèmes et Lettres*, 3 vols, Paris 1960–70, Introduction

594 K. Strohecker, *Der senatorische Adel im spätantiken Gallien*, Tübingen 1948 (Sidonius Apollinaris *et al.*)

594 P. Langlois in *Reallexikon für Antike und Christentum* 8, 1972, 632–61 (Fulgentius)

594 P. Langlois in *Reallexikon für Antike und Christentum* 4, 1959, 230–50 (Dracontius)

596 J. Fontaine, S. Lancel, P. Langlois, A. Mandouze and H. Brakmann in *Reallexikon für Antike und Christentum* Suppl. 1 1985, 134–228 (African literary history)

596 M. Rosenblum, *Luxorius. A Latin Poet among the Vandals*, New York 1961

596 H. Happ (ed.), *Luxurius*, 2 vols, Heidelberg 1986

596 P. Langlois in *Reallexikon für Antike und Christentum* Suppl. 1, 1985, 225–8 (Corippus)

596 Corippus, *In Laudem Iustini*, ed. Averil Cameron, London 1976, Introduction

597 J. Fontaine in *Reallexikon für Antike und Christentum* 5 1962, 398–421 (Ennodius)

597 K. Thraede in *Reallexikon für Antike und Christentum* Suppl. 1 1986, 553–73 (Arator)

597 W. Meyer, *Der Gelegenheitsdichter Venantius Fortunatus*, Göttingen 1901

598 W. Fauth, *Eidos poikilon*, Göttingen 1981 (Nonnus)

600 *Musaeus*, ed. Th. Gelzer, London 1975, Introduction

601 H. Gerstinger, *Pamprepios von Panopolis*, Vienna 1928

602 P. Friedländer, *Johannes von Gaza und Paulus Silentiarius*, Leipzig 1912

603 G. Downey in *Reallexikon für Antike und Christentum* 4 1957, 921–44 (ekphrasis)

604 B. Wyss (see note on p. 572) (Gregory of Nazianus)

INDEX